RELIGION, REDEMPTION, AND REVOLUTION:
THE NEW SPEECH THINKING OF FRANZ ROSENZWEIG
AND EUGEN ROSENSTOCK-HUESSY

Religion, Redemption, and Revolution closely examines the intertwined intellectual development of one of the most important Jewish thinkers of the twentieth century, Franz Rosenzweig, and his friend and teacher, Christian sociologist Eugen Rosenstock-Huessy. The first major English work on Rosenstock-Huessy, it also provides a significant reinterpretation of Rosenzweig's writings based on the thinkers' shared insights – including their critique of modern Western philosophy and their novel conception of speech.

This groundbreaking book provides a detailed examination of their 'new speech thinking' paradigm, a model grounded in the faith traditions of Judaism and Christianity. Wayne Cristaudo contrasts this paradigm against the radical liberalism that has dominated social theory for the last fifty years. *Religion, Redemption, and Revolution* provides powerful arguments for the continued relevance of Rosenzweig and Rosenstock-Huessy's work in navigating the religious, social, and political conflicts we now face.

WAYNE CRISTAUDO is the deputy head and an associate professor in the School of Modern Languages and Cultures at the University of Hong Kong.

WAYNE CRISTAUDO

Religion, Redemption, and Revolution

The New Speech Thinking of
Franz Rosenzweig and
Eugen Rosenstock-Huessy

UNIVERSITY OF TORONTO PRESS
Toronto   Buffalo   London

© University of Toronto Press 2012
Toronto Buffalo London
utorontopress.com

Reprinted in paperback 2022

ISBN 978-1-4426-4301-7 (cloth)
ISBN 978-1-4875-5482-8 (paper)

Publication cataloguing information is available from Library and Archives Canada.

We wish to acknowledge the land on which the University of Toronto Press operates. This land is the traditional territory of the Wendat, the Anishnaabeg, the Haudenosaunee, the Métis, and the Mississaugas of the Credit First Nation.

University of Toronto Press acknowledges the financial support of the Government of Canada, the Canada Council for the Arts, and the Ontario Arts Council, an agency of the Government of Ontario, for its publishing activities.

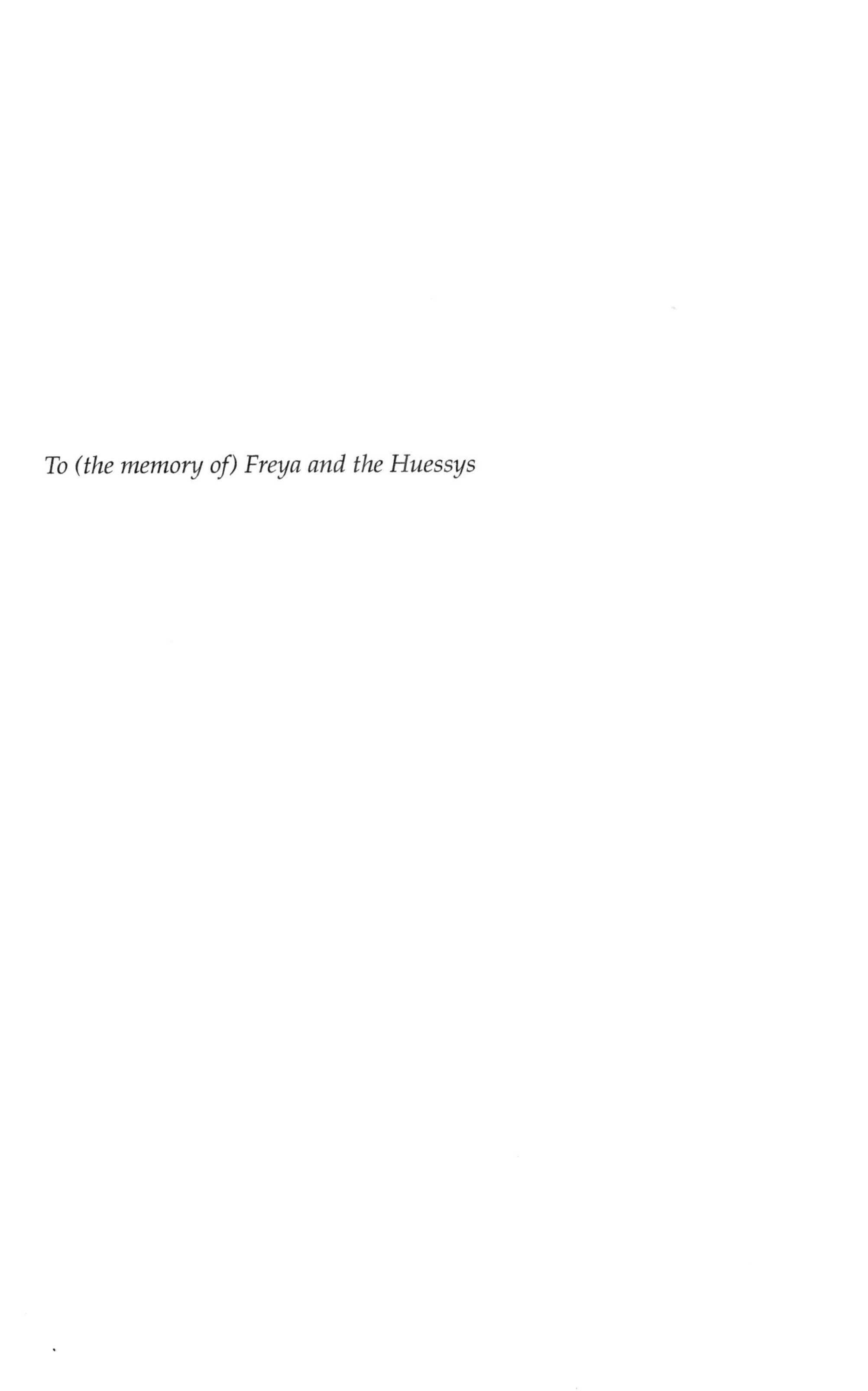

To (the memory of) Freya and the Huessys

We are the internal foe; don't mix us up with the external one! Our enmity may have to be bitterer than the enmity for the external foe, but all the same – we and you are within the same frontier, in the same Kingdom.

Rosenzweig to Rosenstock-Huessy, 7 November 1916,
Judaism Despite Christianity

I have here a thick volume of theological biographies . . . Franz Rosenzweig is included. So am I. But I'm not mentioned in his life and he isn't mentioned in mine. One can do that, I suppose. Life goes on more comfortably without the effort of the truth. But the senselessness of this volume is really astonishing. Franz and I overcame the division in faith. That, however, will only be conceded 50 years after my death.

Letter from Rosenstock-Huessy to
Freya von Moltke, January 1970

Contents

Preface   xi

Acknowledgments   xxxv

Introducing Rosenzweig and Rosenstock-Huessy and Their
'Common Life's Work'   3

1 Which Spirit to Serve? The Stirring of the Living
Loving God   34

2 The Basis of the New Speech Thinking   57

3 Grammatical Organons in Rosenstock-Huessy
and Rosenzweig   82

4 On God as an Indissoluble Name and an Indispensable
Pole of the Real   114

5 The Sundered and the Whole: Rosenzweig's Distinction between
Pagans and the Elect   137

6 Rosenstock-Huessy's Incarnatory Christianity   184

7 The Ages of the Church and Redemption through
Revolution   230

8 The Modern Humanistic Turn of the French Revolution in
Rosenstock-Huessy   255

x Contents

9 Beyond the Idol of the Nation, Part 1: Rosenstock-Huessy
in the Aftermath of the Great War 279

10 Beyond the Idol of the Nation, Part 2: Rosenzweig
on Hegel 292

11 Beyond the Idol of Art, Part 1: Rosenzweig and the Role of Art
in Redemption 310

12 Beyond the Idol of Art, Part 2: Rosenstock-Huessy and Art in
Service to Revolution 325

13 Beyond the Prophets of Modernity: Rosenstock-Huessy and
Rosenzweig on Nietzsche and Marx 370

14 Rosenzweig on Why Allah Is Not Yahweh, the Loving,
Revealing, Redeeming God 401

15 Rosenstock-Huessy on Islam, Confucianism, Taoism,
and Buddhism 416

Conclusion: Pagan, Jew, Christian – or, Three Lives
in One Love 455

Postscript 458

Notes 460

Bibliography 562

Index 577

Preface

This is the first book-length comparative study of the social thought of two friends and dialogical disputants, Eugen Rosenstock-Huessy and Franz Rosenzweig.[1] Both men believed they were launching a revolution in how we think. Rosenzweig called this revolution 'the new thinking'; both also referred to it as 'speech thinking' because it rested on the premise that speech, rather than reason or the mind, is the real basis of thinking. For both men, speech was primarily a creative, revelatory, and redemptive power, and not merely or essentially a descriptive one. Concomitantly, speech, for them, was not simply about cataloguing or itemizing the world as if it were 'all that is the case' – to use Wittgenstein's formulation from the *Tractatus*. And it was not only about how we respond to the world – as if it were solely some mere object in itself – but also about how we respond to, call upon, or command one another to make the future and to respond to the past. To emphasize how important responsiveness is as a condition of speech thinking, Rosenstock-Huessy urged that the *cogito ergo sum* of Descartes – which he believed had done so much damage with its mind/body dualism and its mechanistic picture of life – be replaced by the much more archaic *respondeo etsi mutabor* – 'I respond though I will be changed.'[2]

Our orientation through life is bound up with the powers of life that we respond to and hold most valuable, the powers we are ruled by, or – what is essentially the same thing – the powers we serve. Rosenstock-Huessy and Rosenzweig held that all people seek orientation throughout their lives and are thus responsive to powers greater than themselves. Those powers we serve are our divinities, and thus we are ever part of a triadic order of God(s), Man, and World. Both men demonstrate that despite various philosophical attempts to dissolve these three originary elements or poles of reality into one ground of existence, this triadic ordering of life's most fundamental sources is the most elemental condition of human orientation. In a climate where anti-foundationalism is widely held, one might also add that Rosenzweig and Rosenstock-Huessy *noticed* these triadic poles of appeals and eschewed metaphysics. For their part, anti-foundationalists criticize metaphysics but do not escape the need for appeal, and within their social analyses we encounter more often than not a hidden moral or ethical appeal, one that is predicated on the spectral presence of the self (albeit ostensibly utterly historicized and socialized) as well as on their continuity with the anthropological turn in Feuerbach, Marx, Nietzsche, and (notwithstanding his own later turn and radical ontology) the Heidegger of *Being and Time*.

To know someone's faith, we need merely observe what and whom they serve – that, too, illustrates the nature and source of an appeal. Friedrich Jacobi, a contemporary of Hamann and Hegel, argued more than a century earlier than Rosenzweig and Rosenstock-Huessy that faith is an existential condition and, it follows, not something with which philosophy can dispense.[3]

Given this book's title, a clarification needs to be made before we proceed further. Unlike Rosenstock-Huessy, Rosenzweig refused to use the word 'religion' in *The Star of Redemption* to describe either Judaism or Christianity. Even applying the word 'faith' to the relationship Rosenzweig depicts between Jew and Judaism is somewhat problematic: for him, the Jew is not a *believer* in something; rather, the Jew *is* something.[4] And in his essay 'The Jewish Person' he writes that 'we are the people of faith, and the people of doubt . . . There is, so to speak, no believing Jew, just as little as there is a disbelieving Jew.'[5] However, Rosenzweig's understanding of religion and of the *hiatuses and relationships* among Judaism, Christianity, and the pagan religions is a major theme of this book. Faith, then, in the sense I am using the term – a sense that accurately encompasses that relationship between human beings and their God(s), which Rosenzweig and Rosenstock-Huessy are concerned with – is a mode of orientation through life, a way of participating in life based on people's responsiveness to what provides ultimate orientation.

Faith in God(s) is part of the human condition, even for those people who think their own reasonableness is their 'God' and who do not realize the act of divinization in their own act of faith. In this regard,

Rosenzweig and Rosenstock-Huessy both argue that the Jewish and Christian faiths, whose God spoke existence into being and whose love held out the promise for the future redemption of the world, differ from other faiths in two closely related ways: they alone explicitly seek redemption, as opposed to joining with God or nirvana or some other end. And they do so, according to both men, because unlike other faiths, they take the word (and grammar) as the *organon* of the soul and society.

The development of the New Thinking, which took its keys and clues from grammar, had as its correlate a revival – and thus a new interpretation and appraisal – of Judaism and Christianity, whose respective meanings and importance had, according to both Rosenstock-Huessy and Rosenzweig, largely been lost sight of by modern men and women.

Rosenzweig's magnum opus *The Star of Redemption* remains one of the most important and widely hailed works of Jewish philosophical theology ever written. And while it had only a few readers during the Weimar years, they were generally good readers. Moreover, Rosenzweig's founding of the Jewish *Lehrhaus* (Adult Education Centre) in Frankfurt and his role in helping German liberal Jews find a way back to their faith helped him become one of the most important figures in German Jewry in the interwar years. While his philosophical reputation was always formidable, his non-Zionist vision of Judaism seemed to lose some of its relevance after the Holocaust, when for the majority of Jews, making Israel a homeland became a matter of the highest priority.[6] However, *The Star of Redemption* has found a growing readership again, in no small part due to the impact of Levinas, and the late Derrida's growing preoccupation with the messianic. In addition, the revival of theopolitics, largely brought about by the resurgence of Islam as a political and social force impacting on the West, has again made Rosenzweig's thought timely.[7] It should also be said that Rosenzweig has, over the years, also had an impact on Christian theology. The great Dutch theologian Kornelius Miskotte was deeply affected by *The Star* and even tried to persuade Karl Barth to read it.[8] Many Rosenzweig scholars, especially in Germany and the Netherlands, are Christian theologians.

Rosenstock-Huessy, by contrast, at least up until now has had very little impact on Christian theology. This is largely because, though much of what he says about Christianity is completely orthodox, everything he says about it flies in the face of a conviction widely held by Christians and non-Christians alike – that Christianity is a religion of transcendence, with a transcendent God and a transcendent end of the soul. For Rosenstock-Huessy, this view of Christianity is a combination of legend (which, he argues, is how most truths first express themselves), a 'childish' view of faith that takes literally those truths which – at least until we forge adequate names to express them conceptually – can only be conveyed metaphorically, and a surfeit of Greek theology and philosophy that through the ages has threatened to swallow up key components of the Christian faith and tradition. Moreover, just as Rosenzweig (as we will see more fully later) had argued that the modern member of the Christian nation is more interested in God supporting his or her own will, Rosenstock-Huessy is well aware just how many people in the modern world – and not only members of the Christian faith – are driven simply by the wish that some Other will provide the pleasures of life. Thus in a rather contemptuous aside in one of his undergraduate lectures, he says that

> the superstitious part of all the churches, all the religions, the idiots, consist of these 90 percent of the populace who have the idea that their prayers must be fulfilled. So they go to church . . . and ruin the real religion by saying that Jesus, or Buddha, or whoever it is, is just an automat for the fulfilling of their own wishes. So they just use these people as a means for aggrandizement of their own little private will.[9]

What is almost unique about Rosenstock-Huessy in modern explorations and appraisals of Christianity is that his emphasis revolves entirely around incarnation being its real meaning and achievement. In *The Christian Future* he summarized his position this way: 'Christianity is the embodiment of one single truth through the ages: that death precedes birth, that birth is the fruit of death, and that the soul is precisely this power of transforming an end into a beginning by obeying a new name.'[10] In addition, unlike so many theologians who want to save Christianity by bringing Christians back into the Church, Rosenstock-Huessy explicitly says that '"saving" Christianity is unnecessary, undesirable, impossible, because it is anti-Christian. Christianity says that he who tries to save his soul shall lose it. Our supreme need is not to save what we smugly presume to have, but to revive what we have almost lost.'[11] He also calls for a new form of Christianity, a Christianity of 'Hope.' He calls this new form of Christianity a 'listening Church, [which] will have to unburden the older modes of worship by assembling the faithful to live out their hopes through working and suffering together in unlabelled, undenominational groups, thereby [ready] to wait and listen for the in break of a new consolation which shall redeem modern life from its curse of disintegration and mechanization.'[12] In these respects it is not misleading to take up a term he used, the meaning of which should become apparent later, and say that Rosenstock-Huessy writes for a 'post-Christian Age.' It is precisely this shift in emphasis away from transcendence toward incarnation, and his reading of the Christian faith in the context of the post-Christian Age, that makes his appraisal and interpretation of Christianity so interesting and so timely.

Rosenstock-Huessy's impact on Christian theology has been almost negligible.[13] The same cannot be said about his indirect impact on Jewish theology, which, *incognito* and through Rosenzweig, he has affected significantly. In a letter to his cousin Rudi Ehrenberg, in which (it appears) he first wrote the sentence that would become the epicentre of his entire life – 'I am, after all, remaining a Jew'[14] – Rosenzweig reflected on the conversation he had had with Ehrenberg and Rosenstock-Huessy in Leipzig on the night of 7 July 1913. Rosenzweig declared that Rosenstock-Huessy 'messed up [not only] my whole of idea of Christianity, but also of religion as such and thereby also of my own religion.'[15] And he did not do this simply with an argument – though Rosenzweig seemed completely disarmed by Rosenstock-Huessy's contention that if in the midst of overwhelming suffering he were confronted with a disputant who could not see the point of his religious position, he would simply go into a Church and pray.

This simple gesture, as Wolfgang Ullmann astutely notes, was effectively the same riposte as Paul made in I Corinthians 1 to Hellenistic wisdom – it is a response that eschews any attempt to rationally justify one self to the other. And what to the believer is the most decisive act of faith is to the Greek mind an act of cultural folly and 'a [religious] scandal.' Rosenzweig indicates that prior to this conversation of 7 July, he had arrived at a position of objective historicism and spiritual relativism, based on 'social ideas, historical worldviews, nationalism, and the real conditions of labor' that he had developed earlier with his and Rudi's cousin, Hans Ehrenberg, in what they had called the Baden-Baden Program.[16] What struck Rosenzweig like a bolt of lightning was that this brilliant friend of his, who had been his university teacher, could defer to and find his sustenance in the Christian faith. He could do so because he *saw through* the philosophical consensuses of his age. Living in spiritual trust of a greater power than the mind,

Rosenstock-Huessy could bypass the truths of the present age and awaken Rosenzweig to a power that rang across the ages. Rosenzweig's reassessment of religion in general, and more specifically of Judaism and Christianity, had its inaugural moment on that night.

To be sure, Rosenzweig had already sensed the enormous sociological and historical importance of religious faith. To Hans Ehrenberg, in September 1910, he had spoken of his desire to liberate the twentieth-century power of belief from the religiosity of the nineteenth century, adding: 'We emphasize the practical, the fall [*Sündenfall*], history [and] we see God in every ethical occurrence, but not in the completed whole, in history . . . No, each act becomes sinful, when it enters into history . . . and therefore God must redeem man, not through history, but really . . . as God in religion.'[17] But as Ullmann has rightly argued, Rosenzweig saw religion in the context of a tragic and dualistic view of life stuck between the inhospitable understandings of history as being 'the eternal return of the same, or the Manichean battle between the empire of light and the empire of darkness.' And, again as Ullmann picks up, this fitted the early project he planned of writing a book to be titled *The Hero: A History of Tragic Individuality in Germany Since Lessing*. Recalling that evening in Leipzig, Rosenzweig himself would relate that he could have maintained his position had he dogmatically stuck with his metaphysical dualism of God and the devil, but 'the first sentence of the Bible' hindered him in doing so. That is to say, he simply could not accept that creation was intrinsically bad – God had created the heavens and the earth, and as Genesis continues, God saw that His creation was good.

Rosenstock-Huessy's proposed gesture of prayer was that of a man with faith. His faith stood in close relationship to his medieval studies of history and law, which had demonstrated to him that not all history was formed in the Greek template. Rather, it had been shaped by many collective acts of faith, and the laws of peoples all reflected the various faiths embedded in their speech acts. As Ullmann has noted in speaking of Rosenstock-Huessy's early writings on constitutional law, they had 'generalized Savigny's 1812 thoughts on a grammar of law, emphasizing the consciousness-forming power of law and speech.' The following formulation, provided in 1943, neatly encapsulates what would be the guiding maxim of all of Rosenstock-Huessy's historical studies: 'Language is the vehicle on which history invades the animal life of man. And the study of history and the study of language are one and the same study.'[18]

What Rosenzweig took away from the conversation of that July night would, as I have said, lead him to put his faith in that of his forefathers, now understanding it as if for the first time. Rosenstock-Huessy's anti-Greek gesture showed Rosenzweig how rooted he was in Israel. It also seems that on that night, an important role was played by the Letter to the Hebrews – the epistle on which Rudi Ehrenberg was then writing an interpretation and to which Rosenzweig had referred him. Rosenzweig says that 'he had post-dated the Epistle to the Hebrews, not exactly for 18 centuries, but for centuries, and thus had engrafted the Epistle to the Hebrews onto the living branch of Judaism in the 20th century.' Ullmann's summary of its significance provides an excellent account of what was happening:

> From this letter it emerges that Rosenzweig projected Paul's parable of the olive tree from Romans 11 onto the Epistle of the Hebrews as a whole. Just as the Christians are rooted in Israel, so is Rosenstock's Christianity of the Epistle of the Hebrews rooted in the contemporary life of Israel. I believe Rosenzweig wants to say the following: Where Paul teaches a unity of Jews and heroes, with Christ as purpose of the whole growth of the olive tree in mind, the Epistle to the Hebrews induces us to see in the act of incarnation, which happened in Abraham's offspring, the embodiment of what is indissoluble in humankind. Hebrews 10, 25, which was interpreted by Rudolf Ehrenberg, then becomes a warning not to abandon the synagogue of humanity donated by Christ. Because in light of the eschaton such abandonment must have catastrophic consequences for individuals and humanity as a whole.
>
> This makes the Leipzig conversation an event in the history of religion. He, who in the full indulgence of an idealist inheritance and who was convinced in an unbreakable faith in philosophy to have adopted a position of tragic classicist religiosity beyond Judaism and Christianity, comes up against a Judeo-Christianity which not only points to an end to Christian assimilation of Renaissance humanism, but also a type of scholarly work which has opened up new land. That new land lies far beyond what was known to university-trained minds whose thoughts were formed by theologians and philosophers from the 12th century.[19]

Ullmann's essay makes the important point that whereas Rosenstock-Huessy and Ehrenberg were able to convince Rosenzweig of the value of the Christian scandal, Rosenzweig took an even more scandalous and absurd position by making Judaism the greatest scandal of the post-Hellenic world of the twentieth century. Noting that the Christians teach that none come to the Father but through Christ, Rosenzweig responded that the Jew is already with the Father and therefore has no need of Christ to reach the Father. Thus did Rosenzweig take the *great turn of remaining* a Jew, thereby ensuring that the position of the Jew vis-à-vis the *eschaton* must ever remain fundamentally different from that of the Christian.

Rosenzweig's decision to 'remain a Jew' would completely transform how Rosenstock-Huessy himself thought. The event is a remarkable example of speech thinking, of a dialogue completely transforming the lives of the participants in ways previously unimagined. It would lead to what is perhaps the greatest Jewish–Christian dialogue ever undertaken – the correspondence between Rosenzweig and Rosenstock-Huessy in 1916. That dialogue, combined with Rosenstock-Huessy's painful acceptance of the passionate relationship that developed between Rosenstock-Huessy's wife Gritli and Rosenzweig,[20] inspired Rosenzweig to write *The Star of Redemption*. Less well known is that it would be the most important spur to Rosenstock-Huessy's own life's work. But all of this suggests that speech opens us up to the *incalculable*, and God's ways are incalculable. That is why both Rosenzweig and Rosenstock-Huessy eschewed all the variants of Greek and modern thinking, which emphasize planning, predictability, routines – all of these, from the perspective of Rosenzweig and Rosenstock-Huessy, synonyms for graceless living when they become substitutions for life.

Like Rosenzweig, Rosenstock-Huessy was born into a 'liberal' Jewish household. But whereas Rosenzweig's mother openly resisted Rosenzweig's decision to become a Christian,[21] Rosenstock-Huessy entered the Christian Church without parental struggle. As he would state in his autobiographical reflections, his decision to become a Christian stood in the closest relationship to his interest in speech as a vital power. Moreover, because of his early insight that speech is fundamentally incarnatory, he believed that the Nicene Creed was simply true.[22] Rosenstock-Huessy spent the greater part of his life trying to show the truth of Christianity's power. His answer to the question, 'What is the potency and truth of Christianity?' (like Goethe and Nietzsche, Rosenstock-Huessy equated potency and truth)[23] is, I think, one of the most interesting and arresting explorations of the roots of Western culture ever undertaken. He draws an arc that reaches from Christianity – which he argues was a solution to a crisis of ancient forms of social existence – to the great revolutions of the past millennium. He further argues that the great revolutions – even the atheistic revolutions, such as the Russian and the French – were all eschatological and hence informed by the universalistic messianic faith, hope, and love that are the inner truth and dynamism of Christianity. Furthermore, the Western revolutions have, in their sequence and cumulative effect, compelled us to become neighbours on a shrinking planet. The two world wars were, for him, the irrefutable confirmation of this, just as they were, for him, a confirmation of the failure of modern humanism, as well as of the need for Western men and women to forget the widespread 'nonsense' (his view of it) that they thought they knew about the Church and Christian faith and to re-envision that faith as the creative and messianic force he argued it was.

The personal relationship between Rosenzweig and Rosenstock-Huessy and the 1916 correspondence between them about Christianity and Judaism have been addressed in various chapters and articles; yet no previous book and very few articles have explored their thought as part of a common project. Given how many studies on Rosenzweig proceed by way of comparing him to someone else,[24] this is somewhat surprising, especially since – even by Rosenzweig's oft-cited account – no one else influenced him as much as Rosenstock-Huessy. Just as important, no one ever responded more profoundly to Rosenzweig's most important ideas than Eugen Rosenstock-Huessy. Indeed, I will argue that Rosenstock-Huessy's argument about Christianity and revolution is the most important complement to Rosenzweig's thinking that has ever been written. That Rosenstock-Huessy uses a citation from Rosenzweig, from their 1916 correspondence, as the frontispiece to his German study of revolutions, *Die europäischen Revolutionen und der Charakter der Nationen*, is a clear signal to his readers that his examination of the European revolutions closely reflected the dialogical method that Rosenzweig had mapped out with him.[25]

While many studies have been done on Rosenzweig and the New Thinking, what exactly is *new* in his thinking is often – perhaps invariably – overlooked precisely because few studies have taken seriously Rosenzweig's claim that *The Star of Redemption* was part of a project that was bigger than Rosenzweig himself. The large number of comparative studies on Rosenzweig and *others* suggests an intuitive grasp of what is meant by 'New Thinking.' But the approach taken in most of these comparative works, as in books devoted to him alone, is far more often ensconced in a paradigm that has evolved since the Second World War and that has been embraced by social theorists and academicians in the humanities and social sciences. This paradigm – these consensuses – have been given their current shape by a generation that was radicalized in the 1960s and 1970s by the widespread injustices it perceived. Those injustices – consequences of the persistence of capitalism, colonialism, racial and sexual inequality, and so on – were for that generation an indication that fascism had not ended with the Second World War and that its vestiges were manifesting themselves in a range of social areas – especially those involving class, race, gender, and ethnicity.

It would take us too far afield to examine all of that paradigm's contradictions and nuances or to explore it through the various social theorists who have contributed to its formation.[26] Here I simply wish to identify how the New Thinking differs from what are fairly widely held beliefs that arise from the desire to identify and eliminate lingering forms of fascism in the West. In drawing attention to these differences, the key point I wish to make is that the New Thinking is not another conservative attack on what can very broadly be referred to as radical liberal social thought; rather, its emphases and preoccupations point to a very different kind of thinking. Moreover, its differences are especially useful for dealing with issues that do not easily fall within the ensemble of problems that the 'radical liberal paradigm' was designed to solve.

First, and perhaps most important, the New Thinking centres on love: on the commandments to love God and one's neighbour. How that love is achieved is unspecified. But that love is the most important of life's powers: everything is based on the inherent truth of revelation and on the power that makes redemption possible. Generally speaking, the dominant radical liberal paradigm is concerned with ensuring fair and more equal power relations. John Rawls's *A Theory of Justice*, though not always welcomed by those with more radical agendas because it is not radical enough, made liberties, wealth, and rights (which he extends to mean entitlements and opportunity to hold desirable forms of office) the basis of the good life. (This was, said Rawls, a thin concept of the good, for it is up to people themselves to decide what is their good.) None of the New Thinkers are concerned in any fundamental way with those things. Rawls's work was essentially a politically motivated distributive project whose goal was to create a more just society. That such a society could be selfish and loveless and futureless and spiritually dead was not a concern for Rawls.[27] Indeed, Rawls, who was much more consistently liberal than many other more communitarian-minded radical liberals (such as Rawls's old sparring partner, Michael Walzer), had to pointedly emphasize the priority of the right over the good and the undesirability of various Aristotelian efforts to depict a good community. While not all radical liberals saw themselves as Rawlsians, they did share with him a fundamental concern about social inequalities and the desirability of political and social intervention.[28]

Second, the New Thinking is not just not primarily political, it is also not primarily ethical. It is concerned with love as the power of powers, and it looks to specific acts of love as sources of salvation. In keeping with this, it emphasizes responsiveness and dialogue; it validates a range of human qualities that find little or no room in the radical liberal paradigm – weakness, uncertainty, unpredictability, unintended outcomes, catastrophe, providence – and ultimately it reaches for a theological vocabulary because no other vocabulary captures quite so precisely the conundrums of the human condition or the best solutions for them. It places less weight on the power of conscious intention and individual action (prior to post-structuralism, Rosenzweig was often mistaken for an existentialist, but his project is thoroughly social – though that does not make him a post-structuralist either).[29] It places greater weight on the vast array of historical processes that make up our past and on the role of providence in realizing our divinely promised future. Its interest in salvation is collective, but it has no faith in collective political bodies such as the nation or the state or even, more loosely, 'the people' in the political sense of that term. The New Thinking emphasizes unintended consequences, incalculability and miracles, and the importance of membership in communities that are open to God's love and miracles.

By contrast, the dominant radical liberal paradigm wants to immediately change social behaviours and is open to new forms of collective action; but by and large, it tends to take powers such as capitalism, the state, class, gender, and ethnic or racial identity as determinative, albeit also as plastic enough to be transformed by radical social action. It is not always clear within the paradigm how important morality is; until the de Man and Heidegger scandals, for example, French social theory was – and not without cause – often accused of nihilism.[30] Note, though, that since these scandals, the paradigm has trended toward the more overtly ethical. Evidence of this is how Levinas has been plucked from relative philosophical obscurity (outside of France, at least) and assigned the role of a 'supplement' to the radical liberal paradigm, even though his Jewish theology does not always easily accommodate itself to that role. Increasingly, the dominant paradigm has found itself deployed in all sorts of ways that push more and more in the direction of demands for moral purity (by contrast, Rosenstock-Huessy would simply describe himself as an 'impure thinker') and the importance of establishing one's own political position as credible and one's opponents as discreditable. This explains the transformation in academic literary studies over the past two decades or so, so that today's 'critic' is interested mainly in exposing the 'power politics' of a text. This explains, too, the proliferation of laws relating to discriminatory or socially unfair actions or behaviours (sexual harassment, hate speech, etc.); to the steps being taken to forbid names that would make people feel uncomfortable; and to other steps to ensure that students do not read material that is racist, or sexist, or similar. Yet it is hardly surprising that the radical liberal paradigm has not prevented modern societies from becoming increasingly litigious, or that perceived social injustices must be rectified through legislative channels.[31] That resort to the state is quite contrary to the original character and emphases of some of the paradigm's more important theoreticians (e.g., Althusser and Foucault) indicates that contradictions inevitably arise within any social theory when it becomes politically applied.

That Rosenstock-Huessy and Rosenzweig identified more with church and synagogue, respectively, tells us where their differences of emphasis lay. Both were more interested in the deeper 'cultural' bonds among peoples and in the much more patient labour that must take place over many generations so that it will be possible for peoples with deeply conflicting sources of the sacred and the self to be able to inhabit the one social time.

One further difference should be mentioned, and that is the difference between a paradigm that emphasizes suffering and one that emphasizes oppression. It may seem small, but it opens up a world of difference. The dominant liberal paradigm emphasizes oppressor and oppressed, even if oppression is structural rather than personal. Those who advocate for the oppressed do not need to be themselves oppressed. One can be a spokesperson for the oppressed if one can deal with oppression abstractly, which is why university departments are full of people driven to protect the oppressed who do not share many or even any of the experiences of those groups on whose behalf they speak.[32] I do not deny that such speaking can sensitize a community to various evils or injustices. But to come from a position of suffering is something else altogether. It is to come with a soul that has been shaped in a certain way, hammered and bent, scorched and violated, possibly broken, possibly stronger and even, sometimes, paradoxically, more beautiful. In response to violation, the self may shut down its conscious mind so that it can cope; or it may dwell upon avenging the pain; or it may, as I have just suggested, become full of compassion and take its pain as instruction in the wisdom of the world. Souls, however, don't respond to suffering in this last manner simply because they have been told it is good to do so. Souls are strange and unpredictable. They *may* respond to love, but unfortunately, not always, especially if they have been broken too early. Even God cannot make a soul love Him.

The New Thinking emphasizes human suffering and the common plight of sufferers. When Hans Ehrenberg wrote in *Autobiography of a German Pastor* that 'I was a member of a nation defeated in war and which passed through two revolutions in my lifetime . . . Some of us have faced the Beast from the Abyss; we have been in hell and come out again. We bear the scars and the wounds of the conflict in our minds and on our bodies. That is why there are differences between you and us,'[33] he was providing an important clue to the New Thinking. So was Rosenstock-Huessy when he wrote of *Out of Revolution*:

> The idea of this book originated in an experience we went through in the trenches: that war was one thing to the soldiers of all nations and another thing to the people at home. The attempt to found a new future for the united soldiers of Europe, that is, for its manhood, on the common experience of the World War can only be successful if this generation that was killed, wounded, weakened, decimated by the War can bequeath a lasting memory of its experience to its children. Scholars cannot demobilize until the World War has reformed their method and their purpose in writing history.
>
> I, at least, shall not demobilize until I have made my contribution to that common enterprise of humanity.
>
> The plan of writing the book in this particular way was conceived in 1917, on the Battlefield of Verdun.[34]

What I am suggesting would seem to contradict Rosenzweig himself, who in October 1916 wrote to Hans Ehrenberg in an oft-cited letter that he had experienced so much in 1913 that the world would have to perish for the events of 1914 to have an impact on him.[35] But this letter was written before Rosenzweig revealed how shattered he was by Germany's defeat. Moreover, it was in the face of that defeat that Rosenzweig realized that Germany looked like it was about to become deeply anti-Semitic. As I discuss at length in the chapter on Rosenzweig and Hegel, the combination of his faith, the war, and Germany's defeat had slammed shut the door for Rosenzweig on any of the options that tempted so many of his contemporary Germans to find salvation through politics.

Furthermore – and this is essential for everything in this book – the New Thinking arose from a particular moment and was a highly specific and particular response to what we can call, without exaggeration, the singular catastrophe of the last century. Indeed, the political tensions that have developed from the military and geopolitical breakdown of Western European imperialism, the hegemonic militaristic and economic role of the United States, the continuing struggles of the Russian Empire, the ongoing fallout of the break-up of the Ottoman Empire, the as yet unfilled void and chaos left in much of Africa by Europe's withdrawal and flight from its colonies, and the reconfiguration of China's imperial character in the modern world are all part of a very long wave.[36] The New Thinkers were completely disillusioned by the humanist faith that had driven their contemporaries into the Great War. Furthermore, though far from gleeful about Germany's defeat, they did not wallow in the rancour and bitterness that would spur so many of their contemporaries into fascism and yet another war. Indeed, being among the defeated and deciding not to carry on a futile fight provided the New Thinkers with a useful vantage point that the victors did not have (or rarely had unless traumatized by guilt) – that is, the capacity to examine their own part in the catastrophe. Moreover, the fact that they had been educated at universities in Germany and were steeped in German philosophy contributed to an approach to thinking through the great questions of past and future that retained an eschatological dimension. It also instilled in them a certain desire to achieve completeness.

I am suggesting, then, that much of the difference between the paradigms is explicable in terms of their positionings with respect to the catastrophe that spanned the two world wars and their aftermaths. The radical liberal paradigm was created in the penumbra of the Holocaust, by a generation that had to deal with the guilt, of either their parents being complicit in it (as in much of Europe), or of their parents being involved in colonial acts of war or annihilation (e.g., the atomic bomb). In the United States, the Vietnam War, the legacy of slavery, and treatment of Native Americans that at times verged on the genocidal made it hard to escape the conclusion that the Second World War had hardly solved the problems plaguing humankind. Indeed, both in Europe and in America it was difficult for any young person with an education, a conscience, and a soul not to feel that stopping at Nazism was a convenient delusion. The brutalities of the postwar world were real enough; and whatever was said by conservative and more moderate liberal critics, the radical liberal paradigm was and remains an expression of genuine solidarity and hope.

The New Thinking, by contrast, was developed by people who had been in the First World War and who had a horrible and accurate *presentiment* that terrible forces were swelling in Germany that had to be stopped. *The Star of Redemption* and a number of Rosenstock-Huessy's works were written to prevent what was to become Germany's most terrible act, an act that would cause the great trauma that would in turn shape the West's social and political vision for most of the rest of the century.

In the nineteenth century, Dostoevsky wrote that 'we are all responsible for all.' And the corollary of this is that we are all guilty. When Dostoevsky expressed this he was enunciating a Christian principle that he hoped would save Russia. But he had just as surely given the formulation of how we are all shaped by unintended consequences, and how catastrophic evil comes from not seeing what we are doing as we each seek our own ends at the expense of others. That formulation was not completely inaudible to the radicalized youth of the 1960s and 1970s, and thus the structuralist and post-structuralist or deconstructionist strategies disclose how easy it is to be complicit in fascism. In the aftermath of fascism, it was possible to focus on who was directly responsible for the Holocaust, and the answer was easy enough – the fascists were. But the Holocaust also grew out of the failure to properly resolve the First World War. It grew out of the failure of the victors to realize that by making the Germans the exclusive bearers of the guilt for the Great War, by not conceding the ubiquity of guilt in that catastrophe, they were unintentionally – albeit no less directly for that – contributing to the conditions that would spawn fascism. The children whose parents fought in the Second World War generally knew very little about the First World War. This lack of knowledge has been fateful in shaping the radical liberal paradigm and has played no small role in its faith that if it can track down and expunge the vestiges and privileged sources of fascism, be they the wealthy, white people, men, heterosexuals, or Anglo-Saxons – social evil will be eliminated. In this respect, that same paradigm continues in the tracks of Rousseau and Marx, who were convinced that once the source of social conflict – for them, private property – was eliminated, humanity could live in peace. Conversely, an eye that has been shaped by an understanding of the forces that created and moved beyond the First World War is capable of realizing that the powers of catastrophe are much more complicated and ubiquitous, that they are formed over long spans of time, and that they can only be dealt with over a protracted period of time.

Finally, while the radical liberal paradigm often drew on Marx, it was always liberal. Its orientation was always shaped by the importance of equality and social freedoms (thus, while some briefly fantasized about Mao, the paradigm was never Stalinist). Though I do not dwell in this book on the instances where Rosenstock-Huessy's analysis of revolutions fits into the radical liberal paradigm, I think, after reading the chapters dealing with the French and Russian revolutions (the latter I mainly discuss in the context of art), one will better see how deeply informed the paradigm is by the messianic impulse of both those revolutions. Again, though he is not a New Thinker, Derrida's late writings on hospitality, friendship, and the messianic move beyond the radical liberal paradigm into areas contiguous to the New Thinking. Derrida would even write an essay in which Rosenzweig figures[37] along with Hermann Cohen and Kant, which explores the theme of German–Greek–Jew. Derrida, for all his interest in Jewish tropes, would always remain too 'Greek' to really enter into the same realism as those of the New Thinking.

The liberal character of the contemporary paradigm is what now forces us to consider its limits – which is not the same as saying that its legacy is completely finished or that it won't continue to adjust and adapt and be transformed. What most threatens this paradigm today is the ongoing fallout of the great catastrophes that antedate the paradigm and that cannot be comprehended by resorting to its favoured categories. And those categories are most visible in the revival of Islam as a political power – a power, moreover, that is largely unresponsive to the ethical and moral aspects of the radical liberal paradigm: neither women's rights, nor gay rights, nor ethnic rights concern it.

Generally, Islam seemed a complete irrelevancy after the First and Second World Wars. Few social theorists showed any interest it,[38] which was perhaps why it surprised many that Michel Foucault rushed to Iran to sing the praises of the revolution and – to the constant embarrassment of his disciples today – touted it as a kind of prelude to modern utopian politics, before sense took hold of him again. He ended his days more a radical liberal than a revolutionary; he even publicly bullied those who dared express their fears and concerns about the direction of the Iranian Revolution.[39] But even if the real reasons why the Islamic Revolution was so important escaped him, and had nothing to do with his radical democratic and Sorelian view of politics, it is to his credit that he sensed the enormous importance of the convulsions in Iran. Since the Rushdie affair, 9/11, and recent bombings in Europe, Islam has been forcing itself into the consciousness of Western intellectuals, and there is a small industry of writers who argue that Islamism is not steeped in traditional Islam at all, but is a reaction to modernity.[40] I agree that Islam reacts to modernity, but we cannot overlook the traditional points of disputation and difference between societies and people that have been swept up in the tides of the Christian and secular revolutions and those that were far more stable in their social relationships over long spans of time. If we fail to take seriously the widespread commitment to a theocratic state, if we fail to understand what such a state means and to appreciate the social stability it offers (e.g., through *sharia* law), and if we fail to understand the importance of the hierarchical relationship between the sexes in Islamic societies, we will end up doing precisely what George Bush and Tony Blair did when they overthrew Saddam Hussein and immediately set out to establish liberal democracy in Iraq. That is, we will simply be projecting liberal values onto Islam. And in doing so, we will be overlooking what Rosenstock-Huessy argued made the West so distinctive – that is, its revolutions and their subsequent global spread. The outgrowths of those revolutions, such as the nation-state, international commerce, and the world wars, are forcing us to become global neighbours, which, in Rosenstock-Huessy's time-driven social thought, means that 'distemporaries' are becoming contemporaries. But what precisely is the task before us, and how are we to achieve it?

It is one thing to emphasize the need for dialogue between the West and Islam, and in so doing to acknowledge the large number of peaceful Muslims living in the West. This gives hope that the task can be accomplished. But it is another thing to assume that the traditional directives and social roots of Islam, which are precisely what Islamists appeal to, can immediately and neatly be grafted onto the West – or vice versa. This is yet another example of the difference between a kind of thinking whose idealism is visible in the assumption that thought itself is the biggest obstacle to social change and the New

Thinking, which sees the flesh as the consequence of generations of labour of the word.

To summarize, the West today is confronted with the momentousness of Islam's political presence and the belated need to make sense of it. Moreover, Islam has forced the West to consider its religious roots in ways that very few social theorists twenty years ago ever thought would need to be done. This is forcing thoughtful people in the West to think in far greater spans of time than the post–Second World War generation has been accustomed to. It also means that we cannot engage with the theopolitical problems confronting us by taking concepts forged mainly out of the ideologies that originated in the French and Russian revolutions and that dominated so much of the twentieth century. As I argue later, the great virtue of Rosenstock-Huessy's social thinking is that he ascribes so much importance to taking 'social time' seriously, and thus compels us to question how we relate to 'distemporaries' if we seek to become 'contemporaries.'

Because Rosenzweig and Rosenstock-Huessy always thought of politics in terms of theopolitics, and because they took faith seriously as a primary geopolitical force, they were always aware of Islam as a geo- and theo-political presence. Both had fought in a war at a time when the Ottoman Empire still existed. When the Ottoman Empire was in its final convulsions, Rosenzweig would write:

The contradictions will now be played out and they remain:

Judaism and Christianity
Judaism and Islam
Church and People.

In the coming millennium the surface of world history will be the battle between the West and the East, Church and Islam, Germans and Arabs. Fundamentally the world will remain one.[41]

These are remarkably prophetic words, especially if we take the reference to Germans and Arabs as sequential – that is, as adumbrating the Second World War and the role of the Middle East in the postwar period. Few of Rosenzweig's contemporary Western social thinkers were envisaging any such future battles; almost all his contemporaries thought that future conflicts would have to be viewed through much more modern notions, such as classes, races, or nations. The legacy of this has been the overwhelming predominance of class, race, gender, and ethnicity in radical liberal social theory, and the complete and utter unwillingness – until the most recent of times – to take Islam seriously as a way of world making, let alone to seriously explore the roles that Christianity and Judaism have played in shaping today's world. Inevitably, the belated need to adopt a post-Holocaust ethics and the rise of theopolitics have combined to reawaken social theorists to theology's importance.[42]

I place so much weight on Islam in this work in part because the respective analyses of it by Rosenzweig and Rosenstock-Huessy deserve serious consideration. In general, Rosenzweig's critique of Islam has been all too swiftly dismissed without being given a proper hearing by people who suspect that this is Rosenzweig's residual fascism. The radical liberal paradigm does tend to think that we are all capable of fascism – and we are. But not at every stage in our life, and in any case, fascism is but one of evil's modes. I see nothing in Rosenzweig, after his 'conversion,' that ever led him to deviate from the centrality of the commandments to love God and one's neighbour. And it must be said that he was deeply conservative in his political instincts and that he could, it seems, be quite fanatical in his private dealings (see, in the next chapter, Gritli Huessy's observation about Rosenzweig's treatment of his wife). Moreover, he emphatically did not share the radical liberal faith in democratic politics, believing – and rightly so – that the collapse of the German Empire would fan the flames of anti-Semitism.[43]

Let us now summarize this rather long but still sketchy preamble, which will entail a detour into the differences between the New Thinking and the radical liberal paradigm. This book takes seriously and wishes to explore in depth some concepts that fly directly in the face of some truths of the radical liberal paradigm. Let us also add immediately, that one cannot simply assume that because Rosenzweig and Rosenstock-Huessy differ from certain political consensuses of the paradigm, they must be guilty of conservative moves and positions of the kind that the radical liberal paradigm has sought to expunge.

In particular, let us pause on two 'scandalous' ideas held by Rosenzweig and Rosenstock-Huessy respectively, which are central to this book. The first is that the Jewish people are God's elect. That anyone can be God's elect is surely a recipe for fascism. Yet perversely – and I like to think of the New Thinking as an array of perversities of liberal and conservative positions – in Rosenzweig it is not. The radical liberal paradigm tends to emphasize the emancipatory importance of difference, but not difference that might not fit its liberal framings. And there is nothing liberal about 'divine election.' But if the radical liberal paradigm is correct, then Jews should drop the central belief in their chosen status and be ready to serve equally any other God. Indeed, the radical liberal paradigm contributes to the destruction of the differences that Rosenzweig rose up to defend for Jews. It does this because it has no sense of the demonic – it sees identities where there are explosive differences that can create hellish futures. Despite the pronouncements of post-structuralist thinkers such as Derrida, Lyotard, and Deleuze – all of whom emphasized singularities and shades of difference that supposedly made all the difference – it fails to grasp that the Nazis took the Jewish concept of election and transposed this concept into a world view of hatred and power politics. It had to kill the very truth that it had 'stolen' and deformed, the faith in God's love at the centre of the meaning of divine election, which in its hands became the 'master race.' The living, loving God of the Jews prohibited all 'the values' that ultimately explain why Nazism was a gigantic death wish grounded in idolatry, as was evident even in its insignia.

The second scandal is Rosenstock-Huessy's emphasis on a 'universal history.' Even more scandalous, it is a reading of history that privileges Christ and the Church. Rosenzweig, at least, had his attack on totality, which manages to make him compatible with the general pluralistic ethos of the radical liberal paradigm, provided his reliance on election is not let out of the bag. But Rosenstock-Huessy's view of history is so sweeping and out of fashion that I know my work is cut out for me. (Though strangely enough, Marx has managed to stay in good enough grace and – as I think will be evident later – compared to Rosenstock-Huessy, his reading of history is almost cartoon-like in its lack of detail.) But to the swift dismissal of any such thing as a universal history, I can only respond that the arguments in its favour stretch from the recent crisis in the global financial system, to Islam as a major political issue in Europe, to two world wars, with the most unnerving thought that all of these things are part of an unfinished process that may still lead to further massive calamities – more international terrorism, supranational and imperial trading, political commercial bodies that operate in a world that is technologically linked despite all the massive differences within it (all intrinsic to Rosenstock-Huessy's view of history). I can only urge my readers to consider what is being said by Rosenzweig and Rosenstock-Huessy and to put their objections on hold until the case has been entirely heard. Excessive moral zeal does few of us any good. And the arguments we explore here ultimately require thinking more about *everybody's* complicity and shame, thinking beyond blame logic, and looking more closely at unintended consequences – that is, not even trusting the morally good, and not thinking that social and political interventions are the most important acts we can undertake, and instead thinking in terms of long processes that are shaped by creative acts of love.

The paradox of the New Thinking is that it rests on old faiths. And the fact that Eugen Rosenstock-Huessy and Franz Rosenzweig came to those faiths after having been born into liberal Jewish families is very important. One aim of this book is to explain why their respective revivals of Christianity and Judaism are of such social theoretical importance – why, that is, despite the revival of old faiths, Rosenzweig and Rosenstock-Huessy's thinking through these traditions was considered 'new.' This will, in turn, require clarifying why two brilliant young men steeped in the tradition of Goethe and Nietzsche decided that the humanist and secularist direction of philosophy culminating in Nietzsche was unsustainable.

Toward the end of his life, in his abrasive 'Prologue/Epilogue' to the 1916 correspondence that took place with Rosenzweig, fittingly titled (by Rosenstock-Huessy) *Judaism Despite Christianity*, Rosenstock-Huessy declares that the 'real event' of the letters was the shared perception/conviction 'that the "objectivity" swindle – swindle is perhaps too kind a word, since it implies that the culprits at least know what they are doing – was seen in its murderous impact upon the Western World.'[44] What, he continues, united the Jew and the Christian was the havoc caused by their common enemy, 'the self-styled "humanists" of all descriptions and dispensations.' The 'idols' served are, according to Rosenstock-Huessy, 'relativism (in which not even Einstein believed), "objectivity" (largely spurious at best), [and] abstract and nameless statistics.'[45] For Rosenstock-Huessy, 'objectivity' and relativism are two sides of the same modern coin, forged in the humanist spirit according to which the God pole of reality has become meaningless. Insisting on its discovery of the truth (the truth of the all is one [Spinoza] or of the all rests on the I's self-certainty [Descartes]), modern philosophy's point of departure has been to lock in a shrunken understanding of the spirit. Modernity is a great contradiction, consisting on the one hand of the unprecedented technological and administrative harnessing of corporeal powers and on the other hand of a plethora of souls in disintegration, the weakened personalities of men and women who are 'no longer [being] certain of the sources of integrity.'[46]

Rosenzweig had expressed himself in somewhat similar terms when he wrote to Rudolf Hallo in 1923 that 'the important point "today" is that European culture itself is threatened with collapse and it can only be saved by supra-European, superhuman powers.'[47] Judaism, he noted, 'is one of those powers.'[48] The battle that Rosenzweig and Rosenstock-Huessy were fighting as a Jew and a Christian respectively was against humanism's naturalistic view of the world.

Both Rosenzweig and Rosenstock-Huessy believed that the major weakness of secular humanism was that it failed to grasp the real historical, cultural, social, and existential meaning of Judaism and Christianity. In a letter to Rosenstock-Huessy on 9 September 1918, Rosenzweig had said that the difference between the *geistig* (in English, 'spiritual,' leaning heavily toward the mental or intellectual, as in Hegel's use of *Geist*) and the *geistlich* ('spiritual' in the sense of sacred) was 'our only theme.'[49] He continued: 'Why else are we so infuriated by Hegel? Merely that he doesn't know this distinction. The classification of religion as a branch [of mind/*Geist*] actually comes from him. That's exactly what you taught me.'[50] The source of that distinction was a 1916 essay by Rosenstock-Huessy, 'Die beiden Reiche der Kultur' (Both Realms of Culture), which was included in his book of 1920, *Die Hochzeit des Kriegs und der Revolution* (The Wedding of War and Revolution).[51] In that essay Rosenstock-Huessy had argued that the moderns had elevated the standing of the intellectual spirit (*den Rang des Geistigen*) at the expense of the soul and the sacred spirit. In so doing they had threatened to asphyxiate the freedom of the soul, thereby ruining the inspired power that had ruled the world until modern times. 'The spirit of the intellect [Geist],' he had argued, 'has actually wanted to make even "religion" a mere subdivision of mind/spirit [*Geist*].' His penultimate sentence summed up well the thrust of his argument: 'The entire philosophy of religion and comparison of religion directly strived after that to destroy the ecclesiastical, spiritual love of freedom through the law of mind/spirit.'[52]

If Rosenzweig summarized what he and Rosenstock-Huessy were doing in terms of this 'paltry' linguistic difference,[53] I am tempted to say that this book is a commentary on that distinction. For in it I hope to underscore what Rosenzweig and Rosenstock-Huessy saw as more fecund and powerful in the old faiths of Judaism and Christianity than in the new faith in abstract freedom and equality.

Here let it suffice that both saw that, though the pioneers of the modern scientific, social, and political revolutions had promised to enhance the powers of men and women and bring them into a great new future, the moderns had lost their moorings, because in the main, they did not grasp the differences between the powers that had been discovered and activated by pagan, Jewish, and Christian ways of self- and world-making. Hence the moderns failed to comprehend not only the great tributaries of history – and hence some of the most important and vital components of the modern revolutions themselves – but also how we have come to be who we are, and hence how we may become whom we can be.

Both men's sensitivity to the collective soul-making forces of Judaism and Christianity and Islam was formed in the turbulence of what Nietzsche had termed the shadow of God's death. Nietzsche had seen that Christianity had left in its wake a large array of 'values,' most notably the values of faith in truth as an emancipatory power, and faith in social equality, which he saw as streaming through a range of social and political movements such as feminism, liberal democracy, socialism, and anarchism. Nietzsche thought that these values would die along with the God who gave them birth. And though Nietzsche had spoken many times of how things turned into their opposites, perhaps nothing would have shocked him more than the thought that some of the most brilliant minds of the next generation, including Rosenzweig and Rosenstock-Huessy, who had supped off Goethe and had deeply absorbed his own work, were convinced that the God he had pronounced dead was, indeed, a spectre, as he had rightly said, generated by an otherworldly flight and a fear of life, and was not the loving, living, revealing, redeeming God they worshipped. Moreover, they held that the living God was as vital and eternal as He had ever been, even if there had been a great pagan revival in what had previously been termed the Christian nations. For Rosenstock-Huessy and Rosenzweig, the most important existential act was not an act of private spiritual resolution, but the greater socio-historical one involved in grasping the meaning of and hence surrendering to His powers, thereby harnessing His past interaction with us and the world for our present and the future.

To some extent, I have been forced to write a work that simultaneously can introduce readers to Rosenzweig and Rosenstock-Huessy while trying to clear up some confusions that I think are shared by a number of writers on Rosenzweig. (I have come to suspect that with a few exceptions, readers of Rosenzweig's *The Star*, like readers of Hegel's

Phenomenology or Joyce's *Finnegans Wake,* consist almost exclusively of scholars who have written books or articles on him.) I ask patience of those few readers who are familiar with both and who could easily dispense with the more introductory sections of this work. The balance, in terms of space allotted, of the book does veer more toward Rosenstock-Huessy. This is mainly because he is so unknown and there is so little available on him in comparison to Rosenzweig. It is also because I have decided not to go through what may well be the richest part of *The Star*, the detailed discussion of Jewish festivals and rituals. The reason for this is that I think it very straightforward, and there are many readers of *The Star* who simply avoid the more philosophically elaborate and complex of the first two parts of *The Star* and who take their nourishment from these magisterial sections. Conversely, there are many writers on *The Star* who seem to focus exclusively on its philosophical sections and thereby miss what I consider to be the all-important context as well as the ends to which the philosophical arguments are being advanced. The context and ends will be the focus in my analysis of Rosenzweig.

As large a book as this is, I am acutely aware of how much more could have been written on the two, and I do hope that this will be a spur to further studies on them, as well as on Rosenstock-Huessy in his own right. Just as a genuine understanding of Marx or Heidegger is capable of generating all sorts of inquiries and uncovering new things about the past and present, I think that the real fruits of Rosenzweig and Rosenstock-Huessy will lie in future studies that apply their insights and suggestions to areas as diverse as religion, politics, law, and art. The New Thinking, as I have suggested, is a paradigm, and it was never finished by Rosenzweig, Rosenstock-Huessy, and the others who thought under its signature.

Acknowledgments

In 1995 I met Freya von Moltke, Mark, Frances, Raymond, Mariot, and the late Hans Huessy, all of whom received me into their homes and hearts with such grace and generosity that I wish to dedicate this book, however inadequate it is, to them. I would also like to give my deepest thanks to Harold Stahmer, who in 1995, when I visited him in Florida, not only insisted that I read Franz Rosenzweig if I were going to write on Rosenstock-Huessy, but also gave me a copy of William Hallo's translation of *The Star of Redemption* and Nahum Glatzer's *Franz Rosenzweig: His Life and Thought* to ensure that I did so. The full extent of my debt to him became clear when his initial suggestion took hold of me ten years later. In Michael Gormann-Thelen, I have found a friend whose brilliance, diligence, and ability to discover buried information and to explore new lines of connections among thinkers usually firmly separated provides me with constant delight. Without him this book would have been much, much poorer. He has provided more commentary and information than I can possibly thank him for, far more than I have been able to acknowledge throughout. My deepest thanks also to my undergraduate Greek teacher Mike Dyson, whom I will always remember with gratitude and fondness; to my PhD supervisor Paul Corcoran, who had enough faith in me to open the academic door for me; to Clint Gardner, David Bade, Norman Fiering, the late Page Smith, Bill Caine, the late Cynthia Harries, Leo Harries, the late Harold Berman, Dick Schaul, the late Rudolf Hermeier, Gottfried Hoffman, Lise van der Molen, the late Rivka Horwitz (with whom I at times disagreed, but for whose suggestions I have been deeply rewarded), Paul Caringella, Chip Hughes, who made just the right contact at the right time, Chris Hutton, Mano Mora, Dawn Roberts, Elfed Roberts,

Matthew del Nevo (who has read most of this and has been a marvellous spur to carry on), Renate Cullman, Roland Vogt, Kendall Johnson, and Ari Akermann. Thanks also to the Toronto team I have worked with of Wayne Herrington, Doug Richmond, and Matthew Kudelka (for a great editing job); to the generous organizers of the Rosenzweig conferences I have attended in Germany and Israel; and to the many students who were part of my Rosenstock-Huessy reading group, which lasted for about eight years at the University of Adelaide. I am also indebted to my dear friends who have supported me through so much – Jennifer Buckley, Lelani B. Paras, and Wendy Baker. I especially thank the University of Hong Kong, which saved me from bankruptcy, and Heung Wah (Dixon) Wong, my close friend and former Head of School, who has created extraordinary opportunities and support as well as the fantastic working environment of the School of Modern Languages and Cultures. I also wish to thank the Dean of Arts at HKU, Kam Louie, for his support in creating a first-rate faculty. Also, Zena Cheung, Shirley Chan, and Christy Ho from the School Office, and indeed the entire office and support staff of the school, for their incredible help and support. Also a big thank you to Len Husband at the University of Toronto Press for being open-minded enough not only to consider but also to support the project.

I am also grateful for access to unpublished materials from Rosenstock-Huessy's house in Four Wells, to the Rosenstock-Huessy archive in Bielefeld, and to some material on Rosenzweig at the Leo Baeck Institute. All material from the archive at Four Wells will be referred to by *; any from the Rosenstock-Huessy archives at Bielefeld by #; and Rosenzweig material at the Leo Baeck Institute in New York by §.

Finally, a personal note: two things have compelled me to write a book on Eugen Rosenstock-Huessy and Franz Rosenzweig. First, Rosenstock-Huessy changed my life – though he was long dead when he did so. My book *Power, Love, and Evil: Contributions to a Philosophy of the Damaged* could not have been written without him and without the personal and intellectual meltdown I experienced at the same time that Rosenstock-Huessy's work entered my field of vision, initially through the array of footnotes I found in the first volume of Harold Berman's *Law and Revolution* as I was library browsing during my first year as a university lecturer. This work, which began as an act of gratitude on my part to Rosenstock-Huessy (it was meant to be a short book – so much for intentions), has given me the opportunity to develop some important ideas that I touched on in *Power, Love, and Evil*.

My expressions of gratitude will be incomplete unless they take account of the fact that Rosenstock-Huessy saw his work not in isolation, but rather as a partnership with Franz Rosenzweig, his former student, whom he considered to be wiser than himself. Most people who have encountered Rosenstock-Huessy's name have done so in the context of his influence on Franz Rosenzweig. My path was the opposite, and it was many years before I came to see the power and the beauty of Rosenzweig; though not before having initially been repelled by a philosophical style that prevented me from coming to terms with his great work *The Star of Redemption* for more than a decade as it sat on my bookshelf, periodically being taken up in hand, only to be summarily laid down again. I had no idea that having read Rosenzweig, a new world would be opened to me and I would relearn almost everything I thought I knew about Rosenstock-Huessy. I hope that something similar to what has happened to me in my relationship to Rosenstock-Huessy will also happen to those who are already deeply familiar with Rosenzweig but have not known Rosenstock-Huessy.

My decision to write this book was driven by my conviction – in no small part due to the revival of theopolitics that has accompanied the re-emergence of Islamism – that Rosenzweig and Rosenstock-Huessy profoundly understood the nature of faith in world- and self-making and that their relevance continues beyond that of many better-known and more influential thinkers. Through reading them I came to accept that the secular thinking that reaches from Spinoza to Marx and Nietzsche to Heidegger and beyond is extremely limited in helping us understand how we make the world and where we as a species are going. Thus I wish in this book to underscore why Rosenzweig and Rosenstock-Huessy took a different path, one that can help us reappraise – for want of a better term – faith and philosophy. I have concluded that Rosenstock-Huessy's claim that we must all live our lives as Jews, Christians, and pagans in one is true – even if, unlike Rosenzweig and Rosenstock-Huessy, I was not born a Jew and, unlike Rosenstock-Huessy, I have not considered myself a member of a church since I left my Catholic boarding school, not hostile, but thoroughly divested of any desire to participate in it ever again. Nevertheless, part of what I do in this book will show why I think this formulation of our having to be Jew, Christian, and pagan in one is so valuable.

RELIGION, REDEMPTION, AND REVOLUTION:
THE NEW SPEECH THINKING OF FRANZ ROSENZWEIG
AND EUGEN ROSENSTOCK-HUESSY

Introducing Rosenzweig and Rosenstock-Huessy and Their 'Common Life's Work'

Few figures in the interwar years exercised such an important influence on Germany's predominantly liberal Jewish community in its rediscovery of the power of the Jewish heritage as Franz Rosenzweig. When he died in 1929, Jewish German newspapers mourned his passing. Ernst Simon in his obituary wrote: 'Franz Rosenzweig is the harbinger and messenger of a new time, of our future, even if its roots are still in the old earth.'[1] And in the mid-1930s, as the terrible fate of European Jewry was becoming increasingly imminent, the same newspapers celebrated the posthumous publication of his correspondence. Thus, for example, Eugen Tannebaum greeted that work with these words: 'Precisely in our days is Franz Rosenzweig the right accompanist for the journey, the journey home to Judaism.'[2] In *Autobiography of a German Pastor*, while the Second World War was at its height, Hans Ehrenberg would simply state: 'Rosenzweig rose to a high level of achievement in both life and work, and the Jews of Europe came to regard him as a leader and a saint.'[3] For many German Jews, Rosenzweig's role in establishing the Jewish *Lehrhaus* was perhaps his greatest contribution to Jewish life, though some would argue that his efforts as a Bible translator were also of great significance.

Today, Rosenzweig's reputation as a philosopher is based largely on his critique of totality and on his systematic conveyance of truths originating in Judaism. The contiguity of his faith and thought, his acts and deeds, has resulted in his *Star of Redemption* becoming what he expressly said it would be: a gift to the Germans (and beyond) from the Jewish people. Indeed, no work of twentieth-century philosophy has succeeded so powerfully in expressing such rich Judaic content as Rosenzweig's *Star of Redemption*. Martin Buber, his friend and fellow Bible translator, expressed this point well when he contrasted Rosenzweig with another of Rosenzweig's friends, his teacher, the acclaimed neo-Kantian Jewish philosopher Hermann Cohen: 'The religious reality of Judaism has entered into both works, but in [Cohen's] *The Religion of Reason* it appears as a systematic setting forth of principles, in *The Star of Redemption* as a life process.'[4] Shortly after his death, Rosenzweig was hailed for having provided the first Jewish modern system of philosophy, in contrast to Cohen, who had simply brought philosophy and Judaism together.[5]

Buber was just one of many of Rosenzweig's contemporaries who recognized his philosophical importance. In his short essay 'The Fireside Saga,' Walter Benjamin – a secularist who was, nonetheless, the most self-consciously Jewish of Marxists – said simply, and without bringing the issue of Jewishness into the matter, that Rosenzweig was 'a great contemporary philosopher.'[6] Elsewhere he noted: 'I ought to investigate the way in which my concept of origin as it is developed in the work on *Trauerspiel* and in the Krauss essay, relates to Rosenzweig's concept of revelation.'[7] Shortly after Rosenzweig's death, Benjamin's close friend, Gershom Scholem, would deliver an important speech at the Hebrew University of Jerusalem, 'Franz Rosenzweig and His Book *The Star of Redemption*.' That speech now serves as an afterword to Suhrkamp's German edition of the book. In it he stated that 'the entire Jewish world is as if folded into this book.'[8] By then, in the early 1920s, Margaret Susman had written a perceptive and appreciative review that hailed Rosenzweig as a powerful and original thinker.[9] Certainly the mood of existentialism had created a receptive arena for appreciating a philosopher who had broken with Idealism and who had demonstrated a path that enabled him to step out into life. Thus, in the 1930s, Elsa Freund would write an important philosophical introduction to his work, *Franz Rosenzweig's Philosophy of Existence*, and Karl Löwith would write an essay favourably comparing Rosenzweig with Heidegger. Recent insightful comparisons with Heidegger have come from Peter Gordon and Richard Cohen.[10]

Rosenzweig has also had an impact on some of France's most important philosophers, most notably Emmanuel Levinas, who declares in *Totality and Infinity* that Rosenzweig's presence is to be found on every page. Hilary Putnam and Paul Ricoeur have engaged seriously with him.[11] Rosenzweig's reputation in North America is rising, as can be seen from the many new translations of his work, including Barbara Galli's recent translation of *The Star of Redemption*.[12]

In recent years, the publication of Rosenzweig's *Gritli Briefe* has revealed another factor that contributed heavily to Rosenzweig's most important work as well as to his life becoming what it was. That factor was the love given to him by Rosenstock-Huessy's wife Margrit, 'Gritli,' who during the writing of *The Star* was his daily inspiration. Those letters also reveal that Rosenstock-Huessy accepted, albeit with pain and insecurity, the love between Rosenzweig and Margrit, both of whom emphasized that their love for Eugen was to be honoured in their love for each other.[13] There is no reliable full-length biography of Rosenzweig or the Rosenstock-Huessys, so what we know about this love story is rather truncated. It can best be pieced together from Rosenzweig's published letters, as well as some unpublished ones (some are in the Rosenstock-Huessy archives in Bielefeld and at Four Wells, his old home in Norwich, Vermont), and from stories told by those who knew them.[14] The discussions I have read of the relationship between Gritli and Franz tend to omit the central reason why, after Rosenzweig's marriage to Edith, the friendship between the three, which had continued during the first part of the marriage and had extended to Edith, came to an abrupt end. (This, though, can be pieced together from unpublished correspondence between Eugene and Gritli and the Gritli Letters.) It seems that the shame of committing adultery with a Christian woman, and the humiliation this meant for Edith – especially once he had taken a leading public role in the German Jewish community – eventually became so great that he resorted to self-denial about the depth of their relationship.[15] The last straw came when Franz asked Gritli to return the letters he had written to her. The Rosenstock-Huessys refused to return those letters; and given how both Rosenzweig and Rosenstock-Huessy insisted on truth coming from the life lived, rather than from the thought about it, Rosenstock-Huessy's refusal was, I think, the most authentic response to his request. What Rosenstock-Huessy had accepted as a secret 'sacrament' between the three had, through Rosenzweig's actions, become something shameful. As well, Rosenstock-Huessy felt that he and Gritli had been humiliated by Rosenzweig's gesture of denial of the importance of their friendship. Yet it is also true that this breach was overcome and that to his last days, Rosenstock-Huessy would remain deeply devoted to his friend, insisting that Rosenzweig had taught him more than any other living man. Edith would eventually burn the letters from Gritli, only to watch this secret made public shortly before her death – a cruel confirmation that the spirit of truth does not like to be repressed.[16]

The publication of the *Gritli Briefe* shows just how significant the Rosenstock-Huessys were in Rosenzweig's life.[17] But even before this love affair became public, it was common knowledge among Rosenzweig scholars that Rosenstock-Huessy played a pivotal role in Rosenzweig's development. Rosenstock-Huessy had become a professor of law by the age of twenty-four and had been Rosenzweig's teacher, and Rosenzweig encountered in him a man who had a profound knowledge of history and law, who was as steeped as he himself was in Hegel, Goethe, and Nietzsche, yet who believed that this tradition was full of weaknesses – that the living God had not died and that proof of His presence was in our language, our institutions, our laws, and our calendars, and, more generally, in the historicity of our daily life. Many studies now allude to Rosenstock-Huessy's role in drawing Rosenzweig into a way of understanding the truth and creative power of faith that resulted not in his conversion to Christianity – a conversion that Rosenstock-Huessy and Rosenzweig's cousins, the Ehrenbergs, had hoped to see – but in his embracing again the faith into which he had been born. Some studies of Rosenzweig also acknowledge Rosenstock-Huessy's general importance to Rosenzweig's intellectual development. It is impossible to overlook this, given that in *The New Thinking*, Rosenzweig credited Rosenstock-Huessy as the single most important influence on the 'New Thinking,'[18] a style of thinking that he explicitly stated was not unique to his philosophy but rather was a revolution in thought/ speech that was being undertaken by the Ehrenbergs (Hans working in philosophy, Rudolf in biology), by Victor von Weizsäcker in medicine, by Buber's *I and Thou*, by Ferdinand Ebner in *The Word and Spiritual Reality*, and by Florens Christian Rang. (All except Ebner had published in *Die Kreatur*.)[19]

To Rudolf Hallo, Rosenzweig repeated his claim in *The New Thinking* that he would not have written *The Star* without Eugen.[20] To his doctor, Richard Koch, he confided that 'it was Rosenstock-Huessy's misfortune that I stole all his best ideas.'[21] Even Rosenzweig's mother told Rosenstock-Huessy in 1924, after receiving a copy of the latter's *Angewandte Seelenkunde*, a book that had originally been written as a letter to Rosenzweig in 1916, 'I believe that Franz knows full well what he brought forth in the *Stern* is yours. He is still speaking of his ill-gotten gains.'[22] Shortly before his death, Rosenzweig repeated this assessment when he wrote to Rosenstock-Huessy that he had learned from no one else so naturally or forcefully.[23]

Given Rosenzweig's public acknowledgment of his debt to Rosenstock-Huessy, and the high esteem he expressed for him, it is somewhat baffling that except for a few commentaries on the 1916 correspondence – and more recently, the Gritli Letters[24] – Rosenzweig scholars have barely begun to explore what was clearly the most significant dialogical relationship in Rosenzweig's life. And to be blunt, very little in the extant explorations shows that much effort has gone into reading Rosenstock-Huessy carefully, though a handful of scholars have provided some insightful discussions of the two from the Rosenstock-Huessy 'side.'[25] (That there were two conferences on Rosenzweig and Rosenstock-Huessy in 2008, one at the Johann-Wolfgang-Goethe University in Frankfurt and one at Dartmouth, indicates that this deficit may soon be addressed.)[26]

There are many reasons why Rosenzweig scholars have failed to look more closely at Rosenstock-Huessy. One is simply that Rosenstock-Huessy is difficult to treat on purely philosophical terms – something that can be and, indeed, often is done with Rosenzweig. Moreover, it is hard to imagine two more different stylists than Rosenstock-Huessy and Rosenzweig. Philosophy must be digested, not merely read. Paradoxically, and usually, philosophies are digestible *because* they are hard to read; one cannot simply read Heidegger, Hegel, Kant, or Rosenzweig – one must struggle with them, and one absorbs their meaning through that struggle. Rosenstock-Huessy, on the other hand, is extremely easy to read. But precisely because one grasps the meaning of every sentence without effort, it is hard to digest how his insights cohere into a radical re-vision of what we think we know. Similarly, Rosenzweig is extremely dense philosophically, and his system exhibits a diamond-like precision in its key concepts and structure; whereas Rosenstock-Huessy is a more 'explosive,' associative writer – indeed, Rosenzweig once said that Rosenstock-Huessy's first book *Königshaus und Stämme in Deutschland von 1014 bis 1250* had been spat out like a volcano.[27] Rosenstock-Huessy's ideas race in different directions across the pages, as associations accumulated over the course of a lifetime's study are summarily released.[28]

In spite of what I have said about digestion and reading, there is often room for disagreement about what the overall significance of a philosophy is, even if one has absorbed many of its parts. I generally disagree with how Rosenzweig's 'system' as a whole is interpreted. And missing the purpose of the system in turn effects the 'weight' of the system's different elements and arguments. Even so, Rosenzweig's architectonics are always visible, even if not always weighed correctly. In Rosenstock-Huessy, by contrast, the overarching system and its patterns are much more difficult to pin down. He seems to have taken a deliberate decision about his style. At any rate, in the work he considered his magnum opus, *Die Soziologie*, after having described himself as a 'post-aphoristic and post-systematic' thinker, he adds that 'this style presupposes the strictest, most pedantic system. In my thinking, I first elaborate my system. But only at first. Thereafter, I decisively turn my back on the idolization of my own offspring of thought.'[29]

It is also telling that Rosenzweig could essentially include all his major ideas in one book, and that Rosenstock-Huessy could never do so, even in his massive two-volume *Soziologie*. Yet unless one has read Rosenstock-Huessy's works on revolution or his two large volumes on speech, *Die Sprache des Menschengeschlechts*, one will fall well short of anything approaching a comprehensive understanding of his 'system.' Indeed with Rosenstock-Huessy, the sheer volume and range of his corpus is indicative of a thinker whose ideas could never adequately find one dwelling place. While he himself summed up his 'system' under the rubric 'the cross of reality,' it was ever an open system. Rosenzweig's system, by contrast, is closed.[30] This is in keeping with their respective visions of Christianity as ever open to the times and their requirements and of Judaism as the eternal cycle.

Rosenstock-Huessy suggests that their respective systems reveal something about the two men themselves as well as their relationship. Thus the comment to Georg Müller, in a letter of 8 March 1958, by Rosenstock-Huessy, when he had just turned seventy and had finally published his system: 'Franz Rosenzweig, who had been overwhelmed by writing his *Star*, and feeling the price of his sickness and ecstasy, said of that work, "One is only allowed to write such a work at seventy." I, who was ready [to write my system] in 1925, through the guidance of grace, was so retarded that only now, at the age of seventy, am I presenting my life's work. The secret of this exchange of roles is great.'[31]

In fine, scholars who have cut their teeth on Rosenzweig are more than a little perplexed about what exactly to do with Rosenstock-Huessy. And given how much of him one must read to see what is genuinely going on, he is rarely examined in much depth at all.

Besides which, Rosenstock-Huessy was, as Adam Zak has said, a *'minor inter minores.'*[32] In America he found himself almost completely isolated, and in 1948 he wrote to Georg Müller that no one had heard of him there, except perhaps as a Christian philosopher whom no one needed to read. Martin Marty's opening sentence to his review of Rosenstock-Huessy's *The Christian Future – or The Modern Mind Outrun* was a pretty accurate assessment of the effect Rosenstock-Huessy and his books often had on academics who came upon them. *The Christian Future*, Marty declared, was 'a strange book by a strange author.'[33]

Yet for all Rosenstock-Huessy's obscurity, he has not been completely unread or unadmired.[34] In Germany, his books were reviewed in newspapers after the Second World War, partly because it was known that he had travelled in important intellectual circles. He was also a central figure in the Patmos circle with Buber, Joseph Witting, and Viktor von Weizsäcker and a cofounder of the journal *Die Kreatur*, which included works by the above three as well as by Christian Florens Rang, Leo Schestow, Ernst Michael, Nikolai Berdyaev, Margaret Susman, Ludwig Strauß, and Rosenzweig. The same journal published Benjamin's *Letters from Moscow*. Rosenstock-Huessy's role as a cofounder of the Academy of Labour at the University of Frankfurt, and his pioneering role in establishing work service programs, earned him a reputation outside academe. These projects were, for Rosenstock-Huessy, part of his effort to inculcate in youth a sense of communal engagement, an effort he continued with somewhat mixed results in the United States with Camp William James.

Rosenstock-Huessy did not fit the dominant intellectual climate. In the postwar years, he maintained that the widespread reliance on what he called the fourth generation of Feuerbachians (neo-Kantians, neo-Hegelians, neo-Marxists) was lamentable. He felt that his own 'conversion to the full life of the spirit dated from the First World War,'[35] and he thought that many of the émigrés to America had not fully assimilated the experience of the Great War. He was especially scathing of Bloch.[36] He was also highly critical of Heidegger and furious at Karl Löwith for remaining beguiled by the very thinking he saw exemplified in Heidegger and contributing to National Socialism.[37] He also found it astonishing that atheists were so blind to the hells that their thought-ways had helped foster and to the deeper meanings of religious terms. In 1966, in one of the few references he makes to important postwar social theorists, he criticized Adorno and Habermas, along with the German journalist Carola Stern:

> Isn't it right to say that from 1789 to 1917 the devil has been abolished as the last remainder of theism? Hence it's important that we take our stand against this atheistic talk which has abolished the devil. This woman

> Carola Stern is absolutely certain, twenty years after Hitler plus the Jews, that evil is not incarnated. Those fellows Habermas, Adorno etc. are just as certain that believers incarnate evil.[38]

Yet in America he also found a few influential readers and supporters. Just before Rosenstock-Huessy's death, W.H. Auden wrote a short preface to *I Am an Impure Thinker*. Years earlier, Auden had included an unusually large number of aphorisms from Rosenstock-Huessy in his Viking edition of memorable phrases, prompting one reviewer, so the story goes, to comment: 'Who is he, this Rosenstock-Huessy?' On learning of Rosenstock-Huessy's death, Auden wrote 'Aubade' in his memory.[39] Rosenstock-Huessy was also admired by Jacob Taubes, who wrote a number of letters to him during the 1950s, and he was highly esteemed by Reinhold Niehbuhr, as well as by the political scientist Carl Friedrich, who helped him find work in the United States, at Harvard (where he lost his job for taking religion too seriously and for bringing 'God' into the History Department). In what must seem the most unlikely match of minds, the political scientist Karl Deutsch – whose method typified the match of structuralism and behaviourism of 1960s political science – wrote a foreword to Rosenstock-Huessy's *Die europäischen Revolutionen*.

One of the people Rosenstock-Huessy most admired was Paracelsus, a pioneer in science and a heretic in the eyes not only of some traditionalist Christians – who viewed his integration of magic, alchemy, and astrology with medicine and his faith with alarm – but also in the eyes of the swelling humanist tradition, which, having cast out Aristotle's books, had become enamoured of a rediscovered pagan book-world.[40] Like Paracelsus, Rosenstock-Huessy always found himself on the outside, and he never successed in integrating himself with any major stream of academic investigation – something that he describes with great pathos and autobiographical candour on the last page of *Out of Revolution*. His two-volume work on sociology is so unlike any other work of sociology ever written that it has had almost no impact on members of that discipline; not surprisingly, it has never been translated (though Jurgen Lawrenz, thanks to Dixon Wong and the School of Modern Languages and Cultures at the University of Hong Kong, has now taken up the task). Very occasionally, it appears on university curricula in Germany and Austria, and the sociologist Dietmar Kampfer took an abiding interest in it and Rosenstock-Huessy.[41] There was also his two-volume collection of writings titled *Die Sprache des Menschengeschlechts*

(The Speech of the Human Race), which was as harsh in its assessment of Fritz Mauthner[42] as the *Soziologie* had been on Weber ('the embodiment of the decline of the German university');[43] that, as well as its silence on Saussure and structuralism, and its contempt for the linguistic atomism that predominated in Anglo-Saxon linguistics and philosophy of language, provided ample excuse for yet another field of academic inquiry to ignore him. He had slightly more impact (how could it have been less?) with *Die europäischen Revolutionen*, which in Germany comes up from time to time for discussion (e.g., in Wolf Gruner and Wichard Woyke's recent *Europa Lexicon: Länder, Politik, Institutionen* by).[44] And while the philosophical community has generally never heard of him, one of Germany's best-known post–Second World War philosophers, Peter Sloterdijk, has said that he considers 'Rosenstock-Huessy ... the most important of all theorists of revolution,' as well the 'most meaningful speech philosopher of the 20th century,' more so even than Witgenstein, Derrida, Heidegger, or Searle.[45] The American volume on the European revolutions, *Out of Revolution*, which is less theoretical, includes some different material, and presents its case in reverse order to a German version, was, however, castigated in a review by the historian Crane Brinton. For Brinton it belonged in Cloud Cuckoo Land, along with Hannah Arendt's *On Revolution*.[46] Nevertheless, that work left an abiding influence on Rosenstock-Huessy's student Harold Berman, whose two-volume work *Law and Revolution* is steeped in his predecessor's thematics. Page Smith, author of the eight-volume *People's History of the United States*, was another student who tried to draw people's attention to the power of his teacher's thinking.[47] In Germany, Rosenstock-Huessy's work on revolution has also impacted on some major social historians, such as Reinhart Koselleck, Heinrich Winkler, and Werner Abelshauser.[48]

There is also the problem of how exactly to categorize Rosenstock-Huessy. The German theologian and philosopher Michael Theunissen, in *The Other: Studies in the Social Ontology of Husserl, Heidegger, Sartre, and Buber*, rightly sensing that Rosenstock-Huessy was neither a theologian nor a philosopher (both often terms of opprobrium for Rosenstock-Huessy), said of him that he 'is from the ground up a jurist, sociologist, and historian.'[49] He continued: '[As] a jurist, Rosenstock-Huessy hopes for the permanence of the dialogical from the binding character of the law, as a sociologist from the spiritual substantiality of institutions ... and as a historian from the "time-worn" relations in which the later generation has to meet the claims of the earlier.' Insofar as Rosenstock-Huessy's precursors undoubtedly included Vico, whom he admired tremendously, as well as Giuseppi Ferrari, the nineteenth-century editor of Vico's works, there is some truth in this classification. The deployment of three disciplines to ensnare him ('from the ground up') merely points to the difficulty of the task. Not to mention, one of his three major works, *Die Sprache des Menschengeschlechts*, doesn't fall comfortably into any of the three categories. For his part, Rosenstock-Huessy was contemptuous of Theunissen's treatment of him.[50]

Though Rosenstock-Huessy's work roams far and wide, Rosenstock-Huessy never doubted that his desire to create new forms of community, to change the education system by bringing students and workers together, and to restructure the workplace, were as much part of one calling and project as his studies on Egypt, Greece, Christianity, the tribes, the nations, the law, and every other topic he addressed in his writings. Like Rosenzweig, he saw scholarship as a contribution to life. He held that ideas are nothing without incarnation and that everything he did was all part of one life lived in devotion, service, and prayer.[51]

One other factor has probably contributed to Rosenstock-Huessy being relegated to the sidelines in discussions about Rosenzweig. Simply put, Rosenstock-Huessy has been perceived by scholars and devotees of Rosenzweig as an apostate who wanted Rosenzweig to convert to Christianity and who could never accept Rosenzweig's decision to remain a Jew. Elsewhere I have shown how wrong this description of events is,[52] but I will quickly run through again why this is both wrong and unfair.

If Rivka Horwitz's account is true, perhaps part of the blame for this lies with Nahum Glatzer, author of the work that first brought Rosenzweig to a non-philosophical specialist English-speaking audience, *Franz Rosenzweig: His Life and Thought*. As Horwitz tells the story, 'Glatzer presented Eugen Rosenstock-Huessy in an improper way. He devoted very little room to him – only a few pages – whereas in reality, Rosenstock-Huessy had been a major figure in Rosenzweig's life. Glatzer admitted to me that he had done this on purpose.'[53] Horwitz's account of Glatzer may or may not be true; what *is* certain is that the Jewish apostate and Christian convert Rosenstock-Huessy has been unfairly accused of anti-Semitism by friends of Rosenzweig on the basis of nothing more than the 1916 correspondence, in which he and Rosenzweig argued vehemently about their respective faiths.[54] The charge is especially pernicious given that Rosenstock-Huessy would himself have ended up in a concentration camp had he stayed in

Germany because he was, in Nazi eyes, a Jew. Rosenstock-Huessy also believed that his Jewish mother's suicide in Switzerland was a consequence of her fear of Nazism's spread.

Whatever Glatzer thought of Rosenstock-Huessy, he could not completely ignore Rosenzweig's life-changing conversation with Eugen Rosenstock-Huessy in 1913. Anyone familiar with Rosenzweig's *Star* can see that it was during the dialogue of 1916 between him and Rosenstock-Huessy that many of his most important ideas – which had taken shape earlier, and which would find their way into *The Star* – were sharply honed: the Jews as the eternal people who live in God's truth and who are the goal;[55] the Christians as the people of history, as being ever on the way; the Christian hatred of the Jews for their stubbornness;[56] Christianity's role as a force for Judaizing pagans;[57] Western civilization as a form of Johannine Christianity;[58] Rosenzweig's critique of Islam;[59] the danger and value of movements that attempt to 'take the Kingdom by force'[60] and hence his ethics, and the basis of his theory of art;[61] and – an idea that would be decisive in convincing Rosenstock-Huessy that he had made a major error in thinking of Jews and pagans as a unity – the Jew as the 'guarantee of the reality of the Christian world.'[62] So it is not surprising that Rosenzweig would later declare that he could not have written *The Star* without Rosenstock-Huessy. Furthermore, the central importance given by Rosenstock-Huessy to language and the calendar (rightly acknowledged by Altmann)[63] as the key to social practice was also of fundamental importance in shaping Rosenzweig's method and *The Star* itself. Indeed, the very idea of him fitting his thoughts into the symbol of the star was conceived in reaction to Rosenstock-Huessy wanting to present his own ideas as components of a symbol, the cross of reality.

At the same time, Rosenzweig did more than any other living person to challenge and inspire Rosenstock-Huessy. The latter admitted as much to Georg Müller in 1960, when he listed '1920: Rosenzweig as author of the *Star*' as the first of the three dates that marked his entrance as a 'spiritual person into the world' (the second and third being 1923: *Angewandte Seelenkunde* and 1925: *Soziologie*, Bd 1).[64]

And contrary to myth, far from being despondent about not converting Rosenzweig,[65] Rosenstock-Huessy was delighted that he had learned something he would never have known had Rosenzweig simply become a Christian. In 1916 he wrote his two 'litanies' as 'a seal' to the conversation. Together he and Rosenzweig had reached a 'common front,' even though they, as Rosenzweig put it, remained 'enemies within the kingdom.' Rosenstock-Huessy characterized that position in this way – albeit with his own Christian inflexion: 'God is the Cross and is David's Star [and] the Christian realm, the Sanctum of the Jews are one, though two figures of the spirit.'[66] Rosenstock-Huessy believed that this conclusion had been made possible by Rosenzweig's decision not to convert to Christianity, and that together, their dialogue had built a new relationship between Jews and Christians that could have enormous consequences. Before Rosenzweig's 'conversion' to Judaism, Rosenstock-Huessy had believed that the Jews were like pagans and would be swallowed up by history. Rosenzweig had shown him he was wrong: the Jews would never be superseded by Christians. Rosenstock-Huessy was not ashamed of admitting his mistake, and in 1946 in *The Christian Future*, he would argue that Christianity must be supplemented with truths articulated through the founders of Judaism, Buddhism, and Taoism, telling his audience of a Jewish friend who thirty years earlier had 'refuted my own misunderstanding of Judaism.'[67]

Because of the enormous historical importance of the 1916 correspondence – such was his own estimation – Rosenstock-Huessy, almost as soon as he arrived in America, was determined to publish those letters, even though others, including Edith Rosenzweig, felt that the material was too explosive, especially in the wake of the Holocaust.[68]

The essence of Rosenzweig's argument about the relationship between Jews and Christians was developed and refined in *The Star*. It went as follows. First, the Christians are utterly dependent on Jews for their own survival: 'About us the Christians cannot be in doubt. Our existence guarantees for them their truth.'[69] Second, and closely related to the first point, Jews and Christians do God's work together. The Jew as the eternal people is the elect who dwells like the coal in God's fire; the Christian is the ray that goes out into the world. *The Star*'s most majestic formulation of this relationship comes in what has often been taken as one of the greatest statements of Christian–Jewish reconciliation ever written – and its greatness is in no small part a result of the uncompromising insistence on the difference that is defended and maintained at the very moment that Rosenzweig articulated their concordance under God:

> Before God therefore, both, Jew and Christian, are workers on the same task. He cannot dispense with either. Between the two he set an enmity for all time, and yet he binds them together in the narrowest reciprocity. To us [Jews] he gave eternal life by igniting in our heart the fire of the Star of his

truth. He placed the Christians on the eternal way by making them hasten after the rays of that Star of his truth into all time until the eternal end. We [the Jews] see therefore in our heart the true likeness of the truth, but for that we turn away from the temporal life, and the life of time turns away from us. They [the Christians], on the contrary, follow the river of time, but they have the truth only behind them: they are certainly guided by it, for they follow its rays, but they do not see it with their eyes. The truth, the whole truth, belongs therefore neither to them nor to us. For though we indeed carry it in us, yet for this reason too we must sink our glance into our own inside if we want to see it, and there we do see the Star, but not the rays. And belonging to the whole truth would be that one would see not only its light, but also what is illuminated by it. They however are destined all the same for all time to see what is illuminated, not the light.[70]

But for Rosenzweig, what is all-important is that Christians and Jews concur on the supremacy of the commandment of love, of the God of love and the commandment to love. This, as we will see more fully later, makes them peoples of redemption and revelation. Nevertheless, according to Rosenzweig, there is a parting of the ways. Christians, by rejecting the law and creating a tension between love and the law, show that they do not grasp it. The law 'in its multiplicity, and strength ordering everything, comprising everything "external," that is all the life of this world, everything that any worldly jurisdiction may conceivably comprise, this law makes this world and the world to come indistinguishable. God himself, according to Rabbinic legend, "studies" in the law.'[71]

Besides the dispute about the law, there is the irreconcilable issue of the messiah. Bluntly, the Christian worships a false messiah. Concomitantly, for the Jew, the messiah is always to come, whereas for the Christian he has been and will come again. According to Rosenzweig, the sin of idolatry in Christianity is compounded by complacency: all Christians know who the messiah is, and it is not him or herself, whereas 'no Jew knows whether he himself may not be the messiah.'[72]

Note that Rosenzweig does not deny the possibility of great acts of love by individual Christians. On the contrary, the saint is an essential Christian type, as is the priest, and the two are not to be confused with each other. But that they are fundamentally different types is part of what Rosenzweig sees as Christianity's essentially divided character.[73]

The momentary irruption of love is not alien to the pagan, either. What Rosenzweig unequivocally denies is that the Christian deficiencies, unlike the Jewish dangers or temptations of denial, disdain, and mortification of the world due to the inwardness demanded by God, are surmountable.[74] The Christian dangers are these: 'that the Spirit leads onto all ways, and not God; that the Son of man be the truth, and not God; that God would become All-in-All and not One above all.'[75] For Rosenzweig, Christianity is in its essence prone to idolatry and riven. Its faith, love, and hope pull in different directions and lead inexorably to a 'spiritualization of God, apotheosis of man, [and] pantheification of the world.' At any given moment the Christian is drawn to one of these poles, while the others disappear. But this rivenness is precisely what, for Rosenzweig, characterizes the natural and its prototype, the pagan. What Rosenzweig is saying, then, is that Christianity never overleaps the pagan half of its origin; it never truly or completely grasps the unity of creation, revelation and redemption, and God, man, and world – that All, which is reality as opposed to the abstract All of idealist philosophers, and which forms the basis of the life of every religious Jew. The Christian too often lives in the same fractured – that is, diminished – manner as the pagan. But what may preserve that life from being torn apart is remaining focused on the eternal radiance within it. That radiance is the eternal radiance of God, which is the essence of the Jewish faith.

This theme will be taken up again more fully later, but it forms an essential part of the backdrop to our discussion. For now, I mainly wish to highlight that despite the differences between Rosenzweig and Rosenstock-Huessy, there was a fundamental concurrence between them regarding the respective roles of Jews and Christians and their mutual dependency. For if Christians are dependent on the continued existence of the Jews – as opposed to a mere historical one – for a sense of their own mission, it is also true that Rosenzweig held the equally important belief, as far as his 'system' goes, that the work of Christianity as a historical power ultimately spreads the truth of the Jewish faith. Thus, for him, thanks to Christianity's mission of universalizing the word of revelation and spreading the prospect of redemption, the Jewish people are a hidden intrinsic force in history, an embodiment of truth, who make of Christians their servants. Taking the image from the eleventh- and twelfth-century Jewish poet Jehuda Halevi, whose works he translated into German, Rosenzweig argues that the Jews are the seed, but with the aid of Christianity, the rest of humanity forms the tree that continues to produces the Jewish seed:

Here let it be written in Yehuda Halevi's own words: God has his secret plan for us, a plan that is like his plan for a seed-kernel that falls into the earth and seemingly changes into earth, water and manure, and nothing remains of it by which an eye might recognize it; and it is yet, on the contrary, precisely it that changes earth and water into its own essence and gradually decomposes their elements and transforms and assimilates them to its own matter, and so it forces forth bark and leaves; and when its inner core is made ready, so that the new developing likeness of its former seed may enter into a new corporeality, then the tree brings forth the fruit like the one out of which its seed once came; in this way the instruction of Moses attracts each who comes later, truly transforming him in accordance with himself. Although seemingly each rejects it. And those peoples are in preparation and being made ready for the Messiah, for whom we are waiting, who will then be the fruit, and all will become his fruit and confess him, and the tree will be one. Then they praise and they venerate the root that they once despised, of which Isaiah speaks.[76]

I have not yet presented the critical and all-important reasons why Rosenzweig is convinced that the Jews are the eternal people, that they are God's elect, or why he says that only the Jewish and Christian faiths are attentive to revelation and are committed to redemption. The clarification of this is an essential part of this book. Here I mainly wish to underscore that Rosenstock-Huessy and Rosenzweig were both transformed by their dialogue and that Rosenstock-Huessy's life was dramatically and permanently changed by what Rosenzweig taught him about Judaism, just as he dramatically and permanently changed Rosenzweig's life (a) by showing him that faith makes peoples, and that the faiths of peoples are a far more important key to social understanding and social meaning than philosophy, and (b) that the task of the Christian faith is – to employ a formulation of Rosenstock-Huessy – to make 'contemporaries of distemporaries,' to bring those whose 'potencies' pertain to a different 'body of time' into a common time where all peoples can live under the law of love (revelation), but without losing what nourishes them. This does not mean that identities are not dissolved in engagement and solidarity – love always requires dissolution; nor does it mean that one group is unaffected by the presence of the other, or that one group has the key to all the times and to the powers that have been responsible for bringing new possibilities, 'new times,' into existence. Rosenstock-Huessy calls the future society that can create a concordance out of discordant times a 'metanomical society.' In *Speech and Reality* he describes what is in effect the key to his entire social analysis:

Metanomics . . . might be interpreted as the search for the omnipresence of God in the most contradictory patterns of human society . . . All men are different. In this latter proposition, I feel that we are in the center of all social problems of the future. The paradox of the human being in society is just this: that man is a separate unit with separate interests, and that he is a fellow with identical interests as well . . . The vision of the social teacher is metanomical. He knows that the economics of society differentiate us incessantly; the variety of mankind is perplexing. By metanomics he reclaims man's power to identify himself with others despite these differences. The equilibrium between the special social sciences in which man appears to differ, and the social philosophy which make him appear eternally the same human being, is the secret of all research in the social field. We cannot give up one side of the social paradox, either by identifying all men as being the same, or by allowing them to become so different that they lose their power of identifying themselves with others. Peace is the term which expresses the existence of this paradox in society: that different people by having peace together, are identifiable.[77]

His emphasis on time-bodies as a cluster of powers is one of his most important contributions to social theory. And it is central to the difference between Judaism and Christianity – for Judaism does not undertake to unify the times, but rather (Rosenzweig insists) to be the eternal people. Rosenstock-Huessy's decision to be part of a 'body' dedicated to unifying the times is largely, then, why he remained a Christian, *despite* seeing the power of Rosenzweig's arguments against Jews becoming Christians – viz. that the latter could not offer the former anything they didn't already have. That both men stayed who they were *in spite of* changing who they were was, for Rosenstock-Huessy, an enormous part of the power of the exchange with Rosenzweig. As he would write of the 1916 correspondence:

Much nonsense has piled up about this 'existential' correspondence. Some people speak of it as though it turned Eugen into a Jew, away from his Christian faith, and over the years some very foolish letters have been written to him on this account. And even now, years after his death, Franz is criticized by some for having 'conceded' so much – too much! – to

Christianity. Such interpretations, sometimes amounting to indictments, reflect serious misunderstanding on the part of those who offer them.[78]

The point was developed in 1968 in *Ja und Nein: Autobiographische Fragmente*, in the chapter 'Billardball?' which commenced with the poem he had also published and translated in *Judaism Despite Christianity* and which restates the importance of the relationship between the two. Most significantly, he reflected on the difference between what he and Rosenzweig had and the circumstance in which Nietzsche found himself: while Nietzsche, he said, went mad because the intensity of his truths was too hard to bear alone, he and Rosenzweig did not need to go mad – they shared a creative harmony born out of conflict. (Though he was also convinced – and he repeated on several occasions – that Rosenzweig's amyotrophic lateral sclerosis was the price he paid for the nervous energy expended during the composition of *The Star of Redemption*.) Thus, he says,

the biographies of the two correspondents can best be understood as a junction, the one provoking the other. That this is so could be documented very fully indeed, but it is doubtful that any documentation could convince modern humanists so accustomed as they are to treat biographical facts in a completely individualistic fashion, of the thesis that two men, Eugen and Franz, exchanged life rhythms in the course of their encounter from 1913 to 1918. The arsenals of modern historiography and biography have not yet developed tools for such an interpretation ... *Franz and Eugen did exchange with each other certain fundamentals of their life rhythm in mutuality*, and – must it be added? – quite unintentionally, in total unconsciousness. Individual purposes or intentions were subordinated to a large extent to a process of re-creation or transformation brought about by a most unwanted, even abhorred, exposure to each other.[79] (italics in original)

In the 1916 correspondence, in a thinly veiled comparison between himself and Rosenzweig on the one hand and Kant and Rousseau on the other, Rosenstock-Huessy conveyed the depth of his appreciation of Franz Rosenzweig. Kant, he says,

collaborates in all his own work unconsciously with his opposite number, his spiritual better half who he knows, is at work at the same time. All of Kant's 'Critiques' acquire a bright gleam of illumination only if one sees that his [*sic*] vis-à-vis, i.e. Rousseau, doesn't lie in an abandoned corner of his mind but is his equal; nay, as in every proper marriage, his better half.

This half, of whom one secretly dreams, but with whom one cannot treat if one is writing for a school and for school children who have lessons they must learn – this half in Kant's case is there, and consciously there.[80]

One can also gauge just how important *The Star*'s impact on Rosenstock-Huessy was from the following remark to Gritli about the progress of his *Soziologie* in 1924: 'It is really becoming *The Star* popularized and translated into Christian German, just as Franz's Jehuda translated *The Star* into Jewish.'[81]

But it wasn't simply a private gift that Rosenzweig had given him. In his 1921 review of *The Star*, Rosenstock-Huessy declared publicly that all Christians should be grateful for what Rosenzweig had taught them:

The Christian is overwhelmed by the same belief and the same love as the Jew . . . The complete width of the gulf between Jew and Christian revolves around the fact that only at the end of days is a reconciliation possible and not a moment before. But the great event in this lies in the fact that the Christian as seen by the Jew is also taken into account as intrinsic to the Jew's own essence of belief.

Thus the Christian becomes something that he wasn't before: he becomes resolved in himself. Christianity, torn and sundered in itself, seemed to slowly distance and divide itself. In objection and resistance, however, it finds its essence. In the Jew the believing Christian can suddenly find himself as an unquestioned unity, as Christian par excellence. Churches, confessions, sects rise from the middle point. Suddenly there is an unambiguous point of belief, a specific Christianity, because there arises again – after the Zionist degeneration – an unambiguous questioner of faith: a prophetic Jew.

His form, which steps next to us, produces, then, not merely static electricity which animates every strange geniality, rather he becomes a permanent condition of our souls. We experience a melt-down of the conditions of our being. Our life basis simplifies itself and through that simplification is rejuvenated.[82]

Perhaps, though, Rosenstock-Huessy's most telling political statement about the importance of Jewish life for the Christian peoples came in 1935, when he briefly returned to Berlin from his self-imposed exile in the United States in order to write a preface to the section dealing with the 1916 correspondence between him and Rosenzweig for Edith Rosenzweig and Ernst Simon's edition of Rosenzweig's letters.[83] Referring to Barth's work of 1933, *Theological Existence Today*, he says that the correspondence concerns itself with the 'eternal, typical suprapersonal questions of existence of Jews and Christians in the midst of the nations of the world [*Völkerwelt*] regarding their "theological existence today."'[84] The preface makes it clear that he thinks the dialogue between Christians and Jews is by far the most important question of the day in Germany.

This political gesture of Rosenstock-Huessy's begs comparison with Karl Barth's response to three cries for help concerning the Jews in 1933.[85]

The first cry was from Rosenzweig's cousin and fellow New Thinker, Hans Ehrenberg, himself a Jewish Christian pastor, who implored Barth in 1933 to intervene in the Jewish–Christian question. Barth responded by saying that the most important question of the time did not concern Jewish–Christian relations but natural theology. Ehrenberg was deeply disappointed by Barth's answer, and he registered a firm disagreement about what the greatest struggle within the Church was, while begging him to show more fraternity and understanding. It should be noted that Ehrenberg had been deeply impressed by Rosenzweig's *Star of Redemption* and the way in which it radically reshaped Jewish–Christian relations. And his position was precisely the kind of response that followed directly from the way in which Rosenzweig and the New Thinking generally had come to reconstrue Jewish–Christian relations.

Second, in the autumn of 1933, Elizabeth Schmitz wrote to Barth in deep despair about the fate of her Jewish friends. She had by then intuited that anti-Jewish legislation would lead to the death of millions of Jews. Barth replied that he wanted to remain in Germany, and thus he could not involve himself in the Jewish–Christian question. He said that the Church was not in a position to work on behalf of the Synagogue and that it had to first find its way back to its right denomination.

Third and finally, there was the Jewish Christian Maria Ambrosius, who asked Barth what the Church could do concretely to help Jewish Christians. To Ambrosius's suggestions of various forms of resistance, Barth responded they could serve no purpose. The Church, he said, could do little or nothing to interfere with the Jewish politics of the state. He urged her to understand that the Jewish–Christian problem was part of a greater problem and the Church could only pray for God's intervention.

Of course, Barth eventually spoke out against National Socialism. The point here is that from Rosenstock-Huessy's perspective – which we discuss in more detail later – Barth's hesitancy came down to his mistaken view of the Christian God as a transcendent one and of the Church as a place of purity for communing with this remote Absolute. It is not that Rosenstock-Huessy belittled either prayer, or waiting, or hope; but his interpretation of Christianity always emphasized action and the importance of its timing.

Rosenstock-Huessy's position, then, as outlined in his preface to the correspondence, was essentially one of reconfirming the central position of Jews and Christians as laid out in *The Star*. Yet Rosenzweig, in *The Star*, was all too aware of the history of the Church's persecution of the Jews, and had alerted readers to this in his formulation of the 'eternal hatred of the Christians toward the Jews.' For his part, Rosenstock-Huessy sharply separated the desire to convert from the fanaticism of persecution. In this he was a genuine Protestant, and while he seriously considered converting to Catholicism, he was more true to Luther's insistence on the conscience than even Luther himself, whose *On the Jews and Their Lies* not only was as disgusting an anti-Semitic tract as has ever been written, but also completely undermined the entire principle of conscience, and hence the primacy of faith, on which his Reformation was based. Indeed, one might add that Luther's failure to accept the Jews (which, as all Luther scholars point out, was in ugly contrast to his earlier more positive relations with German Jews) is important for understanding why Jews were often so welcoming of secular humanism.

Rosenstock-Huessy would always remain convinced of the Augustinian orthodoxy of the two cities, the City of God (which we access through our love of the neighbour who is made in God's image) and the City of Man (based on the love of the self). One simply cannot understand why Rosenstock-Huessy interprets the Church as he does unless one keeps this distinction ever in mind. This difference also provides the cornerstone of every internal critique of the Church. The distinction rests on not equating the outer with the inner Church, the earthly Church corrupt with the heavenly aspiring selfless Church. Rather, it means not equating what is done under the sign of the cross with the reality of the cross, not equating what is done in God's name with the love that God commands. A person's faith is never visible from what they say they are doing but only from what they are *really* doing. And a person who unconditionally served Hitler might well have done it with a Bible in hand or from a pew, but only a fool thinks that the devil is not present where holy signs are displayed. Indeed, the devil loves to hide behind holy signs because such concealment enables so much damage.

In keeping with this, it is, for Rosenstock-Huessy, impossible to be both a Christian and an anti-Semite. For to be an anti-Semite is to have hardened one's heart so that the divine radiance cannot enter one's soul. Likewise, he held that Jewish persecution by Christians had always arisen when Christianity succumbed to its pagan elements. Though to be sure, one must concede that he never – as far as I know – comprehensively considered the extent of official anti-Judaism within the Church, including its common presence in major figures of the Church, and the dangers of its social legacy.[86] His position, which he repeated persistently, was that anti-Semitism was a pagan act directed by hostility toward the self-certainty of the Jews as God's elect and by the promise of future redemption. Jewish persecution, he said, is pagan hatred of 'the Beginning of things for the End.'[87] And: 'There is permanent hostility between the wisdom of the serpent and the naivete of Adam. There is permanent hostility between worshippers of the birth of forms and the beauty of things and worshippers of the living God, with his fire burning high above the shapelessness of man's soul.'[88]

In keeping with this position, he held that Jewish persecution by the Nazis was the outgrowth of the same *furor Teutonicus* that had accompanied German nationalism and that had been behind the wave of religious persecutions in Germany in 1825, 1872, and 1933. Each time, he said, Protestants, Catholics, and Jews were all persecuted, but on each occasion one particular group bore the brunt of the attacks. If the latest purge was by far the worst, it was in part because the evil of persecution of faith itself had become an acceptable tactic of German politics, with each subsequent attack going further back in history to expunge the living God and His history so that the myths and gods of the pagans could take their place again. In other words, German political anti-Semitism was, for Rosenstock-Huessy, a reassertion of political paganism. To draw attention to the fact that Hitler had wanted to rid Germany of Christians once the Jews were finished does not excuse the so called Christians who facilitated, who were complicit in, or who stood by as the Holocaust was carried out. Anyone who reads *Mein Kampf* can see that the view of life expressed therein, with its *Weltanschauung* of different peoples in an all-or-nothing, life-and-death struggle, and with its naturalistic God of destiny, is no more Christian than it is Martian.

Hitler might not have been an intellectual, but he knew that Jews and Christians shared something that the Teutonic mythical world he wanted to revive did not encompass, viz., a God who commands 'love one's neighbour' and who does not permit idolatry of the very sort that was essential to Nazism's requirement that the German people place all their faith in a man who would be their saviour.

For Rosenstock-Huessy, then, there was no doubt that Nazism was setting out to expunge the God 'who beckons us from the end of time as the *common* destiny of man.'[89] The Teutonic myth lover found this God of the future 'an abomination to him because he is not found in the past,'[90] just as the revealing loving God of Jews and Christians was an abomination to the Nazis because those who love and serve Him know that the Nazis are idolators – they serve forces of death. There were many 'Christian' dupes who did not understand their faith, but the Nazi leadership certainly knew its enemies. Thus Rosenstock-Huessy says that the living revealer God was 'quite logically . . . denied by Hitler, whether he comes as the messianic God of Israel, as the Founder of the Church, or as the speaker of the Sermon on the Mount.'[91] That Hitler could be supported by the German churches indicated, to Rosenstock-Huessy, how pagan, how Teutonically tribal, how rotten, and hence how unrepresentative of the City of God the Church had become in Germany in the years following the Great War.

How the Jews are treated is, then, for Rosenstock-Huessy, a sign of the genuineness of the Christian faith of a people, a cipher of its openness or closedness of heart, a heart that either would or would not tolerate this 'stranger among the Gentiles.'[92] In *Out of Revolution*, he wrote: 'The Jewish question is not solved and will not be solved in a day because its very meaning is that it must be solved every day.' And he reminded his readers that 'there is no absolute guarantee against the hardening of our hearts. No institution, no pope, no priest or theologian can prevent the relapse of man into his natural indolence.'[93] And repeating Rosenzweig's point that the Jew is a reminder to Christians that their Christianity is always in danger of sliding into paganism,[94] he noted that 'many pagans use Christianity as a veneer.' This point was implicit in Rosenzweig's characterization of the expansion of the Petrine Church, which often converted pagan bodies rather than souls.[95] To summarize, for Rosenstock-Huessy, Hitlerism combined the mechanisms of modern humanism and naturalism with pagan invocations of tribal spirits – and the concoction was as heady as it was deadly.

After the Second World War, Rosenstock-Huessy would publicly criticize Niemöller for what he called his anti-Semitic Christianity, arguing that 'without Judaism, Christianity becomes a sort of Fichte's philosophy of the blessed life, becomes a befogging of concepts. And without Judaism, paganism becomes an orgiastic moment, a senseless chain of Dionysian stupors and Promethean flashes of lightning.'[96] Repeating Rosenzweig's idea of the Christian dependency on the Jews, he said,

> maybe there cannot be a living Church in Germany, because there are no Jews. Of course he does not understand the impact of the question how there can be Christians without Jews. There may well be church-goers and state churches and prelates. But can these gentlemen perpetuate Christianity? Christianity is mission. Christianity *fit, non nascitur.* Without mission, state churchliness must freeze into the ugly visage of the devil. Since the Jews have disappeared from Germany, who is hoping for the church? Niemoeller is not a Christian because he calls himself one but he would be one if he would learn to understand the other faith.[97]

As Alexander Altmann's introductory essay for *Judaism Despite Christianity* rightly points out,[98] Rosenstock-Huessy thought that one of the most important contributions of the French Revolution to the messianic mission of the Christian faith was that it emancipated the Jews. The analysis from beginning to end is saturated with Rosenzweig's ideas, at times citing Rosenzweig directly – 'the Hebrews are like the coals in the heart of the fire, powerless in the hands of God' – and repeating a central image of *The Star*: that the Christians are 'the rays sent out from the central fire, which actually transform the world. As coals in the heart of the fire, the Jews are prisoners of God.'[99] Again paraphrasing Rosenzweig, he says that the Jews are 'unable to form an earthly political order, a national organization, a worldly culture.'[100] And he repeats Rosenzweig's argument that the Jewish community has 'nothing to do with war between geographical units.'[101]

Rosenzweig had also convinced Rosenstock-Huessy of the fundamental importance of the triadic distinction between Jews, Christians, and pagans – a distinction that was vital to understanding the different powers available to humankind – powers that would be lost if the three 'types' were dissolved into 'one common humanity,' just as (Rosenzweig had also shown him), the dependency of Christians on Jews would be lost if Jews simply became Christians. Though just as surely, Rosenstock-Huessy believed that if we could separate the three and understand the uniqueness of each, it would be possible to embody three in one.

In 'Die jüdischen Antisemiten oder die akademische Form der Judenfrage' (Jewish Anti-Semitism or the Academic Form of the Jewish Question), the German version of which is included in *Das Geheimnis der Universität* (The Secret of the University), Rosenstock-Huessy pointed out how tempting it was for intellectual Jews to embrace humanism in their desire to break with their Jewish origins, noting that Marx and Freud had not only embraced 'Greek sciences' but had found it necessary to attack Judaism to show the full extent of their humanist credentials. It was Rosenzweig, he wrote, who had first shown him that we could never understand our past, present, or future if we did not comprehend that the Jew, the Christian, and the pagan were three fundamentally different and irreducible grounds of appeal and that each of these three was an eternal vessel for the one Spirit that was something more than mechanical life.[102] Moreover, their dissolution into a common human was part of the triumph of the same mechanical orientation of life that culminated in the Holocaust.

Indeed, the buttressing of Rosenzweig's triadic distinction against its humanist dissolution had been central to Rosenstock-Huessy's struggle against nationalism, fascism, and Bolshevism – the modern humanistic forms of political organization that were so dangerous for Germany in the 1920s in the aftermath of the Great War. This indicates, too, that he was motivated so strongly by Rosenzweig that he, a Jewish apostate, had attuned himself to an alternative form of apostasy – the conversion to secularism. This was central to his essay of 1924, 'The Dismantling of Political Lies,' in which he noted that the Prussian apostate and conservative Friedrich Julius Stahl, the French republican Léon Gambetta, and Marx were all Jews, and in which he maintained that they had embraced the 'ultra' positions of modern social and political life in their eagerness to distance themselves from the synagogue: Stahl, ultra-statism; Gambetta, ultra-nationalism; Marx, ultra-socialism.[103] Regarding Marx, he would write in *Out of Revolution* (which would repeat most of his ideas about Jewish anti-Semitism from 'Dismantling') – albeit hyperbolically – that we find 'the greatest libel against the Jews ever published in any language by any anti-Semite, in his attempt to disclaim his Jewishness.'[104]

The 'Dismantling of Political Lies' also points out that Hitler and Ludendorff seemed to have no idea how their own anti-Semitic burning desire for revenge had been embedded and fused in the triad of nationalism, statism, and socialism, each component of which had Jews among its most prominent leaders. The more general point of the essay – evident in its title – was that Germany needed to smash the political lies that had arisen since the war and thereby prevent that alliance of nationalism, statism, and socialism that would drive Europe to self-destruction. This essay resonated with themes that Rosenstock-Huessy had developed in an even earlier essay of 1919, 'The Suicide of Europe,' in which he also coupled Jews and Christians. Here he repeated – as he would on many occasions – a story that Rosenzweig had mentioned in the 1916 correspondence (and that he would repeat in *The Star*): when Frederick the Great remarked that there was not the slightest evidence for the truth of Christianity, a pastor retorted that the Jews were the proof of its truth.

Finally, in an essay of 1917, 'Ehrlos – Heimatlos' (Honourless – Homeless), in the context of warning about the dangers of nationalism and statism, Rosenstock-Huessy had repeated the core point in Rosenzweig – that the Jews are not a territorial people but a people of the spirit: 'So that the spirit of Israel must spread over the world, it must be disembodied, its vessel must be broken.'[105] Furthermore, 'a people has become disembodied so that the whole world can be clothed with its spirit; only its soul is left. The Jews thus are the only people who may be allowed, without mockery, to use the much too frequently misused expression of a national soul. Because the national soul is its entire expression.'[106]

That so many Rosenzweig scholars seem not to know that Rosenstock-Huessy took so much from Rosenzweig and applied it in fascinating ways is perhaps of no real importance in the general scheme of things – one could find far more examples of common ground between the two, and Rosenstock-Huessy's work is so replete with phrases from Rosenzweig's corpus that there is little point in discussing them all. What I think is far more important and what I wish to focus on in this book is that the two were part of a common enterprise that made a major contribution to social theory, one that cannot be properly grasped if either Rosenzweig or Rosenstock-Huessy is taken in isolation. Rosenstock-Huessy made this point to Emil Blum at the time of Rosenzweig's death, when Blum approached him to write a short obituary. Rosenstock-Huessy replied: 'Franz Rosenzweig and I have a common life-work to achieve. I can't take my leave of him by means of an obituary simply because he happened to die.'[107] That he would hold this opinion throughout his life is evident from the letter I have drawn from in the frontspiece of this book.

Rosenstock-Huessy and Rosenzweig entered into a dialogue on the openness of the possibility of change, but that dialogue could not have occured unless they emphasized their differences and recognized them as such. They did not want to conceal their differences in order to arrive at some pre-known (liberal) harmony that would destroy who they were. Yet they were willing to talk and talk, to provoke each other, each demanding that one see the other, thereby risking a transformation that would change the very ground of possible harmony as well as their own existence.

In this respect we might return to an earlier point: that the encounter between Rosenzweig and Rosenstock-Huessy demonstrates the process of dialogical thinking. Such thinking awakened Rosenzweig to a path he had thought closed to a philosopher – that of faith. Then it turned out that Rosenzweig's path taken was not the one that Rosenstock-Huessy had hoped for. Then it transpired that Rosenzweig, by taking that unexpected path, would become Rosenstock-Huessy's great philosophical teacher and accomplice. It is this last all-important act in the 'dialogue' that is so often left out of analyses of the 1916 correspondence between the two. It did not mean that either changed faith, but each understood far more about his own faith and hence his own life's task because of that dialogue.

The triad is the truth of the two – for that is the spirit that is summoned by the presence of the two and that calls and pulls the two into new regions of their own selves and the world at large, thereby activating a new power that is always more than one ever realizes is possible. The aim of dialogical thinking is to produce the not yet, that which the one could not produce, the third that is the future conjured up unawares by the commun(icat)ion of the two. This third is the real truth of the two ones. It is out of their control, and this is why it is not a Platonic variant. When Plato uses the dialogue form, it is to bring things to order, to bring the speakers before a higher law – the 'tribunal of reason,' to use Kant's famous and telling formulation of how the philosophical tradition has generally constructed reason's role and nature. To be sure, there are times in Plato when this does not succeed. But it is interesting that when it does not succeed – as in the *Protagoras*, where Protagoras is dumbfounded rather than convinced, or in the *Republic*, with Thrasymachus' irritable departure, and most dramatically in the *Gorgias*, where Callicles, the most dangerous interlocutor in the

Platonic corpus, is left to stew in his absolute defiance – Plato shows that where disputation is not dialectical, the shadow speech forms of poetry, sophistry, and oratory generate deadly chaos.[108] Unlike in Plato, the dialogical thought of Rosenstock-Huessy and Rosenzweig is based not on the desire to bring things into order, but rather on the desire to give birth, to deliver a new creation.

Again, the comparison with Plato is inevitable, for giving birth is precisely the quality that Plato wants to underscore as key to Socrates's greatness. Yet Socrates, while a midwife, knows exactly what it is he wishes to give birth to: wisdom and virtue. With Socrates, the journey always begins toward a form that is partially known but not yet fully understood. By contrast, Rosenstock-Huessy and Rosenzweig begin and remain active within the unknown, the mystery, the contingent, the trust or faith in what constantly defies accepted wisdom and convention. This claim may seem strange, given that both stand under a greater body of belief – the Church and the Synagogue – as well as under the God that gives both institutions their meaning. Yet faith in a living, moving God, rather than in an implacable source of truth such as reason, always forces one to the outer edges of existence and the periphery of social consensus, which is one reason why so many divergent points of view may be found among members of the Church and the Synagogue, and why, as well, some of the very best must leave their Church or Synagogue to express a truth that later generations will feel so naturally that they can barely hazard why its original formulator was deemed a heretic.

The creative and redemptive component of dialogue is akin to love – indeed, real dialogue is one of love's forms. The story of the dialogue between Rosenstock-Huessy and Rosenzweig is one in which difference strongly held does not lead to violence but instead becomes a source of creativity and more love. Such difference does not recoil from one criticizing what the other holds most sacred. Difference is treated cheaply, and life foolishly, when it is considered reprehensible merely to articulate and draw attention to the most serious sources of what makes one who one is. But is this not precisely the mindset that the living God tries to break apart – or, to put it less theologically, that life consistently shows is deadly? And this I think is a common error in academic thought today, which calls so loudly for difference in the abstract, but in practice pays it so little respect.

Rosenstock-Huessy remained committed to redemption of all that can be redeemed, and that is why he was a Christian. Rosenzweig's decision to 'remain a Jew,' on the other hand, was not undertaken to stop Christianity performing its 'mission.' Though here we must emphasize a point that is central to both of them and that is developed later: that twentieth-century Christianity is predominantly secular, and that its nineteenth-century proselytizers weren't so much Harnack, Troeltsch, or Schweitzer, but men who considered themselves atheists and who did not realize how deeply Christian they were – men like Schopenhauer, Marx, and Nietzsche. Rosenzweig believed that the Jews were the eternal people, the elect. But what does this mean for the non-Jew? To appreciate the importance of this question, one must bear in mind that while Rosenzweig was indeed interested in German Jews reschooling themselves in their tradition while living in, but not being exclusively constituted by, their liberal/Christian environment, he was not interested in converting Christians or pagans to Judaism. He was, though, interested in Christians appreciating and respecting Jews, and through their respect and appreciation becoming better Christians, and not becoming anti-Semitic racists and pagans who would thereby lose sight of the promise of redemption. Both Rosenzweig and Rosenstock-Huessy believed that Christians are Christians to the extent that they are dedicated to building the body of Christ throughout the ages. Christianity would thus be always in process as long as there was a single soul outside the Church. And when Rosenzweig insists that Christianity is not the bearer of eternal truth, Rosenstock-Huessy concurs with him – for he held that we are creatures whose redemption is revealed over time. Thus Rosenstock-Huessy refused to recognize any other eternity except as he saw it *lived* by the Jews; and he refused, as did Rosenzweig, to take the Greek/Platonic timeless ideal as a representation of eternity. Eternity is Jewish and the source and centre of life; disembodied immorality is Greek and pagan, a delusion and a projection.

The 'enmity' between Christian and Jew is as unbridgeable as the hiatus between time and eternity. Yet there is also concordance, and this concordance had been exhibited not as an argument or an idea but in the common task and love between Rosenzweig and Rosenstock-Huessy – the love and greater truth transpires despite the refusal of each to enter some third dominion of worship, some logical resolution. Both think that such a dominion or logical resolution is impossible. Tension and dispute are essential to the 'deal,' precisely because both are living witnesses of a truth that refuses to dissolve completely into the truth of the other. This is the classical recipe for the tragic. Yet it is not tragic – it is the opposite of the tragic, a promise of greater life for both parties precisely because of the failure of resolution and the intensification and persistence of a tension due to a knowledge that the one needs the other as the arrow needs the bow's resistance and the archer's strength.

In his autobiographical *Ja und Nein,* Rosenstock-Huessy summarized their different paths: 'My teaching takes its point of departure from the cross of reality in lived time. Rosenzweig, however, took root in eternity where man, God, world and the same eternal paths appear.'[109] That is, indeed, the fundamental difference: the name of one is forever connected to a work *The Star of Redemption,* the name of other to a method that unites a vast corpus of books and also the name of a lecture series, the cross of reality.[110] The cross places suffering at the centre of existence – it shows us that we make our hell by violating the victim; the symbol of the star emphasizes luminousness and gives hope to those who suffer and look upwards; reality includes all phases; redemption, likewise, includes all phases, but the eye is directed toward the end of the process from the beginning. The cross draws us into the centre. The cross is a work of humans, though God then uses that cross for a divine purpose; the star is no human work; it is by its nature something beyond humanity, something we must look up to if we are to see it. Rosenzweig's great work with its three 'volume' headings 'Elements, Paths, Form' is, as he says, suggestive of astronomy.[111] That looking up to the heavens instantly reminds us of our finitude. The star occupies a place in the heavens. The cross is an event in time. The star, though, becomes the Star of David. The cross reaches out and up into the heavens, but also outwards toward the earth. For Rosenzweig the follower of the Davidic Star has remained most true to that promise in the lifelong prayers, rituals, and feast days that are but the expression and engagement with the repetitions of the eternal across generations, the eternal presence in and through time that finds itself re-enacted by members of the one line stretching from Abraham to Moses to the end of time.

But the heavens are not implacable – they revolve. And Rosenstock-Huessy noted the meaning that the revolving planets of heaven would come to have for the Christian peoples – revolution. For those peoples took their understanding of how life on earth should conform to the promise of the heavenly father by bringing a world out of joint back into accord with the planetary order that fulfils the promise of the love that, in Dante's majestic formulation, 'moves the sun and other stars.' The story of the Christian peoples is as much the story of revolutions as of implacable command, or rather of the implacable command requiring the disruption of the loveless hells that are built through selfish and blind pursuits.

The cross is the intersection of four paths; the star the intersection of two triangles. But these two triangles finally form, as the conclusion of *The Star* emphasizes, the human face, and thus the star becomes human, becomes the messiah. But whose face? That remains unknown for the Jew, who waits in anticipation that this person may be the Messiah. But it must be said that Rosenzweig overestimates the Jewish uniqueness of this state of 'unknowing,' for it is also the condition in which every Christian has been schooled to believe. The beggar who stands in need before one may well be Christ returned.

In *The Star of Redemption*, Rosenzweig gave the cross its due – it was the means of the historical unification of the world, and thus it took the word of the living God outside of the tribe of Israel, though it did so ever imperfectly and ever at the risk of succumbing to idolatry. Rosenzweig, for his part, became a model for his fellow Jews – a beacon, if one will – before the Holocaust. He did not live to see the German churches swear their oaths of allegiance to Hitler and once again enter into that eternal hatred of the Jew, a hatred that he said in *The Star* was integral to Christianity. This would have disappointed more than surprised him. Rosenstock-Huessy left Germany immediately on Hitler's coming to power. He knew that fascism was rotten to the core. He would live a long life, and he would continue to try to perfect his sociological and historical analyses of a universal history, a history of explosions, ruptures, wars, revolutions, and changing social formations, institutions, and human types, a history whose only justification was that it slowly built the all-too-precarious bridges between peoples while burning into their memories the need for mutual love – a history, in other words, that expressed, for him, the truth of suffering as the basis of redemption symbolized by the cross – but a cross, as he came to concede, that also was illumined by the eternal star.

For Rosenstock-Huessy and Rosenzweig, the naturalist or mechanistic revolution at the basis of modern secularism did not allow for the cultural connection between time and collective faith as a repository of speech. Together and in different ways, one as a Christian, one as a Jew, they undertook to rectify the deficiencies of a way of thinking that had cut us off from our history and our future. They did so by reopening a path of thinking and acting grounded in speech, love, invocation, liturgy, and incarnation, and not primarily the mechanisms of nature, pure thought, or any one of the world's essences that some philosophy or other has invented. That endeavour was designated the New Thinking or 'speech thinking,' and it would lead Rosenzweig to his reconstitution of Jewish–Christian relations. The post-Holocaust transformation of Christian–Jewish relations – at least from the side of a Christianity aware of its failures and complicities in the Holocaust – looks astonishingly like the kind of appreciation of Judaism that Rosenzweig had wanted from Christians. Rosenstock-Huessy would configure the cross of reality so that Christianity would become but one of its four 'directions' of orientation. While Rosenstock-Huessy always placed Jesus at the centre of history, as early as 1925 he was writing about how Jesus' founding act required integration not only with the other founding acts of Abraham but also with those of Buddha and Lao-Tse.[112] Each had opened a front of reality to which modern men and women must respond if they were to survive and flourish in the modern world.

1 Which Spirit to Serve? The Stirring of the Living Loving God

Despair and crises are to the twentieth and early twenty-first centuries what mathematics, the clock, and light were to the seventeenth and early eighteenth centuries. Twentieth-century social thinking of almost every hue is shaped by anxiety about the flattening out of the world, the increasing atomization, specialization, bureaucratization, and general shrinking of the spirit or soul or life-world that is the accompanying price of modernity's material success and domination over nature:[1] thus its images of the iron cage, the panopticon, one-dimensional man, and finally Agamben's *Homo sacer*. Though perhaps the most compact image summarizing twentieth-century fears and confirming Nietzsche's pronouncements of God's death is Kafka's Gregor Samsa's waking up as a bug. For Europeans the nineteenth century was apocalyptic, yet the mood was manically hopeful; the twentieth century, on the other hand, slowly came to realize that it had nothing to hope for – it picked up Montaigne's and Rousseau's doubts about civilization itself and the preference of the 'primitive' or the Other as its attempts at salvation became increasingly horrendous, worse than nothing. Godot's non-arrival signalled a far better state of affairs than the arrivals of Hitler or Stalin or Mao. Heidegger's 'Nothing nothings' was the metaphysical cipher for twentieth-century philosophical aspirations as Aristotle's unmoved mover was for the Greeks, who would – not surprisingly – take that 'unmovedness' into themselves in the form of Epicurean *apatheia*.

Despair is understandable and can be a sobering device against metastatic faith in false idols. Though despair can also be dangerously reactionary and debilitating. The New Thinking, at least in its Christian inflection, placed itself under the sign of John of Patmos and (as we will discuss more fully later) under the hope in God's love that was its central directive. Its hope was thus never misplaced in the politics of immediacy and was ever conceived as a power radiating over a very long time.

When the spirits of modernity were in their preliminary stages, Shakespeare (in *The Tempest*) and Milton (in *Paradise Lost*) repeated a fundamental founding truth that Luther had brought against Erasmus to articulate: we are always in bondage. The elevation of the self, the ego, the I – which is found in so many modern foundational gestures, from Renaissance aspirations of the will, to liberal understandings of state and governance, to Cartesian metaphysics, to Kantian moral theory – is nipped in every bud by these two masterpieces of psychology and language. Elevation of the self is the satanic (Milton); the powerful self is one who serves the right lord/power at the right time in the right way (Prospero's lesson) because human freedom is always servitude.

When Nietzsche, repeating a formula already coined by Jean Paul and repeated by Hegel, pronounced God dead and declared the advent of nihilism (again he was echoing someone else, this time Jacobi and his critique of mechanism and idealism), he knew that human beings needed something to place themselves in service to. Likewise he saw that the 'I' / the ego / the self was an epiphenomenon rather than a sovereign. Thus to the extent that Nietzsche called himself a disciple of Dionysos he was articulating something that would disappear from the mechanists' horizon of visibility, viz., the insight that unites all peoples who invoke God/s – that it matters what we divinize and whom we serve. Generally, this insight had been lost on modern mechanists, who focused exclusively on forces as essentially numerical and corporeal. Though in the ancient world, even when there was an emphasis on the corporeal basis of reality, there was a recognition that we stand in service to forces we summon or are summoned by. Thus, to take perhaps the most compelling example, the ancient atomist Lucretius summons Venus and places himself in her service as he relates the story of the world (*On Nature*).

Nietzsche saw that his contemporaries had the choice between service to the dead God of Platonism and Christianity (which for Nietzsche were one and the same) or the god he had rediscovered, Dionysos, the god of the vine and life's rejuvenation. Nietzsche's reasons for God being dead followed precisely the same train of thought that Spinoza (the thinker Nietzsche belatedly realized was his precursor) had already set out – the dissolution of God into nature and the concomitant elimination of transcendence and final causes, the historical reading/ reduction of sacred texts, and the the prohibition of miracles. Nietzsche does point back to a more archaic understanding of the self as formed by its sacrifices and devotions, yet even in him there is something of the self's own aggrandizement that gives it a peculiarly modern and (notwithstanding his protestations against Romanticism) romantic character, most visible in his dubious elevation of the aesthetic as a means of giving life its purpose. Mechanism and Romanticism, Descartes and Nietzsche, as different as they are, belong to the same *gestalt*. Thus at the conclusion of the first volume of his *Soziologie,* Rosenstock-Huessy notes that the motherless Descartes and the fatherless Nietzsche represent the two one-sided poles of modernity with its undertones of life construed as mechanical reproduction (Descartes's insight) and its overtones of redemption as artistry (Nietzsche's 'art is worth more than truth').[2] In between are the vast wastelands of spiritual despair – the widespread lovelessness of everyday life that neither gadgetry, nor art, nor 'freedom' has been able to satiate.

Rosenstock-Huessy's and Rosenzweig's appraisals of faith – and of post-Nietszchean theology in general – were symptomatic of the widespread turn from mechanism, and of the reawakening to human life as being formed by powers it responds to. In spite of the nature of their faith, it was an appraisal that Nietzsche had encouraged. For from the moment each undertook to become who he was, he was driven by this question: Who or what should I serve? The starkest way to formulate their question is this: Should I serve the powers that created the modern age or should I serve another power that promises salvation/redemption? The powers of the modern age had long had an aura of escalating doom and despair, captured by Edvard Munch's *The Scream* and the proto-Expressionist tortured presentiments of James Ensor and Vincent van Gogh – they were the very powers that led to the catastrophe of the First World War.

To the mechanist, the question seems silly because the source or ground of the real is manifestly deaf or indifferent to such questions. Yet when the question is given a moral shape and posed as 'Should I behave ethically or selfishly?' the modern academic mind feels no discomfort – which is somewhat strange, if not inexplicable, and only goes to show how Kantian the modern soul really is. From a strictly mechanistic/naturalistic viewpoint, however, such as the one adopted by Spinoza, the question and its answer dissolve into the flow of bodily forces and are but ciphers of those greater forces. For those with more noble hopes for the species – who shirk from the fascism of force itself being the answer to life's purpose, though they foresee equally as grim prospects regarding what life itself has to offer – Kant is still the most pervasive (compelling?) of spirits. Kant did not want to challenge science's sovereignty over nature, but he knew that the question of life's meaning is one we may well ask without being able to answer it with anything more than a rational faith in reason's own ideas. For him this is the supreme elevation of freedom – and indeed, of ourselves as participants in a rational kingdom; it is the touchstone of our dignity and the foundation of our hope. Whether such a response is dignified or sadly, even pathetically, quixotic is worth pondering as we canvass why Rosenstock-Huessy and Rosenzweig wanted no truck with such a widely held modern answer. Neither was convinced by Spinozian/Nietzschean nihilism or by Kantian stripes of moral idealism; yet they were no less tempted by the hybrid that, until rescued by Levinas's incorporation, typified contemporary (North American, British, and Australian appropriations of) post-structuralist politico-ethics, with its surreptitious moralizing and up-front emphasis on power.

Levinas certainly raised the game of what is meant by ethical, in no small part by infusing a Greek concept with Jewish content. Without undertaking a detailed comparison with Levinas, I will simply state that neither Rosenzweig nor Rosenstock-Huessy can really be understood by those – however well intentioned – who accept without fuss the moral or ethical formulations of life's most urgent questions. For neither Rosenzweig nor Rosenstock-Huessy was looking primarily for a moral or ethical answer to the questions that burned in them – though Rosenzweig does have 'an ethics,' which is an offshoot of his primary questions and which can briefly be formulated as 'love the neighbour who is there and not the neighbour you want to be there.' (Observe here that the matching of the Davidic star with the human face at the conclusion of *The Star* obviously anticipates Levinas.) That is why *some* of what Rosenzweig says will be emphasized by readers whose day job is to find moral solutions for our trials and journeys. (And to some extent this is also true of Rosenstock-Huessy, who in volume 2 of his *Soziologie* also explicitly relates the countenance of the face to the nature of speech and thus to what he takes to be the basis of our common humanity.)[3] But unlike philosophers and social theorists who pour over the differences between *Sitten, Sittlichkeit,* and *Moralität,* or questions about whether moral choices can be moral according to their deontological, utilitarian, or consequentialist framings, Rosenzweig and Rosenstock-Huessy do not commence with a distinction between moral and immoral principles and their impact on life. Their questioning, much like Nietzsche's, takes its first cue from life itself with all its potentials and sources. This refusal to stand upon the moral or ethical as such stemmed from their conviction that Nietzsche was correct to the extent that there is no such place – for us at least – to stand outside of life. And to attempt to do so would merely reflect the residue of philosophical Idealism, which refused to accept yet persisted in holding such a faith in such a non-existent ideal space. Many academic writers have devoted themselves to carving out this space and then identifying the rules that make it possible, and attempt to instruct us all how to live, and deal with how human beings should conduct themselves in accordance with the moral/ethical ideals and legal and social standards that they as philosophers have identified – which is all well and good for those who share this faith. But what is it really faith in? And why should anyone share this faith? Kant at least knew that he had to identify the bounds of reason and then protect its majesty with all his might – but who now believes in reason's sphericality? And as for its majesty? Once reason is accepted as something *within* life rather than sovereign *over* it, its pretensions are irrecoverable. Today anyone who wants to present himself as a magistrate because of his mastery of reason's majesty only makes a spectacle of himself as well as his reasons. To watch the daily academic sideshow of one group 'discovering' an ethics, or theory of justice, that all should comply with, even while another group stresses with equal vehemence that we *are* our identity, and that the lifeways and *ethoi* of different groups are fundamental for the group's resilience and hence are not to be judged on 'our Western/bourgeois/masculinist/whitey/heterosexual culture's terms,' only brings to the fore the deep and irreconcilable tensions within a paradigm that wants peace and anthropological pluralism but is clueless how to achieve it.

When another of the New Thinkers, Hans Ehrenberg, in his autobiography wrote that he would always think of himself as a student of Dostoevsky, who was the first to introduce him to the real meaning of John's interpretation of Christianity and St Paul – 'the Christ who sits with tax collectors, prostitutes and murderers is the Christ of Dostoevky's writings' – he added an important insight that I think applies to the New Thinkers generally: 'The religion of morality of Western civilization and the religion of duty of the categorical imperative, "Prussian" religion, find a common grave in Dostoievski.'[4] One can see exactly what he is getting at when he writes, in that same work, that in Britain, Hitler is thought of solely in terms of civilization or morality, and adds that this misses the whole point of the extraordinary powers he summons and channels, what Ehrenberg calls his 'black magic,' something all too visible in the ceremonial stagings of the Nazis' nighttime rallies.[5]

One major reason why the New Thinkers lost faith in moral reasoning as an important compass point was that like Nietzsche, they thought much more in terms of the powers or energy of life. And the priority of love in the New Thinking is simply misunderstood if its energistic nature is not grasped – all part of their common reaction to the mechanization of modern life as killing spirit and body. To be sure, the importance of life as energy is most transparent in the biological, medical, and psychological studies of those New Thinkers, such as Rudi Ehrenberg, Richard Koch, and Viktor von Weizsäcker, whose writings were more overtly biological, medical, or psychological.[6] Their work, however, finds strong resonances in Rosenstock-Huessy's comment in *Heilkraft und Wahrheit* where, as if anticipating the attacks by Foucault and Deleuze and Guattari on the psychiatric profession, he compares the 'bestial character' of the pseudo-Platonist psychoanalysts who throw people into the asylum with that of the pseudo-Aristotelians who burn witches at the stake.[7]

The biological and medical studies of the New Thinkers also stood in the closest relationship to their faith. This is powerfully expressed by Rosenstock-Huessy in an unpublished paper titled 'Biology and the Life of Life,' in which he says:

Man's biological problem is to bury the non-living materials of his conscious life, to secrete in time the corpses of his intellect. We could live the good life if we could establish a permanent process of burying the unliving corpses of our intellectual, moral, social, religious life in time.

Christianity when it came into the world, undertook the task of offering a life freed from the corpses of death. St. John expressed this idea very clearly when he said: the word of life became flesh. Life now was manifested. And he drew the line of demarcation very clearly between 'life' on one side and its fictitious semblances which in fact were messengers of death on the other . . .

Christianity offered to man a corrected form of life. That is its only interest and endeavour. It brought back into life the man who cometh after me although he had gone before me. For he was before me. Those who believed in the name of this everlasting man got power to become children of God. They now were sure of not only eating and breathing and marrying in time but also of passing through the processes of the conscious life in the right order and at the right moment. The words they spoke, the superstitions . . . the ideas they conceived of themselves and of others, acquired now a biological carefulness. The circulation of the stream of life did no longer exclude the highest province of life, the mind's processes. Here too, a perpetual secretion and separation was set into motion.

Christianity offered not a theoretical course in biology but it offered the biological process itself. And here our modern weakness is obvious. Christianity is broke today because we think of it more or less as a theology, a doctrine, as a correcting lesson in morals, rarely as the corrected form of life itself . . . Biology may waken us from slumber. Let us draw new inspiration from the biologists and their interest in the processes of perpetual change. Life is change.[8]

Such a comment as this, and indeed, the general emphasis on energy and the powers of life, is what lies behind the fundamental formulation of love being stronger than death that underpins the meaning of redemption for Rosenzweig and Rosenstock-Huessy. Indeed, the title of one of Rosenzweig's books, *The Little Book of Sick and Healthy Human Understanding* (to translate the title literally from the German to better make our point), places his understanding of where our thinking fits in the greater schema of life itself.[9] In the case of Rosenstock-Huessy, his writings refer constantly to energy and power and their various cognates, and he was always deeply interested in the biological and physiological – something that can be easily overlooked in the way he explores speech. But while grammar is the *organon* of his work (as we will discuss later), grammar is also ultimately embedded in life itself. The Nietzschean similarities are again all too obvious. Though it was not Nietzsche whom Rosenstock-Huessy constantly deferred to and often wrote about in this respect, but Paracelsus, of whom he and Richard Koch wrote, in 1923, that 'his living value lay in the fact that he, as a knowing, willing human being, wanted to come to terms with the world as it is, not with a simplified artificial world.'[10] Some five years later, in *Das Alter der Kirche*, to which he devoted a lengthy section on Paracelsus, he favourably compared Paracelsus to Barth, Gogarten, and Franz Werfel, criticizing the latter for their dualism, which, he said, would ever ensure that divinity and the earthly never meet, so that God can be kept 'chemically pure' – and irrelevant.[11]

The assessment of Koch and Rosenstock-Huessy that we have just cited came from their introduction to their edition of Paracelsus' *Five Books on the Invisible Sicknesses*, under the more general title *Sickness and Faith* – a fitting enough selection, from the persective of the New Thinking. *Sickness and Faith* was the first volume in the Frommann's philosophical paperbacks edited by Hans Ehrenberg (the series was titled *Natur und Mensch* [Nature and Man]).[12] Throughout Rosenstock-Huessy's life, he would refer often to the importance of Paracelus as a founder of the new kind of science (though to be sure, that new science carried some of the more superstitious baggage of its time).[13] In the second volume of his *Soziologie,* Rosenstock-Huessy emphasizes the importance of Paracelsus as a founder of the new science that made Descartes possible (though unlike Descartes, Paracelsus would not create a new metaphysics that has contributed so much to the mechanization of modern life with its accompanying spiritual and physical brutalities).[14] We will return to Paracelsus when we look more closely at Rosenstock-Huessy's adaption of his teaching of the five spheres of life in the chapter 'Das Zeitenspektrum' ('Time Spectrum') in *Heilkraft und Wahrheit;* here I simply want to point out that in contrast to any dualistic and hence moralistic readings of reality, Rosenzweig and Rosenstock-Huessy are thinkers about energy in general, and about the energy of all energies, love, in particular. That love's power over death is the source of revelation and that its transference and expansion by means of the love of the neighbour is the source of redemption is central to Rosenzweig's understanding of the meaning of Jewish life, not just for the Jew, but for the rest of humanity. It is no less central for why Rosenstock-Huessy understands planetary consciousness of the present times as the fulfilment of the Christian mission to take revelation into the pagan world and to find salvation in the realization that the tree of humanity is one (to take an image that he often uses). If love is the power that binds God to His people and His truth to all peoples, it is important to fathom what it is, and not simply to equate it with the moral will, even if the moral will may at times be placed in love's service.

The following passage from *The Star of Redemption* expresses the key difference between modern thinking grounded in moral freedom and the hope expressed by moral faith in the ethical kingdom to come – that is, by the widespread modern idealist faith that so pervades our world – on the one hand, and faith in love's creative, revelatory, and redemptive energy, which is the much more archaic command that drives Rosenzweig and Rosenstock-Huessy, on the other:

Love for the neighbour can be commanded and it must be commanded. This love derived its origins from the mystery of the oriented will. Only the form of the commandment makes visible behind that origin the presupposition of love received by God, and this presupposition distinguishes it from all moral acts. Moral laws dare not content only to be rooted in freedom – as love toward the neighbour also wants it – they actually do not want to recognize any presupposition other than freedom. This is the famous requirement of 'autonomy.' The natural consequence of this requirement is that the laws destined to determine this act lose all content, for any content would exert a power which would ruin the autonomy; one cannot will 'something' and yet will only 'in general'; now, the requirement of autonomy demands that man only wills without conditions, absolutely. And because the law does not lay hold of any content, neither does the singular act ever attain any certainty. In the moral domain, everything can be moral, but nothing is so with any certainty. In contrast to moral law which is necessarily purely formal, and hence not only ambivalent, but infinitely ambiguous as regards content, the commandment of love is clear and unambiguous in its content, and for this love which springs from the orientated freedom of character it needs presupposition that is beyond freedom . . . 'God ordains what he wants': but because of the content of the order is to love, the divine 'already done' precedes what he ordains. Only the soul loved by God can receive the commandment of neighbourly love so as to fulfil it.[15]

Though this is a powerful statement of Rosenzweig's position regarding the importance of love over morals or ethics, as early as 1906 he had noted: 'As if pure ethics could ever produce a religion or provide nourishment.'[16]

Like Rosenzweig, Rosenstock-Huessy trusts the creative and redemptive power of love far more than any moral laws of the mind, telling us in *Der Atem des Geistes* (The Breath of the Spirit) that 'love is not bound to any law.'[17] In the same work he dismisses moralist readings of history: 'All moralizing history prides itself on holding that we should be able to learn off by heart the small and great basics of life like the catechism. If only we did that then we would not make any mistakes, and all would think and say the same thing.'[18] He is even more blunt when he says that 'true action is not responsible to so called ethics.'[19] Though such bluntness and such mistrust of any final court of moral appeal provided by reason does not mean that either Rosenzweig or Rosenstock-Huessy is blind to evil as a real force (as opposed to a merely immoral one), or of the need to battle it. On the contrary, evil is too powerful for our merely moral and reasonable means. In *Out of Revolution*, Rosenstock-Huessy states the difference between the struggle against evil as a slow process over time, involving the catastrophes and the violence of the great revolutions, which have yielded freedoms unknown to earlier peoples, on the one hand, and the idealist moral approach, on the other:

> The moralist and the creator live in different tenses. This is usually overlooked; yet if we mix the ethical with the political aspect of life we shall never be able to do justice to our own best actions. Every soul that faces reality is perfectly aware of this distinction and acts accordingly with the best of consciences. Only if a man tries to take his stand outside the world, as the philosopher of ethics does, he deliberately and constantly neglects the triplicity of past, present and future. It is a great secret, unknown to children or adolescents, but one which is revealed and becomes familiar to everyone who grows up to full manhood, that our ideas about good and evil are one thing, and the right time to introduce a change for the better is another. The idealist who thinks anything can be good outside of time and space only makes a fool of himself. Timeliness is everything. Reality is 'good' when it proceeds timely; it is bad when too late or too early. 'Good' and 'evil' themselves in their deepest sense mean ripeness and immaturity. Any man who looks around him finds a great many desirable points which might make for the improvement of his environment. It is a wise man who realizes that it will take all his energy to carry one per cent of these good and desirable points into reality. The rest of the 'good' is excluded. Reality is closed to the empty pretensions of the 'always' idealist. Reality seems to hate the abstract good with the intense hatred the first Christians felt toward their idealistic rivals, the Gnostics. Real life can certainly never hate 'the' good, but it does hate the abstract idea of the good. It has always spat out the abstract, and always will.
>
> Real life's only approach to a fuller, better form of existence is through necessity and timeliness. Bring a thing into fashion, create a fresh interest, make it timely, and, as a climax, let it be clear that it is inevitable and necessary – and it will be incorporated into the lists of reality.[20]

Love and hate or fear – that is, love's lack – unlike merely moral ideas, are for Rosenstock-Huessy overpowering forces that build up and tear down worlds and epochs. In *The Christian Future* he writes simply: 'Love and its lack are behind all serious conflict.'[21] And in *Out of Revolution* he says:

> Political order is not meant for happiness or the full life or the greatest happiness of the greatest number. That is the cant of public-minded privateers who know nothing of the outdoor life of the pioneer, beyond good and evil, driven by the angels and demons of love and fear. Revolutions come as a positive effort when the fear of a complete breakdown of order preys so terribly on the bowels of men that only a great courage and a great love can open the way to a new equilibrium of powers.[22]

It might seem that talking of love and revolution in the same breath is a long way from the love of the neighbour that drives Rosenzweig, but the reality of love's absence is precisely what enables us to see the truth of the connection between love and life in the first place. Rosenstock-Huessy and Rosenzweig did not accept the sovereignty of the autonomous will or self; nor did they accept that either nature or the mind, or any other 'sacred' designate reached by philosophical consensus, had to be complied with as the ground or touchstone of truth. They respected life – and love as a force creating or founding life, circulating within it and redeeming it.

Just as Rosenzweig and Rosenstock-Huessy did not serve the spirit of ethicists or moralists, they also refused to serve the other, perhaps even more dominant 'spirits' of their time, which called for and received such widespread attendance.

One of the greatest spirits of the modern era, one that demands and receives the service of countless millions, is natural science, that spirit that rules modern industry and technology. Both Rosenzweig and Rosenstock-Huessy did indeed see their work as guided by the scientific spirit, at least in the German sense of science as *Wissenschaft*, which is as appropriate for the human sciences as for the natural ones. And as we suggested earlier, they saw that a reconstitution of the natural sciences was intrinsic to the New Thinking. But for both of them, the scientific spirit was a secondary or subordinate spirit. The title of Koch and Rosenstock-Huessy's edition of Paracelsus, *Sickness and Faith*, makes this clear: faith is essential in every scientific endeavour, and our spiritual illnesses, which have bodily manifestations, may also stem from our idolatry, our misplaced faith in powers that consume and deplete us.

Many philosophers in the Anglo-American-Australian tradition have been content to serve as under-labourers to natural science; this has been much less the case in Europe. This may be symptomatic not just of suspicions about science's role in the technologies that have contributed to the world wars fought on so much of European soil; even since Kant, it has been recognized that science means little without human freedom – that is, without being placed under some higher purpose. Nietzsche made the point that science always needs one more Other to defer to – and that remained true whether it was money, or humanity, or progress, or morality, or communism or some other political program. Rosenstock-Huessy made much the same point in *Hitler and Israel, or On Prayer,* pointing to scientists' need for social direction and observing how the lack of scientific faith in prayer did not eliminate the human need to pray so much as it depleted the capacity to discern between monsters and gods – a capacity that positive science was not especially well equipped to deal with. Science's interpolation into the social world had made many things better, but even by the beginning of the nineteenth century, Enlightenment progressivism was in bad enough repute to have spawned an entire movement that wanted to distance itself from it. The Great War would spawn others – Expressionism, Dadaism, and so forth.

Rosenzweig had begun his studies in medicine, but he wanted more. He was simply too restless, too driven by questions of the spirit, to accept that the natural sciences could answer them. But more important, he and Rosenstock-Huessy, along with countless others, saw that while the natural sciences may provide some goods, the injection of natural science into a metaphysics was disastrous. And indeed, it was this injection accompanied by the imprisonment of living forces within a mechanistic view of life that Rosenstock-Huessy and Rosenzweig saw as a fundamental problem with humanism.

Rosenstock-Huessy was not an admirer of Adorno. But when Adorno argues that 'technical-administrative measures' are intrinsic to the fascistic dimension of the modern project itself, his point of view is identical to Rosenstock-Huessy's criticism that the crime of modern humanism is that it reduces living souls to numbers and mere objects.[23] The modern reductivist logic of control dissolves life and human beings into one overarching entity – 'nature.'[24] Undercutting a view of the world as composed of living creatures, with each creature having been created to play its part in the symphony of creation and receiving its special name, modern humanism permits the raw matter of nature to be excavated, manipulated, commodified, circulated, thrown away, given a number instead of a name, and exterminated if of no use or 'value.' Indeed, as Descartes, Spinoza, and all the mechanists rightly claimed, we better understand 'nature' by not using names and using mathematics instead. When mechanists extract the concept of finality from the world in favour of a more truthful – that is, scientific – understanding of nature, there is no reason why a human life should be more nor less than that of an ant, or a bacterial cell, for that matter. That the term 'human resource' is a part of our everyday use shows how deeply rooted mechanism is and how little we have learned about the conditions, and the role of the names we use, that have made the twentieth century so horrific.

Hitler's description of Jews as bacteria in *Mein Kampf* is simply mechanistic logic injected with his own hatred. Even though the Nazis had expelled Einstein, Nazi Germany generally had no problem fitting mechanistic science into its ideological horizon. Likewise, physicists and chemists seem to have been just as ready to join the party as members of the other professions. And most disturbing of all, as Chris Hutton has demonstrated in his groundbreaking studies of Nazi race theory, the popular view that race theory in Nazi Germany ran through its science is not even true. After 1935, the term 'Aryan' was a linguistic rather than a racial category. And what is almost never appreciated is that the Third Reich's racial anthropology had far more in common with international 'scientifically accepted' standards and conclusions than not.[25]

Philosophers themselves sensed that mechanism could be horrific. Sade would paint the problem with sexually charged ghoulish *jouissance*, and Kant would provide a definitive (if not enduring) formulation – the categorical imperative – and moral grounding in the rational will to distinguish between our moral aspirations and the blind forces of mechanism. He was, nevertheless, sufficiently connected to a tradition of providence, albeit in the more vulgar Enlightenment sense of progress, to argue that those blind and dangerous forces could be interpreted as contributing to historical progress. It did not take long before the 'rational will' needed to be refined if it were to endure. To this project, Fichte applied himself. He was delighted at his efforts, only to have Hegel wreck the enterprise as he looked toward the reality of *ethical life* to provide the reason that a formula could not. After Nietzsche, all bets were off, and it was only with Levinas that the continental tradition (Anglo-Saxon philosophy, in the main, seemed to think such concerns the result of monstrously deformed human energies and brains) could feel that some kind of ethical solution had been found. It is not surprising, perhaps, that Levinas's 'solution' rested on inspirations from Rosenzweig and Judaism and on a renunciation of the naturalistic/mechanistic view of the world that had created the problem in the first place.

While this hostility to mechanism and humanism is intrinsic to understanding both Rosenzweig and Rosenstock-Huessy, it is the latter who repeatedly returns to this theme. To take a rather typical example from a lecture by Rosenstock-Huessy:

> Nature is a minus-concept. It is not a plus-concept. That is, nature is the decision to look around the shifting universe which can be dealt with without the risk of destroying your own existence, your own life. Nature is at every one moment of human history that which can, if worse comes to worst, be expendable. The word 'expendable' at the end of a naturalistic era, has become even the expression for human beings . . . Its coincident with concentration camps, and with gas chambers, and with the idea that man has no name, that a member of the concentration camp doesn't have to be spoken to, and that they are just corpses. We live in a wonderful world where the natural scientist has created the impression that man can be treated, and manipulated, and be known without having any say-so, without being connected with the man who deals with him through the power of the universals, of those gods, divine powers which both invoke together, to whom both pray, under whose guidance both put themselves, which always entails that the psychologist or the sociologist or the concentration camp engineer is not beyond the man whom he puts in the burning furnace or on the table . . . of experimentation . . . that's very serious[26]

And when he adds to his American audience that 'this country is just as natural-science ridden as Russia,' he is emphasizing just how ubiquitous this mind-set is.

Of course, humanity did not need modern science or a concept of 'nature' to kill on a large scale. But instead of simply extending our lives, enabling us to enjoy the fruits of the earth, and freeing us from the burdens of labour, as Descartes excitedly proposed in the last of his *Discourses on Method*, the concept of nature has facilitated technologies that, while not rectifying the passions of the human heart, do hasten the speed and expand the scale of killing. 'The greatest of all wars,' as Rosenstock-Huessy reminded an audience on the eve of another great killing spree, 'was the quickest of all wars. It was marvellous how quickly scientific implements could kill hundreds of thousands of men. In 4 years the destruction was over.'[27]

For Rosenstock-Huessy and Rosenzweig, the Great War seemed to supply the proof of just how thin were humanism's bulwarks against the dangers besetting it from within. This suggests why neither Rosenstock-Huessy nor Rosenzweig could devote himself to liberalism, for liberalism left open the end of the soul's existence, which might well be a wise political choice. Neither man was interested in undermining such liberal basics as the rule of law and the right of voluntary association; indeed, both saw such freedoms as fruits of Judaism and Christendom. Yet neither Rosenstock-Huessy nor Rosenzweig – with his passion of the soul – stopped with what could be achieved through political organization, any more than either man stopped with what commercial organization could achieve. And just as science defers to another, so too commerce.

Rosenstock-Huessy, whose father had been a banker, was much more interested in how the commercial and working classes could find genuine means of cooperation so that the hostilities between classes could be ameliorated, in such a way that common human needs did not simply dissipate in an increasing social atomism and its accompanying anomie, mass addictions, and multiform alienations. Marxists, then and now, saw any proposed cooperation between labour and capital as a flight of fancy at best, and at worst as a betrayal of working-class interests. But as we will examine in a later chapter, Rosenstock-Huessy was as little convinced by Marxists' economic arguments that society could flourish with capital's elimination as he was by their view of human history as driven primarily by class struggle.

Insofar as neither science nor commerce nor liberalism had any great appeal to them, neither Rosenstock-Huessy nor Rosenzweig was untypical of those with vaulting philosophical or *geistige* (which they most definitely did have as well) and *geistliche* ambitions. During their generation, the principal spirits (apart from God) that battled for the attention of hungry young men were the nation, art, and communism (which, unlike liberalism, was at least in its early formation an untried promise of total salvation for humanity). Indeed, in some very fundamental ways, these – along with commerce and modern technology – were the formative secular powers of the twentieth century, and we will discuss them more fully in later chapters. Generally, though, Rosenzweig and Rosenstock-Huessy saw faith in politics and faith in art as the two perennial pagan faiths – as the two great competitors for the soul of the modern. Rosenzweig makes this point well near the conclusion of *The Star*:

> Those eternal gods of paganism in whom paganism will survive until the eternal end, the State and the arts, the former the idol of material gods, the idol of personal ones, are shackled by the true God. If the State might well claim the highest place in the universe for the world, and art might for man, and if the State might dam up the river of time in the era of World history, and art try to drain it off into the endless canal system of experience – so let them! He who sits in heaven mocks them . . . As long as both State and art, each for itself, need to be regarded as omnipotent, just so long they each also, and rightly, claim all of nature for themselves. They both know nature only as their 'material.' Only truth, because it circumscribed both, the State in eternal life, art in the eternal way, could free nature from the twofold slavery and make it one again, in which State and art might now receive their share, but not more.[28]

If none of the great modern spirits were strong enough to make minions of Rosenzweig or Rosenstock-Huessy, there remained the one spirit that had for so long been seen as living and alone worthy of total veneration (albeit, at times, through intermediaries). That spirit was the living God, a term widely used, though Rosenzweig insists in *The Star* that his God is more accurately and precisely designated as the God of the living and the dead.[29] Certainly, at the time Rosenstock-Huessy and Rosenzweig were becoming who they were, many educated people viewed God as irrelevant – as the equivalent to a kind of tooth fairy (United Kingdom),[30] or as dead (Germany), or as a mere vestige of superstition that the powerful resorted to as a tool of exploitation (France). This was why the new spirits of the modern – the nation, art, science, communism, democracy, commerce – were so widely held to be self-evident. Given how certain so many nineteenth-century thinkers were of God's demise or irrelevance, it is hard for many to fathom why in Germany in the early part of the twentieth century, a generation arose that was untouched by what it saw as the vacuous moral pieties of nineteenth-century German theology, but that insisted that there was indeed a creator and redeemer God, a living, loving presence who was the spirit of all spirits. Moreover, that generation's conviction was not based simply on a philosophical flight from reality, as those atheists hold who still see the world mainly through the mechanistic arguments and victories of the seventeenth and eighteenth centuries. On the contrary, a new theology was brewing that was greatly the product of philosophical questions and insights regarding the nature of the real.

The theology that was to emerge in the twentieth century – including the theology to be found in Rosenzweig and Rosenstock-Huessy (who came to hate the word *theology*, seeing it very much as a medieval solution to a medieval problem that was no longer his)[31] – was far closer in spirit to those radical rejections of naturalism that as can be found in philosophies as disparate as the phenomenologies of Brentano, Husserl, and Heidegger and the existentialisms of Sartre and Camus and Marcel and Unamuno and the dialogical revolts of Ebner, Buber, and Bakhtin. By then, Kierkegaard had long since written his *Concluding Un-Scientific Postscript*, a work that remains a masterful demolition of naturalism and idealism; meanwhile, Nietzsche's work oscillated between a raw physiologism (which, with great disingenuousness, most of his Parisian post-structuralist and North American readers simply deny is there) that valorized life/nature in his metaphysics of will to power, on the one side, and a view of truth as symbolic constructionism (albeit ever symptomatic of a will to power), on the other.

In tandem with the break with naturalism was the pressing question of existence and meaning, which also wrested the matter of religion from the confines of mechanistic reduction that united Spinoza, Voltaire, and – at least in his reading of Judaism and Christianity and Buddhism – Nietzsche. Again, Kierkegaard was a decisive figure. Throughout his corpus, but most notably in *Either/Or*, he had argued that the ethical life and the aesthetic one were ultimately unsatisfying for someone consumed by the search for life's ultimate meaning. It followed that for him, politics was yet another poor sort of religion. Like Nietzsche after him, Kierkegaard loathed the poverty of spirit that he saw as the product of Christendom. But Kierkegaard, like Dostoevsky, had a view of Christianity that could not have been more remote from Nietzsche's. For him, Christianity was not an easy choice for the weak and the resentful who hate life; rather, it was striving for something stronger and more real than culture, which was the phantasmic end of Nietzsche's love. (What is culture compared to one's very soul?) For Kierkegaard, the Christian was not someone who turned his back on life, but someone who wanted to intensify life by intensifying the absoluteness of its meaning as well as his own individual meaning and actions. Nietzsche knew of Kierkegaard through his admirer, the Danish art critic George Brandeis, who could see there was an affinity between the two – which indeed there was. It is just that Nietzsche contented himself with attacking Christendom and could only ever see Christianity as a force hostile to life and as preoccupied with flight into another world. It is not hard to see that Kierkegaard's view of Christianity demanded precisely the same kind of resolve and strength of soul that Nietzsche admired.

A similar appreciation of Christian spiritual resoluteness is found in Dostoevsky, who interprets the Christian faith in resurrection not as a symptom of *hostility* to life, but as *love* for life. Thus for him, Christian faith in life after death is not the response of a kind of life needing to project itself into the beyond to enhance its power because of its weakness here. Rather, the superfluity of feeling and awe for the overflowing power of love's presence, as exemplified in Elder Zossima in *The Brothers Karamazov,* is what makes one believe in immortality: one loves life so much that one does not want it to stop. Likewise, *ressentiment* leads to nothingness, not an afterworld, as in Smerdyakov in the same novel, who hates life so much that he wants to bring everything and everyone, his own self included, down into the deepest darkness.

Though Nietzsche's influence was ubiquitous in Germany at the time Rosenzweig and Rosenstock-Huessy were developing their thought, and as the examples of Dostoevsky and Kierkegaard demonstrate, by no means was Christianity visible solely to philosophically passionate minds through Nietzsche's lens. Indeed, Rosenzweig and Rosenstock-Huessybelongedtoanotinsubstantialgroupofbrilliantyoung people – a group that included Karl Barth, Rosenzweig's cousins Hans and Rudi Ehrenberg, Dietrich Bonhoeffer, and Paul Tillich, all of whom were convinced that the God of philosophers that Nietzsche had pronounced dead was indeed a vampire devouring life energies who was widely worshipped within Christendom. This GOD was as rotten for them as it was for Nietzsche, and was just as vacuous – and this dead GOD of the philosophical idolaters was an It, not a He, not a living power, a Lord who issued commands.

From Nietzsche, Dostoevsky, and Kierkegaard, then, that generation had accepted that the life lived conveys its truth – and Nietzsche had shown that the idealist moralistic God had created pathetic lives, just as Dostoevsky and Kierkegaard had shown that the living God had fuelled extraordinary lives. But Dostoevsky departed drastically from Nietzsche by virtue of his prophetic conviction that recent attempts to make a Man-god were producing twisted, tortured, and despicable souls. And his more modest understanding of human capacity and its inevitable failings tied in closely with the insight that we are all responsible for all, that we are all weak, all sinners – all of these, of course, Christian sentiments that are a far cry from Nietzsche's celebration of unbridled innocence and the aristocratic carnivals of cruelty he wished to revive for modern Europe (post '68, Nietzsche has lost these appetites). There were those who followed Nietzsche's fantasy about supermen, but Nietzsche's greatest legacy to the group of (non-fascist) post-Nietzscheans was not so much about supermen, but about his exemplification of a life lived in terms of his own truth.

The revival of Christianity and Judaism, then, by those who had also been exposed to and influenced by Kierkegaard and Dostoesvsky, was not that a generation simply wished to retreat into a pre-Nietzschean philosophy; rather, that generation was not convinced that mechanism captured the true depth and range of human potential, and that that range of powers could not be tapped without reference to a power powerful enough to incorporate lived experience. When I have stressed the Christian side, it is not because a Judaic one didn't exist – indeed, at the time, there also was a reawakening of the philosophical possibilities inherent in Judaism. In terms of Rosenzweig's development, the great philosophical example on the Jewish side was Hermann Cohen, who had set out to find reason in the concrete lives and writings of the Jewish people. Thus did the most attentive of nineteenth-century Kantian scholars move from philosophy and Kant back to his own Jewish faith, seeing in the community into which he had been born the very source of moral reason that Kant had sought to find within reason's own orb. Notwithstanding the persistent admiration that Cohen had for Kant and the linkages he saw between philosophical idealism and Judaism (to this extent remaining pre-Nietzschean), Rosenzweig was a great admirer of Cohen, seeing in him the embodiment of a philosopher of conviction – this most post-Nietzschean trait of traits. But more than that, while it was the heat that had been generated within his circle of friends by the Ehrenbergs and Rosenstock-Huessy about Christianity providing the continuous proof of lives lived in service to a power that reached across generations and that demanded acts of solidarity and love and complete authenticity, Rosenzweig had the example before him of Cohen that this, too, was true for contemporary Jews, not just Jews in the past.

While we will look in more detail in a later chapter at Rosenzweig's argument for why philosophy had been irrevocably drawn into a compact with theology, it is worth supplementing the above discussion of the revival of interest in the living God with Rosenzweig's excellent (if somewhat abstract) summary in *The Star* of the general theological spirit current in Germany that had emerged out of the ashes of the Enlightenment's torching of theology. He points out that just as philosophy 'had felt its ancient throne falter'[32] with the reactions to idealism by Schopenhauer, Kierkegaard, and Nietzsche, theology 'saw itself forced to carry out the evacuation of the line it had held for thousands of years and to take refuge in a new position in a further retreat.'[33] And just as he depicted how philosophy had found itself breaking apart the old dead 'All' of reason with the singular self-conscious (what he defines as the meta-ethical) irresoluteness of the new philosopher, he finds the new theology, commencing with Schleiermacher, certain of the reality of the hope in 'the coming of the ethical kingdom,' and caught up in the latest Enlightenment[34] – the historical enlightenment – shredding its past faith in miracles and emphasizing instead its faith in future redemption, and thereby remaining in step with the eighteenth-century Enlightenment dream of moral progress. The void left by the collapse of historical theology was for Rosenzweig filled by lived experience. And the theology based in 'lived experience' filled its adherents with a conviction of the reality of revelation but with a vanished trust in and need for history. However, according to Rosenzweig, if the new theological rationalism had lost its interest in history, this was not at all the case with philosophy. History had remained part of philosophy's essential brief because the historicity of man was not something placed in opposition to his existential commitments and bearing. This point is testified to by the entire approach of *The Star*, as well as by Heidegger's *Being and Time* (a work, of course, written after *The Star*, but one that seems to have attracted Rosenzweig's interest). In other words, and to use a theological term – which was itself illustrative of how theology had seeped into philosophy – creation (as history) had remained within philosophy's province. And insofar as theology was becoming ever more conscious of its dependence on philosophy (now governed by its emphasis on creation and historicity), if it were to have any 'scientific' (*wissenschaftliche*) credentials or credibility, 'now it is creation itself that is the portal through which philosophy enters the abode of theology.'[35]

In sum, Rosenzweig and Rosenstock-Huessy shared the conviction that the living God was real, that he had not been slain by either philosophy or the Enlightenment. His light was far brighter than that of a project that had already collapsed into the romantic myths and cults of the nineteenth and early twentieth centuries with its race science, its theosophy and occultisms, its charade of social evolution, its nationalisms – the panopoly of its idolatries. This, at least, was what Rosenstock-Huessy and Rosenzweig were convinced of, as were the thinkers who became part of the Patmos group and most of those who contributed to the journal *Die Kreatur*. To be sure, each was part of a broader current or body of Jewish and Christian faith. Both revivals were, however, either cut short or drastically changed by the Holocaust. The Jewish revival that Rosenzweig was engaged with would be overshadowed by the importance of finding a homeland for Jews; the Christian revival would have to account for what it meant to be a Christian after the Holocaust. Moreover, in the case of Rosenstock-Huessy, his particular approach to a Christian revival was so 'this sided,' so anti-transcendent, that he has remained little more than a footnote to a theology that was far better received among twentieth-century Christians. Though Rosenzweig, at least, was touched by Rosenstock-Huessy in a far more profound way than by Barth or any other contemporary Christian theologian, which may at the very least encourage us to take seriously Rosenstock-Huessy's contribution to the post-Nietzschean revival of Christianity. For Rosenstock-Huessy the living God required that we see the great mutability *and* discordant continuity of His forms of collective life – the living proof of the Holy Spirit who restlessly finds new forms/bodies of love. This took him on a different path from most other twentieth-century theologians who have become part of the twentieth-century canon of theology. And he was determined not to allow the different path to be captured under the conceptual net of theology – which is precisely why he did not have the ready-made audience that Barth and his colleagues had.

For Rosenzweig, philosophy and theology stood at a new crossroads, one at which each could benefit from the other. As Rosenzweig wrote in *The Star*, theology 'calls in philosophy . . . to throw a bridge from Creation to Revelation, a bridge on which the connection may take place between Revelation and Redemption . . . not a sort of reconstruction of theological content, but in its anticipation or, more accurately its foundation, the exhibiting of the preconditions on which this content rests.'[36] The bridge that is thrown and that Rosenzweig refers to draws on material that Rosenstock-Huessy had first alerted him to and that had formed the basis of the New Thinking[37] – namely, grammar and word. Creation, Revelation, and Redemption meet in language itself; they are not 'ideas' but modalities of being that spring from our lips – 'the fruit of lips,' to use a title from one of Rosenstock-Huessy's books, which he had taken from Proverbs (13.2) and Hebrews (13.15). For speech creates, reveals, and redeems, as we are illumined by the truth of God's providence – by the fulfilment of the promise, grammar, that lies incubating in the soul's register:

> Linguistic morphology became our organon of revelation as a real entity *vis-à-vis* the original idea of language, which had become our methodological organon of creation. Thereafter, however, the grammatical forms in their own turn thus again arrange themselves according to creation, revelation and redemption. Revelation is after all at once revelation of creation and of redemption, for it is founded on creation in cognition but directed toward redemption in volition. And language as the organon of revelation is at the same time the thread running through everything human that steps into its miraculous splendor and into that of its ever renewed presentness of experience.[38]

When Nietzsche had said, in partial despair, that we cannot get rid of God because we still have faith in grammar,[39] little did he know how profoundly correct he was, at least for Rosenzweig and Rosenstock-Huessy. Both men have faith in grammar, and the idea that language is an obstacle to reality is, for them, but a vestige of naturalism's blindness to the way in which we make and respond to our world.

As we will see in more detail later, grammar is at the heart of Rosenstock-Huessy's understanding of society and history; yet he does not provide a dense and systematic explication of grammar as a thread to trace the spirit of the living God's presence and rationale in the Bible. Even so, he insisted that the spirit of the living God was common to Jews and Christians and that this spirit was what made genuine communication possible. This was the kernel of his contribution to the volume that was prepared for Rosenzweig on the occasion of his fortieth birthday. In it he said that the Jews are the one people who do not need the concept of the Holy Spirit because the spirit of Moses is such a presence with them: 'Now, was not the spirit of Moses holy, since God communicated through him?'[40] He added that the same spirit that spoke to Moses is always present when there is real communion between man and man: 'Wherever mankind is coined definitively there is God . . . Thus, it should be self-evident that the Holy Spirit is the spirit of man in finality. He is in each sacrifice, in every conversion, in every selfless devotion.'[41] This spirit that reaches from Moses to the Trinitarian formulation to its humanistic formulation, 'the spirit of man,' is precisely the opposite spirit to that found in the view of life in which everything miraculous can be dissolved into the mechanical forces of life. The God of the living and the dead, then, for both Rosenstock-Huessy and Rosenzweig, is the spirit who demands service and who replenishes. This is the spirit that not only creates but also redeems while all the other multifarious spirits, also demanding absolute service, are limited in what they create precisely because they fail to replenish and redeem.

2 The Basis of the New Speech Thinking

At different times, notwithstanding their frequent outbursts against philosophy, Rosenzweig and Rosenstock-Huessy would both speak of their philosophical innovations and address the other as a philosopher breaking new ground. 'I philosophise in the form of a calendar,'[1] declares Rosenstock-Huessy in a 1916 letter to Rosenzweig; in another letter, the latter tells him: 'You have never – I mean to say during the last few years – been to me anything other than a philosopher; I have always felt that the jurist and historian were only incidental tendencies. The jurist and historian would have been at best interesting to me; the would be philosopher has become the cornerstone of my life.'[2] And to Gritli, Rosenzweig would say of Rosenstock-Huessy: 'His method, if anything, is more philosophical than natural-scientific.' Then there is Rosenstock-Huessy's claim in his lecture 'Philosophy and the Social Sciences' of 1942 or 1943 (the exact date is unclear) to the American Association of Philosophy that no other topic than 'philosophy and the social sciences was more central to his work.' And in *Speech and Reality* that he is writing a 'grammatical philosophy of man.'[3] Generally, though, Rosenstock-Huessy was so often disparaging of philosophy that Adam Zak even contends that Rosenstock-Huessy had given up on the rejuvenation of humanity through philosophy because he didn't believe in the rejuvenation of philosophy.[4] Certainly he repeated insistently that philosophers were ignorant of time and incarnation. And in the *Soziologie* he makes it clear that after much struggle he thought his work best fell under the rubric of sociology. One might add, though, that the first volume of his *Soziologie* might well be termed a philosophy of social space, and the second volume a historical anthropology.

As for Rosenzweig, he himself would state bluntly, in *The New Thinking*, that *The Star* was a 'system of philosophy.'[5] He makes much of the fusion he has created between philosophy and theology. There can be no question that of the two, Rosenzweig was happier to be called a philosopher. Note also that in terms of style, he proceeds more like a philosopher, and that philosophers (outside the Anglo-American tradition, and Putnam's admiration for Rosenzweig notwithstanding) are generally happy enough to accept him as one of them.

Yet Rosenzweig also told Gritli that *The Star* was 'no philosophy.'[6] And in 1916, Rosenstock-Huessy told him, in what I think is as pithy a description of what Rosenzweig is doing methodologically in *The Star* as has ever been written: 'You yourself taught me this with regard to philosophy, in that for you philosophy is already dead. But what else is the "history of philosophy" but the process of washing out the dye of Greece, just as the "state" is the washing out of the *corpus iurus*.'[7]

But it is also true that the following position of Rosenzweig applies to both: 'We recognize the problem of system in the Idealists (the way of philosophizing as the real crux of philosophy), but it doesn't control the form of our philosophy as it does theirs: we don't want to be philosophers when we are philosophising, but human beings and so we must bring our philosophy into the form of our humanity.'[8]

If Rosenzweig was more conciliatory toward philosophy and theology than Rosenstock-Huessy, he was ultimately revolutionizing them both from within. To some extent, this might well be because his story of Jew and Christian was a story about peoples, and God is discussed primarily in the context of peoples. For his part, Rosenstock-Huessy remained largely outside theological circles, often using the word theology as a pejorative term – for example, 'Christianity is broken today because we think of it more or less as a theology, a doctrine as a correcting lesson in morals, rarely as the corrected form of life itself,'[9] and 'I think most people today so completely mistake theology for religion that the only . . . salvation for you would be to throw out all your theology, all your cheap reasoning about things you have no understanding of and no access to.'[10] For him, religion was always a first-order activity, whereas theology was second-order. Thus in the *Soziologie* he writes: 'Today people confuse theology with religion. The Greek nature of theology, its secondary rank, its lagging behind the life of the soul, of the history of the church, its worldly character is not understood. Theology observes the realm of God with the eyes of the public, with the eyes of the second circle, the audience.'[11]

Rosenstock-Huessy was hostile to 'God' becoming a source of philosophical discussion instead of the creator to be supplicated, invoked, and responded to; and hence he has, with some exceptions, genuinely remained outside theological and philosophical circles. Rosenzweig, by contrast, was embraced by philosophers and theologians. In large part this was because he 'pitched' *The Star* to both philosophers and theologians, arguing that the rejuvenation of each lay in its receptivity to the potency of the other:

> Philosophy today requires, in order to be free of its aphorisms, and hence precisely for its scientific character, that 'theologians' do philosophy. But theologians in a different sense, of course. For . . . the theologian whom philosophy requires for the sake of its scientific character is himself a theologian who desires philosophy – out of concern for integrity. What was a demand in the interest of objectivity for philosophy will turn out to be a demand in the interests of subjectivity for theology. They complete each other, and together they bring about a new type of philosopher or theologian, situated between theology and philosophy.[12]

What is special in Rosenzweig's critical engagements with philosophy and theology is that the very elements that are so central to the vision he develops in *The Star of Redemption* were originally excavated by way of his critical reworking of philosophy (in Part One) and theology (Part Two) of that work. More precisely, the critique of philosophy in Book One yields him God, Man, and World as forming an implacable triad of irreducible parts, as the basis of our sources of appeal; whereas his engagement with theology leads to the superimposition of a second triad, Creation–Revelation–Redemption, on this initial triad. Together, Rosenzweig will argue, these two triads form the six poles of the authentic possibilities of life.

Given the complexity and deftness of his critique of philosophy in *The Star*, it is important to look at that critique in some detail. While we will also consider Rosenstock-Huessy's critique of philosophy, it is fair to say that his is less systematic than Rosenzweig's. Yet together, both were certain that philosophy's greatest deficiency was its idealism and that that idealism blinded people to reality.

In a letter to Eugen and Gritli on 28 March 1919, Rosenzweig wrote: 'We must each one of us free the world from this self-imposed appearance of the supra-terrestrial [*Uberweltlichkeit*] with which idealism has laminated it.' Rosenzweig and Rosenstock-Huessy never agreed with

Nietzsche that Christianity was populist Platonism. On the contrary, both thought that the original Jewish and subsequent Christian understanding of life offered an approach very different from the metaphysical dualism of mind/soul and body of the Greek philosophers. To be sure, one can find affinities with Platonist or neo-Platonist dualism in Paul, and at various times in Christianity it surfaces strongly. But that is, for both Rosenstock and Rosenzweig, a corruption brought about by the phantasm of the philosopher's All being venerated, at different historical times, at the expense of the God who loves, who speaks, and who is not an All but a one, or more precisely a 'this who is' – an 'I am' – among other ones, 'thises' who exist.

For Rosenzweig, philosophy does have its uses, but those uses can only be perceived clearly once philosophy is shorn of its idolatrous tendencies. For Rosenzweig, the great danger of philosophy is that it substitutes the ideal 'All' for reality. As everyone who has looked at the opening of *The Star* knows, Rosenzweig traces the origin of the attempt to know the 'All' – that is, the origin of philosophy – in the fear of death; and from that follows the fear of the flow and transition, the instability of the fleeting multiples of life, which the philosopher rises against. Philosophy consoles by ridding the world of its instability. Its voice is a comforting one of knowledge.[13] Yet according to Rosenzweig, this is a spectral strategy, and indeed a suicidal one, for it leaves the world divested of – the world. This strategy placates the terrors that life throws at human beings by enshrouding everything in something that can be thought, that can be known: philosophy weaves 'the thick blue haze of its idea of the All [about the earthly].'[14] What we all know is that death is something in life; but, says Rosenzweig, when we morph everything into its One, into its All, into its act of cognition, we are reconforming the conditions of living to conform to the logic of the All. Of course, from the very start, philosophy divided the source of that All into two possibilities, material or ideal; Rosenzweig, however, grasps that the nominal subject is far less important than the totalism that the philosopher seeks to impose on everything. The world, though, stays the world, and 'the fear man feels, trembling before this sting always cruelly belies the compassionate lie of philosophy.'[15]

Rosenzweig asserts against philosophy: 'We do not want any illusions. If death is something, then no philosophy is again going to make us avert our eyes with its assertion it presupposes Nothing.'[16] Philosophy, though, is a supposition. Even when it presupposes nothing, it presupposes the capacity of its potency, and that presupposition is at the expense of the world's messiness and flow, which we live with day in and day out in our speech. The healthy human understanding, he tells us in *The New Thinking*, has always thought in the way that he justifies in *The Star*.[17] But our age is suffering from a pathology of its thinking owing to its overreliance on philosophy. Its last gasp was Hegel, who attempted to show how everything fitted systematically within reason's orb, how the logic of heaven and of earth could be delineated in its dialectical development. The defiant stands of Kierkegaard, Schopenhauer, and Nietzsche, in which each asserts his individuality in his own unique way and with his own unique emphasis, converge, for Rosenzweig, in a kind of philosophy that forces philosophy to open itself to selves that will not be constrained by reasons; it really makes no difference whether those reasons are Platonic ones about the good, Aristotelian ones about the good life and the mean, Kantian ones about moral obligation, or Hegelian ones about the ethical life. These men stood up against philosophy and its enclosures. Yet *with* philosophy they opened up and broke what heretofore had been philosophically secure in terms of the sphericality of what would be contained therein – even if philosophers disputed about the precise nature of the content: 'every ethics ended by emerging again in a doctrine of the community that forms a part of being.'[18] But when the ethical is confronted by the living personality that will not be swallowed up, says Rosenzweig, the ethical must yield to the meta-ethical, something more, something that defies the unity of reasoning, that indeed *must* defy it in order for it to be aware of its own life.

This 'self-contained unity' of the personality has rebelled 'against this totality that includes the All in its unity . . . and insisted on withdrawing as an individuality, as an individual life of the individual man.'[19] The personality is a living and unique force; the All that may have been dynamic, but spherical, is robbed of the unity of thinking that it ostensibly encapsulates.[20] (The constant references to reason as spherical that reach from Parmenides to Plato to Aristotle to Kant and Hegel illustrate precisely this All against which Nietzsche and others have turned.) The personality that demands that its own existence make its own necessity more than the merely ethical, more than the sphere in which all personalities are required to comply with thought's or the law's requirements, is itself part of man's expansion of his own meaning over and above what philosophy can dictate; in just the same way, so too is the world's contingency something that requires philosophy's recognition of a role more humble than pronouncing upon the All.

That role must take account of the reality that is not contained but that requires our systems always be subordinate. This had been Schelling's major objection to Hegel, one that had been absorbed and repeated in different ways by Schelling's students, Feuerbach, Engels, Kierkegaard, and Bakunin (who used precisely this objection against Marx's claims about communism). Hegel had declared that his system articulated the internal necessity of reason's dynamics, and his proof lay in the demonstration of the dialectical development of the content of the logic: the sciences of nature and the world of spirit.[21] For Hegel, the form and content of the sciences, and hence (of all we know and can know) of nature and the world spirit, are generated out of logic's immanence. From the Hegelian stance, our nature as spirit is akin to the oak tree contained in the acorn, so that freedom, spirit's development, is the genesis of the forms of ethical life (family, civil society, state) and spiritual life (art, religion, philosophy). Against this, Schelling had reopened the case for philosophy not just being the servant of forms already interpolated into the system of Reason itself (which, if Hegel were right, would be equivalent to Hegel's philosophy), but a philosophy that had to take seriously the irruptions of spirit whose presence was discernible in humanity's narratives and mythologies. What is real is not so thanks to systemic relationships occurring within an overarching Idea, as Hegel has it; rather, the real is the contingent – the positive, the 'that which is there' as opposed to the negative, the 'that which is the result of abstract reasoning.' The systematization of the negative enables the elaboration of predications of the already known to be attached to the subject or substance. Hegel succumbed to the temptation to take the completed as the condition of the next; perhaps he said something true about the systemicity of scientific knowledge, but his 'spirit' kills spiritedness, the incalculable is always philosophically explicable – as Hegel himself said, after the event! Seen thus, the philosopher, in Hegel, is akin to the priest or pastor who administers the last rites over the dead and provides a reassuring speech for the dead person's loved ones and relatives. Such a way of thinking equips us poorly for the ruptures and surprises of the real that is the positive.

The positive brings with it a range of potencies that chart new courses and open up new and unpredictable horizons. Schelling's dark ground leaves our reason always playing catch-up with life's next mystery; and the history of mythology and religion is, for Schelling, the attempt to deal with these mysteries insofar as they are positive, insofar as they arise out of experiences. Myth and religion cannot simply be wrenched from the world of which they are a part and placed in a laboratory and then be expected to function in the same manner as they do when they are part of a larger ensemble of meanings and understandings; they are aspects of 'a world' – they resonate and activate. Their reality cannot be gauged apart from the lives and activities they inform. This is the delusion of all naturalistic philosophies. And this is why it is just another form of negative philosophy – for it begins with abstractions that remove us from the reality it seeks to understand – and not what Schelling calls a positive philosophy, which deals with the reality at hand, the positive presence. One can identify in Schelling some similar concerns that are central to phenomenology and its critique of naturalism and its concept of the 'life world.' But that the experiential is the whole experience, its positiveness is not something that began with phenomenology; though it is central to Schelling and to the New Thinking, except that in phenomenology the transcendental subject occupies the same impartial observer status of subjectivity as in naturalism (which, of course, is why Foucault, for example, did not want his position to be seen as having anything in common with Husserl). Husserl's debt to Descartes and relentless attempts to put the Cartesian turn on a more rigorous and attentive footing does indeed bring 'the life-world' to the attention of science, but that world must still be situtated within a philosophical vocabulary that is still heavily steeped in mechanism. Thus from within the perspective of the New Thinking the egoic certitude of the transcendental subject of Husserlian phenomenology may be dissolved in exactly the same manner as the naturalistic bias of the 'object.' As Rosenzweig writes in *The New Thinking*:

> For experience knows nothing of object; it remembers, it lives, it hopes and fears. At best, the content of memory could be understood as an object; [but] then it would be precisely an understanding, and not the content itself. For [the content] is not remembered as my object. It is nothing but a prejudice of the last three hundred years that, in all knowing, the 'I' must be present; thus that I could not see a tree unless 'I' saw it. In truth, my I is only present if it is present; for instance, if I have to emphasize that I see the tree because someone else does not see it, then, certainly, the tree is in connection with me in my knowing. But in all other cases I know only of the tree and nothing else; and the usual philosophical assertion of the I's omnipresence in all knowing distorts the content of this knowledge.
>
> Thus, experience does not experience the things, which certainly become visible as ultimate matters of fact through thinking about experience;

however, what it experiences, it experiences in these matters of fact. And that is why it is so important for a clean and complete presentation of experience to have set out these matters of fact purely and to have opposed thinking's tendency to confuse [experience] in advance.[22]

Toward the end of *The New Thinking*, he says that if any ism can be said to pin down this philosophy, which is the contrary of all ism thinking, it is

> absolute empiricism; this, at least, would cover the characteristic behaviour of the new thinking in all three areas: the preworld of the concept, the world of actuality, the superworld of truth. That behaviour, which knows [itself] to know nothing of the heavenly except what it has experienced – this, however, it actually [knows], no matter how philosophy may slander it as knowledge 'beyond' all 'possible' experience; and of the earthly too [it knows] nothing that it has not experienced – but about [what it has not experienced, it knows] absolutely nothing whatsoever, no matter how philosophy may praise it as knowledge 'before' all 'possible' experience.[23]

As with Rosenstock-Huessy, Rosenzweig's attack on 'philosophical idealism' is also an attack on all thinking that purports to grasp the essence of reality under one optic or overarching referent.[24] Rosenzweig's critique of idealism, then, must be seen in the context of something more than itself. Idealism is a family member, and it is the family of isms that is at the base of the sick understanding. That sickness has been identified with philosophy, that thinking that 'separates [man's] experience of wonder from the continuous stream of life, isolating it.'[25] Idealism is the original ism: the other isms are its progeny.

Rosenzweig takes the cue of Nietzsche and others in seeing that the law is there for man and not man for the law. This, too, is how thinking and reasoning operate. They are part of what we do, but we are more; they help us, but they are not *us*. To merely place ourselves under their submission is to diminish ourselves by making us beholden to a phantasm of our own making. Thus Rosenzweig says that just as his philosophy takes a 'meta-ethical' standpoint, it also takes a metalogical one. It is not one that denies all value to logic, but it notes that logic is not reality itself: the rules of logic are the rules of logic – they do not control the world as such; they are a part of the world, not an outside entity that possesses it: 'The metalogical in the world makes of logos an "ingredient" of the world and wholly evident in the world, such that the world possesses it, and not the reverse.'[26] Additionally, 'for the world, truth is not law but content. Truth does not prove reality, but reality upholds truth. The essence of the world is this upholding (not the proof) of truth.'[27] To make his point, he uses the example of our thinking being akin to a wall on which one may hang a painting. While one can only hang the painting if the wall is there, the wall does not determine the painting that is to be hung on it; it is separate from the painting itself. The problem, he says of the tradition that reached from Parmenides to Hegel, was that it took wall and painting as one: 'the wall had been painted in frescos, if therefore wall and picture constituted a unity, then the wall is a unity in itself, and the picture is in itself infinite multiplicity, a totality shutting out the outside, that is to say: not unity but oneness – "one" picture.'[28] Our situation in the world is a series of encounters, of trials and tribulations, and we do not know our next encounter or trial. They emerge, and we are in the situation where 'the world had quite simply become non-absolute.'[29] This radical openness of the world is easily missed, were one simply to reintroduce a totality that would restore the philosophical systematization of the world that has been unravelled by post-Hegelian thinking. Hence Rosenzweig insists that the world not be deemed as 'nature,' because nature is but another name for the kind of absolute that metalogical thinking requires us to break from. Thus Rosenzweig leaps back behind the 'consensus' of the moderns (and their Greek predecessors) that nature is an adequate designator of the world's essence and defers to the biblical tradition that makes of the world something created, a 'creature.'[30] The leap from world to creature is a linguistic one, a transference of the name. Given, as we will discuss below, how all-important names are for Rosenzweig and Rosenstock-Huessy, this change of name is highly significant: it is one further move in the New Thinking's attempt to overturn the naturalistic-based domination of names in modern times. The pervasiveness of the irrelevance of names and their subordination to concepts is one further indication of how much twentieth- and twenty-first-century philosophy remains within an older paradigm. When he announces this transition from world and nature to creature he is expressing not simply *his* philosophy, but a fundamental change of orientation that is part of the New Thinking generally. Thus too will Rosenstock-Huessy say: ' "Nature" is precisely what things are not, rather they are creatures, creations which have been called into life. Their names, even when they change, remain part of their allotment as creatures in God's six-day week. They are what they are named, and they are named what they become.'[31] In 'Liturgical Thinking,' he remarks that 'the term "natural" is precisely a mental sledgehammer which reduces this glass of water, "O creatura aquae," to the Hades of H_2O.'[32] The name *Die Kreatur* for the journal that united those committed (to various degrees) to New Thinking was an indication of the common recognition that the dissolution of living creatures into the label of the world and nature was intrinsic to the crises of their times.

The New Thinking, or 'speech thinking,' was not ever something that could begin or end with philosophy. Indeed, Rosenstock-Huessy proposes in *Speech and Reality* that speech thinking should revolutionize all the social sciences. Speech thinking is a thinking devoted to transformation or – more precisely – the redeeming of the world and the self; and it was always conscious of its difference from other philosophical currents of the age. Marxian, Hegelian, Kantian, and even Nietzschean based philosophies have little or no idea about speech thinking; Husserl and Heidegger, who approached it in their break with naturalism, even so remained philosophically focused in a manner that kept them separate from the New Thinking. In twentieth-century philosophy, much has been made of language's importance by structuralists, by post-structuralists, and in some areas by analytic philosophers. (Some post-structuralists, like Deleuze, are thoroughly enmeshed in naturalism, and happily so – for that plane of possibilities is far from exhausted.)[33] The extremes of what Bataille calls limit experiences and ineffableness, Dada's privileging of nonsense, and the Surrealists' preference for a philosophy of the dream over the tyranny of the rational, at one end, and, at the other, behaviourists, analytic philosophers, and (on the other side of the channel) Habermas, with their faith in rational discussion (which should not be mistaken for a dialogical principle – Habermas does not participate in the New Thinking) all occupy a plane that does not address what the New Thinking does.

Hilary Putnam has sought to introduce Rosenzweig and hence the New Thinking to new readers through the avenue of Wittgenstein. I think it worth pausing here on Rosenstock-Huessy's criticism of Wittgenstein (and his passing comment on Husserl) in his entry on Wittgenstein for *The American Peoples Encyclopedia* to bring out why, notwithstanding his interest in language, Wittgenstein remains firmly within another philosophical paradigm.

While Wittgenstein had passed from the logical atomism of the *Tractatus* to the 'language game' Gestaltism of the *Investigations*, it is not clear how attentive Rosenstock-Huessy was to the change that had taken place in Wittgenstein's thought. That said, the charge of relativism that Rosenstock-Huessy brings against Wittgenstein in his encyclopedia entry is the standard one brought against the Wittgenstein of the *Investigations*. Moreover, when Rosenstock-Huessy makes the accusation, he is no more appealing to a Platonic absolute than he is to a natural, atomized entity. The truths that function absolutely for Rosenstock-Huessy are not 'objects' or 'ideas,' but events. Events are formative, bringing with them all manner of experiences and new names that are part of our re-creation – we are plastic creatures constantly being reshaped by collective catastrophes and triumphs.[34] Language, then, is not something that proceeds regardless of these collective experiences; rather, it is inseparably connected with them. Moreover, it is not as if language is freely laminated over our experiences, as Wittgenstein seems to suggest in *The Philosophical Investigations,* in which he reproaches the Augustinian theory of language as based on a correlation between word and thing, in favour of a more 'functionalist' view of language in which it is no longer clear what (apart from a shared commitment to the rules of a 'language game') enables transformation between communicants to take place. For Rosenstock-Huessy, the experiences that accompany an event are of such a magnitude that they *compel* a response. He would return to this difference again and again – and he was especially scornful of the distinterested orientation of the philosophy of language that commenced with mere descriptive phrases to try and grasp the character of speech. In *Die Sprache des Menschengeschlechts* – which was essentially a retrospective collection of his writings on the social and psychological power of speech – he added a footnote to the republication of *Angewandte Seelenkunde,* in which he pointed out that this work, which had originated as a speech letter to Rosenzweig in 1916, was intended to 'ward off (*Abwehr*) all philosophy of language.'[35] The difference between the two approaches is bluntly stated in that same work:

This superficial philosophy posits an artificial network of expedient sewer technology as the essence of the fountainhead of speech which erupts so overpoweringly in men. So it confuses the ability to speak with the necessity to speak. Everything a person has to do, he and his equals also can do. The ordinary person in us can do only what others have had to do. When a person is confronted by the need to speak, however, he no longer sees speech as a tool by which he can make himself understood. Rather, he is seized by speech because things demand to be understood by him;

because a man wants to be fully comprehensible, or because God wishes to become audible to him.[36]

One of Rosenstock-Huessy's most important thoughts is that catastophes are the cauldrons of real speech because they force us to respond, and they do so by making us change our language so that we can get out of hell. Our alternatives in hell are 'leave' or 'perish'; our freedom resides in our ability to avoid catastrophe by being responsive and hence acting early enough, before accumulating forces break out, bringing with them large-scale terror and misery.

To conduct a schoolmasterly examination of sentences as one searches for the perfect unity of meaning (early Wittgenstein's faith) – and then find that examination wanting (late Wittgenstein) – is, for Rosenstock-Huessy, an intellectual game of little or no value. Hence, at one point in his 1959 lecture series on historiography, he erupts against 'all these logical semanticists – Mr. Wittgenstein and Mr. Reichenbach – it's just so absolutely silly, because they take any one sentence and try to analyze. But to speak means . . . to be so much alive that you know that you will survive – you pass through the horizon of the event.' For Rosenstock-Huessy, time, world, truth, and speech are far more important and resilient than Wittgenstein realizes. And while late Wittgenstein's 'guerrilla' attacks on his former philosophical allies may indeed expose logical atomism's deficiencies, it tells us actually very little about us as speaking animals. Significant, too, is the deft linkage that Rosenstock-Huessy makes between Wittgenstein and Husserl. Indeed, it is interesting that both Husserl and late Wittgenstein hold out the promise of something more than their logically atomized naturalistic forebears or former associates, but their procedures hold them back from entering into the 'speech-scape' of the New Thinking. Again it is a rather lengthy citation, but it is a comprehensive statement of how Rosenstock-Huessy sees the differences among the kinds of projects that he and Wittgenstein and Husserl are engaged in:

Wittgenstein's approach to philosophy, which is in terms of the theoretical aspects of language and mathematics, excludes from consideration the actual truth or falsity of any statement; that is, the truth or falsity of a statement is determinable solely in terms of the logical system (the 'language') within which the thinker thinks. Further, the things that are likely to be of greatest interest to living human beings in time – those that require decisions and action – are outside the scope of logic and linguistic analysis except insofar as statements are made about them, in which case the statements alone may properly and meaningfully be considered in the abstract.

Thus the whole realm of life as actually lived is left to accident, to habit, to the power of church or state, or – as in Wittgenstein's case – to a type of mysticism. For Wittgenstein, philosophy is no more and no less than the analysis of statements in terms of other statements; what a living person does or should do about any statement is not the province of philosophy as conceived by Wittgenstein and the various schools of logical positivism and linguistic analysis that were to be so decisively influenced by him.

Language in this context is considered nominalistically; that is, words and other symbols are arbitrary, neutral objects to be manipulated at will. The idea that words and other symbols have a reality of their own, or that they are, or can be, active and actuating powers that derive from, preserve, foster, and even make human history – that may bring people together or plunge them into war – is not acceptable to Wittgenstein, Russell, and others of like mind; but that words do have such power is acknowledged backhandedly in their irritated concern with linguistic 'disease' – the fact that people persist in responding actively to sacred and historically revered names (God, Abraham Lincoln, and so forth) despite 'irrefutable proofs' that such behavior is logically absurd. Opponents of positivism have pointed out that the positivists' expressions of irritation are, in terms of logic, entirely absurd, since the fact that logicians and rationalists become angry at what they regard as illogic and unreason suggests that logicians and rationalists, as living persons, respond illogically and unreasonably to at least the 'sacred names' of Logic and Reason.

Wittgenstein's endeavors paralleled those of Edmund Husserl, whose phenomenological method is essentially a way of clarifying and manipulating ideas and images in the mind without reference to their truth or falsity, or to their implications for the world of action – except insofar as these implications themselves become ideas in the mind. Both approaches were formidably challenged by various existentialists, who acknowledged the usefulness of Wittgenstein and Husserl and their schools in the perfection of scientific method (in the natural sciences), and their value in countering the excesses of Idealism, but who recognized that the total neutrality of Logic and Phenomenology leads one ultimately to embrace an Absolute Relativism that is as much in error as the Absolute Idealism of Hegel and his followers.[37]

Now as I have said, some of this, on first inspection, seems not to fit the Wittgenstein of the *Investigations* – for surely there he is sensitive to the circulation of words and not to their atomized meanings. However, while Wittgenstein points to the importance of the community in which language circulates, he has done very little to show which bits of language do what and how they are important. Indeed – and here it seems to me that Rosenstock-Huessy is absolutely correct – what Wittgenstein has really done is demonstrate how clever he is against the logical atomists; but if one isn't a logical atomist, he has little more to offer. (This is similar to post-structuralism's trumping of structuralism; if one didn't think much of structuralism in the first place, then the pyrotechnics and implications of a work like *Writing and Difference* would be far less thrilling.) Wittgenstein is, in other words, determined by what he wishes to negate, imprisoned by his foe, much as Hegel claimed that Kant's concept of freedom was imprisoned by the very mechanism that Kant had sought to refute with the free will and the concept of autonomy.

So if we place Wittgenstein and Husserl back in the pack with other twentieth-century thinkers who were striving to overcome the suffocating burdens of their traditions by opening up new philosophical byways, another thing they share besides not being dialogical thinkers is that none of them take seriously the possibility of the living God, which means that none take seriously what was absolutely serious for Rosenstock-Huessy and Rosenzweig. Neither Wittgenstein's mysticism, nor Heidegger's Being, nor Husserl's openness to experience – which does indeed facilitate a potential reconciliation with religion – really touches what they touch, because none of them seek to connect with and hence revitalize – or be revitalized by – a living tradition. None think about truth as primarily incarnation, a point that is at the heart of why Rosenzweig and Rosenstock-Huessy study peoples and not merely ideas. And hence not one of the non-speech thinkers just mentioned takes entire collectives of peoples as meaningful powers of world making, except insofar as they wish to found a new pathway of being in the world. Yet the very desire for novelty is precisely the truncation that Rosenstock-Huessy and Rosenzweig are suspicious of, for it wipes away millennia of human experience. Thus, for a moment to take Husserl and Heidegger, while they are at one with Rosenstock-Huessy and Rosenzweig in their opposition to the asphyxiation of the life-world through the moderns' excessive faith in natural science (what to the New Thinkers is idolatry), both are obsessed with their originality – again something that is absolutely foregone by Rosenstock-Huessy and Rosenzweig, whose attachment to Christianity and Judaism is an attachment to collective life.[38] Vast is the anthropological oversight of philosophies that seek a kind of 'year zero' beginning (again Husserl's passion to 'out-Cartesianize' Descartes, or Heidegger's monstrously egotistical desire to show always how someone else – apart from a few fortunate Greeks he is ready to hold up as his equal – has gone for a being rather than Being, and the same game was carried on by young Derrida, who found all before as phallologocentrism). Such claims to novelty may be great career and status moves, but they ignore the overwhelming majority of human beings and movements alive today, not to mention pretty well all and everyone that existed up until the triumph of secularism in the reflexive sites of the Western world in the last century.

To the extent that the young Wittgenstein wanted to rebuild the world from solid foundations, he too was engaging in a philosophical response to the Great War. But as I have suggested with Husserl, all such attempts to begin again foundationally reproduced the very Cartesian heritage that had contributed so much to the crisis in the first place. This is why Rosenstock-Huessy and Rosenzweig broke with any foundationalist projects and why they were so disconnected from those philosophies – and why also, I venture, that as long as those philosophies had widespread appeal, the New Thinking remained largely invisible or, at best, of interest only to a minority.

The dialogical approach of the New Thinking breaks decisively from Cartesianism by taking the same exit from it as Vico had used almost two centuries earlier – by going back into history. Indeed, insofar as the catastrophe of the Great War was created by history, there could be no question of simply pretending it was not there or trying to avoid the forces that had created it. Certainly the idea that one could do this philosophically, without attachment to some great storehouse of powers gathered over the times, was for both the dangerous fantasy of idealism. It is in this hue that we can appreciate the power of what can too easily be seen as rather innocuous, viz., Rosenzweig's proud announcement to Rosenstock-Huessy, which is often interpreted as the original formulation of the New Thinking. As we mentioned earlier, this is the passage that Rosenstock-Huessy used as the frontispiece for *Die europäischen Revolutionen*:

> I believe that there are in the life of each living thing moments, or perhaps only some moments, when it speaks the truth. It may well be, then, that we need say nothing at all about a living thing, but need do no more than

watch for the moment when this living thing expresses itself. The dialogue which these monologues form between one another I consider to be the whole truth. That they make a dialogue with one another is the great secret of the world, the revealing and revealed secret, yes, the meaning of revelation.

In the previous paragraph he had written of Rosenstock-Huessy:

You think much more in a direct way with your own head, whereas I have an inclination (I often fear it myself, like Penelope) to shove the whole of history between myself and the problem, and so think with the heads of all the participants in the discussion. Otherwise I should *not* believe myself (though strangely enough I believe other people when they think directly). Hence, the dialogue method that so annoys you.[39]

That Rosenzweig supposed that Rosenstock-Huessy was 'annoyed' by the dialogue method might have stemmed more from the two men's personal interactive styles rather than from any substantive differences between them: Rosenstock-Huessy was more unconstrained in his speech, a force of nature, more explosive; Rosenzweig was somewhat more controlled, more cautious, more reserved, more superficially polite, but also the master of the surgical strike. Hence more than fifty years later, when Rosenstock-Huessy edited the letters, he could not refrain from setting the record straight:

Eugen annoyed? Perhaps a bit now and then, but certainly not by the 'dialogue method,' which was then, so to say, in the process of being invented – or at least perfected for their purposes – by the two correspondents. Eugen's annoyance, insofar as it existed, was with dialectic, rather than dialogue, and the latter was an approach that Eugen had himself adopted long before these letters were written. In this paragraph Franz was conceiving of 'dialogue' as his thinking 'with the heads of all . . . in the discussion,' which is not a bad way of thinking but is 'dialogical' only to a very limited extent. In the paragraph following, however, his conception of dialogue broadens somewhat, pointing in the direction of dialogue such as that exemplified by this correspondence in its entirety, and the dialogical method espoused in Franz' essay on 'The New Thinking,' in 1925.[40]

In any case it was Rosenstock-Huessy who as early as 1912 had expressed (and was censured for doing so in his doctoral dissertation) the sentence that was to prepare the ground for speech thinking: 'Speech is wiser than the thinker, the self who believes in thinking, where he thinks, though, he only "speaks," and consequently assuredly believing in the authority of the stuff of speech: it leads his concepts unconsciously forward into an unknown future.'[41]

As we have also just suggested, in Rosenstock-Huessy's understanding of speech thinking one cannot underestimate trauma and shock. Catastrophes are the collapse of worlds and the language that has woven them – the sources of appeal and authority. This is why he says that

> the shaken or traumatised [*erschütterte*] man always experiences himself in time, not in space, because he is traumatised, when he says something shocking. Speech thinking doesn't have anything to do with the linguistics of the old style, because it positions itself as traject and preject, rather than object or subject . . . The word leaders [*Wortführer*] of speech thinking are thus people, who have become speechless from a shock; they aren't thinking idealistically about a question.[42]

Rosenstock-Huessy singles out not only Kierkegaard and Nietzsche (as does Rosenzweig) as precursors to the New Thinking, but also Feuerbach, who had made love and dialogue the real bases of community in his *Principles of the Philosophy of the Future.* (Rosenstock-Huessy describes these three thinkers as 'seismographs of catastrophe').[43]

Thus, speech thinking even in its early stages was being applied directly to the Great War. And in 1917, in 'Das Geschichtsbild der europaischen Parteien' (later to appear in *Die Hochzeit des Kriegs und der Revolution*), he writes that the meaning of that war did not lie in any one particular viewpoint accessible to any of the parties engaged in it in a manner that exemplified the orientation of speech thinking. Rather, each participant was driven by its own past – and most significantly, by other wars.[44] Likening war to speech, Rosenstock-Huessy argued that in both activities, conflict generates meanings beyond what is visible to the individual participants. Each is swept along by its own past. Years later, he made this pithy formulation in his Lectures on Greek Philosophy: 'Nobody is the source of truth. We are all only in the metabolism.'[45] In 'Das Geschichtsbild,' after citing Heraclitus – 'Conflict is the father of all things' – he continues: 'Speech demands of us that we learn to hear speech and counter-speech and weigh each against the other.'[46] 'The wrath of free speech' is more than just sitting around comfortably, rationalizing about things or bitterly complaining about one's external enemies. A great part of Rosenstock-Huessy's life's work, the study of revolutions – but also, indeed, the study of how new social formations are generated out of the implosions and catastrophes suffered by peoples, who are crushed and sent to hell by the trajectories of their pasts – is based on this all-important aspect of speech thinking.

In moments of crisis, people are trapped in a vise between the known old and the unknown new, and speech is what makes escape possible by opening up a new time. Speech and time stand in the closest relationship, for the word is the Spirit's breath, the promise and call toward a future where love stands another chance – and the toxicities that turned the world into hell. I want, here, to quote at length from various sections of the first chapter of Rosenstock-Huessy's *Das Geheimnis der Üniversität* (The Secret of the University). It requires no commentary, and if it were well known or easily available (it can only be found in English on the Norwich DVD of his collected works), I would not be quoting it at such length. I do so here for a number of reasons: because it illustrates so well the centrality of catastrophe and trauma in Rosenstock-Huessy's social thought; because it expresses a truth that once correctly appreciated has the power to radically change social theory; and because it will greatly help us grasp a central tenet of this book – that the post–Second World War paradigm *needs to* be supplemented by the model of the New Thinking that grew out of the Great War. Only after we have done that will we be able to perceive and think clearly about the inner unity of the two greatest catastrophes of the twentieth century and thereby orient ourselves toward the future. (Note also that Rosenstock-Huessy's concluding nod to Rosenzweig at the end of this quote confirms, once again, the depth of their allegiance):

Science . . . only generalizes what has already been revealed to the sufferer as the truth, dares not use political motives as evidence. But on the other hand the great philosophers who in each generation re-created the universities grew out of suffering and more exactly out of war . . . No philosopher ever sat down as if in a classroom to answer the questions of his predecessor. To consider the history of philosophy in this way is insanity. Descartes grew out of the Thirty Years War. He has remained its eternal Privat-dozent. Kant became a philosopher after the Seven Years War. Schopenhauer came to meditation on the battlefields of Napoleon. The Franco-Prussian War forced Friedrich Nietzsche out of mere philology. Wars are parts of the future whose meaning must first be brought to light in the ensuing peace. For Wars bring unheard of suffering. And everything unheard-of belongs to the future. War destroys the 'present' of the previous peacetime. In war and in nature there is no present only future and past. The next present is created after the war. This creature is called . . . the various classes of adults who already suffer under the ruling regime or pattern of life represent the future.

In Europe each war gave birth to a new philosophy. Paracelsus, Cartesius, Locke, Kant, Fichte, Hegel, Schopenhauer, Nietzsche are not the natural men. Theophrastus von Hohenheim, Descartes etc. are the sons of the catastrophes through which they suffered, of the revolutions which towered above the wars and peaces of their times. Therefore when we are confronted by a subsequent catastrophe their philosophy must be changed, must be lived down.

As long as a philosophy represses its true source it threatens the schools which carry it on with obsolescence. Every new war should lead to the conscious burial of the philosophies of previous war epochs. Germany, overloaded with philosophies and rich in universities, lacks exactly this power to bury. Today there are still Hegelians, Cartesians, Kantians. This state of affairs has no rhyme or reason inside a 'Polemology' of war. The first commandment of the new science runs: the modes of thought of every previous catastrophe must be buried. For otherwise those who fought this war cannot discover their own language. In the United States the situation is exactly opposite. No new philosophies were built into the American universities after each war and no ossified thought distorted her spirit. But for this very reason the war philosophies in America never became fruitful in their own time. Not once have they achieved even as much as their transitory validity. They have never entered the realm of speech. Too little abstraction of war occurred in America. German history succumbed to abstractions of single wars which were mistaken for eternal truth. The little eternity of a peaceful period was mistaken for eternity herself. Consequently our Polemology demands a new working through of catastrophes for the entire Western World. Catastrophes force upon us time-nourished, time-geminated transitory truths. 'Sense to nonsense, health to plague' is the methodical principle of the new Polemology, the lesson of thought born of sorrow. (See Franz Rosenzweig, Das Neu Denken [The New Thinking], in *Kleinere Schriften*, Berlin 1935.)

May we recognize in the two World Wars one single fratricidal struggle! And may this War enter that realm of truth whence the University derives her teachable science![47]

Speech born out of crisis, speech that proceeds on the basis of disagreement and conflict, is, for Rosenstock-Huessy, something creative – it produces something more than could have been produced had there been agreement from the outset. The two parties to the dispute are not part of a zero sum game in which the one proven to be 'right' has won and the loser is quite simply wrong. A response has been demanded, and that response is the creation of the new. Conflict produces growth. Hence, concludes Rosenstock-Huessy, one needs one's enemies just as light needs shade.[48] It is in this context that Rosenstock-Huessy says: 'The hateful speaker doesn't hate his enemy, but rather loves him much more.' In other words, the biblical injunction to love one's enemies is not simply a kind of Kantian moral rule highlighting a purer moral will, but a truth about human growth, about the bounties that enemies provide.[49] It is also an important insight into how Rosenstock-Huessy came to grasp that life is an ongoing process revelation. Rosenzweig would say that he learned from Rosenstock that 'revelation is orientation'; and in his later autobiographical work *Ja und Nein,* Rosenstock-Huessy would clarify how revelation, orientation, and speech correspond and how we are recreated in correspondence:

> The double character of revelation consists in the way in which it allocates to the speaker as much as to the people whom the speaker sees before him, a new and at the same time a determined place . . . Revelation is orientation. Orientation is a correlation between at least two new poles; one may call it a 'correspondence,' because this relationship between two letter writers is today more likely to be understood than between two speakers. In a correspondence two speakers respond in such a manner that the longer it continues the more each correspondent becomes polarized in his own character.[50]

In his 1954 lecture series Four Disangelists, Rosenstock-Huessy would make the same point, applying the example of the Warrior Code in the context of the Cold War:

> There's no enmity between decent soldiers. Even if you shoot the other man, there's no hatred. Only civilians think this, up behind the lines . . . Decent soldiers have always loved their enemy. So has Grant loved Lee . . . We would have now a wave of unemployment in this country, no prosperity, except for the fear of Russia. Thanks to Mr. Stalin, we have kept awake. It's wonderful. Just, you see, have a good enemy, and you are taken care of. But your friends, beware of them. They put you to sleep. Do you wish to abolish the reality of enmity in this world? Don't make yourself ridiculous.[51]

It is interesting to contrast what Rosenstock-Huessy is saying here with the perspective of Carl Schmitt, whose name is forever associated with the idea that the polarity of friends and enemies is the essence of the political. Rosenstock-Huessy knew and corresponded with Schmitt before leaving Germany in 1933. He was bitterly disappointed by Schmitt's support of the Nazis, believing that Schmitt had sold his soul for survival's sake. On one occasion, Rosenstock-Huessy referred to him as 'the Talleyrand of Hitlerism'; on another, he applied to him the same, and even blunter, term as he had directed against Heidegger: 'scum.'[52]

Schmitt may well be right in identifying friends and enemies as the common polarity in many political regimes, but Rosenstock-Huessy's thinking is not the common (or more bluntly, 'pagan') political one – it is the Christian one of 'love thine enemy.'[53] Such a teaching draws its strength from the perception that the spirit is a power whose mode of entrance into one's life is unpredictable; it comes from where it is least expected. We are rejuvenated through crisis and catastrophe, and our enemies are part of that rebirth. Hitlerian politics is the demonic inversion of this truth, for it uses fear and hatred deliberately, to generate the conditions in which to bind one's friends together. This sort of bringing together requires a separation of the Other that is absolute – indeed, that is an act of total extermination. In this sense, too, the modern tribalism that was National Socialism and fascism was the essence of the demonic – a term that expresses the triumph of death over life. The triumph of life over death, the verification that love is as strong as death – which is the secret of revelation expressed in the Song of Songs (8.6), as well as the core of Rosenzweig's section on revelation in *The Star* – is the real end of the New Thinking, the redemption of life through the activation of all possible potencies. Such an activation is in love with life, life at its most expansive and proliferate, life in its completeness that is beyond the plane of the merely natural. It refutes the naturalist prejudice that the world of symbols, signs, and spirit can be collapsed into nature with no real loss. To close oneself off from other peoples, other tribes, other nations, other spirits, is to defeat life. This is why, as we enter deeper into the future and as our social formations become ever more complex, we expend so much more energy in our efforts to learn about our past, to learn about other ways of being human, other life formations: 'The entire history of the [human] race forever tries to recover all lived life.'[54] In times of war, life confronts itself in the petrifications that have developed over time. War is the means of breaking through petrified lifeways that refuse to enable love's expansion. War is the evil that forces more love from people, who learn in terror that the world they have made is still insufficient in its love; the lesson to be learned in life is ever the lesson of our failures in love. The attainment of universal peace, the Jewish arrival of the Messianic age, the Christian Second Coming, is the real task of the New Thinking. For Rosenstock-Huessy, and no less for Rosenzweig, speech and love and the overcoming of death are not randomly disconnected bits of life – they are aspects of one and the same process, just as 'death is not overcome through not dying, but by our loving beyond it. Only the love, which forces us to speak, does not stop.'[55] 'In speech we overcome death.'[56] And speech is how we reorganize the universe:[57]

> No language is communication with others only, it is communication with the universe. We try by speaking to communicate our experience of the universe to our fellow men; by listening, reading, learning, we try to get hold of their experience of the universe. To speak means to reenact cosmic processes so that these processes may reach others. In every sentence, man acts within the cosmos and establishes a social relation for the sake of saving the cosmos from wasting acts in vain. Man economizes the cosmic processes by making them available to all other men. Man, by speech, establishes the solidarity of all men for the acceptance of our universe.[58]

For both Rosenzweig and Rosenstock-Huessy, language is proof that love is continuous from the source of creation through to living beings. Language is the thread between Creation, Revelation, and Redemption. The intense dialogue between the loving enemies – Eugen and Franz – was, for both, a confirmation of the truth of the fecundity of the enmity between Christianity and Judaism, in the sense that both saw, in their own experience, how their differences had acted as a spur to their own genius, how it formed them in solidarity, and how it demonstrated to them the dialogical nature of truth. That speech was the transformative act enabling us to see the line that radiates from our own existence to the world and to God and to Creation, Revelation, and Redemption was fundamental to Rosenzweig's *Star of Redemption,* as it was to Rosenstock-Huessy's corpus.

Both knew that by taking speech seriously, they would have to break with the idea that language is merely a tool of the mind, and that the mind is a thing apart from speech, something that simply makes use of speech to communicate what has already been fully realized within the thinker/speaker. The paradigmatic linguistic diagram of language seen through this philosophical prism can be found in Saussure's *Course in Linguistics* (which was published, significantly enough, in 1916).

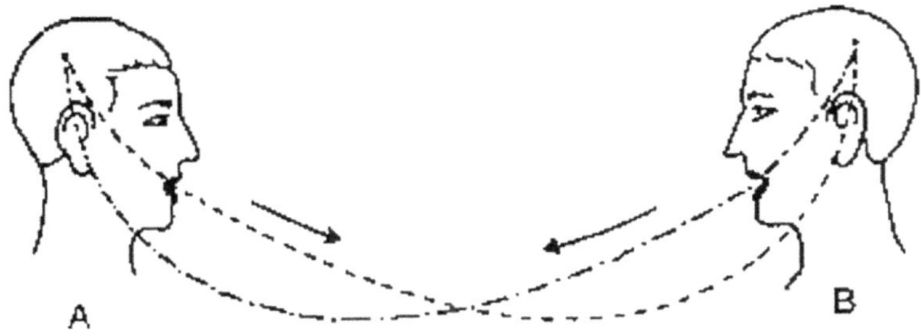

This way of conceiving of language is quite simply, for both Rosenstock-Huessy and Rosenzweig, the triumph of philosophical dogma in the field of linguistics. When Rosenstock-Huessy writes in *Ja und Nein* that 'who sees language as a tool to express thoughts must misunderstand all these forms because language is much more the means of creation, to project us into the world to come [*ein Nach wie Vor*], hence the first thing language must achieve is bringing all grammatical forms into alignment with each other,'[59] he is encapsulating a highly important truth about speech: that it has a transformative power between the speakers. The corollary here is that those who see language as merely a tool to communicate what the mind already knows are working within an utterly false paradigm and closing themselves off from the transformative quality that is precisely language's gift to us. And when we close ourselves off in that way, we end up adopting a far more hierarchical, blocked, and control-bound stance toward the real. That stance, in turn, feeds the illusion that the mind is sovereign. This faith in the mind's sovereignty is, of course, the Cartesian dogma of the modern – a dogma from which both Rosentstock-Huessy and Rosenzweig break. Thus in *I Am an Impure Thinker*, Rosenstock-Huessy writes: 'I have been the sworn enemy of philosophical idealism all my life because it separates mind and body, spirit and incarnation. I prefer a child to an idea, and Lincoln to any abstract principle.'[60] In another essay – in an analysis reminiscent of Heidegger, at least in its procedure – he argues that the transformation of the defilement of the *logos*, from the living fire of the word to the *noetic* substance of Aristotle to the ratio of Aquinas, has as its consequence the race theory of Gobineau. At the root of the transformation is misplaced faith in mind and essences and a failure to understand the real nature of speech as a creative force. As he writes: 'The scandalous [and terrific and unheard] claims of the thinkers consist in this: that first they think, and only after that do they misadvisedly or treacherously disclose what they think to us with the help of speech as their tool.'[61]

We see precisely the same kind of rejection of philosophy's tendency to make language a mere tool in *The Star*, where Rosenzweig likens philosophical language to 'the silent realm of the [Faustian] mothers,' whose speech is 'no more than the merely ideal possibility of understanding.'[62] For Rosenzweig, the philosopher's indulgence in the solitary act of speech creates the illusion of being able to encompass 'the All' with philosophy. The deficiency here is that soundless speech (i.e., thought) is merely 'ideational.' Language, says Rosenzweig, 'is nourished by this life; and this life nourishes it and yet it is distinct from all this life by the fact that it does not move freely and arbitrarily on the surface, but sinks roots down into the dark foundations, buried beneath life.'[63] Idealistic logic, that logic which unites philosophers from Parmenides to Hegel, by contrast is said to transform 'the living into a realm of shadows.'[64] The miracle of life, life-giving speech, is smothered by the dead hand of the already, the preordained, as thought moves from 'species to individuals, from concepts to things, from form to content,'[65] and the given 'must be there in a chaotic and gray obviousness until the sun's rays of its spiritual form make its colours sparkle.'[66] For Rosenzweig, 'idealism lacks naïve trust in language. [Idealism was in no way disposed] to lend its ear to this voice, to answer this voice which resounds in man apparently without reason, but is all the more real because of that. It asks for reasons, accountability, calculability – everything that language could not offer it, and for its part invented logic, which provided all this.'[67]

As he writes in *The New Thinking*, it does this because it takes its own moment of timelessness for life itself, but that is merely a moment in a longer chain of actions, a moment in which calm, control, and predictability enter:

> Thinking is timeless and wants to be; it wants to establish a thousand connections with one blow; the ultimate, the goal, is for it the first. Speaking is bound to time, time-nourished; it neither can nor will abandon this, its nourishing environment; it does not know in advance where it will arrive; it lets its cues be given by others. It lives in general from the life of the other, whether the audience of a narration or the respondent in a dialogue, or the cospeaker in a chorus: whereas thinking is always solitary, even if it

is happening in among several 'symphilosophizing' partners: even then, the other merely raises objections which I myself would really have to raise, – which is the reason why most philosophical dialogues, including most of Plato's, are so boring. In actual conversation, something happens. I do not know in advance what the other will say to me, because I myself do not even know what I am going to say.[68]

And there is a final component of language that is essential to both Rosenzweig and Rosenstock-Huessy, one that is key to their entire orientation as Jew and Christian. It was profoundly and succinctly put by Rosenstock-Huessy: 'We speak because we wish to enhance the love that has befallen us.'[69]

3 Grammatical Organons in Rosenstock-Huessy and Rosenzweig

According to both Rosenstock-Huessy and Rosenzweig (in *The New Thinking*), the turning point of the New Thinking was, as we have mentioned, Rosenstock-Huessy's speech letter of 1916, which was published with some revisions in 1923 as *Angewandte Seelenkunde*. In his footnote to it in *Die Sprache des Menschengeschlects* (unfortunately not included in the English translation), Rosenstock-Huessy says that this letter opened the way out of the Alexandrian grammar and into a speech teaching of incarnation.

It may seem a rather curious idea that the source of so much philosophical error can be traced to an obscure school of grammarians. Yet Alexandrian grammar was *philosophically* designed as the systematic distillation of the grammatical underpinnings of the (originally Greek) sciences of philology, history, jurisprudence, and philosophy. Rosenstock-Huessy maintains that, to the extent that so many practices, sciences, and institutional framings of the modern world are outgrowths of processes fermented in and shaped by the reflexive forms of philosophy, 'we ourselves become structured by grammar'; he goes so far as to say that 'most men are shards of broken grammar.'[1] Thus he conceived his criticisms of the Alexandrian influence of grammar as part of his desire to open up new vistas for the social sciences – vistas that would represent us in our unpredictability, in our heat and light, in our aspirations, frustrations, and loves and hates, and not primarily in our calmer, reflective moments. He saw, then, that the chief defect of Alexandrian grammar is one that has carried throughout the social sciences – it suffers from a grammatical overreliance on the disinterested mood of the spectator and the specifically *anti-dialogical* character. It is noteworthy that this insight makes Rosenzweig and Rosenstock-Huessy's New

Thinking operate on a very different plane than, say, Peirce's semiotics. For while one can – as Michael Gormann-Thelen has done in a highly stimulating paper – draw attention to similarities between Peirce's triadic logic and Rosenzweig, the most striking difference between Peirce and the New Thinking is that Peirce simply takes for granted the stance offered by the disinterested – more precisely, *indicative* – mood as that portal through which truth is transported. By contrast, Rosenstock-Huessy and Rosenzweig – to somewhat different ends and thus through somewhat different emphases – conceive of grammar as a living body in which every mood and element is as much truth's servant as any other, even though each has its allotted role to play. For Rosenstock-Huessy, a semiotics like Peirce's reveals itself all too clearly as the blood relation of the Alexandrian pedagogy and its underlying prejudice and blindness.

Rosenstock-Huessy maintains that, as a time-making and time-saving activity, the Alexandrians broke language down into simple elements whose continuity is artificially fractured from the grammatical foundation of speech. With their systematic representation of grammar, the Alexandrians dissolved formal and informal speech (in Rosenstock-Huessy's terms, primary and secondary speech). Perhaps most disconcerting from Rosenstock-Huessy's perspective is that in Alexandrian grammar the vocative and imperative are little more than appendages, whereas both these speech forms are for him intrinsic to our social and personal existence. This type of formal speech – the kind that founds constitutions and institutions, declares laws and wars, and so on – is fundamentally different in kind from the sort of communication – informal speech – that we find in species that do indeed make signs among themselves but that have not invented a way to use their communication to conserve and traverse time. Rosenstock-Huessy is especially perplexed and irritated by linguists who equate speech with the communications of animals (which, by the way, do show signs of soul and tenderness), but who also fail to see that what makes us are our institutions, which are all premised upon what he calls formal speech – foundings, laws, oaths, declarations, and the like.[2]

For Rosenstock-Huessy, the Alexandrian emphasis, like the philosophical one that wishes to be a 'conductor' of the sciences, misses the point that speech is not primarily a descriptive process but a creative, revelatory, and redemptive one. In his lecture 'Make Bold to be Ashamed,' Rosenstock-Huessy makes the point that 'whenever we have the courage to speak the real thing, then we do not use metaphor; we don't use simile. But we suddenly create bodies, physically touchable, sensible things, events, which we can then describe.'[3] Only when we really pay attention to this incarnatory quality of speech – which is emphasized in both Rosenstock and Rosenzweig – can we appreciate the radical nature of the New Thinking. Many appraisals of Rosenzweig and Rosenstock-Huessy have talked about the importance of 'speech' in their thought, but these appraisals can mean nothing when we do not understand 'speech' as embodying, world weaving, 'enfleshing.'

Indeed, it is precisely this lack of the word becoming flesh that typifies the spiritual hollowness of so many areas of modern life. 'Dream a better world,' says a poster in my workplace showing a starving child. That poster is meant as an incitement to action, but the word 'dream' somehow typifies the phantasmagoric quality of the impotent 'remedies' of modern life – a quality that is even stronger when it comes to spiritual diseases. In *The Fruit of Lips,* Rosenstock-Huessy made the telling contrast between the power of meaningful speech and what happens so often in an age during which machines and mechanized systems are seen as the solutions to our needs: 'Because the word "freedom" has replaced the experience of freedom, "goodness" the experience of getting better, "kindness" the experience of falling in love, "adjustment" the experience of a personal commitment, every effort should be made to make the mind conscious of the grammar of meaningful speech.'[4]

Rosenstock-Huessy had traced this process of the empty word replacing its meaningful deployment back to the process of *gnosis*, which he tells us is 'all over the world today.' *Gnosis*, he says, is caused by people who try 'to think the new life without being touched by it first in some form of call, listening, passion or change of the heart.'[5]

For Rosenstock-Huessy, Alexandrian grammar assists that deadening process because the forms of activation are asphyxiated by their isolation. Language, like spirit, is circulatory, and for Rosenstock-Huessy that is no less the case for grammar than for anything living. But the Alexandrian table lays out a list of tenses and moods as if no necessary relationship existed between them; and invariably one commences with the mood that governs scientific inquiry, the indicative mood, and its conjugation. From his perspective, such commencement only highlights a system's closed circuitry, the manufactured nature of the approach. It assumes that a certain orientation toward reality is the most truthful; then it seeks to treat grammar as a spreading out – without any real sense of why – from that orientation. But for

Rosenstock-Huessy, this original orientation and grammatical foundation is simply not true – at best, it builds on a part of the truth, that is, the part that deals with finished or recurring experiences; it wants to make a root of a branch. Contrast this impersonal and disinterested perspective with what Rosenstock-Huessy says about the vocative in *Angewandte Seelenkunde*, where he points out that

> a person's being addressed by his own distinguishing proper name precedes any thinking about himself the 'I' may do. Accordingly, the shortest principal part of a verb (in Semitic, as well as Indo-Germanic languages) is the 'you' form of the imperative: go, come, listen, be, become. Only after hearing that does man respond – defiantly, self confidently – 'I am I, a man who is distinguished by a proper name, unlike the classifiable things of the outside world: trees, tables, stones, or houses.' This makes it clear to him that he can answer yes or no, that he can resist.[6]

Throughout his corpus, he repeats this point and elaborates on it in great detail. Indeed, it would be no exaggeration to say that Rosenstock-Huessy never completely finished his 1916 speech letter to Rosenzweig, for it was rich and broad enough to occupy him with its nuances for a lifetime. Whereas, then, the New Thinking emphasizes that we make ourselves and our lives and hence our communities and world as responses to calls, requests, and addresses – and Rosenstock-Huessy's speech letter was an answer to a behest of Rosenzweig – Alexandrian grammar begins in an abstraction, as if abstraction activated the deep structure of the process. In other words, Alexandrian grammar provides a deep structure, but it does so by robbing grammar of its vitality, of what makes meaningful speech; it is to creative human action what a corpse is to a vital life. In the same way that death comes at the end of life, the analysis of an event by the disinterested spectator/observer orientation is seen by Rosenstock-Huessy as the conclusion of a process: 'In the first instance one hears a name called out above one, then one communicates with another, who participates in the same named group as him. In the third we report, everything that has been done and has happened under this name; we report, we explain and we establish what is happening. Finally we oversee everything and compare and draw the sum of everything into a logical system. We analyze.'[7]

Of course analysis may well be useful and enable us to prevent certain kinds of dangers. Indeed, analysis is an essential component of a complex scientific world. But it also requires that the real it interacts with already fit its conceptual net so that an analysis may take place. Just as the anatomist does not care whose corpse is to be dissected when teaching or learning about how the body functions, the Alexandrian grammarian does not care who is speaking or what is said. Yet the world we make and the self we become both completely depend on who is addressing us, how we are being addressed, and what is being asked of us. First of all, 'the reciprocal salutation through names is thus the creation of a common life . . . A million words are senseless, if one who is spoken to doesn't know in which name he is being addressed.'[8] Second, 'vocatives create the preconditions for reciprocal communication; whereas nominatives and other cases take their place inside of communication. The vocative provokes the conversation.'[9] Third, 'the vocative means: turn around and face me; we want to talk with each other for a while. Such a summons, invitation, challenge, introduction sets men in motion. The other cases enable all the named to have their place. The vocative, however, turns them around!'[10] In contrast to this:

> The abstract madness of the school grammar explains the last grammatical creation: the declarative sentence 'these are' as the beginning of speech. But it's only a conclusion, behind which it has to be started again from the beginning. From the declarative sentence nothing ensues for the future. That's why no knowledge of nature helps us to answer the question how we should live. The bible with its 'let there be light' and 'there was light' has the experiential demonstrable grammar. Imperative (prejective), conjunctive or optative (subjective), preterite or perfect (trajective), neutral indicative (objective) are grammatical necessities arising out of times and spaces. A higher scientific grammar can exist because from now we can see the modes, the tenses, persons in a completely different way to the Alexandrians.[11]

Much twentieth-century thought is preoccupied with the danger that the great machine will destroy our animality, as well as with the need for us to reassert that quality in the face of asphyxiating forms of life, which offer great utility and material resources but cost us our feelings and energies. For Rosenstock-Huessy and Rosenzweig, it is precisely our human qualities that are being destroyed by the relentless grind and increasing disassociativeness and anomie of mechanized life. The 'human' lies specifically in the world that we make as creative revelatory acts of ourselves. Human beings are constantly in danger that new powers will become mechanical routines and thereby turn us into the living dead. Marx's account of alienation was an accurate telling of how widespread this process was in nineteenth-century industrialized societies. But there are a million ways to become routinized, mechanized, anodyne, and eventually zombie-like. True speech is always speech that awakens us – speech makes the self and the world more than they would otherwise be. By contrast, energies that are applied mechanically are extractive energies; they turn us into 'resources,' into things that are to be utilized for the construction of other things that are indifferent to our own potency. The pyramids are the paradigmatic example: wherever human beings exist solely to create such edifices, they are slaves. That is why Rosenstock-Huessy tells us: 'Thus we discover the founding act of life as the shaking up or shock [*Erschütterung*] of a man so that he is finally activated and called upon to join in the formation of history in his own name.'[12] 'In every healthy society,' he reminds us, 'one is inducted and introduced [*vorgestellt*], because life continues as a chain of people and things who have been introduced/ represented [*Vorgestellten*]. That's how one enters history, in so far as one asks after my name and then one acclaims the other . . . The human world does not consist of "will and representation" but rather as love and introduction/representation.'[13]

As we can see in these extracts from *Ja und Nein*, Rosenstock-Huessy views speech in its incarnatory character. Though I have provided a number of quotations from a relatively late work of his, they are but nuanced restatements of the dialogical perspective that he developed against the Alexandrians, one that led him in the *Angewandte Seelenkunde*, for example, to tell us:

Modern superficial language, on the other hand, sees only something calculable in the plural: one plus one plus one. But 'we' is not a plural in the sense that 10 chairs or 10 apples are. It was not 10 oxen which first shouted 'Te Deum laudamus,' but a 'we' which was made up out of different first, second, and third persons: out of a father, a child, brothers and sisters, a bridegroom, a servant, a mother, a maid, a guest of honor, a beggar, a congregation, a household, a family. They all can find themselves in the hymn of praise of the three persons of the plural, we, you, and they, 'Father, we praise thee, praise the Lord. The heavens are praising the glory of God.' This means a 'we' doesn't just cover up a bundle of identical, uniform 'I-s.' That already is practical exploitation of the 'we' by the marketplace. A 'we' doesn't even cover the bonds between 'you-s' and 'I-s' who have found one another. That was the special function of the archaic 'dual,' nowadays submerged in the plural. In the genuine original plural, however, in the sense of a praying congregation, of all communities filled with faith, of any religiously alive original cell, in the original plural, a piece of the world – that is of some third person – has been fused together with pieces of 'you-s' and 'I-s.' Primal grammar fuses God, man, and world into a resounding we.[14]

Thus far I have discussed Rosenzweig and Rosenstock-Huessy's commitment to a grammatical method as if their positions were more or less identical. So it needs to be said here that, while Rosenzweig's deployment and analysis of language crosses over with Rosenstock-Huessy's – for both insist that philosophy has largely proceeded in ignorance of the grammatical method, whereas the Jewish and Christian faiths are followers of the word – their positions do diverge quite significantly. That divergence is symptomatic of their respective journeys and acts of faith. Rosenzweig's interest in grammar is primarily in keeping with thrust of his life's work and revolves around the nature of the eternal people and their relationship to Christians and pagans. That is to say, Rosenzweig wants to demonstrate how the collective openness to the experience of Revelation and Redemption is, in fact, an openness to language. Rosenstock-Huessy, by contrast, is mainly interested in exploring grammar as an *organon* for reconfiguring social science in order to abet what he calls the meta-ethical or metanomical society. As he writes in *Speech and Reality*:

> My own direction of thought, probably, will have to be listed as the meta-ethical search for a synchronization of mutually exclusive social patterns of behaviour, as the 'metanomics of the great society' which must contain contradictory ways of life. My grammar of assent, my grammatical organon, is devoted to the task of supplementing the statute law of any given society with the metanomics that explain and satisfy our enthusiasm for the synchronization of the distemporary, of old and young, black, brown and white, government and anarchy, primitive and refined, highbrow and lowbrow, innocence and sophistication, all at peace in one human society.[15]

The requisite balance of unity and diversity that is necessary to allow distemporary lifeways and social forms to coexist on the same planet – and for Rosenstock-Huessy, striking that balance is the great challenge facing the human race – can only be achieved if we attend to the diverse speech streams that have enabled the formation of the multifarious time-bodies that are to be found forming and occupying a common collective space. As he writes in *Out of Revolution:* 'Let us go back to the unity of man's history and yet listen to the inimitable variety of his original tongues. For when God said, "let us make man, historical man, the varieties of man" He let all these varieties speak for themselves.'[16] Thus the emphasis on language stands in close relationship both to his understanding of what the Christian faith is (viz., the formation of a Corpus Christi) *and* to a metanomical order that is only possible to the extent that it can cooperate with the un-Christian. Thus he tells us that 'the chief duty of any member of the Corpus Christi is to strengthen the other forces of humanity,'[17] including the un-Christian: 'the unChristian forces play their part in the process of reimplantation of every branch of mankind into the one tree which is the perpetual effort of our era.'[18]

As is clear in *Angewandte Seelenkunde,* and as he worked out in a multitude of ways throughout the *Soziologie* and elsewhere, Rosenstock-Huessy constructed a grammatical framing of the different vistas of human formation that made philosophy only *one* of humanity's expressive and creative modes. As noted earlier, he was opposed to any idolatry of art or of natural science. And a major part of that, we can see now, is quite simply that we are constantly engaging with different fronts of reality as a consequence of accentuating different aspects of our expressive powers. Thus it is no accident that even a society as steeped in natural science as our own is no less garlanded by the arts. So it would be foolish to make natural science – or the arts, for that matter – the tribunal for all we are and should be, but it would be equally foolish to allocate that task to philosophy. We need all the powers we have, and speech is the clue to the range of expressions and needs of our souls. Yet, insists Rosenstock-Huessy, these different modes and ranges are fundamentally indebted not only to the soul being more breath-like than mind-like (the mistake of so much post-Cartesian thinking) but also to that soul being grammatical in character. Thus he sees that on closer examination, the different ranges of expression – and hence at the different aspects of life they give birth to – are also symptomatic of the different grammatical characteristics of the soul.

Art represents the place of the first person plural – the person of transfiguration and apotheosis – in the whole of our spiritual and intellectual life. But art contains as well the whole wealth of the three singular persons, in lyrics, drama, and epics, for instance. This is no more of a contradiction than the fact that cells can recreate whole organisms. On the contrary, it shows that we have indeed made a discovery. We have come to an understanding of the uniform origin of the life of the soul and of the peoples.

The fields of learning can also be broken down into sciences of the world in the narrower sense of knowledge of space, of nature, and of numbers and measures; as well as into sciences of the 'I': logic, philosophy, criticism; and into the teachings about the 'you' and how it should conduct itself: jurisprudence, ethics, and history. Philosophy, in which the intellect lets everything revolve around the 'I,' starts with the assumption of eternal freedom. Natural science, emphatically revolving around the 'it,' starts with the principle of laws. Jurisprudence, however, (and ethics with its emphasis on 'Thou shalt,' or 'I shall'), proceeds from legislation, from statutes which are fought over, drafted, and issued, one way today, but differently tomorrow! The body of legislation changes in its turn through the three grammatical forms of becoming, of being, and of application. The 'I-s' and the 'we-s' rule the political hurly-burly of legislation, of deliberations, of resolutions, of approvals and disapprovals, of the tally of votes, and the results of votes.[19]

In one of the last books he published during his lifetime, *Speech and Reality*, Rosenstock-Huessy densely brings together his ideas about grammar being a register of the soul and the source of much of our social formation. He does so, in part, by connecting the tenses of past and future – what he respectively designates as trajects and projects – with the orientations of subjectivity and objectivity and with the expressive forms and social formations that these and other grammatical orientations generate. For Rosenstock-Huessy, then:

The whole intellectual life of a nation must reflect this balance of power between:

command	prejective
song	subjective
history	trajective
calculation	objective

And indeed, the subjunctive of grammar, in the life of a great nation, is represented by music, by poetry, by all the arts. The equations of our calculating logic are spread out in all the sciences and techniques. The

trajective, linking us with the living past, lives in us through all the traditions. The prejective is represented by prophecy, ethics, and programmatic
movements.

The neglect of any one of these formations as a means of generating
action and hence truth ultimately disempowers us, leaving us stranded.
For Rosenstock-Huessy, societies have evolved and stratified the way
they have in terms – at least in some of their most recurrent modalities –
of social expression; and they have done so not haphazardly but as a
result of grammatical pressures, which are quite simply the pressures
of the forces of the universe itself requiring life's own furtherance.
The following extract provides the essence of his grammatical view of
society and is straightforward enough not to require further commentary in a book of this nature (as opposed to a monograph devoted to
Rosenstock-Huessy's grammar and social science). Though long, it is
little-known enough to warrant inclusion:

The four great professions:

lawyers	(trajective)
preachers	(prejective)
artists	(subjective)
scientists	(objective)

are nothing but expanded forms of human grammar. Any society contains
them, regardless of labels. They are a constant because our relations to
time and space are constant. All the time and all over the place, we decide
what is past and what is future, what is part of us, what is facing us.

The whole intellectual life of a nation – literature, legislation, politics, sciences, song and slang – is subject to a grammatical analysis of its health.

1. Imperative	Politics
2. Subjunctive	Literature
3. Recording	Ceremonies, history, customs, holidays
4. Analytical	Sciences, statistics

The four types of cognitive sentences: song, command, calculation,
story, we may call macroscopical phenomena because they all occur in
any individual's own sphere daily; they are enlarged to telescopical

magnitude when we think of the whole world's literature, the whole social world of orders given and obeyed, the whole universe of scientific
facts, and the whole firmament of rites and traditions. On the other hand,
they become microscopically small in the particles of the isolated sentence.
When the grammarian dissects a Latin phrase, he has a minute cellular
structure under his scrutiny. But it is one and the same life of the spirit, in
its phases, which, we have before us in:

1. verbs	imperatives	politics
2. adjectives	subjunctives	literature and arts
3. nouns	narratives	tradition
4. numerals	indicatives	sciences

Because we are constituted by all these forms and forces, it is, for
Rosenstock-Huessy, an act of towering stupidity to take one grammatical mode as the benchmark for life itself; yet this is precisely
what philosophy, theology, and natural science, at different times and
throughout the ages, have often sought to do as they have taken the orientations necessary for dealing with one aspect or front of life (and ourselves) as the essence of life (and ourselves). They have, as Rosenzweig
expressed it, been guilty of 'ism' thinking. In this respect, he repeats
Rosenzweig's claim that the ideas of the metalogical, meta-ethical, and
metaphysical are necessary stepping stones for escaping from the isms
that have been the corollary of the triumph of Idealist philosophizing
and natural science.

Closely related to this interpretation, and freeing us to attune ourselves to the soul's grammar as well as to the speech streams that constitute our deepest needs and that give rise to the world in which we
participate, is Rosenstock-Huessy's belief that throughout the greater
part of the European experience and until the complete severance from
it by natural science, religion played a fundamental role in binding together the different potentialities of human experience. It did so on the
foundation of the shock and trauma of suffering. It is for this important
reason that speech thinking must take note of the reality of religion and
not simply dismiss it, as the Enlightenment *philosophes* did, who viewed
it as the root of all phantasms – whereas to the contrary, phantasms
thrive everywhere, as Adorno and Horkheimer (not to mention Hegel
and the Romantics) had to remind us, even in the Enlightenment's own
light. Religion has at various times been so phantasmic in its expression
and development because of the degree of truth it has had to convey

and also because of the range and nature of the powers it has sought to bind and help transport over the ages. Rosenzweig avoided the word religion in *The Star* when speaking of Jewish and Christian life; and Rosenstock-Huessy sometimes said that Christianity is no religion, though in *Angewandte Seelenkunde* he would write a passage that would spur Rosenzweig's grammatical analysis of Creation, Revelation, and Redemption in *The Star*:

> We hardly need to say that the third part needed to make up a community of 'we' is the self-consciousness of an 'I.' 'I-s' suffer. Bodies that pray – be they bodies of people, households, or 'I-s' – start praying because they are sick, because they are suffering. An 'I-s' suffering loosens the tongue, just as the shock of a 'Thou,' and the amazement of an 'if' do. And if more than just one, or another, or the third of these things befalls the soul, if all three come together, then all single forms of grammar are suspended. This is the language of prayer and worship. That is why the language of religion towers above the languages of science, art, and law-giving. It is the crown of languages because it leads the dance of the three grammatical persons, of the jubilance of 'we-s,' of the humility of 'you-s,' of the amazement of 'theys.' Religion in its daily life is just like art or science, a mere container of language. Primal words which erupted once, to be established and pronounced, are preserved in religion, as in other areas of life. 'Religion' is only distinguished by the fact that its shrine preserves transformation itself, the secret of transformation.[20]

If Rosenstock-Huessy was prepared to make religion 'the crown of languages,' he also emphasized that the religious appeal to another world has its roots in language and that rationalist attacks on religion are primarily about language: 'Not religion but language forces man to distinguish between this world and the real world, the world as we know it and the genuine, or better known world. The crux of theology is a crux of language, and all our rationalists are not protesting against religion but against speech.'[21]

Rosenstock-Huessy's interest in grammar is richly suggestive of an approach to what, notwithstanding Rosenzweig's philosophical objections, we can for the moment – in keeping with Rosenstock-Huessy's point – call the religious traditions. But it was Rosenzweig, not Rosenstock-Huessy, who explored the peoples of revelation and who argued that their uniqueness is captured in part by the grammatical accentuations that guide their existence. While doing so, he continues his critique of philosophy, in a manner similar to Rosenstock-Huessy, for its unwarranted faith in the mind's capacity to stamp itself on the chaos of existence and to create an order that is more truthful than what language itself provides. And as he first explores the grammar of the *logos*, he does this by contrasting the life/thought ways inherent in that attunement to grammar with life/thought ways (Islamic and Idealistic) that might easily be mistaken as similar, preferable, or deeper.

For Rosenzweig, this involves a further critique of Idealism, especially that variant of it which attempts to explain the creation of life as a form of generation. For Rosenzweig, generation is not genesis; the Idealist account of generation, for him, falls far short of an understanding of Revelation and Redemption.[22] For him, such an account fails for the elementary reason that it tries to provide a proof where no proof is forthcoming about the why of the world's existence on the basis of its being. (Anyone familiar with Rosenstock-Huessy can see that he, too, avoided such 'philosophical' topics.) For Rosenzweig, the world's being does not point back to a *before*; and humans originally bestowed the term 'Creation' not as a scientific hypothesis but rather to designate how interaction with the world and ourselves is experienced. Only then could it become something that is part of a greater process in which life's meaning is experienced as a process of Revelation. 'Creation itself,' Rosenzweig tells us, 'is not demonstrated by the world . . . It is not possible to believe in Creation because it provides a coherent explanation of the riddle of the world. He who has not yet been reached by the voice of Revelation has no right to accept the idea of creation, as if it were a matter of scientific hypothesis.'[23]

While some philosophical schools have sought – unsuccessfully, contends Rosenzweig – to explain the universe as something created, it is undeniable that Creation, when applied to ourselves and the world, like Revelation and Redemption is at the very least a *word*. Yet a unicorn is also merely a word and an image with no existential counterpart – though, recalling Hegel's famous dismissal of Kant's distinction between a real thaler and a mere concept of one, we can apply Hegel's insight and say that the very concept of a unicorn is predicated on its lack of existential import, just as a thaler that cannot be cashed in is not – contrary to Kant – in any sense a real thaler. But true as this may be, Creation, Revelation, and Redemption are not like unicorns – they aren't things in any sense of the word; rather, they are ways of orientation that – as Rosenzweig reminds his readers – have been closed to philosophers but are the staple of theologians. But aren't they only words? Yes, Rosenzweig allows, but not just any words – they are words that orientate, that build or form lives, that have formed two peoples or nations – the Jews and the Christians – and that have purported to form a third – the Muslims. Words, then? Yes, but for Rosenzweig, 'language is truly the wedding gift of the Creator to humanity; and yet at the same time the mutual possession of the children of men in which each has his particular share and finally the seal of humanity in man.'[24]

For Rosenzweig, then, we are woven in words, and we find in language itself the very processes of Creation, Revelation, and Redemption that we ascribe to God. The miracle that is man's soul, however, is but the light of God, as Rosenzweig reminds his readers near the end of the introduction to Part Two of *The Star*.[25] Just as we may reveal some secret to another person, and just as we may reveal part of ourselves in and through our exchanges and encounters, our promises and veilings, our lies, and so on, and just as our words set something in action, and just as an action may be redeemed – all processes of everyday life – there is for Rosenzweig a coherence and a promise at the basis of language/speech, a truth we can discern in how our own lives are constituted by the vast array of signs that have contributed to our formation.

The Star, as we have said, and which we will return to again, provides a detailed analysis of the signs of orientation – God, Man, and World, and Creation, Revelation, and Redemption. The exploration of the first triad was not one that showed us what we could be – indeed, it showed repeatedly (again, as we will explore in more detail later) the limits of a world, a self, and (a) God(s) that were unable to achieve the kind of coherence and fulfilment that a people is capable of achieving. The limits and incoherence, for Rosenzweig, of peoples whose horizons stop at the poles of God, Man, and World stem simply from an inability to understand life as a process wherein Creation, Revelation, and Redemption are on offer – and that is, according to Rosenzweig, in large part because of a failure to attend to the promise of grammar. On the other hand, for Rosenzweig, the peoples who hearken to the relationship between Creation, Revelation, and Redemption are the peoples that have found these three potentials through their willingness to be open to experience; they have connected the original three poles of orientation of God, Man, and World.

By constrast, according to Rosenzweig, philosophers leap to make sense of the chaos of existence by trusting their speculative capacities, whereas the Jewish people have trusted experience and its grammar more than their analysis; they have recorded and followed what Rosenzweig claims in his analysis of Genesis 'is the treasury of verbal forms of creation.' He emphasizs this point by asking, 'Doesn't the Creation take place in the word? Didn't God say?'[26] And 'the word that creates the whole of Creation irrupts, as the first action word of Creation, the "God said."'[27] For Rosenzweig, all of this reveals the depth of Jews' responsiveness to the God who speaks the truth of Creation while revealing the redemptive dimension of life. Such responsiveness of the Jewish people has nothing to do with a conscious argument, as if it were a kind of collective theoretical consensus of a like-minded community, (again) as if the conference or seminar room were the basis of community orientation. Communities emerge and evolve through shared experiences, the shared joys and traumas of life. Which is also to say, yet again, that Rosenzweig's *Star*, unlike so many other works of philosophy, does not set out to convert people to a way of seeing reality so that they may act differently, or more morally; rather, in that book he is recording what the different peoples of the world respond to – at least those that interest him for the purpose of his task at hand – and why they are what they are. Certainly he has a stake in liberal Jews, who, just like he once did, see what heritage they lose by failing to appreciate the story they belong to. Thus, for the non-Jew, the value of *The Star* is that it enables an appreciation of the Jewish mission and the Jewish God.

Rosenzweig is certain, then, that the path he is walking has been trodden for generations. For him, it is quite simply the path of the word of God, for the word is the place where God is present and active and in our mouths. (And just as Heidegger had philosophy speak Greek and German, the God of Redemption, for Rosenzweig, seems to speak Hebrew and German.) For him, the word reaches from Genesis to the Song of Songs to the Psalms – it is the path, then, of the Bible, which is also a sign of God as Creator, Revealer, and Redeemer and what, according to Rosenzweig, the Jewish people *qua* people *are* to the extent that they live in response to such a God and his word:

> We are describing the path that we believe in with the words we trust. To believe in the path is a difficult thing, for we never see anything but the single point where we are living; but language is the truly 'higher' mathematics, which reveals to us, ever since the singular point of the lived miracle, the entire course of the believed miracle. And to trust it is easy, for it is in us and around us, and when it comes to us from the 'outside,' noth-

ing other than it echoes from our 'inside' toward the 'outside.' The spoken word is the same, whether it is listened to or said.[28]

In Book One, Part One, of *The Star*, in the chapter 'God and His Being or Metaphysic,' Rosenzweig had argued that all beings are originally thought and spoken of by means of affirmation (yes), negation (no), and the connection between the yes and the no – that is, the connective 'and.' Thus, he continues, 'yes,' 'no,' and 'and' are three silent accomplices of language – they are the conditions of any language.[29] In Part One of *The Star,* Rosenzweig is searching for a language prior to language, for the elements that enable human beings to find the most elementary orientation within existence as they encounter a self and the world and the ground extrinsic to the self and the world (a Creator). The affirmation, for Rosenzweig, finds its simplest grammatical component in the predicate adjective – which he interprets as 'the nothing but assertion'; while the negative is in the 'substantive subject,' which is the 'nothing-but-object-of-the-assertion' – that is, a definite decision that the subject is not another one, but this one being referred to. The connective 'and' enables the sequence of words that form a sentence to take place. The movement of 'yes' and 'no and 'and' is the same mathematical movement that Rosenzweig sees as necessary for any being to be a 'this' and not a 'that' and something that can be connected with something else. Thus he sees that emergence and passing away have both linguistic and mathematical aspects that are basic to the world in which we exist. And just as with the infinitesimal, 'nothing' is not an absolute – rather, it is part of a function; and the 'nothing' is not an entity that can be known as 'nothing' – rather, it is meaningful only insofar as it is part of a relationship in which something is affirmed. This is why Rosenzweig – quite rightly in my view – insists that 'the Yes is the beginning. The No cannot be the beginning; for it could only be a No of the nothing; but this would presuppose a nothing that would be negatable, that is to say, a nothing that had already decided on a Yes.'[30] (The point, though grammatical, is similar to Sartre's argument in *Being and Nothingness* that 'non-Being exists only on the surface of being.')[31] And the 'and' 'is not the secret companion of the particular word, but of the sequence of words. It is the keystone that completes the vault of the cellar above which is erected the edifice of logos, of reason in language.'[32]

While, then, the foundations of language, for Rosenzweig, commence in the silent functionality of emergence and withdrawal and connection, its miraculous nature is part and parcel of Creation as such, whose utmost possibility is to participate in the process of Redemption. It is this next step that is probably the most densely argued and cryptic movement in *The Star*. And it is an argument whose difficulty is only compounded by being broken up under the headings of Creation, Revelation, and Redemption and then squeezed into the various symmetries on which Part Two of *The Star* is organized so that the discussion of grammar proceeds along with his discussion of Islam, his critique of Idealism, and his elaboration of his theory of art. Though Rosenzweig never tells us exactly why he has organized his material the way he has, it is most likely that the discussion of Islam preceeds that of grammar so that we can better contrast – and thereby break through – this false Revelation, which for Rosenzweig, contrary to Judaism and Christianity, from the outset construes itself as religion. Rosenzweig will hammer this home, smashing to bits all outward manifestations and false showings of Revelation, which he claims (for reasons we explore more fully in a later chapter) are essential to Islam. It is false, for Rosenzweig – as we will see when we examine this point in detail – in the same way that the Enlightenment is false. False, because it does not heed the truth in Revelation that is inherent in grammar. Rosenzweig insists that we view grammar as more truthful, more elemental, than art and philosophy; yet when art is attentive to and subordinate to the loving God, we can see how the truth of grammar is crafted in the Book of Books, is made 'art,' made the highest art. This, too, will be explored more fully in our discussion of Rosenzweig on art.

While Rosenzweig's claim about grammar providing an *organon* in *The Star* is a bold one, his argument is extremely cryptic and so dense that it would require a monograph, at least, to unpack and test it. The kind of glosses provided by Mosès and Samuelson in their commentaries on *The Star* strike me as unilluminating and unconvincing, for they only reinforce the opaqueness of the thornier, more puzzling, or more dubious aspects of his grammatical analysis.[33] No doubt this grammatical analysis – at least in the section on Creation in *The Star* – strikes many readers, as it does me, as thoroughly contrived. One might add, as some sort of defence (though it does not really help), that *The Star* is an extraordinary contrivance, a contrivance that wants to make a *virtue* of contrivance – how could one think one belonged to God's chosen people unless one responded daily in a manner of certainty, a certainty that others call faith, and that indeed *is* faith, a faith seeming confirmed by one's continuance and by the rituals and festivals that give meaning to this continuance? But is this not itself the contrivance of contrivances? Radiant or dazzling? Illuminating or blinding? To the philosophical (Greek) mind, this is utter madness, a madness already played out by the first prophet in his willingness to sacrifice the very condition of the fulfilment of the promise, his only son. In *Fear and Trembling,* a Christian spelled out for us moderns just how absurd and insane this is – so insane that Christians replay the whole thing by transforming the story of Abraham into a story about God, with God not just finding the sacrifice but *being* the sacrifice, and then testing the whole human race in the very manner that Abraham had been tested. True as this is, it does not overcome the opaqueness or contrivance of Rosenzweig's grammatical analysis.

If Rosenzweig's argument about grammar seems contrived, matters are not helped by the speed and lack of explication with which he undertakes the grammatical derivations on which he bases his entire argument. So it would hardly help to simply follow him through what he refers to as his 'successive synoptic tables drawn up by means of the root words.'[34] What is more important for our purposes is to note that the grammatical analysis that Rosenzweig undertakes throughout *The Star* is reminiscent of nothing so much as Kant's strategy in *Critique of Pure Reason,* in which it is obvious that Kant starts from the fact of Newton's physics, *then* identifies the principles that have no empirical counterparts so that he can *then* identify the categories of the understanding, without which there could be no pure principles of pure reason, principles that make physics possible. Yet Kant, in taking this approach, presents the argument as if he has already come across the categories. Anyone who has studied *Critique of Pure Reason* knows that cannot be so, because the logical tables from which he makes his adjustments in order to hit upon the table of categories can only help him once he has already decided which principles of pure reason must be explained. And only after that can he possibly know how he will then reconfigure the logical forms in such a way that they can become forms of a possible experience, become categories and not remain mere logical functions. By proceeding as he does, Kant bewilders his readers, who can only wonder how on earth he can simply hand down the table of categories, as if he had just received them from on high the way Moses received the Ten Commandments. (Anyone who has read how Kant's immediate contemporaries responded will notice how bewildered they all were – I suspect that only Hegel thoroughly grasped what was going on.)[35] Matters are only made more confusing by the way he quickly modifies some of the traditional logical lexicons in order to help readers get from the logical table to the table of categories. It is only once we have got to the principles of pure reason themselves that what had seemed a purely capricious act in the name of pure reason shows itself to be a brilliant and insightful contrivance whose veracity stands and falls with the veracity of the principles of Newtonian mechanics – principles that he quite rightly sees are the *conditions* (which are not to be confused with the content) of (Newtonian-based) scientific laws and explanations. Kant commences with the facts of the successful application of mathematics to the universe and the descriptive and great predictive power of Newtonian physics; for his part, Rosenzweig commences with a fact that is, for him, also a 'miracle' – a miracle that is the thread of Creation, Revelation, and Redemption, viz., the miracle of the Jewish people and the book that provides them with their orientation.

Rosenzweig, then, like Kant, already knows precisely where he wants to go when he does his grammatical derivations in the sections beginning with the 'Grammar of the Logos' and continuing through to 'Idealist Logic.' In the 'Book of Creation,' it is evident that what he wants to get to is the book of Genesis, and he could not have dreamed of the synoptic trajectory he undertakes for the grammatical forms without already having had Genesis in front of him. To be sure, the extent to which we readers will be impressed by these sections of *The Star* depends largely on whether we are convinced by his 'successive synoptic tables' – which are all the more obscure precisely because he does not present them as tables! Though he does not say so, it is pretty clear that he expects his reader to draw up the tables – but a table is after all a table, not an argument. In any case, not until we have seen the analysis of Genesis that he provides can we see that he really is attempting to show that 'the ways of God and the ways of man are different, but the word of God and the word of man are the very same.'[36] In the analysis of Genesis, Rosenzweig writes,

One sentence runs through the whole chapter which relates the work in the beginning. A sentence that that occurs six times and consists in a single word preceded only by a colon. This sentence is: Good!: it was and it is and it will be – 'good.' Creation resides in this divine Yes to the existence of the creature. This 'good' is the word of the end pronounced aloud for each day of Creation, because it is nothing other than the silent original word of their beginning.[37]

But if Genesis provides Rosenzweig with the grammatical clue to the beginning of the grammatical key to Creation, there is also a sentence that provides him with the complete formulation of life's purpose as a redemptive process. That sentence he calls 'the genealogical sentence of Redemption, the roof on the house of language.' It is, he continues,

> the sentence true in itself, the sentence that remains true in any sense it is taken and from any that it might come. That two and two are four is what can become non-true, for example when it is taught to a parrot that begins to 'say' it: for what is mathematics to a parrot? But the sentence that says that God is good, even in this most absurd case of all where language utters it, could never become a counter truth; for the parrot too was created by God, and all things considered, his love applies to it, too. All the other linguistic forms must be capable of connecting to this sentence.[38]

In other words, Rosenzweig is indeed following the grammatical thread, but he knows exactly where it will lead. His reliance on grammar to demonstrate the connections among Creation, Revelation, and Redemption is not something he has begun in the dark; on the contrary, he has begun it in the light – in 'the let there be light' confirmed by the genealogical sentence that tells us 'God is good.'[39]

The 'path' that leads from Creation to Redemption – from 'in the beginning' to the communal prayer during which all are invited by a living community to give thanks by singing, in praise, that 'God is good' – must, claims Rosenzweig, begin with the word that 'leads from the primordial, inaudible Yes to begin with.' Such a word he calls a root word – that is, one that attracts a cluster of other words around itself as living growths, just as (he sees) the root sentence has living, loving, redeeming sentence upon sentence, spurring on living, loving, redemptive deed upon deed gathered around it.

A root word, he says, cannot be too concrete, precisely because its concreteness implies a vast negation, 'an infinite negation, hence implying the And of the so and not otherwise.' Rosenzweig contends that he is not dialectically presenting 'a grammatical development, not outlaying an immanent order,' but instead describing 'an order that is brought to grammar from outside . . . from the role that language plays in relation to reality.'[40] As opposed to the noun – which, he says, must first be extracted from the flow of qualities, which are then relegated to the surface or attributes of a substance or subject – there is the most elemental quality, a *root*, which is simple affirmation, this is 'so,' which is 'exclusively assertion and nothing else': 'The positive value judgment is nothing other than the primordial Yes become audible. As is shown in other respects by the usage of many languages that say: "Fine!" or "Good!" in order to say "Yes."'[41]

For Rosenzweig, 'the pronoun is much more pre-noun than pronoun';[42] that is, it is a sign that indicates the vagaries of what lies before it – not an abstraction from what is known, but something that precedes our knowing, a kind of probing into the substratum that is the noun: 'What it is remains problematic. Only the indefinite article gives an answer to this "what": it is a representative of this or that genus; and only the definite article seals all this great process and shows that it has been accomplished: "the" thing is known.'[43]

Note that insofar as Rosenzweig has emphasized the qualitative nature of the real in the most elementary encounter of self and world, he has not made a substance of 'the good' as Plato and neo-Platonists have done. For he is looking for the start of a grammatical thread, and a noun is not a thread but an end. Where Plato and his others enclose the alpha and omega in the noun 'the good,' Rosenzweig wants to trace the thread – or, to use an even more apt metaphor, to ride the grammatical wave wherever it may lead – which, he is convinced, leads into the word that binds the body of Jewish believers. In fact, it too leads to 'good,' but good as a 'seal' rather than a substance, an adjectival seal of existence and a promise of more and better, not a closed principle waiting to be defined by us. The 'what is' of the Platonic disposition is, for the New Thinking, a kind of chloroform that anaesthetizes living processes so that the philosopher can master them. The speech of the living God, by contrast, releases and affirms living powers, and we in turn name life's process, not so much as an act of mastery but as acts of remembrance, of fear and awe, of mourning and celebration, so that our names reveal the past to the future and serve as warnings and gifts. Perhaps it is not surprising that Rosenzweig's argument about goodness being intrinsic to existence is reminiscent of Augustine, but that only testifies to the guidance that both received from Genesis.

The grammatical key of the Bible is, then, for Rosenzweig, precisely the grammatical key that befits the genuinely 'objective,' for 'it is the past tense which enables us to see what a thing is "objectively": it completes the objectivity of the becoming just as the thingliness defined by the article completes that of being.'[44] Furthermore, 'God created. And the world, that which was created? It "was"; this word, too, ceaselessly resounds. As the Psalms sums it up: "He spoke and it was!" '[45]

As in Genesis, in which the past tense had become for Rosenzweig the crown of Creation, as the alpha was also the omega, and as the Good creator looked out on the good Creation and there was the promise that that creature would later sing God's praise, 'good' is, as we have said, never a closure, as it was for the Platonists; on the contrary, it is always an opening to more, a promise of more. For Rosenzweig this shows that Revelation has need of Creation and that the No of Redemption is the power that ultimately sanctifies and preserves what is worth affirming; the No, for Rosenzweig, is absolutely what is required for Redemption, for *only what is charged by love redeems*, while Creation is all affirmation, affirmation of all that is, including even the killing of love. Redemption, on the other hand, judges and extinguishes love's killers and the false love's killings, which is why it cannot simply be Yes to all of creation's destruction. Redemption is grasped only by those who follow through Creation beyond the merely natural and the reasonable, who recognize that the good is the promised open end of the good Creator, the loving Revealer, the responsive Redeemer. The promise points to the fact that the 'better' is the opening up of a new realm. As we have suggested, that realm is love's realm. The Song of Songs is, for Rosenzweig, the expression of relationship, the power of soul upon soul, the power that requires the address of one to the other; but such love is still only a step on the way, a step toward the fulfilment of God's command that He be loved, toward the command that we love our neighbour. Love as attribute spreads in this way and reveals that it is indeed as strong as death. And how does it continue? By taking creation further and seeing what may survive within this commandment – by seeing what through this commandment is charged and becomes part of the eternal that is Redemption.

The Christian, too, is privy to these commands and has taken heed. But these are not the eternal people – they move past redemption for themselves and journey ever forward toward the redemption that is like Hegel's bad infinite, always there is more time to fulfil the journey, ever there is beginning, ever a gap. But all the while, Creation continues; and the pagans are, as we have seen in Rosenstock-Huessy, the peoples of Creation and part of the chaos until they step onto the path to Redemption. The Christian brings these other powers onto the path, seeking to redeem them and to bring more brothers and sisters into

Christianity's fold. This is not where Rosenzweig can go: his people have remained committed to the eternal – embodying it, doing God's bidding, following the thread – and this culminates in their life, not the life of other peoples, not the pagan life that comes and goes and that may be reconfigured on the plane of the commandment to love one's neighbour. It is the life that has been decreed for this particular people, as Rosenzweig described so powerfully in the Urzelle:

> So the organizing concept of this world is not the universal, neither the Arche nor the Telos, neither the natural nor the historical unity, but rather the particular, the event, *not beginning or end, but rather middle* of the world. The world is 'infinite,' both from beginning and from end. From the beginning infinite in space, toward the end infinite in time, only from the middle arises a limited home in the unlimited world, a bit of ground between four tent pegs, which can be stuck further and further out. Viewed from this perspective, beginning and end are also transformed for the first time, from limit-concepts of infinity to corner posts of our worldly estate, the 'beginning' as creation, the 'end' as salvation.

This, then, is why Rosenzweig believes what he believes and thinks what he thinks. This is what makes him who he is.

Rosenzweig and Rosenstock-Huessy both take grammar as central, to Jewish and Christian life respectively. Even so, it is clear that their procedures differ quite markedly. Rosenstock-Huessy's grammatical analysis commences with a situation and action – hence the imperative mood, because of the precariousness of life and the urgency of continuance and of establishing chains of command over time. Thus his analysis emphasizes the relationship between actions and the fronts of reality we are attempting to orientate ourselves through, on the one hand, and the aspects of life that are, thanks to language, being passed across generations, on the other. His focus on grammar does not suggest as clearly as Rosenzweig does a dichotomy between inner and outer. In this respect, Rosenzweig's analysis is more 'philosophical' than sociological. Nevertheless, Rosenzweig explores how elements of language form not just an action but a people, who, being attuned to the innermost depths of Creation, follow the word to what is beyond Creation and thereby see themselves as responding directly to the command of a living and loving God. The respective grammatical approaches of Rosenzweig and Rosenstock-Huessy reproduce their central difference – the quest to dwell here in eternity, versus ongoing temporal expansiveness. This difference was spelled out by Rosenstock-Huessy in *Ja und Nein:*

> Franz Rosenzweig received from me, as he never became tired of confirming his entire life, the teaching of the You which precedes the I. But he didn't follow the path I took into the cruciformed reality; instead he stepped with his *Star of Redemption* into the heart of revelation and established a dialectical teaching about speech.[46]

He adds that Rosenzweig's teaching

> was an existential answer and a rejoinder to my own teaching on speech and its history among men. In the mean time this book has become as celebrated as it has been infrequently read. It is an incandescent subjective confession, intelligible only as an answer to my word. Since the years 1913 to 1923, which we spent together, there has arisen a doubled teaching of speech; the one has been laid out by me, the other dialectically added by Rosenzweig. All future teachings will, however, express themselves as either Christian or Jewish or pagan. Speech is Trinitarian.

Given that the New Thinking was a collective effort, I do think it important to introduce at this point another New Thinker, Martin Buber. It is not simply because Buber was one of them. Rather – and this will strike most readers as a strange claim to make about this famous Jewish thinker – it is because Rosenstock-Huessy saw Buber as a representative of pagan humanism and hence as a rejuvenator of this third pathway. I also wish to draw attention to Rosenstock-Huessy's critical engagement with Buber to signal the importance of Rosenstock-Huessy's formulation of living three lives in one: Jew, Christian, pagan. It is important to add here that Rosenzweig, too, understood that both Christianity and paganism had formed him. And for him, from this, there was no escape. But his role as Jewish philosopher and teacher, and his robust demarcations between Jews, Christians, and pagans, combined with his desire to make sure there could be no confusion as to what is what, he was less interested in emphasizing the unity of the three-in-one life than in highlighting the differences between them. Rosenstock-Huessy was as insistent on the need to see these differences as Rosenzweig, but he also realized that the task of his times was to demonstrate an inner and necessary unity between them. To this end, Buber was genuinely important to him, both as an example of what he did *not* think and as an example of how thinking such as Buber's, nevertheless, had an important place alongside his and Rosenzweig's.

In the section we have quoted earlier from *Ja und Nein*, after stating that Buber represents the third way of speech thinking,[47] Rosenstock-Huessy adds that Buber stands beside the Idealists, and he identifies Buber as expressing a teaching consistent with the Greek and academic mind. That he takes Buber as representative of the pagan/Greek mind is as striking as it is paradoxical. Not only was he Rosenzweig's co-translator of the Bible into German, but his tales of the Hasidim, his devotion to the cause of Zion, and his writings on evil and the Holocaust, not to mention *I and Thou*, would all seem to mark him as a major Jewish thinker, perhaps the quintessential one. I have already expressed strong disagreement with Ignaz Maybaum's cursory and libellous labelling of Rosenstock-Huessy, but his judgment concurs with Rosenstock-Huessy's when he writes in *Trialogue between Jew, Christian, and Muslim* that 'Buber was never a synagogue goer. Those who did not read his learned essays and books and knew him as he lived among his fellow Jews were convinced he was an agnostic; true, a committed Zionist, but otherwise an un-Jewish Jew.' (And Rosenstock-Huessy knew him personally.) Maybaum also writes that Buber 'preaches humanism, the Humanist-Ideal, as the German expression goes, but makes humanism the means to propagate his branch of nationalism.'[48] Which, however, does not stop him from also making this point: 'Buber is the great, perhaps the greatest Jewish personality of the years before and after the holocaust.'[49]

Rosenstock-Huessy's assessment of Buber is in many ways a summation of the core characteristics of what he sees as the difference between Christian speech thinking and humanist speech thinking. In *Ja und Nein* he makes the difference rest on the sequence of the title of Buber's major work – which at first glance seems trivial, for what does it matter where one commences, with an I or a thou? But given the general critique that Rosenstock-Huessy has of Alexandrian grammar and the importance that sequence plays for him in the formation of social processes, and hence of grammar as social *organon*, it should not surprise us that Rosenstock-Huessy places so much weight on this critique, coming back to it on many occasions, for example, during his 'St Augustine by the Sea' lecture of 1962:

And since he [Buber] put the 'I' first, people have not understood there . . . are not two people, only, but that you begin as a 'Thou,' and then grow up to be . . . an 'I,' and then later a 'we.' It's terribly important that you should see that you yourself have to run through the stages of grammar in every one act. When you are integrated into a society, you begin with understanding the command. In this moment, an imperative . . . Somebody has to extinguish the fire, so we all shout, 'Fire, fire, fire!' Somebody who is obedient to this call, runs out, and brings the water hose, and begins to extinguish the fire. Others remain indifferent, and this act does not touch them, and they remain outside history, so to speak, because they do not feel that they should respond. Responses make people. Anybody who hears the vocative, 'John,' and who follows the vocative is in the state of being born as a person. But he has to take upon himself this humiliating experience, that somebody else creates him into what he has to do. We are not self-makers of ourself.[50]

He later developed this criticism in *Philosophical Interrogations* at greater length, with a response by Buber.[51] Rosenstock-Huessy brings together all the core elements of his thought in his comparison with Buber, and one sees how important the difference is between the thinker who takes time, speech, and history as the triadic rubric under which he operates and the thinker who pauses at 'the encounter' of the *I and Thou*. Buber's work shimmers with references to the mystical moment. The grammatical moves that Buber makes in *Between Man and Man* – with its chapters 'The Single One' and 'What is Man' – bear witness to his readiness to accept the eclipse of the living name by the pronominal or the creature's dissolution into Man (Rosenstock-Huessy asks not 'what' but 'who' is man?). Buber's Zionism (which he intended to temper with goodwill and humanity toward his Arab neighbours) displays a political need that, notwithstanding Rosenzweig's later concessions on this point, pulls Judaism (perhaps for inevitable historical reasons) back into the pagan world of the state and its concerns. What is more, Buber's early work *Ecstatic Confessions: The Heart of Mysticism*, in a gesture of spiritual ecumenicalism and political tolerance, brings together Jews, Chinese, Christians of all ages and hues, Gnostics, Buddhists, and Muslims into a common humanity by making mysticism the cornerstone of religious experience. For Rosenstock-Huessy, Buber may well be one of the great religious humanists of the twentieth century – but he also believes that from Buber in particular, and from humanism in general, one will not learn the core of Christian thinking. Hence he comments in *Philosophical Interrogations*:

The real gulf or gap between Buber's and my way of thinking is our approach to the historicity of man. To me, any word spoken makes sense only if testifying to the spiritual coexistence of three or more generations. To speak means to live backward before one's birth and forward beyond one's death.

To be named establishes one into a time sequence with at least two epochal and decisive breaks: the death of the person who named me and the death of myself, the career of a name which is meant to survive any physical destruction.

Pluri-aged is my thought; single-aged is Buber's. This also happens to be the distinction between socialism (with its as yet liberal, i.e., single-aged conception of the social order) and communism (with its religion like pluri-aged approach to the reproduction of the social order and within the social order).

Buber as well as myself is perfectly aware of this dividing line between these two approaches. To me, no individual and no individual generation seems capable of making any experiences of history. *Man*, the individual, cannot do more than realize the experience of his five senses. Sense, common sense, is not the travesty of the democratic superstition, that is, the identity of perception for fifty or a thousand individuals at the same time. It is the power of a dynasty of generations – at least three or four to pool their energies around one and the same experience and for making one and the same experience. For instance, the Constitution of the United States of America is that incorporating tool through which the nation is made *at all* capable of registering certain domestic experiences over one hundred and fifty years! In foreign affairs, the United States has not created any such incorporating 'spine'; hence Americans are unable to develop common sense in this area; they are incapacitated for making any experience in history: *vide* the ruin of World War I 'experiences.' These many experiences of 1918 never became an experience of the United States.[52]

I cannot help but comment on a number of points made here that go beyond Buber and that touch on the importance of Rosenstock-Huessy's assessment of humanism *per se* as well as the very humanist nature of contemporary political problems. The problematic character of contemporary politics is sharply disclosed by Rosenstock-Huessy's distinction of a thinking that takes account of intergenerational processes and the fruits of love and evil as they grow over time (what he sees as the essence of Christianity). Together with his humanist thinking, this longitudinal view may well provide, in schools and universities, a subject called history, but that subject's grammatical emphases remain rooted in the more static modalities in which space takes priority over time and in which science and contemplation take priority over genesis and future building. It is truly astonishing that with so much academic radical critique of the injustices/immoralities of unequal power relations, and of those 'victims' as Derrida puts it (summing up the contemporary non-conservative politicized academic mind), 'be they victims of wars, political or other kinds of violence, nationalist, racist, colonialist, sexist, or other kinds of exterminations, victims of the oppressions of capitalist imperialism or any of the forms of totalitarianism,'[53] the discourse remains resolutely oblivious to how evil must be fought *through* and *in* time. Thus, for example, the thrust of the postmodern political emphasis on the local – a response to a reality that Rosenstock-Huessy had himself noted and drawn attention to in 1938 in *Out of Revolution* – has rarely evolved into an appreciation of the power of the institutional innovations that have characterized the greatest achievements of Christianity.[54] In part this can be seen as a further residue of the left Hegelian anti-institutionalism that is so characteristic of post-Leninist and post-Stalinist left critique. But it is just as much a massive blind spot arising from humanism's paradoxical openness to everything past and contemporary, so long as what flows *into* humanism conforms to the matrix of its extratemporal moral stance – or, more broadly, what Rosenstock-Huessy calls the Greek mind.

For Rosenstock-Huessy, humanism typically provides a moral stance to condemn evil and folly, and those who see themselves as more moral can hope to seize political power and implement better policy; the pooling of energies across time is, however, a much more consuming project. The appeal of religion is to a sacrificial requirement. It is built around awareness of how energy is transferred across bodies, not merely as ideas. To see the difference, consider, for example, how many truckloads of books and academic articles were written in the 1960s and 1970s about capitalism and its evils, each calling for its overcoming. Yet outside the essentially spent force of Leninism (and I can't think of any Western academic of note who is a Leninist, though Žižek is theoretically one), acts of incarnation are largely absent as the system motors along imperviously. The radical critic is reduced to calling out into the wilderness for people to take political action (here, see Žižek's recent missives on the financial meltdown of 2008). It is as if almost *any* activity is better than nothing. The elevation of literary theory to an act of political intervention was a godsend to academic radicals who faced the prospect that however political they wanted to be, they had been relegated to writing about politics. Not surprisingly, Marx's economic base/ideological superstructure distinction had been sufficiently – if somewhat surreptitiously – overturned by Gramsci and Adorno such that one could still be a Marxist (and a member of a mindset) even without belonging to a revolutionary body. I am not saying this to make a point about the lack of moral rectitude of critical social theory, but to emphasize what in fact is a basic Marxian point that at least in part concurs with Rosenstock-Huessy – viz., whatever one's intentions, actions are modulated by the underlying institutional and socio-economic forces that the speaker inhabits. In more Marxian language, whatever one's conscience, the modern university is a bourgeois institution and the kinds of actions open to those within it remain constrained by bourgeois parameters. Concomitantly, the isolated nature of the bourgeois subject at the heart of bourgeois ideology finds itself replicated in what is, effectively, the 'brain trust' of bourgeois society.[55]

In contrast to the plight of the contemporary critical intellectual in the modern university, the Church was rebuilt/reformed every time one of its members stepped into the world in a new and exemplary way so that others followed. It was, and largely still is, a common belief among its members that 100,000 volumes calling for action do not amount to one millionth of the potency of St Francis's simple embrace of a leper; real historical creation is made by an action that makes a difference because of the specificity of its rightness. The timeliness of an action is ever the answer to the ubiquitousness of the evils we must confront. St Francis did not call for others to act – he *himself* acted, and his action demonstrated a type of action that others could do. The saint is not a saint by virtue of having a cleaner moral conscience (pure Kantianism) but by virtue of opening a way for others to follow. Thanks to him or her, they now see how to follow and how to participate in life in a way that saves them from their frustration, from the self-contempt arising from their own impotence; and that in turn contributes to the salvation of other souls. Of course, by the time of Luther this was so often phantasmic that the entire practice was dropped by the evangelicals; but by praying to saints, people hoped to strengthen their resolve and summon the powers of God so that they could participate in the process of salvation. The prayer to the saint was but a moment in the process of incarnation. By contrast, the never-ending calls for better ethics and political transformation from the university citadels today are empty precisely *because* nothing new is being incarnated, no new holes in the walls that enclose our hearts and energies have been found, and no acts brave or splendid enough have been undertaken that others feel inspired to follow.

For Rosenstock-Huessy, this failure of contemporary humanism as an incarnatory power stems in part from the level of abstraction and the grammatical priorities of humanism, which, having happily elevated the Self, finds itself rather powerless unless it acquires just the kind of power the society respects. For all their differences, Rosenzweig and Rosenstock-Huessy and Buber respect the hidden powers as among the greatest. Jewish and Christian power – and this is just as true of all pagan inventiveness as well – begins with acknowledgment of powerlessness: the greatest contributors to the future have, by acts of love and service, turned their powerlessness *into* something. Even so, Rosenstock-Huessy thinks that Buber's seemingly innocuous placement of the 'I' in its relationship to the 'Thou' has unwittingly reproduced the kind of abstractions that – as I have sought to show – plague the academic mind, even those minds that most strongly desire social transformation:

> *Ich* (I) and *Du* (You) are to me fictitious abbreviations for the real pluriaged, named, 'nationalized' and century bound real person. To me, pronouns are *omissions*. To Buber, they suffice. If you look into my *Züruck in das Wagnis der Sprache*, you may find ample proof for my thesis that pronouns are neither here nor there. You are Mr. Friedman and Maurice Friedman long before you are I or Thou. This, today, goes unrecognized. Liberalism and humanism have perverted the relations of names, nouns and pronouns. Buber had no reason to fight this centennial tradition. Hence, his reconnoitering into the I and Thou was not felt to be ruinous for the whole humanistic and naturalistic traditions about man – as being 'naturally himself.' To me this is nonsense.
>
> For me, *time* is indivisibly three in one; Future, Past, and, as their victor, Present are only simultaneously given. They are, trinitarian, prismatic aspects of one and the same whole: Time. Time is given to real man (not to the abstraction called 'physicist') as one in three: (1) the Times I enfold myself; (2) the Times which have preceded my consciousness; (3) the Times which follow after I am dead. Buber, on the other hand, accepts the phenomenon of time in its reduction to an inarticulate, logically indefensible, present.[56]

Buber's answer is a dignified account of his own position, but whether it really comes to terms with Rosenstock-Huessy's critique is

another matter. After praising Rosenstock-Huessy for having concret-
ized the teaching of the historical nature of man, 'about which we have
been basically and emphatically instructed in the epoch of thought beginning with Hegel and ending with Heidegger,' 'as no other thinker
before him as done,'[57] he says that while he accepts that this is one side
of man, it is not 'the most important and decisive reality.' In a statement
that shows a fundamental continuity between his earliest mysticism
and his mature dialogism, he tells us that behind language and history,
there is a greater mystery of the person, and that this mystery holds
him in greater deference than the name:

> Out of his [Rosenstock-Huessy's] valuation of the proper name – which
> I regard as an indispensable and unsatisfactory symbol of personal
> uniqueness – there follows for Rosenstock-Huessy the so-to-speak bio-
> graphical equation of two deaths: the death of him who named me, and
> my own. That is an Old Testament manner of thinking to which I cannot
> adhere; it is, at any rate, already relinquished by the Gospels, where the
> giving of the name is no longer an important biographical act and changes
> of name are no longer undertaken by God or the people, but the person.[58]

That Buber takes as a fact the person's capacity to self-name seems to
me less a refutation by the Gospel of the importance of naming, in the
manner of Rosenstock-Huessy, than a new realization of the power of
renaming, and the sealing of the power of the one who undergoes *meta-
noia* with a new name. Nevertheless, it is less my brief here to assess the
debate between the two, than to highlight the difference of emphasis
and why Rosenstock-Huessy sees Buber – the Jew, who here quotes the
Gospel in order to affirm that his faith is 'in the life of individuals, and
in the life of the human race, where the historical bursts open and the
present reveals itself' – as a contributor from the academic/humanist/
pagan wing in a trialogue in which each wing discloses truth. And let
us be clear, despite the relentless nature of Rosenstock-Huessy's critique of idealism/the Greek/the academic/the Gnostic/the humanist/
the pagan mind and Buber's 'fit' within these formations, he resolutely
held that the truth is only disclosed as an alliance of the Christian cross,
the Israelite experience of eternity, and the 'Gnostic genius.' (I might
add, to reinforce this, notwithstanding my critique of so much radical
social theory, that it does not mean that it does not expose true injustices.) For Rosenstock, these three types must always exist, and we are

diminished without all three. Moreover, as he tells the story, this was understood by the members of the Patmos circle:

All three ways of speaking from now on have to be cultivated. So just as there have always been the clergy, intellectuals, and the merciful Samaritans, as three, who glow and to be sure in completely different ways. And as there must be priests, professors and artists, so must there always be Moriah, Patmos, Eleusis, and Rosenzweig and I, with our friends from the Patmos circle, for that reason envisaged three publishing houses which should bear these three names. Only Patmos came out of it. Schocken was a moment of the Moriah publishing house. And the group from the Creature anticipated Eleusis.[59]

What is highly significant about Rosenstock-Huessy's claim that he, Rosenzweig, and Buber have each articulated a path of speech thinking is that all three were born Jews. And on the basis of what we have said thus far about Rosenstock-Huessy – especially regarding how he sees the relationship between the creative power of the word and its role in history – it is probably that Miskotte would not be alone in recognizing that 'as a Christian, Rosenstock-Huessy remained Jewish in his whole habitude of mind.'[60] Rosenzweig went back to the heritage of his birth to make that explicit; Rosenstock-Huessy moved away from that same heritage but – after struggle and torment – embraced it as a living force in the form of his friendship with Rosenzweig; and Buber moved away from Jewish ritual yet embraced Judaism and lived it as an idea – that is, he lived it as intellectual humanists live things, in his Zionism, in his books and speeches and moral gestures and affirmations. And for a while, at least, in the years after the Second World War, at a time when the very best in humanism was so desperately needed to contemplate the extent of the depravity that had befallen us when our common humanity was denied, his was the voice that commanded the largest audience.

4 On God as an Indissoluble Name and an Indispensable Pole of the Real

The names God, Man, and World preside over a series of other names that receive their sense from being predicated on the grounding name. The grounding name does not dissolve back into another grounding name without the domain of meaning becoming lost. 'What is there,' asks Rosenzweig, 'sufficiently external to God, yet despite its externality so inseparable from Him that it belongs to Him – what is there sufficiently "extrinsic" to reach across to that which is without?'

> It is His name. To utter God's name is entirely different from uttering the name of a man or a thing. True, they have something in common; the name of God, His proper name, and a term of designation are not identical with the bearers of these names. But except for this they differ widely. Man has a name so that he may be called by it. To be called by his name is for him an ultimate distinction. God does not have a name so that he may be called by it. To Him it is irrelevant whether His name is called or not; he heeds him who calls Him by His name as well as those who call Him by other names or those who speak to Him in nameless silence. He bears a name for our sake, so that we may call Him. It is for our sake that He permits Himself to be named and called by that name, since it is only by jointly calling upon Him that we become a 'We.'
>
> And thus the name of man remains a proper name and clings to him; He keeps the name bestowed on Him. God's name, however, is subject to change although at any particular instant, it is conceived as a proper name.[1]

This is the essential accusation that Rosenzweig and all the New Thinkers level at atheism: it fails to see that its act of deicide is an act of self-mutilation, for the greater part of man's narratives about life's meaning, according to the atheists, amount to nothing more than his fears and fantasies and the like – Epicurus had said this first, and it would be repeated with gusts of laughter at the wretchedness of our condition by Rabelais, and with sobriety, sombreness, and sadness at what we have made of ourselves by Spinoza.[2] Yet those very actions have been what have made us and still do for those millions upon millions who continue to take their orientation from that speech, who refuse to comply with a particular philosophical nomenclature about life and its purpose. That Kant knew that the idea of God had been deployed in natural science, morality, and providential readings of history was evident in his argument that God must be preserved as a regulative principle of reason and as a rational principle of practical reason. Of course, Kant's God is so spectral that he could not even last a generation, and his younger contemporaries were already reinstating Him as the Absolute – a reinstatement that Rosenzweig saw in Hegel's case as vacuous and that in any case was also dismissed as ridiculous by the next, more radical generation of neo-Hegelians.[3] Though it did make a brief come-back in the neo-Kantianism of Hans Vahinger, who is mocked in *Understanding the Sick and the Healthy* for following Kant in asking us to believe that we will act on the 'as if,' as if we ever did and as if we ever could: 'Act as if you were paying: You'll see the cashier will be completely satisfied,' says Rosenzweig witheringly.[4] The 'as-if' is but one more attempt at Idealism, the substitution of a rationalized essence for the names that have been generated out of historical experience.

After Rosenzweig's initial philosophical excavation in *The Star of Redemption*, God (like Man and World) is first and foremost a name whose content remains to be filled, a nothing that becomes something. How does it become something? How do we know its nature? In the way that all things become something for us: through their historical presence, through their emergence over time, and through the collective experience we have of them – which is to say, through their *names*. Modernity is a series of isms piled upon isms, of philosophical constructions vying to impress us with the purity of their insight into the real. But such insight requires the curtailment of connection with our past and indeed with all 'distemporary' peoples who do not share a humanistic, naturalistic, or mechanistic basis. Our language, by contrast, is living, and the echoes of past names, decisions, and faith course continually through our everyday world. But mechanism and naturalism would like to curb that, ever fearful of the superstitions that have caused so much horror and havoc in Europe. Thus do we find in Locke and Spinoza a clear recognition that for the new world of knowledge to be right, the names must be used correctly. For Spinoza, our imagination must be subordinate to our understanding and our understanding must follow the sequences of nature; while for Locke, all representations (except merely logical ones) must be traced back to their empirical source. The same attempt at an *Aufbau* persisted into the twentieth century with the logical positivists and logical atomists, including Carnap and the young Wittgenstein. But modernity – or rather, its systemic philosophical constituents discernible in its administrative, legal, and technological components – is merely a particular configuration of an ism. In this sense there is significant overlap with Heidegger's deconstruction of modern metaphysics by the New Thinkers. But one of the problems with Heidegger – something that Rosenstock-Huessy addresses directly in his *Zurück in der Wagnis der Sprache* and in 'Heraclitus to Parmenides' in *I Am an Impure Thinker* – is that Heidegger, terrified of the world's abstractions, retreats into the very linguistic terminus, the dead end of abstraction itself: Being. The original, though unpublished, title of 'Heraclitus to Parmenides' was 'Death by Abstractions.' Of course, Heidegger knew that Hegel had said that Being was nothing, and he had seen this as a key deficiency in Hegel. But Heidegger's attack on Hegel is no less due to the fecundity of life than Schelling's or Feuerbach's. His settling for Being is a decision to stand in the openness of what he calls 'the that which region,' so that it is not instrumentalized, technicized, logicized, and just part of the machinery of the earth's exploitation and our mechanization. Its strategy, born out of Germany's despair, is one that was never overturned in his *Kehre*,[5] one that retained the disconnectedness from history in spite of all his talk of historicity, one that patterns the decisive act of resolve and authenticity in *Being and Time*. That is, Heidegger prefers the most pronominal of pronominals, that which is least connected to a name, and – as he says in his own words – he waits for a new god. Heidegger's awaiting a new god, who is nameless, on an earth from which the gods have fled is indicative of just how barren is his landscape of possibilities. To be sure, there are times in life when a gesture of prostration is all that is left, but to make this the defining philosophical gesture is to render oneself completely impotent. For all his talk, then, of being beyond metaphysics, Heidegger is so afraid of repeating its gestures and moves that he is imprisoned by it. He is still, for all that, primarily a philosopher, and far less a *Mensch* exercising 'common sense,' trusting in names (and Heidegger notwithstanding, one need not be a humanist to be a human being).

For Rosenstock-Huessy and Rosenzweig (as with Heidegger), life is indeed murdered by metaphysics. And like Heidegger, they saw that our compartmentalizing of the world and ourselves into essences does indeed do tremendous harm to our environment and all parts of us – our relationships, our communities, and so on. But unlike Heidegger, they stressed that we are naming beings, and – here the departure from Heidegger – that names are more primordial and vital than Being. This is also why Rosenstock-Huessy has Heraclitus take Parmenides to task – two thinkers whom Heidegger insisted were really part of the greatness of Greek thought before its Platonic descent. As his Heraclitus says to Parmenides: '"Being" is the scalp of the divine acts and the political names. This scalp hangs dangling on your belt, to hell with your "pronoun," to hell with your "pro-verb" "being." Or we shall all find ourselves in hell.'[6] Of course, with philosophy we are able to make great strides in knowledge, we are able to group things together, build systems; but Rosenzweig and Rosenstock-Huessy, likewise Adorno and post-structuralists emphasizing difference, are keen that life itself not disappear in this movement. A name locates, summarizes, emphasizes an event that has been or will become; a name orientates through its specificity. Names are a fire in the memory of the group, and as long as they flicker with life, they are able to act on us over time. As Rosenstock-Huessy says:

> The political power of names makes people circulate. Names signify our division of labor. They make room for a man and a thing. The 'throne,' the 'hustings,' our 'tongue' as Greeks, the 'eye of justice,' the 'thunder of Zeus,' those were all names whose invocation made people move out or in . . .
>
> Names make no sense unless they stand in mutual relation. Mother is not mother unless she may call, under the law, somebody the father. Brother is brother to a sister. And unless he calls her sister and she calls him brother, the name is worthless. The general and the sergeant, the master and the apprentice, the army and the navy make room for each other, in the wonderful whole of names. All names belong to this holon, to society. No name is good without the others. The Pan of the universe drives people panicky, that is they lose speech. The holon of the city gives everybody a name in such a manner that everybody else now can be named by him, too.[7]

In the first of his *Letters to Cynthia* (Harries), he emphasized how the name is the political means by which time triumphs over space. This is a central theme in his *Soziologie*, whose two volumes' titles can be translated as *The Dominance of Spaces* and *The Fullness of Times*. The map is not a geographical entity but a historical one, something all-conspicuous when one looks at different maps at different times where names and places are political creations, signs of the triumph of a political temporal body over a designated space.

On the other hand, a pronoun is a way of not being precise about location, emergence, faith, hope, love, and so on. 'Pronouns are a compromise between the real name of a person or a thing and the pointing finger while such person or thing is within the reach of our sense of perception. To call a spade a spade is one thing; to point to the spade while it lies before us, which simply requires the gesture and a "there!" is a totally different act. One is the act of naming, the other is an attempt to reduce naming to its informal minimum.'[8]

When Rosenstock-Huessy gave his lectures on Greek philosophy, he paused at book 2 of the *Iliad,* where Homer recalls the ships and the names of the places and commanders of the different armies of the Greeks. 'Homer's heart,' he said, 'is in following the first impressions also in the physical, in the real life, you see. He's not systematic. He's anti-philosophical. Can you see this? Because a philosopher must have all his material gathered before he can subdivide it, you see. Therefore it's always a second impression, it's an afterthought.'[9] And whereas philosophy does need the information of the names, 'poetry never thinks about all the people who come under the same name, but poetry has to keep the individual names of every one city here.'[10]

Plato was the last classical philosopher for whom the names of speakers played an important role in the inquiry for truth; significantly, when Hans Ehrenberg provided his work on Fichte and Schelling from the perspective of the New Thinking, he made a point of drawing attention to the importance of the names of his interlocutors.[11] Plato was overawed by the man Socrates, thus himself verifying incarnation over idea; even so, his philosophical legacy was formed around the primacy of definitions, concepts, and ideas. Rosenstock-Huessy says in the same lecture, 'that's the terror of Platonism, that we are all his ideas.'[12] It is no accident that in providing the template that would shape the next two thousand years and more of philosophy, Plato not only attacked the poets but also, in the *Cratylus*, ridiculed the idea that names have originally profound meanings embedded in the etymology of words, so that the more thoughtful person will know more about reality by tracking down the etymology of names. Like a well-known section of the *Protagoras* where Socrates gives an interpretation of a poem by Simonides that only goes to show that someone can turn anything into anything, the *Cratylus* attempts to show that the elevation of names is a sophistic game of the same order. Names proliferate, and the understanding goes off on a wild goose chase during which the essence of things is missed. It is no exaggeration to say that the shape of Platonic philosophy is dictated by the shadow family it wants to bring under its control if not silence completely: the family of poets, orators, statesmen, and – the one Plato most persistently returns to – the sophists. The lack of stability of meaning, for Plato, meant that we all live in a delusory flux. From Rosenzweig's and Rosenstock-Huessy's position, this assault on the sophists is overdone. It is not that either Rosenstock-Huessy or Rosenzweig has sympathy for the relativism of the sophists – for them, the sophists are playing games. But if they play games with language, that is the fault not of language but of a wilful perversion. And the game playing cannot be stopped by the philosophical police. The perversion that must be made by philosophy in order to halt sophistry is no less perverse than the disease it wants to cure. Yes, sophistry plays games with words, but that is indicative of what people at play can do. For Rosenstock-Huessy and Rosenzweig, that delusory flux is nothing other than life itself, and while it is understandable that Plato was seeking to be rescued from the hell of the internecine struggles within and without Athens, the way out is the wrong way, because it involves asphyxiating the very processes that enable us to be most alive.

What Platonism does, and what all philosophies that follow in its wake do, is underestimate the depth of common sense of the named world and overestimate what the philosophical or logical mind might be able to do if it reigned over human reality. And much of modernity has been shaped by just this victory of philosophy over common sense. In *Understanding the Sick and the Healthy*, Rosenzweig, looking at modern men and women as sick patients, sees a major part of the problem in the way they speak about and thereby kill life. For Rosenzweig, modern humanity, 'our patient,' has been seduced by philosophy into losing all faith in common sense and the everyday world. Modern man has lost his 'God given right, his privilege as a man, of conferring names. He had lost faith in the continuity of names and of other things; he had renounced his human privilege. And it was because he did not believe in the divine quality of language that he became uncertain of the names which he and others assigned to things.'[13]

In sum, then, Rosenstock-Huessy and Rosenzweig both reaffirm the huge significance of one of humanity's most primordial acts – the act of *naming* in the face of philosophy's misconstruction and trivialization of that act. In the philosophical scheme of things, naming is merely a haphazard act, a sheer pretence at knowledge, mere opinion, like everything else that is done without sufficient deference to the strictures laid down by philosophy. What this means is that each particular ism, each specific philosophy, must be dissatisfied with the various and vast regions of reality that have been named that do not conform to what would satisfy the squinting vision that wants all of reality deflected through the prism of its ism. An ism has its ground in its isolation of a specific something that is part of reality, so it is not the case that there is nothing true that lies behind Idealism or its various subspecies; rather, its untruth is visible in its overextension.

The plurality of our experience is something that can be, momentarily, 'thought away' but not lived away or spoken away. Speech draws us into the multiple somethings by virtue of its constant imposition of differentiation within integration, a differentiation of arrangement, context, assumptions, or codes depending on who is speaking or listening. Naming is that act of speech that is a response, a command, and a question, all three: it is a *response* to situation and previous namings, a *command* in that it is a laying down of a way of seeing or understanding, and a *question* in that it is asking whether others will also see the previously unnamed in the way the new name suggests. Rosenzweig, in a remark that could just as easily have been made by Rosenstock-Huessy, tells us that language 'neither can be, nor does it want to be, the world's essence. It only names the things of the world. Adam gives names; words find their way to things. To utter a word is to affix a seal as a witness of man's presence. The word is not part of the world; it is the seal of man.'[14] And Rosenstock-Huessy says bluntly: '*To think means to introduce better names.*'[15] Philosophical (i.e., Idealistic) thinking takes place after an event, in the quiet and stable recesses of the mind; whereas Rosenstock-Huessy identifies the imperative as the grammatical mood that captures our most fundamental (*not* our exclusive) relationships. The imperative is what makes possible the chain of survival and growth. The name is closely related to the imperative, for the '*name is the right address of a person under which he or she will respond.*[16] And in *Understanding the Sick and the Healthy*, Rosenzweig writes:

> Each word, as soon as it comes into existence, requires the strength of continuation and the capacity to traverse the river of time so that it may finally become the ultimate word. The word of man, an initial word uttered by man, joins that which was ultimate from the first, the word of God. The intention of language to form composite designations and double names, its capacity to create such designations, is shown by the way things obtain a name whenever someone confronts them. To name is the primal right of all men, a right which they are forever exercising. The one condition required is that the creator of the name actually confront the thing. At this stage the name is only a cognomen. And then also the person, or persons, to whom the originator of the name exhibits the thing, must be present. Thus Adam performed the act of naming, and so also do his offspring.
>
> In addition to these names, a thing has names which it does not receive. It already possesses them. They also may have been 'cognomens,' at some moment uttered for the first time. However as soon as they are spoken, they adhere to the thing. From then on the thing goes by that name. The thing possesses equally the right to keep the name it has, and to receive new names. Whoever gave the old name may be absent or even dead; in spite of this the name he gave still clings to the thing. And furthermore each new name must come to terms with the old ones. The thing gathers names. And indeed its capacity to do this is inexhaustible. It is a man's privilege to give new names. It is his duty to use the old ones, a duty he must perform, though unwillingly. His obligation to pass on the old names, to appropriate them and translate them into names he himself designates – this creates the continuity of mankind. Mankind is always absent. Present is a man, this fellow or that one. The thing, however, is tied to all of mankind by language and by its inherent law of transmission and translation. These linguistic laws require that each new word confront the old.[17]

If God is the name that Jews and Christians have traditionally given to the Creator, the Revelator, and the Redeemer, the reality of God is, for Rosenzweig, something we can grasp through naming itself. Of course, the name of God has so developed that it could be mistaken for a complete nothing, a misnomer. But only if one either forgot about history or wished to free us from its tyranny – which was precisely what Spinoza wished to do when he founded modern theological criticism. Spinoza's historical biblical criticism was the corollary of his pantheism, and these two were his philosophical contributions to the foundations for the modern secular world, which would relegate God to man and his imagination, or world (God = Nature, ergo God does not exist in His own right). Spinoza intended biblical criticism to show how an overexcited imagination lacking in understanding led to the creation and interpretation of a history that was out of tune with whom we really are, in exactly the same way that our misunderstanding of the natural world was out of tune with nature.

The Star of Redemption tackles the problem of the *what* of God in the context of its larger project and the elements that constitute it; in *Understanding the Sick and the Healthy*, Rosenzweig succinctly makes the case against the modern variants of atheism, including pantheism and anthropocentrism. After saying of Schopenhauer that he is to be commended for being the first philosopher to openly acknowledge his atheism and thereby making atheism respectable, he writes: 'Our knowledge of our various "gods and idols" seems at first to consist of nothing but fanciful imagery. But, it is maintained, these creations of ours may have no foundation in reality whatsoever. They may have been created by fear, lust, creative instinct, a desire to explain, etc.'[18] So the question is: Are the gods nothing really, merely ciphers of something else, a projection of fear and fantasy, our imagination activated by our fear? When posed in that way, he continues, the question has two possible answers, both of which rest on the assumption that 'something' exists behind the appearance 'which is altogether different' from what appears:

> [Either] there is a fantast concealed behind our phantasmagoria who indulges in fantasies 'within ourselves,' very much like raving children in certain types of delirium appear to be possessed by an alter-ego which seems to be their nature and yet is not their true self. Or they conceive of a phantom-reality existing behind the images we see, in much the same way as a frightened child transforms a white sheet into a ghost, or the design on the wall-paper into a gorgon's head.[19]

The 'nature is god' story of Spinoza, says Rosenzweig, is 'explained by the white sheet that produced them. But the sheet is not the sheet, and God forbid that the world should not be the world. The sheet and the ghost are "essentially" one; the world is God (in essence). Mother, having embroidered and hemmed the sheet, is quite well aware that her sheet is really her sheet.' What astonishes Rosenzweig here is that the world that is the world has now been transformed into what it is patently not. If God is disfigured by being equated with the world, Rosenzweig's line of attack is to emphasize that the world also is disfigured: 'To be God, the world must be shelled and husked, deprived of its reality. Heaven forbid that the world should be an ordinary, natural reality.'[20] The point is simple but irrefutable: nature is invoked as the substance, but it is distinguished from the signs of its articulation. This is precisely what Spinoza does when introducing the distinction between understanding and imagination, between nature as it can be known scientifically and nature as it is experienced. Rosenzweig continues: 'The spirit of Spinoza's concept of nature was rarefied by Goethe and Herder. It was this deified "nature" robbed of all natural qualities, not Spinoza's *deus sive natura* which became the God of the enthusiasts. The effect – the statement "God is the world" can be made only if the world is nothing.'[21]

Quite simply: How, if we really accept that nature is the All, can we trust a philosophy of nature that does not accept as nature a supposed part of nature – namely, man's nature, his signs and gestures and names and behaviours? That is, how can we trust a philosophy of nature that cannot absorb man's nature except by treating it as an embarrassment, a mistake? To restate, Rosenzweig stands with Schelling on the facticity of the world – our world with all its myths and religions and ways of creating.

After dealing with the pantheists, who dissolve God into nature, he turns to those who dissolve God into mind. For Rosenzweig, this is tantamount to making 'Man and man's prostrate mind . . . the essence of God. Thus the mind of man has won a promotion.'[22] For Rosenzweig, to dissolve God into any of the other names is always to fall prey to a diminution of the world of our experience – that is, the diminution of world and man. Yet this diminution occurs under the act of elevation and overreach. This is the fear that is addressed in the Bible from the very beginning, for God has as its corollary the reminder of human finitude. To transform God into mind, which as we have seen is the transformation of man and his mind into God, means to abandon the awareness of limits that best enables the mind to play its part in our life. The Hegelian account of the evolution of mind or spirit in the world is rightly interpreted by Rosenzweig as meaning that 'God Himself is mind, evolving and unfolding.'[23] What follows from this, says Rosenzweig, is that 'God is not.' Insofar as God is not, man is also not. Man, like mind, must wait to become. Until that moment he is just a step on the way, a contingency contributing to the appearance of essence (a position identical to Spinoza's). In this respect, Rosenzweig anticipates that critique – which would become widespread in the twentieth century – of any evolutionary model that devalues lives and cultures which fall outside the perceived peak of the evolutionary model. (This places him in step with the '68 paradigm and the more general defence of indigenous cultures – which only makes it that much harder for those in the paradigm to deal with his 'more troubling' positions on paganism.)

In effect, then, Rosenzweig's emphasis on the moment takes the moment as of infinite importance. From this position, the Hegelian view of the world devalues our infinitude in the moment, deferring our reality to a later historical moment. The living God has not been comprehensibly encapsulated in this story; rather, He is eliminated, along with real existing man in the range of his capacities. In this way, Rosenzweig contrasts the view of man that exists when seen in relationship to his God with the man of the Hegelian and evolutionists' narrative:

> Man is privileged to have everything that he needs to be a man. He is in possession of the moment. And as for the rest, God and the world assist him here. He is in possession of the moment and so has everything. Thus he is enabled to fulfill the commandment given to him because the command is for the moment and always only for the moment. The person which he confronts represents the whole world and the very next instant man's eternity. But the notion of development deprives him of being human – a privilege which is also a duty. Evolution takes the place of man. That human mind, which was proclaimed to be the essence of God, is consequently not the true mind. It is rather a mind deprived of its human privileges, a mind annihilated.[24]

Again we are left holding nothing, because a something was exaggerated, essentialized, 'deified' as a consequence of our inability to trust the world into which we have stepped.

The other position which dissolves God that Rosenzweig considers and refutes is that God refers to everything. But that, too, is simply another attempt to conjure away the name and the potencies activated by humanity's confrontation with that name. To summarize, each position is but a variant of reason's attempt to ensnare the All – the very act that Rosenzweig has sought to eliminate with his meta-ethical, metalogical, metaphysical examinations in *The Star*.

In *The Star*, Rosenzweig had arrived at the metalogical through the argument that if the *logos* is a component of the world and not just something belonging to reason, the world as world looks very different from how it looks to the naturalist who has taken the word and hence ourselves out of it, or the Idealist philosopher who has made it synonymous with reason. A very important consequence of this is that once thought has been released from the philosophical strictures of rational necessity, nothing that has been named can merely be dismissed (or indeed, assassinated) for failing to fit into the truth that has been allowed by the All. The philosopher is forced to come back into the world and join the rest of us, and there he or she finds the 'stuff' that human beings talk about.

Rosenzweig makes a similar point in his justification of the meta-ethical over the ethical – a point that had led him to praise Nietzsche for making the 'first philosophical refutation of God where God is not indissolubly bound to the world.'[25] (Likewise, he protects the 'metaphysical' from any total dissolution by reason into an ism.) Now just as the meta-ethical enables man to be more than the *ethos*, and the metalogical makes the world more than the *logos* while not denying that the *logos* is part of the world, the metaphysical for Rosenzweig is a reference to what is more than the *physis* of the ancients or the 'nature' of the moderns. Insofar as God is the name of the creator of *physis* or nature, the term 'metaphysical' was never meant to equate God with nature, as it was made to do, for example, by Spinoza. At the moment it did, the living God was dead in the hearts and minds of those who made the equation. But what is it that denies the existence of the living God? The man and woman who believe that the name 'God' addresses a living reality do not do so because of a philosophical argument, but because such a name as God, and only such a name, befits a particular part or aspect of their experience; only the invocation of or supplication of what is summoned by this name and what calls us by our name allows this to make any sense – for insofar as the name 'God' is an active ingredient in our world and self, that name makes us who we are. The metaphysical in this sense, for Rosenzweig, cannot be foreclosed or prohibited by reason; reason simply does not have this power to say what does or does not exist. And because the living God was never equated with the world, those denials of God's existence that seek verification in the world cannot make sense. (Kant had argued as much, but his understanding of 'God' precluded any God other than a philosophical concept of God, which is to say that his understanding, too, was defective because of the initial mistrust in language, or mere lack of understanding of naming. That had been Hamann's criticism of Kant's *Critique of Pure Reason*.) The divine freedom that is the essence of God may defy the totalizing logic of philosophers who do not know what to make of this 'being' who is obeyed and worshipped and not just thought or argued about.

Rosenstock-Huessy correctly grasped that the trajectory of *The Star* was a deeply personal one. It was the movement of someone who is developing and defending not only his right to existence, but also the glory and mission of a people's being within a horizon that – for Rosenzweig – had been crushed by the dead weight of a dead philosophy. The dead weight and the dead philosophy were, for Rosenzweig, the idols of secularism – science, logic, nation, art, and the like. Thus he saw it as his task to demonstrate that these forces are not ultimate but secondary powers. The truth of Rosenzweig's situation was that German liberalism would not be strong enough to protect the being of his people. Its failure, in part, was philosophical and not merely political: a philosophical failure in that its subjects and conditions were abstractions. Hence, for example, liberalism is a grand ethical system, but because we are meta-ethical and our enterprises are metalogical, liberalism will always find its logic questioned by those who refuse to be merely situated within its matrix (or 'imprisoned,' as Foucault's later image of the panopticon would have it).

Now whereas a contemporary philosophical reader of Rosenzweig might find little difficulty in moving from his account of the breakdown of the ethical into the meta-ethical and the dissolution of the totalizing logic of philosophy, the move to metaphysics will make many baulk. Matters are not eased by Rosenzweig's bold (cheeky?) claim that 'meta-ethical man is the fermentation that breaks down the logical and physical unity of the cosmos into the meta-logical world and the metaphysical God,'[26] which he follows up by turning Nietzsche into a negative theologian. But Rosenzweig wants to get to God because his people stand under that name and are meaningless without that name; their meta-ethical existence cannot be affirmed without a metalogical stance, and that metalogical stance is meaningless if the highest name under which they are *formed* is said to be unreal. The atheistic philosopher who declares that the power behind the name is unreal is, for Rosenzweig, simply showing us something about what he or she takes as real; and this does not convince Rosenzweig, because the name 'God' was never subject to the same conditions of the real as man or any other thing in the world – even though it is in the vaguest of senses a 'this and not that.' In Kantian terms: the fact of the Jewish people is indisputable – 'How are they possible?' But it is not only the Jewish people whose existence has been formed by their faith, their worship, their appeals, their obedience and defiance; until the triumph of the secular state, still masked under deism with the French Revolution, all peoples were so formed. God and gods were a positive presence – to repeat, real forces in the formation of all peoples, and thus Rosenzweig tells us that 'the gods in whom a living world believes cannot be less alive than this world itself.'[27]

When in the introduction to *The Star*, then, Rosenzweig moves from meta-ethical to metalogical to metaphysical, he is really following the inverse sequence of the highest grounds of appeals that have emerged historically. First there were gods and God, then there was reason, then there was the philosophical outcry of those living souls who refused to be suffocated by reason's all-encompassing claims. He has to begin at the end because his educated reader is more than likely much more of a contemporary of Nietzsche, Schopenhauer, or Kierkegaard than of Plato or Moses. As concerns our own individual existence, it would matter little where one started in the triad of meta-ethical, metalogical, or metaphysical. But if we wish to deal with the positive presences of God, Man, and World, now liberated from their engulfment in reason's deadly sphericality, then we need to do so on the basis of their reality. The that-ness of their existence is undeniable if we proceed historically or existentially and follow the trail of names, not prohibiting from the outset a being deemed to be irrational. Their sheer that-ness, their sheer participation with the world, as things named as vital presences, as facticities bestowing historical meaning, yet as ultimate sources of appeal, leads Rosenzweig to say that he wants to restore the three great philosophical objects of God, Man, and World that Kant had reduced to nothings (for knowledge) – but not 'as objects of rational science, but precisely the reverse, as "irrational" objects.'[28]

These irrational objects, then, are what Rosenzweig says are to be taken as the new foundation for philosophy. He has chosen the word 'foundation' deliberately. God, Man, and World form a triad of bases, of grounds, of sources. None, though, can be the source of All. The formulation 'All = All' was the philosophical *hubris* that revealed itself as vacuous because it kept out the particular propulsions of the three irrational objects.[29] These propulsions for Rosenzweig are emergents; thus, to seek a higher ground from which to survey them is to misunderstand what they are – there is nothing before them, because they are the elements to which we have historically appealed in order to make – and make sense of – our world and ourselves. The only higher ground is the non-ground of nothing, and 'our voyage of explanation advances from the nothing to the something.' Such a nothing is not an emptiness: there is no essence of nothingness that we can talk about, point to, or address other than as a 'not this.' Nothing, then, is but the 'empty being, being before thinking,'[30] a 'slumbering' that reason cannot penetrate.

Rosenzweig sees this appreciation of the nothing as an important philosophical breakthrough in Herman's Cohen's work on the infinitesimal:

> The differential combines in itself the properties of the nothing and of the something. It is a nothing that refers to a something, to its something and at the same time a something that still slumbers in the womb of the nothing. It is, on the one hand the quantity that is dissolved in that which is without quantity, and then, on the other hand, it has, as 'infinitesimal,' and by this right, all the properties of the finite quantity, with only one exception: precisely this property of the quantity. It is in this way that it draws its strength that founds a reality, at one time from the powerful negation with which it breaks the womb of the nothing, and yet then equally at another time from the calm affirmation of all that borders on the nothing, to which it remains, in spite of all, itself bound as infinitesimal. It thus determines two paths that go from the nothing to the something, the path of the affirmation of that which is not nothing, and the path of the negation of the nothing.[31]

The theological resonances of this are obvious and are highly instructive in what they say about the body of the faithful, the Jews and the people who created philosophy, the Greeks. The biblical God simply emerges, hovering over the waters. There is no attempt to establish where He dwelt or what He was doing before He spoke the different bits of creation into existence, including heaven and earth. Greek philosophy, for its part, had prohibited the idea of such genesis. Thus Plato's demiurge in the *Timaeus*, for example, must look to a pre-existing something, the ideas, and work with a pre-existing something else: matter. Likewise, Aristotle comes up with a doctrine of four causes, notwithstanding his critique of Plato's two-world model, which, though formal, is but a variation on the 'nothing will come from nothing' dogma. And Aristotle's doctrine of the unmoved mover provides a theological ground that is ultimately beholden to reason's own ability to establish that such a first cause must exist. There are no end of books that discuss the beginnings of philosophy by equating the story of Genesis with Greek origins as examples of the speculative mind, but such works miss the fundamental point that there is *nothing* in the Bible that is of *any philosophical worth;* there are wisdom teachings, but philosophical doctrine is as absent as the presence of a philosophical figure. This tradition continues in the Christian Bible. However, by then there is a consciousness of the pronounced difference between Jews and Greeks, and this leads Paul to warn against the temptations of philosophy (Colossians 2.7–9). Indeed, the closest we have to philosophy in the Bible are Job's friends who try to discover the why of Job's plight; and what this amounts to is that their speech is empty. One should not underestimate the ferocious necessities and despair that drove Greeks to philosophy: Socrates' search for virtue and the good *polis* was as much a response to the Peloponnesian wars and the *coup d'état* of the thirty as it was a product of a culture of disputation within the courts, as it was a response to his own *daimon*. However, the writers of the biblical book of Genesis do not seek to demonstrate the existence of God or to rationalize about His nature, as Plato does when he uses the term 'theology' in the *Republic* (for the first time in history, as far as we know) while seeking to demonstrate which qualities must be divine and which cannot be. The god, for Plato, cannot change his form, cannot be angry, cannot be supplicated – indeed, cannot be like Yahweh. Yet Yahweh is worshipped; He has his people. Is He to be dismissed as non-existent because He is not reasonable? His fruits are there for all to see, and had His people served other gods, they would have other fruits and themselves be other fruits. Furthermore, one may seek to destroy the Jewish people and all they stand for, but they – as everything genuinely incalculable, that is, miraculous – emerged as something out of nothing.

This is related to another important distinction between Jewish experience and the Greek speculative mind. Yahweh does create Adam, but He does not know what Adam will do – nor, indeed, does he know what He will do in response to Adam or anyone else. Once Greek philosophical thought become enmeshed with the interpretation of the Bible within Christendom, theologians would dispute the issue of freedom and election on the grounds of God's omniscience and twist themselves into knots trying to reconcile a fundamentally Jewish narrative with a Greek philosophical matrix. But Rosenzweig is not interested in entering into such historical thickets; his task is to show the meaning of the people of the star and how their reality is comprehensible.

While the *manner* in which Rosenzweig demonstrates the triadic necessity of God–Man–World is uniquely his own, that triad was no less important to Rosenstock-Huessy. He knew that Rosenzweig had already done the labour of demonstrating the triadic interpenetration of these three uncollapsible poles of reality. While, then, he refers to it often throughout his work, I will just mention two important discussions of it in Rosenstock-Huessy. The first is in his essay 'The Soul of William James.' Rosenstock-Huessy admired (though not uncritically) James, and in this essay he points out that James was struggling to find the way out of the limits of naturalism. Through his reading of Charles Renouvier, James had come to see the legitimacy and necessity of free will, which he had originally closed off through his dogmatic mechanism, and he credits Renouvier with freeing him from the tyranny of monism and attuning him to pluralism. According to Rosenstock-Huessy,

> like the 'enlightened' men of the 18th century, James possessed an uncanny and sometimes absurd curiosity about anything and everything under the sun. He also was quite sure – at least most of the time – that all that man could say dealt with 'things' in the universe. It was left to the generation after James to show that man and the world and God are not reducible to each other, and that they can not even borrow language from each other. Yet James belonged, with Bergson, to the generation that sought deliverance from mere worldliness and mere things. Though he actually defined man as 'a thing which,' he at least disliked that state of affairs.[32]

For Rosenstock-Huessy, the negative side of James's legacy was a blind, polytheistic pluralism that left people bereft of real orientation, and a misplaced faith in the masses:

> James' 'Will to Believe' ushered in the revolt of the masses, because it withdrew from our faith in God its prop: God's faith in Man. The masses are plunged into night when the word 'faith' is made dependent on human will, instead of meaning that God holds us in the palm of his hand. The Greek and Hebrew word for faith means God's faithfulness and trust. Your belief and mine is but the poor reflex of God's faithfulness to all of us together. If God did not keep his promises to mankind, nobody could talk to anybody else with any hope of success. Hence, we may admit that a pluralistic universe, with a finite, object-like God in it, is the American

edition of all the heresies that devour Europe before our eyes. They also teach that 'will to believe' in any kind of God or in many gods, instead of in the true God who does not trust in one man or one nation, but in us all, and thereby unites us.

However, the dangerous crest of this wave may soon pass, because the generation that followed James will correct his misinterpretation of God. God is not a concept but the right name; and the whole Bible is nothing but the search for God's right name. On the other hand, Man is not found except in his conversation with his brothers. God and Man are not found as long as we use language about 'things,' 'world,' 'nature,' certainly not in laboratory tests. Henry James senior could not reach the world because he started with God. William James could not reach God because he started with things. The third corner, man, of the triangle God-World-Man, James did reach, but only by 'giving up logic squarely and forever'; in other words, James made a break between World and Man, but did not make the same break between the universe and God. The principle, however, is the same. Neither the right names for God nor the vital dialogues of Men can be deduced from concepts used for the things of this world. Concepts cannot be 'experienced,' words and names can. Man makes the world work, not pragmatically for his own ends, but as the faithful servant of some higher design and purpose, in honor and valor, with the eyes of the soul wide open.[33]

There is a lot in these two paragraphs, but here I wish to highlight two things that are central to the orientation of the New Thinking in general, and to Rosenstock-Huessy's development of it. First, and at the risk of simply restating the point already made about Rosenzweig, the sign 'God' refers to that which human beings serve, what they respond to, that which calls them. All societies are formations under some highest voice of appeal, an appeal that comes not just *from* 'Man' but is addressed *to* 'Man.' This is as much the case with democracy and its appeal to 'the people,' or republics with their appeal to the nation, or communism with its appeal to 'the future classless society,' or National Socialism or Italian fascism with their appeals to 'the will of the Führer or the Duce,' as it is with the Jewish nation with its appeal to Yahweh, the Christian nations with their appeal to Jesus Christ, the Muslims with their appeal to Allah via God's messenger, and so on. Despite atheism's claims that we are godless, such a claim arises from the fact that atheism is a philosophical doctrine. The gods, though, are not philosophical constructions; they are no more born out of the philosophical mind than babies are. Polytheism exists where there are many and conflicting calls upon us; the faith in the living God arose when a group, the Jews, could discern out of the chaos of conflicting commands one voice above all others who spoke of His promise and His love and of the World and Man being part of a common creation, *His* creation, in which He too intervened and which he wished to Redeem.

The second point is that James as a product of the naturalist revolution remained embedded in the world of things. His faith in free will was a way for him to conceive of humanity as more than just stones and gases and vegetable life; but the name of God had become alien to him, and that name, to repeat, for Rosenstock-Huessy was not primarily a concept but a name whose invocation was as important as the action undertaken under the presence of the trail of its significations. Polytheism often makes its way back into human experience not only as a serious option but also as the most desirable option, as it did in the eighteenth century and then in the twentieth century in the writings, *inter alia*, of Carl Jung, Joseph Campbell, James Hillman, and now – in a new wave – Regina M. Schwartz,[34] Jonathon Kirsch,[35] and Michael York.[36] In part, this testifies to the fact that polytheism expresses something true (something not denied by Rosenzweig or Rosenstock-Huessy). It is also due to the political horrors of idolatrous monotheism at a particular socio-historical moment. But the new benign version of polytheism is highly selective, and the new polytheists fail to pay due attention to the pandemonium and horrors of polytheism gone disastrous. Hesiod in his *Theogony*, for example, amply set out why the Greeks took the philosophical path toward a search for one overarching source of harmony and justice, while Nikolai Berdyaev, one of the contributors to *Die Kreatur*, made a powerful case that the nationalism of the Great War and its subsequent fascist forms were returns not only of paganism, but also of polytheism.[37]

The other discussion of God–Man–World that I wish to pause on in Rosenstock-Huessy comes from *Out of Revolution;* in some ways, it is one of the pithiest formulations of his 'social philosophy.' First, he essentially restates what Rosenzweig has sought to defend in *The Star*:

God–man–world are the three eternal components of spiritual life. Any process of thought, speech or inspiration must restore the tripartite order between divine question, human answer and subject matter. The triplicity is inevitable since any serious question is beyond the individual that is struggling to answer it; any theme, on the contrary, is beneath the man who is analyzing it. Names, of course, are ambiguous. The name God may degenerate into a mere word, the 'world' may be proclaimed God; but the mechanism of the three levels is present in every breath of life. No attempt at replacing them by calling everything divine, or everything worldly, or every power social or human, stands the logical test. Where there is no question, no standard, no command, no conscience, God and man both disappear and only brute nature remains. When we put all the divine power into man by worshipping society or humanity, man's truly human side evaporates into dust, and God and world remain the only realities.[38]

For Rosenstock-Huessy, and Rosenzweig for that matter, there is no question that the word God has little or no resonance for many people, but that is because they have lost touch with how peoples used to speak of God and gods, human beings and the world. A god was the name given to an inescapable hidden power, a power forcing us to respond:

> The power who puts questions into our mouth and makes us answer them, is our God. The power which makes the atheist fight for atheism is *his* God. Of course God is not a school examiner. . . . Man never gives his real answer in words; he gives *himself*. The gods whom we answer by devoting our lives to their worship and service ask for obedience, not for a lip-confession. Art, science, sex, greed, socialism, speed – these gods of our age devour the lives of their worshippers completely. They trace every line in the faces of their servants. Yet servant and master are never the same. The asker and the answerer remain different units. I summon you to 'love me,' 'obey me.' You answer this with an 'I will' or 'I will not.' But the I which urges you to react, and the you which reacts, more or less reluctantly, are not in command of the same powers. The 'you' that answers has not the same weapons at its disposal as the 'I' that presses you for an answer. God's questions come to us through the meek yet irresistible forces of heart and soul; our answers may rely on the thousand devices of our intellectual and social equipment. The I that asks me to seek the vital truth of an issue is in command of all the good angels of truth.[39]

Rosenstock-Huessy sees that in the ancient world, the response to life's demands was a triadic classification into heroes, citizens, and subjects or slaves; and that the 'objectification' process, the transformation of the world into a collection of things, was a certain moment of a process:

In the old days the hero who asked us a question of life and death, and wrested a vital answer from us, was called a god. The human being within ourselves that was willing to listen to such a question, to obey its impact on heart and conscience, and answer it, was called man. The slave, who could not listen, had neither name nor gender, nor speech like the men who could. He was a thing. What then was a 'thing'? Any thing involved in the dialogue, any content of question or answer, was a thing, *id est*; whatever was treated as a theme was an object, a part of the objectivated world. In this sense God Himself, when treated as the helpless and analyzed subject matter of discussion, as the Divine, becomes a 'thing'; but any part of the world, sun, earthquake, crisis, revolution, can become a god when we feel that it is a power urging questions upon us.[40]

We can ask questions to nature, but because nature in itself does not simply put questions in our mouths, it is inappropriate to simply dissolve ourselves completely into nature, as the metaphysicians of naturalism and mechanism did, in that doubled move made originally by Descartes that leaves a way out by elevating the subject to sovereign. With Kant, the noumenal self is a sovereign with an empty throne, and in some ways, that is more honest than with Marx and Nietzsche, who promise so much to man as communist or as superman, but only by virtue of having him 'not yet.' As we have already suggested, the modern naturalist metaphysicians commence with a grammatical orientation (taken over by philosophy) that already asks after the essence of something, thereby already 'objectifying' it. The triumph of philosophy that occurs with the development of a scientific culture is also a transition *within* philosophy. Thus Spinoza and Descartes, Bacon and Locke – with Leibniz being the salutary exception – all continue the humanist attack on Aristotle and on doctrines of final causes so that nothing can escape the naturalizing of things, the 'worlding' of all things so that the way out for those who still want to assert human freedom (which doesn't include Spinoza) is a means for man's divinization. Rosenstock-Huessy tells us:

The old meaning of the word 'to ask' included the ideas of command, demand, search, and question. When the modern mind began its scientific adventure, it limited the verb 'ask' to the sense of a purely intellectual process. By this lowering, it became possible to ignore the difference between the divine 'I' that asks and the human 'you' that endeavours to answer.

Descartes fell into an heroic fallacy when he identified the majestic 'I' of the God in his soul, who asked a response from him, with the responsive 'you' from which the answer is wrested. He labelled the two interlocutors with a single ambiguous term, 'ego.' This self-conversing personality is an invention of modern times. Neither Plato nor Aristotle knew anything of such a chimeric 'Ego,' who was neither God nor man; but Godlike and yet anthropomorphical. On the one hand, all the real distinctions between men – sex, age, colour, race – were neglected; the 'Ego,' so we were told, transcended them all. On the other hand, the really superhuman powers, those veritable 'I's,' were denied.[41]

Modernity, then, for Rosenstock-Huessy, is inseparable from a crisis of language or speech, a crisis in which large sections of humanity have lost their capacity to see themselves as responsive creatures because they have accepted the phantasms of modern philosophy's ego, something that – as Kant said so truly – is nothing but a mere Idea of Reason, though it would have been more accurate to refer to this as an idea sculpted by a group of people dependent on language who believe they are reason's high priests. Milton's depiction of Satan as the great windbag was a brilliant and insightful one of egocentric humanity in its infancy, from a man who saw the vacuity of the creature who mistakes itself for God and who creates from his Self a very hell. (That Milton is so frequently read as being on the side of Satan only shows the grip that this idea of the self's sovereignty has on the moderns.) The great irony is that the living God was rejected as a superstition by philosophers who were seeking to ensure that humanity would never again succumb to superstition; yet what has transpired is that humanity has simply discovered another superstition to bow to. In the same way, Eve in *Paradise Lost*, having been told that she would be a god once she had eaten the forbidden fruit, after tasting the fruit immediately bowed down to – a tree! In her act of disobedience, which was supposed to divinize her, she became *less* than the creature she already had been. To the naturalist, talk of gods is a gigantic step backwards; to the New Thinkers, it is a reconnection with the human race *as it is*, not an imaginary one that has been severed from its narratives, its rituals, its own 'skin,' but *as it is* and, to the extent that the triad of pagan, Jew, and Christian is added, also *as it can be* in the fulfilment of itself in the Messianic age to come. In this important quotation from Rosenstock-Huessy, we have an excellent example of how he attempts to bring together Jew, Christian, and pagan elements and how these connections to the eschatology of Marx and Nietzsche's view of 'man' are still visible, albeit in the context of a broader historical and religious vision:

> In the Bible there are two names for God: one is grammatically a plural, Elohim; the other is the singular Jahve. The Elohim are the divine powers in creation; Jahve is he who will be what he will be. When man sees through the works of Elohim and discovers Jahve at work, he himself begins to separate past from future. And only he who distinguishes between past and future is a grown person; if most people are not persons, it is because they serve one of the many Elohim. This is a second-rate performance; it deprives man of his birthright as one of the immediate sons of God.
>
> In the Sistine Chapel of the Vatican, Michelangelo shows God creating Adam, and keeping in the folds of his immense robe a score of angels or spirits. Thus at the beginning of the world all the divine powers were on God's side; man was stark naked. We might conceive of a pendant to this picture; the end of creation, in which all the spirits that had accompanied the Creator should have left him and descended to man, helping, strengthening, enlarging his being into the divine. In this picture God would be alone, while Adam would have all the Elohim around him as his companions.[42]

5 The Sundered and the Whole: Rosenzweig's Distinction between Pagans and the Elect

Despite various attempts to skirt the issue, if Rosenzweig's triad of pagan, Christian, and Jew has no merit, then *The Star of Redemption* is almost entirely worthless. Certainly its purpose no longer has anything to do with its structure or with Rosenzweig's motives for writing the book. It becomes just a disconnected set of philosophical insights that lack inner coherence. So let us state bluntly: in *The Star,* Rosenzweig wished to identify the differences among pagans, Jews, and Christians, and he attempted to demonstrate the following: what was unique about the Jews; what united and divided Jews and Christians; and what separated these biblical faiths from all other faiths and hence peoples who had been shaped by the living energies and powers they summoned, supplicated, and responded to. It is true that his analyses are sketchy, and he himself thought that what he had written on Islam was too scant and that its scantiness was the most serious weakness of *The Star.* He had, of course, no inkling that his analysis would be dissolved into his own polemics and then dismissed out of hand because of a liberal pluralistic orthodoxy that had extended itself to religions. Furthermore, in his discussion of religions, unlike Rosenstock-Huessy – whose Christianity led him to engage with religions for a very different project – he does not pause on what virtues each may have. That has no relevance for him. He is driven by these questions: Does a religion teach the truth of Revelation – the law of God's love and the commandment of neighbourly *love* (not to be equated with social justice)? And is that religion dedicated to Redemption? As he expressly said, he did not intend *The Star* to be a philosophy of religions. And he worried greatly that what he took to be the uniqueness of the Jewish life, intrinsically bound to the Revelation and promise of Redemption of the loving God, would be lost in the morass of other calls and energies then arising in the West, such as theosophy, anthroposophy, and movements inspired by Eastern religions.

I will be analysing Rosenzweig's critique of Islam in great detail in a later chapter. But I think it worth pausing here to examine the most hyperbolic criticism of Rosenzweig's analysis of Islam – the one levelled by Gil Anidjar – in order to show how Rosenzweig can so easily be wildly misrepresented in present-day social theory. For really, wild claims like Anidjar's could just as easily be levelled at Rosenzweig's discussion of *all* religions that he sees as non-revelatory. And Anidjar's polemic has the merit of expressing – with great directness and impeccable clarity – the real reason for the fear, embarrassment, and hostility displayed by scholars who admire Rosenzweig *except* when he talks of faiths other than Judaism and Christianity.

In an interview on his work, *The Jew, The Arab*, Anidjar stated that

[Rosenzweig's] relation to Islam must be treated in the same way, and as exclusively, as Heidegger's relation to the Jews (in other words, Heidegger's relation to Nazism). Someone asked how I could draw such an analogy since Rosenzweig never said that Islam should be eradicated, or that Muslims should be exterminated. I reminded them that Heidegger had also never said that Judaism should disappear from the face of the Earth or that Jews should face extermination.'[1]

The accusation is built on the comparison between a non-Zionist thinker, a member of the Jewish religion, which has no history of systematic Muslim persecution,[2] and a philosopher who publicly endorsed the leader of a political party that repeatedly and publicly espoused the expulsion, dispossession, and murder of the Jews. (So much is clear to anyone who has read *Mein Kampf*. That Heidegger, like so many others, probably never read it, is no less damning.) It seems that Rosenzweig's unforgivable act was to make a number of serious philosophical criticisms – albeit at times resorting to polemic (though his pales beside Anidjar's) – about the shortcomings of Islam's understanding of Revelation and Redemption, in order to demonstrate the difference between Judaism and Islam.

In *The Jew, The Arab*, in the chapter provocatively titled 'Rosenzweig's War,' Anidjar claims that Rosenzweig is declaring war on Arabs. The accusation is a sheer fabrication: Rosenzweig not only never says he is declaring war on Muslims or anyone else – indeed, a core part of his case that the Jews are God's elect is that they do not engage in Holy Wars. And anyone with even the most elementary knowledge of *The Star* should know this. Add to this Anidjar's very telling slip when he (unlike Rosenzweig) equates Arabs and Muslims. In fact, a common criticism of Islam – one that Rosenzweig does *not* make – is that the centrality of the Arabic language to Islam makes it a religion of Arab imperialism. Anidjar does not even pause on the fact that there are far more Muslims outside the Arab world and that not all Arabs are Muslims. For what it is worth, Rosenzweig did not especially 'like' Islam, but from his reading – which extended to learning some Arabic – and from his few meetings with Arabs, he thought Arabs '*herrlich* [wonderful]' and 'genial.'[3] That is to say, he never thought that a critique of Islam was a critique of Arabs, let alone an 'exterminatory gesture.' But then again, Anidjar is attacking Rosenzweig for something he neither said nor did. But is this not the typical procedure of the politically staged trial? And what Anidjar is doing under the guise of intellectual criticism is staging the intellectual's equivalent of a political trial.

Another jarring aspect of Anidjar's 'critique' – the showstopper in a political trial (and, let us be blunt, Anidjar deploys the same sort of tricks that made Vishinsky such a successful prosecutor in the Soviet Union) – is the accusation that Rosenzweig's argument naturally leads to extermination, as if it were an inevitable next step in Rosenzweig's argument.[4] One might just as well accuse Anidjar of wanting to murder Rosenzweig – though Anidjar's real point here is that he is morally more 'pure' than Rosenzweig, for he only wants to destroy his foe's character (i.e., not his life). Anidjar purports to be a philosopher, yet what he is really attacking is the very act of philosophical criticism. He seems to think that criticism of religious beliefs is 'exterminatory' by its very nature. Yet if he said that Rosenzweig's 'followers' wanted to exterminate 'followers' of Idealist philosophers, or that 'followers' of Hegel wanted to kill 'followers' of Kant, or that 'followers' of Kant wanted to kill 'followers' of Leibniz, or that 'followers' of Leibniz wanted to kill 'followers' of Spinoza, and so forth, no one would take the accusation seriously. And even though followers of revolutionary thinkers such as Rousseau and Voltaire and Marx have been revolutionary and murderous, their critiques of social injustice are not simply dismissed (at least by other philosophers) as valueless or untrue because of the killings done by their followers. More to the point, unlike Rousseau and others, Rosenzweig never for a moment calls for the radical overthrow (let alone elimination) of a group of people.

Yet Anidjar believes – as do those who have taken up his criticism of Rosenzweig – that those who criticize Islam are guilty of inciting murder. (Unwittingly, were Anidjar right, he himself has provided the basis for an argument for executing critics of a faith.) But the singularity of Anidjar's accusation suggests that this is all a rhetorical trick; and like all ideologues who hermetically seal their own group from criticism through the rhetorical gesture of equating critics with murderers, he is reproducing the very fascism he is claiming to expunge.

Carl Schmitt's division of the world into friends and enemies – very important not only to Anidjar but also to much of contemporary social theory – *might* be a way of assessing what often occurs in politics, but it is precisely the miracle and the deviation from the norm that dialogical thinkers strive for in their critical encounters.[5] The miracle is made possible through speech – it is the new opening that free speech can create. Rosenzweig and Rosenstock-Huessy were able to arrive at what both thought was a new space for Jews and Christians because they never surrendered what they took to be non-negotiable, even while learning something from and about each other. Anidjar's rhetorical gesture ultimately seeks to obscure the fundamental differences, which we elaborate on in later chapters, between Islam and Judaism, as perceived by a thoughtful Jewish person who has studied a religion, Islam, that has always set itself up as superior to Judaism.

This has been a lengthy preamble, but I feel that it would have been useless to proceed further had I not sought to open a clearing for Rosenzweig to be heard, and had I not engaged with the most extreme formulation of the common radical liberal critique of Rosenzweig.

I also think it absolutely necessary to do one more thing before we consider Rosenzweig's arguments for distinguishing between the pagans and the peoples of Revelation and Redemption, and that is orient ourselves more carefully to the structure of *The Star*. Few works are so directly determined by their structure as *The Star*. Moreover, because of its extreme stylistic density and ellipticism, *The Star*'s whys and wherefores are often very hard to grasp, at least on first encounters. Without for a moment suggesting that the schema offered here exhausts all of that book's questions and motifs, it is fair to say that *The Star* devotes itself mainly to the following questions and answers:

Introduction and Book One

Why has philosophy failed to grasp the important truths from which all the peoples of the world have taken their orientation? Because at least until post-Hegelian philosophy, its Idealist view of reality had been incapable of seeing the truth known to all pre-philosophical peoples – that God(s)/World/Man are three irreducible poles of reality.

Why are the pagan peoples pagans? Because they do not grasp the interpenetration of the three irreducible elements in such a way that they are open to the other three elements of Creation, Revelation, and Redemption. Hence they do not form their lives, at least as a collective, under the powers of the Creator, Revealer, Redeemer God of love.

Book Two

What does philosophy have to learn from theology? That its claims to completeness are limited unless they have recourse to Creation, Redemption, and Revelation. Ancient idealisms (specifically, neo-Platonism) attempted to account for creation, but their view of creation was limited by their idealism.

(a) What are the meanings of Creation, Revelation, and Redemption? (b) Where are they first disclosed? (c) And how are they related? (a) Creation includes not only nature but also, for human beings, the living word (grammar) and art, which are essential aspects of it; Revelation is the truth that 'love is as strong as death'; Redemption is the command that we are to love our neighbour. (b) In the Bible, specifically in Genesis, the Song of Songs, and the Psalms, and the Jewish people. (c) They form a triad that can be seen as superimposed on the first triad. Taken together, they form a unique way to be in the world and to make the self and one another.

Are Revelation and Redemption to be found in Islam? No, Islam is a parody of the peoples of Redemption because what it offers as the redeemed life is really but a particular approach to natural (i.e., pagan) life, not a departure that is also a fulfilment of it.

Book Three

Given that there are two peoples dedicated to achieving Redemption, and hence two peoples claiming election – one by birth, the Jews, and one by conversion, the Christians – what are the essential differences between them, and what do they have in common? The Jews are the people of eternity, the Christians the people of history. These differences are transparent in their different festivals and rituals and calendars – hence *The Star*'s detailed examination of them. As the above quote about Jews and Christians expresses, these two peoples are yoked together for a common purpose. But Christians are ever in danger of re-lapsing into their pagan origins.

It is very clear from all this that the importance of Jewish election is a central theme of *The Star*. That in turn is what makes it necessary for Rosenzweig to engage with Christianity. Earlier, we emphasized the common tasks of Jews and Christians; that said, *The Star* is uncompromising in its depiction of the Christians as 'lost.' In a letter of 1919, Rosenzweig would bluntly tell Rosenstock-Huessy that '*The Star* rests completely on one assumption, that Christianity is a lie.'[6] Rosenzweig is saying here what he clearly thinks is the truth of the Jewish life – that the Jewish person should speak out – for such is the truth of why one should *remain* Jewish. Yet he is not in the slightest bit interested in converting non-Jews to Judaism. Judaism, as he reads it, is *essentially* a 'blood matter.' That is why Rosenstock-Huessy was so elated when Rosenzweig told him that their friendship was a triumph of spirit over blood – he believed that their dialogue opened a new way for Jews and Christians.[7] For most of its history, Judiasm has had next to nothing to do with conversion. (And indeed, if any pagan were to consider conversion after understanding *The Star*, it is far more likely to be to Christianity, the redemptive religion that does indeed require converts, and that is – for Rosenzweig – the best redemptive hope for pagans, even though privately, Rosenzweig found Christians nauseating.) He does indeed want to show Christians why they should desist from anti-Semitism and honour the Jew in their midst (a very urgent task in post–Great War Germany), and he wants German liberal Jews 'to come home' – and 'home' will not be reached by going to Jerusalem, but in the daily practice of the Jewish life and involvement with its calendar. Some contemporary readings have wished to make it so, but *The Star* is not a call to a particular kind of radical and hence voluntarist action (hence nothing to do with post-structuralist political concerns); instead, it is a reminder to a people to know who they are and to understand what benefits and challenges flow from that condition. Nor does it involve a 'critique' of other nations – for other nations are simply 'other nations/peoples.' What he says about pagans, though it has often been interpreted in this light, is not even really a critique – and it certainly does not ask pagan peoples not to be pagans. It can only even be *conceived* as a critique if one first of all shares Rosenzweig's conviction that Redemption – not nirvana, not comfort, not alleviation from suffering – is the purpose of Creation.

And he would be in no doubt that the very criticisms he now provokes show how *Christianized* (in the Johannine form we discuss later) academic culture has become, at least in some very important respects – for it is Christianity that seeks to universalize the teaching of Redemption. All of these aims give *The Star* a peculiar, almost unique quality. Let us now analyse *The Star*'s demarcation of the Jewish life from pagan religions.

We recall that the introduction of *The Star* undertook to show that the philosophical or Idealist understanding of life is inadequate because it has superimposed an All upon it – only for that All to crack under its own weight as philosophy struggles out of its orb and opens itself to the metaphysical, metalogical, and meta-ethical perspectives. What emerges from *The Star*'s introduction is a concurrence with the consensus of humankind that God, Man, and World are genuinely distinguishable – that they are three fundamentally different and hence irreducible poles of appeal, and sources and sequences of events, histories, and names – and are not the result of a philosophical deduction of life as we experience it. Rosenzweig refers to God, Man, and World as the great three 'irrational propellants' – the great powers under which we have traditionally formed our life and (for much of humanity) still do. By far the most important part of his 'philosophical analysis' is completed in *The Star*'s introduction, and later, he will rejuvenate that analysis after showing how desperately philosophy needs theology if it is ever to attune itself to lived life rather than to life's delusions.

In Part One of *The Star*, Rosenzweig explores the metaphysical, metalogical, and meta-ethical, no longer as mere philosophical forms of analysis, but as content-filled positivities. What he believes he shows, however briefly, is how the planes of the metaphysical, metalogical, and meta-ethical within the great civilizations of China, India, and Greece leave these three primordial elements of the All – God, Man, and World – as elements. As mere elements, they fail to form a *real relationship*. The philosophers had indeed *thought* about the three elements – now taking one (the Ancients' and Middle Ages' elevation of God), then the other (the naturalists' elevation of World), and then the other (the anthropological turn of Feuerbach, Marx, and Nietzsche) as sovereign – but only by destroying their nature altogether, thus making them the subject of the philosopher's own brain and thereby depriving them of their own positive content. All peoples who haven't been deluded by reason see and understand that life is a creative process. But in their designation of the three greatest powers, not all peoples strive to coordinate each with each. They lack, says Rosenzweig, an 'And.' The attribution of the 'And' to these great primordials would involve not only a reconfiguration but also a transformation of everything that made these civilizations – however magnificent and powerful (pagan terms of appraisal having nothing to do with redemption – loving God/loving the neighbour is the authetic Jewish/Christian appraisal) – disappear or close in upon themselves until they were forced, by encounters with the outside world, to become part of the history of humankind. That a person is transformed through what he worships, and that what he worships is the voice he responds to in his world building, is I think why Rosenzweig commences his analysis of the metaphysics, metalogic, and meta-ethic of the pagan with the metaphysical. In fact, the analysis of each plane brings out the homological nature of the contents of God, World, and Man. This is no doubt redolent of Hegel, but not untrue for that.

In each book of Part One of *The Star*, 'Die immer Währenende Vorwelt' (The Everlasting Primordial World), Rosenzweig begins with the bits and pieces – 'the positivities' – of what has come to light in God, World, and Man. In each case, while exploring these elements he deploys the same formulation – that is, '"about" or "of" God/World/Man we know nothing.' In each he stresses that he is not engaging in projection, that he is not bringing these religions and peoples all under the same 'discursive regime,' as those would do who believe there is a fundamental essence of religion or 'religious experience' – as those would do who believe in a 'perennial philosophy' (a very telling phrase, from Rosenzweig's perspective, for it guarantees that what will be counted as religion fits the philosopher's demand).

In a neat and not untypical gesture of symmetry, Rosenzweig delays his formulation a moment longer in the case of the World when he writes of God (para. 2, as opposed to para. 1), and a further moment in the case of Man (thus para. 3), as we move toward what we seem to know more obviously,[8] which is not really true, for we are a mystery to ourselves, just as the World and God are mysteries that reveal themselves over time. Yet they all pass, or emerge, from nothing to something, not because the nothing is a substance, but because it is what has not yet become discernible as a proper something, a nothing of our knowledge: 'We do not know a one and universal nothing because we have rid ourselves of the All. We only know the individual nothing of the individual problem.'[9] In each case though, what has been left out (what does not fit in the philosopher's vision of the All) is precisely what Rosenzweig thinks of as significant.

Rosenzweig's procedure in Part One can easily baffle the reader – and again, few commentaries on *The Star* are very convincing or helpful because they seem not to have grasped Rosenzweig's reasons for his procedure. This is mainly because he expresses himself cryptically and writes with almost unparalleled philosophical density. Yet there are, in fact, two things governing the procedure.

One is an attempt at disclosing the character of these raw propellants – a character he designates as conforming to the muted language of mathematics rather than living, loving speech. This seems very odd indeed. And it remains odd unless one realizes that he is taking this approach in order to later contrast peoples inhabiting a protocosmos of isolated or disconnected elements with a people whose cosmos is relational. In other words, he wants to demonstrate the particular discovery or attunement of the Jewish people to how life's powers are orchestrated and integrated, not in the (Greek) manner as an orb, but as a continuous opening of love (Levinas's defence of the open infinite picks this up). We are accustomed to associating the word becoming flesh with Christianity, but if it is a Christian formulation, it was prior to that a thoroughly Jewish idea, and the formulation merely betrays the Jewish roots of the first Christians. For God speaks the world into existence, and the Jews are the enfleshment of his creative word.

This part of the procedure is thoroughly formalist, for it too is preparing the reader for the importance of how peoples are formed by their attunements to the God(s) that call them to make themselves and their world.

The first aspect of the procedure is difficult, and the rationale behind it is only apparent once one understands the book as a whole. Rosenzweig knew that it would be a challenge for the reader to keep going in order to *get to its real end*: the depiction of the Jewish life, the establishment of the Christian dependency on Jewish existence, and the separation of divine tasks. That this division of tasks gives Jews a reason to engage with their Christian neighbours is no small thing, for it enables Rosenzweig to reconcile his faith with his (Christian) environment. But it should be said, too, that the pagan is also indispensable insofar as the pagan is ultimately a natural creation. Rosenzweig saw that the Christian recognizes this in the requirement that to be a Christian, one cannot simply be born a Christian – one must *become* one, must be baptized. The Jew is indeed born a Jew, but he is born always into a pagan world. Again, Rosenzweig's entire edifice falls if his argument for the Kingdom to come is transposed onto the State of Israel. That Israel is at war with its neighbours is, from Rosenzweig's very orthodox point of view, proof that it is entangled in the pagan energies of the state.

The second thing he is doing is identifying certain 'facts' about Greece, China, and India that point to reality as such if they are not viewed under the optic of Revelation and Redemption.

We need, then, to keep both aspects of his procedures in mind as we consider more closely why he says what he does about traditions that do not follow the path of the 'ever renewed world.'

Book One of Part One of *The Star* deals with metaphysics. And near the beginning of that book he states, in a formulation whose resonances are unmistakably those of Schelling: 'We are seeking God, as we shall later seek the world and man, not as one concept among others but for itself alone in its absolute factuality – if the expression is not misleading precisely, that is, in its "positivity."'[10]

The original positivity, for Rosenzweig, is the affirmation itself, its being, a Yes. For Rosenzweig it is first and foremost an affirmation that contains within it infinite possibility. The emergent, then, is the negation of nothing, the not-nothing, which is 'an affirmed infinity,' the affirmation that is the same propulsion that separates the infinitely large and infinitely small from the nothing, the differential that makes the something that Kant, in his chapter 'Anticipations of Perception' in *Critique of Pure Reason*, had called intensive magnitude. This presence is the affirmation – the Yes, says Rosenzweig, to cite it again – that is 'the original word of language, one of those which makes possible – not sentences, but to begin with, simply words that go into sentences, words as elements of the sentence.'[11] Every thing that is not nothing carries with it this initial affirmation, and when Rosenzweig writes that 'the first yes in God establishes the divine essence in all infinity. And the first Yes is "In the beginning,"'[12] he is suggesting that the experience of knowledge and the experiences of existence are experiences of manifestness, whereby the original emergent is the expression of its own freedom and infinitude.

But why, the naturalist would ask, will this emergent not be a piece of nature, a cell from which all others will unfold and develop up to and including the idea of God? For the simple reason that we have already discussed in the last chapter – because there is no All that reason can simply enfold within its totality. Thus God, too, is not a name in which all is immanent, at least not the living God whose trail is being tracked by Rosenzweig, or the God or gods of other peoples; only the philosopher's God, a God born of Idealism rather than collective experience, does that. Only the assertion that there can be nothing outside of nature forces one to forgo the question of the meaning of the name 'God,' but such an assertion brings with it the automatic dissolution of the world as we know it, and its replacement with a counterfactual world that has no interest for Rosenzweig. What interests him is the awareness of that power that freed itself from the nothing through an act of its own affirmation, its Yes and the No of its response to the nothing, that it would not be that: 'God's freedom is quite simply a tremendous no.'[13] Moreover, God is originally really nothing but this original freedom – a freedom that he says is finite in itself,[14] leading to infinity: infinite arbitrariness that nevertheless exists in this relationship to the nothing, this nothing, that is not a substance, but that again nevertheless is characterized by its inertness: 'So the arbitrariness, neither summoned nor attracted, seems able to fling itself upon the essence. But when it approaches the essence, it falls under the spell of the inert being of essence.'[15] The relationship is a relationship of struggle, of pull and push, attraction and repulsion – all resonances of Schelling's account of God's creation – and Rosenzweig designates 'this point, in contrast to the divine power and arbitrariness, as the point of divine necessity and destiny.'[16]

This tension between infinite freedom and necessity and destiny is the matrix on which the name of God is played out. It is, as we have seen, a grammatical as well as a historical story; and this, for Rosenzweig, is what gives it its real significance. God, for him, is what emerges out of the triad of the three elements that enable any speech at all – affirmation, negation, and conjunction. With these three elements that seal (yes), that differentiate and have power over what is simply noted (not this), and that develop ('and') speech to unleash, so too God is first of all something that is conceived in speech by the speaking animal that we are and that seeks orientation within the reality in which it is immersed. That the God(s) live is the fundamental fact on which Rosenzweig's analysis rests. The stress and strain between divine freedom and subjection to necessity are played out over and over in stories of God or the gods. That there is so much more to the name of

God, in terms of what he reveals of Himself over the great time span of the existence of the Jewish people, and that people will come to see so much more in this freedom than is at first manifest, is of great importance to Rosenzweig, but this is not something originally widely experienced. He sees that originally, human beings are struck by the vitality of the powers of life emergent, of free, unpredictable vital omnipotent energies – Gods: 'They are nothing but alive. They are immortal. Death lies beneath them.'[17] There is no relationship between God and Man because the gods are self-enclosed, because *they are gods*. If they were not, they would be less. And later we see how important this implication is – other peoples (i.e., non-Jews) are captivated by this separation from these overwhelming powers and their own death.

These gods do not escape the tension between infinite freedom and necessity or fate, but that tension is combined in a 'mysterious unity.' The mythic world is an enclosed one of arbitrariness and fate. Rosenzweig's highly compressed discussion of Greece, China, and India is indeed sketchy, and certainly there is much more scope for nuance and elaboration. And anyone who wanted here a comprehensive survey of the religions of the world is going to be rightly dissatisfied.

Furthermore, if Rosenzweig were doing a *horizontal* analysis, attempting an analysis of the lines of power, beauty, and complexity generated within each civilization or socio-historical formation – that is, if he were simply doing a comparison on the basis of *culture* – his analysis would be far from adequate and of very little value. This other project, which is not Rosenzweig's, is precisely what is being falsely projected onto Rosenzweig by his more 'liberal' readers, who feel deeply uncomfortable with a hierarchical comparison of religions and cultures. Their discomfort is based on fears of colonialism and its accompanying political and social chauvinism. The fear expressed in such criticisms is quite rightly based on a hostility to Enlightenment ideas of progress, which are complete anathema to Rosenzweig. Furthermore, if Rosenzweig was merely doing what Rosenstock-Huessy did – that is, showing the contribution to universal history by the various social complexes, and which loves held them together, and which catastrophes, fears, and hatreds drove people to found new formations to transport themselves into a new time – his sketches would also be deeply unsatisfactory. But he is not doing any of this; it is simply not his brief.

Thus, Rosenzweig's analysis of the metaphysical horizons of China, Greece, and India – more broadly, the non–Judaeo-Christian world – while a vertical one, is driven by this fundamental question: Is there anything to suggest that God or the gods are conceived of as *redemptive* forces? It is not whether men or women of a later age, who have been so historically and culturally influenced by the presence of the redeeming God, want them to be redemptive, nor whether the gods feel pity, nor whether they intervene when prayed to; rather, it is whether, with these peoples' depictions of God or the gods, there is anything to indicate a redemptive call to action from the god/s toward His/their creation that would result in the triple-Redemption of the world, the self, or even (and highly significantly) God Himself. When the question is posed that way, one might reply, quite rightly, that Rosenzweig was extremely unlikely to find the Jewish and Christian God being feared, praised, or worshipped in China, India, or ancient Greece, and that he takes his readers on a search for the Jewish and Christian God knowing that He will not be found where he is not wanted, needed, or present. Exactly. That is very much the point of this first book of Part One of *The Star*, which is why someone who understands the project and details of *The Star* can only be baffled by the politically and ethically motivated – not to mention wrong-headed – asides directed against Rosenzweig for his treatment of other cultures and religions.[18] Neither Greeks, Buddhists, Hindus, Taoists, and Confucianists, nor (before encountering Christianity) tribal peoples, nor, for that matter, Muslims, want redemption or to be God's elect in the sense that Rosenzweig means. On the contrary, they absolutely do *not want* these things; though Rosenzweig might add they don't want it because it is not an option that is visible from the array of elements available from the 'everlasting primordial world.'

To appreciate why others may not want election, let us leap forward for a moment into the fire of what being the 'elect' means. For this alone shows why choosing to respond to the revelation of love is such a hard path, and nothing like the childish view of love that bombards us constantly in our daily diet of television shows, movies, popular songs, newspapers, and magazines with their sweet, deceptive, and unnourishing-as-candy portrayals of love. To be God's elect is to be forced to live a certain way, to be rootless to the world, though anchored to God and one's own. It is not always, and not in each individual case, but nevertheless time and time again, to be called – or, more often, to be forced back into the fold by those who hate the very existence of the Jews. To be God's elect is not to have an easy life. On the contrary, it is to be ever connected to what may not too improperly be called the dark side of God and His steadfast commitment to the Covenant; though one must add that God is experienced as a darkness or as an absence when humanity closes out His love. When His love is shut out by iron walls of will when selves turn to other gods and to other far more beguiling powers – at those times, God's love cannot reach the world and selves. From Rosenzweig's perspective, this is inevitably what happens when Creation is left alone in its own tumult, without hope or faith in the possibility of Redemption: because life as it is (i.e., unredeemed) seems bad, death is better or so good that nothing could be better except perhaps more of it – which is, as we will see, precisely why he thinks Islam does not understand the real meaning of Redemption.

Jews are 'the remnant,' that which the world will not fully absorb into its history because the Jews are eternally God's. For Rosenzweig, being loved by God means having to bear the agony of love's lack and the persecution of anti-Semites – people who do not see the divine in the face of the Other, who do not see that we are made in God's image, and who love sin and themselves more than God and His commandment. Being God's elect is living in the harshness of love's commitment, 'suffering for God's sake,' just as in the teaching of the Shekhina:

> God's coming down to men and his dwelling among them, is explained as a separation that occurs in God himself. God himself separates him from himself, he gives himself away to his people, he suffers with its suffering, he migrates with it into the misery of foreign lands, he wanders with its wanderings . . . Because the suffering of the remnant [i.e. the Jews], the constant separating and having to be eliminated, all this now becomes a suffering for God's sake, and the remnant is the bearer of this suffering.[19]

Being the elect, then, has nothing to do with getting all the candy, or all the goodies of Creation (the typically childish and hence the most naive pagan view of 'heaven'). (This is not to equate the pagan with the naïve – there is nothing naive in the strictures and practices of yogic, Buddhist, or Taoist paths.) Election is to be enmeshed in God's love; but that love is not a magic wand guaranteeing a morally good world order. To repeat a point raised earlier, God cannot force people to love Him. The commandment to love Him is an expression of wisdom and love and not merely megalomania or caprice. For the failure to do so is evident in the world we make when we love derivative and disconnected powers that, lacking connection to the creative and redemptive source, destroy us. We are God's creatures, but the world we inhabit is also our creation. And its human horrors are our creations. Thus when it is said, for example, that evil is the disproof of God, or that the

Holocaust is proof of God's non-existence, it is clear that the speaker is rejecting God, seeing in God a kind of Santa Claus figure; and no doubt, for many, that is what He is. But this is not how Rosenzweig or people who take the living, loving, redeeming God seriously ever think of Him. For them, God's love radiates eternally. The world and selves that we make are made either in compliance with or in rejection of this love. In an important sense, disbelievers and serious believers in the loving God share a sense of ethical responsibility (hence Levinas can appeal to both audiences). Both are correct in their view that only the deluded think that some magic will fix everything up. The televangelical and New Age views of the world – which posit that the Higher Self or God or some mysterious power is just waiting to hand out new cars, houses, stashes of cash, and the like to the pious – is as stupid and contemptible as it is remote from everything Rosenzweig is talking about – which, in part, is why he does not even seem to have considered that his illness had any bearing whatever on his faith; it was just another circumstance that life had thrown at him.

Where the (so-called) atheist and the faithful differ, in Rosenzweig's sense, is in their respective constructions of the grounds of life, and as we have stressed throughout, in their respective understandings of peoples, history, and speech as real forces. Rosenzweig's *Star* is very much a love story, and though it is a story of a blazing light, it is not a story guaranteeing a happy ending for the individual – indeed, this is really faith's gamble. Rosenzweig's response to this gamble is beautifully articulated in the 'On Being a Jewish Person':

> Trust is the word for a state of readiness that does not ask for recipes, and does not mouth perpetually 'What shall I do then?' and 'How can I do that?' Trust is not afraid of the day after tomorrow. It lives in the present, it recklessly crosses the threshold leading from today into tomorrow. Trust knows only that which is nearest and therefore it possesses the whole. Trust walks straight ahead. And yet, for those who trust, the street that loses itself in infinity, for the fearful rounds itself in imperceptibly into a measurable and infinite circle.
>
> Thus the Jewish individual needs nothing but readiness.[20]

Rosenzweig is contending here that the Jews are God's elect – that they have a unique place in the world and a unique call stemming from a unique covenant with God. But the meaning of this has nothing to do with cultural, nationalist, or religious chauvinism, all of which express the inversion (the demonic depiction) of the meaning of being God's elect.

If there is one criticism that might stick, it is this: it is preposterous to conceive that a human being can by mere birth be part of an elect group. Besides which, consider how little there is to gain from this faith in terms of the world's treasures. One can well imagine Larry David (probably the most astute observer of the antagonisms between Christian and Jewish manners in North America) with his trademark smile pointing to the ridiculousness of our situation, giving his familiar catch phrase 'pretty, pretty good' as the answer to the question, 'How does it feel to be one of the elect?' And one can just as equally see him yelling out to his manager or anyone nearby if he were reading *The Star* – 'Hey get a hold a this guy – I'm part of the elect,' only to realize five seconds later that life goes on in the same catastrophic way as ever. In other words, the simplest and potentially the most accurate criticism that can be laid at Rosenzweig's feet is not that he is a religious warrior paving the way for the extermination of other faiths and cultures, but that he is seriously deluded – which is, in effect, Richard Rubinstein's criticism. But if he is, so are all followers of Jahweh. All he can point to – indeed, all *anyone* can point to – to demonstrate the power of his faith is his life and the Jewish world of which he is a part.

Thus, even though in Part One of *The Star* he does not elaborate on the nature of Redemption – because in keeping with his systematic approach (very thorough, very German), he does not have the elements to talk about it – he wants his readers to understand that Redemption is not the retreat back into the nothing, that it is not an abnegation of life, that it is not something mystical, that it is not something otherworldly, nor is it anti-worldly, or 'anti-mindly,' for that matter. This, then, is also why, in the section on metaphysics in *The Star*, Rosenzweig is also looking for elements that support the name 'the Living God'; it is why he says that those elements are mostly absent in Eastern religious experience, which he was well aware was being hailed in some Western quarters – especially in theosophy and anthroposophy – as a superior form of spiritual practice;[21] and it is why, in antiquity, the gods formed the basis of the mythic, which in turn formed the basis of art: 'the spirit of the myth found the realm of the beautiful.'[22]

His criticisms of the religions of China and India are not due to a misunderstanding of what human possibilities and energies and responses to life they emphasize; rather, it has to do with their not being based on linkages between God, Man, and World that would open their adherents to the law of love that is revelation. Certainly he is polemical – not respectful in a liberal sense – but, while he could have been more nuanced, he is not mistaken regarding what powers these religions concentrate on. He is not mistaken when he says that the Chinese heaven is an immanent or totalizing conception, that it is all-encompassing, and that its gods control life. Nor is he wrong in saying of Brahminism that it rests on a vision of silent omnipotence and that it does not command its faithful toward redeeming one another, but rather draws them into its own silent power:

> China's Heaven is the concept raised to the world-embracing, of divine power which without pouring forth over the divine essence and thus being configured in the divine vitality, arranged the entire universe into an enormous ball of its ruling arbitrariness; [it] is not as another thing, but as a thing that contains in itself, a thing that 'inhabits' it; nowhere does the graphic sense of the idea of immanence become as clear as in this Chinese deification of the vault of the heavens, outside of which – is nothing. And just as China's God is exhausted in going from the nothing to the all-embracing power, so, too, for India's God on the road between the nothing and the pure, all-penetrating silence of the divine essence, of the divine nature. The sound of divine freedom never penetrated into the silent circle of the Brahmin; so it itself remains dead, although it may fill all life and absorb all life into itself.[23]

In both cases, Rosenzweig wishes to emphasize how the affirmation that is breaking out of nothing by that living power which is witnessed by the Greeks as a bursting forth of divine forces or gods and by the Jews as the living God, is seen and experienced by the Brahmins as well as by the sages of classical China as more of a negation than an affirmation; it is a negation that renders impossible that other affirmation, which Rosenzweig equates with the affirmation of the living God, the God that wants Redemption of the world, of Man, and of Himself. As we have already stated, a defining feature of the living God is the *desire* and need for this triple-Redemption. Concomitantly, the search for stillness, or acquiescence in the eternal flow, as opposed to the entreatment of Redemption and the irruptiveness of a God that comes upon something weak and broken in order to redeem it, is seen by Rosenzweig as a reaffirmation of the proto-cosmos itself at the expense of the path to configuration. It hankers, in his terms, for a return to what is prior to life, for a blocking out of the voice that wants more life, not only horizontally on the plane of Creation, but also vertically on the plane of Redemption. (This talk of planes is not to be confused with a neo-Platonist chart of planes of consciousness, or with astral, etheric planes of the stripe that found their way into theosophical and anthroposophical circles in the latter part of the nineteenth century in Europe and that now appear in New Age movements and books.)

Redemption, for Rosenzweig, is as remote from otherworldliness as it is from mysticism, as it is from 'expanded states of consciousness.' When Rosenzweig talks of Redemption he is talking about and experiencing qualities *of* and *within* life that have been ecstatically transformed by love. Redemptive love, though, is not just love of God or gods or of one's tribe or family or group (these are 'natural'); such love is also love as experienced *from* God and *for* the neighbour, whoever that neighbour might be and in whichever way that love might be required to be expressed. The law of Redemption, love thy neighbour, 'the embodiment of all commandments,'[24] does not specify the *how* of love precisely because love is as unpredictable as the loving revealing God who gives love and who commands that love be given to Himself so that He can love more, and to one another so that the cosmos itself will be more full of love.

Redemption thus grasped is nature revived and transformed through more love. The direction expressed by the power of Heaven or the Brahmin Self or Nirvana or the Tao is a contrary direction, a contrary movement that affirms the original nothing and the desirability of that nothing and its various tropes. That the loving God will not be stopped, that the loving God presses forward with His command, is why, for Rosenzweig, all of these religions of escape, of the affirmation of nothing, are somewhat countered in the Asian world by the more proliferate and life-affirming energies that typify natural life or creative paganism and that are to be found in the more populist 'primitive' myths and gods and rituals of Asia:

> [But] only because this last abstraction [the nothing] of all divine life is unbearable to the living Self of man and to the living worlds of the peoples, and lifeless pallor of the abstraction – in short, because it is the destiny of the Buddha's and Lao-tse's disciples that a flourishing paganism grows again over the unyielding stone blocks of their non-thoughts, only for their reason in spite of their fascination, the ears of men are inclined to become receptive again to the voices before which those men once fled in order to hide in the spaces of Nirvana and Tao, where sound does not

reach. For only where there is life, be it a life intoxicated by the gods or one that is hostile to God, only there does the voice of the Living One find an echo. In the empty room of non-thought, into which there flees the fear of God that did not muster up the courage to be in awe of God, that voice gets lost in the void.[25]

Rosenzweig might be taken to task for not appreciating what incredible potencies lay incubating in that region where life and nothing conjoin, where the slowest breath and wake-like sleep, the meditation of the yogi, not to mention the astonishing capacities that the attunement into this region opens up for the body, and the clarity of Buddhist or Taoist calm, can create in the tumult of the world, and hence the importance and sheer blessedness of such moments of peace. But, given his brief, the criticism is completely beside the point. A more potent criticism of Rosenzweig would be that these are actually strategies for a fuller life and that they are part of the means of our Redemption. This, indeed, is how these paths are now often interpreted in the West. But there are two issues here. One is to restate that the real touchstone from Rosenzweig's perspective is whether (a) these religions opened up communal lifeways that did not lead to nirvana or some silence or resting place, and (b) whether this was visible in the communal shapes they formed. Another is to make the point that Rosenzweig is limited to focusing – albeit briefly – on original religious social *Gestalts*, but that the meaning of these *Gestalts* transforms over time and social circumstance, so that they may not have initially contributed to – or even have been intended to contribute to – Redemption in Rosenzweig's sense. This later position is, in fact, that of Rosenstock-Huessy, who is interested in all the basic *Gestalts* of the human condition as contributing to the one 'economy of salvation.' That is why he came to see that Buddhist withdrawal and Taoist submissiveness to the Tao and their mutual renunciation of desire and worldliness are, contrary to Rosenzweig, strategies in life's enhancement, concluding that the modern cross of reality must have a Buddhist and Taoist component.[26] And while Rosenstock-Huessy was no specialist in world religions, his approach was to emphasize that 'there's always something in any one of these various religious doctrines which is very reasonable, very sensible.'[27]

But such matters are important once one accepts that the purpose of Redemption is to recharge all regions and potencies of creation with love, to share and to build through temporal and spatial communities all the fruits of humankind, and to bring all to the banquet (all of which very much form Rosenstock-Huessy's brief). This must not, however, be confused with the disentanglement that is driving Rosenzweig to look for those original forces of creation and hence the original fields or complexes of cultivation, which are themselves not merely creative but also expressive of Revelation and Redemption themselves. In this respect, then, Rosenzweig notes the 'superiority' of the Greek cosmo-theology – 'even if the mythological gods did not live beyond their realm surrounded by walls – they still lived,'[28] – because it strives, albeit unsuccessfully, to break out further into life, to reach higher into it, to spread itself more, to provide the linkages between God, Man, and World, which in turn would make possible the intergenerational linkage between neighbours of the Synagogue and the Church. The linkages are what enable the original triad to be elevated into eternity in its conjunction with the triad of Creation, Revelation, and Redemption.

When God, World, and Man are not seen in their unity as a path, as opposed to an idealist substantive unity that is not path but identity, thought easily becomes dazzled by those powers that are rightly seen as divine, and a confused rationalism emerges where Man confuses himself with God and God's absolute power cannot deign to descend lest somehow He in this process be confused with some lesser power. The closed world of myth, says Rosenzweig, is reproduced in the closed God of the mysteries and the philosophers; in the longing to be or merge with God, Man and World are lost:

Already the theology of antiquity which was oriented towards myth, had fallen into an uneasiness that pushed forward to go beyond the self-satisfied sphere of myth and seemed to demand that reversal of that which is simply living into the generator of life. But with regard to the violence of the mythical view, it is a wonder that the attempts in this direction in the mysteries and ideas of the great philosophers always strove to put man and world into the sphere of the divine: exactly like myth, then, they possessed only the divine. The autonomy of the human and the worldly disappeared, both in the mysteries to do with deification and in the concepts of love and yearning, which permitted the philosophers to bridge over the abyss; these concepts never led from the divine to man and worldly things, but it was always the reverse. This is true of the Greeks in their loving quest for the perfect, and of the Indians in their love of God. It would have seemed to be a restriction of God, of the God on whom one was priding oneself for just now having elevated him to the one who includes all things by amassing on his one head all the noble qualities of many gods, if one had wanted to entangle him again in the passion of love. It may be that man loves him; but his love, God's love for man, could be at most an answer to the love of man, the just reward then, and not the free gift which extends its blessings beyond all norms of justice, not the original divine power that makes choices without constraints, or even anticipates all human love and makes the blind see and the deaf hear. And even where man believed he had attained the highest form of love, like in those circles of the Indian friends of God, by renouncing, for the sake of God, all that belonged to him, all desire and all longing as well as all ascetic efforts, awaiting God's grace in complete surrender – even here this surrender was the performance achieved by man, and not first the gift of God. In other words, God's love in the first place was not for the hardened one, but for the perfect one.[29]

Rosenzweig's redemptive vision is, then, one in which God, World, and Man become as full as possible. Any approach to life that sacrifices one at the expense of the other is seriously deficient. The God who reaches out and into the lack and deficiency of man is, for Rosenzweig, precisely the revealing loving God who is not entombed by the rigidity and limited understanding of love of those who confuse power with deficiency (the deficiency of a god who only loves what is *worthy*). 'It is precisely these lost ones, these hardened ones, those uncommunicative ones, that is to say the sinners, whom the love of a God had to seek, a God not merely worthy of being loved, but who himself loves, independently of the love of men.'[30] Almost everything else that follows in *The Star* about God can be found in embryo in the section 'The Twilight of the Gods' from Book One of Part One of *The Star*: for it contains all the elements of his critique of Idealist religion, the mysteries, the religions of India, mysticism, Islam (without yet mentioning it), and even Christianity. The fork in the road that ever renders impossible complete reconciliation between Jew and Christian turns on the issue of whether a man who has lived and died is God – or more accurately, from the Christian side, a member of the trinity that is God.

If, then, as Rosenzweig claims, in antiquity God 'keeps his nature for Himself,' it follows that how World and Man are construed will differ fundamentally from how they are framed vis-à-vis the absence of the living loving God and the presence of other forces that interact with both in a completely different manner. In Rosenzweig's exploration, the elements of the proto-cosmos are also developed as symbols. For him, this is a way of displaying the formal differences and hence the errors that accompany failure to see the triad of God, World, and Man as a path. Thus the symbolization of God as that universal is $A = A$, the symbolic equivalent of 'I am that I am.' Whereas the emergence of God out of the nothing suggests an original yes and no of some original 'one,' if we take the world as it is and not as enfolded within thought that supplies it with a unity; it is the infinitude of its proliferateness; 'oneness' is everywhere pluralized, yet everywhere there are particularities. Of course, once the world has been summoned under the law, once its particulars are regimented into the sciences, then the world may assume a unity of order, one substance, as Kant had insisted was essential for our reason – the first 'analogy of experience is a condition of there being laws of nature.' In such cases, Rosenzweig contends, the symbol of the spirit of the world is ' $= A$.' 'It is the symbol of the spirit of the world. For this would be the name we would have to give to the logos that is spread and amalgamated everywhere and always in the world, both the so called "natural" world and the so-called "spiritual" one.'[31] But, says Rosenzweig, 'really what is dismaying in the world is that it is not spirit.' It is a ceaseless emergence of particulars, a plenitude of 'ever renewed convulsion of procreation and giving birth' – 'each new thing is a renewed negation of the nothing, something that has never been, a beginning for itself, something unheard of, something "new under the sun."'[32] Whereas, he says, 'hidden in the universal is a need for fulfilment, a turn to application. In the particular there is nothing like this . . . There is no need for anything, neither of direction, nor of force – not even against its like . . . Its force is only the blind weight of its being. According to our terminology, its symbol is simply B, the naked sign of individuality, without an equal sign referring to it.'[33] He continues:

> The particular . . . bursts in, and so it is there. It is not the 'given' – a mistaken designation in which is reflected the error of all the pre-metalogical philosophy of the world; it is not for nothing that its systems again and again arrive at an impasse at this problem. It is not the given; 'givens,' once and for all, are sooner the logical forms in the simple and infinite validity of their Yes; the particular is a surprise; not a given, but a gift ever new; more precisely, a present, for in the present the thing offered as present disappears behind the gesture of presenting.[34]

Yet for all this infinity of miracles, one can still see in the particulars a common character of belonging: that they are in the world. This world can be interpreted as a logical necessity, as the universal that wants to swallow life up and bring it all under the authority of thought: the logical forms, those 'precious ancient vessels, always ready to hide the wine of new harvests in their fat bellies,' as opposed to more fecund aspects of the *logos* – 'the spontaneous beast[s] . . . that break into the gardens of the given to seek their nourishment there.'[35]

Logos and world can work in the most life-enhancing of manners; the *logos* can become a means for life overcoming death in the form of the name, a force that otherwise would have been activated, all played out as forces are in the Animal or Plant Kingdom once they are spent and consumed in the world of human beings, where the *logos* is present and can be resummoned and trigger off new events. That is why Rosenzweig likes the term 'spirit of the world' or 'soul of the world'; it is not the universal *logos* bringing everything within its fold, closing all in upon itself so that calm is restored to chaos and the philosophical legislator can make pronouncements upon the world and God and man by making all conform to the dictates of reason. Rather,

> the logos brings about the unity of the world only from within; the unity, as it were not as its outer form, but as its inner form . . . The logos, thus again turned into the soul of the world, can do justice to the miracle of the living body of the world. The body of the world no longer needs to stay there as a mass of undifferentiated 'given,' full of chaotic agitation, ready to be seized and shaped by logical forms; phenomenon, a flow that sweeps down on the calmly opened womb of the soul of the world and unites with it to shape the organized world.[36]

One would be very mistaken if one did not see the magnitude of the difference between the ways in which *logos* operates in these cases. In the Idealist deployment, the 'already known' always will take pride of place over the 'not yet known,' the 'not yet' once it is rounded up and corralled within the configurations already made available to the world by the master thinkers of the *logos*. In the case of the *logos* being seen as bringing unity from within, a path is being forged so that the proliferateness of the world, one's openness to the miracle of particularity, contributes to the creation of an even more miraculous world. The loving God and the living World go together, first by the living World not blocking out the possibilities of the miracles of the living God and then by the living God finding an openness for the flow of gifts into the earth. World, of course, is not just natural world; it also includes the spiritual and human world, which is why Rosenzweig talks about the proto-cosmos of the social world in this book.

Rosenzweig's insights throw an important light onto how the modern world simultaneously is so fecund with respect to the kinds of things it makes available through technology even while imposing all manner of administrative standardizations, rigidities, and controls that hold back the living world. Without in any way wishing to take Rosenzweig as an apologist of free market forces, it is evident to me that his distinction between the living and 'grey' *logos* of Idealism is analogous to Friedrich von Hayek's distinction between taxonomic and catallactic systems of order. The former is akin to a military exercise and involves the allotment of tasks and the subsequent collection and coordination of information on the basis of a general directive, while the latter is not planned but grows; it opens up our creative powers by leaving unspecified who does what with whom and how, in the awareness that more information is not only gathered but also generated in the interaction that provides the basis for further creations. It is also analogous to Deleuze and Guattari's comparison between arboreal (tree-like) logic, in which the universal digs down into and thereby colonizes the territory of every subordinate, and the logic of the rhizome, which defies laws of connectivity, deterritorializing as it rambles, aimlessly roaming and blowing wherever it goes.[37]

However, whereas Hayek's discussion of catallaxy is applied primarily to the economy and law, and Deleuze and Guattari's is part of a call to radical political action that can open new lifeways in a world increasingly being captured and colonized, Rosenzweig's account of the metalogical leaves its deployment open – for as concerns the World, all that Rosenzweig is seeking to do is show what it is like when seen as living and as not subjected to the Universal. At the same time, he is aware that our world is made not just by an infinitude of ones and differences but also by composition, by integration and transference, by the pooling of energies and the subsequent reception of pooled energies. The species is a pool of energies or potencies, and so – potentially at least – are the forms of its development: its peoples, its states, and so on. Whereas the logic of Idealism interprets, in its arboreal-like logic (to use Deleuze and Guatarri's term), the path of the Universal down to the particular so that A = B, the metalogical process of Rosenzweig moves over the course of its life in the opposite direction, and hence its symbolic formulation is B = A. The Idealist formulation that placed the

Universal as the ground of the particular was A = B, thereby ensuring that there was nothing more in B that was not already in A. Rosenzweig thus notes that the same thought processes – which deprived the living God of life by the false rationalism and fear of God that had God as only being God were He not to bring His majesty down to Man – form the logic of Idealism: the Universal would not be Universal if it were to let the particular run free outside of its reign. Indeed, for Rosenzweig, what such thinking misses is that particulars become more integrated into Universals as they grow. Certainly not into the one Universal of the Idealist *logos;* rather, the particular's potencies, so open at birth, become channelled into the formations of its development as it moves into the geographical, historical, social, and economic formations that facilitate someone becoming whom he or she is. The particular is not merely the compliant material that receives its stamp from the Universal (it is alive), but something in which the line from particularity to universality always keeps its particularity: 'many roads lead from the parts to the whole; indeed, strictly speaking, each part, insofar as it is really part, really "individual," has its own road towards the whole, its own trajectory of descent.'[38] The particularity is always moving and thereby transforming the content and nature of the Universal.

As in Rosenzweig's exploration of the configuration of the metaphysical, his book on the metalogical is preliminary; it provides the formulation of an element, but an element severed from any links with the metaphysical or meta-ethical – an element, then, that is more real, more generative, than the vapid shadow of Idealist logic but less capable of the reality it could be when open to sources outside itself. What Rosenzweig is saying, then, is that just as the metaphysics of antiquity was one in which God was closed off from the World and Man, the metalogical view of the ancient world is likewise limited by its closures. This is true, in different ways, for East and West. In ancient Greece, the philosophical contribution to cosmology, at the microcosmic *and* macrocosmic levels, was thwarted by the limits of the metalogical. So this is an interesting move that Rosenzweig makes: in the introduction to *The Star* he had sought to establish the metalogical by freeing it from the All and by making it only one of the three elements of the All; whereas in his analysis of the metalogical in Book Two of Part One, he is showing how, in the cosmological thought of Plato and Aristotle, the vestiges and limitations of the metalogical still shape their thought:

Even Plato and Aristotle do not teach, within the world, any emanatory or an active relationship of any sort between idea and phenomenon, concept and thing, genus and individual, or however else the opposition is seen. Rather, here there appear the remarkable notions that things 'imitate' the idea, that they 'look' toward it, 'long' for it, 'develop' toward it, which is not cause but 'end.' The idea rests. The phenomenon moves toward it. It seems to be exactly the meta-logical relationship.

The difficulties unresolved by the ancients are obvious in this interpretation. They are expressed in part in Aristotle's polemics against his master, but he himself did not master them. Against Plato's theory of Ideas, Aristotle in effect sets in motion the idea of infinity; beyond concept and thing, a concept of the possible relationship of the thing to the concept must again be posited and so on. But against this concept of infinity, the metalogical view of the totality of the configured world in general is disarmed, and Aristotle's cosmos is just as finite as Plato's is. It is precisely there that we see the limit of the isolated metalogical idea. Aristotle evades the problem by a *salto mortale* into the metaphysical. For his divine 'thinking of thinking' is just thinking only of thinking; that it might also be thinking of the unthinkable is expressed and fundamentally rejected; divine thinking can only think the 'best,' that is to say only itself. But this a-cosm of his metaphysics makes it incapable of exactly what it must realize. It must – as doctrine of final cause – present the principle of the world. But as a result of its purely metaphysical essence, it is a principle only to itself.[39]

So for Rosenzweig, the metalogical world is a closed world. And this is as evident in the metaphysics of the ancients, which is a closed metaphysics, as in the enclosed mythic world of antiquity and in the art of antiquity, which depicts humanity as closed off from the love of (the) God(s). The comparison in the above quotation between Plato and Aristotle and the emanationist theory – which had not been developed until neo-Platonism had absorbed the radiances of Jewish and Christian thought during the Roman Empire – well illustrates for Rosenzweig the blockages in ancient cosmology that prevent it from being ingested and revived on its own terms, without a radical transformation, into a more vital cosmology. Among ancient philosophies, the emanationist theory is the only one that finds its developed form in the neo-Platonist systems – most notably those of Plotinus and Proclus, by way of the early Christian Gnosticism of Basilides and Valentinus, and earlier in the Jewish philosopher Philo of Alexandria. The dialectics among neo-Platonism, Christian Gnosticism, and early Christian thought are important ones; and while, yet again, they are dealt with rather sketchily in *The Star*, I think they serve as a powerful confirmation of Rosenzweig's broader argument about how the Jewish eternal fire radiates throughout the world thanks to the spread of Christianity. It is not that the emanationist theory is correct, for Rosenzweig; indeed, for him it is not. But as he shows in Part Two, Book One ('Creation'), in his further exploration of Idealism, it is at least a serious attempt to account for the miracle of life that occurs within Creation. But for Rosenzweig, because of the limitations arising from the strictly metalogical purview of the ancient philosophers, emanationist theory is incapable of bringing its elements into a sufficiently integrative combination. Its failure, for Rosenzweig, is symptomatic of a world that encloses itself because it is unable to redeem itself.

Later, of course, the Greek world is redeemed. Aristotle's cosmology will be redeemed in the Middle Ages. Though it will be condemned to death again, and Plato's Pythagorean views will be redeemed in their deployment against Aristotle. Likewise, Stoic and Epicurean mechanistic ideas will be redeemed. The Renaissance is itself part of the redemptive process of Christianity's march through time and space. This is not simply, as Burckhardt and Nietzsche argue, a return of the pagan; rather, it is a redemption whose roots are in the Christian mission itself. Rosenstock-Huessy draws attention to this aspect of Christianity in its redemption of Greece during the Renaissance:

> Jacob Burckhardt never became tired of showing that Greek thinkers could not change the slightest little thing in antiquity. There was no superstition lacking; thinkers name no children. They thought of the good, the beautiful, the divine, the true as ideas, with the transformation through times and spaces of mankind. Only 1500 years later, after the word again had become flesh and the four acts of incarnation had rolled by, thus not until the Renaissance of Greek thinkers from 1500 to 1900 did the books of the Greek 'thinkers' live as forceful political movements. Because the word was in the position to become flesh, modern political forms were able to emerge out of Greek thought.[40]

To repeat, what is happening here is the application of Jewish means to Creation itself, and that application involves selection and rejection – the No – of Redemption.

Earlier we referred to Rosenzweig's description of his methodology as 'absolute empiricism.' This points clearly to his ability to delineate patterns within the lived horizon of a group and within a philosophy or body of belief. His ability to do this has rarely been matched; ironically, given Rosenzweig's antipathy toward Hegel, it must be said that in the history of philosophy, Hegel is one of the very few to also possess this gift.

What we wish to emphasize here is that this reconstitution of the ancients reflected the kind of pluralism or polytheism that is widely celebrated today; what is being celebrated, understandably so, is the fecundity of Creation and the marvels of cultural achievement. However, both Rosenzweig and Rosenstock-Huessy wish to alert their readers to the ground on which this pluralism has taken hold. The deployment of counterfactuals in our reading of history is so widespread that it is barely noticed, especially in politically driven discourses that wish to redeem the repressed (as I have already indicated, a thoroughly Christian gesture, though made with Idealist means). That said, Rosenzweig and Rosenstock-Huessy were not interested in counterfactuals, but in forces of activation – that is, in real powers as they appear, die, return to life, and are replenished. And both Rosenzweig and Rosenstock-Huessy saw that this unified approach to life, to which they both subscribed, was Jewish in origin rather than Greek.

The living God, living World, and living Self are allied by their commitment to life – that is, to a particular *modus operandi* in which each is elevated. Through that mutual elevation, different spheres of life across time and space also are activated and energized.

As we suggested earlier, idolatry occurs whenever the god served merely *consumes* life and does not *bestow* more life on the World or the Self; *or*, when the form of the World thereby made does not replenish the Self or God; *or*, when the Self formed does not replenish and revitalize the World and God. The forces from metaphysical to metalogical to meta-ethical are correctly aligned when the triad itself is expansive. In antiquity, however, the metalogical element of the proto-cosmos, like the metaphysical one, failed to contribute to the kind of expansiveness that Rosenzweig seeks. Its lacks were conspicuous in the role of art, in the diminished lives of slaves and women, in wars among city-states, and so forth. This was evident, for Rosenzweig, in how the relationship between social particular and social genus was 'solved' in the ancient world at the level of social formation; that is, the solution was one of absorption and diminishment, in much the same manner as ancient gods absorbed the energies of their followers at least in the face of the genus. Even in Judaism, until God provides the sacrifice, there is the following [mis]understanding about the relationship between Man and God:

> People, State and all forms of community that Antiquity knew are lions'
> dens: the individual clearly sees the footprints going in, but none coming

out. Strictly speaking, man comes up against the community as a whole, of which he is only a part, and well he knows it. These entireties of which he is only a part, these genera of which he is only a representative, reign as absolute powers over his moral life, although they are in themselves in their turn only particular cases of the genus State or the genus people in general. Just by reason of this being closed to the outside, and this unconditional characteristic within, those communities become the singular essence configured throughout, which a little careful reflection will inevitably compare with the work of art.[41]

Rosenzweig compares modern representative states that have been Christianized – and thus, for Rosenzweig, touched by the living God of the Jews – with ancient states, pointing out that in the former, representation is undertaken in order to increase the power of individuals, whereas those individuals disappeared into ancient states, much like bricks into a building: 'only a body can have organs; a building has only parts.'[42] Though he was not addressing totalitarian modern states, it is clear from his analysis – and Rosenstock-Huessy expressed this on many occasions[43] – that totalitarian states reproduced the idolatry of the ancient world: self-consciously so in fascist regimes, and increasingly so in the evolution of Leninism into Stalinism.

We have emphasized that modern cosmology resuscitates elements of ancient Greek cosmology on the basis of a range of concepts (notably 'the infinite') that are still 'locked up' in metalogical reasoning. In a similar vein, modern non-totalitarian and non-dictatorial states are a fusion of factors. These include constitutional forms (a point correctly made by Rosenstock-Huessy in 'Polybius, or the Reproduction,' which was included in *Out of Revolution* and *I Am an Impure Thinker*) and political representation and rights, which have grown on Christian soil. Rosenzweig is well aware of this, and throughout *The Star* he discusses Christianity's role in taking pagan forms of art and the state and reinvigorating them spiritually.

This combination of liberty and universalization, this capacity to see the world as something that should be the kingdom, a place where the plenitude of the Self meets the plenitude of God – a capacity that is so essential to Judaism and Christianity – is for Rosenzweig precisely what is absent in the disconnected metalogical view of the world. Hence even in most universal form, the empire of Augustus, the world remains 'a closed world, a world appeased and satisfied in itself.'[44] The metalogical view of the world was felt by the ancients themselves to be a massive constraint. This was visible, Rosenzweig points out, in the antics of the Sophists, who wished to assert the sovereign power of man; Protagoras's 'Man Is the Measure' was the formulation of this aspiration. However, the Sophists' revolution had no real effect on the development of the ancient world.

Regarding the 'non-plastic world' of Asia, Rosenzweig draws attention to those characteristics of Eastern thought that he thinks indicate how the world was prevented from rising to the glory that Redemption would have enabled. Thus he is struck by the Buddhist doctrine of 'Maya,' which makes of world a mere illusion; and by the caste system of the Brahmins, which, much like ancient states, swallows one up so that it 'includes' someone, 'not like a community, but like a universality that is superior to him.'[45] Life in such cases, according to Rosenzweig, is thwarted because the miracle of the particular is dissolved into the *explanandum* before its particularity can flourish. What need is there of flourishing if life is Maya, if a life is there to serve a hierarchy, or if the world generated by knowledge and desire is being generated by something that would be better done without? This is why, for him, there is a certain sameness about Eastern thought, a sameness that he sees in the Buddhist dissolution of the Self in all things, in the oneness of the Brahmin, in the world hymns that 'begin in the greatest individuality and die away in colourless universality,'[46] in Indian tales of the origin of the world, tales that give birth to a 'a legion of juxtaposed, learned pseudo-myths, each of which, under cover of a legend of origin, actually developed a system of categories, water, wind, breath, fire and all the rest,' which 'are not elements of a reality, but ways of explaining the world away and thereby taking us away from the world.'[47]

Also, for him, the Confucian tradition of ancestral worship becomes more abundant than meaningful as a redemptive path, sharing as it does the polytheistic tendency toward proliferating and diffusing life's powers and human cognizance of them. Likewise he tells us that Lao-Tse's series of negations, 'not to rule, not to dominate, not to prescribe nor proscribe in overly busy calculations, but to be oneself, like the root of things, without doing and without not-doing,' do not provide a basis for the second triad that concerns him.

Just as the metaphysical and metalogical blocks of the world remain, for Rosenzweig, mere elements until they are conjoined by an approach to life that can see their interconnections and thus fathom their potentialities in relation to one another, the disconnected meta-ethical view of life is ultimately frustrating. Thus depictions of the proto-cosmic view of the Self are but variants of the problem with the proto-cosmic view of God and the World. The symbolic formulation of the meta-ethical understanding of the Self is B = B, a formulation that encapsulates the specificity accompanying the Self as closed off from the radiance of the Universal, or A. Recall that while the metalogical view allows for humanity reaching up to God, it does not work both ways. One is reminded of Homer's depiction of Zeus in the *Iliad* when he pities the carnage and brutality of men in battle. He knows that humans are there for the gods' pleasure, and he is forceful and powerful; nevertheless, he must weep and stand by and give way to fate's decree when his son Sarpedon is slain by Patroclus.

As Rosenzweig notes, that the Self can also be seen as something in the World was behind the Kantian insight of the dual Self as *noumenon* or mere Idea, and as empirical or what appears in space and time. In Rosenzweig's view, however, Kant does not develop this insight's potential because he loses sight of the Self at the very moment he makes it: for the Self is, after all, experienced *by* the Self *as* a Self. At this stage, he is not talking of its richness or paucity – only its facticity, which as Self is to find itself with limited freedom, a 'finite freedom': 'not freedom for action, like God's, but a freedom for willing; not free power, but free will.'[48] The Self's nature is, for Rosenzweig, a defiance: the Self is capable of becoming a fuller, more real Self and not simply remain aware of its brute and suffering animality. The Self must become a Self, instead of remaining the raw presence and potentiality of a creature, mere personality; 'the Self is the lonely man in the hardest sense of the world. The "political animal" is the personality.'[49]

> The less he is still individuality and the harder he becomes as character, the more he becomes Self. This is the transformation of the essence which Goethe achieves in *Faust*: at the beginning of Part II, he has already lost his rich individuality and just for this reason appears in the last act as a character of most perfect hardness and utmost defiance, truly as Self a faithful image of the ages of life.[50]

For Rosenzweig, the history of the World, the history of God's Revelation, and the history of the Self form a unity that is the openness of each to each and that gives the Self its genuine humanity – that is, it is a fulfilment of the potentials generated by loving openness, as opposed to the rawness of the consciousness of its animality and location. That triple-history is the result of a dynamism and openness that develops only after we abandon the disconnections of the sort that we find in the meta-ethical, metaphysical, and metalogical elements of antiquity: in China and India. Just as the living God remains imprisoned by the metalogical view of the God, and just as the living God strives to break out of the tombs of disbelief in Him – tombs that are part and parcel of the metaphysics of the mythical, the ancestral, Nirvana, and the Tao – Rosenzweig depicts the Self's struggle to be more than the meta-ethical understanding enables it to be.

The meta-ethical concept of the Self is limited, then, according to Rosenzweig, by its succumbing completely either to the particular forms that absorb it; or to a complete dissolution or act of negation – a retreat to the nothing out of which it emerges; or to tragedy. None of these is, for him, a happy solution. Nietzsche had sung the praises of the *Book of Manu*, finding in it a model for future philosophers who wished to re-establish an order of rank dedicated to the cultivation of higher types, and hence too the deployment of lower types as the scaffold on which these others could rise. Rosenzweig saw in Vedic and Hindu literature – and the quotation below suggests that he had the *Book of Manu* very much in mind – a spirit that petrified the Self's development precisely because it preserved a caste system that was held together by staunch hierarchical relations, and also because he saw the specificity and range of controls over human behaviour to retain the social order as utterly incompatible with the redeeming, loving God. That Hinduism has itself been forced to confront these issues in modern times indicates that it, too, has been swept up by the long waves of revolutionary forces of the Messianic dimensions of the West and their disruptive course:

> India never arrived at the identity of the Self that displays its defiance in all the characters; the Indian man stayed stuck in the character; there is no world more rigid from the point of view of character than that of Indian poetry; there is no human ideal which stays as much a prisoner of all articulations of the natural character as does the Indian ideal; it is certainly not only to the sexes, or the castes, but even to the ages of life that a particular law of life applies; the highest duty is that man obey this law of his particularity; not everyone has the right or even perhaps the duty to become a saint; quite on the contrary, it is forbidden to the man who has not yet established a family; even saintliness is here one particularity among others, whereas the heroic is the same universal necessity of life for everyone.[51]

He sees Buddhism's reactions to the possibility of the Self's development as a retreat from the grim prospects that seem to lie before itself.

Yet Buddhism, in its own way, is a liberation from the available stultifying possibilities offered by the Hindu caste system. But for Rosenzweig, the historical context of Buddhism's spiritual positiveness is offset by the solution it adopts – not a shaping of a people *qua* people determined to go into the world to energize itself and its neighbours in love, but a retreat, at least for those who follow the way of the Buddha. For Rosenzweig, Buddhism's very prospect of reaching out for development and fulfilment is overlooked in favour of the solace of the nothingness of nirvana, which, from the perspective of a thinker who is pursuing a way of Self-making in which love recharges life, is tantamount to preferring death. (Here, too, one might contrast this with Rosenstock-Huessy's point that, placed in a different social context with a different set of tasks, Buddhism's way is capable of overcoming the depletion of powers caused by the West's frenzied and voracious appetites.)

Rosenzweig is propelled by the same drive to life and by the same rejection of nihilism that one finds in Nietzsche, which is why it is not surprising that both view Buddhism as a kind of nihilism. Something similar to Buddhist nihilism is, as we saw above, also found by Rosenzweig to exist in Chinese indigenous traditions and in the 'self-concealment' of the follower of Lao-Tse, whose 'love is like himself nameless and hidden.'[52] As with the Buddhist reaction to Hinduism, the Taoist reaction to Confucianism, for Rosenzweig, carries in its path of flight the all-encompassing totality of the structure it wishes to escape from. The exodus of the Jews was not primarily a refashioning of the Self and the creation of a new type in an environment in which selves were like bricks to be placed in service to the imperial mortar. It was a *physical* exodus that gave the Jews opportunities for re-creation that never could have occurred had they remained within the pyramidal powers of the Egyptian Empire. Buddhists and Taoists were certainly able to turn their souls in another direction, but this constituted a 'dropping out' rather than the creation of another kingdom. That the Jews would also build another kingdom, before eventually being fated to be kingdomless in this world, is central to Rosenzweig's (pre-Holocaust/pre-Israel) vision.

Against these nihilistic traditions – nihilistic because they find the nothing as the aim of existence – Rosenzweig explores the tradition of the Near East, which, in the tale of Gilgamesh, provides us with our first example of tragedy. *The Epic of Gilgamesh* is, for Rosenzweig, a tale of the entrance into the Self, into its 'cries and silences.' According to Rosenzweig, tragedy is the expression of the enormity of the Self's predicament, which is a fundamental dissatisfaction with its metaphysical

and metalogical environment, a dissatisfaction with the lack of fulfilment and connection in one's inner and outer life:[53] 'By being silent, the
hero dismantles the bridge that links him to God and the world, and he
tears himself away from the landscapes of personality, which, through
the spoken word, marks out its limits and individualizes itself in the
face of others in order to climb into the icy solitude of the Self.' One is
trapped by forces from which there is no exit and which one realizes
exist only when it is too late.

Tragedy is valuable for Rosenzweig in a way that the contemplative/
meditative strategies of Buddhism, Taoism, and yogic practices are
not: because it expresses the intolerableness of the absence of redemption, whereas Buddhism and so on simply cut off the desire to seek
redemption.

I repeat again that none of the traditions that Rosenzweig is discussing here is interested in pursuing what Rosenzweig wants. In the case
of Buddhism, for example, it is obvious that Rosenzweig – and Jews
generally – are caught up in Maya, and the Self he is seeking is a Self
whose personality is fully developed. Buddhism traditionally never
wanted to find such a Self; and from a Buddhist perspective, such a
search smacks of essentialism. Yet the Self that Rosenzweig has in mind
is not essentialized, for its fullness is meaningful only to the extent of
its openness to grace, to its refusal to be petrified through constant attendance to the loving God who ever demands new tasks of the Self.
While, then, Taoists and Buddhists – at least traditionally – do not want
what Rosenzweig seeks, Rosenzweig is polemical because he wants to
underscore for his readers the extent of his difference from them.

Let us return briefly to his discussion of tragedy, to highlight why
he thinks the Greeks are closer in spirit to the Jews – though nevertheless different from them. What strikes Rosenzweig about tragedy in its
various forms from Aeschylus through Sophocles to Euripides is that,
despite the formal transformations surrounding the drama and dramatic dialogue, the will remains enclosed; and unlike modern drama,
which involves a redemptive moment, a winning over, 'a bridge where
one will breaks and guides another,' there is 'no bridge to any outside,
even if this outside is another will.' Ancient tragedy displays the tragic
condition of the hero and simultaneously immortalizes that hero in
his or her suffering. The name Oedipus rings through the ages just as
Gilgamesh's name was writ on brick, and it draws the spectators, in
their fear and pity, deeper into their own Selves. Art brings depth to the
Self, but in his depiction of the meta-ethical and the tragic and artistic

nature of that aspect of the All, Rosenzweig deliberately accentuates what Idealists and moderns often fail to do: the limits of art. We will explore more fully later why Rosenzweig did not worship at the altar of art; here, though, let us anticipate his critique by showing how he designates its deficiency in the ancient world's conception of the Self:

> The realm of art provides the soil where the Self can grow everywhere; but every Self is again an entirely solitary singular Self; art nowhere creates a real plurality of Selves, although it creates everywhere for Selves the possibility of awakening: the Self that awakens knows still only of itself. In other words: in art's world of appearances, the Self remains always Self, it does not become – soul.[54]

The proto-cosmos that Rosenzweig depicts in the three books of Part One of *The Star* is, in sum, a depiction of 'three monisms'[55] – a 'polytheism,' a 'poly-omism,' and a 'polyanthroposism' – sundered and splintered, what he calls an 'orgiastic pell-mell of the possible.'[56] Another way of saying this is that the pagan world is rich in creative possibility but thwarted by the fact that there is another plane of life that it does not know how to access; its gods are as condemned to extinction just as its worlds and its Selves are condemned to nothingness (the East) or tragic isolation (antiquity). The facticity of the three elements nevertheless survives in the sciences of theology, psychology, and cosmology, which point toward the implacability of this original triad of Rosenzweig, whose three elements become manifest in the historical sequence of the gods that preceded antiquity, the Self formed in antiquity, and the World after the decline of antiquity.[57]

The first part of *The Star*, then, is a philosophical anthropology in which the irrational prototypes have become visible, as have the real historical limitations of their potencies as long as they remain sundered. But equally important are the limitations of the grounding fragments that the All of philosophy has allowed. Are God, Man, and World the only All that we are permitted to deploy philosophically in our desire to live as fully as possible? History shows us this is not so; the Jewish and Christian and – more problematically, as we will discuss below – Muslim peoples are living proof that they have been formed through their relationship to God: He reveals Himself to His creation, and in turn they act out of faith and hope in Redemption. Thus, too, the creations of these peoples – and they themselves, across the generations, as much as their works, are *creations* – are undeniably real. Reality is disclosed and generated not simply by thinking but also – as theologians know all too well – by faith.[58] This reality, which is demanded by the philosophical commitment to reality rather than by ideals and counterfactuals, is the basis of Rosenzweig's philosophy and also forms the basis for theology, in much the same way that God, Man, and World form the poles of the philosopher's All, having been freed from the Idealist 'block' in which they have been entrapped.

The symmetries between Parts One and Two of *The Star* continue with the shift of the ground that makes philosophy and theology, respectively, possible: the shift in philosophy from the philosopher's rational All to an All that reveals itself in the actual analysis of the original prototypic elements of theology, psychology, and cosmology has as its parallel the shift in theological ground. The traditional basis of faith had been the miracle, but theology became embarrassed by its former 'favourite child.' This embarrassment, Rosenzweig points out, was due largely to a fundamental change in the meaning of 'miracle'; nowadays it is akin to a magic trick, a shabby deception. Prior to the Enlightenment's paradigm shift whereby miracles came to be construed in a purely pagan manner, as things that violated nature's laws, 'the miraculous character of miracle rested . . . not on its divergence as regards the course of nature predetermined by laws, but on the fact that it was predicted. Miracle is essentially sign.'[59] The real miracle, for Rosenzweig, is not magic: 'magic and signs are on different planes.'[60] Hence the Torah demands the death of the sorcerer who 'attacks God's Providence and wants to snatch, bully and force from it, by trickery or by force, that which is unforeseen and unforeseeable of it, that which is willed by his own will.'[61] Theology has found itself so entangled by such misconceptions about its own powers that it has been duped by the 'paganizing' of the concept of the miracle.

At the time Rosenzweig was writing *The Star*, the pagan revival among the Christian peoples had released the cruel gods of the nations, which acted just as savagely as the gods depicted in Hesiod and Homer. The gods were entrapped in their 'furious self absorption,' to use Bernard Knox's apt description in his introduction to Robert Fagles's translation of the *Iliad*.[62]

For Rosenzweig, the pagan energies unleashed after the Great War were not an attractive proposition, and the desire for that unleashing suggested to him a miscomprehension of the struggle that was (and still is) required to give those energies more benign forms. Rosenzweig in *The Star* is appealing to precisely what fails to find a thorough articulation and enfleshment in the pagan view of world, viz., love at work from every source: creative love, revealing love, redeeming love. It does not mean – and this is very important – that individuals may not have heard and responded to the loving, living God.

> Should God have waited for Mount Sinai, or even Golgotha? No, as little as paths lead from Sinai or from Golgotha, on which He can be reached with certainty, so little can He have denied himself [the possibility of] encountering even the person who sought Him on the trails around Olympus. There is no temple built that would be so near Him that man might take comfort from that proximity, nor is there one so distant from him that His arm could not reach even there. There is no direction from which He could not come and none from which He had to come; there is no block of wood in which He may not once take up His dwelling and no psalm of David that always reaches His ear.[63]

But does His Revelation, which is 'always present,'[64] find peoples over great time spans – other than originally the Jews and then, problematically, Christians – gathered and formed by the double-triadic path? For Rosenzweig, the answer is clear: No. There is no anthropological or socio-historical evidence of such peoples, even if at times there were small groups that perhaps lived thus. Does being included in that formation make one a better person, less inclined to 'sin'? For Rosenzweig, the answer is again unequivocal: No. The history of the peoples of the path (the Christians) and the peoples in and of the fire (the Jews) is the history of their flights from Revelation as much as their response to God's commandment to love. But just as 'revelation does not destroy genuine paganism, the paganism of creation; it only lets the miracle of reversal and renewal occur within it,' so Jews and Christians – the latter thanks to their Jewish core if it does not completely relapse into paganism – find themselves mysteriously ever pulled back to God, whose call is registered in their circumstance, speech, and rituals, their very being. Rosenzweig's own return – like that of other contemporary German liberal Jews – to an understanding of the meaning of the Covenant and the role of the Jewish people within it, was living proof of this.

That love is as strong as death is what is revealed, and the law of love of the neighbour is the law that redeems the world. For our love reactivates what will bring back to life what has been dead. God is not love, as Rosenzweig reminds his readers, but He loves, He radiates – He is light or illumination that may even awaken love in the dead heart. Part

Two of *The Star* concerns itself mainly with the theology that breaks down into a delineation of the ways of the real Creator, Revealer, and Redeemer of the Jewish and Christian peoples and into the false or pseudo revelation of what is essentially a pagan view of creation power in the de-formed versions of Creation. According to Rosenzweig, the true theology is one that leads us to the truth that God is the truth; such a truth is not primarily cognitive but lived. Yet what can be cognized is the God that is not truth because of the truncated view of His nature, His world, and ultimately the selves He creates. The false theology, for Rosenzweig, can be detected by a closer inspection of how Creation and its Creator are represented in their ground. Rosenzweig provides the following definition of God as Creator, which forms the counterpole to limited, truncated, defective understandings of His nature: 'God the creator is essentially powerful. His creative work is therefore omnipotent, without being an arbitrary act. The God who is visible in creation can do all that he wills; but he wills only what he wills by nature. In this formula, which for us is so plainly obvious, all riddles are solved which the idea of creation, as far as God is concerned, could give rise to.'[65]

This definition of the essential attribute of God as power only truly holds when Creation is rightly understood in its fullest possible sense. In the first instance, that means that Creation is not a once and once only event but an ongoing process until the 'end of the world' or 'the end of times':

> The Creation of the world only needs to find its end in Redemption; only from there, or seen retrospectively, from whatever point such an end would be placed, and seen from there the creation of the world and absolutely be 'Creation out of nothing.' Facing this world the metalogical world view would really have to be 'nothing' that is to say something absolutely incomparable with the created world, something unbound, something which has disappeared along with its interests.[66]

Redemption is the promise of *Revelation*, that 'the world is destined from the beginning to come alive.'[67] The redemptive end – this full vitality where 'existence must be alive through and through'[68] is the 'Kingdom.' Perhaps an even better formulation of Redemption occurs in a lecture of Rosenstock-Huessy when he says: 'To buy back man from his falling into the worship of deader things, compared to more living processes, this is redemption.'[69]

What, then, Rosenzweig is invoking in the idea of the Kingdom is a particular way of seeing and being in life. It is not everyone's way. It is not a natural way. From the natural way of seeing things, it looks all wrong, and that is why Islam and the modern and the pagan conspire in their different ways to be rid of this nonsense (the modern)/infamy (Islam). But this madness is shared by Jew and Christian, and it is the madness of its perception of time and eternity, of past and future, and the integrity of things within eternity, and the futurity of things within the present. I say *madness* because it is an insight that requires the capacity to *see* eternity in the temporal through the coming true of the promise of Redemption:

> The Kingdom, the vitalization of existence, comes from the beginning; it is always coming. So its growth is necessary. It is always in the future – but in the future it is always. It is just as much present as in the future. Once and for all, it is not yet there. It is coming eternally. Eternity is not a very long time. But a tomorrow that just as well could be today. Eternity is a future. Which without ceasing to be future, is nevertheless present. Eternity is a today that would be conscious of being more than today. And to say that the Kingdom is eternally coming means that its growth is no doubt necessary, but that the rhythm of this growth is not definite. Or more exactly that the rhythm of this growth does not have any relationship to time. An existence that has once entered into the Kingdom cannot fall back outside again; it has entered under the sign of the once-and-for-all, it has become eternal.[70]

Eyes that are trained to see other things will not be able to see that something 'has entered under the sign of the once-and-for-all.' The transformation of the world through love, its great Redemption, is not something most people either see or believe in. The world contains enough regular catastrophes to confirm that no such process exists. But for Rosenzweig, the peoples that genuinely hearken to the revealer God and who see and live the path of the eternal configuration, who do not succumb to the isolation of the three towering elements of the proto-cosmic, who do not fall into the pagan traps of idolatry of the mind or idolatry of the state or idolatry of art or (as in Islam) idolatry of the simulacrum of Revelation, hasten to realize this kingdom by living in eternal anticipation of its arrival by already living in it ritualistically.

'The creature' is the name that Rosenzweig, like Rosenstock-Huessy and a number of their contemporaries, took as the appropriate one for this living component of Creation. To recognize oneself as creature is to recognize oneself part of continuous Creation and 'from its point of view being created would be self revealing as creature.'[71] The theological corollary of this act of recognition by the creature, for Rosenzweig, is 'the idea of divine Providence.' 'This providence renewed every morning is thus what is really meant in the idea of the creature.'[72] As creature there is a complete dependence upon Creator, and this is so for the whole of Creation, and for Rosenzweig this dependency is the fundamental meaning of providence. All creatures exist in need of the Creator. They are incapable without the Creator's presence, and His presence is always and everywhere, not only sometimes, not only for those who are brave, or morally good, or smart; intelligence, courage, even goodness are ways of viewing the relations between the gifts of God or the gods that, when seen as self-sufficient ends, are but pagan elevations of powers of the Self, and hence are delusions destined to lead to ruin.

The Creator's beneficence is for all creatures. Redemption is redemption of the Universal, not simply the particular. In fact, Redemption is thus because Creation itself is but a stage on the way to Redemption. If one fails to recognize this then one is working with a fundamentally deficient understanding of Creation. This, according to Rosenzweig, is blocked out in Islamic theology as well as in Idealistic theology. Leaving Islam aside until a later chapter, the basic problem with what he calls Idealist theology is that its various platforms to explain Creation – generation (Plato/Aristotle), emanation (the neo-Platonists), the Self of modern Idealism – have all failed, and thus Idealists have transposed their faith from logic and thinking to Spirit and art. They do this, Rosenzweig tells us, because they simply are not able to move deeply enough into Creation and enter into the revelatory and redemptive dimensions that ultimately give it its real meaning.

Creation, Revelation, and Redemption are each directed at a particular dimension of time: Creation, to the past – the world has been created; Revelation, to the eternal present; Redemption, to the outer limit of time, the future. As he says in the concluding section of Part Two, 'The Threshold,' the Book of Creation dealt 'more about the world, hidden in Providence and daily renewed, than about the Creator'; the Book of Revelation 'more about God's love than about love received by man'; and in the Book of Redemption, more about 'the act of love of man for the neighbour . . . than about the growing life of the world.'

And if . . . after the descent into the originally created primordial world and after that ascent through the manifest world, we then know which sight awaits us there. There we shall see man, born of woman, totally redeemed from all singularity and self-seeking into the created image of

God; the world, the world of flesh and blood, and stone and wood, totally redeemed from all thinglines into nothing but soul; and God redeemed from all the work of the six days of Creation and from all loving anxiety about our poor soul, as the Lord.[73]

The 'image of God,' 'soul,' and God Himself redeemed constitute what Rosenzweig calls 'the illumination.' In Creation itself, it might on first examination seem that these 'ends' are not evident. Certainly, if one simply delimits one's horizon to nature as such, this might well be the case. But as we have said, for Rosenzweig, our understanding of Creation itself is curtailed if we do not grasp that it is but a step on the way, a way that – as we have already suggested – is opened up to us, if we but pay attention, in the very structure of grammar itself.

The truth that is revealed is very simple and affirms that Creation does not stop with death. Yet again, I emphasize that there is nothing phantasmic or spectral in what Rosenzweig is saying; he is saying – or rather repeating, providing an exegesis of the formulation from the Song of Songs – that 'love is as strong as death.' As creatures, we find that death is everywhere around us, a promise and a certainty. We recall that in the very beginning of *The Star*, Rosenzweig had held that it was from the fear of death that philosophy had retreated into the All, had locked itself up in its own 'mind' and proceeded to develop and substitute essences for life. With its stories of immortality or essential materiality or reward in the afterlife, philosophy had found a series of manoeuvres to avoid death, to make it palatable through its denial. But, for Rosenzweig, the value of death is that it points to something more than Creation – to love itself, which takes us into the heart of the eternal present.

As keystone of Creation, death imprints everything created with the indelible stamp of its condition of creature, with the words 'has been.' But love declares war on it. Love knows only the present. It lives only out of the present, aspires only to the present. The keystone of the dark vault of Creation becomes the foundation stone of the bright house of Revelation. For the soul, Revelation is the lived experience of a present that, though resting on the existence of the past, does not dwell in it; on the contrary, this present walks in the light of divine countenance.[74]

That love is the decisive factor in Revelation simultaneously indicates the potential of the World, the Self, and God and His meaning. This last point is extremely important for appreciating why the God of

Revelation, for Rosenzweig, must not be confused with other 'Creator' Gods who can thus be termed living gods. But this God is full of a particular promise to the World and to the Self, and to simply assume that all gods make such a promise, or that all 'religions' are based on this same promise, is to betray a profound confusion about what God and gods do and how our capacities are developed in service to what we worship and love. Liberty first appeared in the West in the form of religious tolerance, as an act of desperation and necessity when Christendom itself could not find sufficient consensus about the will of God. That atheism would appear to be a more peaceful prospect than faith was drawn to the public's attention by Pierre Bayle; while the movements of pantheism and deism, the predecessors of modern atheism, became the 'natural religions' of philosophers and revolutionaries who wanted to free Christendom from political strife and to awaken humanity to the 'self-evident truths' of the equality of God's children.

The liberal pluralistic faith that is now as 'self-evident' as deism was to Thomas Jefferson, contains however, one major defect – it assumes that all wish for the same World and for the same Self. The God worshipped is the cipher to the World, and the Self made for our will is responsive and not – as the German Idealists held – creative in itself. Now the God of freedom and equality and the I and tolerance and mutual respect and social justice may be a well-meaning God, but it is a relatively young God. And though its characteristics are discernible offshoots from the older creator, revealer, redemptive God, its differences from the God of Jews and Christians is conspicuous in its lack of love. Such a God is definitely not a Lord, in some circles a She, incapable of entering into a relationship, more an idea than a person, and rarely referred to as a God – so it seems that the appropriate designation for this God is 'It.'

In love, the lovers dissolve and become not a nothing, but something much different and much more than they were originally. The God of love is that power which takes whoever is capable of receiving His love beyond all other attachments. This is why for Rosenzweig, the Jewish faith is not attached to state or tongue; rather, it is ever in, and ready for, God's loving acts. And that is why even the real Christian cannot love his or her nation or culture or class or race and so on as God. The God of liberal pluralism wants all people to hold such groupings, insofar as they are capable of conforming to equality, which cannot be done where privilege reigns. But the venerability of the past, of an origin, of a bond that ties – this is pagan, and if worshipped too much is always ruinous. God binds but He also breaks bonds. He rules over the living and the dead because death is intrinsic to His way: there can be no Creation without death, nor Redemption. And He demands death of habits, of entire lifeways or cultures. Death is the condition of Redemption. Again, but what of the Jew? Is the Jew not the ultimate example of holding on to tradition? And here is a central paradox of Rosenzweig's: the Jewish tradition is the tradition that is outside of history, that is ever prepared for the eternal, while it lives historically, but it lives to respond to the present and it can serve the world in which it exists – thus Rosenzweig could be a German patriot, loyal but not fanatical, because as much as he served a worldly power to the extent required, he saw that that worldly power, and any service to it, was always inferior to the power of the living, loving God.[75]

As we saw in our discusssion of Creation, the eternal God as depicted by Rosenzweig is all-powerful and providential, a continuous creator – but He is also the God of Revelation who loves, and this love must be appreciated for what it is and not simply assumed to be something that all Gods promise. Indeed, in Rosenzweig's thought it is important to appreciate the strangeness of such a gesture – a strangeness that may not be so conspicuous to peoples whose life-worlds have been shaped by this God whose shards are widely dispersed, albeit unconsciously, in their hearts and minds. 'All the demands put on the concept of the Revealer converge toward love: the love of the lover, not that of the beloved. Only the love of the lover and this giving of self once again in every moment, only this love gives itself in love.'[76]

If one wishes to serve a God who does not love like this, then one is not serving the God that Rosenzweig holds to be the God of Revelation, and one will thus not be open to Revelation. For it is not a question of saying that this or that group should be punished or despised or harmed or treated as second-rate because they do not serve this God: none of these things have anything to do with why Rosenzweig is writing *The Star* – though he thinks that groups are punished and ruined by the very forces they worship; indeed, these things have to do with the politics of those who do not serve the loving God or who know what the loving God demands. But to speak the truth of what the loving God is and in what that love consists is for Rosenzweig the only possible way one can reveal His truth, which is 'nothing other than the love with which he loves us.'[77] To put this another way, Rosenzweig has nothing in common with political liberalism because he most certainly thinks there is a God who is the true God and a way that is the way of truth, and that not all ways lead to that true way (nor is his teaching strictly speaking a politically conservative one – it is not a political teaching at all). But the true way for the Jew, as opposed to the Christian traveller, is to live ever in the moment of God's love, and that means not mistaking Him or His love for someone or something else:

> The love of the lover is implanted in the moment of its origin, and because it is so, it must deny all other moments, it must deny all of life; in its essence, it is unfaithful, for its essence is in the moment; and so, in order to be faithful, it must renew itself every moment, and every moment must become the first glance of love. Only through this totality in every present moment can it grasp the whole of created life, but through this, it really can do it; it can do it by traversing this whole life with ever new meaning and by shining its rays and its life upon now this and now that single thing – a progress that begins anew every day, and never needs to come to its end; at every moment, because it is wholly present, it thinks it has reached the highest beyond which there is none higher – and yet, each new day it learns again that it has never loved as much as today the part of life which it loves; every day loves a little more that which it loves. This constant increase in the form of permanence in love, in that and because it is the most extreme non-permanence and its fidelity is devoted solely to the present, singular moment: from the deepest infidelity, and from this alone, it can thus become permanent fidelity; for only the non permanence of the moment renders it capable of living every moment as new and thus of carrying the flame of love through the vast nocturnal-and-twilight-kingdom of created life. It increases because it does not want to cease being new; it wants always to be new in order to be able to be permanent; it can only be permanent by living entirely in the non-permanent, in the moment, and it must be permanent so that the lover may not be merely the empty bearer of an ephemeral emotion, but living soul. This, too, is the way God loves.[78]

And in another passage, he emphasizes that 'love is not attribute, but event'; its fecundity, eternal presence, and continuous dimension is 'as strong as death.' The nature of His love makes this God what he is as opposed to another God:

> 'God loves' does not mean that love belongs to him like an attribute, like the power to create for instance; love is not the fundamental form, the solid, immovable form of his countenance of the dead person, but the evanescent, never exhausted change of expressions, the always new

light that shines upon the eternal features . . . 'God loves': this is purest presence whether it is going to love, or even whether it has loved –
what does love itself know of this? It is enough for it to know one thing:
that it loves. It does not extend into the immensity of infinity, like the attribute; knowledge and power are omniscience and omnipotence; love
is not all love; Revelation does not know of any father who is universal
love; God's love is always wholly in the moment and at the point where
it loves; and it is only in the infinity of time, step by step, that it reaches
one point after the next and permeates the totality with soul. God's love
loves whom it loves and where it loves; no question can touch it, for each
question will one day have its answer in the God loves, too, even the questioner who is forsaken by God's love. God always loves only whom and
what he loves; but what separates his love from an 'all-love' is only a 'not-
yet'; it is only 'not yet' that God loves everything besides what he already
loves. His love traverses the world from an always new impulse. It is always in the today and entirely in the today, but every dead yesterday and
tomorrow are one day swallowed into this triumphant today; this love is
the eternal victory over death; the Creation which death finishes and completes cannot resist it; it must surrender to it at every moment and thus
also ultimately in the plentitude of all moments, in eternity.[79]

This love that is revealed as what overcomes death, this love that is
ever present, moves. And this same movement is required in Redemption, this triple-Redemption of God, Man, and World in which God
finds His fulfilment by bringing 'the day of the world to a close beyond
Creation and Redemption': 'Man and world fade out in Redemption,
God completes himself . . . God becomes that which the human spirit,
in its temerity, constantly sought everywhere and affirmed everywhere,
yet without ever having found it, for this was not yet: the One and the
All.'[80] But such a Redemption, the completion, requires that God be
loved and that His world likewise be loved. The lack of Redemption is
the lack of love's fulfilment, love's not yet being completed. In this respect, there can be no Redemption without the Self's openness to God's
love and the Self's willing participation in furthering God's love in the
world. God's love is a present for the soul, but the Self that is closed
in on itself is not open to receive that gift which enables its growth.
Yet God's own completion requires that its beloved recognize His love.
Again, it needs to be stressed that this way of seeing things is far from a
universally acknowledged way of seeing the relationship between Creator and creature; but it *is* Rosenzweig's, and he sees it as an essential

part of the redemptive story of the Jewish and Christian peoples. Thus he writes of the creature's faith in God's love being

> the silent brightness of an immense Yes, where the love of the lover, which always denies itself, finds that which it could not find within itself: affirmation and duration. The faithful belief of the beloved acquiesces to the love of the lover, bound to the moment, and reinforces it so far as to make it a lasting love. This is the counterpart of love: the faith of the beloved in the lover. The faith of the soul testifies, in its faithfulness, to the love of God, and it gives to it a permanent being. If you testify to me, then I shall be your god, and otherwise not – these are the words that the Master of the Kabbalah puts into the mouth of the God of love.[81]

Only by being responsive to the loving God can the soul be open to love's redemptive power as a force that is as strong as death. Thus, 'when the soul confesses before the face of God and with this confesses and thus attests God's being, then only does God, too, the manifest God, acquire being: "When you confess me, then I am."'[82]

The God of love, then, is the God revealed, the God known by the hearts of His faithful to be the condition of their love, and known to be real by virtue of His love and by the life that is lived in that condition of love. The Redemption of the World, the Redemption of the Self, and the Redemption of God Himself are not three separate processes but one and the same process.

The three original irreducibles of God, Man, and World, which as we have seen may be overcome in God's completion, can not be overcome in their origin; they are the past that cannot be eradicated or escaped. What in pagan traditions remain ensconced in separateness or lead to the ultimate affirmation of the I (modern Idealism and modern bourgeois society) or God's implacable majesty (Islam), are for Rosenzweig vitally interdependent in the triadic axes of Creation, Revelation, and Redemption of biblical peoples so that the Self is redeemed by God if it is but open to God. The World is redeemed by the Self that transfers the love of God into loving acts of the neighbour, to each and every neighbour, not just the beautiful or good ones, not the ones of one's own clan or even of one's own faith, but *all* ones.[83] The Redemption of the World is the charging of life with love, and it requires that each creature be loved, which is what the God of living love reveals, and that that creature love in turn; the commandment to love one's neighbour is the commandment 'that accompanies all the single commandments and that alone removes from them the rigidity of laws and makes them living commandments.'[84]

The redemption of the World, then, is not one that skips groups or generations, not one that can be based on the omission of this one or that one, not one that can be based on the sacrifice of the present for the future, as Nietzsche's Zarathustra calls for (thus does Rosenzweig see him as zealot and sinner in one).[85] Indeed, Rosenzweig was acutely aware of the hunger for the kingdom, the Messianic drive that could so easily take on Gnostic turns and create hell on earth because the Redemption of the world that can only be built upon neighbourly love becomes divorced from the source of its possibility turning into a tyrannical imposition undoing the very goal it seeks to realize. As he says of the three towering forces of modern political thought: 'Liberty, equality, fraternity – changed from heartfelt words of faith into the slogans of the times and were taken into in the inert world with blood and tears, with hate and ardent passion, in battles that have not ended.'[86]

This, then, is what Rosenzweig offers his readers – a look into the meaning of the Jewish God, the Jewish world, and the Jewish Self. He does it through a sequence of comparisons, comparisons developed through the construction of the forms that he sees become whole – Jewish – or at some crucial point thwarted. Christianity is limited by its endless attachment to time, though this attachment to time is also part of God's plan. This aspect of God's plan would be the focus of Rosenstock-Huessy's work. And it would be this aspect that is responsible for what on first inspection seems – and indeed is in many ways – the opposite of Rosenzweig. That God, like life itself, commands, works, and instructs through paradox is not something unknown or ever denied by these inimical co-workers.

6 Rosenstock-Huessy's Incarnatory Christianity

Just as Rosenzweig's writing all revolved around the meaning and truth of Redemption as a force in the world and his main focus was (the peoples of) Redemption – those who embody it (Jews), those who strive for it (Christians), those who parody it (Muslims), and those who lack it (the rest) – Rosenstock-Huessy's writings all revolve around the prospect of salvation over time, a providential reading of history or *Heilsgeschichte*. And for him, 'human history . . . is a process of the salvation of the world and the conversion of the pagans by the Word.'[1] This sentence sums up why he is a Christian and why he thinks that universal history has its basis in the Christian faith.

Before addressing in detail Rosenstock-Huessy's account of Christianity, I think it important to make some more general statements about two closely related concepts – sin and providence – that are so important not only in Rosenzweig and Rosenstock-Huessy (and his interpretation of the meaning of the total revolutions of the last millennium), but also in Judaism and Christianity generally. In the modern era, sin and providence are usually treated as belonging exclusively to theology. But this fails to appreciate that these 'names' were not 'invented' by theologians or a priestly caste (contrary to the Enlightenment story of religion as the invention of a class of clever deceivers). Rather, the names referred to experiences of everyday life, and indeed there would have been neither Judaism nor Christianity had people not had these experiences.

First, sin. Given our earlier comments about morality, it might not be surprising that I suggest that sin should not be confused with what – at least in the mechanistic and post-mechanistic philosophies – we usually mean by immorality. Once again, the point is clear if we proceed by way of a comparison with Kant. Kant had so infused morality with intention that he insisted that consequences are irrelevant to morality. Not all modern moral theory is Kantian, but Kant's move is in keeping with the elevation of the sovereignty of the Self and its freedom as a great modern moral value. The great divide that separates the ancient understanding of sin from the modern understanding of morality is obvious to every modern adult whose education has been primarily secular and who opens the Bible for the first time to find a morally repellent God ruling the show: He not only destroys entire cities and peoples, but on one occasion even destroys almost the entire Creation. He also punishes children for the sins of the father; and on a smaller scale, he destroys Job's life on nothing more than a bet to prove a point. When William Empson completely bowdlerizes Milton by making *Paradise Lost* a mighty act of subversion of a cruel and tyrannical God, he is being a modern moralist, one who claims that Milton is one too.[2] Except that Milton saw the world through the Bible, not through moral concepts of desert and deservingness, and he saw the greatest of sins as pride, with pride's central act being the Self's divinization – all of which is to say, that Milton thought in contrary ways to the modern.[3]

If we want to understand the biblical God, we first need think of how life is actually experienced instead of how we want it to be – that is, not how it would be if it conformed to how reason would make it, if reason were given a chance. Only when we drop those concepts that don't tell us about life as it is, but rather about life as it would be if it were humanist and 'reasonable,' is it possible for us to see that what human beings do in their selfishness and indifference is indeed something that is paid for by their children and grandchildren, irrespective even of how 'pure' their intentions were. We would also then concede that entire peoples do indeed perish if they lack the powers to persist into the future, if their actions corrupt and corrode. Sin is, *inter alia*, that which depletes the powers that give us future, and its consequences drag all of us, the righteous *and* the unrighteous, into its evil maw. The righteous are 'saved' in the future of the living who honour and still take nourishment from them, but rarely in the catastrophe of the present. That is how powerful evil is. Where people are not given the opportunity to be unrighteous, where they are victims, there may be a greater chance of finding the righteous, but evil sullies almost everything. That is why when Abraham was challenged by God to find fifty righteous people in Sodom, he could not do so. Evil is viral. Human beings, in the main, flourish or perish as communities; and even in flourishing communities, the broken form micro-communities, which unattended (i.e., unloved and left alone) produce damaged souls that 'break in' to the safer and more lovable worlds of the 'blessed.' That was, I think, the point of the book and recent film *The Reader*, which generated so much misplaced moral criticism. Schlink was not trying to exonerate Hannah, who as a young woman had been a brutal prison guard, because she was illiterate; what *The Reader* powerfully demonstrated instead is that people can easily slip into the machinations of the world's evil before they have any idea that they have done so, thus throwing away their lives along with the lives of those they have helped destroy. This was one of the great lessons of the Holocaust that took so long for people to see – that it was ordinary people who did the most heinous things, people who in another social environment would never have dreamed that they would be complicit in such evil. That was why, after the Second World War, so many Germans were in complete denial about their complicity in Hitler's Germany. Evil makes accomplices of all but the most righteous – it 'infects' the young and the innocent before they have any idea of who or what they are. Thus does a community, no less a creature than a single person,[4] become a raving beast and its members bestial members of a single organism.

The moralist strategy of dealing with evil is to try to stop the possibility of evil before it happens and to invoke the just law after if happens. But the hiatus between law and morality, as well as the hiatus between the law's intention and the dirty penumbra of its application, are interstices where evil ever grows. The problem is not (*contra* the philosophers) that people do not have a good enough moral theory to guide them; rather, it is the threefold one that we constantly do not *know* enough about, or do not *care* enough about, or do not have sufficient *control* over, what we are doing. And no amount of saying we should will change this. Very often one of these lacks (e.g., lack of care) is closely associated with suffering, of people suffering so much that to escape their pain they will do anything to release themselves from it. Here the carelessness is one side of a bipolar condition – the other pole is all about care, but only care for one's own self, one's own kind. People who do terrible things are often extremely sensitive – far more sensitive than most – but what could be the basis of empathy and hence magnanimity is often the condition of its lack, because it is directed only at one's own self. This is why, when a community or a person is damaged, those who do the breaking or damage, irrespective of their intentions, are unleashing forces for which others will suffer.[5]

The lesson is repeated so often that it is stupefying how it seems to go forever unheeded as peoples ceaselessly rely upon the triumvirate of moral rectitude, the law, and reparations in order to do what those powers never do – stop evil from spreading.

Sin is, *inter alia*, poisonous energy or social toxicity that is the social and toxic effluence of selfishness and – what is but a synonym – carelessness, indifference toward others. This may sound very similar to Kant, who also sought to attack selfishness; but sin is the norm of human life because indifference and carelessness – along with insufficient understanding of ourselves and our world – are our daily diet irrespective of how moral we might be at times in our day. Our moral moments are those times when we wake up and try to pay attention, but we can no more be ever morally awake than we can live without sleep. It is true that if we can be 'good enough,' attuned enough, we can stave off evil within a community for a while. But human experience shows that this is an endless task with mere moments of relief. When Camus wrote *The Myth of Sisyphus*, he thought he was describing the human condition – and perhaps he was, at least as the pagan (which he explicitly said he was) saw life. But he was describing, even more astutely, how we live with evil – as he had done in his other great study of evil, *The Plague*.

It is telling that Kant had conceived of moral improvement asymptotically, as something we are always striving to achieve but never quite reach. Though he provided a more sophisticated account of moral striving than the believers in historical progress, both his and their thinking (in spite of his insistence that morality was based on a reasoning beyond time and space) was steeped in the mechanistic metaphysical notion that space and time constitute the essential operative conditions of a power and that those conditions can be mapped out so that cause and effect can be plotted in some linear or sequential fashion. This certainly gave us much hope in what knowledge can do. And it is true that for all sorts of things, it is helpful. But its greatest power – the dissolution of quality into quantity – also rendered it a very limited approach for understanding human beings, who are as driven by the past of memory as they are by hope for and faith in the future. Human actions do not simply push and pull like bodily forces. Often they lie fallow, seemingly dead to the memory, only to have been revealed to be incubating as they become reactivated in times of crisis and fear (Kant conceived of freedom as leaping into a causal sequence, but not as living powers, which he construed mechanistically). Aspects of an act may stay 'on hold' for decades or centuries before lurching back into existence. A sin, like an act of charity, may occupy its own time frame, and the time taken for its 'expenditure' is unpredictable. It is hard enough, then, for us to place our faith in knowledge even if, as Descartes promised, we have a right method to align the mechanisms of life within a common spatial and temporal matrix that enables us to order the processes of nature so that we can eventually survey and rule them.

Sin, then, is often hidden, and its power grows in its hiddenness. And it is because of this hiddenness that sin can easily sidestep justice and law – at least in any other than a divine sense – until it is too late for law and justice to do anything about it. The really big sins, the ones that don't just end up in personal catastrophe, a personal death or loss, but in the collapse or death of a community, a state, an empire, a people, are protected and driven by self-destructive myths and legends, by phantasms. And phantasms are the incubators of sin. Moral orders – even reasonable ones – may well be phantasmic; only those who believe that reason is sovereign over life have difficulty seeing this.

It is not knowledge taken as something in itself – as a force of curiosity or an instrumental end – that prevents sins. A parent may treat a child with duty his or her whole life and contribute to rearing a hateful, resentful child who lacks what duty can never supply – love. But this is true of entire social strata and groups. Societies whose different groups and strata cannot love one another – or, what amounts to the same thing, who cannot find ways to dissolve and join at least parts of themselves into something greater – live on the edge of perilousness, if not in outright conflict.

It is the power of the right kind of love at the right time that prevents sins – but love is not always effective in the way we hope it is. As with evil, love follows its own time. And an act of love may have little impact at the time of its birth, especially in the maddening conflagrations of evil – love, too, can incubate, waiting to be resummoned by need and memory. As for the loving act, whereas philosophy has generally required wisdom for goodness, love's needs can be performed equally as well by the village idiot as by the university philosophy professor – indeed, it is often harder for the latter to have an openness in his or her soul to know what that act might be; for being full of mind might well hinder the heart's responses to love's need of the moment. To be sure, knowledge may help a loving act, but it does not give us the love to *perform* the act, and it operates on a plane that is far distant from the radiances of life that we rather dismissively call 'instinct' – as if we had much of any idea what 'instinct' is.

All in all, though, we find ourselves ever confronted by the consequences of not acting in accordance with the possibilities of love and the fruits of Redemption. We constantly act blindly and wilfully – which are two sides of the same coin – and we end up in the midst of catastrophe, be it the catastrophe of a broken heart, a broken life, a broken community, or a broken empire. The scale may vary, but the processes that lead to the breakage are unleashed every second of every day with the greatest of ease. And because the consequences of greed, lying, pride, and all the other 'sins' are not always visible, people trusting their small eyes and small minds think no further of the consequences. A sin is not over because someone admits moral culpability or starts being moral or even stops sinning (if such a thing were possible, as I clarify below). By the time the evils have accumulated to such an extent that they break lives and communities apart, there is no longer any sense of where they have come from. Thus evil takes all by surprise except for the prophet, who is deeply attuned to the sins of the time and who senses the cries of the future generations that have been condemned to perish on their account.[6]

Sin, then, is the poison that leads to the breakdown of a world or self (for a self is but a smaller world) – or what is the same thing, it is the breaking forces circulating in the world. And its perpetual generation and circulation is the proof that we are less than the creature who, according to the teaching of Revelation, is created in the divine image. From the perspective of the teaching of Revelation, our divinity is our birth promise and destiny, and the span between the two is our history, the panoply of acts whose powers, if rightly tapped and rightly learned from, may help us fulfil our destiny. This is why, for Rosenstock-Huessy, our divinity is attained only after sin has brought us to ruin and despair. We act ever in ignorance, and the act once done cannot be undone. But it can be redeemed if instead of continuing to repeat the acts that lead to catastrophic consequences, we learn from our testimonies and memories and channel our energies into new forms of life.

What I have just been describing is, I believe, the real meaning of original sin – and while Jews generally hate the formulation, because of all sorts of other baggage it often carries, both Judaism and Christianity accept human weakness and brokenness and the sufferings that flow from them as their basis – and Rosenzweig is most explicit on this. And despite Augustine's excessive focus on concupiscence – and again, *contra* some of Augustine's formulations and focus – original sin is not merely bound up with carnality *per se*, but with weakness and fear as well, and with the will's trust in the weaker power (the self) over the stronger (the self's creator and redeemer, God). Indeed in *Heilkraft und Wahrheit*, Rosenstock-Huessy clarifies the point that the real opposition that Christianity made to concupiscence was not against the flesh pure and simple as sexual desire. Rather, he says, the flesh condemned by Jesus was 'the persistent wanting of our intentions' (*das Dauernwollen unserer Absichten*) – 'flesh,' he adds, 'in the Bible means the will, not pleasure.'[7]

In 'the kingdom' of the messiah, the pain of injustice and carelessness will be gone (if it hasn't, there is no 'kingdom'), but until then the world is constantly built of pain upon pain, blind act upon blind act, and wilfulness and selfishness.

When Schopenhauer spoke of *The World as Will and Representation*, the truth he expressed (signalled by the very title of the work, as well as in the disposition that was a response to the terrible reality he confronted) was, despite the work's seeming non-Christian and Eastern character, talking about the same thing – that is, the ceaseless toxicity of the social effluence of (selfish, i.e., self-enclosed) desire. (This is also why Rosenzweig could see that Schopenhauer's philosophy, notwithstanding his self-proclaimed atheism, reeked of Christianity.) Indeed, Hinduism, Buddhism, Judaism, and Christianity all concur that willing selves (for Jews and Christians, desiring heedless of God's commandment to love) lay behind the evil of the world. Where they differ is in how they deal with this insight.

It is a perfectly understandable response to wish to flee this horror, through an escape to nirvana or to a morally pure location of the pure moral will. But that a reaction is understandable does not mean it is successful. And the alternative flight paths of the mystic and the moralist show their inner relationship: the one is a solo journey, so its success is singular and hence it leaves the world exactly as it left it, and if all behaved like this then the world would be transformed; the other provides no singular relief, but creates a community of like-minded wills, and again, if all behaved in conformity with the moral stance then the world would be transformed. Here, *if only* is the common core. But the world remains with its policemen, judges, jailors, and criminals alongside its mystics and moralists. The moralist might provide better information about who should be judged, taken before the law, and sent to prison, but this is not Redemption.

The faiths of Rosenstock-Huessy and Rosenzweig, on the other hand, are built around love as the power of Redemption. Love does not – indeed *cannot* – stop every evil, or careless or brainless or inattentive act. Love's power comes from what it breathes into the world it finds and from adding one more thing into the world. Love ever finds itself working within the admixture of wilfulness and selfishness, of 'the warring members' of the flesh.

Providence is the name we give to what love does with this 'stuff of sin.' Providence is the promise that grace, that God's radiance, does not stop because evil has succeeded for a time in walling it out. Providence is not something we can see like a tree or lake; rather, it is something we may bear witness to if we have a certain kind of comportment (to borrow Heidegger's term). It is not visible to the eye of all – no rational argument will prove its existence, any more than an argument can suffice to create a tree or manufacture a car, because providence, like grace, is something that is only noticed by those who are attuned to it. Providence, not morality, is the real opponent of evil, the real subverter of evil – and as evil is a perennial accompaniment of life – until life is completely redeemed – its victory is always over a *particular* evil, not evil as such. Only when love is fully formed, when we are fully capable of receiving and transmitting the love that radiates constantly and is continually blocked, will evil be no more. This is the cornerstone of faith in Redemption. The experience of providence is born of the experience of hope; faith, I think, comes later.

Providence is the confirmation to the faithful that evil's successes, however frequent and terrible, are partial. Faith takes its cue from the experience of life building upon life; it attunes us not to time's healing capacity (for time does not heal), but to love's radiance through and over time so that even the most horrific evils leave traces of God's eternal presence responding to the clamor for Redemption – victims cry to heaven to be heard, are properly mourned, and take their place as guides to the future.

This point, notwithstanding its different emphases, has affinities with Emil Fackenheim's famous argument in *God's Presence in History* (an argument that also appears in Emmanuel Levinas's equally famous essay 'Useless Suffering') that if Jews were to cease to believe in God, they would become accomplices of the Nazi endeavour to eradicate them from the earth.[8] For both Fackenheim and Levinas, the appeal is to distinguish between the evil that seeks to crush and destroy and the perpetuity of the presence of what deserves and is worthy of love, the great refusal. To be sure, their point seems to be primarily a moral one, but its efficacy comes from the truth it recognizes: that we must honour and mourn those who 'uselesly suffered' and not sit back in our indifference – for such indifference is the very wall of the hard heart against the God that would enter with His love and transform and redeem us and put an end to useless suffering.

And it is the same truth that is central to Rosenstock-Huessy's argument. For his is an appeal not to what we *think* we are doing, but to what is being done constantly in the world around us: the living spark of the divine refuses to die so long as we draw breath. This is why human beings constantly return to the sites of injustices and pay tribute, why the dead refuse to be silenced. Evil *impresses* itself upon generations; to be sure, its perpetrators may not lose any sleep over their brutality, but eventually the living must come to grips with the price of death that has been the very condition of their own existence. This coming to grips by the living of the price of death is an element that finds itself embedded in the concept of providence. Furthermore, evil is not something that we can pretend is not there; we cannot simply pontificate about it to try and stop it, or reflect upon it after it happens – as if it simply ceases with an execution or defeat of the 'sinner,' again whether 'individual' or group or nation. The effects of evil are as seed in the earth, with which the world continues to be made.

Thus seeds of the Holocaust had to be tended long after the destruction of Nazism. And those seeds refuse to recede into nothingness; they have left an impression on subsequent generations, which are now more alert to racism as one of (the d)evil's forms. Those youth of 68 were made by Hitler and spent much of their lives killing him. (Freudians may well find here what their master had expressed through the symbols of sexuality, which are simply hard truths of generational creation and the interplay of life and death.)

That human beings are so slow to learn about evil may be disheartening, but we can only work with what we have. And that is the world at the moment, and its ground, just as the earth we walk on is the result of decay and corpses, which does not mean that we cannot take our bearings from the horizon of the future. Idealists of every stripe are able to provide proscription and postures because they are beyond the world's evil in their mind, but while Rosenstock-Huessy emphasizes how we live off martyrs, a moral pronouncement made from a safe place is not to be equated with a martyr's action.

This also stands in the closest relationship to the fact that it is only *after* we act that we have the material of life – again, when we act we rarely know what we are doing. Purity or goodness of intention matters for little in the world we make. The vision of life here is the exact opposite of Platonism (and Platonism's most recent manifestation, a real ubiquitous sickness of our time – managerialism).[9]

The Platonist believes that life should follow the plan. Plato, at least, thought that God was the original planner as He looked to the stable ideas and perfect forms – and this idea would often be attached to Christian thinking. But it is the opposite of everything that Rosenstock-Huessy understands as Christian. It allows no room for grace or providence, and it suffers from the delusion that our puny brains can build the future exactly as we want it to be. It makes this mistake because it fails to make the most elementary distinction between creaturely and merely bodily existence. Thus intoxicated by the kind of scientific precision that enables rocket ships to land on distant planets, and nuclear power plants (mostly) to be successfully operated, they think that social existence can be replicated with the same amount of success, in utter violation of what every parent learns about the hiatus between their plans and hopes for their children's lives and the actual lives of their children.

An excellent example of the completely contrary way that Rosenzweig and Rosenstock-Huessy think, relative to the purist way that moralists and planners think, was expressed in a conversation between the musicians and producers Brian Eno and Daniel Lanois. As Eno says,

what would be really interesting for people to see, is how beautiful things grow out of shit, because nobody ever believes that. You know, everybody thinks that Beethoven had his string quartets completely in his head. They'd somehow appeared there and formed in his head, and all he had to do was write them down and they would be kind of manifest to the world. But I think what's so interesting and what would really be a lesson that everybody should learn is that things come out of nothing. Things evolve out of nothing. You know the tiniest seed in the right situation turns into the most beautiful forest, and then the promising seed in the wrong situation turns into nothing, And I think this would be important for people to understand because it gives people confidence in their own lives to know that that's how things work.[10]

Now the 'shit' or 'nothing' that concerns Rosenstock-Huessy is that of the great social catastrophes, revolutions, cataclysmic events driven by hatred of one order and love for something better – both being sufficient for men and women to cut off their connections with the world in which they live and to leap into one they can only hope and pray for.

Let us now return to Rosenstock-Huessy's broader argument about Christianity in order to better grasp how it enables us to see its providential relationshionship with revolution, bearing in mind that what we have is sin, love, providence, and 'shit.' And therein lies our salvation.

For Rosenstock-Huessy, to understand history as the history of salvation requires that we understand the basic collective forms of the world's peoples and how they form a common history. Thus in the second volume of his *Soziologie, Die Vollzahl der Zeiten*, he focuses on the major types of social association that have emerged historically and the different creations that each type has generated. For him, the most elemental of these types are the tribes, empires, nations, and publics (*Publikum*), with their masks, temples, geniuses (poets, philosophers, legislators), prophets, saints, and – in the second millennium – revolutionaries and, most recently, nihilists.

For Rosenstock-Huessy, what makes human beings unique is that they are not merely territorial creatures; they are also temporal and speaking creatures. Hence the accumulation and transference of power is not solely – or, once properly grasped, even primarily – a matter of conquering space (whether through seriousness or play – the peacetime managing of space);[11] it also entails creating bodies of time, incarnating these through founding, endowing, and reproducing – processes that would be impossible without grammar.

Moreover, Rosenzweig focuses almost exclusively on three types: Pagan, Jew, and Christian. Whereas Rosenstock-Huessy, while utilizing the same triad when appropriate, is also interested in drawing out what is the unique creation of each human type. He is concerned with how we are heirs to all these types and how we may incorporate them into ourselves without tearing ourselves apart and without their power being utterly dissipated, in order that they can form some kind of concordance. Thus, Rosenzweig rightly emphasizes the historical and temporal character of the Christian faith; while Rosenstock-Huessy sets out to show that the mission of the Christian faith is to make contemporaries of distemporary forms of life.

For him, then, war, revolution, and social catastrophes were not simply a matter of spatial or territorial rivalries; much more than that, they were the result of collisions of the times, of peoples and their institutions formed over and by the different needs and longings, loves and hates, that had fused them into their various temporal regimes. To some extent the humanist dream has been to make a unity of all peoples by bringing them into the muted flow of uniformity that shares one moral law and a 'reasonable'/scientific view of the world. For Rosenstock-Huessy, humanism's failure to achieve this, at least in a way that would provide genuine concord among distemporaries, is largely due to its failure to take time seriously as an essential component of life.

Of course, the Romantics had exposed the unsatisfactory nature of the solution, though they had only touched part of the problem and part of the solution. They valorized myth and archaic or exotic lifeways but had no real idea of how concord among distemporaries might be possible; instead they simply fell back, as Herder did, on Enlightenment universalism to glue together the discordances of contrary lifeways. Not surprisingly, it would degenerate into nationalism. And after nationalism and the ideologies of the twentieth century have failed, we now have a mish-mash of the Enlightenment emphasis on rights plus Romantic nostalgia for premodern forms of life plus faith in economic growth and environmental sustainablity.[12]

What is needed is to discern what is living and what is dead in different traditions. In theological terms, all must be judged to see what is worthy of Redemption. But this judgment is not something that exists in a purely spiritual location; rather, it occurs in every great revolution and catastrophe when one age passes judgment on another. In this way, Resurrection and the Last Judgment stand in the closest relationship to each other and are, for that reason, intrinsic to history itself. For just as Resurrection meant the resuscitation of historically spent forms of life so that their powers can be tapped for generations to come, the Last Judgment refers to the decision either to 'resurrect' a dead form of life or to let it die. Thus in his 'Faculty Address on The Potential Christians of the Future,' Rosenstock-Huessy says: 'And I know of the Last Judgment as a reality because I have seen Last Judgments passed on Proust's France, on Rasputin's Russia, on Wilhelm II's Germany, President Harding's America. Similarly I believe in resurrection of the body because I see resurrections of bodies, all through history, on earth. Any genuine soul will be incarnated time and again.'[13]

Heaven, hell, and Resurrection – as we have suggested with sin and providence – are terms that long ago lost their true meaning for many people who understand these terms 'religiously,' even though in everyday parlance they often function well enough. The point about hell is well made in *The Christian Future*, when Rosenstock-Huessy tells the story of Woodrow Wilson's daughter, who, having overheard her father say that hell is a state of mind, rushed downstairs to tell her sister that her father had lost his faith. But as Rosenstock-Huessy continues:

It is natural for children to think that Heaven and Hell are places in space, because they can only picture in external terms what they have not yet experienced. But Wilson's remark was strictly orthodox, and by no means an instance of modernist fudging. Jesus said both that his kingdom is not of this world, and that it is in our hearts. And Origen wrote before A.D. 250: 'I have commented on this [prayer] "Our Father who art in Heaven," in order to abolish the low opinion of God held by those who place him locally in the heavens. Nobody is permitted to say that God dwells in a physical place.' And if 'God in Heaven' does not mean something in space, neither by implication does 'the Devil in Hell.'[14]

Likewise, on the question of heaven, Rosenstock-Huessy says it is not the playground of singing choirs – 'heaven is the spoken, promised future . . . Our Father in Heaven means the God who is still to come.' And it is 'everything . . . which preserves its own name inside the family of men.'[15] Thus it stands in the closest relationship to the importance of speech and the names we call upon to orient ourselves. Again in his Lectures on Comparative Religion, he makes the point well when he says that 'the Kingdom of Heaven is something very definite, something very alive. It is peopled by all the names which you think are sacred, which . . . mustn't disappear in reality from this earth.'[16]

Conversely, he thought that the Greek faith in immortality was simply a piece of childishness, one that he believed was tolerated by the Church because it did no real harm to its mission as long as Christendom was united by a common commitment to making the world on the basis of sacrificial love:[17] 'The Church has always allowed the childish to see things childishly, and has forbidden clever people to sneer at a child's belief. But it has with equal energy forbidden children to dabble with the adult understanding of the Creed.'[18] Moreover, he saw that this literalist and childish view of such central terms of faith had become more prevalent since the Reformation.[19]

But he also saw that even the disciples at times thought in these childish terms. Truth enters the world in times of panic and catastrophe as 'a mythical frenzy.' Only experience teaches people to distinguish between legend and reality. Rosenstock-Huessy conceded that even Jesus' disciples went through this:

Christianity has made the discovery that man needs frenzy and passion to achieve anything. The misunderstanding of the Disciples, their devotion for the Lord . . . their squabbling over the seats in the kingdom of Heaven, were inevitable. They had to do this in order to learn . . . So their myth, while Jesus was on earth [was] . . . a complete misunderstanding. Everything. Not only Judas. Peter just the same, and [e]ven John . . . discusses ways seats will be in Heaven, in the sky . . . so with everybody. There is no way of growing, except by going through the myth, through your mythical period.[20]

For many interpreters of Christianity, the fact that even those involved in the origins of Christianity spoke mythically and believed in legend discredited it from the beginning. Truth is often spoken about as if our talents, our fully formed natures, and indeed, the qualities we require for the natural sciences to exist, could have emerged fully formed from day one of creation. For Rosenstock-Huessy, this naturalistic delusion was part and parcel of Descartes's 'farewell' to history. From his perspective, this was like looking at an infant and holding forth on all the reasons why he or she would never be able to do what adults do. Truth is not like an object in the world or the mind (as materialists and Idealists would have it) waiting patiently and fully formed to be espied; it grows with us. Thus just as every living creature commences in infancy before reaching adulthood, we grow into truth. Moreover, as we said earlier, for humanity to fathom truth it cannot simply take one modality of speech as the one and exclusive vista onto reality.

This is why Rosenstock-Huessy also says, when pointing out that Christianity's legendary dimension does not make it untrue: '*To omit the legendary form of truth is to suppress truth.* As a human being, I need the legend, the myth, the ritual, the poem, the theorem, the prophecy, the witness, the sermon, every one of them.'[21]

The fact that apart from the apostles, and perhaps a handful of others, none of Jesus' contemporaries could have predicted the potency of that life for the ages to come is indicative for Rosenstock-Huessy of the way in which a truth grows over time. Moreover, it is not something divorced from faith, hope, and love, but absolutely dependent on those powers. And this is true even of the sciences – the truths accessible to natural science could never have been formed had it not been for the sacrifice of scientific pioneers and for the love and faith and hope of those who followed in their wake.

To summarize, then, Rosenstock-Huessy saw Christianity as a living power, not as a set of logical propositions or a moral code. This, he says, was what the Church understood, and hence why, for all its many faults, it was so powerful: it realized that its mission was to carry us across and unite us through the ages and in so doing participate in the salvation of the world as all became members of the one body of Christ. The completion of that task would be the salvation of the world, the salvation of the times. Christianity is not a narrative about isolated acts of goodness and isolated souls performing acts of love that somehow are observed and rewarded by God in the afterlife; rather, it is about how singular acts of love are life forming, how lives gather and form around the actions of those who love life – who love it so much that they are fearless of death and are willing to die into new life. Love redeems the world by contributing to dead or spent things being awakened, being reconstituted, where possible, within the revealed law of love. This stands in the closest association to Rosenstock's sociological orientation – he does not deny that a person cannot break out of the social mould. This is no mechanistic determinism; he is simply taking cognizance at a deep level of the forces and pressures that are involved in human action and human formation. In this respect it is the salvation of the human race that is his major concern, not simply this person or that person. Indeed, for him it is the salvation of all that forms the completed body of the risen Christ. Thus in his lectures in Munich after the Second World War he would declare, citing Gregory of Nyssa: 'Humanity should become God. But that cannot happen without all other human beings becoming God.'[22]

This is also why it is providential and not egoic or individualistic. And it is why Rosenstock-Huessy can at times be so sharply critical of Kierkegaard – 'that grim and grisly monster without confession and without Church,' as he described him one in letter to Rosenzweig.[23] To Walter Lowrie, the North American scholar and translator of Kierkegaard, who had irritated him immensely by implying that his ideas were essentially those of Kierkegaard, Rosenstock-Huessy responded: 'Not the individual but the nations being God's children . . . everything I touched was social, legal, ecclesiastical, collective. Not philosophy, but the grammar of society therefore is my twentieth century theme . . . My Revolutions of the Christian World are the psychoanalysis of the Nations of Europe. And so in every respect, have I been forced to live with, to call forth, to be reborn through groups, not single [individuals].'[24]

The history of the Church was, then, for Rosenstock-Huessy, the history of the pouring of God into man.[25] I mentioned earlier that as a very young man, Rosenstock-Huessy believed that the Creed was simply true. He believed this because he believed that what it 'guaranteed' in its three articles was 'our trust in the unity of creation from the beginning (God the Father made all things in heaven and on earth), our liberty to die to our old selves (given us by God's Son, who implanted the Divine itself in human life by living as a man, and dying, yet rising again), and the inspiration of the Holy Spirit which enables us to commune with posterity and start fellowship here and now.'[26]

Thus, incarnation is not secondary to the Christian faith – it is its central activity. For without an understanding of incarnation as the movement from God to the patriarchs to the prophets to Christ to *corpus Christi* to the *eschaton,* we can understand nothing of the real miracle of faith and must remain ensconced in legend.

For Rosenstock-Huessy, it was the third article of the creed that confirmed the centrality of incarnation to the Christian life: 'From now on the Holy Spirit makes man a partner in his own creation. In the beginning God had said, "Let us make man in our image" (Gen. 1:26). In this light, the Church Fathers interpreted human history as a process of making Man like God. They called it "anthropurgy": as metallurgy refines metal from its ore, anthropurgy wins the true stuff of Man out of his coarse physical substance.'[27]

It is as an anthropological process that Resurrection is to be understood, not as a mythic tale, and not – as some of the pagans believed – as the metempsychosis of the soul. Nor can it be understood if we think purely in terms of mechanical reproduction, the eternal return of the same:

> The body 'is sown a natural body; it is raised a spiritual body' (I Cor. 15:44). 'The corrupt body does not return in its first nature, for it is not the corrupt seed that returns as grain. But as from the seed of grain there rises the ear, in the same manner there is in our body a raison d'etre, in the power of which, if it has not been corrupted, the body rises in an incorrupt state.' So a human type will rise again only in so far as it is 'not corrupt.' It has to be purified, and nothing but the pure metal will show in the resurrection.[28]

This process, then, requires an act of faith of foundation and acts of love of receptivity – founding, endowing, and succession. Together these form a process of Resurrection that in turn contributes to the world's Redemption. 'There are,' says Rosenstock-Huessy, 'countless illustrations of the resurrection of the body in Christian history':

St. Francis, for example, died without offspring, but Franciscan humanity has flourished ever since, and not only in his Order. The Franciscan way of life, immortally portrayed in The Imitation of Christ, became daily bread for the lives of countless Christians of all denominations, even the most radical Protestants. The Franciscan type guided the political life of medieval Italian cities. The 'Third Order' spread over all Europe and counted among its members even the Habsburg emperors, who, in death, humbly deposed their titles before the majesty of the Franciscan spirit. Finally, in Abraham Lincoln, Francis of Assisi celebrated his secular resurrection in America. When Lincoln, as President and Commander-in-Chief of a victorious army, walked into Richmond in 1865, on foot, without escort, St. Francis had conquered the powers of this earth. In Siberia, in Egypt, people would whisper that old Abe, a new type of man, had appeared in the world. Here, ruler and servant were blended into one. Such men are epoch-making in the history of the human species. The relation of Lincoln to St. Francis was unconscious. It was not imitation but genuine succession, revealing the power of a soul that had tried to come into the flesh ever since St. Francis set the example.[29]

In his remarkable essay 'The Twelve Tones of the Spirit,' Rosenstock-Huessy describes this process as the genuine 'good news' about life – that it is stronger than death and that the species is thus not doomed to tragic repetition:

SPIRIT AND LOVE ARE STRONGER than death. Hence, we cannot do without them unless we condemn ourselves to sterile futility. For to love means to become fruitful, and to be inspired means to overcome and to limit death. When the body dies, the spirit remains. The spirit proves itself to be divine whenever the trails blazed by creative, loveable lives are travelled by deliberate successors, heirs, pupils, followers, or when devilish trails are renounced and abandoned by warning posts: No trespassing! Hence, the ultimate test of the spirit is the heritage of newly acquired faculties which future generations gratefully receive and accept.[30]

According to Rosenstock-Huessy, these twelve tones of the spirit are the stages of the spirits' conquest of death. But just as the Greek philosophers failed to grasp this because they believed in a rational soul that survived death, and just as the secular mind of today is blinded by its social atomism, Christianity had grasped the relationship between life and death. It defied the natural view of things, and it showed that the spiritual order is the reverse of the natural sequence, much as Copernicus did when he reversed the view of the cosmological order:

> While in 'nature' birth seems to precede death, and life is described as the sum of all the processes this side of dying, the Spirit reverses this order of naturalism.
> In nature, birth precedes death;
> In nature, life tries to shun death.
> In the spirit, death precedes life;
> In the spirit, the founder's death guides his heirs' lives.[31]

While I can only repeat the sketch he provides in *I Am an Impure Thinker*, what is important for my purpose is to draw attention to the fact that Rosenstock-Huessy is exploring the process of incarnation as a social fact that we are in danger of forgetting and that he sees as central to the Church's sacramental understanding of life. On the verge of death, the testator passes his or her command into the future. The stage of testator – the last stage in a full life – stretches back through the ages that have constituted this last gesture of life. Of the phases of life, he sees that they break down into four stages, beginning in childhood with the necessity of obedience so that one may be inducted into a social order through to adulthood and eldership. The phases of childhood, adulthood and eldership are further classified as three main types – the artist, the fighter and the universal priesthood of believers. That is to say, the artist retains the perspective of youthful vigour necessary for social rejuvenation, the fighter provides the critical input so that the society does not petrify through its conserving tendencies, and the aged provide a social consolidation through laws, education, its warnings and its testates.

Thus does he list the twelve tones of the spirt from the stages of age down to youth:

> testator
> prophet or warner
> teacher or educator
> leader or legislator
> sufferer or perseverer
> protester or rebel
> critic or analyst
> doubter or despondent

player or singer
learner or wanderer
reader or conceiver
listener or obeyer[32]

In this list one can immediately recognize various social types. What Rosenstock-Huessy has done – which is more interesting than merely observing these types – is see them in a sequential relationship that takes account of the different stages on life's way, to borrow Kierkegaard's title. He does not mean that every youth, or every elder, traverses these stages in a strict sequence, but he does think that 'each tone of life should be given one period of life for its full cultivation.' And he also maintains that the triumph of spatial thinking over temporal thinking – which has grounded and accompanied the triumph of mechanistic metaphysics and humanism – has jumbled up any sense of the sequences of spiritual and social development.[33] A healthy society will contain all these types and will induct people into these phases of life, thereby creating a concordance over time.

Rosenstock-Huessy is here listing the most general phases of social development, and his resting of those phases upon the testator is another example of his connectedness with premodern ways of thinking. While testatorship is not specifically Christian, the view that life involves different sacramental stages was indeed central to the Church's sacraments. Similarly, the traditional Christian view of life built upon the power of a testator to open a new way of life. This is what, I suggested earlier, the saint was, and what a world was that required we pray to saints. Every great inventive act of the human spirit requires sacrifice, and those who love the opened path enough, and who are ready to follow, replicate their lives in the model provided by the 'the founder,' the patron 'saint.' As I also suggested earlier, this was as true for scientific innovation – which Rosenstock-Huessy discusses at length in *Der Atem des Geistes* and in the final chapter of the second volume of the *Soziologie* – as it is for any other spiritual act of invention. Thus Rosenstock-Huessy writes in *The Christian Future*:

A new soul, a fresh originality of the human heart, thereby survives the man or nation in which it came to birth and incarnates itself in a spiritual succession of typical representatives through the ages. For there are definite new phases of human existence never lived before, which arise at particular birthdates and, if they are genuine, they force themselves upon man's plasticity with such impressiveness that they don the bodies of later men and women in turn, and shape them into the same type.[34]

To summarize, let us restate our earlier point that Rosenstock-Huessy's Christian vision is based on incarnation and that it is thoroughly anti-transcendent. Rosenstock-Huessy reads the Christian heritage as this sided, yet commited to a better world to come. Rosenstock-Huessy views Christianity as a force for human survival whose success lays in having enough members who turn their backs on a world gone rotten, and who strive to create – with God's grace – the world promised by the father, the world without end, not in the sky but in the future. It does not interest itself in a moral order to judge this one, and thus it dispenses with a primarily moral overview of life; but it does judge this world from the future to come. This last point may seem but a variation of the same thing, just using different words – which is essentially how deists such as Kant interpreted religion (i.e., as a means of moral education).

But the difference becomes clear enough when we reflect on the Christian concept of repentance, which has no real importance in the several moral variants of Platonism. Platonists may welcome it when the immoral person proceeds on the path of virtue, but the only way they can integrate this act into a greater cosmic order is for the soul to continue 'to spiritually evolve' after death, either by returning to earth (thus Plato's interest in metempsychosis, as is evident in the *Phaedrus*, the *Phaedo*, *Gorgias*, the *Republic*, and the *Meno*) or by continuing through other planes of existence (the neo-Platonist story). Kant's argument for the immortality of soul – one that wishes to satisfy the needs of reason and that makes immortality an idea of practical reason, but that does not want to insult the intelligence of observers of nature – is but a variant of Platonism. And in morals, Kant was explicitly a Platonist.

The Christian position does not need to resort to a Platonic world to give meaning to repentance. The interweaving of souls across the times means that a single action may be of infinite worth. But again, this is an experiental idea, one that flies in the face of a dogma of Greek rationalism, which only allows so much power in the cause as in the effect. Christianity conceives of the everlasting soul as a power continuing to activate other souls, which draw inspiration from it – indeed, sometimes (as in the example of the good thief) from a single moment of a life. Thus does Rosenstock-Huessy favourably cite Althusser's teacher Jean Guitton: 'The unsurmountable abyss between Greek and Christian thought is the Christian rehabilitation of the unique and temporal event. The moral order is general and abstract to every philosophical or Greek mind. In Christianity the time of every human existence receives a superior quality in its smallest fragments.'[35] Unlike Platonism, Christianity sees everyone, no matter how well educated or smart or even good, as a sinner. (In three of the gospels, Jesus reminds us to call none but the Father good.)[36]

Given how anti-transcendent this understanding of Christianity is, it is understandable that Rosenstock-Huessy would be criticized by those who interpret Christianity in more Platonist tones. Thus in his 1946 review of *The Christian Future* for *Church History: Studies in Christianity and Culture*, Karl Löwith claimed that Rosenstock-Huessy had secularized and vaporized Christianity and that his ideas were essentially closer to paganism (especially Goethe's).[37]

Rosenstock-Huessy saw criticisms such as Löwith's as due to a complete inability to understand the connection between the Christian, the pagan, and the Jew, and the widespread tendency to project Greek philosophical abstractions – soul, immortality, timelessness, the good, and so on – onto Christianity. Rosenstock-Huessy, who was very critical of Löwith in his private correspondence to Georg Müller, simply could not understand how Löwith could not see the connection between modern philosophy and the murdering machines of modernity. In this respect, he shared a deep affinity with Heidegger, for he saw that Platonism had provided the original template for the intellectual breaking up of the world in a manner that prefigured the possibility of a technicized view of life (though unlike Heidegger, and much more in the spirit of Nietzsche, he saw Plato as the student of Parmenides). Thus, Löwith did not see that his view of Christianity's core concepts was but the vapours of the Platonism that had done so much damage. For Rosenstock-Huessy, people like Löwith only had the foggiest idea of what Christianity is; they thought it was a fog – they saw the words and the symbols that constituted it but not its essence. Rosenstock-Huessy realized all too well that the Church today – and not only today – is full of people like Löwith. But he also well realized that the Church ever was and still has other members, members whose faith is but the blood and bone of their sacrifical love and a commitment to Redemption based upon their sacrifice.

A much more important theologian than Löwith was Karl Barth, and Rosenstock-Huessy had eagerly awaited Barth's *Letter to the Romans,* only to be bitterly disappointed once he had read it – and he incurred Barth's irritation by telling him so.[38]

Rosenstock-Huessy maintained that Barth's failure to understand that the Church existed to incarnate the spirit was yet another continuation of Greek reasoning. By then, Barth had rightly smelled Rosenstock-Huessy's anti-transcendence. And Barth responded by asking him whether he saw the unity of *Geist* (spirit/mind) and soul, people, and state as supra-terrestrial. Referring to I Corinthians 15, he asked Rosenstock-Huessy directly whether the 'transcendent' powers belonging to God were meant for humanity. Rosenstock-Huessy's response strongly suggests why he thought Christianity was true and why he thought that Barth was actually a Platonist playing with Christian symbols:

> Hasn't salvation come into the world? Hasn't God taken pity on us? Does Paul speak of the transcendent powers of a new eon or of a Father who lives up there 50 million kilometers away or does he speak of the Son of God who became man. Christ became flesh, thus we live in his name which is the addressable and effable name of God. Thus has God revealed himself. Where's the transcendence in this?[39]

Elsewhere, in a letter to an unknown recipient dated 18 February 1920, Rosenstock-Huessy said with a touch of disdain that Barth had written a 'purely intellectual (I) "book of experience" [*Erlebnisbuch*] . . . For him the questions of theology are themselves experience.'[40] Furthermore, 'his book is *art pour l'art* in pure culture,' and his Christ was 'merely a buzz word.' 'Sins, death, especially Easter and resurrection – he asserts them constantly, but he only asserts them. And just what is asserted, is just as easily disputed. I dispute the lot. The more I read Barth, the more mythical his Christ becomes to me, which is to say the more doubtful.'[41]

For Rosenstock-Huessy, Barth simply had no idea of the time needed for Christ's power to work its way into the world: 'It took a complete millennium, the first one, so that he could attract monks and martyrs. And then it took another one so that he could appeal to the rest of us, ever new parts of the world had to be supplied and won by Christ through the power of love, the power of resolution (all which remains stuck in Barth's dead Christianity).'[42] Barth, he said, had failed to grasp that 'we only come to eternity through time. First we have to emphasize that we are time men and time comrades. Only through that are our thoughts refined to supra-temporality.'[43] Barth, he added, did not really understand that 'the secret of Abraham can only be brought out after Christ has lived – and only a man of a new bond may formulate what the old cancels out.'[44]

I think it highly significant that Rosenstock-Huessy saw Barth as (a) a Greek systematic thinker and (b) someone who had not ingested the significance of the Great War. Comparing the Patmos group with Barth, he wrote:

> We experienced the First World War, but he didn't. That is not meant as a complaint against Barth . . . We should only speak of experience [*Erlebnis*], if our thinking experiences a new date. Barth occupied himself with the World War as with other world affairs. Whereas, with us, the World War gave us a new marching route, a new time calculation, a turning away from theology and philosophy out of obedience toward the path of salvation. Damnation was decisive for us; for Barth it remained just a theme, an objective fact.[45]

Rosenstock-Huessy also said that the most brilliant critique of Barth had been expressed by Rosenzweig, in a letter to Buber dated 20 February 1922. In that letter, after expressing disappointment that Barth had only recognized Christian revelation, Rosenzweig compared Barth unfavourably to Kierkegaard: 'Behind each paradox of Kierkegaard one senses biographical *absurda*, and for this reason one must *credere*. While behind Barth's colossal negations one senses nothing but the wall on which they are painted, a whitewash wall, his immaculate and well-ordered life . . . Not that they are unbelievable; but it is, after all, an indifferent authenticity.'[46] Elsewhere Rosenzweig expressed essentially the same argument as Rosenstock-Huessy: 'After a long drought, today we have a theology, mostly protestant, that leaves nothing to be desired as to the accuracy. We have it now: that God is wholly other, that to talk about Him is to talk Him away, that we can only say what He does to us.'[47]

Rosenstock-Huessy thought that Barth's great partner in dialogical disputation, Emil Bruner, was just as mistaken as Barth.[48] As in his critique of Barth, he saw that the hostility to the Roman Church was based on a moral stance that had transported both men out of that history, which extended from Christ to Luther and Calvin and into the morally safer climes of post-Reformation theology. But for Rosenstock-Huessy, this was once again a failure to see Christianity as a process of incarnation. Hence he said that if Brunner were right, 'I could not teach the incarnation in history.'[49] Just as Barth had wished to appeal to God's absolute otherness in order to separate Him from the more bloody and gristly works of the Church, Brunner needed to separate His moral purpose from the grounds of His existence.

For Rosenstock-Huessy, as we have already noted, this was a fantasy, one that might make us feel better about ourselves, but at the expense of our understanding of how we become who we become. It was all part of the same atomistic/egoic way of thinking that disconnects us from reality. Reality, for Rosenstock-Huessy, is always connected – from past to future and from inside to outside. That is why reality is a cross and why suffering is of its essence; and that is why, for him, Christianity is not a theological solution to a problem, but a deep insight into life and the role of sacrificial love in the integration of time, speech, and history:

> Brunner's view of Church history is the old partisan view of Anti-Roman 16th century historiography now extended to all established Churches en bloc: Constantine swallowed the Church, Christianity became fictitious. It is untrue for two reasons, one subjective, one objective. The subjective reason is that Emil Brunner owes everything he believes, not to some 'source' Christianity but to the martyrs and saints and the dogmatic 'quibblers,' and the monks and Fathers who all 'succumbed to the temptation' and went fictitious in Brunner's terms . . . A man who exploits a heritage of the times from 300 to 1100, simply by his speaking of 'State,' and 'Church,' and 'dogma,' and 'Christ,' cannot bury seventeen hundred years by terms like transformation and fictitious and temptation. The itch to kick against that which made us, is unworthy of our short time of grace during which we are still able to discuss our faith. Objectively, the simple facts as known by every child are these. In 300 and 400, the Church was not swallowed by the emperor, but the Church as the salvation of all sinners, swallowed the greatest sinner of all, the man-God Caesar. Only 'Protestants,' in quotation marks, may shun the simple question: What else could she do? Christians cannot, because the Church was founded for sinners. But if the Church had to baptize Constantine or his successors, as they asked for it, then by this divine dispensation two steps became imperative: 1. With a man-God, Caesar, not on the altar but in the pew, the dogma of the Trinity had to make it impossible for Arius and his like ever to confuse this former man-God in the pew with the God-man on the altar. All the dogmatic quarrels about the Trinity were the immediate consequence of Caesar's baptism. In other words: the Church *did not 'succumb to the Constantinian temptation* as Brunner says, but overcame

it by concentrating on the trinitarian dogma as long as the emperors were dangerously powerful from Nicea to Chalcedon – The real temptation being Caesar's divinity, not the established Church. 2. Since the ecumenic emperor now sat in his pew, as a believer, in Spain as well as Nicea, in Trier as well as Byzantium, what else could he do but convene ecumenic councils lest he be forced to worship in contradictory Churches, one and the same man? Actually, this is what happened. The rest is simply protestant myth.[50]

That Christianity cannot be understood apart from the Ages of the Church is fundamental to Rosenstock-Huessy, for Christianity must constantly fight against earthly encrustations. That is why he finds Brunner's account so crude and misleading. The Idealist is fine when it comes to identifying corruption – what to *do* about it is the issue. Then there is the matter of providence – which is always left out in declinists' views of life (and just as stupidly assumed in every new step by progressivists) so that a crisis is not simply the final entombment, the ultimate victory of death over life. But Rosenstock-Huessy believes that God (albeit over time) 'rewards' those brave spirits who are prepared to walk away and who with their love and sacrifice create a new way out. Thus, for example, he does not deny that the Church was imperilled in the fourth century when it became the religion of the empire. But what he can't stand about such accounts of the Church is that they overlook that the importance of incarnation is not an aberration within the faith that was so important to so many of the Church's leading figures and indeed for much of the Church's self-understanding – all of course but the continuation of the very process of God sending his son into the world, of the son sending the apostles into the world, and then of the apostles sending bishops into the world, and so on. Moral critics who judge the Church from a transcendent vantage point of absolute purity – that is, idealists – are paralysed by the darkness and horrors done under the sign of the Church, yet it was precisely because there *were* men and women prepared to step out of the darkness, who refused to let the Church putrefy *in toto*, that the institution could continue for so long. Thus, for example, the armchair humanist critic of the Church will, with a sweep of the hand, wipe out centuries of human endeavour and struggle, and the hundreds of thousands of people who sacrificed themselves in their deeds of love and service within the fold and power of their faith, by focusing on events such as the massacres of the Crusades and the Inquisition. True, these actions were shocking, and they will ever bring shame to the Church. The humanist who condemns everything about the institution might, though, as well condemn *all* our institutions – for none of endurance are free from bloodshed and iniquity. But the point for Rosenstock-Huessy is not that peoples steep themselves in blood – ever and ever again – but that history does not end with those acts of carnage and horror, and that, for example, a St Francis arises in the Church's dark hour, or a Dante, or a Thomas More, a Johann Huss, a Luther, and that they leave fruits for posterity that we still live off.

It is not a question of simply abdicating any moral compass when we reflect on past events – indeed, over time the very names of events possess moral significance. But the tragedy of the human situation is that our moral consensuses are generated through the horrors that are intrinsic to the events being played out. On the cusp of a new event, which is by its nature an unprecedented constellation of forces, those who really grasp the workings of evil within it are invariably in a minority – if they were not, the horror would not break out. In comfort zones, we can all be righteous – but the comfort zones, or what Rosenstock-Huessy designates as 'play spaces' – have been created after the evil has been defeated (such defeats, of course, are but momentary). And as people have vanquished a particular evil, a particular constellation, and thus have arrived at an entire new constellation of names, all redolent with moral significance, the following generations easily succumb to the delusion that the 'play space' always existed. This is essentially what Brunner and Barth and their like fail to see. The struggles that were carried out within the Church after it had been thoroughly Romanized changed Europe and eventually the world in all manner of ways that have enabled freedoms we take for granted (Rosenstock-Huessy's reading of European revolutions is predicated on this). Yet they talk as if somehow, quite magically, our freedoms would have appeared out of thin air.

To be more specific, where Brunner dismisses the Church because of its Caesarian corruptions, Rosenstock-Huessy devotes a long section of his *Soziologie* to the lives of Augustine, Anthony, Hieronymous (St Jerome), and Athanasius,[51] each of whom opened up new pathways of life just as Moses had opened up a new pathway by his and his people's exodus. Indeed, for Rosenstock-Huessy, Anthony's flight into the desert – years before Constantine's conversion – became a turning point for monastics and ascetics, one that would provide a potential counteraction to imperial corruption. By going into the desert, Anthony and 'his successor monks served the same God in the desert as the Christians in Rome, or Byzantine.'[52] God lived *there*, in the desert, not just in the empire. Indeed, because the imperial centres of power were so spiritually corrupt, He was even *more* present there.

 Like the peoples of tribes, the monks were free to wander unencumbered by the city's protective walls. But, notes Rosenstock-Huessy, unlike tribal peoples, those monks were also off the track of the warpath (a pathway we discuss later and that he sees as intrinsic to tribal life, and whose importance, power, and need for survival most moderns simply do not fathom). The monks were unarmed and – again like the peoples of tribes, who are governed and guided by the spirits of ancestors – they followed the precarious and unknown trails of the 'Holy Spirit,' driven by their faith in God's love.[53] What is astonishing, a real miracle, is not that one man would go into the desert but that so many others would take to this form of life for so long, and that the most powerful people on earth would look to such people and the cells and wildernesses they inhabitated for their own spiritual direction:

> In the areas of the ancient Roman empire, from 400 to 1100 thanks to this colonisation by hermits, the difference between habitat and bush, between the inhabitable land [*Land*] and uninhabitable land [*Unland*] had progressively disappeared. Increasingly the tribal warriors learned to abandon the safety of the wilderness around their huts. Thus increasingly the settlements in what had hitherto been waste land became the norm; this 'inner colonisation' thus wore down the borders and boundaries and transformed the no man's land into the best land. The next centuries saw the disappearance of the great demarcations between one people and another. The margraviates of Brandenburg, Silesia, Namur, Ostmark, Lausitz, the Scottish-English and the Bavarian – Lombardic, the Steiermark, and Transylvania were left open for settlement in the High Middle Ages. New orders of monks such as the Cistercians and the Praemonstratensians mastered the clearing (Überwindung) of these wider uninhabitable lands. Anthony's faith was still alive in them, the living soul would have to move there where the existing property arrangements had not yet penetrated. Only in this way would God's history unfold.[54]

Rosenstock-Huessy well realizes that in our post-Christian age, most of us have long forgotten the traces and weavings of St Anthony in the world we now inhabit. But this is not, for him, the point, any more than it is the point that people quickly forget the sources of great catastrophes, finding it more comforting and intellectually easier to embrace abstract moral reasoning and blame some individual, or some group occupying a particular social location at a particular time. Which allows them to ignore the fact that great social explosions do not occur without a long gestation – long enough, that is, for potencies, resentments, and frustrations to accumulate until bursting point.

For him, Anthony's tracks (and the tracks of those who followed in his) are of considerable importance, even if forgotten – for they have enabled us to see our world traced on the map of the heart of one who does not centre his being in a stable and rigid identity. Thus those who are opposed to Eurocentrism or to any kind of national/imperial centrism, who are able to hear our common humanity in the cries of common suffering and who are able to push nations to the periphery, have much more in common with Anthony and the monastics than they realize.[55] Of course, Rosenstock-Huessy never tires of pointing out that, however we chronicle our history, the relationship between past and present is not simply sequential. History is full of leaps, and he welcomed developments in quantum physics as a naturalistic paradigm that might help historians throw off the causal mechanistic view that blinds us to how deeds incubate, die, and become reborn.[56] Of course, we cannot grasp the importance of this vision of the world – a vision that was part and parcel of the monastic retreat – merely by looking for 'causes.' The point is not that our contemporaries who are opposed to nationalist or imperialist chauvinisms have been 'anticipated' by the monastics, nor is it that they are directly influenced. Though if you follow Rosenstock-Huessy correctly, the connection is real albeit not immediate. What had an immediate impact on Western people's lives during Rosentock-Huessy's lifetime (and on ours ever since) were the explosions of the two world wars. But as he spent much of his life arguing and demonstrating, those wars were the culmination of a thousand years of revolutions. And those revolutions, which we will explore in more detail later, were set in sequenced motion by a revolution within the Church and the Holy Roman Empire: the Gregorian Revolution. That revolution was not caused by Anthony, Athanasius, Augustine, or Hieronymous, but all four were vital to the task of building and shaping the institution from which Europe, the West, and now the world continue to this day to march toward universal peace – or at least those members of the Church who hope, and 'pray,' and work, to achieve it, irrespective of tribe, nation, or denomination.

For Rosenstock-Huessy, 'the second defender of the growing realm of God against the nonsense of a Caeserisch privileged imperial Church' was Anthony's biographer and follower, Athanasius. For forty years he moved from one land to another to escape the Diocletian persecution of Christians – Anthony had quite literally shown him a path to survival. Athanasius' great contribution was that of dogma, the dogma of 'the same being or nature' (*homoousia*), as stipulated in the Nicene Creed, where the Son is of the same being/nature or substance as the Father. That term was central in the dispute with the followers of Arius, who, by emphasizing the Son's humanity at the expense of His divinity, were undermining the uniqueness of Jesus' power. For Rosenstock-Huessy, the question of divinity only makes sense if we know what a god is and how widespread were (and are) both the language and the practice of divinization. Athanasius' position – which also became the Church's orthodox position – was the Trinitarian one, which to latter-day humanists looks utterly baffling, if not laced with supersititon. But this is largely because the different worlds are woven out of different ways of speaking. The triumph of humanist speech is not the triumph of the cessation of divinization: the cults of Stalin, Hitler, and Mao – and in a less brutally political but no less revealing way, the cults of celebrities today – remind us that the practice continues. To borrow Wittgenstein's 'language-game,' for the humanist at the reflexive level 'there is/are no god(s) [except man]' proceeds as if all divinization is foolish/wrong – though the tendency here is to use substitute words such as *charismatic*, or *leader* (in Germany), or *the great helmsman* (in Maoist China). But the language does not stop the process of worship and surrender. Indeed, the dissolution of the term 'god' from meaningful everyday speech may actually blind us to the idolatry that develops when the only thing that can properly be said about processes like Hitler or Stalin worship is that 'they are taking this man for a god.' Athanasius' emphasis on the divine nature of Christ, and on the Son having the 'same nature' as the Father, is intended to fasten all eyes upon the importance of what was achieved in Jesus' life and death. Athanasius and the opponents of Arius believed that the triumph of Arianism would undermine the spiritual and social galvanization that was the Church's mission in terms of providing an alternative/opposition to the state. Had Arius triumphed over the Church, the divinization of Caesar, of the state and its ruler – that is, of the great pagan storehouse of forces – would have remained intact.[57] According to Rosenstock-Huessy, those who focus on the corruption of the Church from Constantine on are neglecting the great revolutionary struggles that the Church unleashed precisely *because* it was not so completely capivated. To summarize, making Jesus of the same nature as God was intended to put an end to such acts of divinization. As Rosenstock-Huessy would say in his lectures, the whole point of Jesus being God was to put a stop to the idolatry that is the inevitable result of our habit of (false) divinization: one God has been, and now we can stop doing this. In effect, Jesus closed the list of man-gods:

> Since the Creed was addressed to both Jews and Greeks, it had to deal with the minds of each. The first article sides with Jews against Greeks. Sky and earth are not the domains of separate deities, for in the beginning God created both. The second article sides with the Greeks against Jews to the extent of saying that one man was God. To a Greek, this placed Jesus in the list of sons of God, from Hercules and Achilles to the Divus Julius and Titus of his own day. But as the Christ, the only begotten son of God, Jesus closed the list, ended the era in which scattered individuals could receive divine honors.[58]

The following account of Athanasius' critique of Arius from the Lectures on Universal History represents well how Rosenstock-Huessy saw the entire problem experientally (again, the methodological thread of 'absolute empiricism') and how (a) his view of Christianity and Jesus was scrubbed of any Platonic encrustations, while (b) being based on a reading of the Church as essentially sharing his position:

> Arius is the Unitarian. He says, '. . . the qualities of God are unique, no man is God; therefore let us call Jesus "god-like."'
>
> Now Athanasius put against this two proofs. One: Jesus is true man, and true God. Of course He's a man in His own right. He had a poor digestion probably; He breathed, He had to sleep, He sweat[ed], He had fear, He had hopes, He loved. He wasn't immortal. And He died, very much so . . . And He was in His mother's womb. And He is . . . completely a human being. Don't forget this. Otherwise this whole discussion becomes nasty.
>
> I have heard people discuss . . . this whole story, in the way as though . . . Christians said that Jesus was a god. No. He's Perfect Man, and Perfect God. As to what God has done to Him, he is God. As to what He has lived Himself, He is man. From His death, backwards-looking, it's God who is on the scene, all the time. As from His birth forward-looking, it's man acting out his own human life all the time . . . True Man and True

> God means that Jesus' life can only be understood when faced both ways, from His birth to His death, and from . . . His death to His birth. If you do not make this cross the crucial position of man . . . Christ cannot be understood. He is man, in the direction from His . . . birth to His death. He is God in the direction from the Crucifixion to His birth, because then you can say that the God in Him was born, . . . the man who could go to the Cross.[59]

Such a mission as that undertaken by the formation of the Nicene Creed is indicative of the precarious position that the Church was in, and indeed the dangerous choices open to it if it were to survive.

As Rosenstock-Huessy emphasizes, the strategy of Athanasius, which weighed heavily on him throughout his life, was a dogmatic one that, through the subsequent interpellation of the *'filoque,'* would have fatal results for Church unity.[60] Rosenstock-Huessy reminds his readers that the term is not biblical but Greek, 'borrowed from the schools of the world.'[61] For Rosenstock-Huessy, the very word that is so important to Athanasius' influence is laden 'with original sin for he who speaks it reflects on God. And who reflects on God, at that moment stands in opposition to God.'[62] Yet in speaking thus, Athanasius found himself in the same situation as Paul had encountered when (as is described in Acts) he attempted to convince the Athenian philosophers of his time about the truth of the Resurrrection. Intellectual speculation is, for Rosenzweig, always the sign of a certain intellectual idleness: when things are really important, there is neither need nor time for speculation. And just as we are made and remade by catastrophes, God is meaningful only in the moment He is summoned and encountered; once He is placed under chloroform for dissection (i.e., analysis), he is already a corpse. For Rosenstock-Huessy, many traditional Christians are complicit in this grotesque act of simplifying God; one might even say that this is one of faith's greatest tests – that we not give in to childish longings for mythic redemption. In 'The Terms of the Creed,' Rosenstock-Huessy writes:

Logically, the Creed lists Father   1.

Son   2.

Holy Ghost   3.

Empirically, God enters our lives not as the Creator of our embryonic physique when we are begotten – but at the break-through of our little mind into the courageous affirmation of our allegiance. Hence

1. Spirit
2. Son
3. Father

is the experienced order. The childish talk in our Churches about God the Father makes me blush. Our God Is the Father to whom the Son had to say: God, oh my God, why hath thou forsaken me. But our Sunday school teachers make God out as the Father of Father's day, in plain English, as Daddie.[63]

Anthony and Athanasius represent for Rosenstock-Huessy one dyadic set of forces that would travel across the times against the imperial usurpation of the Church; Jerome (a.k.a. Hieronymous) and Augustine represent for him another. Briefly, Jerome's significance was in the creation of the Vulgate, the Latin version of the Bible. He had understood that a fundamental insight of Christianity is that what cannot be translated cannot be redeemed.[64] Just as Rosenzweig had seen that the Jews illustrate that God's love is unencumbered by His people having neither language nor state to root them, Rosenstock-Huessy sees that the power of Christianity is from its inception involved in translation – from Aramaic to Greek, to Latin, and with the Reformation to the vernacular. To anticipate a later point, there is a stark contrast between the Church and Islam regarding the issue of God and language and the centrality of translation in the Christian tradition, on the one hand, and the Islamic desire to ensure that the Koran is learned in the original word of God, on the other.

Rosenstock-Huessy tells us that the canon of the New Testament is 'itself a chain of magnificently faithful and magnificently free translations.'[65] The combination of fidelity and freedom in this sentence is as precise as it is telling. For it is precisely the purpose of faith to enhance freedom – the Spirit is this very freedom of love's power. Jerome 'showed that any language is a sheath for the sword of the spirit, but not the sword itself.' Thus he 'defies the . . . language of his own day; he becomes a great translator. That the spirit has to be retranslated in every generation, and in every generation, and every day, every word that we speak should be . . . a fresh translation of the spirit.'[66]

This is also why Rosenstock-Huessy insists that the gospels were never intended to be four attempts to faithfully reproduce one story that could be enclosed in one text (what Rosenstock-Huessy considers the fable of the text). Indeed, those four must break down if taken in this way (a point we consider more closely below). There is, he says, 'only an evangelical symphony in four sentences.'[67]

But it was the fourth of these four Church fathers, Augustine, who most directly influenced Rosenstock-Huessy. For it was Augustine who first conceived of a history of salvation, who made of history not simply a chronicle (as Greeks and imperial peoples did), or a story of God's elect (as the Jews did), but 'the history of humankind dedicated to one theme: "how does love become stronger than death."'[68] Thus Rosenstock-Huessy wrote of Augustine what is perhaps the key to his entire corpus:

> The scores of this composition, the histories, must be paraphrased in so many editions as there are generations [*Geschlechter*] of humankind. For the composition is recomposed in each generation by those whose love overcomes a murder or a death.
>
> So history becomes a great song, Augustine's Carmen Humanum; in its every line, perhaps every tone, becomes a lived human life. As soon and as often as the lines rhyme, love has once again become stronger than death. Then from out of absurd contingencies, from adverse circumstances, from silent events of epoch-making necessities, in which a lengthy ingested illness is finally confronted, crossfertilized [*eingekreuzt*] and consequently overcome.[69]

For Rosenstock-Huessy, Augustine was one of the last great examples of personal confession – the Church would subsequently convert entire peoples. And it is this fusion of perspectives, of individual and collective Redemption – his *Confessions* and his *City of God* – that makes Augustine such a remarkable figure for Rosenstock-Huessy, in that he was the first to envision a universal history. He is not, for Rosenstock-Huessy, primarily the writer of a philosophy of history, or a theologian – two types who may well possess shadowy features of Augustine; rather, he is a conscious creator of the future, whose mission is to bridge past and future through an institution that is open to all and through a vision of the past in which all members whose love is stronger than death are seen as essential contributors to the body of loving souls who together compose the goal of Redemption. For the Church has been wherever human beings have placed the God of love over their own egos, their own purposes; it has been wherever they have served love – with its requirement that sacrifice and desire be balanced – instead of bowing to the rule of selfishness. (Affinities with certain Hindu, Taoist, Sufi, and Buddhist de-essentialized views of the self are strong indications of how their coexistence with one another and with Christianity is both possible and an essential task of the future.)

The *Heilsplan,* the plan of salvation, is of a goal to come, the realized City of God, humanity in its completeness – the realization of its inherent divinity, in which each soul is a verse and a bearer of the entirety of history, because we realize that different histories belong to us – that all of history has the power to shape us if we are plastic enough in our responsiveness, sensitive enough to the living God who has spoken through the Ages and through *all* the forms of human association, that is, through all the bindings of love. There no complete isolation because the term is an oxymoron – just as we cannot be complete *in* isolation. The times chase each other – future catches up with past and in so doing ingests it into further future. And as we learn more of the past and it becomes part of our future, we *learn* – not in any conceptual sense, but in the day-to-day praxis of our common circumstance. The *Soziologie* is very much an attempt to tell of the common circumstance, to enable each person to see the tribal, imperial, Jewish, Greek life as having a certain shape and limit that was its past and that now finds itself reconfigured as empires and tribes, once outside of the world, become conscious of the Jewish God and the Christian historical march. As their presence is impressed on the consciousness of the Christian peoples, they change that consciousness, much as Marx had said when he maintained that the conquered change the habitus of the conquerors.

Rosenstock-Huessy's *Heilsgeschichte,* then, is a love story, the story of love's mutually expansive and integrative power. This and this alone is the real significance of the Bible, the Church, and history – they all tell and at the same time provide important contributions to the content of the story. Moreover, Rosenstock-Huessy learned this story from Augustine: '"Who loves, has faith and hope doesn't need anything else, scripture would become then a means for instructing others" (*De Doctrina* 1, 39[428]). "Love and do what you will" is another phrase of his.'[70] That this story of salvation is often hellish, even genocidal, is not in question. For evil is, as Augustine so astutely understood, love's resistance and misdirection (the constrictions of divine powers in an enclosed and thereby en-helled self).[71] And elsewhere, Rosenstock-Huessy cites (it seems wrongly) a phrase once commonly attributed to Augustine: 'unity in necessity, liberty in doubt, charity in all things,'[72] which he sees makes 'Augustine [the] ancestor of us all.'[73] He is ancestor of us all, not merely in having a 'view' of history but in understanding the unity of our plight and being possibly the most important architect ever of that unity. Of course, he deferred to Christ, finding in him the source of salvation. And he saw that he never could have envisaged such a unity of purpose unless Jesus Christ had died to bring humankind together as neighbours under the Father's love.

While, then, Rosenstock-Huessy's understanding of Christianity is utterly anti-Platonist, and in thorough defiance of those multitudinous vestiges of Platonism that, he saw, are so active in theologians such as Barth and in Brunner's moral critique of the Church, one of the features of his understanding of Christianity that is so interesting is how it connects with pre-Christian (anti-Western) tribal and imperial peoples. That is to say, his view of universal history, while based on Christianity as a constellation of powers that have been integrated through the Church, is not only not Platonic, but also not Eurocentric, at least in the usual way that Eurocentricism has been conceived, which is, as the extension and encapsulation of other lifeways through a colonizing logic of Western (philosophical) reason. Given that Rosenstock-Huessy makes the European revolutions the 'engine' of the second millennium that has brought us into the third millennium, this might seem a strange claim to make. But while he argues that the explosions of Europe have been essential in an economy of salvation, there could have been no Christianity without the social formations that enabled its birth. Not only that – and this, too, is part of his opposition to modern humanist and Platonist templates – but he also sees that these lifeways provide much of the material with which Christianity must work. A big part of the problem with humanism and Platonism is that their power largely derives from their abstractness, and abstractness moves us *away* from life. For managing and controlling dead things, this is very useful, but turned upon living creatures such a process is constantly in danger of killing the spirit – redemptive life needs living powers to reactivate dead ones.

Thus his *Soziologie* and his numerous courses on social history all induct readers and students into Christianity by first awakening them to premodern life. To be sure, a person can only know so much. But he had a profound knowledge of Egypt, Mesopotamia, Rome, Greece, and European tribes, and he had read widely about tribal peoples in anthropology. True, of other empires he seemed far less well read – or at least he said little, though he often alluded to other imperial societies such as China. But his main comparative interest was in the broader structural patterns that pertained to them and in the integration that had taken place over the ages. Most important, he was constantly trying to break down his readers' and students' humanistic/modern Euro-American–centred way of seeing the world. And he thought that any version of Christianity that was built on primarily Greek or modern naturalist and humanist concepts could only understand the Church's history through a blend of morals, legends, and myths, while remaining oblivious to the phantasmic character of the building blocks of modern naturalism and humanism ('self,' 'subject,' 'nature,' 'object,' 'mind,' 'body,' etc., none of which are concrete realities).

That, too, is why he could so starkly contrast biblical thought with Greek thought, while making the point that only sometimes and at certain places in Church history had Greek thought completely held the upper hand – for example, in the formation of scholasticism, and in those places where it hung on tenaciously (nowhere more than in Paris when it was at its most rotten, as we will examine in detail later). In his approach to Christianity, nowhere does he project from modernity onto tribes and ancient empires; rather, he situates Christianity in the context of the Roman Empire – that is, with its Jewish origins, its surrounding tribal interactions, and (last but, if not least, certainly not first) its Greek intellectual bits. To understand Judaism, he digs deeper than Rosenzweig, insisting that one must first understand what Judaism reacted *against* – the imperial life of Egypt. Thus he wrote a substantial amount on Egypt, not only in the *Soziologie* but also in *Die Angeschriebene Ewigkeit: Briefe nach Kairo* originally written in English as *Letters to Cynthia*), which takes up a considerable part of *Die Sprache des Menschengeschlechts*. In a short essay in *I Am an Impure Thinker,* he even contrasts the spiritual importance of the Egyptian symbol of the *ka*, 'the power behind the throne and life giving genius,' with the impotence and distintegrative view of the modern ego or self, heavily criticizing von Bissing and Breasted's work in Egyptology for its modern Eurocentric projections.[74]

But he also insists that to make sense of Egypt, one must first understand the life of the tribes against which Egypt defined itself. This inevitably brings with it a certain sense of historical 'progress.' For he is interested in demonstrating the crises of limits of human association – crises that build new flight paths and that create a common history. Let us leave aside for the moment the politically volatile concept of progress, and just say here that Rosenstock-Huessy was as contemptuous of the Whig view of history as pretty well everyone else today. But just as Kant sought to explain how mathematical physics was possible, Rosenstock-Huessy had a simple question on hand that needed to be answered: 'How were two world wars possible?' Which can also be translated as, 'How is that we have become conscious of being members of the one planet?' There are, of course, many different answers to this, or parts of a single answer. Where, then, does one start, and how much detail does one provide? Again, there is inevitably disputation about which events ought to be emphasized when trying to answer this question. Rosenstock-Huessy's answer can be faulted for minor historical errors (he makes occasional errors of date, location, etc.), and one can dispute the significance he attaches to some events. That said, his most compelling argument relates to his major methodological contribution, which may be said to have four aspects: (a) the role played by the great European revolutions of the last millennia; (b) the role played by Christianity in precipitating those revolutions; (c) the porosity he ascribes to Christianity, that is, how it absorbed potencies from the great storehouses of living powers of empires, tribes, city-states, and that engimatic diasporic people whose God they responded to (or appropriated, depending on how one reads it); and (d) the radicalness and novelty of Christianity's reconfiguration of those powers. These four aspects taken together are essential for understanding his interest in Christianity and the historical role he ascribes to it and its entire centre, Jesus.

It would take a book every bit as long as this to present the details of Rosenstock-Huessy's account of Jesus. Ultimately, that account is inseparable from the arguments he provides about the social intersections to which Jesus' life and death were such a radical response, and from his emphasis on how so much of Christianity's power came from its location – that is, from the geohistorical intersection of tribal, imperial, Greek, and Jewish lifeways. All of these, he believed, were simultaneously at crisis points at the time of Jesus' birth. In the case of the tribes – and this will be explained more fully in a later discussion of the tribes in the context of Islam – he always held that tribes that had survived in their pure forms (as in the Americas and Australia) were limited in their powers of resistance precisely *because* they had found a way to disassociate themselves for so long from the greater catastrophes that had brought or forced so many of the world's tribes into imperial lifeways. I say this to clarify the reference to the Sioux in the following description of the fourfold crisis from *The Fruit of Lips*, in which he makes his case schematically and succinctly, stressing the impact and response to the crises of different forms of life rather than their enduring contributions, which he discusses at length in the *Soziologie*:

When all this had been said, when the Sioux had spoken and the Chinese, the Greek and the Jew, one world came to an end. This was and is the complete cycle of antiquity:

1. Listeners to the spirits of the dead created Ritual.
2. Listeners to the sky-world and the cosmic universe built the temples.
3. Listeners to laws and cities already achieved became poets and artists.
4. Listeners to the future became prophets.
5. These four phases of speech were unified and superseded in Jesus. And because of this action, he is called Christ. Christ is the fruit of lips of antiquity.[75]

And:

Jesus is the heir of antiquity. He filled and fulfilled the four 'listening posts' of
Child of the ancestors in tribes,
Child of the times in empires,
Child of nature in Greece,
Child of revolution in Israel.[76]

Christianity had sided with the victims of each of these various social formations. Those whom the major social forms of the ancient world had excluded and repressed, those 'souls' that had been left un-activated except to satiate the needs and desires of their masters, and then to die, were the powers appealed to and marshalled by the earliest Christians.[77] In *The Fruit of Lips*, Rosenstock-Huessy writes that Jesus 'by being the voluntary victim at the feast . . . becomes the first victim in the world who can speak. Nobody has ever spoken in this role. But victims, though mute were essential.'[78] And: 'In the mass, the first victim invites the others, the partakers, of the service in which they themselves are the offerings.'[79]

And it took four gospels, each reaching out into a different part of reality for the message of the Lord, each accentuated in its own unique way by each gospel writer,[80] for that message to be given. Again from *The Fruit of Lips*: 'The written Gospel is the luminous track left in the dark from Christ on Golgotha to the Church of James in Jerusalem, to the Church of Peter in Rome, to the Churches of Paul all over the Gentile World and finally to John and to the Island of Patmos.'[81] Schematically, he sums up the different roles of the four gospels as involving four dramatic actions:

Scene One: Matthew, the tax collector, digs beneath the figures and concepts of his accounts and discovers the full power which human words may acquire when they, as his seed, are spoken on a man's way to his death.

Scene Two: Peter, the 'boorish fisherman,' is placed in the center of the last Western sky-world, in Rome with The God-Man Caesar, with the astrology of her temples, with the hieroglyphs. Here he proclaims the true temple, the Word, and the true hieroglyphs of this temple, the ministers of the Word.

Scene Three: Luke, the Greek physician, versed in the art of healing, is placed in the Jewish medium of 'No' to the physical world and of fear of contamination with physical idols, and places this No between the natural law of Jews as well as Gentiles, on the one side, and the new creative Yes of the Christian.

Scene Four: John, the prophet of Revelation, comes into the Greek cosmos, and frees their art and poetry by making God's poetry his theme. He asks, how does God write a poem?[82]

Christianity was a social body, but it had also insisted on the uniqueness of each soul in its relationship to God and, through that relationship, in the uniqueness of the gifts that each in its service could provide to others. Christianity was thus from its inception polymorphous, polyphonic, and polychromic and hence could and did appeal to peoples of every sort of social formation. Philosophy, on the other hand, always emphasizes one capacity above all others – that being our capacity to know – and one type – that being the philosopher. That is why the enlightened philosophers criticized the Church for not being philosophical, for the barbarism of its missionizing. But anyone who knows anything about Church history knows that it did not spread throughout Europe through the sword. The fanatics of the Crusades and the Inquisition, and the missionary zealots who supported the Conquistadors (to take three of the worst creations of Christendom) were different creatures from the slaves who gathered in catacombs, or the monks who went deep into unknown forests armed with nothing but faith. Christ had taught that we can enter the kingdom only by each of us being each other's servant. Again, from *The Fruit of Lips:*

Outside the Christian era, we are particularized into the shabby half-ness of one sex, one generation, one place, one class, one intelligence, one individual separated-ness. Inside the Christian era, every hearer of the word who links up with one single underdog, any one team composed of speaker and listener, of battered victim and baptized good Samaritan, together makes epoch.[83]

And:

> If he says that we all together are the Son who shall become as divine as the Father, he will find inside this history his own line which just he and he alone is asked to speak. The We who shall be who they shall be, do not consist of dumb animals. These 'We' cannot contain anybody who remains just anybody. Everybody must enter inside and into the 'we' in his appointed hour, in his power of becoming somebody, this definite person.[84]

If Christianity's power came from its siding with the powerless, the Church's success was not by way of its purely philosophical appeal to a morally pure vantage point that ever sighs at humanity's endless errors and crimes. The Church was a way to work with what powers were on earth and in heaven, and it summoned them to form the body of Christ, and with that to reactivate energies thought dead and useless, just as the earliest Christians were the riff-raff and useless dross from some godforsaken dump full of religious lunatics in the Roman Empire.

It was the same riff-raff that believed in the Second Coming, which, for Rosenstock-Huessy, was none other than actualizing of the City of God. It was the messianic fulfilment for which the Jews wait and pray, which they recall, dwell in, and anticipate in their daily services, rituals, and festivals. But for the Christian, it can come only through time, only through faith and action done in love. When Rosenzweig said that 'there is no history at all of the Kingdom of God'[85] and that 'the history of the Church is as little history of the Kingdom of God as is the history of the empire,'[86] he was speaking as a Jew. But through a Christian lens, he had indeed spoken of the most Christian orthodox of distinctions – the one between the heavenly city and the earthly city. This distinction, as we have indicated already, is also of fundamental importance to Rosenstock-Huessy. Indeed, without it one will never understand how he could talk simultaneously about the pagan *and* Christian nature of European nations. For this dualism ever alerts one to distinguish between what is part of the real and eternal kingdom and what is part of the delusional and ever disintegrative kingdom of the love of self. The

Augustinian distinction is more often than not interpreted as a dualism confirming deeply Platonist philosophical tendencies. But Augustine's view of providence had little to do with the Platonic teleological cosmology precisely *because* it sought to demonstrate not only how evil or sin may be incorporated into the whole of creation for some good (even Plato suggests this, in the *Laws*), but also how over time the body of faithful will succeed – 'thy kingdom come on earth as it be in heaven' (Plato never breaks with the cycle, which is most evident in the *Republic's* constitutional typology).

The history of salvation, though, is indeed one in which the dark human side is operative precisely because that *is* the nature that must be transformed. We are born in sin, but sin is also our teacher. It is what creates the crises that force inventiveness of the spirit and openness to grace, that compel us to found institutions erected on and devoted to principles that emerge as their response, in our efforts to close off one form of hell.

For Rosenstock-Huessy, that we can have a sense of there being a world, that we can have a planetary consciousness, that we can see the world from the victim's perspective, that we can possess a sense of the solidarity of the suffering – these are the real miracles, not fairy tales. But such miracles would, he holds, not be possible had there not been a completely different approach to reality than is evident in all other forms of human association prior to the Church and to its mission of pursuing the full number of the times.

For Rosenstock-Huessy, Christian faith is the expression of the truth of the powers of faith, hope, and love. And Christianity is a fruit-bearing tree. Its fruits are the different bodies and institutions that are formed to contain the Holy Spirit. This, in a nutshell, is why Rosenstock-Huessy found any kind of ahistorical reading of Christianity to be but one more example of the ubiquitousness of Greek abstraction in modern life – specifically, the Greek (philosophical) perversion of Christian teaching. Jesus was Lord of the aeons, for he had recognized that on their own, none of the ancient types of humanity or the lifeways within which they were formed could help us survive. Jesus was neither priest, nor prophet, nor king, nor poet, nor a tribesman, nor a man of empire, and while born a Jew, he refused to remain bound by Jewish law. But he had understood that we can be all things in all – indeed, this was our God-given promise. He had, says Rosenstock-Huessy in the *Soziologie*, combined the four calendars: of the seasons (our imperial or Egyptian heritage); of the family (the days that effect us personally); of birth and death days (days on which we are compelled to commemorate either founding or mourning); and days of spiritual enjoyment, and holidays (literally, 'holy days').

Rosenstock-Huessy's study of Christianity is ultimately a blend of anthropology, sociology, and history combined by means of his grammatical orientation, which for him was closely bound up with the method he described as 'the cross of reality.' He conceived it largely as a way for us to understand the temporal as well as spatial nature of reality, so that we could break from the monchromatic, sequential time model that he saw as dominating the social sciences. Thus in the *Soziologie*, he explicitly rejected Schelling's formula from The *Ages of the World* that 'the past is known, the present cognized, the future intimated' (which students of Rosenzweig have rightly claimed is also repeated by Rosenzweig), because it remained trapped in that model.[87]

Rosenstock-Huessy's most elaborate account of 'the cross of reality' runs through much of the first volume of his *Soziologie*. In Part One of that volume he investigates how the various schools of sociology have tended to be marshalled into one of the four fundamental orientations to reality that correspond to life's spatial and temporal dimensions: inwardness (as in reflection or subjectivity), outwardness (as in action or objectivity), trajective (from past forward), and prejective (from future backward, as in all goal-orientated action). When we take these separately, we fail to see that they intersect and cross over – that is, we fail to see that they form a cross.[88]

In his conclusion to Volume One of the *Soziologie*, he also defends his argument that we are ever situated at a crossroads within reality. This is in the context of his exploration of the importance of fourfoldness in mythical thought.[89] Here, his thinking had been anticipated by Kant's fourfold table of the categories – that is, Kant had grasped that the consitutents of thinking that had been identified and tabulated by Aristotle could only be deemed genuine components of human understanding if they applied to more than just thought; they had to be conditions of a possible experience, and hence spatially and temporally applicable. With his categories of the understanding, Kant had gone beyond the law of contradiction of logic. But even more important, he had, according to Rosenstock-Huessy, transcended the oppositions and tensions that typify mythologists (who invariably find themselves imprisoned in one of these four vistas), and metaphysicians (who emphasize subjectivity and objectivity), and Romantics (who privilege the past), and utopians (who privilege the future), by showing how categories of understanding work cooperatively in thought so that we can make adequate judgments about experience.[90]

In the context of epistemology, as good a definition as any of what Rosenstock-Huessy means by the cross of reality comes from some straightforward passages from *Speech and Reality*, *The Christian Future*, and an unpublished essay on epistemology, 'Dr. Johnson's Cat and the Assimilation of Reality: An Exercise in the Functioning of the Cross of Reality.' The first of these passages emphasizes how our speech is governed by this fourfoldness, what he calls its cruciform character:

> When we look at the four statements once more, they show man in a very obvious situation, and this situation is nothing but the situation of any living organism within a living universe.
>
> Whenever we speak, we assert our being alive because we occupy a center from which the eye looks backward, forward, inward, and outward. To speak, means to be placed in the center of the cross of reality.

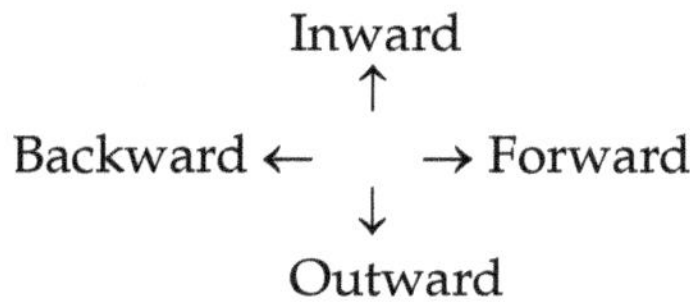

> Four arrows point in the four directions in which any living being is enmeshed. A human being, when speaking, takes his stand in time and space. 'Here' he speaks from an inner space to an outer world, and from an outward world into his own consciousness. And 'now' he speaks between the beginning and the end of times.[91]

In 'Dr. Johnson's Cat,' he emphasizes that in wanting to know something, we must be aware of the different directions that our knowledge may take us and thus remain centred in an orientation that enables us to empower ourselves on all of reality's fronts, so that we are not depleted through one-sided and contradictory visions of reality:

> The assimilation of reality by our understanding takes place in a gradual manner. Man has to use a number of glasses in order to become acquainted with reality. Each pair of glasses represents the world to us in a different order, a different arrangement. And not before we have passed through

the four aggregate states of which the glasses are sympathetic, can we pretend to know. Each separated step of getting information through one pair of glasses only is a preliminary step. A student learns external data, a child repeats solemn formulas, our will for power thinks in Imperatives and a mystic poet revels in inner ecstasy.

Each of these four types uses another entrance into the house of wisdom. Most of them are pretty fixed types and never hear of other doors in the house. The first impression is final. The rationalist always remains the eager student on the bench, the conventionalist is satisfied when he conforms with society, the British colonial, the Junker, the Fascist are at peace when they shout their commands into the face of reality and the mystic soul meets his God in silence, because all cling to their one and first doorway as final. I am afraid, we cannot abandon our claim for all the entrances to the house of reality. For on each doorway one indispensable form of truth is disclosed. It would not suffice to say that the glasses of the four methods of approach are of a different colouring though it may be true that the light differs widely.[92]

A somewhat similar point, albeit not so clearly epistemological, about the dangers of being pulled in different directions by our grasp of reality comes from *The Christian Future*, where he writes that we are lost if we cannot adjust to these different poles of reality and that

man's life, social as well as individual is lived at a crossroads between four 'fronts': backward toward the past, forward into the future, inward among ourselves, our feelings, wishes and dreams, and outward against what we must fight or exploit or come to terms with or ignore. It is obviously fatal to fail on any front – to lose the past, to miss the future, to lack inner peace or outer efficiency. Would we run forward only, all the acquired qualities of character and civilization would vanish. If we look backward exclusively, we cease to have a future. And so on.

Yet it is equally obvious that no individual can move adequately in all four directions at once. Therefore life is perpetual decision: when to continue the past and when to change, and where to draw the line between the inner circle we speak to and the outer objects we merely speak of and try to manipulate. Hence both mental and social health depends on preserving a delicate mobile balance between forward and backward, inward and outward, trends. Integration, living a complete and full life, is accordingly.[93]

The final quote, from *The Christian Future,* emphasizes how suffering itself is involved in the forces of space and time:

> Our existence is a perpetual suffering and wrestling with conflicting forces, paradoxes, contradictions within and without. By them we are stretched and torn in opposite directions, but through them comes renewal. And these opposing directions are summed up by four which define the great space and time axes of all men's life on earth, forming a Cross of Reality.[94]

That this fundamental feature of reality is depicted by way of an analogy with the crucifixion demonstrates that Rosenstock-Huessy was *committed* to his participation in reality. This was why (a) he finally settled, after much unease, on depicting his work as sociology; and (b) he was convinced that sociology was the one discipline among the human sciences whose practitioners were invariably dedicated to diagnosing the sources of social diseases and suffering. In this he found Saint-Simon to be the father of modern sociology, for he had powerfully grasped the 'primary fact of suffering' and had made it the cornerstone of his social thinking. Rosenstock-Huessy also saw Saint-Simon as attempting to 'renew the treasures of clerical Christianity, and to transmute them into the language of science, of the thought of the future, of general human applicability.'[95] Rosenstock-Huessy's own sociology would follow in that vein, and he would deliberately place his work under the authority of Saint-Simon. Both, he said, based their Christianity on it being the 'science of sinners . . . and suffering human beings,'[96] not on any dogma. Hence what he says about Saint-Simon is an important clue to his own method:

> Saint-Simon is not the slave of the latest social problems. He does not harp on particular principles, or summarily trace everything back to labour, or economics, or Christianity. He sees the first-hand-ness of various forces of creation untraceable to one another and yet presented to us as one uniform creation. 'Saint-Simon was still learning when he died. There is nothing to show that he had arrived at his final position' (E.M. Butler, *The Saint-Simonian-Religion in Germany,* Cambridge 1926, p. 10). It was for this reason that he was able to cry out on his deathbed, *'L'avenir est à nous!'* Most men end as they begin, as isolated individuals: this à nous is the proud fruit of his sufferings, and that is why I acknowledge Saint-Simon's authority.[97]

The centrality, then, of the fact of suffering in conjunction with the fourfold pulls and intersections of space and time, combined with the attempt to overcome that suffering by bringing (to slightly modify Shakespeare) the times into joint is what he sees as the power and truth of the Church. How it does that, though, is ever dependent on the times in which it finds itself, in the same way that what it in turn becomes is dependent on its times and on the mission that is necessary for those times. Again, this is Augustine. Though it is easy to miss this because most people do not think of the Church through its Ages, but as one block.

7 The Ages of the Church and Redemption through Revolution

Rosenzweig and Rosenstock-Huessy both agree that the Church could only be appreciated as a historical body, and that we could only make sense of it if we understood the major ages that constituted it. While Rosenstock-Huessy would write a work (with his friend Joseph Wittig) entitled *Das Alter der Kirche*, it was Rosenzweig who originally argued, in *The Star of Redemption*, that the Church consisted of three ages.

The first of the ages of the Church, for Rosenzweig, was that of the Petrine Church. He sums it up thus:

The messengers of Peter's successor crossed the *lines*: they went out and taught all the peoples. The Church no longer sets any outer limits for itself as the empire did; it is on principle not satisfied with any border, it has no knowledge of renunciation. As it outwardly throws its protective cloak around the destiny of the whole world, so, too, within its bosom, no one may remain only for himself. It demands of everyone the immediate sacrifice of his Self, but it fully returns this to everyone in its motherly love; each is a precious and irreplaceable child, always unique in spite of all others. Hence, through it, the individual's life depends immediately on the life of the whole world. The bond that ties him, like the Mother Church itself, to the destiny of the world is love. In the missionary's love for those who still sit in darkness, the pushing back of the outer borders takes place, the enlarging of the outer, visible edifice; in the visible sacrifice of pious work, in the visible offering of the material or spiritual good deed, love which unites man with it and thus with the whole, also exists in the heart of the Church. In this way the Petrine Church creates a visible body, at first for itself and the men who are its members and inasmuch as they are its members; but, afterwards also for the world outside, which it gradually

pervasively shapes and rules, in the empire's union over the kingships
of the nations; in the edifice of classes and professions with regard to the
individual, it finally annexes man, too, to itself, insofar as he is still outside
and remains outside, and yet with this also incorporates him in it.[1]

According to Rosenzweig, while the Petrine Church missionized an
external world, it could only deal with paganism by defending itself
from it, by closing it out. But reality – and the powers of the human
soul are as real as any 'object of nature' – is not something that can
simply be quietly entombed forever. The Christian world closed out
all sorts of talents and capacities and powers. Thus, to take an example
not advanced by Rosenzweig, the entire approach to *eros* in the pagan
world was feared, attacked, and closed down by the Church Fathers,
and a new type – the monastic – was created and favoured. Yet *eros*
would return and would have to be dealt with. Originally it returned
in a spiritualized form; but so overwhelming was its return that it gave
birth to the still enduring myth of romantic love, and a new type, the
troubadours, came into existence to sing of the beauty of the beloved.

To make his point about the attack on paganism, Rosenzweig uses
the example of the ecclesiastical closure of the philosophical schools.
He could just as easily have mentioned any of the art forms that had
flourished in Greece and Rome and that had all but died out for a thousand years. The powers of the pagan world's past continued to lurk
in distant memory – or in records left unread for centuries. But when
there was a willingness to re-engage with pagan powers – from the
late Middle Ages, through the Renaissance and the Reformation, up
until the time of Goethe – the Church, says Rosenzweig, had to reinvent
itself, so that it was driven no longer primarily by a 'love' that would
incorporate members into its visible body, but rather (and this would
underscore the change in psychic power required by the new challenge
at hand) by a *faith* that would seek actively to transform pagan powers
by engaging with them.

The subsequent Pauline Age of the Church was identifiable by the
role played by interiority and invisibility within the Church. During this
age, the Church attempted to win the spiritual battle against paganism
in the world (as well as the paganism it saw everywhere in the visible
Church and its head) by resorting to the inner powers of conscience,
soul, spirit, and mind. The proof of the power of faith in God or of
God's love was no longer to be demonstrated by visible achievements.
But in this very re-engagment with paganism, however tenacious its

faith in its ability to transmute the powers of everyday life (which are essentially what pagan powers are), the Church exposed itself to the danger that it would be swamped by the world's pagan powers:

> These are the centuries where the world unity established by the Petrine Church seemed to shatter on all sides, where pagan configurations came to life again everywhere, where the nations sought to overturn Christianity, the States the empire, individuals the classes, and well-known people the professions. The Christian world body seemed again to disintegrate for these three centuries, in fact four centuries, counting the aftermath; this was the price of the success of the Christianization of the soul, the conversion 'a posteriori' of the now awakened pagan spirit that had never quite died. When this period ended, there was no longer a twofold truth; faith had succeeded where love had to fail: the baptism of the soul that is without a world, the invisible, recollecting. The soul now brought to God its whole memory, its whole content, as the invisible offering (like in the Petrine Church, it brought its whole presentness, the context of its action) and received it back from him in the invisible gift of faith. Hence the soul was now freed of all fences and walls, and it lived in the unconditional. But it was 'faith alone' that had led it into this life. It was the soul alone that lived it.[2]

According to Rosenzweig, both the Petrine and the Pauline Church were torn by unsustainable dualisms: the former by faith and reason, the latter by inner and outer, or spirit and body. And just as reason had pulled faith in its train into a new age where it could truly be active, as it was for the Reformers, the Reformers' or Pauline Church, according to Rosenzweig, found its resolution and completion in the recognition that a life is both body and soul, and that the inner man and the institutions that house him must all be expressions of the freedom that is his birthright and destiny. That destiny is to be found in the world, so the world must be able to sustain and nourish the spirit.

Goethe's prayer of hope and destiny is the great modern articulation of the modern self's sense of destiny in the world, of an assuredness that one's inner life is bound to 'the whole of worldly life,'[3] and of the capacity to pray to it. There is still love and faith behind this prayer – they are not negated, but they do find a completion and a reconciliation in hope.[4] For it is hope in the future, a prayer of hope, that one's existence and one's (inner) freedom form part of the interlocking spirits and body of the world, of that microcosm (and Rosenzweig uses that favourite phrase of the Renaissance, which was drawn from the pagan 'mysteries').[5]

Rosenzweig's discussion of Goethe stresses that he is 'the great pagan and the great Christian' and that his prayer is as much one of unbelief as of belief, for it places himself and his own happiness at the centre of the universe – 'my will' be done, not 'thy will' be done. Yet the *mine* and the *thine* are united in the hope behind the prayer. This is why Rosenzweig also says that the prayer is one of unbelief *and* belief. The prayer that expresses the underlying sensibility or orientation of soul of hope is what defines the Johannine Age. For this reason, Goethe is said to be the Father of the Johannine Church.[6] Now, says Rosenzweig, this prayer is,

henceforth prayed by every Christian, even if in distinction from Goethe it is not his only prayer. And henceforth, the peoples, too, and all the secular orders of Christianity say this prayer. They all know now that their life must be personal life and is inserted precisely as such into the movement of the world; they all find the justification of their existence in the vitality of their destiny. We see Christian peoples appear only now, whereas in the Pauline era there were worldly authorities, and in the Petrine era nations subject to the one Holy Empire. States and tribes needed a complement to their lives, the one finding it in the faith of the individual and the steward-ship of the Word, the other in the Empire and in the visible Church; it is only thus that they could be sound fertile soil for the sowing of Christian-ity. Only now do the peoples have complete vitality in themselves: since then every people has known and believed it has 'its day in history'; and if they still need an earthly completion beyond this, then also the purely worldly, really all too worldly concept of 'society' gives it to them.[7]

Of the Johannine Completion, Rosenzweig also writes:

The Johannine completion does not have a specific form; it is simply not a piece anymore, but only completion of the till now incomplete work. Therefore it will have to live in the old forms . . . The Johannine Church itself does not assume a visible shape of its own. It is not built; it can only grow.[8]

If, then, Goethe's prayer is but the prayer of a future built upon a hope that is the completion of the love and faith of the preceding ages, Rosenzweig also notes that Goethe's prayer also borders directly on [that of] the prayer of the sinner, who presumes himself free to entreat everything, and of the fanatic, who thinks that, for the sake of the distant One which the moment of the prayer indicates as essential to him, everything other than this One, everything nighest, must be forbidden to him.[9]

That is to say, the prostration of oneself before God, the act that is undertaken in the knowledge of our deficiency, of our dependency on powers beyond our control, of our wish to work with what is higher, easily slips into an act of *hubris*. The subject might want everything now (the sinner) – cf. the righteous man, who waits for the proper time to receive the gifts that he will be ready to appreciate – and might be so sure of how to get it (the fanatic) that he brushes aside those nearest to reach his goal. This new supplication, then, easily creates sinners and fanatics. Or to express it in more secular terms, Rosenzweig is saying that there are three ways that modern men and women stand before their future: the first is Goethe's, or the Johannine way of hope and service and destiny being united; the second is to be driven by one's own selfishness (the sinner); and the third is that of the zealot, the fanatic, who is ruthless enough to sacrifice all and sundry to bring about a better future. In contrast to Goethe, Rosenzweig sees Nietzsche's Zarathustra as the prototype of a sinner and fanatic in one, 'an immoralist who smashes all the old tablets, and a tyrant who overpowers his neighbour as well as himself for the sake of the next but one, his friend for the sake of new friends.'[10]

The revolutionary fervour of the age in which Rosenzweig lived was, then, seen by him as the result of the false messianism that is at the root of Christianity and that, because it is false, is incapable of preventing, and indeed has accelerated and facilitated, the diabolical outbreak of sinners and fanatics. This is the antithesis of the messianic politics that the stateless Jew embodies. The fanatical pursuit of false redemption delays the redemption that is the object of messianic politics. What Rosenzweig calls 'the entreatment of the kingdom' is, among the moderns, a sickness. And for Rosenzweig, the utopianisms of Rousseau, Tolstoy, and Bolshevism, no less than Nietzsche's tortured call to the higher men and philosophers of the future, are symptoms of the modern cultural sickness. And the doctrines of such utopians cannot provide the cure, as is evident, for him, in the failure of each to live his utopia.[11]

The Messianic age, by contrast, comes from God. But that age is prepared by the day-to-day work done for, and by the love given to, 'anybody' who is the neighbour. The Jews know how to wait in preparation of the messiah, and they must be ever prepared. In a letter to Gertrud Oppenheim, Rosenzweig wrote that 'every act must be done as if the fate of eternity were to hinge on it. Because one never knows whether it weren't to hang on it.'[12]

What Rosenzweig has done here – albeit in sketchy form – is make the claim for the evolution *and* continuity of the orientation that reaches from the Petrine to the Johannine, from the early Christians to the modern as exemplified by the father of the new Age, Goethe, who is both a pagan *and* a Christian. Yet the modern Christian is *also* pagan.

Rosenzweig's depiction of the three ages of the Church is, then, part of his attempt to throw light on what he sees as the character of modern Christian peoples, which includes his contemporary Germans, most of whom do not realize what in them is part of their Christian heritage and what is part of their pagan heritage. Christianity is, then, not simply or even primarily to be confused with one of its former ages – and this, for Rosenzweig, is precisely the confusion to which most modern Europeans succumb. Yet it is significant that by and large, this is not how educated Muslims think. They most definitely think, with Rosenzweig and Rosenstock-Huessy, that Europe is Christian. That it has not escaped its roots by becoming superficially secular does not mean that its people do not belong to a wall-less Church. The values of its states, its myths, and its approach are still saturated with Christian creations.[13]

The converse of this is also true – that people who do indeed associate themselves with the Petrine or Pauline Church are pagan in all manner of ways they don't suspect – for example, in their estimations of physical beauty, wealth, the mind, power, or any of these 'natural' goods.

For Rosenstock-Huessy, the proof of the spread of Christianity was the Great War – a war that was also, for him, a concoction of pagan energies. Briefly, but this is to be developed at length later, the modern nation was a Christian creation in its original (French) messianic mission and in its overthrow of all that blocked and poisoned the creation of the kingdom. And it was pagan in its idolatry of the nation. For Rosenstock-Huessy, its most Christian act was also its most radical act – the reconciliation between Christians and Jews in the form of Jewish emancipation. And that could only occur by making the gesture under another sign – that of *humanitas*. And the return of the pagan came with the very undoing of that gesture in the Dreyfus case. That undoing was the beginning of modern Zionism and much of the subsequent conflict that has plagued Israel and its neighbours. That the nation-state now is simply accepted as the 'natural' order of things is indicative of how powerful this new form of a people as nation was. Its global reach was clear and obvious proof of the French Revolution, whether the particular nation-state was democratic or not. Indeed, Rosenstock-Huessy emphasizes that no constitution is simply one type and that what the ancients classified as the basic constitutional types – monarchy, tyranny, oligarchy, democracy, polity – are but various means of dealing with the different fronts of reality.

For Rosenstock-Huessy, until the Great War, it was meaningful to speak of peoples untouched by Christianity. Thus in the *Soziologie* he writes: 'Until 1911 there were the twins of Egypt, the Chinese Emperor. There were and are stone-age tribes, there are academics and Israel exists. All these exist as if Christian calculation of time had still not occurred.'[14] But for him, this all ceased with the war. From then on, all peoples were pulled into the same combustive power of revolution that had created the nations and the great revolutionary ideologies of Europe and eventually the world wars. That is to say, all the peoples of the earth were pulled into the one economy of salvation. Hence he writes that 'the division between pre-Christian and intra-Christian nations has stopped or must stop.'[15] The economy of salvation is another way of saying that all people on the entire planet have been forced to become neighbours – even if they remain enemies. And this is why the Christian cannot stop at the formulation of love thy neighbour. For the universality of the Christian mission makes a neighbour of everyone, but it also recognizes that the commandment to love must be active in a world in which enmity is a constant reality.[16]

If, then, we talk of Rosenstock-Huessy's Christian social thinking, it is important to bear in mind that he is not interested in resuscitating pre-Johannine forms of Christianity. This makes it hard for self-designated Christians – who are invariably more ensconced in pre-Johannine incarnations of the Church, whether Catholic or Protestant – to accept that Rosenstock-Huessy is a Christian at all. Central to his work is that he wants to instruct his audience in the processes that bind us into a common era, the ones that have brought us to a common path and a common task. For him, even though there is more knowledge of history today than at any other point in the past, he sees ever fewer people thinking in terms of historical waves, and ever fewer people being able to see life as a temporal process that conforms not to mechanical time but rather to the ruptures and new paths opened by events. In Volume Two of his *Soziologie*, he wrote that he called the first volume the *Die Übermacht der Räume* (The Dominance of Spaces) because the overwhelming majority of twentieth-century men and women were unable to rise above their horizon of time and grasp the greater stream to which they were being subjected.[17] Few historians or sociologists have ever taken seriously the idea that 'spaces are projected times'[18] – an idea that, when heard carefully, forces us to think about social existence in terms of the tides and streams of time that form it and not simply in terms of the synchronization or delineation of spatial forces. Rosenstock-Huessy has an uncanny ability, most evident in Volume Two of his *Soziologie*, to show the features of a time body as if they were a living creature. And this is exactly what he believed – that times are bodies that are creaturely: 'the tides of time in which we participate, day and year and age of life and century, are creatures like violets, roses, oak trees, high mountains.'[19]

In *Out of Revolution*, Rosenstock-Huessy reminds his readers that in the year 1000, not one of the modern nations existed; they were born out of the five hundred years of clerical revolutions that commenced with what is more widely known as the investiture conflict but what Rosenstock-Huessy calls the 'papal revolution,' or the 'first clerical revolution.' This is in reference to the conflict during which Gregory VII sought to assert his spiritual supremacy over the Holy Roman Emperor, Henry IV – a conflict that transformed the most powerful man in Europe into a humble penitent shivering in the snow at Canossa, waiting to be accepted back into the flock of the faithful by Christ's living representative. For Rosenstock-Huessy, this event – which is part of the curriculum of any student of political theory, but which is all too frequently skipped over so lightly in discussions of European history – 'was the most general and intensive social earthquake Europe has ever seen. It shook the only stable, unblemished and respected symbol of unity: the economic, racial, religious, and moral unit of palace and manor. It emancipated the sons, clergy, knights, and servants of every manor in Europe. By a revolutionary act the pope set up a new balance between economic particularism and spiritual universalism.'[20]

At the heart of that conflict was Gregory's enforcement of the celibacy of the clergy, which had been established to put an end to the nepotism and widespread corruption in the emperor's clerical appointments, as well as to prevent Church property from becoming a means for personal or familial gain. By creating an institutional counterweight to the emperor's power, Gregory established the basis for what would later, with the impetus of the Reformers, form the cornerstone of modern freedom – the division of Church and State. Gregory VII's reform involved raising Paul's status above Peter's and casting himself as a follower of Paul; in so doing, he set up the Church as a Church Universal – no longer was it merely the Church of Rome.

The movement from Church visible to Church invisible, from Petrine to Pauline Christianity, had its embryonic moment in Gregory's clerical revolt, as Peter's Church became but one of the Churches under the Pope's 'Pauline presidency.'[21] Though of course, its Petrine form was to emerge victorious as Rome increasingly asserted itself politically. The pope would become one territorial ruler among others; and by Dante's time, Pope Boniface VIII (whom Dante puts in hell) had enthusiastically embraced all the worldliness that Gregory had renounced so strictly. In so doing, Boniface dragged the Church back into the psychic squalor that had first led Gregory to stand against the emperor.

Nevertheless, Rosenstock-Huessy rightly draws attention to the revolutionary arc that spans from Gregory to Luther and that leads to Paul overcoming Peter once and for all. One need only review Dante's attacks on Church corruption and avarice – including his damnation of numerous popes and cardinals, and his hostility to simony – to see that, notwithstanding the plethora of differences exacerbated by the shape and pull of the respective forces and semantic fields of their different ages, he and Luther were part of the same revolutionary movement. Thus, while under Luther, the heavens would need to revolve again (revolution, Rosenstock-Huessy reminds his readers on the first page of *Die europäischen Revolutionen*, was originally an astronomical, not a political term), Gregory's rejuvenation of the Church would only be completed once the very condition of priests' spiritual supremacy (celibacy) had been dropped so that they again took their place in the world. That, though, is the very requirement of a revolution, and indeed of the Holy Spirit itself: that we must ceaselessly renounce the external forms, the institutions, habits, and so on of the spirit in order to be true to the divine spirit and thus enter more deeply into God's love. And just when the Reformers were certain that Paul had triumphed over Peter, Paul's followers had to deal with the fact that the Middle Ages had already – in the visions of Joachim of Flore – prepared for his successor, John the Evangelist, the disciple of love. 'Paul,' as Rosenstock-Huessy informs and reminds his readers when speaking of Joachim, 'was not mentioned in this great vision of the future.'[22]

For Rosenstock-Huessy, then, the monumental nature of Gregory VII's revolutionary program as outlined in the *Dictatus Papae*, where he made himself 'the spiritual seismography, not of Italy, but of the whole world,'[23] was the beginning of a chain of revolutions, all of which were united in their 'absolute programme for the whole of mankind, and a vision of a new earth,' each believing itself 'to be the vessel of eternal, revealed, definite truth,'[24] each an attempt to 'readjust the equation between heart power and social order,' to 'bring about the Kingdom of God by force, and reach into the infinite in order to reform the finite.'[25] For Rosenstock-Huessy, Western civilization – and to an important extent the entire planet, for the West has exported its revolutionary potencies as manifested in its speech, values, institutions, technologies, discoveries, conquests, communications, trade (for good and undoubtedly also for ill) – has been formed out of the collisions between love for the kingdom and the subsequent eruptions of violence, whose accompanying hatreds have been directed at the obstacles to love's fulfilment. *Out of Revolution* and *Die europäischen Revolutionen* are devoted to recountings of total revolutions that were local neither in intent nor in effect: 'They all believe themselves to be the vessel of eternal, revealed, definite truth. Only reluctantly do they come back to the old earth. Every revolution makes the painful discovery that it is geographically conditioned.'[26]

I mentioned earlier that we easily take for granted social forms such as tribes and empires – and now even nation-states – as somehow simply 'there,' that is, as natural; yet each of these forms arose to solve a problem. For Rosenstock-Huessy, the great revolutions have no less impressed themselves upon humanity, have no less been absorbed into our *habitus*, than these other social forms. While some of these revolutions will be examined in some detail, at the outset what is of fundamental importance for Rosenstock-Huessy is how each was created and what its legacy is. Though none of them have resulted in peace on earth as such, each has helped open up a new cluster of powers, thereby rendering utterly unnecessary our defeat by a multitude of forces that constrict us. This is clear from a chart he drew up that he described as 'the ladder of potentialities for progress' (see page 240).

The sentence he provides underneath the table should clear up any notion that he thinks that such freedoms can never be lost: 'These, then, are the stakes of our present struggles.' And he warns that the progressive, in 'his insatiable thirst for newness may suck the blood out of the institutions on which he wholly depends for his progress'; and he calls on 'the conservative to recognize the fact that his old institutions will decay if the sap of the tree is not given a new outlet into the timely institutions of today.'[27] For Rosenstock-Huessy, 'the pedigree of revolutions shows that each tried to realize one neglected or imperilled potentiality

Century	Liberties	Protecting principle	Corresponding institution
20th	Freedom for growth, health	Public character of labour	(Perhaps adult education, decentralization of industry?)
19th	Freedom for talent, thought, genius, speech, creativeness, to compete	Public character of private ideas	Copyright, patents, a written constitution
17th	Freedom of endowment	Public character of wills	An independent judiciary
16th	Free choice of profession, no vows for children	Public character of education	Public schools
13th	Freedom of competition between teachers	Public character of the sciences	Universities
11th	Freedom of movement for the men in the professions	Public character of civil life, (truce of God)	Judges of the peace, public prosecution of crime

of the life-cycle, and stressed its importance by establishing one great national institution to take care of the reproduction of these special processes and types. Each Revolution started permanent cultural processes to mould a specific character out of plastic humanity.'[28]

The final point we wish to make in terms of the general schematics of his analysis of the great revolutions is probably the strangest suggestion that is made anywhere in this book: that a correspondence can be found between Hugo of St Victor's eight orders of the sacraments of divinity and the ideologies of revolutions. Given how bizarre this may seem, and given also that he barely even attempts to justify the correspondences, I do not want to dwell too long on it, for it is not as if the rest of the book would collapse without it. In what follows, I am more interested in representing what I think is an interesting idea – a piece of insightful imagining – than in trying to argue that it must be so. That said, much of the initial bizarreness of the schema vanishes if we simply bear in mind, first, that Rosenstock-Huessy thinks the Bible is essentially a massive socio-anthropological compedium created over more than a thousand years, and that its value is to be found in the depths of its insights into human nature and human needs and divine longings. Second, that this is how men like Hugo of St Victor, St Francis, and the like read the Bible. Third, that needs and longings can be lexically ordered. Fourth, that the lexical ordering is one that can only unfold over time. Fifth, that the total revolutions were all attempts (largely successful) to overthrow one fundamental obstacle to our humanity/divinity – attempts that are outlined here. The dates listed in the following chart refer to flashpoints of the total revolutions, and to the American Revolution, which he argues was a half-revolution (like certain other ones, such as in Sweden and Spain), and also to the founding of All Souls' Day, which for him was what set the whole revolutionary enterprise in train.

Thus he is saying with this table that the institutionalized vision of the Last Judgment (All Souls' Day) triggered the revolution within the Church (the Papal Revolution); that the rejuvenation of the Church could only continue by a return to the New Testament (the German Revolution of the Reformation); that the liberties and entitlements that Englishmen had held to be true since 'time out of mind' had to be accessed not by the pseudo-reformed Anglican church, nor by a repetition of Luther's New Testament, but by an appeal to an older body of revealed truth, the Old Testament; that the appeal to the law of nature, which was at the heart of the American Revolution, was made in order to legitimate the birth of the new, which in turn involved an identification of the New World with the biblical plight of Noah; that the political empowerment of the creative productive classes in France required overturning not only the first and second estates but also the Church itself, which was so rotten in France as to be unsalvageable, hence the appeal to a new, genuine, and uncorrupted humanity whose first father was Rousseau's new Adam; and, finally, that the Bolsheviks, not content with the Robinsonade Adamite bourgeois man of the French Revolution, appealed to the most basic aspect of our social beings – its pre-Adamite sheer materiality – as well as to the essential importance of production and reproduction rather than bourgeois novelty and inspiration. For Rosenstock-Huessy, all of these diverse revolutions sought to overthrow what had been obstructing essential powers of humankind and preventing them from flourishing, and to replace them with different arrays of powers devoted *to redeeming* the following (now in

HUGO DE ST VICTOR	REVOLUTIONS	CHAPTER
1. Creator		
2. Creation of Matter	1917	IV
3. Freedom of Will and Fall of Man (Adam)	1789	V
4. Natural Law (Noah)	1776	XV
5. Old Testament (Israel)	1649	VI
6. New Testament	1517	VII
7. Church	1075	X
8. Last Judgment (Resurrection)	998	IX[i]

[i] *Out*, 548.

reverse order): our material conditions; our creative freedom; our natural rights; our own kingship; our own inner priest; our solidarity not with the corrupt earthly powers but rather with the mother Church, which would create the new man (the real end of the Papal Revolution, which continued through the Renaissance and is so visible in its art); and finally and originally, the solidarity of all of God's souls. The Russian, French, English, German, and Italian revolutions can each be formulated, says Rosenstock-Huessy, by a slogan that provides the key to what the particular revolution held to be of utmost importance – that is, the new type it wanted to emancipate – and that shows how each built upon the preceding revolution by broadening its constituency beyond the limits imposed by its predecessor. This is evident in the following table from *Out of Revolution*:

> Russia: Every proletarian a capitalist.
> France: Every man of talent an aristocrat.
> England: Every gentleman a king.
> Germany: Every Christian a priest.[29]

Though he does not include it in the table, *Out of Revolution* also provides the material for the two earliest revolutionary slogans: 'every human creature a soul' (Odilo of Cluny's original revolutionary program), and 'every soul a member of the Church' (the Gregorian Revolution, which would spread into the Franciscan Revolt). Each of these slogans, says Rosenstock-Huessy, 'presupposed a clear vision of territorial unity, of God-given borders which considerably modified the rational constitution.' That is to say, each revolution could only be realized by curtailing the extension of its totalizing claims. Thus, 'every proletarian a capitalist; yes, but within one economy held together by the Communist Party. Every talent an aristocrat; yes, but within an indivisible nation. Every gentleman a king; yes, but within the United Kingdom.' He continues:

> The real progress and the tragic blood-shed of each revolution were both caused by the paradox contained in this 'yes, but.' The clue to the success of the English, French and Russian revolutions was that none of them bribed the respective supporters at the price of diminishing the size of the body politic; they all reached out for a political organization bigger than anything attempted before. The Commons shook off the yoke of the Congregationalists because the Congregationalists would have dissolved the united Anglican Church. The French beheaded the Girondins because Federalism would have dissolved the central power of an individual France built up in royal Versailles. The Russians killed the Social Revolutionaries because these people loved the Russian village and would not have had the hardness of heart to sacrifice it to a united economy for all Russia.
>
> In all these cases there is some comprehensive, uniting force – kingdom, nation, economy – which is upheld in the face of the ranters and romanticists. Something pre-existing and preciously united is reformed and transformed by the revolutionaries in order that everybody may participate in the circulation of its blood.[30]

Rosenstock-Huessy's analysis of revolution thus stresses the cumulative and progressive chararacter of the great European revolutions of the past thousand years. It is very notable that Rosenstock-Huessy is deeply at odds with a declinist 'discursive regime' that is widely touted in modern social theory. Yet, on the one hand, the modern discursive regime's commitment to freedom and equality (palpably Western norms) is equally ubiquitous; and on the other, its sensitivity to the multiplicities of colonialisms (which are one more variant of fascism) makes it generally extremely unhappy with any suggestion or possible implication that the West's powers are so valuable that they should be universalized. One might say this is part of its own revolutionary heritage: Rousseau (the anti-progressivist dimension of the French Revolution arising from a reaction to civilization's rotteness) plus Marx (the Russian Revolution, the progressivist faith in productive forces and humanity's creative capacities). A major part of Heidegger's role in the radical liberal paradigm (though he is not in any way a liberal or a democrat, nor is he a political left winger in any way, shape, or form),[31] and an important part of that paradigm's appeal, relates to the dystopian, declinist story of the West – a story that dovetails quite neatly with a century of two catastrophic world wars and that finds continuation in Foucault and more recently in Agamben. This paradigm also finds itself far more receptive to Walter Benjamin's bleak view of history, while retaining its hope in a better future – which brings back to mind the aptness of Rosenzweig's insight that hope is the theological residue of the Christian faith that holds the modern 'Church' together. Derrida's 'messianism without religion' is the formulation that best attempts to enfold the 'effectivity or actuality of the democratic promise' and 'the communist promise' with 'this absolutely undetermined messianic hope at its heart, this eschatological relation [i.e. the relation to the final event or last judgment] to the to-come of an event *and* of a singularity, of an alterity that cannot be anticipated.'[32] In other words – as with Benjamin – hope in the future *in spite* of history. Benjamin and Derrida, unlike Rosenzweig, wanted to take this most fundamental of Jewish truths outside of the framework of religion and into political engagement. This may well be honourable, but it is prone to the same kind of criticism that Judaism makes of Christianity – that it is idolatrous. Or, to say it another way, it dispenses with Jewish election by appeal to a new universal, and hence it is a variant of the Christian. (Derrida's desire to bring Islam into the loop absolutely fits the paradigmatic emphasis on dividing the world into fascisms and non-fascisms. Because Islam is the predominant religion in previously colonized parts of the world, it is treated as a 'victim' of fascism. Such is Derrida's logic, though it is utterly Eurocentric and entirely neglects non-Western colonizers such as the Ottomans and the kinds of earlier imperial conflicts that were hardly all symptomatic of Western conquest or victory.) But whereas Judaism, as Rosenzweig rightly says, finds its eternal solace not only in the promise but also in the divine love behind the promise and in the concrete body of its people, the new paradigm is in danger of being but a spectral variant of Kant's moral theology – albeit with the added force of the weight of the Shoah. But increasingly as time recedes, it is sustained by people whose faith is transformed into 'mere ideas.'

One other problematic feature of the paradigm is that we must build *with* something. This is the essential point of Rosenstock-Huessy's and Augustine's view of history and sin. We act in sin, constantly; what we *do* with it, though, is the real test of what we have learned through faith. This is the real key to understanding that Rosenstock-Huessy recognizes (like conservatives) that revolt is a terrible product of a diseased society, as is war. But – and here he sides with the revolutionaries themselves – what is rotten cannot be upheld. The revolutionary act, though, is only meaningful at the right time. The dominant radical-liberal social theoretical paradigm favours revolutionaries over conservatives, yet it is deeply opposed, and with good reason, to any appeal to the moral superiority of the West. Radical-liberal social theorists are, in Rosenzweig's language, the priests and priestesses of the Johannine Church. (Less appealing, to the more cynical, is that their moral self-assuredness often renders them rather quick to judge those who do not read the world the same way as they do.)

In contrast to the more voluntarist (and hence post-Kantian) aspect of the radical liberal paradigm is the notion of a universal history formed by revolution (common, despite various differences, to Marx and Rosenstock-Huessy) that is not in any way based in any faith in moral superiority, but rather is the response to common necessities of survival.[33] Revolutions are not the products of holy men and women, people with 'good ideas'; far from it – they are social explosions that occur because the world's evils are so heavy that explosion is the only way that a new future can be made.

On the other side, there is the bias that for a long time dominated the political left and the Whig view of history. It is the one that tends to completely downplay, if not completely ignore, the great emancipatory strides made by the Church in the Middle Ages, focusing almost exclusively instead on the more secular achievements of the Russian and French revolutions and on an especially dubious interpretation of the Renaissance as a predominantly secular event. In *Out of Revolution,* Rosenstock-Huessy takes issue with what he calls the 'French myth' that has led so many to simply ignore so much of medieval history and the Church's changing role:

Today all our schoolboys and schoolgirls are taught a 'French' myth. Not by a contemptible trick, but through the naive faith of three or four generations, what we may rightly call the 'French' periodization of history was created – unknown and inconceivable before, but now believed, worshipped and learned by heart in every civilized nation. All the former total revolutions had done the same. Odilo of Cluny re-erected the great framework for one united history of all mankind, believers and infidels. Joachim di Fiore distinguished successfully, first, an ecclesiastical history of the

Christian centuries before him, and, second, a post-ecclesiastical, i.e., political, spiritual and cultural history for our millennium, beginning in his own time. And Luther's disciples separated what they labelled the Middle Ages from modern times. All these three divisions are of permanent value. They are all unforgettable. The same is true of the French contribution to mankind's recasting its memory time after time. The French invented the period of the 'Renaissance,' beginning about 1450 and ending in 1498 or 1500 or 1517.[34]

The above quote can be bookended by the following, also from *Out of Revolution:*

All our antecedents are twofold: Roman and Christian on one side, national on the other. The first millennium created our Roman and Christian past, the second, by restoring Roman Church and Christendom, created the Christian nations. Without dropping the term Middle Ages, this clear distribution of two different millennia cannot be taught to our children. If our children cannot learn some simple facts about the last two millennia, they will give up and follow the line of least resistance. Sacrificing all chronology, they will place prehistory, ten thousand years B.C. before their own past. The skulls and bones of primitive man will act as an historical charm and nobody will penetrate into the thicket of facts about our real past.[35]

The revolutions of the West began, then, long before the French Revolution for Rosenstock-Huessy. And the Renaissance itself was the outgrowth of a process that had begun centuries earlier. According to him, at the root of the programmatically growing character of the total revolutions of the West was something rarely realized – that they were fundamentally Christian in their character, that even the ostensibly and virulently anti-clerical French and Russian revolutions were driven by the messianic promise that was the rationale behind the *corpus Christi:*

The French and Russian revolutions are results of the Christian era. They depend upon it, they complete it. Christianity is not a mutual admiration society. It may allot to a certain form of life the necessary area in which to establish its own realm. The chief duty of any member of the Corpus Christi is to strengthen the other forces of humanity and thereby to assure the later co-ordination of the Russian antitheistic form with the rest of the Christian community. The economic unity of the world will probably offer an opportunity for co-operation between forces of life which are consciously Christian and others which suppress their Christian inheritance for the sake of restoring one single vital phase. Still the un-Christian forces play their part in the process of reimplantation of every branch of mankind into the one tree which is the perpetual effort of our era. During the last millennium the scattered nations of the whole earth were remoulded into parts of a whole.[36]

While the adequacy of the proof of this claim can only be gauged by examining the evidence supplied throughout the whole of *Out of Revolution* (and *Die europäischen Revolutionen*), the following, albeit rather lengthy passage provides a thorough summary of the argument:

So definite is the revolutionary process of the last thousand years bound up with the unification of thought by the common possession of the Bible that every revolution passionately claimed a special section of Biblical history as the classical text for its own drama.

The popes of the Gregorian Revolution, from Victor II to Eugene III, clearly recalled the last chapter of Biblical history: the early centuries of the Church, during which the very canon of the sacred book had been fixed and developed. The Guelphic leaders, Saint Francis and his followers, as well as Innocent III, lived the passion and cross of Christ and His disciples. Luther, by enthroning the '*Predigtamt*' of the German '*Geist*' [Spirit] as the controlling power of secular government, restored the prophetic office of the time of Elias, John and Jesus. Cromwell's and William's England reinstated the Judge's function and the divine voice of public spirit which had ruled Israel before the Kingdom of David. France went in for the period before the age of revelations – natural man, the God of nature and the rights of Adam before the Fall. And Russia and we contemporaries of Bolshevism delve deep into the pre-adamitic and pre-historical forces of labour, sex, youth, primitive tribes and clans, hormones and vitamins.

This exact sequence, an inverted Biblical chronicle from 300 A.D. back to the first days of life on earth, was traced by revolutionaries who thought themselves completely free, individual and independent and original, and who violently opposed the terms and slogans of every other revolution, preceding or following. Yet they were all under the invincible spell of 'One Universal Language of Mankind.' The vigour of this epic unity, binding the national revolutions was tested by our investigation of the American vocabulary. Half-way between the English and the French, America might not have shared this biblical retrogression. But this was not so at all. We found in the pamphlets and sermons of the War of Independence the figures of Noah and his sons symbolizing the new cradle of nations in these United States! Noah, Shem, Ham and Japhet, taking their places exactly between the Puritan Judges of Israel and the Rousseauist 'Adam,' bear witness to the unity of 'language' throughout the Christian era, in spite of all national languages.[37]

For Rosenstock-Huessy, the benefits that have come out of the great furnaces of rage and social upheaval have extended far beyond the borders of the area in which they have occurred, and their circulation has drawn human beings across the planet into an evolving composite of common institutions. What superficially has so often been rendered as a story of progress in which humanism and rationality triumph over 'unenlightened' belief and superstition is indeed a story with some 'progressive' elements (but not without loss and ever in dangerous proximity to imminent catastrophe) – that is, it involves the forging by violent revolution of those elements that have contributed to humankind's realization that it shares a common fate or destiny if it is to have a common future peace. While he builds his case in *Out of Revolution* over eight hundred pages (and the *Die europäischen Revolutionen* is much the same length), Rosenstock-Huessy's view of Christianity's role in shaping modern Western society is summed up succinctly in his claim that

> no man is a European who has not been educated by certain church-like institutions in his own country, institutions created once and forever by a revolution which teaches him faith, hope, and love, but mainly love. The languages of Europe are not materialistic facts, but creative expressions of a certain side of the Christian faith, used by a certain political class in a certain section of the continent.[38]

Rosenstock-Huessy often makes the point that what human beings sacrifice themselves to is their God; and that what binds them to that sacrifice is their religion. He does not seek to avoid the word 'religion' for Christians or Jews, as Rosenzweig does; and, also unlike Rosenzweig, he generally does not wish to privilege philosophy and theology above religion. That is to say, he is, *contra* Rosenzweig, far more sympathetic to the word 'religion' as accurately depicting the particular bindings of peoples and their gods (the objects of their loves and sacrifices). For him, then, religion is but another name for the great social acts of love, faith, and hope. Thus he writes in *Out of Revolution* that faith, hope and love, the religious forces of mankind, are not limited to denominational purposes. Faith, hope and love are universal. They are the only real motive forces of history and political life and language, for the simple reason that they alone connect the words men speak and use as means of communication with a real power working in time and space.[39]

In this way, Rosenstock-Huessy is able to bring politics, revolution, and religion into a semantic concordance in precisely the way that such a concordance actually operated for so long in European history. At the same time, he is mindful to draw attention to the distinction in a way that enables him to construct a theory of revolution that brings the experience of revolt closer to the overwhelming powers of life – and hence also to hell or chaos – while interpreting politics as falling within the sphere of governance and law and (subsequently) order. Thus he writes that

> the difference between politics and religion, confused as they are today, can be re-stated simply by the distinction of public and open. At no time can any group exist without religion and without public law. To reduce these two elements into one has often been tried, and never will succeed. Public Law asks the citizen for obedience, religion for worship. Any group obeys politically its legal ruler; but it worships religiously the opening of a new path out of chaos.[40]

If revolution is closer to religion than to public law – the key function of politics – it is also the case that politics and religion share the same basic task of creating a certain kind of person.

Nietzsche had, of course, repeatedly called for the breeding of a new type of human being, and he had seen culture precisely in these terms. The biological and totalitarian implications of Nietzsche's project were so strongly associated with fascism and National Socialism that most twentieth-century Nietzscheans dropped all such talk lest they be mistaken for fascists. Furthermore, there are more than enough references to physiology in Nietzsche for anyone who reads him with an eye to nineteenth-century eugenics to see – despite liberal and postmodern Nietzschean protestations that are highly selective in what they quote to advance their case – how there is indeed a sharply visible line running from Nietzsche to fascism to National Socialism. And while Rosenstock-Huessy was not blind to this connection, he thought there was a great deal more to Nietzsche than that (as we will explore in more detail later).

Most important, Rosenstock-Huessy is one of the very few thinkers who adopts and adapts Nietzsche's requirement of cultural breeding in a non-essentialist, non-(pseudo)biological, and hence non-fascist manner, enabling us to see how history produces a different set of types and kinds; this, too, is thoroughly in keeping with Rosentock-Huessy's incarnationist view of the Church. Of course, Marx – without any prodding from Nietzsche – wants to do this (the 'New Man' was a phrase commonly used by twentieth-century communists, at least until the only Marxists who remained were not communists, but academic cultural theorists). Later we will look more closely at Marx and Rosenstock-Huessy. Here we can say that Marx's problem is the narrowness of his understanding of the essential foundation of social reproduction, that essential foundation being class. With Rosenstock-Huessy the passions of all the different groups of players involved in revolution, and the religion that first gave peoples a sense of historical continuity and faith in an *eschaton* and a new kind of life, have combined to create the nations in which the new 'nurseries' of human reproduction have been formed. As he writes in *Out of Revolution*,

> in the course of history, the branches of the tree of mankind are truly re-generated – ay, by grafting they are really reproduced and changed, and this can only be done by a reconstruction of the great nurseries of men which we call nations.
>
> Revolutions do not create man; they build nurseries, as we have said before, for his reproduction in a certain way and according to a certain type. There is no Christian country and no national character which can boast that it is founded on evolutionary institutions alone.[41]

And a little later in the same work, he again emphasizes the role of the passions, the Church, and revolution leading to the creation of a national type, a new type: 'The successful creation of a new political language by a new class, in a new section of the continent, is called a Revolution; and the territory within which it succeeds and the people whom it transforms are the components of a nation. Nations are the products of Revolutions.'[42]

While Rosenstock-Huessy's work on revolutions is conceived in a religious manner – more specifically, as a Christian *Heilsgeschichte* – what he has done is provide a historical account of the growing circulatory forces that, while now generally read as secular, are but the great milestones in the past thousand years of Christianity's mission to complete its messianic journey. And what he provided in his explorations of the creations and redemptions achieved by the Christian nations was also a more detailed representation of Rosenzweig's sketch in *The Star* of Christianity's historical and universalizing mission. But it was a representation that put flesh on the bones of Rosenzweig's argument, clarifying how the Christian nations have attempted to spread Revelation and Redemption throughout the world at large.

Of course Rosenzweig himself – not to mention Rosenstock-Huessy – risks the accusation (the best intentions from his liberal apologists to the contrary) that his view of history is a variant of Hegelianism, though Hegel's vision is ultimately pagan and tragic. For while Hegel does indeed refute Enlightenment triumphalism, he also eschews the possibility of perpetual peace, and thus the Messianic age of Jewish and Christian redemption of the world. (Surprisingly enough, for all Hegel's opposition to a beyond [*jenseits*] and for all his claims to be Christian, he renounces the very *telos* of a this-sided Christianity.)

There is certainly nothing to guarantee that further catastrophe is not brewing and that Jews and Christians might not be the victims. The living God loves the world and loves the self, but He cannot protect the world from the world; that requires a willingness on the world's part to receive His love. Thus Rosenstock-Huessy writes: 'Mankind always stands on the edge of barbarism and universal warfare; a matter of inches separates it from ruin.'[43]

Likewise, there is no mechanism whereby each stage of progress is superior in every way to what has preceded it. Such progress is primarily an acknowledgment of the capacity to incorporate the lessons of suffering. That is, such an idea of progress relies on an imagined future, or more precisely on faith in a joyous future – joyous because the sources of collective suffering have been overcome. Thus it is that faith in a certain kind of future is bound up with reassembling our past and present in a certain kind of way. The tragic view of life, so celebrated by Nietzsche and rightly seen by him as quintessentially pagan, conceives of neither its future nor its past nor its present in such a way that it is meaningful to talk of neighbourly love; and this is one reason why, in spite of Zarathustra loving the overman, Nietzsche did not speak of such a thing. Faith in an *eschaton* is the condition of a messianic view of history, and a messianic view of history seeks to distinguish between those states of heart and soul and those actions that contribute to endless division and interminable suffering, on the one hand, and those that coordinate, integrate, incorporate into a common future, on the other. As Rosenstock-Huessy puts it in *The Christian Future – or The Modern Mind Outrun,*

Christianity came into a world of divided loyalties – races, classes, tribes, nations, empires, all living to themselves alone. It did not simply erase these loyalties; that would have plunged men into nihilism and cancelled the previous work of creation, and Jesus came not to deny but to fulfil. Rather, by its gift of a real future, Christianity implanted in the very midst of men's loyalties a power which, reaching back from the end of time, drew them step by step into unity.

Paganism thus meant – and means – disunity, dividedness of mankind. This is true historically as well as geographically. Pagan histories are many, not one; each begins somewhere within time, for instance with the founding of Rome or with the Olympic Games in 776 B.C., and ends likewise: the god Chronos devours all his children. So pagan thought almost universally pictures human life as a decline from a golden age in the past toward ultimate destruction in the future. And beyond that it can imagine nothing but meaningless repetition of the same cycle to all eternity.[44]

The resuscitation and reabsorption of pagan life forms into Christendom threatened and often engulfed the Christian. Rosenstock-Huessy points out on several occasions that the Renaissance also meant the revival of slavery; and that the Church itself became the centre of paganism (as Nietzsche himself recounted with glee when he thought of how close Cesare Borgia came to occupying the papal seat). As Augustine rightly perceived, how easy it is for the love of God and the neighbour to be traded for love of the worldly and the self.

If, then, the Jewish experience is to be eternal in history, the Christian experience is to forge a history that opens the rest of humanity to the eternal truth: it travails over time, and the world it builds is over time. Both Rosenzweig and Rosenstock-Huessy saw Christianity, as it worked over time, as a truly miraculous cultural force in its resuscitation and reincorporation of the past. This fundamental Christian characteristic is what Rosenstock-Huessy was referring to in the title of the second volume of his *Soziologie – The Full Count of the Times,* in which, over almost a thousand pages, he demonstrates this attribute of Christianity in detail. He makes the same point more succinctly in *The Christian Future* when he writes about the Christian idea of progress and how it differs from modern distortions of it:

Precisely because Christianity created future, progress is the gift of the Christian era, and it vanishes in proportion as we secede from that era. Of course there were particular instances of improvement in man's estate before Christ, but they remained sporadic, for they were at the mercy of the cyclic character of pagan history, which swallows all its children again so that nothing finally adds up. And only since Christianity unified man's history from the end of time are these pre-Christian achievements of the race being rescued from the twilight of the gods which was their doom. What, for instance, would have become of Greek science and philosophy had Rome simply declined and fallen like Babylon, with no Church to preserve its relics and initiate that recapture of ancient learning which has been one of our glories since the twelfth century?

The idea of progress was not invented in 1789 or 1492. Jesus promised that his followers would do greater works than he had done (Jn. 14:12). The Church Fathers championed progress as the Christian view in opposition to the pagan belief in cycles of fate, with the golden age lying in the past; they proclaimed the resurrection of life and love after and through suffering, whereby God himself made progress in the hearts of the faithful.[45]

The Jews chronicled their history as the history of their covenant with God, of their journey toward the awareness that the kingdom was always with them and that their task was to anticipate the coming of the messiah. Pagan empires chronicled their dynasties; the Greeks chronicled their history; Christianity combined the dynasties and histories of the world's peoples with the Jewish promise. Christ's coming is but the new beginning to the fulfilment that is his Second Coming, and the body of Christ is the Church itself in its struggle – often failing to be Christ-like, succumbing to the energies of the animal, the man, the pagan, and at worst the demonic, as it seeks to remake man as God.

Revolution, then, is part and parcel of this process of Creation, Revelation, and Redemption. Revolutions re-create man on the basis of the desire to found the kingdom; they reveal the harsh truth that love is stronger than death as regimes and institutions that fail to enhance the love between neighbours are condemned to death; and they redeem practices and institutions once deemed dead. Revolutions are one place where everything durable is thrown into the furnace and transmogrified by the ferocious outburst of revolt. What philosophers may calmly contemplate in the safe and sure chambers of the mind takes on deadly and murderous proportions when inserted into the lives of those who are struggling to bring down a hellish order and create a new one that is fit for people who wish to live fully. Thus even something as philosophically derivative as Thomas Paine's *Rights of Man* – which is unimaginable without Descartes's search for a new world, and which pays direct tribute to Rousseau and Montesquieu – is part of a greater array of social and historical forces, each of which brings reasons with it and each of which is never able to be construed simply by reason alone. In revolutions, faith, hope, and love smash against the walls and encrustations of dead habits, dead practices, and suffocating orthodoxies. Yesterday's truths that no longer nourish must be left behind or overthrown lest we perish. It matters little for Rosenstock-Huessy how venerable the institutions are that orthodoxies attach themselves to – they are spirited or they are not, they lift up or they do not, they enhance life or they destroy it. This is even true, for Rosenstock-Huessy, of the Church itself, which is why the Church had to pass through its Petrine, Pauline, and Johannine phases. But in the Johannine phase it is all too easy for people to forget their unity and interdependency, as creatures who not only must share and build in space but who must share and build *across time*.

Thus far in my discussion of Rosenstock-Huessy's analysis of the great revolutions, I have provided only the broadest claims about them, focusing on the more general reasons why he claims they are cumulative and sequential. The real power of his argument can be properly gauged only by a more in-depth account of what he says about *particular* revolutions. Instead of following him in the two sequences he himself provides, I will take a different tack. I will commence with his analysis of the French Revolution, because it was the watershed between the previous Christian revolutions and the secular understanding of politics that is ubiquitous today, and hence between a vast semantic field that once was the ground of social existence for almost all Europeans, and today's even more vast field that has but disconnected pockets which can still think in a meaningful way with that earlier vocabulary. Second, the French Revolution was the one that facilitated the elevation of art over religion and the primacy of the nation as the primary body of social nourishment. In other words, much of the material I wish to discuss in the context of Rosenstock-Huessy's analysis of revolutions will be discussed as part of his attempt to overcome the idolatry of art and the nation – for it is against these two most modern forms of humanist idolatry that Rosenstock-Huessy's and Rosenzweig's 'systems' were primarily constructed.

8 The Modern Humanistic Turn of the French Revolution in Rosenstock-Huessy

One cannot overestimate how important the French Revolution becomes in Rosenstock-Huessy's understanding of history, including its single greatest achievement, its creation of the social possibility for the interpenetration of Jews, Christians, and pagans. It could not sustain this, as the Dreyfus affair showed, but it set us on the way. The great failure of the French Revolution was that it did not concede that it was part of a much greater messianic journey than it realized: that in the place of the Christian semantic field which preceded it and which it abandoned, it created the fundamentals of our more secular, mechanistic, and art-driven age. For Rosenstock-Huessy, the French Revolution's self-construction and accompanying reconstruction of history was perhaps necessary to drive out old parties and forms of Christianity that had become ossified in France, but this came at a cost – it blinded the French (and much of the rest of the world) to the limits of its innovations and stratagems, and it obfuscated the power and endurance of more archaic powers by rendering them redundant, even though they were still vital and, he believed, too important to be cast away.

Rosenstock-Huessy's analysis provides an important key to his understanding of what he meant by Christianity in a modern context, and to why he thought that the humanistic strand of the French Revolution contributed not only to its success but also to much of its unravelling, to the crisis of the Great War, and to some of the most toxic social pathologies of our day.

For Rosenstock-Huessy, the French Revolution was definitely not (as it was for Marx) primarily a bourgeois revolution, even though it did indeed make the bourgeois a citizen, and even though the social discontents in France arose mainly from that class. Rather, the French Revolution was the revolution during which the nation became the bearer of the messianic mission of the hopes of the moderns. The impetus for this came from French civilization having conceived itself as the genuine heir of European civilization, and as the epicentre of Europe. (The Central Powers, Rosenstock-Huessy reminds us, were called 'Boches,' 'Huns,' 'barbarians,' and *autres chiens*,' but certainly not Europeans.) Seeing themselves as the centre of Europe, the French also saw themselves as the embodiment of all that was civilized in Europe; and those values were not Christian but classical – the classical values of democracy, liberalism, and nationalism.[1] For Rosenstock-Huessy, what was so distinctive, then, about the French was how they had driven a wedge between European and Christian identity, thereby breaking with a long-standing tradition going back at least to the defeat of the Muslim invaders by an army of 'Europeans' led by Charles Martel. Rosenstock-Huessy reminds his readers that the French Revolution's positing of Europe and Christendom as two distinct spheres of life had a long prequel:

> The same French who dared to ally themselves with the Infidel Turks as early as 1524, the French whose King Louis XIV locked himself up in his room in a great rage when all Christendom was in glee over the defeat of the Turks before Vienna in 1683, the French who were the first nation in Europe to enjoy the foreign customs of the *Lettres Persanes* and the *Arabian Nights*, now abolished all audible and visible connection between the Christian past and their European civilization.
>
> In the mouth of the Frenchman 'Europe' means a field of action for the philosopher, the artist, the thinker, the democrat, the Republican, the soldier and last, not least, a market for the fashions of Paris.[2]

Three closely connected themes run through this analysis of the French Revolution. One is the all-important point of the messianic tradition taken up by the Jacobins – the blessing that was, albeit too briefly, not just for the Jews but for *all* Europeans. According to Rosenstock-Huessy, the messianism of the Jews had been taken up by the French: 'Messianism, originally limited to the Jews, later communicated to the heathen by the Church, is transferred by the European nationalism born in 1789 to the nations in general, which now enter upon a common race of messianic nationalism.'[3] Rosenstock-Huessy also writes that 'this national messianism of the French had to outbid the messianism embodied by the Jews themselves.

The French could not bear that any nation should be more messianic than their own.'[4] He continues:

> That is why it was not the respectable, kind, well-educated enlightened Jew who was emancipated by the ideas of 1789. Any notion of a selective process for certain particularly welcome and agreeable individuals must be rejected before we can understand the principles of the emancipation of the Jews. The deeper cause of emancipation was the new equality. The last Polish or Russian Jew had the same right to it, from the viewpoint of 1789, as the 'philosopher,' because citizenship was due not only to the actual philosopher but to any man who was capable of using his reason in the cause of humanity.[5]

This touches on the second theme of Rosenstock-Huessy's argument – that the French Revolution was, notwithstanding its multitude of humanist components, a Christian event. To make sense of this great paradox – for the French Revolution was also the most radical overthrow of the Roman *and* reformist church – we need to appreciate not simply how pagan French society had become under the Bourbons, but also this all-important point: paganism had always been vital within Christian societies. So thought both Rosenzweig and Rosenstock-Huessy. Referring back to how the pagan tribes entered Christianity, Rosenstock-Huessy points out that 'many converts hoping to buy and store up Roman civilization, cursed a faith so exacting that no pagan impulses were safe from its challenge.'[6]

More pertinent, though, was the widespread political reassertion of paganism among the ruling classes. Machiavelli's *The Prince* and *Discourses on Livy*, for example, are notorious for their blunt attacks on Christians as effeminate milksops who have no concept about politics being the art that requires princes to lie, and to manipulate appearances to win the love of their people while always being prepared to invoke fear and terror, not just in one's enemies but in one's own people. He maintains that Christianity had weakened Italy and that its inability to deal in brutal reality only created more bloodshed. Furthermore, failure to understand the people's slovenly and resentful nature will always bring ruin down on a principality or republic. Machiavelli was self-consciously pagan, and he was not coy about it: in the *Prince* he insisted that the prince must learn how to be half-beast, and in *The Discourses* he contended that modern rulers should revive Roman festivals and rituals with all their bloody viscera, as a means to remain in touch with their bestial energies.

For Rosenstock-Huessy, Machiavelli's work 'marks the danger of a world which had lost all faith in the Church.'[7] Machiavelli was not a lone ranger: Cesare Borgia was his hero and almost achieved the task that Machiavelli had hoped and prayed for – that is, the unity of Italy (and subsequent imperial expansion). Luther was a younger contemporary of both these men; but for Rosenstock-Huessy, what he fought for connects him to the later revolutionaries of England and France: unlike Machiavelli and Borgia, they had all participated in the same faith against 'the arbitrary powers of princes' that Luther had attacked.[8]

In contrast to Jean Bodin, the political theorist (so esteemed by Carl Schmitt) who provided the pernicious mythology of the absolute sovereignty or divine right of the king that would cause so much havoc in France, Rosenstock-Huessy writes,

> He ignores the religious balance of power between the systematic fight of the learned Christian against the abuses of the church and his fight for the Christian state. Bodin bisects the problem. He is a philosopher. He is not interested in the Reform of the Church. He keeps the visible half, the sovereign prince, who is here to rule his territory without the old bondage of canon or imperial law; but in doing so Bodin cut his own country off from the tree of Christianity . . . And in 1789, when the Catholicism of the King was finally given up, France made the sacrifice, not for the sake of her own miserable sovereignty, in Bodin's sense of the word, but for the sake of a new community of Europe and of all civilized nations. Bodin is the devil of territorial and moral sovereignty stealing into the garden of the Christian Commonwealth.[9]

It had never been a Christian teaching that a king could do whatever he liked to his subjects or that he was God's *representative* on earth, even in Paul's most conciliatory claims regarding Christian subjects and rulers. To be Christ's representative on earth became a peculiarly Roman/papist claim only under Gregory VII, as part of his strategy to rid the Church of its corrupt element in Western Christendom. Ultimately, though, as the reformists would argue, the Church was the body of Christians and was the real representative of Christ's presence on earth.

What, then, Rosenstock-Huessy is suggesting is actually a reapplication of Augustine. Europe, he is saying, was split between two deeply opposed forces – one of which was the body of faithful, the real Church, held together by the only acts that are ever genuinely Christian, acts of faith, hope, and love in service to God; and the other of which is its perennial antithesis, acts of self-love. And he says that at the time of the French Revolution, 'the nations of Europe were on the way to complete repaganization in the eighteenth century . . . the churches themselves were open to this attack.' And most important of all: 'all this was changed completely by the emancipation of the Jews.'[10] The emancipation of the Jews was, for him, *the* Christian act in a time almost overwhelmed by pagan energies.

For the person who thinks that a visible sign or statement or attachment is a key to the nature of a thing, the Christian must remain as invisible as the devil. It is precisely in contradiction to this kind of 'common sense' that the Holy Spirit is divinized in the Christian faith. For the Jews – and this is evident to any reader of Rosenzweig who pays attention – what Christians call the Holy Spirit is but an aspect, or rather the way of the one God. The converse of this importance not to assume that because someone is a cleric or goes to Church, then he or she is a Christian, is that the Christian can sometimes survive only by assuming the most contrary of forms. This is why, as we see later, Rosenstock-Huessy views Nietzsche's attack on the Church as the most Christian act of his time. It is also why he writes – and this seems to defy all common sense – that 'the non-Christian side of French Jacobinism is really its most Christian side. It offers to the Jew a common meeting ground on the basis of humanity, of humanism.'[11] Why does he say this? The attempt to prepare for the second coming is, for him, the Church's universal mission. Acts of faith that do this are genuinely Christian acts; those that are concerned with the self's own enhancement are not.

Curiously, he does not mention what was to become a central feature in Hans Ehrenberg's *In der Schule Pascals:* that Pascal had rediscovered the importance of the Jews for Christianity, that he had anticipated what Rosenstock-Huessy would see as the greatest achievement of the French Revolution – from which, as Ehrenberg says (and Rosenstock-Huessy concurs), there can be no turning back – that Jews, Christians, and pagans, for all their differences, which need to be identified, are also members of the one humanity.[12] For having explored how Pascal had detailed, like Rosenzweig after him, the Christian dependency on the Jews, Pascal – so Ehrenberg tells us – deserves 'the title of the father of ecumenicism.'[13]

Despite Pascal's enormous importance (see below), Rosenstock-Huessy's analysis of the French Revolution is based on two core points: (1) that it continued in the spirit of the Christian task of Redemption that is the unitary principle of the European revolutions, and (2) that it turned against Christianity. Understanding why it did so is thus central to understanding its particular character and hence much of the character of our times.

The French Revolution had as its prequel the German Revolution, which in turn had as its prequel the clerical revolutions in Italy. But in the University of Paris, France had as powerful an institutional interest as Italy, Spain, and Austria – the heartlands of Rome – in *not* responding to the reformers. With a formulation that could only come from someone who sees processes in terms of long waves, who looks beyond the flashpoint to see what wounds fester and incubate in the social imaginary (to use Cornelius Castoriadis's term), and what collective energies swell up and gain momentum over time, Rosenstock-Huessy writes, 'it was the eclipse of mediaeval Paris which was responsible for the French Revolution.'[14]

Paris's medieval power was not straightforwardly political, nor was it due to a great imperial centre or army. Rather, 'Paris was the brain of the Occident, the School of all Christendom, and had neither Gallican nor French limitations.'[15] As the centre of Catholic theology, it was devoted to training people in the 'purity' of the creed. Originally, theology itself was viewed with great suspicion, as were the Aristotelian techniques that sustained it. For it drew attention to the various discordances that had developed over a thousand years of Church teachings, relying upon reason to reconcile the contradictions of the faith, and hence leaning heavily on the rediscovery of Aristotle. The very title of Abelard's *Sic et non* (Yes and No) tells the story of the procedure, as Abelard steered a course through the great intellectual division of the age between realists and nominalists by arguing

> that words are neither real in the sense that the realists contended, nor merely arbitrary constructions as the extreme nominalists maintained. A *sermo*, or expression, is the way a man *must* speak for the time being among men in fellowship. Important words *become* universals by their being accepted as universal, and *used* as such to express *necessary* truths.[16]

Initially, Abelard had been ordered 'to leave the land of Paris,' and he taught first from a tree, then from his little boat on the Seine, and then on the Left Bank, before finally being allowed back into the bishop's school in Paris. Having embraced Aristotle and theology, the University of Paris became the most radical centre of learning in Europe, and most of the great medieval theologians, including Aquinas, studied there. By the time of Luther, though, scholastic theology was like a rotting fish and the University of Paris's innovative glory had long vanished. Aristotle himself had become an object of ridicule to the humanists and reformists. In 1521, when the University of Paris responded to Luther's attacks on scholasticism and on the infection of Christian thought by the pagan philosophy of Aristotle by burning his heretical ninety-five theses, and when, some six years later, it censured thirty-two of Erasmus's propositions, it exposed itself as a purely reactionary force. Some twenty years later, in his own attempt to smash the oppressive powers that he saw in the Church, the education system, and the government – and the general smallness of people's minds – Rabelais would immortalize the University of Paris as a laughing stock. Furthermore, as Rosenstock-Huessy correctly tells us, other universities had sprung up supporting the new ideas, and prior to Luther's great act of defiance, the University of Paris had even alienated the papacy:

> During the democratic movement of the great Councils of the Church the doctors of Paris triumphed over pope and cardinals. This presumption was violently resented. The popes returned from Avignon and re-established their absolute power at the Curia without any regard for the doctrines of Paris (1450–1517). After 1517 the progress of the Reformation destroyed for good and all the scholastic authority of Paris over more than one half of Europe; Wittenberg and Heidelberg and Marburg gained the authority lost by Paris.[17]

Yet the University of Paris refused to accept that the lowering of its station was part of a greater process of human emancipation, and it refused as well to seek concessions from the French Protestants. Its abhorrence of any peaceful compromise with the Reformers led to its role in the St Bartholomew's massacre of thousands of Huguenots. Rosenstock-Huessy states simply that 'the despotism of the most Catholic University of Paris made it impossible for the French Government to come to terms with the Protestants.'[18] Branding Henry IV as a heretic and renegade, 1,300 of its clergymen, headed the Rector of the Sorbonne, went in procession calling for his dissolution as king.[19] Henry had little choice but to crush the Sorbonne. And 'in 1594 Paris ceased to be a royal city.'[20] The University of Paris's refusal to seek peace with the new forces sweeping through Europe, and its opposition to the king's efforts to reconcile the diverse forces that were threatening to engulf

France, were together pivotal to Paris's decline as a power centre. The monarchy abandoned Paris, consolidating its power by turning its interests to ruling ancient Gaul. In the process, however, it paved the way for its own eventual demise, by destroying the estates 'which assembled in 1614 for the last time.'[21]

The absolutization of the monarchy was, says Rosenstock-Huessy, a return to Caesarean authority presiding over Caesarean borders – that is, it was a return to a pre-Christian conception of sovereignty and political order.[22] The new power centre was Versailles. Paris' disfavour, Rosenstock-Huessy tells his readers, was evident from Louis XIV's commission of a monument in the City Hall of Paris in 1645, showing him 'contemptuously treading a rebellious Parisian under his royal feet.'[23] To gain absolute power over Gaul, the king had to negotiate with 'the traditional right of the Frankish regions, embodied in the nobility, dukes, counts and barons,' whose estates divided France into a crazy-quilt of thousands of little scraps of soil, each with its own common laws and customs and privileges. The Fronde, a civil war in France to protect 'ancient liberties,' which flared in the midst of the Spanish-French war, had been fuelled by the revolutionary events across the English Channel and had played into the hands of the king. He eased the discontent in *les pays* by taking its leaders to Versailles. Once again, the unintended consequences of this action were to be fateful for France. For in quelling one conflict, the king created a spoiled, parasitical class of wealthy gentlemen whose privileges were no longer bound up with any genuine political service and who were to become detested by those in France who actively produced wealth.

Meanwhile, the Church rotted within France. 'The priests,' says Rosenstock-Huessy, 'made the French Caesar a bigot.' This was exacerbated by the reactionary religious role allotted to the Jesuits, a foreign religious force that was much hated in Paris:

In 1685, when Louis XIV drove out the Huguenots, the friends of his great-grandfather, Henry IV, he expelled the progressive part of his nation, whose courage alone had made it possible for him to govern the country by 'raison d'etat,' against the 'reason of theology.' The reason of State was overruled when Madame de Maintenon and the Jesuits secured the repeal of the Edict of Nantes by which the Huguenots had been allowed to stay in France. Most of them left France, carrying her best blood into the world abroad; but many of them left – for Paris . . . The edict of Versailles was a triumph for the provincial and royal clergy, and though the Jesuits only joined in the triumph, it unchained the fury of Paris against them as well. As a Spanish order, seated in Rome, to fight English, Dutch and German Protestantism, the Jesuits overruled, so to speak, the Île de France, the old centre of speculation. Having an international reputation as schoolmasters, they were apt candidates to take over the role of the old Catholic Paris for the rest of Europe, but certainly not in Paris itself. Nowhere else was the fight against the Jesuits so much a nationalistic crusade against invaders from outside. From 1590 to 1761 the Jesuits were anathema to Paris. Richelieu had sensed this when he founded the Academy of Paris, to replace the dying Sorbonne, and when he included Huguenots in its ranks from the very beginning.[24]

Religion, and the issue of the Huguenots, then, was the running sore of French religious memory, and the monarchical reliance on provincial clergy, royal priestly stooges, and a foreign reactionary order (which owing to public pressure was exiled from France in 1761) was bound to make genuinely religious souls look for other outlets in France. Jansenism was one such outlet. It provided succour for Blaise Pascal, whose *Provincial Letters* attacked the Jesuits and a 'church' in disrepute and disrepair, 'a church too visible which used reason only for apologetics.'[25]

Pascal, for Rosenstock-Huessy, was more than the author of 'the first great piece of modern French prose'; he also 'condensed into his short life the permanent features of the French character: the cosmological vision of a sensualist and rationalist, the personal courage and faith of a crusader, and the heart of a troubadour.'[26] Furthermore, Pascal had distinguished

1. Sublime Science, on the highest level (his mathematics).
2. Provincialism, to be fought against as the murder of the intellectual life by mere inertia (his *Lettres Provinciales*).
3. Port Royal, the free harbour of the soul, which is not created to be alone (his *Pensées*).

Whereas England and Germany had both resorted to the speech of the Bible to express their hopes in the future and their animosity to contemporary corruption within the Church and state, France had slaughtered and exiled or isolated its Christian dissidents. And by the time it had done so, a new kind of orientation, a new escape route from hell, was being sought in the vast realms of indefinite space by a mind liberated from the intolerable burden of the past. Rosenstock-Huessy's

'Farewell to Descartes,' the title of the penultimate chapter of *Out of Revolution*, was intended by him as a farewell to faith in a scientistic approach to reality, and to the atomized view of the self and the organized reality that was supposed to enable the self's salvation. His critique of Descartes was far from unique in the twentieth century. Husserl's attack on the colonization of the life-world of natural science, accompanied by a reworking of Descartes, was already on that path, though with Heidegger and his post-structuralist admirers there was an equally strong conviction that the elevation of the subject by Descartes was a move whose consequences (as Foucault implies) ultimately turned the entire world into a prison.

Yet where Rosenstock-Huessy differs from Heidegger and others – and from the Dadaists, who were equally dedicated to overturning Descartes's nightmare machine world and the rational self on which it was based – is that his analysis focuses on the fact that Descartes 'regenerates the pagan independence of the individual mind.'[27]

Pascal found the self hateable and the infinite expanse terrifying. For Descartes, by contrast, the radical departure revolved around making this 'hateful thing' – the self – the source of certainty. Descartes dedicated himself to overcoming this fear of the indefinite by conquering it and by discovering all the mechanisms contained therein – for those mechanisms alone could, for him, provide the key for the purpose of our life, viz. human comfort. That Pascal was horrified by such a shallow and unsoulful end, that he suspected this could only lead to a society ridden with despair, terrifying loneliness, and, by implication, addiction, indicated not only the all-important divide between two types of human beings, but also two antithetical faiths: the modern faith that bulldozes the past into oblivion so that its own sovereignty is unimpeded by the burdens of previous generations, and the far more archaic faith that requires building on accrued time.

Descartes's vision of the conquest of nature would be reflected in the great engineering feats of Versailles.[28] Descartes himself had emphasized advances in medical knowledge and the eventual 'victory' over old age, and the alleviation of the burdens of labour. Ultimately the new science he espoused was to be dedicated to making life on earth more comfortable – indeed, comfort is the explicit end of Cartesianism. If the achievement required the creation of a new method and the various sciences which would be reformed by that method, the vision itself had already been expressed by the alchemists, whose roots could be traced back to antiquity, as is evident from the extant fragments of Empedocles.[29] Descartes, for all his hostility to classical philosophy, and for all his methodological transformations, and despite the hiatus he makes between a cognitive subject and the world of extension, had returned to the Greeks' materialist view of nature. In the terms of Rosenzweig and Rosenstock-Huessy, it was one more great pagan revival. This did not, of course, make it bad. Neither Rosenstock-Huessy nor Rosenzweig ever says that something is bad because it is pagan. What they *do* say is that the kinds of powers summoned and directed by the pagan are indifferent to love's ruling presence. This is why Rosenzweig and Rosenstock-Huessy belong (to use Ehrenberg's phrase) in the school of Pascal more than in that of Descartes. It is not that any of these figures are opposed to science, but that the theo-cosmological horizon of the Cartesians (and Baconians) and their successors (including mechanistic antagonists) have completely reshaped the entire semantic field of human self-understanding and the understanding of the world and God.

Even though Descartes desperately wanted – and thanks to Malebranche, he succeeded posthumously – the metaphysics that sustained his physics to be interpreted as a theological contribution, he was hounded out of France by the same scholastic interests that some four hundred years earlier had succeeded in incorporating Aristotle and Catholicism and protecting that hybrid from the subsequent major currents of reform. Descartes attempted to limit his enemies by swearing allegiance to Church *and* state and by providing a metaphysics – which did not fool the schoolmen, who understood that this was putting new wine into old scholastic bottles, as he himself expressed it to his enthusiastic and somewhat reckless 'fan,' Henricus Regius.[30]

In *Discourse on Method,* Descartes had confronted the collision between the radical future to which his thinking lent its support and being a member of a traditional social body with its own conventions and mores by using the metaphor of three houses. The first house is the traditional house of prejudice and old age; the second is the new house of the future; and the third of is 'a sort of temporary appartment to give temporary shelter to the searching mind.'[31] Voltaire was indeed a supporter of Newtonian science against the Cartesians, but he understood that the radical character of Descartes's science came from the wide scope of the mechanistic vision more than from the accuracy of his mechanics. Taking Descartes's idea of the three houses to heart, Rosenstock-Huessy says that Voltaire realized that

the mind of a man who doubts everything, who is independent and enlightened, has already sacrificed his real 'old' house; that to get to the new house it was not enough to borrow a social order in the meantime by simply obeying the laws and customs of a Protestant country. There had to be a certain peculiar formation between old and new, distinctly hostile to the old and unquestioningly devoted to the new. Voltaire, in fighting Catholic and Protestant bigotry from his 'fox-hole,' lived the future life of the age of reason by kindling 'the revolution of minds,' or, as he said in French: 'la révolution des esprits.' Voltaire converted 'revolution,' up to his time the physical rotation of the stars, into an intellectual process. He was not an isolated mind like Descartes, but made himself the grand master of enlightenment, the idol of the European reading world. It was the readers of Europe who had to fill the breach between the old house of tradition and the new house of natural science.[32]

Descartes's *Discourse on Method* had been written in the French vernacular not only to attract a large readership but also to gather an army under his leadership, dedicated to discovering useful knowledge, to promoting the general welfare of mankind.[33] It was 'to replace the speculative philosophy taught in the schools.' *The Meditations*, by contrast, were written in Latin for the schoolmen – that is, for those who made no practical contribution to the improvement of the lot of mankind and who preferred the arid rationalizations of the mind to the grasp of reality.[34] The *Meditations* were an attempt to silence the schoolmen (which it didn't in his lifetime) by reconciling his revolutionary ideas about nature with their more 'precious' longings for the beyond.[35] The beyond he offered them was, as Pascal sensed immediately, arid and devoid of any religious content, for God was construed as irrelevant to everyday life – the mind was equated with the soul.[36] Science and the study of nature (eventually, with Rousseau, to be replaced by *communion* with nature) replaced prayer and communication with an incalculable power that burst into nature. For Pascal, God's every act was a miracle; for Descartes, there could be no miracles (this followed logically from the system itself, but was stated explictly only in his posthumously published *The World*),[37] for if there were miracles, God was a deceiver and ergo, according to Descartes, not God. Descartes did not see fit to mention that the Bible does indeed allow God to deceive his enemies (e.g., II Thessalonians 2.11–12). Concomitantly, there are no logical restrictions on the biblical God, except that humans have the freedom to love or turn from Him, in large part because the God of living love does not give to reason the weight that philosophers, including Descartes, at least up until the meta-ethical (to use Rosenzweig's term) revolution of Schopenhauer, Kierkegaard, and Nietzsche, generally do. And the way they are able to make God conform to reason is by transforming Him into a being and by reducing his qualities to what conforms to reason. This philosophical limit of God is precisely what Rosenzweig would blow away in *The Star*, first by showing the triumph of the metalogical view of the world over the various 'idealisms,' and second by showing how the metaphysical is not a means of encompassing God with a concept we have of Him, but rather a way of opening us to the infinitude of a nature that cannot be exhausted conceptually. The entire point of Descartes's God, by contrast, is to bring it into line with the requirement that is at the very heart of his method – only to proceed with ideas that are clear and distinct. That God is defined as a perfect being does, as he well knew, bring it in line with scholastic thought. Though that the idea is innate directly cuts It – for now God ceases to be a Him and becomes an It – off from experience and leaves It as an object of speculation, not a loving Father. The enlightened will argue that certain similies are being used by the less sophisticated and that certain qualities of reason – Kant, of course, will emphasize God as a moral idea – are being anthropomorphized.

Rosenstock-Huessy, on the other hand, consistently makes the point not only that philosophical language is *not* more concrete, but also that in real communication our names not only describe but also *evoke* and *summon* the mood and power of the the experience itself. Thus he says that in matters of any real importance, there are no synonyms or similes because 'every name was an attempt of man to accompany the course of events with a worthy response to the gifts of time. The energy flowing through time materialised in communal forms whenever he found the right names in which his fellow men could join in a common outcry of faith.'[38] For him, 'any part of language is as real as a daisy or a violet or a pansy or a weed,'[39] while for the mechanists – as we have already suggested – names are just words that obfuscate meaning. Hence for Descartes and all the mechanists, the nameless language of mathematics is the way in which the philosophers of nature may access the truth. And hence also – and by contrast – Rosenzweig's argument in *The Star* restricts the mute world of mathematic language so that it is appropriate only to the aspects of life that can adequately be described by the process of emergence – the process captured/depicted by calculus and not by the creative process of peoples and the living word that leads to Revelation and Redemption.

For Rosenstock-Huessy, names are (to use Rosenzweig's term) what seals communities – communities are held together by the summoning of, response to, and veneration of common powers. This is no less the case for scientists than for members of the Catholic or Jewish faiths and for tribal peoples. Thus Rosenstock-Huessy says that

> a man's religion is in the names which make him act in common with others. There is no other religion. These names may be passing, but in their time they are more incisive and more public and more history-making than all private relations to a pretty face or a blood relation, or to the air and the sky and the sun and the land. For the names decide whether we respect the sister in the woman or seduce her as a female. They decide whether we report to Washington for duty, or retire to the back hills when the draft is enacted. It is true, that all the protestations of modern man are to the contrary. He insists that words have no power, that words have lost their meaning, that this is all verbiage or propaganda.
>
> Yet will he be judged for his genuine religion. And this religion is his relation to the life and death and resurrection of the spirit as expressed in those names which make him behave.[40]

Hence, too, the God who is described as a perfect being in a philosophical argument is, for Rosenstock-Huessy, already a philosophical figment, a dead force, who does indeed render ridiculous any anthropomorphic depiction, which would be a mere simile. Spinoza's 'not to laugh, not to cry, not to hate, but to understand' represents the dispassionate orientation of the student of nature required of the servants of the god of 'nature.'

But when men and women tremble before living powers, not by resorting to philosophy, but instead – as a collective response to the range of forces operative in an experience – by referring to God's wrath or love, and use anthropomorphic language to convey the reality of their experience of the relationship between them and their God, then, Rosenstock-Huessy's remark from his Lectures on Greek Philosophy is most apt:

> first impressions never speak in similes, but mean what they say. The language of the cult, which . . . speaks of God's heart, or God's wrath, or God's right finger, means exactly what it says . . . That's not a simile. That's not a sublime figure of speech . . . We speak of God as we must speak of Him, or we shouldn't speak of Him at all . . . In any real society, there are no synonyms . . . All original speech, if you want to have it this way, is metaphorical. And there is no other speech. If I say that the king has to have a scepter in order to be able . . . to command silence, or that we are

under . . . his hand, or under his care, that's a necessary way of speaking. There is no other way of saying the thing. The law says that he wields the scepter of this country . . . You will never understand speech . . . if you do not understand that first impressions have to be expressed in an unshaken terminology. You cannot say to a child that the father of Jesus Christ is a supreme being without poking fun at the fact that you ask this child to pray to 'Our Father in Heaven.' He is either 'Our Father in Heaven' or He's nobody. He's not 'the supreme being.'[41]

The 'supreme being' was simply a deist name for the perfect, bloodless, unresponsive being of Descartes. Though of course, Descartes's God had – as he was constantly to point out to his opponents – been cultivated primarily in the scholastic philosophy/theology of the University of Paris. Rosenstock-Huessy generally did not think that the scholastics had any relevance today for understanding life. Their philosophical and metaphysical roots were too Greek, even if their objective of trying to resolve the contradictions that had arisen within a thousand years of the Christian faith was a necessary one for the preservation and development of that particular social body in which the originators of scholasticism took part.[42] But, as Rosenstock-Huessy emphasized in *Speech and Reality*, there were also crucial differences between Cartesian philosophy and scholastic reasoning: most notably, scholastic reasoning used logic as an *organon* (instrument), whereas Descartes used it as a metaphysics. As we have implied, his metaphysics served two purposes – to shut down opposition from scholastic enemies, and to maintain a framework of lawfulness in nature. This, in turn, meant dispensing with the scholastics' deployment of two components of Aristotle's theory of four causes – formal and final causes were, for Descartes, as for Bacon and Spinoza, mere projections (Kant would rehabilitate them as transcendental conditions of certain kinds of judgments), and the material cause was useless because of the notion of different kinds of material. All that was required, then, was the efficient cause. Furthermore, scholasticism was bound up with its service to the Christian faith, not to reason as such. Though Descartes (along with Leibniz) is often classified as a rationalist, this can be very misleading. The term 'rationalist' was a polemical label used against Cartesian physicists by defenders of Newtonian mechanics. It did draw attention to a weakness in Cartesian physics, viz. that for all its aspirations, it was burdened by its excessive speculativeness due to its first principles, which, as the 'fact' of gravity demonstrated, were devoid of mathematical support (despite what Descartes himself said about the role of mathematics as providing the distinctness and clarity required by reason). For the Cartesians, gravity was an occult force that flew in the face of the strictly causal modern that Descartes had laid down as according with the rules of correct reasoning; for the Newtonians, gravity, while undoubtedly a metaphysical mystery, was merely a mathematical and hence an empirical fact. Newton could hold himself aloof from the attacks directed at him by metaphysicians calling him an occultist, by simply claiming that he did not deal in hypotheses. And he could indulge in metaphysical claims about the significance of the absolute nature of space and time to support his Arian theology.

But the debates between Cartesians and Newtonians all helped move the focus of theology away from what the scholastics had always accepted as the foundation of their faith – that is, 'the crucifixion,' which Rosenstock-Huessy would later call 'the irreducible datum in experience' of the scholastics.'[43] The crucifixion played no part in Descartes's thinking, even though the 'customs' of his own land made him accept it as true (even though elsewhere he insisted that one should never accept as true what one cannot affirm with one's own reasoning). And, again, even though he would swear at every available opportunity that he was a good Catholic, while taking good care not to live in a Catholic country.

No less significant than God being removed from time and history (which found its appropriate heir in Spinoza's biblical criticism, which was the natural extension of Descartes's refusal to accept miracles) is the Cartesian equation of mind and soul. The radicality of this distinction is often overlooked in the literature on Descartes's metaphysics because so many contemporary scholars have lost any sense of the distinction:

> the Christian church . . . has always maintained that soul and body belong to the individual, but that mind and spirit are not individual qualities. Intelligence gives the individual soul a share in the universal inspiration: that is all. Modern clergymen themselves have forgotten this fundamental truth. By giving way to the famous God of Nature, by abandoning the sharp distinction beween mind and soul, they condemned the soul to be nothing but a mind – God's information bureau. Now it is not our minds but our souls to which God is a secret and a revelation. The mind of the philosopher can know nothing of God. But Cartesianism makes the mind boast that it has through its own power a notion of the Supreme Being, a God of Nature.[44]

Where Descartes's metaphysics were most fateful, then, was in preparing the way for the deist religion of the Enlightenment. Voltaire was the high priest of the new religion of deism. Whereas Descartes wanted to create an army of physicists, Voltaire wanted an army of readers who would enlighten others against prejudice, ignorance, tyranny, and despotism and who would 'hold themselves ready until the material revolution actually occurs.'[45] Men would be freed from superstition by the power of their ideas, and philosophers would be the new high priests of humanity: their love of ideas would save them from the corruption that had befallen those great tyrants of humankind – kings, aristocrats, and priests. They would lead the men of property, whose creativity in the world would be guided by those who imbued them with 'a set of positive values.'[46]

Rosenstock-Huessy notes that, unlike the Russian revolutionaries, Voltaire and his revolutionary contemporaries were neither atheists nor despisers of law as mere ideology. The old wine must be put into new bottles: 'the eternal "ideas" must be kept, but freed from the old institutions which had corrupted them: Church, kings, and customs.'[47] What Voltaire wanted most of all was quite simply the rule of Reason – or, more cynically (though not unfairly), the rule of those who thought like him. But however strong the bourgeois emphasis on individuality, no social change can take place without solidarity, collective resolve, and unity of purpose. If the world was to change, it would not be enough for Voltaire's army of readers to simply read in private. As Rosenstock-Huessy notes, the solution to this problem would involve adapting and then turning to revolutionary purposes an institution that had taught 'God without Church, government without authority, and law without prescription.' This solution was not new – it had arisen in Britain in the early eighteenth century, in the Freemasons' assemblies, as left Whiggism's reaction against the petrification of the Anglican Church.[48] Conspiracy theorists (including the Nazis) have made wildly ridiculous claims about the power of Freemasons, but their lodges were an important means for spreading the ideals of the Enlightenment in eighteenth-century Europe and for bringing together believers in a rational master builder.[49] Also important in Paris were the salons, which nurtured the talents of geniuses and facilitated social contact between men of ideas and their audiences. As Rosenstock-Huessy put it, 'the queen of cities, Paris, has replaced Versailles because her salons have replaced a dynasty of kings by a dynasty of inspired individuals whose candidacies the ladies of the salons have previously approved.'[50] In this role she not only helped elevate the genius as the type to be venerated above all, but also prepared the way for the revolution.[51]

For Rosenstock-Huessy, Voltaire – and the enlightened *philosophes* generally – had followed Descartes in dissolving eternity into space and in embarking on a project of infinite perfectibility. Descartes had set the enlightened on their path by asking all to follow their natural reason and reconstitute all of human knowledge from point zero by breaking every piece of data down into its smallest components and then building up a model, piece by piece, with no unbroken links in the chain of causal relations of the universe. His great analogy for this is in the *Discourse,* where he asks his readers to imagine being lost in a forest (as his generation is) and then suggests that the only hope of a way out is by settling on a direction and then sticking to it. In time one will come out, whereas if one keeps wandering around in circles, one will be lost forever. The path of constant progress has been set. And with it there is a deep conviction that the fundamental antagonisms and polarities of life – notably 'law and love, repetition and surprise, custom and revelation,' which are essential to the Christian understanding of life – are as passé as the dualisms of its institutions, most obviously Church and State, emperor and pope, king and priest, which are expressions of these antagonisms. Descartes was philosophically a dualist, but ultimately his dualism served only to reinforce the monism of science. Kant would fight to save a residue of the dual by the moral law – at the price, of course, of it being but 'a mere idea.'

The Enlightenment gave rise to stage theory – that is, the idea that history is accompanied by increasingly complex forms of social organization. (Rosenstock-Huessy himself might be mistaken for a social evolutionary because he took this idea seriously, but he also saw each stage as having its own pathologies and as capable of collapse.) Note well, however, that stage theory paved the way for social Darwinism, Marxism, and the Whig view of history. The Cartesian beginnings of the Enlightenment required a completely new ahistorical beginning. And the concept of this year zero was to be of enormous importance to Rousseau – and would be encountered again in Foucault's endorsement of the Ayatollah, and most savagely of all in that former student at the Sorbonne, Pol Pot.

Rousseau had baulked at the idea of social progress because he could not accept that the rotting dynasties of Europe and their minions represented any kind of social or moral progress.[52] While Voltaire and

Rousseau squabbled with each other, Rosenstock-Huessy focused on them as a team who 'unconsciously divided their labour,' 'one aiming at the individual, the other at the institutions.'[53] This is somewhat contentious, for Rousseau certainly wrote about institutions. But the basis of his *Social Contract* is the individual whose will established the collective (from which it is often so hard to escape). Rosenstock-Huessy's analysis of Rousseau, at least in *Out of Revolution*, is somewhat one-sided, for it emphasizes freedom and individuality more than equality and solidarity (though he does mention the former). But this is because he is more interested in the Rousseau who had such an enormous impact on France in the eighteenth century, the Rousseau of the bourgeoisie, rather than the socialist Rousseau who condemned private property as the greatest curse of humankind and who so greatly inspired the Romantic movement.[54]

What fascinates Rosenstock-Huessy is that whereas Pascal had looked for a mystical body from which to launch his attack on a rotting France,

> Rousseau had the courage to exhibit himself as the first individual of the new society, the citizen of the future earthly paradise. But his personal nervous fits and ugly acts – he went so far as to treat his legitimate children as natural children and to banish them to a foundling asylum – needed certain auxiliary constructions. Jean-Jacques restored Adam, and Adam was to replace Jesus. Jesus, the first citizen of the city on Mount Zion, was supplanted by the natural man and wife. As pure water – Adam's ale – had existed before the refinements of wine or beer, so Adam himself was the natural man who existed before the original sin of division into classes; when Adam delved and Eve span, who was then the gentleman? The Creator had bestowed on the natural man the gift of freedom.[55]

The opening of Rousseau's *Confessions* – 'I wish to reveal to my fellow beings a man in all the truth of nature, and this man will be myself! . . . myself alone!'[56] – illustrates, for Rosenstock-Huessy, the revolutionary transformation that had taken place. Rousseau had grasped 'man's liberty to change at different stages in his life,' and he was certainly opposed to any institutional or class-privileged attempt to curtail that capacity. Referring to Groethuysen's classic *The Bourgeois: Catholicism versus Captialism in the Eighteenth Century*, Rosenstock-Huessy points out that prior to the French Revolution, sermons often talked of the 'pride of "doing it oneself."' 'Adam was glorified, not merely as a piece of or child of nature, but . . . as a man who masters nature.' He continues:

> Rousseau's gospel fits the owner of land, the owner of property, the owner of capital, the owner of talent, because it sees man in action according to his own free choice. No choice without opportunity. Therefore the 'fair chance' is our real social property and fortune; the simplest expression of liberalism is that everyone shall have an opportunity. Opportunity is the electron in the field of force created by Rousseauism. The agglomeration of opportunities in a few hands may lead to wealth; but the only essential feature is that everybody shall get at least one opportunity.[57]

Having found civilization rotten, Rousseau turned to the noble savage as the yardstick by which to measure its degeneracy. This was, says Rosenstock-Huessy, apt for the situation of France, though the same move helped establish that other great bourgeois icon (much detested and ridiculed by Marx), Robinsoe Crusoe:

> The French, preparing themselves to regenerate Europe, were perfectly willing to place Christianity below the noble savage. For the purpose of turning the scales from Pascal's Christian humility to the creativeness of the man of nature, the noble savage was a wonderful foil. Robinson Crusoe was an even better example because he recovered from a rotten society by setting all the miraculous energies of his brain to work on an isolated island. And since Robinson Crusoe became the model of classical economics, his relation to Rousseau's Adam must be stressed. The whole prehistory of Robinson Crusoe, his upbringing, experience, equipment, standards, count for nothing: all our interest centres in this man who represents society in a nutshell, before the division of labour, that is to say, before the fall of man.[58]

If Descartes had severed the self from extension by making it a thinking substance, and (to Spinoza's chagrin) by looking at language as proof of the self's freedom (even while, in the *Passions of the Soul*, denying this very freedom in our psychological constitution), Rousseau had made freedom the source of this self's nature. In that he would be followed by the framers of the American Constitution and their view of God and life.

Rosenstock-Huessy's critique of Jefferson and Rousseau rests simply (so he says) on common sense: the self is constantly changing, and its freedom is won over time; the self's freedom is not given at the same time as its nature. But so seemingly obvious are the self and nature in today's world that, for many, it is only when pressure is placed on the concepts that one must concede that the self is every bit as unknown as nature – both are merely concepts that we use to make sense of processes. Nietzsche may have prided himself on exposing the unity of self as a fabrication; but to a Luther, Augustine, or Paul, this was no news. The Christian self had always been a multiplicity of forces, a malleable composition of the flesh's 'warring members.' The neat unity of mind and body offered by Descartes was a modern scientistic distinction between subject and object, not an experiential one. Similarly, for Rosenstock-Huessy, nature as conceived in modern times gained its present power in the Renaissance. In his essay 'Liturgical Thinking,' regarding the Renaissance conception of nature, he writes that 'for the first time in the history of thought, dead matter was held to have preceded living growth, in a living universe, too, we may have to cope with corpses. But the mechanical "natural science" after 1500 tried to explain life out of its corpses by making nature primarily a concept of dead mass in space.'[59] Now Rousseau's self, even more than Descartes's thinking subject, has as its content the *a priori* element of freedom that releases it from being merely subject to the forces of nature; but as Kant's system developed – with far greater philosophical precision than anything to be found in Rousseau – this moral self consisted more of its legislative power than of any certitude about its innately good character (Rousseau, we recall in *The Social Contract*, had made freedom depend on our power to give ourselves law).

There is much, much more that Rosenstock-Huessy could have said about Rousseau, about how his Romanticism was closely related to nostalgia; and about how nostalgia is the most modern of moods in an age that romanticizes indigenous forms that remained outside nations until colonization, even while being dedicated to ever greater manipulation of nature and ever more 'excellence' (to take the word that almost every instution of higher learning in the world has sought to wrap around itself, thereby thus ensuring that originality and excellence are antonyms). He could have dwelled longer on the contradiction between individualism and collectivism – how this man who wanted all citizens to formulate and then be bound by the general will, and who wanted to make politics the duty of everyday life, was also the man who despised men and who wanted to be a solitary dreamer. He does note that the writer about child rearing abandoned his own children to an orphanage – a revealing sign of the modern's acceptance of the morally enthusiastic abstract over the self-sacrificing act, of the idea over the actual. And Kant's moral theory of the pure will and the irrelevance of consequences perfects this move, by isolating intention to the exclusion of everything else. This most modern move of Kant's defence of the Self's absolute sovereignty was in strict contrast to the classical philosophers of antiquity, who had noted that intention was an issue to be weighed in an overall assessment rather than a fail-safe mechanism of moral evaluation.

Rosenstock-Huessy could also have addressed the problem of Rousseau's contribution to totalitarian democracy.[60] Rousseau is a fascinating 'world' because of the various contradictions he contains and because he is so free and messed up, like so many of us moderns. Though in his German book about the European revolutions, *Die europäischen Revolutionen und der Character der Nationen*, Rosenstock-Huessy does make a few more points about Rousseau. There he refers to *The Social Contract*, saying that it wants to show that all conventions are unnatural; that only families took root in nature; that no generation has the right to prescribe laws for the next generation; and that the free will must be purified by education so that it can produce the right general will; and noting that the Parisian convention was able to imbue Rousseau's empty general will with the prevailing content of the *Zeitgeist*.

But perhaps the most important point that Rosenstock-Huessy is interested in making is how Descartes, Voltaire, and Rousseau, working together, created a vision of reality in which time was of secondary importance to space. Indeed, as far as Rousseau's politics were concerned, this is what divided him from Montesquieu, who was another important – albeit far more cautious – Enlightenment figure. For Montesquieu was conscious of the resilience of customs precisely *because* they had been formed over long spans of time; it followed that social relationships could not simply be severed at one stroke without a society being thrown into disarray. Of course a revolutionary *welcomes* disarray, preferring it to the grim certainties of the status quo. And what Voltaire welcomed was the building of the house of reason, which would come from the *révolution des ésprits*, whereas Rousseau welcomed the equality that would accompany the freedom he saw unleashed by the Adamite reduction.

Rosenstock-Huessy did not think that the dangerous powers of France arose simply from the elevation of freedom and equality or from the invocation of reasonable requirements against heartlessness and privilege. Rather, it was the abstract character they took on, and their fusion into a fighting army of monism, which he saw as dominating the world between 1789 and 1914. Again, the Great War would provide the vantage point from which Rosenstock-Huessy surveyed the action – that same war that owed so much to the spread (under Napoleon) of French imperial power and Enlightenment ideals, to France's role in the creation of German nationalism, and to the modern form of nationalism that would generate so much turmoil within the Austro-Hungarian Empire, and that would warp reason, freedom, and equality into units and allegiances of units into collective bodies with very real grievances. The monism that came out of the French Revolution is 'found everywhere in the modern world as a principle of wonderful driving power';[61] but while the mechanisms that Descartes and physicists wished to take as the ultimate causes of living processes have helped us invent machines, societies simply do not conform to the same logic. They are living bodies with their own unconscious, their own physiognomies and psychologies, and their own biorhythms (indeed, Rosenstock-Huessy likened what he was doing in *Out of Revolution* to a psychoanalysis of nations).[62]

Rosenstock-Huessy held that 'the crisis of modern history came when nationalism threw itself into a fiery messianic crusade for a common future,'[63] and that nationalism had unleashed the powers that gave birth to the Great War; but he also held that ideas of nationalism, democracy, and liberalism had helped end serfdom in Russia and slavery in the United States.[64] Moreover, nationalism was essential to the establishment of extranational units of social cooperation, which Rosenstock-Huessy saw as flowing out of the total revolutions. And at the centre of all this was nationalism's vision of Europe as the centrepiece of civilization. Even after the seeming defeat of the French Revolution (which Rosenstock-Huessy referred to as its phase of humiliation), the idea of Europe was adopted by France's enemies:

Even the antagonists of the French Revolution soon bowed before the idea of 'Europe.' The leaders of German romanticism, in 1810, founded a review called Europe. The King of Prussia published a summons to arms against the French in 1813 with the argument, 'My cause is the cause of all the men of good will in Europe.' In 1814, when the Allies against the

French began to organize the Continent, they built up the European Concert, without the pope, as a purely secular community of nations. (In 1856 the Islamic Sultan of Turkey joined the European Concert.) The leaders of the emancipation of the Jews called Christian baptism the ticket of admission to European civilization! Another example: in the thirties of the nineteenth century all the non-democratized governments of the old world faced revolutionary movements of young Poles, young Germans, young Italians, etc. All these groups recognized their affinity by calling the whole movement 'Young Europe.'[65]

Rosenstock-Huessy lived to see the formation of the European Common Market, but he died before the EU proper was formed. That latter institution brought about the economic integration that he viewed as inevitable;[66] in addition, though, the EU has made itself a model of 'soft power' – that is, a new politics devoted to freedom, economic security, and democratic institutions. Ultimately it is not simply Europe that the EU hopes to transform, but the world. To that end, it is engaging in all manner of bilateral and multilateral trade arrangements to bring about political and social change. If the EU plainly sees itself as a leader in helping civilize the world, it also is, at best, ambivalent about its Christian past – hence it did not invoke any overtly Christian principles in its efforts in 2005 to develop a constitution. The EU serves as a reminder that France succeeded in separating Europe from Christendom and in tying its faith in liberty, equality, and the nation – indeed, in civilization and its progressive improvement – to the fate of this new Europe.

In our analysis of the French Revolution we have only hinted at another essential ingredient that Rosenstock-Huessy saw fermenting within it – an ingredient that would do much to shape the modern world. That is, the importance that revolution ascribed to art, especially to literature and sensualism and novelty. We will explore these areas more thoroughly in the chapter on Rosenstock-Huessy and art.

9 Beyond the Idol of the Nation, Part 1: Rosenstock-Huessy in the Aftermath of the Great War

Nationalism is a spirit whose significance and forms of expression shift according to a range of other forces. Nationalism may be as innocuous as supporting a sports team and feeling a sense of pride in national cooperation and achievement, as happened in Germany with the 2006 World Cup of Football, when for the first time since the Second World War – that is, six decades later – Germans publicly, joyously, and harmlessly displayed their national pride. Or it can be utterly horrific. Ethnic groups with different linguistic roots may live side by side for long periods in harmony and share their commitment to a common national identity, as in Switzerland. But the violence that accompanied the break-up of Yugoslavia in the 1990s were a shocking reminder to Europeans that nationalism could still be unleashed on their continent. If the end of the twentieth century was driven by a push toward an 'ever closer union' of European nations – as Desmond Dinan neatly formulates it[1] – the cusp of the nineteenth and twentieth centuries was defined by rapid political changes brought about by the spread of democratic ideas, at a time when blind and tottering colonial empires were struggling to contain peoples who wanted more liberty and control of their own affairs. Nationalism was the power that gathered many peoples into nation-states; it was also the spirit that drove Europe and the world into the Great War, with each nation being driven by old enmities, faith in a new future, and cankerous outbursts of unfinished business and festering resentments.

Rosenstock-Huessy, by his own account, had entered the Great War as something of a nationalist and definitely as a patriot; by the end of the war, however, he was convinced that unbridled nationalism was among the most demonic of all spirits. In Germany, this insight was a blessing, for those who weren't cured of nationalism would come to be embittered by it and, with varying degrees of culpability, would within two decades plunge the country and Europe into another war of nations. But even during his nationalist phase, Rosenstock-Huessy's views had been tempered by his faith. Throughout his corpus – and indeed, in Rosenzweig's as well – one notices some affinities with Romanticism (albeit he is not uncritical).[2] And while a degenerate form of Romanticism would foster a degenerate form of nationalism, the original Romantic idea of the nation was itself conceived as part of a greater unity, the unity of the human race. This idea that we are all branches of one great tree, members of one great family – formulations used on many occasions by Rosenstock-Huessy – would play a major role in his theory that the European revolutions amounted to a messianic journey of the nations 'in which every century of our era has fallen less and less completely away and . . . man has become more and more natural, more fully all he was meant to be, from the beginning.'[3] That is to say, for Rosenstock-Huessy the nation and faith were complementary, with the former subordinate to the latter. Furthermore, the latter was lost when the former became its object rather than the living, loving, redeemer God who had created the nations. In fact, what Rosenstock-Huessy saw as the great problem was the idolatry of politics itself. Thus he argued in *Das Alter der Kirche* (The Age of the Church; 1927) that nationalism and democracy were only *apparent* opposites: one was the peaceful form, the other was the 'war-form' of the pagan world. And the pagan world, for Rosenstock-Huessy, was (precisely as it was for Rosenzweig) one in which the sundering of human energies was the inescapable consequence of their sacrifice to idols.[4] And in an insight so often skated over with blissful ignorance by social/political commentators who invoke democracy as a solution to all our ills, he also pointed out that the dangers into which nationalism falls are not ameliorated by democracy; it is a matter of no great consequence whether the blindness of nationalism is driven by a prince or by a democracy – a salutary point at that time in Germany.[5]

Rosenstock-Huessy was mostly convinced that 'the nation' – as opposed to any specific nation – was an enduring form of spiritual development, though the specific constituency and boundaries were fluid, and so were its features of common identity. This openness to the transformation of forms is a central theme in his work and is in large part why he is so sympathetic to the revolutionary spirit; for that spirit is in deadly opposition to all ossifications of the most urgent needs of the human heart and is prepared to risk everything by its faith in a better future viewed from the unbearable hell of its present. Rosenstock-Huessy would state his position succinctly in *The Fruit of Lips:* 'I could not believe in the Holy Ghost unless He had changed His form of expression relentlessly.'[6] For him, the nations were simply the means by which the Holy Spirit was able to expand itself and bring human beings into a common recognition of their shared suffering and hence their need for shared love, faith, and hope. In this respect, human beings needed to be reminded constantly that no matter how mighty an earthly power the nation was, it was a transient and subordinate one. Thus in *Out of Revolution*, he writes that

> the world unrest of today, caused by the great revolution of the World War, should again bring home to us the truth that the nations of Europe are rather short lived: when Austria has vanished from the map. It dawns upon us that the great powers themselves are temporary. Not one of them existed in the year 1000. It took three more centuries before Italy, the first of the modern nations, came into being; and it was not until 1500 that England, Germany, France, Russia, Spain, Poland were moulded to a recognizable degree into 'nations.'[7]

In recognizing the limits of nationalism, Rosenstock-Huessy would often emphasize the urgency of supra-nationalism and the dangers immanent in nationalism. Thus in 1939, in 'The Rise and Fall of Nationalism and Internationalism,' he argued that 'nationalism is wearing itself out. The strain of worshipping national gods at the terrific pitch of recent years is reaching its breaking point.'[8] 'The nation,' he would continue a couple of pages later,

> has been a real stage in our historical growth. National 'types,' music, literature have added to the variety and interest of life. In national units we have exploited resources, discovered new territories and encouraged the development of machinery and the progress of technology. But the nation has passed as the desirable unit of political organisation . . . The new sovereign will be the 'bloc' or continent.[9]

A year earlier he had written in *Out of Revolution* that 'state sovereignty is doomed. Yet it cannot be sacrificed until some other road is open.'[10] Around the same time, he had been calling for 'Europe [to] be organized economically as America and Russia are organized already.'[11]

But what he was emphasizing here was the danger that nationalism would fold in upon itself. People, he contended, needed to recognize that the nation must be cognizant that it could play only a partial role in bringing people into a common future and a common history – which, for him, largely meant mourning in common over shared catastrophes, losses, and sufferings, as well as celebrating shared triumphs: 'Common sufferings create. Common tears restore.'[12] In this regard, what he expressed at the beginning of the Second World War was essentially the same as what he had expressed at the end of the First World War, when he had written: 'With the year 1917 the epoch of state sovereignty has concluded.'[13] And: 'The earth has become round for all times. Time has become unified for all zones. The human race has become one for all times and zones. The bonds of blood, nation, race can never again become Lord over the unity of fate.'[14] In his feverish writings toward the end of the Great War and in its aftermath, he had urged Germans to surrender their faith in the old forms of the spirit such as the kind of imperial state that had led them into catastrophe. The suffering induced by the war, he said, had made it impossible to lean on the two great poles of Germany's spiritual and political body – Goethe and Bismarck, Germany's heaven and hell (though he also pointed out that Bismarck had been driven to provide for the very social and liberal forces he opposed). Now, he declared, Germany must be open to spirits hitherto unattended.[15]

Running through all the essays on the war gathered into *Die Hochzeit des Kriegs und der Revolution* (The Marriage of War and Revolution) is a central methodological tenet of Rosenstock-Huessy's thought – a tenet that is also at the root of his belief that Christianity is not simply a personal belief, not primarily a religion, at least not in the way the word is bandied about today by 'believers' and 'disbelievers'; rather, it is a collective truthful response to the inner workings of the relationship between death and life. That tenet is this: death does not follow from life; rather, death is the precondition of life's rebirth. Thus when he writes that 'the German people has never been so spiritually empty as today,'[16] and 'we are in the night, only in the night'[17] – just two of many formulations in *Hochzeit* acknowledging the desolation of defeat – the question is what Germans are to do with this emptiness. The content and structure of *Hochzeit* suggests that they can be tempted back into their old fate by opting for further national idolatry or idolatry of the Self, and thereby prove Spengler right by committing suicide (thus his 1919 essay, 'The Suicide of Europe'). Such an option might involve going back to Bismarckian politics; or buying once again into the myth of the state as saviour, or adopting Romantic visions of Germanness and its role in the world such as one finds in Steiner or Johannes Müller (both of whom he criticizes harshly in *Hochzeit*); or accepting the demonic offerings of Bolshevism. Each of these options, though, would simply involve resorting to the pagan energies that had created the catastrophe in the first place. Or, a fourth option: Germany could become a nation of education and work and join in the 'family of kindred spirits rather than an Empire, a major family in the concert of the peoples of the world,'[18] thereby playing its part on the messianic journey that first gave the national spirits their task and truth.

In *Hochzeit*, Rosenstock-Huessy made an argument on which he would elaborate for the rest of his life (and it would dismay him that his thesis as well as the mass of evidence he had accumulated for it would be passed over in silence). His argument: the Great War had been the result of one thousand years of history, of all the forces that Christendom had generated exploding in one huge burst and tearing asunder the mighty cumulative spirit of 'Western man' arcing from Jews to Christians to moderns. Christianity, for Rosenstock-Huessy, was a vast storehouse of energy that flowed from a particular approach to time and action, an approach built on the powers of speech, time, history, endowment, and incarnation. For him, the truth of the Church was not something that could be grasped by a philosophical mind looking for logical, moral, or scientific purity – again, all Greek referents or powers, which in their place are powerful and useful, but when worshipped as ultimate powers are inwardly depleting and outwardly devastating. The Church's truth was its power, and above all that power lay in its accumulation and transmission of energy over time. For Rosenstock-Huessy, the Church knew that this had been its mission from the first; only in its degeneracy did it mimic the state and try to rival the state as a conqueror of space.

In *Hochzeit*, against the great modern powers of state, nation, and empire, which had caused the war, Rosenstock-Huessy counters with the Church – a Church freed from the corrosive encrustations of nation and state and empire – as an example of a living time-body whose greatest triumphs had been formed out of neighbourly love. To be sure, he was keenly aware of the modern Church's inability to prevent the war. But how could it have prevented it when there was so little faith in the Church and so much faith in the very powers that had *caused* the war? For Rosenstock-Huessy, the war had shown how absolutely necessary it was to abandon the forces that had created it. And because the blame for this catastrophe, whose complicity involved all the European nations, was being laid on the defeated, Rosenstock saw that Germany, whatever the injustice (perhaps even precisely *because* of the injustice), must be prepared to be the scapegoat so that peace could be fulfilled. He knew that Germany's only opportunity for a better future was *not* to do what seemed so natural in terms of its history and its defeat – *not* to cry foul, and *not* to enfold itself in resentment and repeat the entire catastrophe. If his most serious error as a social theorist was, in *Out of Revolution*, to talk up the prospects for peace in 1938, his potency as a social theorist is clearly evident in the timing and depth of his insight regarding which 'idols' would have to be abandoned by the German people, and in the urgency of his call that they be abandoned. Equally prescient was his awareness of the impact of the war in generating two fateful new modalities of nationalism – Bolshevism, which he saw as a product of Russia's war experience rather than of Marxism; and fascism.

In 'Bolshevismus und Christentum,' also included in *Hochzeit*, he conceded that Bolshevism contained many true accusations against European culture.'[19] But, he argued, it did not do enough to overthrow the idols that had created the crisis. On the contrary, for him, Bolshevism was demonic precisely because it gave the illusion of being what it was not: it purported to offer a universal peace when it required more killing to be secure, and it claimed to be internationalist but was in fact ultranationalist. He would repeat this latter point in *The Dismantling of Political Lies*, in which he wrote that Bolshevism was a Russian solution to a Russian catastrophe and that 'Bolsheviks don't Russify Europe, but nationalise Russia.'[20] That essay made a similar case that fascism was an Italian solution to an Italian experience. Each, though, for him, was built on political lies that were only contributing to future catastrophes. What he did concede to both movements was that they recognized the need to harness the energy of the working classes. And for his part, before he immigrated to the United States, where he would establish Camp William James, he had held various positions with organizations that linked work and labour and adult education. These projects included founding a workers' newspaper at Daimler Benz, becoming leader of the Academy of Labour in Frankfurt, and travelling to England in 1925 to study adult education, before returning to Germany in 1929, when he was elected vice chairman of the World Association of Adult Education. He was also involved in establishing cooperation among workers and student and peasant groups in Löwenberg. His social involvement was reflected in his large number of writings dealing with industry, the workplace, and adult education, such as *Werkstattaussiedlung* (1920), *Im Kampf um die Erwachsenbildung* (with Werner Picht) (1926), *Vom Industrierecht* (1926), *Lebensarbeit in der Industrie* (1926), *Das Arbeitslager,* edited with C.D. Trotha, (1931), *Arbeitsdient-Heeresdienst* (1932), *Der unbezahlbare Mensch* (1955), *The Multiformity of Man* (1973), and *Planetary Service* (1978). For Rosenstock-Huessy, the workers' movement was a hugely important stratum of social energy – too important to be left to the communists and fascists. Both, he said in *Industrievolk*, were doing their best to destroy that energy.[21]

Rosenstock-Huessy's post–Great War social vision was, then, built around his repeated warnings about the dangers of Germany's Nibelungen death cult.[22] He urged that a co-operative Christian community be founded that would be neither nationalist nor overly statist. He knew that German National Socialism would be an unmitigated disaster because it had been born of the resentments and hatreds generated by Germany's defeat, because it refused to accept the reality of world history, and because it indulged in the delusion that Germany could win the next war. In his 1931 essay 'Das Dritte Reich und die Sturmvögel die Nationalsozialismus' (published under the pseudonym Ludwig Stahl), he observed that National Socialism's dreams of restoring German nineteenth-century culture – 'Bayreuth, Lagarde, Fichte'[23] – combined the very forces that had helped drive Germany into war: Hegelian state theory, Bismarck's *Realpolitik,* and Kant's moral imperative.[24] That movement was driven by illusions, and it would end in what it was actually seeking – death, which he maintained was what had been the real basis of German idealism: 'German idealism in its purest form is unfortunately mostly the will to throw away one's life into a great moment . . . Hegel, Kant and Fichte taught the nation's youth to pull together singing into death. To live as a people, as a human being amongst human being – no, that's exactly what the 19th century lacked.'[25] Years earlier, in 'Lehrer oder Führer (Teacher or Leader),' he had attacked the *Führer* ideology as a dangerous mechanistic ideology hankering after a dead unity. The leader, he said, deforms all his followers by making them contemporaries of himself, thereby condemning successive generations to short-sightedness.[26] (I cannot help but note how relevant his criticism is to the extraordinary revival of the leadership cult that has grown up in the past five or so years within managerialist discourse – a discourse whose malevolent features are all too conspicuous to anyone with a historical ear once they are translated into German.)

On the brink of the Second World War, in *Out of Revolution*, Rosenstock-Huessy wrote of National Socialism as 'the stripping naked of Germany, the philosophy of the hammer of destruction swung by Hitler.'[27] As in his earlier analyses, he sought to make sense of the roots of Hitlerism and Germany's new religion of racism (this time to an American audience) as lying deep in Germany's rancour over defeat, in the admixture of its lack of faith and the break-up of Germany's dynastic orders without offering anything in its place:

> The rock of a racial religion is needed today in Germany because its High Magistrates, the sponsors of the free profession of the Faith, are gone. The downfall of the twenty dynasties in Germany necessarily brought on the most terrible outbreak of fear and hysteria: without the dynastic States, the German intellectual attitude of constant Protest has become a nuisance.
>
> A great nation like the German could live without a visible church just as long as the thoughtful criticism of 'every' Christian was balanced by the prerogative of 'every' prince. Then, the unending criticism might produce the sublimation of politics into reform. The World War destroyed this balance by destroying the power centres, and what was left of the Christian's liberty appeared as the sulky grumbling of mud rakers. Without a powerful state, a dreaded sovereign, a victorious army, a possible expansion, the individual German could not sit and sulk or philosophize or protest. He only could crave for a moral or religious unity of sacred character which would alleviate the offences from the outside and the anxieties within the flock. The system of the German Reformation has been destroyed in Germany today.
>
> The three essentials of the Reformation: civil service, universities, music, are of no importance any longer. They have been sacrificed, after the princes fell, by a young generation full of fear, full of superstitions, full of the need for a simple universal faith, and its personification in Hitler. A Storm Trooper like the Potemba murderers who trampled to death a political enemy in the presence of his mother, and who were acclaimed by Goebbels and acquitted by Hitler for doing so, is far away from the civil servant and wise counsellor of his prince; the *Parteischulen* and *Ordensburgen* in which *Mein Kampf* or *The Myth of the Twentieth Century* are studied, are strange contrasts to the Universities of Jena or Heidelberg where the 'Word' of the Bible set in motion the stream of systematic criticism; the Horst-Wessel-Lied is no music.[28]

Given how alert Rosenstock-Huessy was to the dangers of Bolshevism and National Socialism, it is astonishing that some German scholars – such as Rüdinger Safranski, Alois Prinz, and Heinrich Petzet (a Heideggerian) – have suggested, on the basis of a single illogical sentence that they all repeat, that Rosenstock-Huessy was blind to the dangers of National Socialism. It is a sad symptom of how academic truth is easily manufactured and of how a 'minor author' can easily be misrepresented by scholars who wish to use an example to illustrate their point but who do not bother to check their facts.

The supposedly damaging story was told by Georg Picht, the son of Werner Picht, who had for years been a close friend of Rosenstock-Huessy and a member of the Patmos group.[29] Werner Picht had also written on adult education as well as on the military spirit, and he had remained in Germany during the years of National Socialism. Furthermore, Werner Picht had (as Rosenstock-Huessy wrote to Georg Müller) gone astray with the Nazis.[30] It seems that Rosenstock-Huessy never forgave him for this, and he refused to answer his letters after the war. (Gritli, however, did resume contact with Gerda, Picht's wife.) It does seem, however, from a letter that Rosenzweig wrote to Gritli, that Picht was an anti-Semite from as early as 1917.[31]

Besides having a father who had become a Nazi, Georg Picht was a philosophical follower of Heidegger. It is not surprising, then, that Picht would want to make the point that intelligent people had been beguiled by National Socialism. Thus, in his postwar reflections, on the matter of National Socialism, he simply equated Rosenstock-Huessy – the son of a Jewish mother and father – with Martin Heidegger – whom Rosenstock-Huessy had publicly called 'Nazi scum.' But on what was this equation based? It was based on the report that he had once heard a lecture during which Rosenstock-Huessy claimed that the Nazis wanted to realize Hölderlin's dream!

I don't doubt that Rosenstock-Huessy said this. Anyone who has read Hölderlin and who knows anything about National Socialism can see there is truth in the statement. And while Rosenstock-Huessy liked Hölderlin very much and was not a man given to aesthetic idolatry, there is nothing to suggest that he believed for a millisecond that it was desirable or even possible to try to realize Hölderlin's late eighteenth-/early nineteenth-century dream in the twentieth century (as did, say, Heidegger, who liked the Nazis for precisely this reason until he realized the extent of his folly). Just as there was nothing to suggest that because the Nazis wanted a rural, communalized, proud

Germany, their politics were desirable. Nazism was bad not because one could find in it intellectual bric-a-brac from Nietzsche, Hölderlin, Wagner, and others, but because of the jackboots, the idolatry, the anti-Semitism, the book burning, the overthrow of the rule of law, the rounding up of 'enemies' of the state, the concentration camps, the military conquests, the enslavement of the Slavs, and the gas ovens and mass death. Picht's logic is on a par with making vegetarians complicit in the Holocaust because Hitler was a vegetarian.[32]

What makes the discussion especially disgraceful is that Rosenstock-Huessy, while mistaken about Nazism's insatiable expansionist aspirations, was nevertheless a man who stopped teaching the day Hitler came to power and who left Germany almost immediately afterwards. Moreover, he had taken his pen up against National Socialism almost immediately on its appearance, recognizing that it was a death wish and that Hitler was the incarnation of German embitterment and yearnings for past glories. Yet for reasons that defy any kind of intellectual rigour, he is compared with the hapless (or, more charitably said, tragically deluded) Felix Jacoby, a Jewish historian who declared in 1933 that he had been voting for Hitler since 1927 on the grounds that Hitler was to be Germany's Augustus. It is obvious that neither Picht, nor Safranski, nor Prinz – whose added embellishment was to imply, without a shred of evidence, that Arendt had also said this about Rosenstock-Huessy – had ever read any of Rosenstock-Huessy's numerous writings on National Socialism.[33]

A far more accurate picture of Rosenstock-Huessy's impact as a social activist and thinker between the wars in Germany is provided by Klemens Klemperer in his *German Incertitudes 1914–1945: The Stones and the Cathedral*. Comparing Rosenstock-Huessy to the philosophical anthropologist Helmuth Plessner, he observes that

> despite all the nonsense that has been gathered around Gemeinschaft there were two German scholars, Helmuth Plessner and Eugen Rosenstock-Huessy, who during the 1920s gave serious thought to its scholarly usefulness and political integrity. Distinguished and original thinkers, both concerned themselves with the fate of the 'modern machine man,' as Rosenstock put it, especially among the Germans, and thus they came to confront the problem of Gemeinschaft. Both pointed to the problems created by the German encounter with modern technology and the city. But they neither stopped at negative criticism nor abandoned themselves to sentimental Weltschmerz or otherwise backward looking illusions, but

they sought to explore positive and creative ways of facing up to an inevitably modern world.[34]

A little later he continues:

At the center of his [Rosenstock-Huessy's] thinking and doing was his concern about the harmful effects of the precipitate Industrial Revolution, especially on the German 'Industrievolk.' Rosenstock criticized employers for not living up to their social obligations, as well as the Social Democrats for their theoretical commitment to a Marxism that spelled class warfare and atheism. In his vocabulary *Gemeinschaft* was so to speak written in capital letters; it figured even in the term *Volksgemeinschaft*. He did not, however, use these terms, as did the radicals of the Right and the National Socialists, as seductive and in the last analysis meaningless propaganda clichés designed to undermine the democratic order.[35]

There are, however, several other points that need to be made about Rosenstock-Huessy and National Socialism. While Rosenstock-Huessy had warned against it and had absolutely no illusions about its murderous intentions, he made perhaps his worst social prediction on the verge of the Second World War, in *Out of Revolution*, when he stated that National Socialism and Bolshevism and fascism had abolished war in their ideologies,[36] and that 'in the field of foreign affairs, the German Nazi revolution is really going back to the forests of *Germania antiqua*. It needs world peace more than anyone else. The repressed instincts of pre-State existence turn up again and are deliberately fostered. The Germans are anticipating the tribal organization of an economically united world.'[37]

Altmann, in his introductory essay of 1916, criticized Rosenstock-Huessy's position in *Out of Revolution* for being too optimistic.[38] Indeed, Rosenzweig had recognized very early on that Rosenstock-Huessy was given to unreasonable bouts of optimism. Thus in a letter of 1917 he chastised him for 'seeing' what he believed rather than what Rosenzweig saw as the bleaker facts that confronted them: 'For you 1914–1917 is full of atonement and appeasement.'[39] And having castigated him for having already seen heaven on earth, and having wiped away all the isms and spectres that were still haunting contemporary Germans, he added: 'With you, they [the spectres] are already singing in a higher choir, with me they don't have time to sing.'[40] Indeed, while Rosenstock-Huessy certainly tailored his exhortations to postwar

Germans in light of their lack of atonement, it would be also be fair to say that it was his undue optimism that later led him to make his greatest error of judgment. The mistake, however, is perhaps less interesting than the insight that National Socialism's tribalism was a modern reaction to a global economy. Long before postmodernists sought to make sense of what is now encapsulated in the formula 'think globally, act locally,' Rosenstock-Huessy had said:

> With a conscious economic organization of the whole earth, subconscious tribal organizations are needed to protect man's mind from commercialization and disintegration. The more our shrinking globe demands technical and economic co-operation, the more necessary it will prove to restore the balance by admitting the primitive archetypes of man's nature also.[41]

And:

> Economy will be universal, mythology regional. Every step in the direction of the organizing the world's economy will have to be bought off by a great number of tribal reactions.[42]

In point of fact, Nazism was indeed an early political expression of this tendency. Moreover, in further confirmation of the point Altmann made about *Out of Revolution* demonstrating his debt to Rosenzweig, Rosenstock-Huessy made the point that what the Nazis were trying to do by establishing their tribal identity – and what they were manifestly failing to do – had been achieved by the Jews, who alone might succeed in showing the world how to balance 'local interests and the universal welfare of humanity' – which, he believed, addressed the key question repeatedly put to the human race, as well as the thread running through European history.[43] Such a statement was of course an obvious affront and provocation to National Socialists and their sympathizers. Indeed, the juxtaposition may be equally an affront to others, but while the juxtaposition may startle it is not less true for that. And in the following:

> Before any tribe or group can sacrifice reason to the unreal myth and magic of pre-history, its food and shelter must be guaranteed by the peaceful world-wide organization of production. Nazism is premature; it cannot coexist with the potentiality of war. Frightened by the proletarian Revolution, the Nazis are attempting 'a classless nation,' a solution which lies even beyond the Russian society. They are developing the character-

istics of the primitive tribes before they can commit themselves to such an adventure. And the professed pacifism of Hitler hinges upon the fact that the Nazis plan to return into the forests like the Germanic tribes. The Jews, who represent the universal history of mankind, stand in their way. Yet it is perhaps only through the Jews that the world may become a playground for tribal primitivism! Possibly the Jews will contribute more than others to that universal organization of production which makes wars impossible and leads in a world-wide economy. This is the necessary presupposition for the revival of primitive archetypes in different sectors of the globe.[44]

10 Beyond the Idol of the Nation, Part 2: Rosenzweig on Hegel

As with Rosenstock-Huessy, Rosenzweig's view of the nations cannot be separated from the experience of the Great War. Though of course, that view was modulated through his conversion and by the impact of that conversion on his assessment of the meaning of the nations.

For Rosenzweig, the Jewish people were the original nation, but precisely because they were the original nation, the nation chosen by God to embody His eternal promise, they alone among nations were 'already at the goal' of eternity. They were the people who reached from Adam to now, and hence for him the only people who were fully conscious of themselves as being God's elected from beginning to end. And being 'the eternal people' was not simply a matter of will or choice – or of being members of an imagined community, to use a well-known term coined by Benedict Anderson to designate nationalism. On the contrary, Jewish being is a matter of a raw *there*-ness that exists owing to one's birth line, what Rosenzweig calls a 'blood matter' – that is, a reality that does not have to do with volition or choice, but rather is a 'life condition.'[1] Even in his first explicitly 'Jewish' publication, 'Atheistic Theology,' he had focused on the modern dependency and inversion of theology in what he called the 'rationalist deification of the people.' For him, the deification was (as is all idolatry) at the cost of the very essence of revelation: 'Instead of asserting God's becoming human, one asserted His being human; instead of His descent to the mountain of the giving of the law, the autonomy of the moral law.'[2] The perversion was completed in the divinization of race and the people. In 1914 no one could see just how murderous this concoction would be for the German people, but that Rosenzweig had identified the misplaced act of divinization suggests how astute a political brain he had.[3]

Unlike other peoples who come and go, and who require territory for verification and as a condition of their existence, the Jewish nation is a stateless nation (at least at the time Rosenzweig was writing, and as it still is for non-Zionists today), always a nation within another nation, an exiled people on someone else's territory, always having to speak another's language and not just their own sacred tongue. And when he says in 'The Jew in the State' that 'the word state can't be translated into Hebrew,' he wants to reinforce that the Jew 'must be in a state, but because the state cannot be in a Jew.'[4] Jewish life, for Rosenzweig, simply does not want to find its spiritual objectification in the state – it would be lost if it did so – and this, too, separates him from all left-Hegelian political projects, which, like Derrida's, or like Agamben's in *The Coming Community*, use explicitly messianic/Jewish tropes for a complex of 'gestures and practices' that remain ever embedded in a Greek political matrix.

Yet another point of emphasis about the relationship between Jews and states should be highlighted. The Jewish people remain outside history as Jews, yet as men and women who reside within a state, Jews are affected as much as anyone else by the difference between peace and war. Thus does Rosenzweig, a German Jew, write his tale of Jews being a nation beyond war while fighting a war for Germany. Indeed, *The Star of Redemption* generates its tremendous pathos from the future of horror that drives home how necessary it is to redeem the entire world, without leaving a single people vulnerable because they are the elect, the exclusive bearers of the eternal. Rosenzweig's argument is a clever turning of the tables on the traditional animosity toward the Jews for their lack of 'trustworthiness,' for their refusal to swear an oath, which throughout Christendom denied them the same rights as were held by Christian subjects. Yet the Jewish people's peace remains bound to everyone else's success at creating peace. As Rosenstock-Huessy argued, Jewish rights began to spread throughout Europe with the messianic fervour of the French Revolution.

So whatever the differences in emphasis in Rosenzweig and Rosenstock-Huessy, which spring from one belonging to God's elected (the Jews), and the other to a people of conversion and mission (the Christians), Rosenzweig's assessment of the nation-state is steeped in his opposition to the idolatry of the nation-state that played such an important part in the Great War. And his opposition has two aspects – first, that the Jew is beyond the nation-state, and second (as with Rosenstock-Huessy), that the value of nations is that they bear a messianic spirit, which must not, however, be confused by nations perceiving themselves as ends in themselves.

The same restless search for a social form that would transcend the nation-state – a search that was essential to Rosenstock-Huessy's *Out of Revolution* and to his writings dispatched during and after the Great War – was also part and parcel of Rosenzweig's thinking about geopolitics, especially in his writings and letters during the Great War.

As Jörg Kohr wrote in 1916, Rosenzweig was seeking not so much an 'effective overhaul of the nation-state, but a thoroughly reformed cultural nation.'[5] To this end, Rosenzweig wrote what he described as a 'Middle European School Program for Europe.'[6] He urged postwar Germany to join with Austria-Hungary and form a coalition of states (*Völkerstaat*), each state to have its own nations, ethnic groups, languages and religions. Indeed, Austria-Hungary was (the Serbs notwithstanding) already an exemplar of a largely successful coalition of this sort. He thought that the Chancellor of the Reich, Bethmann-Hollweg, and Friedrich Naumann, whose work *Mitteleuropa* had laid out a similar vision, could provide the necessary leadership for such an undertaking. In his 1917 essay 'Globus: Studien zur weltgeschichtlichen Raumlehre' (published posthumously), he expanded this idea into a global ecumenical vision, one that was to include western and southern Slavs, the Magyars, Turks, and Arabs, and black Africa, arguing – again in a manner totally consistent with Rosenstock-Huessy – that the Great War had been a transition (*Übergang*) from an earlier Europe to a coming 'planetary epoch. What we call world history is nothing else than the becoming of the earth into a closed historical space, "one world."'[7]

Rosenzweig's 'Volksschule und Reichsschule,' and 'Globus' were both in keeping with a providentialist reading of history. Thus, when discussing his ideas about war and peace and politics, he told his parents that '*Realpolitik* has justified the kernel of pacifism – the overcoming of the nation state by the coalition of states.'[8] This conclusion is very similar to that of Rosenstock-Huessy. And those two works, like Rosenstock-Huessy's, could also be mistaken as Hegelian – except that by making history an immanent and dialectical process of Reason itself, Hegel had kept only the bare shape of providence while dispensing with its essence – that is, God's intervention. In that respect, Hegel's was a kind of demonic variant of the concept. That is certainly how Rosenstock-Huessy and Rosenzweig viewed Hegel's approach to history.

Indeed, because of the importance that Rosenzweig attached to the Jewish people (or to say it again, the pre-State of Israel) existing outside of history and war, it is easy to assume that Rosenzweig saw little benefit in war and thought much like a pacifist. This, though, would be a fundamental misunderstanding of him. For while there is no war in the kingdom of the end time because a genuine peace reigns, in the interim 'war is no more unethical (or rather unreligious) than peace.'[9] Peace, for Rosenzweig, was not a result of human effort. That is to say, it was not something that could be reached merely by applying a set of ethical rules; rather, it was the direct intervention of God, something that would be introduced by Him through the 'last inconceivable fruitful war.'[10] And again to his parents, he wrote that war was no sickness, because it had nothing to do with nature. By that he meant that war, like art and science, is part of our humanity and not merely an expression of our animality (i.e., our raw nature).[11] War, then, for Rosenzweig, was not a sickness but a catastrophe, a way in which crises reached a head when they simply could not be resolved in any other way. (Rosenstock-Huessy agreed with him that war is a catastrophe, but he also saw it as a disease, as the failure of a community to be healthily unified through speech.) The pacificist, Rosenzweig maintained, viewed war as a sick error, as if what could be achieved through war might be achieved some other way.[12] This stood in the closest relationship to an important insight of his that the good is *not* justice and is *not* something that humans can achieve through rules and organization, because it is not 'objectively measurable,' nor is it objectively 'recognizable.'[13] It is also why Rosenzweig's overall thinking once again simply did not conform to the usual ethical approach to life that believes that good or pure intentions will make the world better. But he did think that the world was meant to be constituted through love, that ethics strives for that, but places too much weight on intention. And intention is ever condemned to not attaining its goals. The position is reminiscent of of Hegel's critique of Kant's philosophy, which for Hegel reveals its flaw through making a virtue of infinite striving, which is synonymous with accepting infinite defeat. Quite simply, for Rosenzweig the mistake of ethics – with the exception of the ethics of revelation, which only specifies that we love, not that our will be done – lies in the false grounds of reason on which it rests.

Rosenzweig believed that during the Great War, the Western powers had been driven by the very (liberal) ethical idea of mutual tolerance, which he saw as typifying the 'materialistic pacifism' that he so eschewed because – and here he cited Goethe – 'to tolerate means to insult.'[14] By contrast, the Germans, he added, were striving for a peace – what he called (rather curiously, in terms of his later vocabulary) 'an idealist pacifism,' which he equated with the messianic and which was dedicated to forming a union of peoples. Good and evil were never pure in the world, and the world was weaving itself out of that stuff: 'Through "good and evil" alone a world other than the one handed to us is made. This and nothing more is what religion says with faith in immortality.'[15]

As is evident from these early writings – and indeed, in his view of the primacy of the Jewish nation as a stateless nation – Rosenzweig was developing ideas that directly contradicted Hegel's political philosophy, which had made the state the objectification of spiritual existence. And he expressed his opposition to Hegel at length in his classic study *Hegel und der Staat* (Hegel and the State).

Hegel und der Staat is an extraordinary book.[16] As a book of Hegel scholarship, it is as revealing about its author as it is about its subject – something that Rosenzweig realized, and to which he subtly alerted his readers in his preface when he suggested that his work belonged in the line of the three previous 'classics' on Hegel by Rosenkranz, Haym, and Dilthey.[17] The one thing these very different appraisals of Hegel have in common is that they are all ciphers of their authors and their times. And they retain their interest far more because of this than because of their 'objective' renderings of Hegel. And like these 'classic' treatments of Hegel, *Hegel und der Staat*, for all its dense treatment of Hegel's texts and surrounding political circumstances, is jarringly unwilling to enter deep into Hegel's philosophical system – or simply not interested in doing so – even though it is relentless in tracking down the changes, developments, contradictions, and comparative nuances in Hegel's writings. Rosenzweig barely touches on the great triumphs that Hegel believed he had won over metaphysics, especially the triumph of making his *Science of Logic* the new metaphysics and thereby solving the key metaphysical conundrums that had driven Fichte's self-asserting/self-postulating ego to complete (and thereby trump) Kant's transcendental deduction. Likewise, he barely touches the brilliance of Hegel's account of the pattern of the metaphysics of the age, in which the restlessness for the beyond (the pejorative, '*jenseits*,' which is dotted all over Hegel's pages) is treated as the depiction of the tragedy of the divided self, with its longings of the heart and feelings (its faith) on the one side and its knowledge (its sciences and hence reason's achievements) on the other. Hegel's identification of the common thought patterns in philosophers seemingly so disparate as Fichte, Kant, Jacobi, Fries, Schelling, and Schleiermacher shows him to be a reader of philosophy with very few peers. For Rosenzweig, at least in *Hegel und der Staat*, such analyses as these might as well not exist. Superficially at least, Rosenzweig's interpretation of Hegel seems so unphilosophical that one might readily forgive readers for questioning Rosenzweig's philosophical credentials and for bypassing it altogether as an important contribution to readings of Hegel's state theory. Indeed, this has been its fate among most Hegel scholars, especially since the Second World War. The entire impetus behind Rosenzweig's analysis seems to have become invisible – which is why, I suspect, the book has never been translated into English.[18]

Yet there can be little doubt that Rosenzweig had an excellent grasp of Hegel's philosophy and its implications. He certainly knew it well enough to make the case that the manuscript he had discovered and published as the 'Earliest System Program of Idealism' had to have been composed by Schelling and only recorded by Hegel.[19] And, of course, he certainly knew it well enough to explode the concept of totality that is so central to Hegel (in the form of the Absolute Infinite) in *The Star*.

But the real issue, for Rosenzweig, in *Hegel und der Staat* had nothing to do with what a great philosopher Hegel was. Rather, it was what Hegel stood for in the context of the world in which he found himself. It is clear from a letter to Rudolf Hallo in 1923 that from the beginning, as soon as he had begun his doctoral research on Hegel (under Friedrich Meinecke in 1912), Rosenzweig considered Hegel's philosophy to be 'damaging.'[20] We also know from his letters of 1916 to Rosenstock-Huessy that he was loath to spend more time on turning the Hegel thesis into a book during the war. And whatever critique he could make and indeed had already made of Hegel did not count for much in the ruins of 1918. Hegel simply belonged to another field of problems and possible answers.

If, then, in 1912 he had belonged to a different field than Hegel, by the war's end he no longer entertained the same dreams he had when he started writing it. Yet as he rightly informed readers in that book's preface, one could easily find a sense of his former sympathies – hence he would say that this book could not have been written 'today, just as little could I rework it.'[21] The book, he also says in the preface, had been essentially completed when the war broke out. Then there had been hope that the Bismarckian state, with 'its inner crampedness and extrinsic stultifyingness,' 'would expand into a free world breathing realm,' whereas now 'an expanse of ruins depicts the place where the Reich previously stood.'[22] As far as German politics being a benign force for integrating the spiritual powers of the people, the whole game of

German nationalism seemed spent. We can see the extent of his despair – despair for Germany, for himself, and for German Jewry – in a letter he wrote to his mother on 19 October 1918, which touched on the Hegel book and on his mother's concern about its possible future:

> In 1914 I never conceived that defeat was possible, at most a Hubertus Treaty,[23] that is a stalemate, and a retention of Bismarckian results. Now everything is lost and the world which I imagined is not there any more. You are worried about the paper shortage for the Hegel book, whereas I'm worried about something completely different – the shortage of readers. Who is supposed to read this book on this bloody [*sic*] German who not once believed in the Holy Alliance, not to mention this unholy League of Nations? Just think of the motto of the Hegel book. That is now like a slap in the face, because Versailles was no step, but rather a temporary high-point. There is certainly nothing more to do. And as for the heroism of the French to fight on after the battle of Sedan, no one could expect more than four and a quarter years or so. That we will lose everything there is to lose is certain. I consider even the Hohezollern to be a write-off. I have only just noticed what a monarchist I am; that's how much this business about Wilhelm hurts me. (Whether he abdicates or not – he *has* abdicated.) What am I supposed to do about the important Scheidemanns of this world! I'm just as significant. I want a *king* . . . The end is terrible. Wilhelm is falling without anyone to lift a hand . . . That we are going to get a transformation of anti-Semitism into democratic clothing is certain.[24]

And the following month, he wrote despairingly about the Kaiser's flight to Holland and subsequent abdication. He was extremely disappointed and cross that Rosenstock-Huessy was working closely with the Social Democrats. On 9 November 1918 he asked Gritli, in a most revealing expression of the different accentuations behind Rosenstock-Huessy's and his own political temperaments: 'What does he want as a Christian amongst the Bolsheviks? Why doesn't he do the natural thing and join the counterrevolutionaries who must be organizing something somewhere.'[25] Two days later, he exclaimed that in the midst of this crisis, he didn't think of himself as German, but as 'Prussian,' and he swore that 'after this experience I'll never again become a democrat.' And over the next two days he again expressed depression at the 'horrible thought' of Eugen sitting with 'the red rabble in some office.' (Rosenzweig's suggestion that he was more bourgeois and Rosenstock-Huessy more Marxist was, I think, a nice, cartoonish summarization of their political positions.)[26]

But what was worst, and what primarily drove his despondency and his 'conservative' politics, was that he thought that a revolution in Germany would merely be an excuse for a pogrom.[27] Nevertheless, there was more than fear of anti-Semitism behind Rosenzweig's conservativism. The way he saw it, the very nature of Jewish life compelled him to carry his tradition with him throughout the ages, and that world view made him fundamentally conservative. 'The Jew,' he wrote in 'Jewish History in the Framework of World History,' is 'emphatically no revolutionary, he is conservative – he is the conservative *tout court*.'[28] Of course, this stands in the closest relationship to his (typically conservative) mistrust of what people do when they plunge into the future driven by what, from his perspective, is always a misplaced search for a political solution to the real ends of human existence.

Hanging over *Hegel und der Staat* are Rosenzweig's deep despondence about the collapse of a strong German nation and his anticipations regarding the terrifying forces of vengeance that would arise from that broken state. On the one hand, in terms of Rosenzweig's prewar vision of politics, he was assessing Hegel and finding him deeply wanting. On the other hand, by the war's end he was evaluating his original aspirations *and* Hegel's defects in terms of the complete collapse of the German national dream. At the time the war started, Rosenzweig had sometimes felt decidedly un-German;[29] but throughout the war, his enthusiasm for Germany's role in *Mitteleuropa* had inspired deep feelings of patriotism, if not mere nationalism; and by the end of the war, he was crushed not only by Germany's defeat but also by what he saw as the implications of that defeat.

No wonder, then, that Rosenzweig had no time for Hegel's philosophical subtleties, which, in the midst of such despair could be little more than pyrotechnics. The book had begun by asking whether Hegel had much to offer the dream of German nation building; by the time of publication, the question had become, 'Did Hegel have anything to say to a world whose ruins he neither foresaw nor helped stave off?' The answer to both questions was a very loud 'no.'

Though he had not intended it during the writing, the preface and concluding remarks made the entire book read as Rosenzweig's funeral oration of the German nation-state and not just – as it had perhaps been conceived under Friedrich Meinecke's tutelage – about the hollow theory of the self and Hegel's equally hollow theory of the state.[30] That it was so conceived seems clear enough from its procedure. The book is one long exercise in mapping out each of the many twists and turns that comprise Hegel's commentary on and response to the political life

around him. And as Hegel wrestles with the world as it is happening –
or rather, as he loses his grasp of his subject and runs off in search of
it again with some new conceptual net to catch it – Rosenzweig records each failing encounter much like a Cervantes reporting on the
'victories' for chivalry by Don Quixote, except that Cervantes loves his
knight errant.[31] For his part, Rosenzweig everywhere gives the distinct
impression of major irritation as Hegel expresses himself with the same
philosophical pompousness and erroneousness every time the world
spirit gives him its new verdict. What also seems to strike Rosenzweig
with each twist and turn is how blind Hegel remains to where German history is going and – more pertinently – what the German people
should be making of their history. In one section, just after he discusses
Hegel's preface to the *Rechtsphilosophie,* with its emphasis on reconciling reason and actuality and the task of philosophy to know the rose
in the cross in the present, Rosenzweig cannot help exclaiming: 'That
is the Rhodes where he "dances"; but "at best" he will be it; he has not
set himself to know the cross of the time, but the rose in it. To know!
Nothing more.'[32] The exasperated disbelief expressed in this outburst is
never far from the surface of Rosenzweig's analysis.[33]

Indeed, between the Rosenzweig who started writing the book and
who (like Meinecke) was more sympathetic to the Bismarckian foundations of modern Germany, and the Rosenzweig who bid its ruin
farewell, exasperation with the book's subject is the major constant.
According to Rosenzweig, Hegel is imprisoned from the outset by
his original theoretical template of politics – a template that reflects
its distinctly German political immaturity. Unlike in England and
France, writes Rosenzweig, in Germany a gulf between the personal-
ethical life and the official life of the state had arisen, leaving an enmity
or indifference between individuals and state. He points out that in
England and France, the Enlightenment was deeply shaped by the state.
This, however, was not the case in Germany, where the Enlightenment
had been mainly a spiritual movement, a community of 'the public of
our classics.' It was not a movement that penetrated deep into society's
roots, and the members of that society remained *alien* to the state rather
than *inimical* to it.[34] One cannot but be reminded of the young Marx's
contention, in *The German Ideology* and *Introduction to a Contribution to a
Critique of Hegel's Philosophy of Right,* that Germany's philosophical success was the result of its social backwardness and that its sovereignty
over ideas was merely the empty ideological prize for revolutionary
impotence. For Rosenzweig, while Englishmen and Frenchmen were

actively forming the bonds that would be central to nineteenth-century nation building, educated Germans were still contemplating the rational spirit of Rousseau, the spirit of experience of Montesquieu, and the political triumphs of – of all places – Sparta![35] These were not much use for dealing with the real issues of politics.

It is not exaggerating too much when I say that *Hegel und der Staat* could well have been subtitled 'How Rousseau's Modern Delusions on the Individual and General Will Misinform German Social and Political Thought.' Indeed, for Rosenzweig, Hegel's thinking about politics never really escapes the Rousseauian formulation of the problem of politics with its abstract polarities of individual and collective; and where Hegel thinks he has escaped, Rosenzweig (almost sneeringly) emphasizes (with shades of Haym's Hegel critique) that Hegel, notwithstanding his contrary desire, does little more than embrace the Prussian conservatism of Karl Ludwig von Haller. For Rosenzweig it is no surprise that Prussia, the German state that depended most heavily on the French Enlightenment for its sense of self, should be the state that not only best fit Hegel's philosophy but also was made of the same stamp: 'Thus one can say that Hegel was the philosopher of the Prussian state, just as one may quite rightly say that the Prussian state of 1820 was a thought of Hegel's philosophy. One is as true and untrue as the other.'[36]

The Prussian state of 1820, however, was not the Prussia that would become the engine of German national power. And Hegel had as little sense of national power as he had of the tapestry of national alliances and movements that would do so much to shape Europe. Instead of following the historical seams of real peoples and real processes of nation building, he made vague appeals to world courts and world history; meanwhile, for him, states remained as individualistic and atomized as Rousseau's collective sovereigns. Hegel had articulated the problems of social life and their answers in the abstract, shuffling bits and pieces of his system as he went,[37] and had come up with the state; in this, he was impervious to the real forces of nationhood that were rising within Germany. Indeed, in each chapter of *Hegel und dder Staat*, what Rosenzweig is really underscoring is how ill-suited Hegel's philosophy was for his genuine German aspirations. Take, for example, this assessment from the second volume: that Hegel had made way for the Restoration after enthusiastically welcoming Napoleon, that 'world soul on a horse.' What Hegel never conceived, however grand and intoxicated his statement about Napoleon having given way to a sober rationalization of the Restoration, was the terrible legacy that Napoleon's imperial excursions would have in shaping Germany's subsequent perception of French power. To be sure, Hegel may be forgiven for not hazarding the shape of Germany's sense of its own national destiny, or the geopolitics of the next century. But what was he doing muddling around in areas of such magnitude armed with not a lot more than his Logic, the newspapers, and Rousseau and Montesquieu, whose political problems were so patently those of another age?

> To the philosopher the state was in such possession of its own roots in the system that he was barely capable of thinking of its subordination under the nation: a people without a state has no history. That a people on account of its history and according to the measure of its history must form itself into a state – this leading thought of later national politics was completely alien to him. In the position of a German Reich, which was not a genuine state, were 'German empires,' which hadn't appeared at best to him to be merely political passages or preliminary forms of state, but as states in the full, and for him complete sense of the word. The territorial-egoistic fear of the king [of Wuertenberg] of a future German total state conjoined at the same point with the philosopher who had faith in the state and respect for the old against every and anything new that was forming itself into the German Reich.[38]

But the entire tragedy (or farce) of a German state on its way to ruin being studied by a philosopher who never quite sees his object with sufficient clarity to help his fellow Germans is summed up in Rosenzweig's concluding remarks.[39] Having noted again that Hegel had taken the concept of will from the eighteenth century and had inserted it into his state theory, he equates Hegel's statism with Treitschke's nationalism, with each dissolving the people into the higher purpose – only for them to be lost:

> Both, the individual like the nation, could become what they are completely in the state – the individual could become only truly ethical in the state, while the nation only become truly a people in the state – in both the individuals and the nation are thus required to sacrifice themselves to the state, the sovereign rights of humanity to the state just like wholeness of the nation; the terrible cut of 1866 happened in these spirits and became . . . born in these spirits.[40]

Much like a Socratic dialogue where the interlocutors are left in a state of *aporia,* suspecting that Socrates is secure in some knowledge that he is not imparting, there is, I think, little doubt that throughout *Hegel und der Staat* Rosenzweig is hinting to his readers at something more important than Hegel.

The real backdrop to the book would only become visible when Rosenzweig was seen, not simply as a scholar of Hegel, but as a name in his own right – and for some, a more important name than Hegel. The real backdrop to the book is, of course, Rosenzweig's own realization about the meaning of Judaism, and the decision to really live the Jewish life – a decision that once taken was not simply an existential decision of absolutely individual importance, of the sort that gives Kierkegaard's philosophy its character. Indeed, it is fair to say that Rosenzweig's decision was a decision *not to be a single individual,* but to be a member of a nation – though tellingly, not of a state (or at least not to the same extent, and certainly not to any Hegelian extent). Indeed, this very polarity between individual and state as totality was what was so wrong for Rosenzweig.

Once Rosenzweig had decided to practise the faith into which he was born, he also accepted that the Jews were the first nation and the people whose destiny it was to be without a state. Even before his conversion, he had insisted that Judaism and Zionism were driven by fundamentally different spirits – indeed, in one early diary entry he even said that Zionism and anti-Semitism shared a common spirit.[41]

It is true that the longing in the Hegelian dream is to give the self more, to give it the entire world insofar as that world is 'actual/ rational,' that is, insofar as the world has a genuine future. Whatever is faulty in Hegel, and as distant as Rosenzweig is from Hegel, they are at one in their awareness of the emptiness of modern freedom in its modern construction. Yet as Rosenzweig's book emphasizes, Hegel's solution was as abstract as the self whose content he wished to fill. Likewise, the construction of the German nation in Hegel is empty. When *The Star* and *Hegel und der Stat* are placed side by side, one sees the strength of the contrast that Rosenzweig wishes to draw between the durability of the powers that guide his thinking and the transience of those of the modern. That Hegel's entire philosophical reputation was based on his analysis being rooted so concretely in the universal and in the actuality of Reason in history makes this contrast even more salient. For Hegel had wagered all on a phantasm whose security seemed so assured – for what could be more assured than the state? – that it had, as Hegel emphasized, become the objectification of the Absolute, had become God in the world. Furthermore, he had gone ahead as if the German people were already awaiting philosophical instruction so that their actuality and rationality would be as one. Thus, for example, on the matter of religion, Rosenzweig emphasized in his analysis of the *Rechtsphilosophie* how deeply embedded Hegel's view of the world was in Protestantism, and he was deeply irritated by Hegel's constant carpings about Catholicism having no historical future, as if the Austrian (and subsequent Austro-Hungarian) Empire had little significance in the nineteenth century. Given how the union of Austria and Hungary had succeeded in creating just the kind of alliance that Rosenzweig had hoped would be expanded and consolidated with its tapestry of different nations, ethnic groups, and religions, it is extremely understandable why he was as unconvinced by Hegel's 'bloodless' (i.e., nationless) state as by his equally 'bloodless' view of Christianity's presence in the Christian nations. For Hegel's Protestantism was but a thin veneer for philosophy itself usurping the role of religion, which was precisely what Rosenzweig could not abide, because it was the substitution of the conceptual for the liturgical expression of life, the latter, for Hegel, being only the incomplete and shadowy intimation of the former.

Unlike Hegel, Rosenzweig had placed his all upon a people dispossessed of the trappings of nationhood, yet who were the nation among nations, the first nation, a nation needing neither a living language nor location nor political integration. The Jews, so often seen by Hegel to be a surpassed people, had not only survived but also lived as an example. The Jewish life was not so much to be imitated as appreciated and valued; its meaning was not simply to be swept over on the grand stage of states. While other peoples needed arms to expand or protect their lifeways, the Jewish people, for Rosenzweig, found their way living in God's presence in their day-to-day, week-to-week, feast-to-feast, year-to-year eternal routines. Theirs was a way of remaining true to the original reason of the nation – the sharing of a common faith in God's love and love of the neighbour. By contrast, the dream of salvation through politics was a shattered one – and while statism and nationalism were ciphers of a genuine hunger for love of community and of neighbour, they were, at the time of *Hegel und der Staat*, in crisis. Nevertheless, from Rosenzweig's perspective, it is evident that his political conclusions pointed to a view of the German nation that was moderate in its claims and aspirations and that was not caught up in the kind of abstract delusions of Hegelian statism. Such a state was imperilled by atomistic disintegration (the danger of liberalism) and was developing in cooperation with mores derived from the more archaic forces of Judaism and Christianity. This cooperation had indeed been achieved momentarily by the support of liberal messianic nationalist movements supporting Jewish emancipation. It was essential that this spirit be captured again, but this time by making liberals aware of their Christian roots and the Christians of their Jewish ones. For his part, Rosenzweig until the end wished to prove that being Jewish and being a good German were not contradictory, but were of his very essence. Thus he asked Rudolph Hallo (to Hallo's surprise) to read at his own funeral the obituary/speech of Ulrich von Wilamowitz-Moellendorfs for Paul Lagarde. Not the least of Hallo's surprise sprang from the fact that Lagarde was not only a Christian but an anti-Semite. Yet Hallo recounts how Rosenzweig had held Lagarde's prophetic character in such esteem and how he so powerfully represented the passion and intelligence of the German people.[42]

That Hegel posed a powerful challenge for Germans was also important for Rosenstock-Huessy. And given the Hegel renaissance that had taken place in Germany in the twentieth century (in the latter part of the nineteenth century, he was considered pretty well dead),[43] it is understandable why Rosenstock-Huessy, too, decided to engage with Hegel. Though Hegel's name appears relatively frequently in his writings, there are two main places where he provides an important assessment of Hegel. One is in the essay 'Hegel und unser Geschlecht' in *Der Neue Merkur*, later published in *Friedensbedingungen der planetarischen Gesellschaft: Zur Ökunmie der Zeit*; the other is in chapter 19, 'The Revolution of German Great Powers,' of *Die europäischen Revolutionen*, where he discusses the Habsburg Empire and Prussia's military state. In the *Merkur* article he refers enthusiastically to Rosenzweig's Hegel book when arguing that Hegel was caught in the contradiction between Idealism and Romanticism and never really broke free from it. For Rosenstock-Huessy, Hegel was both a liberal and a conservative, a man of the Enlightenment and a traditionalist, a figure of spirit and of power politics: 'At the beginning of his work (1802) "Germany is no longer a state." At the end there is the spiritual equipment for Prussia's hegemony and for Prussian power in Bismarck's empire.'[44] Hegel embraced the contradictions of his time. Rosenstock-Huessy is somewhat more sympathetic to Hegel's entanglements than Rosenzweig, but he was convinced that his contemporaries could not afford to view their own crises through the concepts and contradictions laid out by Hegel. 'We also,' he wrote, 'commence with the cry "Germany is no state more." But we are neither idealists nor romantics, and can't be both. We are children of an economic-materialistic "realistic" time.' Idealism, he added, circulated widely in Germany between 1870 and 1914, but it did not change the fact that Germany was building up its army and navy and rapidly industrializing. If Hegel had sought to flee from the accumulating materialism of his time, his strategy, says Rosenstock-Huessy, was blocked for this generation; it was not Idealism and restoration that could offer a way forward for him and his contemporaries, but only an attitude of love and metamorphosis, a metamorphosis 'of a completely technical, completely real world.'

In *Die europäischen Revolutionen*, Rosenstock-Huessy argues a fuller case that Goethe, Hegel, and Schlegel 'embody the German relationship between the nations and the two major state powers of the 19th century.' Such a formulation points to a very different emphasis than one finds in Rosenzweig – Hegel's problem was not that he was so out of kilter with what the Germans were doing, but that he expressed one wing of it that was to prove disastrous. For Rosenstock-Huessy – not surprisingly, given the esteem he typically held Goethe in – Goethe was the most clear-sighted of the three. Having unconditionally rejected the Prussian state as any kind of ultimate, Goethe was open to the spiritual ways in which the Germans could find fulfilment. In his openness, says Rosenstock-Huessy, Goethe avoided being beguiled by the Romantics and their dead ends of Prussian nationalism or old empire. For it was the romanticization of Prussia and the Austro-Hungarian empire, he suggests, that conspired to bring so much ruin upon Germany.[45]

Recognizing Germany's political immaturity, Goethe had looked to futures more fulfilling for Germany than either nationalism or statism; for their part, Hegel and Schlegel had become respective mouthpieces for the existing major powers of the German people, even though millions of Germans were beyond their reach.[46] Hegel and Schlegel, says Rosenstock-Huessy, were 'total thinkers' – and in Hegel's case, it was precisely this aspect of his thought that Rosenstock-Huessy viewed (in keeping with György Lukács) as making him 'the real forefather of bolshevism': 'Prussian state thinking and Bolshevik interpretations of history both lead over the Hegelian right and the Hegelian left back to Hegel. Again and again that's why "Prussiandom and Socialism" have sympathised with each other.'[47] For Rosenstock-Huessy, Hegel was the direct contrary of Goethe insofar as what Goethe saw as a temporary stage of spiritual growth, in Hegel was absolutized and transformed into the goal, as it was equated with Reason in itself.[48] In Hegel's thought, it is not merely the state that becomes divinized – which for Rosenstock-Huessy would be concern enough – but a particular form of it (viz., Prussia).[49] This, for Rosenstock-Huessy, is as crazy as it is sad. Nevertheless, it is highly instructive; for every other attempt to divinize (a form of) the state is bound to meet with failure. And it was precisely this desire to transpose a particular, provisional, temporal, historical form onto the end of things that had been such a disaster for European statists (including left-wing Hegelians such as Bolsheviks) and nationalists. Given that Rosenstock-Huessy's own deployment of the concept of totality was also accompanied by a reading of history as a history of salvation (*Heilsgeschichte*), and hence as providential, in which the nations play their part, it is important to underscore this fundamental difference with Hegel.

In the preface to *Die Hochzeit des Kriegs und der Revolution* (The Marriage of War and Revolution), Rosenstock-Huessy made an explicit and favourable reference to Hegel's teaching of 'objective spirit,' which, though, he inflected through 'a spontaneously exercised use of speech' (*spontan geübten Sprachgebrauch*) of a particular self-contained self-developing power/force in the course of history.[50] But then he added that this idea of 'objective spirit' that absorbs the free will into a higher necessary complex developing through its own laws and necessity is 'actually the theme of the union of Christendom and peoples in the West.'[51] In short, Rosenstock-Huessy did not want to dispense with a concept that Hegel had mishandled (at least from where the spirit was now) in an Idealist and restorationist manner and that had been central to the self-making of Christendom.

In a letter to Rosenstock-Huessy, Rosenzweig made an insightful comparison between Hegel and Rosenstock-Huessy. In it he told Rosenstock-Huessy that Idealism posits a *telos* in the world and then lets the world develop into its *telos* (i.e., it collects the world from its disjointed members, from which it proceeds). Rosenstock-Huessy took up that observation, proceeding from the *telos* but repeatedly subjecting it to analysis. He was perhaps more successful than Hegel because the latter had failed to bring the different purposes into one unifying purpose; the parts refused to be subsumed into the one. What Hegel achieved, according to Rosenszweig, was a teleological artifice, a building – that is, something where the ends are forced into union as they become servants to the whole. But, he continued, Rosenstock-Huessy had achieved unalloyed agreements/alliances (*lauter Bündnisse*), enemies were wed, and the whole had become a realm (*Reich*) in which the parts were not in a hierarchical relationship but in a relationship where 'mastery and service are one and the same.'[52] The references to the wedding of enemies, and to mastery and service, were precisely the biblical ones that had been lost in Hegel's 'rational' account of history, which, for Hegel, was just as much a historical account of reason. That last formulation was also indicative of Hegel's fundamental departure from Christian *Heilsgeschichte*. Rosenstock-Huessy was not at all impressed with Hegel's extremely narrow selection of the 'reasons' around which the Spirit turns and upon which history is made. And given how much Rosenstock-Huessy wrote about Church history and how attentive he was to demonstrating how Christian institutions and practices are embedded both in Europe and in the world, he was even less impressed by Hegel's almost complete lack of interest in the Church.

One other passage in *Die europäischen Revolutionen* powerfully summarizes the meaning of the world wars, and Germany's part in them, in a way that relates to Rosenstock-Huessy's assessment of Hegel. It is also an important example of Rosenstock-Huessy's view of *Heilsgeschichte*, and it is turned against Hegel/Prussia and Schlegel/Austria and Austria-Hungary. The passage draws its strength from a fundamental concept he deploys in his *Heilsgeschichte* – that of endowment (*stiften*). Not surprisingly, the term shimmers with medieval tones. Like so many philosophers (though not Schlegel, whose error in large part came from romanticizing the Middle Ages), Hegel tended to see the Middle Ages as a dark blob that had to be got through in the journey from the modern to the classical world. The passage is also very different in tone from the despondent and despairing one we encounter in Rosenstock-Huessy and Rosenzweig in their post–Great War writings. For this passage appears in 1958. And if in 1918 and throughout the 1920s Rosenstock-Huessy was all too aware that many of his fellow Germans were leading Germany, if not the entire world, back into hell, in 1958 he was more optimistic, at least about Germany's immediate prospects. He saw that Germany's utter humiliation and total defeat had finally killed the rancour and mad flights of fancy that had spawned Hitler. Germany had become a nation among nations, and the nations were aware, in large part because of the Cold War, that they were part of something far bigger than anything Prussia could have prepared itself for.

The world wars threw the middle powers back into the world.[53] The world wars distinguish themselves very clearly from the founding wars of Bismarck. They were carried out over the heads of statesmen. German historians . . . found these great catastrophes, to make no sense according to the picture of history. Naturally. Because they *endow*. To endow is to care for the reproduction of life. To endow means to care for the recurrence of life. Endowment is not only for individuals, but also for peoples then, when they surrender their life for an unknown future. Jesus endowed the Church, because he did not ground it. The world wars endow the totality of the world anew and the Germans as a world people within it, as an organ of a world totality. This endowment liquidates the Europe of 1789 that had placed France in the middle of the world . . . Hegel's and Schlegel's interim solutions have been unmasked as interim solutions, even if as brilliant and true interim solutions . . . The endowed powers of the World Wars establish the unheard of task of functionally integrating a whole, the nation, into a whole . . . the overcoming of the Hegelian left and the Hegelian right has now been endowed.[54]

11 Beyond the Idol of Art, Part 1: Rosenzweig and the Role of Art in Redemption

If arts for art's sake and the Romantic cult of the genius were formulations of the nineteenth century, the value of the artist in the twentieth century was nothing if not ambivalent. With the plethora of movements and manifestos that so typified twentieth-century art, artists certainly took themselves seriously. Dadaism's youthful clownish gestures were accompanied by manifestos whose sentences were no less clownish – but the underlying message that rationality and civilization were murdering machines was a screaming rather than a laughing matter. Whether like the Futurists, or like Breton and the other Surrealists (who wanted to be political leaders), or, at the very least, like Picasso, Aragon, and others too numerous to mention on both sides of the political spectrum, who simply wanted to place their art in service to a higher messianic political purpose, such gestures were symptomatic of how much importance artists assigned to themselves and to their work.

Artists seemed to want to open up human beings to the utopian possibilities that lay within their visual or aural or linguistic reach while simultaneously displaying their own unique genius and individual 'vision.' Dadaism and Surrealism both mocked notions of genius only to ensure that they could reappear again by the use of the very mechanisms they had so debunked – notably, the deployment of the traditional aesthetic space so that the act of aesthetic defiance might still retain for itself an elevated aesthetic status. I think it fair to say that for all the light and heat around art and for all the manifestos that stressed the virtues of one style against another, it is striking how poorly twentieth-century aesthetics succeeded at integrating art into human experience as such. There is a simple reason for that, one that is expressed by both Rosenzweig and Rosenstock-Huessy, which is, that for all its importance, art gains in power by its relationship to some higher power. When men like Tzara, Aragon, Breton, Eluard, and Picasso so deeply desired to show their political credentials, what else were they saying than this? For all their brilliance, and despite what so many artists said about art, it seems that in their desire to please, upset/disgust, and instruct all at the same time, most knew that art was subordinate to a messianic purpose.

Within philosophy there is a similar ambivalence about art – an oscillation between its sovereignty and its subordination. Hegel, for example, was sure of its subordinate role to philosophy itself – for Reason was sovereign, and philosophy its final mode of recognition and expression. For Hegel, art was merely a sensuous representation of the Absolute, something subordinate to the labour of the concept in service to the idea of the Absolute itself. Thus Hegel's system, whose clearest representation was in his *Encyclopedia*, concluded by citing Aristotle's definition of reason or intelligence (*noēsis* or *nous*), from Book XII, Section 7, of the *Metaphysics*, as a (spherical) God in which intelligence contemplates intelligence.[1]

In many ways – and strangely, given the conflict between the death of God and the Hegelian divinization of reason – twentieth-century aesthetics is the triumph of Hegelianism in aesthetics. The paradox is even stranger when one takes into account that so much twentieth-century art wants to subvert the classical triumvirate of the good, the true, and the beautiful. Yet Hegel had correctly indicated that art's future was not so much in and of itself, but rather in its acceptance of the greater reason of which it was a part. This was evident not only in the importance of conceptual art by the end of the twentieth century but also in so much earlier twentieth-century art, which represented various movements and required manifestos. All, in Hegelian terms, efforts that subordinate representation to idea, intuition to meaning. By contrast, and perhaps even more conspicuous within philosophy, is Nietzsche's pithy and telling formulation that 'art is worth more than truth.' This insight had been stirring in philosophy at least since Schelling's *System of Transcendental Idealism*, which declared that 'philosophy attains . . . to the highest, but it brings to this summit only, so to say, the fraction of a man. Art brings *the whole man*, as he is, to knowledge of the highest.'[2] For it is art that brings together freedom and necessity, as Kant had argued in *Critique of Judgment*, albeit without seeing the full implications of his declaration. In Nietzsche's case, we cannot separate this formulation from his fear that we are not getting rid of God because of the grammar.[3] Heidegger and post-Heideggerean philosophies have followed Nietzsche with their emphasis on the ineradicable poetics of truth. The dissolution of truth into discursive formations – so that literary studies are primarily means to explore manifestations of, and strategies for the accrual of, social power – is very much the dissolution of aesthetics into social existence, but equally an offshoot of social life construed as conforming to aesthetic criteria (as is transparent enough in Foucault's and Derrida's deep debts to Heidegger). Not surprisingly, politics is increasingly aestheticized in certain practices both on the right (fascism and Nazism most obviously) and on the left (the style of the '68 legacy).[4] The story, then, of the dissolution of aesthetics into the world is the tale of the world's dissolution into the aesthetic.[5] To list all the names of those who are woven into that story from Nietzsche to Agamben would be a pointless exercise, but it is a large component of twentieth-century social theory. It is also part and parcel of the same story as nihilism tells, again as Nietzsche announced it: the aesthetic trumping of nothingness and the nothingness's trumping of every beautiful thing – the story of Idealism's desperate next step. And early glimpses break through again in Kant's *Critique of Judgment* (a point driven home by Lyotard's work on the sublime). To Rosenzweig, it is also evident that the mistrust of language that is Idealism's stock in trade (according to both Rosenstock-Huessy and Rosenzweig, as we will explore in more detail later) is also behind art's great rise as a sovereign philosophical power. As he says in *The Star of Redemption*, 'idealism came to deify art at the very moment it rejected language.'[6] His description of the thought processes at work from the late eighteenth century on through Nietzsche until today is remarkable in its prescience, revealing as it does Idealism's tendency to want the limitations of its penetration into life to come back to it as the meaning of life:

> Art seemed like an ultimate point and at the same time confirmation of the method of thinking – an 'organon' therefore – and a visible phenomenon of an 'Absolute': this step was in sight and already prepared in Kant, with his allusion to the 'common root.' The trust then that idealism denied the human word, where it did not want to see an answer to the word of God, this trust it accorded instead to a human work. Instead of having faith in the spoken word of the soul, in the revelation of man's innerness, which embraces, bears, and completes all that man externalizes, it made the entire weight of its blind trust be carried on a single limb, torn from the whole of the body of humanity.[7]

Rosenzweig identifies the major problem with every kind of Idealism: a part of life is elevated, and then the philosopher wishes us to surrender to it as if he had identified life in its essence. Likewise, Idealism *always* blocks out the gift that is more than its own methodological dictates about the permissibility of the real. Certainly, art is a welcome addition to truth's arsenal after naturalism has refused to acknowledge what comes to us through portals other than nature itself. But 'art represents only a limb. A limb without which, of course, man would be only a mutilated man, while remaining man nevertheless. It is one limb among others. Man is more.'[8]

Rosenzweig and Rosenstock-Huessy, again not surprisingly, are similar in terms of where they draw art's boundaries – art is secondary. For Rosenzweig, there is no doubt that art is essential to who we are: 'If there were no artists . . . humanity would be crippled.'[9] He is also concerned, as is Rosenstock-Huessy, that art not be taken as a real substitute for real life. He speaks of the beguiling power of music and of the danger of becoming a 'musical person,' a person whose love of music may well deaden him to reality. For Rosenzweig, music is the lyrical art *par excellence* – the lyrical, for him, being 'the self-surrender to the singular moment, the forgetting of one self's own totality and of the multiplicity of things.'[10] Music is likewise the most timely of arts, dependent as it is on sequential flow and on the surrender of the self to that flow with its rhythms and harmonies. That is why, for Rosenzweig, the musical person easily becomes less of a person in this world, governed as it is by its time, than he is when transported into the other, more lyrical, world of music, with its alternative and far more desirable time. The musical composition, he says in one particularly powerful image,

> lets its listener forget the year in which he lives. It lets him forget his age. It carries him in waking body across the dreamers of whom it is said that each of them possesses his own world . . . So he lives a foreign life, no, not even a foreign one; he lives hundreds of lives, a different one from piece of music to piece of music, and not one his own. Truly, the dog that is infernally distressed, because his mistress played the piano, lives more authentically, indeed if this I allowed, more 'humanly' than the 'musical person.'[11]

It should be no surprise that the decision to return to the Greeks for one's spiritual direction, which is so pronounced in German culture, and not only in German eighteenth- and ninteenth-century culture, should be one that elevates beauty and the aesthetic approach to life in general. But for the Jewish life, beauty is but one of its moments – God is not *the* beautiful, even if life lived in God's radiance has a beauty more real than art because it is not confined merely to the moment of artistry. As Rosenzweig says elsewhere: 'Do you perceive what we lost when our grandparents turned their back on the beautiful life, and turned toward a life in which beauty is but an island [*l'art pour l'art*], an isolated phenomena, an idol? Do you perceive what we have to gain, and how we have to be regained? A life that is wholly artwork [*ganz Kunstwerk*], wholly beauty, because it is wholly life, wholly *our* life.'[12]

Rosenzweig's concern is with Redemption, with the life that is wholly alive. Thus art must be seen as something of great value that is nevertheless only really what it is best capable of when it is part of this greater energizing of Redemption. This is the key to what on first spec seems to be the strangest, if not the maddest, of theories of art: that the highest art is applied art – a move that initially seems to take us in the opposite direction entirely from where art has been heading since artists first freed themselves from patrons, courts, and churches. Yet as we have already hinted, this desire for artists to place themselves in service to political goals should at the very least make us consider that Rosenzweig's theory is worth taking seriously, even if we must not lose sight of the fact that the theory is not built around art itself, but rather around the meaning of the Jewish life and the eternal truth of the living God:

> Only the arts that are called applied arts, a name intended as a condescending devaluation but which truly ennobles them, only they, without even losing one spark of their splendour, lead man completely back into life, from which he had departed as long as he indulged in 'pure' artistic treats. Of course, it is they alone that may be able to cure him of that sickness of estrangement from the world that lulled the art lover into the deceptive illusion of the best of health just when he was succumbing to the illness with no resistance.[13]

As for the rest, well, they may take their place in what he calls 'the great burial chambers of art'[14] – museums, galleries, concert halls, and the like, where they may be appreciated/studied with reverence and awe. But for Rosenzweig, this is all to little purpose. He does not deny that art other than applied art may potentially have an incarnatory quality. Indeed, he mentions Wagner in this context, noting that 'it is not Bayreuth that testifies that Wagner and his world are alive, but the fact that the names Elsa and Eva became fashionable names and that the idea of the woman who redeems colored the form of masculine eroticism for decades in Germany.'[15] But the power of the artist, however essential and anticipatory of redemptive life it is, is limited – it is only a relatively short time before the work finds itself relegated to the burial chamber.

With such a view of art, then, it may be much less surprising that Rosenzweig seeks to take his or her reader into the future by reaching back as deeply as he can into the past, back to the creation of the world and man in Genesis. And just as, according to Rosenzweig, Greek art was fractured in its purposefulness by virtue of its fractured understanding of the three great elemental poles of life – God, Man, and World – the real source from which art receives its depths and profundity is, for Rosenzweig, to be found in liturgy.

One cannot underestimate the importance of liturgy in *The Star.* This is evident from the fact that the work is built on three *organons:* mathematics, which facilitates our knowledge of the natural world and the proto-cosmic elements of God, Man, and World; grammar, with which Rosenzweig wishes to demonstrate, by following its leads, how we may transcend our natural understanding and come to an awareness of the second triadic truth about who and what potencies are contained in Creation, Revelation, and Redemption; and liturgy, which is the expression of the truth that is beyond – beyond what we have experienced naturally, and beyond what we have spoken of as coming to be in Redemption. Liturgical forms are 'the light in which we behold the light, the calm anticipation of a world shining in the silence of the future.'[16]

Because of the importance of silence in Rosenzweig's thought, he is at times mistaken for a mystic.[17] Had he been writing a book in which his main point was that the experience of Jewishness culminated in mysticism, he might, like the young Buber, well have undertaken the great attempt to reconcile Chinese, Indians, Greeks, Muslims, Gnostics, and Christians and dissolve them all into the common ecstasy of God's love. But he does no such thing. And not only does he not do that, he is as sharp as he is clear in his rebuke of the mystic:

Mysticism turns into the cloak that renders the mystic invisible. His soul is open to God, but because it opens only to God, it is invisible for the rest of the world and cut off from it. With an arrogant sense of security, the mystic turns the ring on his finger, and immediately he is with 'his' God and has nothing more to say to the world. This is possible only because he wants to be absolutely nothing other than God's favourite. In order, to be so, in order, that is, to see nothing other than the one track running from God to him and from him to God, he must deny the world, and since it will not let itself be denied, he must actually dis-own it . . . He must treat it as if it were not created, but instead put at his disposal, just to provide for needs of the immediate moment when he grants it a glance. This relationship of the pure mystic with the world, which is fundamentally an immoral relationship, is absolutely necessary for him, if indeed he wants to confirm and safeguard his purely mystical state.[18]

Rosenzweig's story is one of life, with its historical, collective, and personal experience and all the temporality it involves. It is, however, one in which the living participate together in that moment of life that crowns all life by having redeemed it. This is where art, for Rosenzweig, finds itself completed as it morphs into its sacred origin as the gesture combining the very elements that bring art into the world. For Rosenzweig, this combination involves three essential qualities: the epic, the lyrical, and the dramatic. The epic is our capacity to grasp the detail in the totality – 'the aesthetic point of unity.'[19] The plastic arts are the ultimate expression of this capacity because they are the representation of the work all at once in space. The lyrical is the self-surrender of the whole to the moment 'through which the detail concerned at any given time becomes a little whole: in this way the whole depth of inspiration becomes open to it.'[20] Time is the essence of the lyrical, and as we said earler, music is for Rosenzweig the art of time *par excellence*. In music, rhythm marshals everything temporally – even in cacophony and utter discordance, space is dealt with through time.[21] The dramatic, Rosenzweig says, 'caps' the epic with its 'material qualities, enveloped by the unity of the form,' and the lyric with its 'spiritual qualities, which shatter the unity of the form.'[22] According to Rosenzweig, poetry is the greatest expression of the dramatic. Indeed, we know historically that drama evolves out of poetry. For Rosenzweig, that it does not emerge out of the plastic arts or music is sign enough that it is beholden neither to (in Kantian terms) the forms of intuition (*Anschauung*), that is, space, the epic domain, nor to time, the lyric domain. Drama is triumphant over both in its capacity to reconfigure the self, who is capable of being incarnated in a new space and time – or more precisely, in its capacity to draw on one of Rosenstock-Huessy's key categories, a time-creating space.

Any reader of Rosenzweig must, initially at least, be perplexed that in his classification of the plastic arts and music he has deployed the first two modalities of poetic evolution, at least in the Greek world. This is indicative of his systemizing 'craftiness' (in both senses of the word). For by deriving his classifications of the non-poetic arts from poetic formulations, he is cleverly supporting the essential point he wishes to make about poetry's lordly role within the arts. 'Poetry,' he says, 'is not a kind of art of thought, but thinking is its element . . . and from thinking, it ends also by putting at its service the world of inner and outer intuition, space and time, the extensive "epic" breadth and the intensive "lyrical" depth. It follows that it is the living art in the proper sense.'[23]

Significantly, also as befits his systemic manner, he does not make the case for liturgy as the apex of the poetic arts where he first discusses tragic man in his section on the meta-ethical in Book Three of Part One of *The Star*. There he alludes to a pathway to Redemption, which was partly open for the Greeks but which they were unable to fully travel. Instead, he delays revealing the nature of the dramatic and the poetic as fully formed potencies until Book Three of Part Two, where the discussion of Redemption as such is underway. This delay allows him to analyse the language of the Psalms. Again, his counterintuitive move is quite astonishing – or more bluntly, a thorough affront to the usual tale of aesthetic development and appreciation. The Psalms are more poetic and dramatic than *Oedipus*, or *Prometheus Unbound*, or the *Oresteia* trilogy? Who would normally take such a nonsensical claim seriously? Perhaps before Rosenzweig, almost no one, except the Jewish person of deepest faith who had either not been exposed to or had not been overpowered by a classical education.[24] After *The Star* it can be seen as a deeply serious proposition by anyone who has followed him into his labyrinth, where he not only makes poetry the highest art (Hegel, too, had gone there), but also makes of the Psalms the highest expression of the highest art (there Hegel certainly did not go). Poetry's greatness, for Rosenzweig, is not derived from the intoxication of its musicality, nor is it derived from the dramatic intensity of feeling awoken in an 'audience' – if that were the case, *Oedipus* must trump the Psalms (which are not for an audience, but for the self that sings them) a million times. Nor is it derived from the synoptic crystallization of the moment in a concept, the epic grasping of the detail in a stroke of metonymic genius. What does concern Rosenzweig about poetry is its 'aliveness' – 'because it is the most alive, poetry is the most indispensable art.'[25] Again, in an affront to what we usually think of poetry, he claims that far more so than painters or musicians, the poet must possess 'a certain human maturity . . . The understanding of poetry is itself already strongly conditioned by a certain richness of lived experience.'[26] Rimbaud and Keats and Shelley and Kleist (the last of whom he mentions two pages later!) all testify to how counterintuitive, how surely (but so surely?) wrong, Rosenzweig is. But Rosenzweig is interested in what poetry has to give us not for our enjoyment but rather for our insight and understanding into how to live life. He insists that if music is what we want, then to music we should go. Much poetry is lyrically great and epically great, but this, for Rosenzweig, is all secondary to what he wants from poetry: 'A beautiful tonality quite alone would be a pure delight to the ear; a beautiful language quite alone would be a phrase. It is only an "idea" that gives life to the poem.'[27] The quintessence of poetry – which is what he most wants to get at, to be succoured by – is something that does not just open us to a truth or beauty of something. What he wants from poetry is this:

> The unarranged breadth of possession and of artistic representation has to be spanned entirely by consciousness in order that for the spectator art will not be a burdensome or indifferent possession of representations acquired accidentally but the precious, inner possession and treasure of the soul, collected over a lifetime and lovingly arranged. So the door of the individual realm of art comes ajar and the way into life opens up.[28]

Rosenzweig takes Genesis, the Song of Songs, and the Psalms as paradigmatic examples of grammatical constructions that illumine God's plan. As such they are steps on the way to their liturgical culmination. Genesis affirms the goodness of existence. Whereas the Song of Songs, built around the insight that 'love is as strong as death,' affirms the completely personal nature of love that connects the two, 'for love always is a matter between two persons, it knows only the I and You and does not know the street.'[29] Then that love expressed in the passionate intimacy of the Song of Songs moves out into the world so that love itself is extended, and there is 'a becoming external of the love that no longer grows in the I and the You, but demands to be grounded in the view of the entire earth.'[30] But over and beyond this, the Psalms are 'the songbook of the community.' They are the affirmation and expression of the 'Kingdom of redemption,' where the I has entered into the 'We all,' a new community 'that God points out to him and whose miseries are his miseries, whose will is his will, whose We is his I, whose – "not yet" is his "yet."'[31] This anticipation that is enacted in the now is, for Rosenzweig, what liturgy is; liturgical forms 'anticipate; they make a future into a today. So they are neither keys nor mouth of their world, but representatives. They represent the redeemed world to cognition; knowledge knows only them; it does not see beyond them; the eternal hides behind them. They are the light in which we behold the light, calm anticipation of a world shining in the silence of the future.'[32]

Liturgy is common to Jew and Christian; but as far as art is concerned, it is notable that in 'The Fire of the Eternal Life' – which is the section where he discusses the Jewish life as it is lived through its practices, holidays, and feasts – discussion of art is absent. Instead he turns his attention to the state and to how the Jews are a people who have transcended the need to form a state. But he picks up art again in his discussion of the Christian. For Rosenzweig, the Jews are the people who live in an eternal present rather than in the chronologies and epochs that are so definitive of the Christian era.[33] Where the Jew is *already* Jewish by virtue of birth, the Christian, as we have noted previously, must be baptized and *believe* or have *faith* in order to become a Christian. And *that*, for Rosenzweig, points to the Christian drive to create a universal social and political order – the same drive as to creativity as such. Christian faith 'is creative in the world'[34] because it wants to redeem the world, and it sees its mission in the *going out* and *bringing others back* into the circle of the faithful. Art, then, in the Christian life, is subordinate; and it is pressed into its missionary character, as can indeed be seen by anyone who studies the history of art in Western civilization.

In discussing Christianity and art, Rosenzweig again ushers in the elements of epic, lyric, and poetic. He strives to show the limitations of the Christian faith – that it is faith rather than being, and that it is movement toward rather than presence, and that it is perpetually beginning and never ending; even so, he showers Christianity with praise in the field of art. For him, Christianity has sought to integrate and resuscitate the arts by harnessing them to a universal sense of spiritual purpose for accessing and representing God, human beings, and His creation. And these representations are, in turn, part of the dynamism that is the corollary of Christianity's mission of accumulation, integration, and universalization. Thus Christianity, for him, integrates the arts within its way of being in the world in a manner that the most artistic of ancient peoples, the Greeks, could not do; for the Greek vision had mere intimations of Redemption, rather than a conscious dedication and understanding of life as a redemptive process. Thus while the

Greeks did indeed excel in the plastic and lyric and dramatic arts, for him the Church is the most triumphant in the epic, Church music the most triumphant in the lyric, and the procession the most triumphant in the dramatic. Most triumphant? Again, this at first – perhaps not only at first – may seem crazy. But Rosenzweig is focusing here on the transformation of lives that the applied arts achieved in the Church, and – equally as important – on how through that application the arts themselves have been imbued with an inner dynamism of form that enables them not only to be involved in the restless search for spiritual succour, but also to constantly adopt and adapt pagan creations for their own purpose. What is true generally of Western Europe – that it is like a gigantic sponge drawing into itself the marvels and exotica of other peoples that it has come across during its missions, trade, and conquests – is true also of the arts, and for the very same reasons. For with the Christian view of life, everything is surveyed and drawn into a sense of historical and spiritual accumulation so that we can see what can be deployed for the greater glory of God, Man, and World. This makes more sense when we bear in mind Rosenzweig's view of the Church as passing through three phrases: the Petrine (Church visible), the Pauline (Church invisible of the Reformers), and the Johannine. For is this not precisely what Western defenders and lovers of lost forms of life are doing? – wanting us to ingest the power and beauty of another way of life? And is this not the most dangerous of tasks? How can this be accomplished without exposing the fragility and delicacy of a 'creature' from another time to the Western time of steel and digital machines – and most dangerous of all – to Western men and women themselves, who are often so unhealthy that they themselves seem to be both machine and simulacrum?

Rosenzweig's theory of art is systematically connected, then, to this view of the three ages of the Church, discussed above. Art itself, as a force for spiritual meaning in its modern sense, also moves from its connectedness to the Church as a visible entity (the Roman Church's contribution/mission), to its dissipation in the everyday world of the Christian community (the Protestant or Pauline churches' mission/ contribution), to its further dispersal into the pagan world as a Christian act *incognito* – an act informed by the singular characteristic of John's gospel, which is charity. And hence just as without the Petrine church there would be no Johannine church, no Goethean Christianity, and without the Petrine Church, which originally drew the arts into its service, without these, then the kind of world that Europeans take for granted along with most of the rest of the world – a world in which art is viewed as essentially a means of communication of the open heart to the open heart, crossing nations and cultures – would not exist. It is indeed largely because of this same phenomenon that philosophy has often, as we suggested earlier, followed this incarnation of the spirit and made of it the Absolute, to use Hegel's term (though not his intent).

Moreover, and rather fascinatingly, Rosenzweig hints that the Church stands in relationship to the arts of the modern as Homer stood in relation to the subsequent development of poetry in the ancient world. For in both cases it is the epic quality that first encapsulates what will subsequently be released into forms in their own right. In Homer, though, the epic quality resides in the scale of the images surveyed and brought together as poetry; whereas in his definition of the epic, Rosenzweig fastens upon the plasticity of the form itself so that it occupies real space rather than (as in Homer) imaginary space. For Rosenzweig, the epic finds its zenith in the space where human beings become infused and energized by the love of God, which then circulates as the two energize each other to go into the world more lovingly. Thus, for him, the significance of the architectural space of the church is that within its domain the human is reawakened into being fully human. Hence it is within the church that the epic is most truly epic, and its function is to facilitate the drawing of the arts into the service of the higher force: the Church. Thus he says that only inside the church do the arts 'waken from their apparent death of those burial chambers their true life.'[35] The church is built 'from the inside to the outside'; it immediately orientates all who enter to the unity of its design and its purpose, which is, he says, 'the most universal one of human life.'[36] The sacred space of the church recharges every object that enters with a new and higher meaning: 'Only objects used in worship, once formed resist any modification of their form; they are simply no longer things like other things; they have become, as daring as the term may sound, "living things."'[37]

Just as the epic, for Rosenzweig, finds its fulfilment in activating not only objects but also living souls within the sacred space of the house of God, the church, as opposed to the concert hall, is that place where the lyric is not an escape or flight from the self into a reality from whence it does not wish to return, because this reality is so paltry in comparison. Rather, in the church this reality becomes the music, and the I and the we join together in song and again energize each other as all exist together in the moment of Redemption here and now: 'whoever joins in singing a hymn, whoever hears a Christmas Oratorio or Passion, knows exactly in which time he is; he does not forget to flee from time, but on the contrary: he wants to place his soul with both feet into time, into the most real time, into the one time of the world of which all individual days are a only parts.'[38]

And finally, according to Rosenzweig, regarding poetry, 'even if it comes by chance to the theatre as dramatic poetical work its aesthetic "ideality" is done for; the true drama is the drama of the book.'[39] That is, like all the arts, if poetry wants to be more than poetry – to be something that activates the living in more than a momentary manner – then 'the poetical work would also have to be freed from the book covers of its ideal world and introduced into the real one, before it could become the leader of a crowd of men into the land of mutual; reciprocal silence.'[40] What Rosenzweig says about the epic and the lyric and the poetic is, of course, hardly a dispassionate observation about the nature of art, and it is highly unlikely to make the poet, any more than the musician or architect, want to apply his trade solely within the confines of the Church. But that is somewhat beside the point he is making. Rather, he is providing a triumphant argument for the superiority of sacral art over the pagan drive to aestheticize existence, thereby enabling us – *all* of us, Jew, Christian, and pagan – an insight into the respective drives of each type. If he does not convince the pagan of the superiority of the applied arts, he does, I think, highlight for the faithful the sublimity of their own pursuit, while underscoring a truth about the Church's role in the evolution of European art. In that it wants to appeal to the faithful, *The Star* is a partisan work, but how could a work of the New Thinking, for all its desire to provide the different poles of discursive formation, not also be a statement of the speaker's faith?

And here the Christian and the pagan must equally see that their position is equidistant from Rosenzweig. For if he shows that Church and Synagogue are part of a common task that transcends the pagan possibility, he also repeatedly insists that Christianity's distance from the goal be attained. And that distance is for him everywhere visible in the respective festivals and holidays of the Church, in such a seemingly trivial fact that 'the dance does not appear in Church.'[41] For Rosenzweig, 'the dance is that art form in which the poetic work . . . climbs out from the book covers into the real world of presentation.'[42] The dance is 'the first gesture,' but within Christendom it is integrated into those activities that take place outside the walls of the church – in processions, marches, and holidays. The dance as such is thoroughly pagan, but the Jewish ceremony retains the dance within the divine service, 'the closed circle of the community,' while the Christian 'opens the circle into a spiral, it bursts open the locked gate, and the procession goes out into the city.'[43] For Rosenzweig, this is but one more confirmation that the Christian is ever on the way, in much the same way that Christian feast days do not encircle themselves around Redemption, but rather in acts of renewal, of baptism, of the birth of the baby Jesus, so that after the service one is ever ready to go out into the world again. Whereas the Jew, according to Rosenzweig, in the synagogue and in his festivals and feasts, is ever brought back into the redeemed circle of eternal life.

And finally, as concerns art, Rosenzweig looks at one more 'tear' in the Christian soul, again a tear between the pagan transmutation of the stuff of life and the complete Redemption at the heart of Jewish existence. The tear is the greatest tear in the human heart, the tear of suffering itself. Rosenzweig accepts that the profundity of the Christian life has to do with its relationship to suffering, which is the cross – but that very symbol and that very realization is the realization once again of the gap. And just as the symbol of the cross is also the sign of the overcoming of suffering by surrendering to it, by 'its configuration,' Rosenzweig notes that this is precisely what art, too, offers: 'Prometheus,' he reminds his reader, 'was hanging on the rock for five hundred years before the Cross was raised at Golgotha.'[44] And

art, too, overcomes suffering only by giving it figurative shape and not by denying it. The artist knows himself as the one to whom it is given to say what he is suffering. The muteness of the first man is also in him. He seeks neither to 'hide' nor to 'cry it out': he represents it. In the representation, he reconciles the contradiction that he himself is there and that yet suffering, too, is there; and he resolves the contradiction without in the least removing it. In its content, all art is 'tragic,' a representation of suffering; even comedy lives from the sympathy of the ever present poverty and defectiveness of existence. In its content, art is tragic, as in its form as all art is comic, and even the most horrible – it represents with a certain romantic – ironic ease. Art as representation is that which is tragic and common in one. This face of Janus of art, that it at the same time heightens the suffering of life and helps man to bear it, lets it become his companion through life. It teaches him to overcome without forgetting. For man is not supposed to forget, he is to remember everything with his heart, he is to bear suffering and he is supposed to be consoled.[45]

What Christianity does is alert human consciousness to the common human core of suffering: 'The lonely soul of pagan stock, for which the ultimate unity of the We does not circulate in the blood, only discovers this unity facing the Cross of Golgotha. Only under this Cross does the soul know itself to be one with all souls.'[46] One might immediately respond that Buddhism does this as well, and certainly Rosenzweig could have nuanced his point better, but at the moment he makes it he has long left the 'religions' of humanity behind and is strictly concerned with the question of Redemption itself, which is not, as we have said, something that for Rosenzweig concerns Buddhism or indeed any of the pagan religions, at least not in the way it he defines it.

12 Beyond the Idol of Art, Part 2: Rosenstock-Huessy and Art in Service to Revolution

It must be said that at times, in comparison to Rosenzweig, Rosenstock-Huessy could express himself with such disarming bluntness that one could easily think he cared nothing for art. In a public lecture in 1966, 'The Lingo of Linguistics,' when he was interrupted by a woman who asked him about the importance of art, he retorted brusquely that art was play: 'What do I care for art? What do I care for art? This is Mr. Cassirer, my dear lady. I have nothing to do with the intellectuals who worship art.'[1]

Certainly, he thought that too much preoccupation with aesthetics – especially when art was taken as some kind of end in itself – was a waste of energy and a complete distraction from the most pressing matters – our survival, growth, and future peace. Moreover, when it came to his personal tastes, he gave rather short shrift to the more famous modernist writers, clearly preferring Dostoevsky to Kafka, Chesterton to Eliot, and Thornton Wilder, whom he called an 'essential contribution to the philosophy of reality,' to James Joyce (in the *Soziologie*, he even quoted Wilder 'that when James Joyce plays on 24 languages as if on a piano, the student of today does not find it senseless').[2] He was generally damning of modern literature's preoccupation with decadence, though also on occasion (Proust, for example) willing to cite it as articulating a world in dissolution, and hence as an important cipher of contemporary spiritual need.[3] Likewise he conceded that Joyce's decision to date *Ulysses* back to 1904 showed 'an astounding instinct for the epoch made by that year in the soul of the European.'[4] He would remind his readers that 1904 and 1905 were the years of the Russo-Japanese War and the first Russian Revolution, as well as the time when 'the world crash began to appear on the horizons.'[5] But ultimately he thought that the problem with writers like Joyce was that a preoccupation with decadence disempowers speech – a point he made in 'A Horse's Block,' the preface to *Die Sprache des Menschengeschlechts*, when he compared Joyce with Churchill:

> One month before the Fall of France, I attended the annual dinner of the Literary Society at our most highly endowed university. I was surrounded by professors of the English department. And so I told them that my son as a new student was required to study Joyce's Ulysses. In this book all human speech of the last thousand years, from the Dies Irae and Holy Mass to the latest slang, ingeniously is blown to smithereens. Was it necessary for a freshman, I asked, to enter the realm of speech by means of an air raid? They laughed at the complaint of a rustic. Suddenly, the ringleader, by some profound instinct, said: 'Joyce certainly is a million times better food for your son than the dead oratory of Winston Churchill's speeches.' – Four weeks later, Winston Churchill was Prime Minister. And soon, he had to form that Life preserver to which the British clung for the next thirty months. He forged it in four words, with the dead oratory of the ages: 'Blood, Sweat and Tears.' 'Blood, sweat, and tears,' never have so few words exhaled so much power, cut out such a far-reaching alley into the future, and borne so much fruit.[6]

He is telling us here that literature's importance can never surpass the urgency of creative speech in our hour of peril. And for him, at its richest, that is what literature is – a creative contribution to our survival and enhancement, and not a mere reflection of an aesthete's private exhilaration. This is why he also says that 'we should give up the superstition, of literary histories, that great men are read and admired for their literary merits alone; as if literature were a water tight compartment where pens and tongues are used for the sake of book writing.'[7]

Rosenstock-Huessy, then, had an interest in art as something closed off from the rest of life's trials. The urgency of his times made him hostile to its art, which revelled in the spiritual death of the West. While 'decadent art' can be a cry of the sick for help in achieving a better future, he thought that far too much Western art amounted to a soundtrack to or anatomical representation of the decline of the West, instead of part of any project to return it to health. For him, one corollary of the West's sense of its own demise was the aesthetic revival of life's primitive and tribal dimensions. It is not that he was unable to appreciate 'primitive' aesthetics – his writings on masks, dance, and ritual, and on imperial lifeways, indicate that he approached these subjects with awe and reverence for what they could tell us about the human condition and the trials of past generations. But he was not romantic about them. And he understood that modern men and women were so sick that they needed a spiritual 'hit,' a kind of soul transfusion.[8] But this, too, for him was symptomatic of a problem that he did not think could be remedied by such art. For him, the modern's fascination with 'primitive art' was largely a kind of sickness, a vampire-like appropriation: having drained the blood out of its own historical forms, the rapacious modern was now looking elsewhere for nourishment. Thus the modern aesthete feasted on primitive art while remaining oblivious to the more brutal hardships and circumstances of tribal experience that had generated that 'aesthetic.' If an appreciation of primitive art opened us to an appreciation of the human condition, then that was, for Rosenstock-Huessy, something valuable; but if it was just one more thing for us to entertain ourselves with, then it didn't, for him, amount to much.

The matter of different forms of art, then, was not a question of arguing about whether primitive art was superior – precisely the kind of argument that didn't interest Rosenstock-Huessy. If that was one's main concern, one was already 'playing.'

Of course, such views of art had nothing in common with the avant-garde of his times or with more radical views of art, and one could argue that his taste was reactionary and that his views sounded a little like the communist and Nazi attacks on 'reactionary' or 'degenerate' art. But drawing such an equivalence would involve overlooking the obvious fact that Rosenstock-Huessy was not the slightest bit interested in politically imposing his taste by banning different kinds of art. Nor was he seeking redemption in the twentieth century through artistic propaganda. And despite the personal classical leanings expressed in his rants at students to get them to read, he was not interested in 'ennobling' the populace by having them observe 'beautiful' or 'heroic' forms. Most important, and much like Rosenzweig, he held the conviction that being intoxicated by art was not a substitute for living one's life. Moreover, again much like Rosenzweig, he saw that in our age, art had taken on an exaggerated importance because the age had been divided between the deeper provinces of art and the more shallow mechanical mundanities of everyday life. For him, it was a terrible indictment that 'the whole of creation is groaning and moaning for the broadening of joy, of youth, of wonder, in an all too well known universe.'[9]

In the *Soziologie* he had made the simple point that art belongs only 'to the shadows of life.' 'Certainly,' he added (again with echoes of Rosenzweig), 'it is among the most lofty shadows, but still it is chained to the triumphant procession of love.'[10] In the second volume of the *Soziologie*, he quotes Goethe's famous remark to his son that the muses are there to accompany us through life but not to lead us.[11] For him, perhaps the key point to be made about devotion to art was that it had not saved the Greeks, who had made art their own particular genius. Other peoples and groups certainly had their arts, but no others, among the ancients, had raised it to such heights of importance. Yet that elevation had not prevented the Greeks from tearing themselves apart. Love's power must be present and active in the specific bonds that form peoples before art can complete us: 'If love already inflames us, the spirit is already enthused, then, that is when it really requires accompanying music. As soon as life has already been elevated toward love the Greek genius is not poison, but medicine.'[12] The Greeks' failure, for him, lay not in their inability to create great art – for clearly, they did have that ability – but in their failure 'to harvest,' that is, to truly benefit from their inspirations.[13] He adds that Romans and Christians were much more successful at creating peace in other spheres of life, and thus could feast off the muses in a way that the Greeks, who had so few protracted periods of peace, could rarely do.[14]

For Rosenstock-Huessy, artist and community must feed each other as the community pushes the artist to new heights. Art, it follows, should be a means of triggering creative capacities in others so that each becomes a divine co-creator. The artist may then open up new prospects and regions of the soul, but only because there are already living souls with whom the artist may commune. Thus in 'Arts and the Community,' an address he gave to the Stuart School of Creative Art in Boston in 1939, he observed that

> instead of breaking mankind up into two halves, artists here and public over there, there must have pulsed through human-kind one unified stream of wonder and ingenuousness and expectation. You, we, I, we all must write poetry, we all must feel like writing poetry, for example. You, I, she, we all must paint, or feel like painting the sunset, and only give up in the face of the tremendous task reluctantly. We all must start to praise God in his creatures and in songs of love. Only when, in this active way, our own expectations are harnessed, can the artist do what everybody would like to have done, himself.[15]

But these comments need to be placed alongside his discussions about art being a mode of expression for people who are in such desperate times that they need 'to manipulate time,' to participate in the creation of another age.[16] What primarily interests Rosenstock-Huessy about art is clear in *Out of Revolution*, where he cites with approval the American artist Abbot Thayer regarding the great political function of art:

Art rescues man from his state of being limited to a point and to a moment. Contrive as you will, your camera cannot exclude the peculiarity of the moment and the place. This is the torture of the intellect, that it is condemned to still-photography. But it longs to see from all points, from all moments, as God does. The bliss of contemplation of a work of Art is this sense of emancipation, of seeing as God sees, and as we may sometimes see. What if it were prophetic?[17]

Yet for Rosenstock-Huessy, art at its most important is more about *forming* than seeing: it is part of the human arsenal of incarnation. This, for him, is clearly visible in the two poets whom he believed epitomized the creative potential of poetry: Homer and Dante.

In the chapter 'The Vowels of the Muses' in *Die Sprache des Menschengeschlechts*, he says that as a 'forming power,' Homer can only be compared with Dante. For each of these poets created a form that enabled him to express 'the All [*das All*] of the souls of their times.'[18] They, he continues, 'encompassed all the powers of their time,' and that is what distinguished them from all other poets, whose gifts are not at issue. Nor can it be disputed that they were part of a great energistic pool of talents and voices, for the fact that they arose from such a 'pool' was essential to their 'originality.' But unlike their predecessors or contemporaries, each created a new form of speech: Homer, 'the epic of the soul'; and Dante, 'the novel of the soul.' Of course, without Homer there would have been no Dante, and Dante's deference to Virgil as both the greatest of poets and his guide through Hell and most of Purgatory is also a deference to Homer. For it was Homer who gave Virgil his epic hero, Aeneas, and who also gave the Romans a sense that their historical past was based in their founder's flight from the destruction of Troy. And for Dante, the future realm of peace, which was to be under the rule of one universal empire, was but the continuation and Christianization of the Roman Empire. Nevertheless, Homer and Dante both stood, for Rosenstock-Huessy, in a unique relation to the overwhelming powers nd problems of the times, and each had founded a new age; sharply put, 'Italians spring from Dante, Hellas from Homer.'[19] In the former case, this importance was bound up with the fact that Italy was the first of the European nations to embark on what would, for Rosenstock-Huessy, be the great sequence of revolutions that was 'the march of the nations' toward the realization of the Messianic age of Jewish and Christian faith. But before we examine more closely Dante's role in the great revolutionary wave that Rosenstock-Huessy saw as the greatest Christian achievement of the second millennium, it is important to dwell on what Rosenstock-Huessy said about the artistic genius of Homer and his role in shaping what he saw as one of the four great 'speech-ways' of life of the pre-Christian era – and one, indeed, that would find itself revitalized in the modern world.

Peoples, tribes, and empires, says Rosenstock-Huessy, are all ways of life that carry within them a particular temporal orientation: tribes are especially reliant on the past because they take their orientation from the dead (a point more fully discussed in the chapter 'Rosenstock-Huessy on Islam'). The realms control and are controlled by the present, and they follow the rotation of the stars so that they know at any time what to do; and the 'nations'/people (*Volk*) have their origins in their faith that they have been promised a great future by God.[20] But alongside the three social forms of the tenses is a fourth orientation. This is a 'space' of timelessness in which play, art, science, and philosophy are possible; and, says Rosenstock-Huessy, it was the Greeks who marked out this space, thereby providing so many of the resources that are so fundamental in the formations, pursuits, administrations, technologies, and entertainments of modern peoples. In yet another schematic tabulation, he depicts the innovations of tribes, realms, nations, and (the people of the) muses:

> Tribes create families – Members bear a name
> Realms create classes – Inhabitants practise a profession
> A nation creates destination/assignation (*Bestimmung*) – Souls come to speech
> Muses create poetry – Men have time.[21]

Regarding the muses, he continues: 'Until today, the Olympic games, Plato and Aristotle, mathematics, and physics and astronomy, tragedy and comedy, have become indispensible elements of education. Because all education creates time for evasion, it permits us play . . . The speech of human thinking (*Gedenkens*) is Greek.[22] Each new science furnishes itself with a Greek vocabulary.'[23]

No doubt other peoples of the ancient world had sung their stories and told their myths, but the Greeks alone raised both the poet and the poetic form to a level of importance beyond liturgy, ritual, or cult.[24] Though as Rosenstock-Huessy notes, tragic drama was liturgical, and the use of mask ritualistic – signalling the tribal side of the Greeks (the city-state, he says, 'reconcile[d] tribes and empires').[25] Concomitantly, in Homer there is neither liturgy nor myth.[26] But it was the great cluster of innovations that made Homeric poetry the equivalent of a new speech-way, reinforcing what, with the city-state, was already a radically new form of human association, one that required a plasticity and adventurousness on the part of its members unlike either the more rigid caste divisions and professions that held the empires together, and unlike what the less 'settled' tribes were able to muster. Contrasting the Egyptians and the Greeks, Rosenstock-Huessy writes:

> If I live ninety percent serious, priestly, warlike and technical like the Egyptians, then my word remains enchanted, imperious and prescribed.
>
> Because the Greeks had to live 80 percent as seafarers, pirates, traders, travellers, colonists, wandering physicians, singers, tradesmen, their word became poly-mythical, rich in variations, and multi-keyed. That is the basic meaning of the word 'poetic,' that the Greek saw himself perpetually forced to choose his own key. He could worship, compare, report, narrate, explain, because he had to speak in 258 cities, now as mayor, now as visitor, now as trader, now as host, now as foreigner. The Greek language is the result of pantomyth, of the infinite choices of degrees of belonging and strangeness, of exodus and immigration, of taking leave and welcoming.[27]

For Rosenstock-Huessy, what was really important about Homer's art was not simply its artistic merit, but that Homer actually created a new type of social body, one that had no parallel in tribes or realms – the public. This type, for Rosenstock-Huessy, was one that we are all too familiar with today, and it is perfectly encapsulated in the expression 'public opinion.' A public is a 'molecule' formed by an initial atomization, by a breaking down of a hierarchical collective into individuals.[28] A public is formed in relationship to an artist or event. But as a member of the public, one's focus is directed toward the stage/site of performance rather than – as, say, in ritual – to other members of this same public. For Rosenstock-Huessy, then, a public was a particular kind of audience – one that did not involve itself liturgically or ritualistically in a 'performance.' The audience was instead transported into a 'free time' where its members could mentally wander back and forth as they heard the tales of their heroes. Thus, for

Rosenstock-Huessy, just as Achilles and Priam created 'a holiday space' in book 24 of the *Iliad* in the midst of a war,[29] Homer created a clearing so that his 'public' could reflect on their heroic origins at leisure. To an important extent, the atomized identity of the members of the molecule, 'the public,' partly reflected the circumstance of Greece itself, an archipelago consisting of a huge number of independent city-states with their own laws, which Greeks could wander between. That archipelago became transformed into a unity during its war against the Trojans, and Homer's great catalogue of the ships – where, as Rosenstock-Huessy reminds his readers, Homer names 265 independent communities[30] – was the original artistic representation of the formation of that unity.

The Greek world, says Rosenstock-Huessy, 'is a generalisation,' and 'a generalisation remains ever dependent upon the particular which she emerges from.'[31] On the other hand, that atomization is also in keeping with the view of the world that we find in Homer. For he was also the first to have a vision of human society being built up of individuals, and thus in his work the sweep of peoples revolved around the dramas of individuals. Our empathy for each of his heroes – most notable in the various and constantly shifting pairings that run throughout the *Iliad* (e.g., Achilles and Agamemnon, Achilles and Patroclus, Achilles and Hector, Achilles and Priam, Hector and Paris, Hector and Andromache, Hector and Achilles, and so on), and the *Odyssey* (Telemachus and Nestor, Odysseus and Circe, Odysseus and the Cyclops, Odysseus and Penelope, etc.) – gives those two works so much emotional power that it enables a new view of what constitutes humanity.

Besides creating a new type of social body, Homer created a new world alongside this world, a *framed* world; and later that frame would take the form of the stage, or the frame of a picture, or a sports arena – in just the same way that Homer has his heroes play their games during an interlude in the Trojan War. What is all-important is that time is suspended, held at bay so that the audience can focus its attention on the event the poet is depicting. And just as the rules of time are held at bay, so are the rules of human association – most notably their sacrificial dimension. For Rosenstock-Huessy, the arc that stretches from our earliest kind of human association – the tribe – through to our most complex and most recent, the nation-state and international blocs of nations – all depend for their survival on members' willingness to sacrifice themselves in times of need so that the collective can survive. Rosenstock-Huessy's commitment to Christianity was to no small extent based on the central role of sacrifice from God to man as a radical/revolutionary understanding of the meaning and nature of sacrifice, of no less social importance than Copernicus' astronomical revolution has been to our understanding of the universe. One fundamental consequence of the revolutionary insight of Christianity is that the sacrificial component has been accentuated in Christianity so that the highest and most powerful of cosmic forces are themselves engaged in sacrifice for the sake of achieving the task of Redemption. It is as if a king is to understand that his death is required so that the collective he rules will not just survive but prosper through the very dissolution of the form that has heretofore protected and sustained all. That is to say, whereas the tribe, empire, and city had required their members to sacrifice themselves in times of need to protect the chief or imperial or legislative power and the form of life over which they reigned, Christianity pushes us to understand that the very form of life – the specific form of human association – may at times itself need to be surrendered. One must die into new forms of life. Rosenstock-Huessy's *Out of Revolution* (and *Die europäischen Revolutionen*) and *Soziologie* are erected entirely on the depiction of these sacrificial moments, which is to say they are depictions of the highest form of love in action. For Christianity's power, according to Rosenstock-Huessy, is that it moves the axis of service away from the traditional act of sacrifice of the heroic toward the absurd act of faith. In the latter, the witness (the martyr) rides death like a wave into the future so that death is the precondition not of preservation but of Resurrection, of transfiguration. Which to no small degree is how Rosenstock-Huessy is able to note a momentous geopolitical fact that is hardly ever appreciated or even seen as noteworthy – that the great chain of total revolutions originated on Christian soil – soil that, he stresses, had been tilled for more than one thousand years.

One consequence of modernity is that it has tended to downplay sacrifice altogether, both in its 'natural' or pagan form and in its Christian form. The idea – which Marxists would ascribe to bourgeois society – that you can have it all, that life is fundamentally about sating pleasure, avoiding pain, and achieving comfort (Descartes's dream realized by a utilitarian calculus), is so widespread in modern societies that only in times of war are most people awakened to the requirement of sacrifice (usually of young men) as a social necessity. Paradoxically – and again, this is a key point in *Out of Revolution* and the *Soziologie* – while moderns live daily off the sacrifice of revolutionaries who died in order to create the institutions that (however imperfectly) protect the rights and freedoms of the members of free societies, they rarely connect those freedoms with the faith of those who died to secure them.

My digression here is meant to underscore what Rosenstock-Huessy in his discussion of Homer was emphasizing about the atomized nature of the public and Homer's role in creating that public. That is, the creation of a group bound together by its self-understanding as a public body – hence the subsequent importance of the Kantian rule of 'publicity' – is an attempt to create a moral communicative order among these atoms (for the modern world completely absorbs the notion of public into its politics).

In his discussion of Homer, Rosenstock-Huessy dwells on the suspension of the sacrificial requirements at the very basis of the creation of a social order – a social order that originally (and repeatedly) created public spaces where the sacrificial order was suspended and replaced by one of play.[32] In the sports arena, the theatre, the seminar room, and so on, we exist in another world, one that requires the suspension of the absolute polarity we are caught up in as we watch others subject themselves to their fates in a different space. In our 'other world,' we occupy a safer, and a more secure, anonymous, and unbonded position as we watch others kill and die.[33] The danger, according to Rosenstock-Huessy, is that in our absorption in the spectacle we will become oblivious to the larger events and the specific bonds that constitute our circumstance.

Closely related to this act of the erection of another world via the frame is another Homeric creation, 'the law of reflection.' What is noteworthy about this law, for Rosenstock-Huessy, is that the 'mirror of art and of thinking invert the direction of time.'[34] The public knows that Achilles will die, and they know that the only reason Book One of the *Odyssey* tells of Telemachus, Nestor, and Menelaus is that this is the story of Odysseus' homecoming; even if Homer tells his stories sequentially, the real sequence has been inverted before the story begins. This inversion of the sequences contributes to the tension that enables the leisured listeners to repeat and relive and review the stories.[35] The public can reflect on and discuss all manner of alternatives – as Plato does, when he damns the entire Homeric mode of life. But he is only able to do so because he too now can share in the cleared and idle space that Homer first created. Plato's debt to Homer is obvious to Rosenstock-Huessy, and he discusses that debt in some detail. For him, most noteworthy is that it was the one totality, the Greek world, that yielded poetry, theatre, philosophy, speculative natural science, sport, and mathematical reasoning about the cosmos. They are, for him, various dispositions that were made possible only by the original establishment – which we first find in Homer – of a new approach to play and time, which is an approach where the second-order activity of play takes on so much importance that it is seen as superior to reality.

According to Rosenstock-Huessy, two other closely related aspects of Homer contribute further to this transformation. One has its roots in the poetic compassion that is intrinsic to Homer's individuation and pairings. The culmination of the poetic compassion takes place, for Rosenstock-Huessy, in Book Twenty-Four of the *Iliad* when Priam and Achilles gaze into each other's suffering: a father looks upon his son's killer, and a warrior looks upon the father of the man who has killed his greatest friend.[36] The mutual compassionate gaze between enemies, between (soon to be) victor and vanquished is, for Rosenstock-Huessy, both a break with the panic that one would expect of enemies from other tribes or realms or nations, and the foundation of an approach to life that those other modes did not have. This moment is, he says, the foundation of humanism.

Throughout, we have emphasized that Rosenstock-Huessy's opposition to humanism was based on what he saw as a misplaced trust in the source and scope of human powers. And we cannot overlook that his critique of Greek thinking was essentially the same as Rosenzweig's – that it wanted to be the All, that it only admitted other forms of life on its terms, for it held it had discovered the true nature of humanity and the world.[37] Nevertheless, the esteem that Rosenstock-Huessy has for Homer also flows into his appreciation of what he sees as the most important insight of humanism:

> Humanism is today misunderstood as the understanding of everything human. No, it is something more powerful. Humanism means, that the inhuman is he who not in the slightest finds himself in another being (*Wesen*), and that he is unhappy who is not recognized in the slightest by another being. Ancient humanism supplies also a description of human luck and a human type with the help of a rule, that no individual human being exists before someone recognizes you as a human being, and before you, in turn, recognize another being as a human being.[38]

For Rosenstock-Huessy, it is precisely in 'this word gaze into [*hinein-schauen*] *eishoran* in Homer' that we find the source of Greek idealism.

'Greek idealism is precisely not the abstract "insight" into any truth. It is the gaze into the enemy in the light of admiration.' This is what gives Idealism its humanity. Indeed, he says, it would be 'inhuman,' and could not stem from Homer, if it did not contain this all-important element. From Homer, then, Plato inherits the capacity for mutually appreciative reciprocal engagement between members of contrary or opposing communities. Hence, for Rosenstock-Huessy, Plato attacks the framework of Homer even while he retains the essential insight of the human being who realizes that truth can only be attained if we commence by considering others' points of view: 'both Homer and Plato give to the subjects of a world of gods, as a second element of existence, membership in "a nature," which he does not remain enslaved to. Included in his "nature" of the Greeks which he can observe, are his enemies, his neighbouring cities.'[39]

The other factor that Rosenstock-Huessy thinks so important in the erection of another world is a linguistic one. Homer, he says, is full of substitutions of more general terms of description for proper names:

> Homer's favourite word is of course the little word 'as.' But 'the one and the other,' 'someone else,' 'somehow,' 'somewhere,' 'anybody' and above all 'something' are his real words of disenchantment. These words transform the god of this city or the rites of this clan into 'a' God and into 'a' rite. From Homer the entire Greek philosophy and science received the new words of comparison, which contain the 'someone,' 'something,' 'how' and 'a.'[40]

Thus when Plato asks after a god that conforms to an essence, his way has already been prepared by Homer, who had previously spoken of 'the,' or 'some' or 'a' god, instead of doing what other peoples had always done, which is supplicate a specific god with a specific name. The essentialism of philosophy is but a further instance, then, of a preceding linguistic abstractness. For Rosenstock-Huessy, this linguistic turn also underpins the mathematization of reality such as one finds in Pythagoras and Plato, who now use this same 'something' to reduce the cosmos to number.[41] For Rosenstock-Huessy, the fact that there is no vocative for the singular *theos* (God) in classical Greek suggests that the word is deployed so that 'one can already discuss the gods in abstentia';[42] instead of a god being a real power to implore, he or she is now merely an 'etcetra.'[43] Once again, a linguistic point finds itself reinforced in the actual content of the poetry so that just as 'the god' is an abstraction, the gods themselves take on a degree of abstractness in the lives of the heroes. This is not to overlook the obvious fact that the gods in Homer still intrude on the affairs of men; rather, it is to underscore that their otherness makes them completely unreliable (a major Homeric theme), whereas humans, in spite of their enmity, are united in their common mortality. 'Only the Greeks,' says Rosenstock-Huessy, 'fundamentally nullified the chasm between holy and worldly speech ... Speech to the god became in Homer still only an idiom for the gods among themselves. However, below men one and the same power of speech is in use, whether they are opening their mouths over things or among the gods.'[44]

In his discussion of Homer, then, what has interested Rosenstock-Huessy primarily is what is unique in his creation, and hence what new approach to social space and time has been received through the ages. Homer represents an extraordinary deviation from the tribes and the realms. Rosenstock-Huessy also contrasts Homeric poetry with the poetry of tribes that do not take the humanist and reflective turn opened up by Homer and who remain enmeshed in one of the great pathologies of the tribes – that is, their susceptibility to cycles of revenge that culminate in a group's eventual annihilation (and it must be said that every social formation is susceptible to a particular range of pathologies).[45] He notes that this is precisely the fate of tribes that is recorded in the *Songs of the Nibelungen*, a saga he calls at one point 'the song of the will to victory and the defeat of this will.'[46] That Wagner and the Nazis would take up the Nibelungen myth is indicative, for him, of the kind of death wish that drove them and how remote this was from Homer's humanism. Yet Rosenstock-Huessy is at pains to point out that while the Greeks opened up a new life/speechway, they did not change tribes or realms.[47] They left a great legacy – 'one can thank the Greeks for free thinking, but not, however, for free action'[48] – but it could only be a legacy because we were already reconfigured in such a way that we could do more with the Greek achievement than the Greeks themselves did.

For Rosenstock-Huessy, that reconfiguration was the achievement of the Christian peoples, who – so he believes – slowly but surely recovered and revived one Greek invention after another, including Homer himself. If, as we have seen, Rosenstock-Huessy is concerned to show the great originality of Homer, how he opened up another way of experiencing time and another kind of human association, his concern with Dante – and indeed, with all artists in the Christian era – has, apart from the vital quality of incarnation, another emphasis altogether. What concerns him is the revolutionary service and impetus of artists. He contends that Homer's emphasis on mutual recognition – the ability to glean the tragic choices of enemies – is an essential feature that is taken over by Dante in his depiction of Guelphs and Ghibellines (and that subsequently is taken over by Goethe in his depiction of the common humanity of Protestants and Catholics). What has changed between Homer and Dante – and this is evident in the very oppositions just mentioned – is that European art is part of a greater current of religious forces. Hence in *Out of Revolution* he writes that 'poetry and fiction and art are always a sequel to religion,' adding that 'Goethe's Faust translated the experience of Luther and of his singing congregation to the unbelieving public of the nineteenth century. Dante, writing as a lost, an exiled, soul, at the end of the imperial period, enables us, who are not contemporaries of the eleventh century, to share the feeling stirred by the introduction of All Souls in 998.'[49]

It is in this light that Dante holds, for Rosenstock-Huessy, a special place in the modern world for artists – one that he sees as analogous to Homer's place in the ancient world. Though Rosenstock-Huessy does not say this, I am tempted to say that the love song that is so ubiquitous in modern society is the greatest of Dante's legacies. For while it is true that Dante did not invent either romantic poetry or the lyric, his investment of cosmic significance in both the love poem and the beloved is echoed in an age in which romantic love and the overwhelming and ever-present expression of the absolute importance of love and the beloved is the soundtrack to modern secular life.

Dante's *Divine Comedy* is built around the Last Judgment – and Rosenstock-Huessy notes that that judgment in Dante 'reveals its moral majesty by showing all the tears and fears of a human heart under the weight of true judgment.'[50] It had, of course, been Augustine who first, and repeatedly, spoke of how the direction of the soul's love acted as weight that transported it to its desired place. The *Divine Comedy* takes this insight of Augustine by reconfiguring divine justice as the physiognomy of desire and by showing how the soul's desire shapes society. The *Divine Comedy* is the greatest alignment of society and soul that had ever been undertaken. But as Rosenstock-Huessy also argues, and as any reader of Dante immediately learns, it had as its immediate political background the schisms and tensions within Christendom that had polarized Church and Empire while (paradoxically) giving rise to a desperate search for universality and unity on earth, which Dante shows as the will of heaven. Thus, speaking of the *Divine Comedy*, Rosenstock-Huessy says:

This poem, begun in 1300, testifies to a much older dualism. The dualism for which the song of Hell, Purgatory, and Heaven was conceived as a high dirge was the dualism of the Roman Empire during the tenth and eleventh centuries. The emperors of the North, from Henry I (1002–24) to Henry VI (1307–13) were the heroes of Dante . . . Facing a changed world, he had to sing the Last Judgment so that the great period when the emperors had acted as judges of Christianity might be eternalized in a work of art. As a simple outline of Dante's vision of the Last Judgment, we can say that he draws a line from everybody's specific and particular existence to his place in the universe which lies beyond the visible organization of earth. His Last Judgment applies the categories of unity and universality to the Beyond, because earthly life is local, parochial, particular, fragmentary. He is obliged to trace everybody's destiny to its last judgment; it is the only way to unite men who are separated on earth. The realm of faith is the only universal and unifying home for the scattered villages of the tenth century.[51]

It is this search for divine justice and for the realization of the *eschaton* on earth that gives Dante's poem and his own role a revolutionary purpose unknowable to Homer, or indeed to any of the Greeks. It is precisely this search that Dante himself saw as unique to Christian peoples and that led him, with regret, to consign Virgil, along with Homer and other ancient poetic and philosophical geniuses, to hell. For what Dante was saying by such a consignment was simply that the absence of the virtues of faith, hope, and love (i.e., the Christian virtues) within the social capillaries condemned even geniuses and pagan saints to ever inhabit a world limited by strife and conflict. Of course, it is not that Dante's world is not full of conflict – but the hope and faith in love for the future and the commitment to orchestrating social forces toward the achievment of a universal peace is what separates them. Dante's consciousness of his revolutionary role and purpose also makes him an important figure, for Rosenstock-Huessy. Dante, says Rosenstock-Huessy, 'dares to conceive for the first time the great idea of revolution':

At the end of his poem he says that one and the same power moves the life of mankind and the life of Stars and Suns. Our actions and movements, therefore, when prompted by love, are near to the constellations and revolutions of the celestial bodies. With this bold equation, Dante transferred and projected our deepest and most human experience upon the sky of the external world. He prepared the reapplication of the world revolution to Society. For Dante made these revolutions of the stars the symbols of life, and their motivation identical with the passions of our own life. No wonder that his century, the fourteenth, is the century in which the main concept of this work, Revolution, was first used by Italian chroniclers to draw a parallel between heaven and earth, between the meteoric changes in the sky and those in the political life of the Italian city-states. But the most important feature of Dante's poem is that it bears witness to the old time when the Sacred Emperor, marching through this world, still paved the road for God's judgment.[52]

But this does not meant that Dante *instigates* the process of revolution. On the contrary, as the above reference to Dante's reliance on older dualism emphasizes, he is but one of the revolutionary forces that have been activated by what Rosenstock-Huessy considers the first revolution that was conscious of itself as undertaking to move heaven and earth – the Gregorian or Papal or Clerical Revolution. And just as two centuries later Luther would remain Dante's ally and contemporary in his uncompromising stance against the corruption and squalor of the Church, Dante was the ally and contemporary of those reformers who had preceded him and who strived to sweep away the injustices and corruption within Christendom.[53] Dante rode on that revolutionary wave, which in turn gave birth to the Italian Revolution – Rosenstock-Huessy also called it the 'Second Clerical Revolution' – and which involved the wars between the papal party, the Guelphs, and imperial party, the Ghibbelines, which in turn yielded what he called 'the garden of the Renaissance.'

For Rosenstock-Huessy, at the centre of the revolutionary process is the attempt to transform the 'whole of the occident into one city . . . Jerusalem'; the establishment of a 'super-local unity' of the constitution of a monastic order; and the feast of All Souls' Day. For him, the importance of All Souls' Day is summarized in this passage: it 'wrote the notion of universality into the hearts of the Christian people.' All Souls' Day is a reminder that all, whether king, pope, or peasant, will stand naked in soul before God to be judged. It 'established the solidarity of all souls from the beginning of the world to the end of time';[54] it was 'the first universal democracy in the world'; it was 'a democracy of sinners, united in their common confession of sins in expectation of the Last Judgment.'[55] Thus he summarizes: 'Europe learned democracy. She learned unity, she learned universality. All Souls is the cornerstone of all our modern civilization.' And thus he sees the pivotal revolutionary importance of a feast day that falls on 2 November, the day after All Saints' Day, and that has long since lost its significance in the West's collective unconscious.[56]

But All Souls' Day was initiated by the abbey of Cluny – a super-abbey, that Rosenstock-Huessy credits with being the 'the first trust, the trans-local corporation: It was they who, for the first time, wrote the idea of super-local unity into the constitution of a monastic order . . . They united monasticism by imitating imperial centralism. As the emperor had distributed public duties among the many imperial monasteries, so did now the abbot of Cluny for spiritual purposes. Cluny incorporated all the "Roman" monasteries which were reformed by it.'[57] Cluny was renowned for its reformist spirit – one abbot, Rosenstock-Huessy informs his readers, 'refused to become pope in Rome,' and Cluny, he continues,

> invented the *treuga del*, the truce of the land. The liturgy of the church was used to restore peace. The week of Easter, from Palm Sunday to Easter Sunday, with Maundy Thursday and Good Friday in it, was taken as a model for daily life. Monday, Tuesday, Wednesday, a man was allowed to fight his kind. But from Thursday to Sunday, Cluny imposed abstinence from all violence. Holy Week was epoch-making in that it divided life again into peace and war, making peace and war definite, abolishing their complete confusion; and ennobling the task of the common knight as a defence of God's peace. The ritual of a king's coronation was extended to the knighting of every soldier of God.[58]

But, says Rosenstock-Huessy, Cluny's 'greatest act was giving to mankind the day of All Souls. It is not triumph and victory, which had been celebrated by the Church on All Saints' Day for almost two centuries but purgatory and mutual suffering and the sin that causes it which is celebrated with All Souls.' And this, he says, was so appropriate because 'the Church in 1000 is no church of saints. It is a church of sinners, who by their blood-ties are all involved in bloodsheds: pious bishops fighting in the imperial army, innocent children being biased by vendetta.'[59] All Souls' Day had given hope to the very least and most oppressed that God's judgment would not forget them – 'it revealed man's dignity, his claim not to be thrown into the fire like a weed, but to be judged'[60] – and that being a king or emperor or pope or cardinal was no protection from God's judgment and justice. Dante's condemnation of popes, emperors, kings, and cardinals to hell (and purgatory) along with history's most wicked was due not to a unique vision or sense of divine justice on his part, but to a widespread faith – held by members of 'an army of Christian soldiers' marching with the 'irresistible faith before their saviour who was their comrade, and is now their judge'[61] – in the power of righteousness and faith that the Church would protect its flock from the rapaciousness of clerics and secular rulers alike. Thus in his discussion of the importance of All Souls' Day and Dante, Rosenstock-Huessy says: 'I hope I have succeeded in overcoming our common notion of the Last Judgment as a mere religious concept without practical consequences. In fact, it was a political agency of the first importance; it attracted the wealth of the people like a magnet, building up an immense property in the hands of a disinterested trustee, the Church.'[62]

For Rosenstock-Huessy, the revolutionary vision contained in All Souls' Day and in its role not only in reforming the Church but also in creating faith in the Church itself as a revolutionary force, has its counterpart in the liturgical aspects of that feast day. The mass, he points out, was a Latin 'plain chant':

> On All Souls, the priest used the real first and last language of our soul, which is before the division of song and speech. The plain song of the mass also keeps alive the oldest of all truths, that language is living and life-giving speech. This language is not to be found in the dead, soundless prose of our daily talk and chatter. We whisper; our language is a dead branch of the living tree of speech. Souls dive into language as into their true element and where they dare commit themselves to the flood of sincere speech, there is no division of language, no Babylonian confusion of tongues.[63]

Rosenstock-Huessy describes in some detail the liturgy that sprang from the founder of All Souls' Day, Cluny's fifth abbot, Odilo. Here he dwells on its crowning hymn, 'Dies irae, dies illa.' The feast and its liturgy are the seed of the 'first revolutionary' who 'set out with a new faith in the meaning of life and death.'[64] Just as the discovery of Jesus and his martyrs created the first millennium by taking a truth of the Jewish people and transforming it into a universal enterprise of salvation, it was Odilo who discovered world history as a universal order and fact, when he ordered the whole religious fraternity to pray for the liberty of *'omnes omnirnodo fideles.'* Up to that time, monks had prayed only for their abbey, their relatives, their friends, their connections. Odilo conjured up instead the universe which lies between *heaven and hell, between saints and sinners,* waiting for our prayers, and which consists of all those who have been, from the beginning of the world to its end.[65]

His 'disciple' Gregory VII, the 'monk emperor,'[66] responded to this call by seeking to clean up and empower the Church by bringing the emperor under the same realm of divine justice as all of God's sinners and sufferers. That the Church would, by Dante's time, be so in need of further rejuvenation that he would urge it to sacrifice its political power to the emperor is not *despite* that revolutionary seed planted by Odilo but as a *consequence* of it; and Dante's *Divine Comedy* is one fruit of that seed, the spread of which is, for him, the spread of the faith of universal justice and universal democracy: 'so called world history became a reality from the moment when All Souls began to work on every man.'[67]

As we saw earlier, for Rosenstock-Huessy it was the Papal or Gregorian revolution that had planted the seed of revolution throughout Europe. The revolution, for him, had rested on the pope's demands that the mobile imperial palace not wall in the papal *curia* or court, and that the papal *curia* replace 'the palatine principle under which emperor and pope shared one and the same chancellor.'[68] The institutional importance of this event can be gauged by this formulation: 'the sequence of European revolutions can be illustrated by a diagram of the imperial palace and its slow dissolution.'[69] For in the end, that 'slow dissolution' of that 'imperial palace' was what marked the emergence of the modern European nations. What had begun with the pope granting every Christian the right of appeal to every Christian soul against the injustices of his bishop eventually required that every bishop regularly visit Rome and face the complaints of his own diocesans in Rome. This revolutionary shift in power, which transformed the office of the pope into a sovereign court in competition with the emperor, 'broke through the forms of personal allegiance which existed in the feudal system of the empire, and established a new system of immediate allegiance between every bishop, every abbot, every Christian and the pope.'[70] The Church, in other words, had under Gregory transformed itself politically into the great protector against imperial and even clerical injustice. And by 1100, owing to Rome's breaking out of the imperial wall, the Church had become reinvented as the Mother of every Catholic individual; and previously the 'emperor's chancery was accustomed to call Rome the Mother of all Churches.'[71] But by 1300, the papacy was so corrupt that Dante (like Marsiglio of Padua) was calling for the complete containment of papal political power. For those who try to encapsulate the meaning of the Church through the periods of its decadence and decay, the widespread faith of the Church makes no sense at all, nor does its artistic celebration, nor does its revolutionary character. But this is like trying to judge someone's potency by contemplating his life exclusively through periods of fever or his stooped, arthritic, and aged body.

When Dante lived, the Church was indeed in crisis, rent asunder through the papacy, and it would remain so for more than a century. Nevertheless, the Church was never simply the papacy, and Gregory's revolution was reactivated and pushed further by the Guelphic revolution of 1200 to 1500, which Rosenstock-Huessy also called 'the second half of the papal revolution.'[72] In his view, a number of core components – some of them fortuitous – contributed to and expressed this revolution and drove it forward:

The invention of a new harness 'which exploited the full energy of the horses shoulder blades' – thus enabling the transportation of hitherto impossible carloads of materials thus changing the landscape as new stone churches replaced wooden ones, stone bridges and an increased number of roads and stone castles were built;[73]

The crusade and scholasticism – the purpose of which was to create the universal solidarity and conquer 'the hell of paganism from inside.'[74]

The introduction of a temporal limit ('a year and a day') to the holding of political office first adopted by the growing number of republics in Italy and then spread throughout Europe as far away as London.[75]

The creation of 'diets' so that peasants were granted citizenship and could join the guilds and minor crafts, hence a new bond of political solidarity was established.[76]

The founding of the Franciscan Order and the establishment of the vow of poverty – poverty was to become as important a sign of integrity in the 'second revolution' against the Church's increasing accumulation of earthly riches in its attempt to make itself the visible power, as celibacy had been for the Gregorians.[77]

And at the centre of all this was Mother Church, even if it capitalized on new inventions or powers mainly by deploying them to draw people into its bosom through greater acts and expressions of solidarity. This new 'power over nature,' which enabled lords of the manor to expand their geographical territories by building castles more remote from their principal seats and having them administered by knaves, brought in its train a need for a new kind of law capable of dealing with the new forms of conflicts and disputations generated by such a reconfiguration of the social map:

> The Church placed itself at the head of the new movement. In the inevitable struggle over the issue as to whether the increased power over nature should finally belong to the old manorial lords or to the other classes as well, the Church turned the scales by establishing itself as a feudal court for the world at large. The very word for the Holy See that is most commonly used today, Curia, is not older than the eleventh century. And it means a centre of feudal law for an army which is no longer living in the home of its military commander but which is living outside on separate estates.[78]

If the initial liturgical impulse had been All Souls' Day, the liturgical accompaniment to this revolution was the feast of Corpus Christi, whose 'order of . . . Service' was composed by Thomas Aquinas, and whose origin was recorded for posterity in one of Raphael's most famous paintings, 'The Mass at Bolsena':

> The feast was made compulsory for the whole Roman world in 1310, and unknown in the Orient, a scandal to any Protestant, the Feast of Corpus Christi commemorates the opus operatum, the real reality of the Church's work of reconcentration. The crusading Church believed in its capacity to concentrate the light of all priesthood in one pope, the thoughts of all saints in one summa, the problems of all fathers in one concord. It believed, therefore, in its right to celebrate this process of reconcentration by one feast, which concentrated the revealing power of a whole millennium of sacraments into the triumphant procession of one bright summer day. Corpus Christi leaves the crypt and choir, the altar and nave of the church building. The crusading Church celebrates in procession. Led by

the Lords Spiritual, on Corpus Christi Day the Church recalls its fight for liberty. The result of the Papal Revolution is well expressed in the text of the service. The faithful pray for protection against the persecutors of the Church; they pray for the pope, 'whom Thou has destined to preside over Thy church.' (This singular – 'Thy church' – would have been impossible three centuries before.) They pray for the new barriers established against the emperor's 'simony' with the words: 'Let Thy church serve thee, resistance and heresies being utterly destroyed, in protected liberty.'[79]

The nearest equivalent that anyone alive in the twentieth century can equate with the impact of the papal revolution is, Rosenstock-Huessy suggests, the Russian Revolution. For what was occurring was a transformation based mainly on the establishment of a universal form of solidarity under the spiritual and political guidance of a body with enough faith, power, and spirit to give it direction:

> From Gregory VII to 1500 the Church was more than the audible and visible Body of Christ. It was, besides, a stormy party of reform within the Corpus Christi, waging war against the mundane decay of clergy and laity by means of Crusades and Doctorates, making its internal treasures visible. Mysteries were unfolded, secrets explained; the ways of life were made clear. The multitude of Sacraments was simplified. Seven sacraments dealt with every Christian's life-cycle from cradle to bier. Baptism, Confirmation, Marriage, Ordainment, Repentance, and Extreme Unction were the recurrent stations of every soul's pilgrimage.[80]

As we have stressed throughout, a large part of Rosenstock-Huessy's undertaking as a historian and social theorist was to show not how we think our liberties *might* have arisen on the basis of imagined solidarities and circumstances, but rather how they actually *did* do so. Thus typically one might construe the French Revolution as the great watershed of freedom (Hegel himself does this), when in fact it was a national event *as well as* a universal event that was the heir of other universalizing predecessors. As a national event, its anti-clericalism was a symptom of the inexorable weakening of France's first estate long after the revolutions in Germany had forced the Church back to its original mission (albeit in the context of a new, worldly emphasis on family and profession), and long after the English Revolution had rid that realm of the political myth of the divine right of kings. That particular myth had taken such a strong hold in France that the people could free itself only by eradicating the monarchy. Thus France had compacted and extended the aspirations of liberty and human solidarity, aspirations that Gregory VII had awakened from his lonely chapel. And the fact that, during the French Revolution, even the clergy had to be sacrificed was not a sign of freedom's awakening, but of what freedom required if it was to break out of ossified institutions:

> The liberty of the Church was and remained the great war-cry for four centuries. Even in the four centuries after the Reformation the liberties of man were only translations of this liberty of the church. The Rights of Man were a translation of the Rights of the Christian people, the Rights of the Christian people were a translation of the Rights of the Universal Priesthood and the Rights of Priesthood were deduced from the Rights of the Trustee of Priesthood, the Pope, against the threats of the Anti-Christ.[81]

The great political conflict leading up to and running through much of the Renaissance between the papal and imperial parties, the Guelphs and Ghibellines, laid the foundations for a new kind of politics, a politics whose hopes would be reflected in much Renaissance art. This is a central line of argumentation in the tenth and eleventh chapters of *Out of Revolution*, where Rosenstock-Huessy emphasizes two of the great achievements of Guelphic politics, one revolutionizing a politics of time, the other a politics of space.

The revolution in the politics of time had to do with superimposing temporal limits on officers of earthly power. This limitation, which found itself reflected in such measures as periodic elections, and term limits for office holders, has its basis in the representative of eternity (the Church) treating society and its governance under the rubric of temporality. And for Rosenstock-Huessy it was *the* revolutionary Guelphic idea of the years between 1200 and 1500:[82]

> The Guelphic city subordinated man's calendar to the church calendar. It forbade the body politic to go beyond the year of the religious soul. This 'Guelphic' concept was so general that it spread over all Europe. The kings and princes took it up for the government of their realms, by giving a temporal share to the estates of the country. I say, a temporal share; for it was the 'diet,' the representative of the country in 'going, staying, and returning' that gave the estates their power. What we have mentioned in little Andorra, can be found just as well in Great Britain.[83]

The spatial correlate of this revolution in a politics of time was the granting of political rights to peasants – that is, the 'Guelphic mixing of peasants and citizens.'[84] Rosenstock-Huessy underscores the radicality of this principle when he comments that 'Dante's antipathy to the artificial citizenship of the husband-man was shared by all the Northern princes.'[85] In Germany, for example, this Italian principle was considered the equivalent to an outright Soviet system. Time after time over the next two centuries, the empire forbade by law the existence of 'pseudo-citizens.' Just as one would find artists in the twentieth century drawn to the Russian Revolution like moths to a flame, artists throughout Europe celebrated this event and in so doing transformed the history of art:

> The great artists of Florence came from her villages. Settignano gave her Michelangelo, Vinci the great Leonardo, Vespignano produced the first painter of the 'stilo nuovo,' Giotto. In exchange, the city gave something to the country which no peasant or knight could have given. The alliance between city and country created what modern man enjoys as landscape. No 'landscape' whatever was in existence before 1200 . . .
>
> Guelphic Italy discovered the landscape as the background of its cities, because the landscape was no longer owned by separate and greedy proprietors. It was changed into the field of political potestas, of 'civilitas.' Landscape became a political and an artistic reality. In looking at the Guelphs and Ghibellines of Italy we are reminded of the difference between the Social Revolutionaries and the Bolsheviks in Russia. Here it was the Social Revolutionaries who were in love with the individual peasant or village. They distributed the land among individual settlements. The Bolsheviks conceived the unifying vision of one Russian economy. The Italian city-state is so small that modern national historians always wonder why the Italians did not unify the whole peninsula in the Ducento. This absurd projection of present-day proportions into the past hinders us from learning by the past where it is really identical with our own situation. The Guelphic effort was as real as modern economic planning, because the economy of the city was something new, something bigger than manorial husbandry had been.[86]

Rosenstock-Huessy analyses a third revolutionary aspect to the Church's recasting of the political landscape. This one was embodied in the figure of St Francis of Assisi, who was 'the coping stone in the vault which was raised by the Guelphic revolution over "the garden of the Empire."[87] It is difficult to overemphasize the importance of Francis and his order, unless one chooses simply to ignore faith and the body of the faithful (the Church) as a historical force for social transformation. For Francis simultaneously exemplified the purity of the spiritual, through his vow of poverty, and his honour of the beauty of the earth, through his hymn to creation. In this respect, he was a forefather of both the Reformation and the Renaissance. Of course, the division between Reformation and Renaissance involves historical labels that do not neatly encompass the contrary processes for which they are so often taken as standing – that is, the pagan revival of the earthly spawning a revival of the arts and sciences, versus a spiritual backlash against Rome's corruption. Rosenstock-Huessy placed Francis in the context of a revolutionary wave whose diverse parts could be seen in their more authentic unity. He wrote of Francis's hymn to Creation:

> When one reads, one understands why it makes an epoch, why Raphael and all the painters of the Renaissance are the fulfilment of thirteenth-century Spiritualism. One understands that there is one stream of life running through the whole period. Henry Thode was right when he said that the Italian Renaissance began with St. Francis. The political and religious life between 1200 and 1500 is a unit, preceded by the Crusades and followed by the Reformation.[88]

Francis's was the necessary reaction of the man of faith to the Church's political success. Just as Gregory had embraced celibacy, Francis embraced the life of poverty. Both had done so against the corruption of Church.[89] Francis was part of the same revolution that had made the Church the symbol of a new hope. In this rather lengthy passage, Rosenstock-Huessy summarizes why and how the revolutionary character of the Church was such a major source of artistic inspiration:

> The triumphant vision of the new political movement in Italy became the 'Madonna in the Landscape.'
>
>   What distinguishes painting after 1300 from all previous art? Perspective. What distinguishes Occidental art from Chinese, to which it owes perhaps the knowledge of landscape painting? Perspective. The gilded background of Byzantine art is exchanged in Italy for a new perspective. The Madonna, the fixed visual centre of the divine service in the church,

is framed by the political vision of the new city-state: the Landscape. The stilo nuovo in painting was what books on planning are today, or what written literature was to the national revolution in France: the expression of a common effort and a common faith. The Mother Church, and the citizen protected by her, were felt to be the centre from which light shone into the darkness of the world. A landscape is the country viewed from within the city. When Petrarch wrote his famous verse, 'Fior, frondiy erbe, ombre, antri, onde, aure soavi,' the painters had blended cathedral and country. A whole territory lay before the charmed eye, delivered from local tyrants, centralized under the lawful power of purely temporal government. The deeply felt opposition between the new temporal and the old local order may help us to sympathize with the enthusiasm of the people whenever a Madonna was painted in the stilo nuovo. Nicolo Pisani is, I think, the first artist to receive special homage from the community for his famous relievos, in 1260. About 1300, Duccio of Siena, an eye witness of the battle during which the Virgin had spread out her mantle of protection, painted a Madonna which was received by bishop and clergy, governors and people, and was conveyed to the cathedral amid the ringing of all the bells. In his verse-subscription to this painting, the artist treats himself as an equal of the city:

Mater Sancta Dei Sis Senis causa requiei,
Sis Duccio vita te quia pinxit ita.

Holy Mother of God,
Be thou the cause of peace to the Sienese;
Be thou life to Duccio because he painted thee thus.

The relationship between the pope and Raphael or Michelangelo exceeds by far the customary relation between princes and artists in other countries. Even in Venice, the proud patrician city, we read in the Cathedral of St. Mark: 'First contemplate carefully and acknowledge the art and labour of brothers Francesco and Valeric Zuccati, of Venice, then judge.' The painter, being an artisan (artista) himself, and being honoured for painting the symbol of the city's liberty, could represent all the crafts and guilds of his community. He was no isolated, impressionable genius like the artist of the nineteenth century. He was the best man in his craft.[90]

There is one other major figure whom Rosenstock-Huessy discusses in the context of the second clerical revolution: Joachim of Fiore. Joachim taught that there were three ages of the spirit: the age of the Father, which was an age of law and fear; the age of Christ and his apostles, which was one of grace and faith; and the age of the Holy Spirit, which was to be an age of love and liberty and of universal peace, a Sabbath of the Church, under the governance of spiritual intelligences, contemplative monastics dedicated to the service and love of God and humanity. For Rosenstock-Huessy, Joachim stood in the same relation to Francis as John the Baptist to Jesus:

> Joachim forecast the end of the existing form of the Church; the Holy Ghost moved on. In his terms, the Virgin Mary had to conceive a new son by the spirit. This son was a new people, with all the power (potestas) under heaven that was promised by Daniel. Here the people's sovereignty is proclaimed to be a seed of the spirit. The year 1201 begins a new era in the history of the world's salvation, which was to be awaited with the greatest anxiety. The prophet dated the great change from the ancient form of the Church to a new form, to the epoch between 1201 and 1260. In his philosophy of history, Odilo of Cluny's great conception of All Souls is kept alive, but with the additional idea of revolutionary change.[91]

Anyone familiar with Dante's *Divine Comedy* will recall the high esteem in which Dante held Joachim, placing him in paradise with the souls who manifested themselves in the sphere of the sun.[92] Indeed, Dante's political eschatology and the hope he invests in the emperor as ushering in an age of universal peace is thoroughly Joachimite. And while Dante places him in the company of Bonaventura, in real life Bonaventura was highly critical of Joachim. As Margaret Reeves has pointed out, 'he was favoured by four popes, yet denounced by the Cistercian Order as a runaway ... His sanctity guarded his personal reputation when his views on the Trinity were condemned in 1215, yet after "the horrible scandal" of 1255 the Commission of Anagni set up by the pope to examine his works condemned the whole "fundamentum doctrine."'[93] Given the revolutionary implications of his teaching, it can hardly be surprising that he was acclaimed as well as feared and hated. In the twentieth century, the political theorist Eric Voegelin argued in his *New Science of Politics* that Joachim had been largely responsible for promoting the Gnostic heresy of bringing heaven to earth, which Voegelin saw as the root cause of the ideological nightmares of the twentieth century. But whereas Voegelin mistrusted millenarian or chialistic visions of history, believing them to be responsible for murderous rampages, Rosenstock-Huessy saw Joachim as a vital link in the transition from the Petrine and Pauline Churches to the final, 'Johannine Age of Christianity.'[94]

> It was a complete revolution of values, taught by the left wing, the Joachimites, and it prepared the way for Luther . . . After the era of the Church will come an era of the Holy Spirit. We find here the temptation of a change in era so characteristic of every total revolution. Joachim calls the future 'Johannine'; Paul being tied up with Peter in the visible church of Rome, John, the Apostle of charity, is made the patron of the new age of pure spirit. Joachim's writings had so great an influence that other books were forged in his name. An *Evangelium aeternum* was published, around which a strong party of so-called Spirituals, especially monks, gathered. The pope's spiritual sword was no longer acknowledged by the Spirituals as the climax of spiritual life. Preceding Wycliff, Huss and Luther, they, the Spirituals, taught that the clerical functions of the Church bore the name of spiritual improperly, and at best figuratively; that the gift of the Holy Ghost came long before all clerical ministrations; and that next to the famous seven gifts of the Spirit, the free utterances of inspiration would still precede the hierarchy in spiritual rank. It was a complete revolution of values, taught by the left wing, the Joachimites, and it prepared the way for Luther.[95]

For Rosenstock-Huessy, then, this great span of time from Odilo to Luther reached through two revolutions before creating yet a third – what is more widely classified as the Reformation, but which Rosenstock-Huessy very deliberately classified as the German Revolution, thereby emphasizing the importance of the political landscape that transformed one more personal stand against the Church's corruption into a major event that simultaneously formed the basis of what would become one of the most fateful of modern nations and that radically transformed all nations by sparking off a great chain of political reactions against Rome's hegemony, which in turn was a pivotal moment in the formation of all European nations. As for the Renaissance itself, it was, he says, 'a sunset,' thus contradicting the common prejudice that it was a secular outbreak and a new beginning. And its artistic triumph was primarily an expression of the revolutionary impulses that swept artists along in its train:

> The Renaissance is the legitimate outcome of a five-centuries-long effort.
> Its painters and architects and poets translate the great inspirations of

Gregory and Francis of Assisi into secular garb and classical forms. But the landscapes of Raphael's Madonnas, and the background of the Caesaric Judge in Michelangelo's 'Last Judgment,' are translations into humanistic terms of the whole hearted effort of more religious centuries. The cynical humanists of the Quattrocento spoke the last word, not the first. They dissolved, they could not construct. They did for Scholasticism what Goethe did for the Reformation: they secularized its mysteries. By Renaissance art, the Guelphic revolution was made accessible to the agnostic and the snob, and to the educated man of modern Europe.[96]

We have gone to great lengths to present Rosenstock-Huessy's argument about the relationship between Dante and the Gregorian Revolution and to describe where Renaissance painting fit into the general revolutionary wave that created Italy. This is because of the huge importance that art began to play in Europe's self-understanding in the time from Dante to Leonardo and Michelangelo. If, as Rosenstock-Huessy maintains, the aesthetic achievements of Italian artists from that arc of time worked very much in tandem with the two Italian revolutions, the great outbursts of artistic achievement in Germany (and subsequently the Austrian Empire), France, and Russia were also closely associated with their respective revolutions. Though he deeply loved Shakespeare, and though he did refer to Milton as 'the poet *par excellence* of the English revolution' in *Out of Revolution*,[97] he did not say much at all about the revolutionary impetus given by England to the arts or about Britain's contribution to the arts. What he did see as powerful about the English Revolution was its wondrous rhetorical use of Old Testament speech.

In the case of the German Revolution, Rosenstock-Huessy focuses mainly on Goethe and on the relationship between Germany and music. On the importance of music and the Reformation, to support his argument that the Reformation in Germany was a great spur to music – one that had no parallel in any other nation – he cites the English work *Music and Puritanism* (1934),[98] which makes the point that 'the church hymn was born with the German Revolution.' 'The non-Lutheran Protestants did not approve of the use of the original hymns in public worship,' he reminds his readers, adding that in Luther's battle against the priests, the layman had to 'rival, not only the prose of a sermon, but the tunes of the mass, which lie between speech and song.'[99]

Just as, for Rosenstock-Huessy, the Reformation could be summarized by the phrase 'the Church invisible as opposed to the Church visible of Rome,' music was the very expression of the invisible power of the spirit triumphing over the visible power of the Roman Church. And just as the life of the spirit was taken into the professions of everyday life as priests and nuns left their monastic lives *en masse,* music became part of the tapestry of daily life:

> The purified Church replaced pictures by music, bodily pilgrimages by singing. 'Luther sang many millions out of the Catholic Church' is an old saying. The German chorale is unequalled in beauty and variety. The German nation, robbed of its visible ornaments, takes refuge in the world of sound. In German an influential man does not 'set the fashion,' he 'gives the tone' (i.e., the pitch). Music became a politicum, a religious institution in Germany. As in the field of learning, where three centuries were dominated successively by theology, law, and philosophy, so German music has three periods, from Luther to Bach, from Bach to Mozart, and from Beethoven to Wagner and Strauss. 'Music and government are like church and state,' wrote Luther himself. 'Potestas ecclesiastica non impedit politicam potestatem sicut ars canendi non impedit politicam administrationem.' Ecclesiastical power does not hinder political power any more than the art of music hinders the political administration.[100]

For Rosenstock-Huessy, if Lutheran hymns set the ground for a new world of music, it was in its secular form that this found its modern fulfilment, in much the same way that Luther's church invisible – which was Pauline in every intent, including Luther's allusions to himself as St Paul *redivivus*[101] – paved the way for the Johannine Church announced by German philosophers. On the issue of German philosophy, Rosenstock-Huessy tells us that modern German philosophers 'all sacrificed the letter of theology to save the spirit of the Reformation for an enlightened world,' that they 'expanded the Lutheran war-cry of "every Christian a priest" into the philosophical principles of "Every man a bearer of the torch"':[102]

> These philosophers – Lessing, Herder, Fichte, Schelling, Hegel, Feuerbach, Nietzsche – and their lesser colleagues, Fries, Krause, Natorp, etc., were descendants of parsons, or former theologians themselves, and clung to the universality of the theology they inherited. Not one of them could be an empiricist, an adventurer on the ocean of scattered data, as an English thinker could. The Protestant philosopher in Germany had to defend a certain system of values. He stood for the universe, for pure learning about the totality of things.[103]

For Rosenstock-Huessy, just as philosophy became the stream through which the Reformation became modernized, music too often became 'philosophicized.' In this respect he saw Beethoven as 'bridging the gulf between Lutheranism and modernity':

> From Beethoven to Strauss, philosophical music led the way. It is true, Schubert, Schumann, Brahms were faithful to the unphilosophical tradition. Felix Mendelssohn, the Christian descendant of a Jewish philosopher, revived with fervent faith the evangelical Bach, and himself composed the wonderful songs of 'Paulus' or 'Elias.' But in spite of all these other trends, the political and religious force of German music was transferred during the century of liberalism to the heroic, the Promethean music of Beethoven. In the era of individualism, Ludwig van Beethoven could become the very genius of music to every liberal, every individual, every self-made man. Any American or Frenchman who is dried up by the formula of his own nationality takes comfort when he listens to the quartettes of Beethoven. Here the Christian soul of man has expressed in undenominational form the universal secret of the child of the nineteenth century, beyond the limits of class or ideology or economics or nationality.[104]

In contrast to Beethoven, Rosenstock-Huessy saw Wagner as representing 'all the passions, prejudices and heresies of the nineteenth century.'[105] Wagner, he said, wanted to bring together Catholic and Lutheran Germany, but not on the ground of what had been achieved by the German Revolution, which had also affected Catholic reform. Like Nietzsche, whom he cited approvingly, he saw Wagner as a Roman relapse – 'Rome's songs without its words, but with its incense.' For Rosenstock-Huessy, then, Wagner was much as Nietzsche saw him: a kind of dangerous tonic for the debilitated, a surrogate religion. In contrast to Wagner's music with its potpourri of Schopenhauerian philosophy and its politics of 'proletarian anti-capitalism and anti-Semitism,' Haydn, Mozart, Beethoven (again), Bruckner, Wagner's father-in-law Franz Liszt, Johann Strauss, and Mahler were all testaments to how Catholic Austria was able to take the musical legacy of the Reformation and make it *the* common tongue of an empire of disparate peoples.

Rosenstock-Huessy's linkage of music to the overthrow of the Church visible is merely one aspect of his analysis of the German Revolution. At the centre of his analysis is the elevation of the civil servant to a religious position. And the importance he ascribes to the revolutionary role of the High Magistrates in Germany offers, I think, a compelling explanation for why the Reformation first took hold in Germany and not in any of the other European countries that had simultaneously spawned strong personalities seeking to throw off Church corruption.[106]

If Hitler was, for Rosenstock-Huessy, the embodiment of the German overthrow of the fruits of its revolution, Goethe was Germany's poetic fulfilment of that revolution. That can be seen as much in Goethe's life as a civil servant as in *Faust*, and as in *Ilmenau*, a celebration of German forests. Speaking of the woods as 'Germany's most popular institution,' Rosenstock-Huessy writes that 'if the German composers have built the invisible church of music, German poets have glorified the natural scenery of the State: its woodlands. In his greatest political poem, *Ilmenau*, Goethe, the most universal poet of Germany, translated Luther's hopes into secular speech.'[107] Germany deeply mythologizes its forests and makes their preservation intrinsic to its identity – a point that Rosenstock-Huessy takes even further during his discussion of Goethe's *Faust,* when he states: 'the German artisan and his relationship to his raw material, is, in every branch of German craftsmanship, very much akin to the attitude of the forester or the father.'[108] We saw in an earlier chapter how important Goethe's youthful prayer of destiny and hope had been for Rosenzweig as a cipher of the longing of the 'Johannine' modern soul. In his section on Goethe's *Faust*, Rosenstock-Huessy adds the next lines of that same poem, which lend strong support to what – in the context of his discussion of the German Revolution's contribution to the German soul's formation – provides a very neat symmetry between artistry and forestry:

'O high fortune, let me achieve the day's work of my hands. No, these are not empty dreams; these trees, now lifeless sticks, will one day give fruit and shade.' He might not see the results, but the future would bring with it a recurrent life. In this there was no vanity or ambition on his part. Goethe is not thinking of immortality, like a romantic hero. His trees neither will nor shall bear the name Goethe. But in their life he will be represented. Goethe also said: 'He who has not begotten a child or planted a tree is no man.'[109]

That Goethe, in his capacity as a civil servant, formulated this prayer while attempting to educate a prince in Weimar, supports another essential component of Rosenstock-Huessy's analysis – that is, the radically new role of the civil servant that was a consequence of the German Revolution. He takes up the analogy between tending to the forest and tending to the details of social life, and he does so in a way that is richly reminiscent of Goethe's own approach to life. Moreover, Faust's world, as Rosenstock-Huessy also reminds his readers, 'is not Africa nor America, it is the present life of a small German town, with meadows and mountains around it, projected into the Greek classical past and into an ultimate vision of the future':[110]

> To plunge into an objective world which follows its own rules but allows you to serve it, is the aim of the true civil servant. He is a layman, but he has a field (Fach). This objective world of 'fields' is no mechanism: it embraces peasants, trees, animals, craftsmen, arts, sciences. It is growing and organic. It is God's world. You cannot mould it arbitrarily to your shape or in your image. The things of creation shall be carried to their destined goal by the help of man. His best inspiration, his knowledge, his training, have to give up their personal character, their *namedness* or fame, before they can penetrate into matter and make the son greater than the father.
>
> This is not a townsman's vision. In the town a man earns his living by his visible labour, sees what he visibly does, and hears his reputation proclaimed most audibly every day. The civil servant in the remote corner of a wooded mountain belongs to an *invisible order*. Without this moral power, no brain trust can build up a civil service free from graft and the spoils-system.[111]

Rosenzweig wants to emphasize the distinction between Goethe and Luther by having them belong to different Churches; Rosenstock-Huessy is more interested in emphasizing the link between them. Having cited Faust's surveying of his last enterprise – the dredging of a marsh to create not something whose fruits are for himself, but 'a prosperous people's home' – Rosenstock-Huessy continues that for Goethe,

> Man's destination is invisible to himself. To the last, Goethe remains a Lutheran in poetry. Faust cannot see his free land and his free people, but he can hear them like celestial music in his ear. The clicking of spades sounds to him like the chorale of a singing congregation; he knows this is the sacrament of atonement for earth, fallen from its divine destination:
>
> 'The crowds are delving, banking, piling,
>   Earth with itself re – reconciling.'

The poets, even the religious poets, must express themselves in a worldly style. Goethe's Faust is a secular chant: it is the translation of Luther into the vernacular. Goethe concentrated in his work the wealth of the German language . . . Literature was, so to speak, his doctor's gown, as Luther had replaced his monk's hood by the preaching of God's word.[112]

Rosenstock-Huessy continues the equation between Luther and Goethe by taking his lead from Wilhelm Rudolf's point that the word *hoch* (high) – a term used to pit the authority of the state and the university in Germany against the visible Church of Rome – became the keystone of Luther's metaphysics, his 'most important word,' playing a 'similar role to that of the "eternal" among his concepts of time.'[113]

If Luther realized his dream of having a Bible in every evangelical home, and if his reform provoked further reform even within the Catholic Church, it was, for Rosenstock-Huessy, Goethe – like Lessing, whose *Nathan the Wise* was a source of non-denominational inspiration – who was able to take the Lutheran message behind the Catholic wall separating Germany. In this respect, while Rosenstock-Huessy sees art as generally subordinate to religion in its capacity to form humanity (though as noted earler, his analysis of Homer suggests that the Greeks were an exception), he nevertheless sees that art can sometimes carry a message into regions where religion cannot enter, precisely *because* its form is capable of preserving and conveying a teaching while transcending the barriers of disputation that are retained when presented through religious symbols. This, for him, was the case with Goethe's *Faust*. The Lutheran message of salvation through faith alone and of the opposition to final forms of spiritual enclosure – the restlessness that runs through *Faust* – could be well appreciated by German Catholics when they were presented in the life of Faust rather than in the theology of Luther.[114]

The transposition from religion to art in the movement from Luther to Goethe as part of the ongoing process of the European revolutions was furthered by the French Revolution. So Rosenstock-Huessy saw it. We have already seen how, for him, the French Revolution was both a continuation of the revolutionary spirit of Christianity and a humanistic reaction *against* Christianity. That revolution's love for and debt to Hellas was carried on by the artistic revival it had generated during its self-construction. As noted earlier, Rosenstock-Huessy argued that the corruption of French Christianity had created a new faith – a faith in the mind's power to rid peoples of superstition, in the power of enlightened men to access clear and distinct ideas and thereby replace priests. The new priest was an intellectual, a philosopher, not in the German sense – that is, not a 'disguised theologian,' as Rosenstock-Huessy described German philosophers – but rather someone who reflected on his own passions and who was 'sincere enough' to apply the force of those passions to his 'creative life.'[115] Rosenstock-Huessy does not say this, but I would note here that French philosophers, from Rousseau to Camus and Sartre (unlike German philosophers), have often also been novelists – an indication, I think, of what the French expect from their philosophers – that they be artists.

But if the new priest was the intellectual/*philosophe*, he was not working merely on his own behalf – as Marxist revolutionaries would remind all and sundry. The essential social situation of France mapped out so clearly by Montesquieu in his *Spirit of the Laws* was that of a productive class without political power tethered to a non-productive but politically empowered alliance. Thus Rosenstock-Huessy argues that the 'creation of a group of intellectual leaders [was] the *conditio sine qua non* of the Revolution . . . An intellectual class had to be trained to help the industrial classes' to create 'the moral atmosphere' that would concur with 'the economic facts.'[116] The elevation of this new class of inspired individuals, and the scorn of birthright and accidental privilege, was brought to the stage by Caron de Beaumarchais in his 1778 play *The Marriage of Figaro*, the final chorus of which proclaimed: 'Incense for twenty Kings / Vanishes with their death, / But Voltaire is immortal.'[117] The ideas of the *philosophes* had become so widely supported and the general faith in the *écrivain*'s social role so strongly accepted that the authorities not only failed to halt the spread of Beaumarchais's subversion but even failed in their attempts to imprison him. Indeed,

> the poet received his pension from the King's privy purse. *Figaro's Wedding* was acted in the presence of the whole Cabinet of the King, after six months of delay, on August 17. At Figaro's observation: 'Since they cannot humiliate *l'esprit*, the genius, they take their revenge by torturing him' – the whole audience burst out in a frenzy of applause.
>
> The climax was reached when, on August 19, 1785, the author was invited to the little palace of Trianon, built in the style of Rousseauism by the Queen, Marie Antoinette. There, in the disguise of shepherds and shepherdesses, the royal family had taken up the fashion of natural life and abolition of privilege. In this environment, Louis XVI, King of France, and Caron de Beaumarchais, banker, citizen, sat down together and saw the other play written by this *enfant terrible*: his *Barber of Seville*. The main part in that play, Rosine, was acted with great charm by the Queen herself, Marie Antoinette. That evening the Bastille was destroyed.[118]

If Rousseau and Voltaire had provided the bourgeoisie with its moral vision to sweep away the rotting vestiges of the past, the *écrivains* supplied the inspiration to inject the present with faith and meaning. That the revolution was 'highly theatrical,' full of 'dramatic events' (as Rosenstock-Huessy says in the opening line of the chapter on the French Revolution),[119] that one gesture after another became a staged historical event, was fully in keeping with the new audience that the theatres of Paris had prepared to become the nation. For Rosenstock-Huessy, this was precisely the purpose of Parisian revolutionary theatre:

> not only did the actors try to play 'the mad day,' but the madness of the Revolution was embodied in an actress who had to play the Goddess of Reason on the Field of Mars in 1794. It was an actor who first wore the costume of a sans-culotte. An actor and an actress infused into the French Revolution a bit of histrionic gesture, ardour of declamation, inspiration and verve. The French Revolution introduced the clapping of hands from the theatre into public life, where it had been unknown before. One wave had to flow from the ocean of theatrical passion into the newly organized nation to foment its new covenant; and it did . . . The theatre changed the audience; it communicated the sentiments of Daphnis and Chloe to the King and Queen of France and the passions of the Great to the *roturier*, the business man. The stage was a training camp for the new equality of citizenship.[120]

In keeping with a revolution whose vanguard gave it its props and grand gestures and articulated its meaning, was the intelligentsia's overhaul of a great church into the 'Panthéon' – 'the place sacred to all gods and geniuses.'[121]

Every textbook on nationalism notes that modern nationalism originated in the French Revolution. But what Rosenstock-Huessy emphasizes – which is no less important for the modern's sense of national self-construction – is how the French invented the idea that 'a language needs a permanent centre of unification' and that that centre is found in literature. Comparing the old concept of nation – 'a geographical subdivision within the Church' – with the modern nation, he wrote that

> a nation was a group of scholars, doctors, and princes at one of the Christian Councils. At the great councils of the fifteenth century the French nation was led by the University of Paris. Now, in the eighteenth century,

the nation had to be organized outside the Church, outside Christianity, in the natural world: the doctors of theology were replaced by the writers and expounders of philosophy, and the estates of France – King, clergy, and nobility – by the Freemasons of reason. These elements formed the 'nation.' Wherever modern nationalism in Europe succeeded in founding a national state within natural borders, literature and the lodge were at its back. The modern nation is therefore not a product of nature but of literature, not a body of mere inhabitants but of listeners and readers of modern philosophy and science.[122]

With France's lead, 'a nation is not a geographical or racial fragment. Nations are divided from barbarian tribes by the one reality of Inspiration. Where a nation organizes its inspiration into an endless stream of literary production it becomes civilized, it counts, it belongs to humanity in the sense of the humanism of the French Revolution.'[123] The messianic purpose of French nationalism thus found itself accompanied by a purpose of civilizing the world. (For Rosenstock-Huessy, 'European civilization is the result of the French revolution,'[124] and the 'world-wide purpose and programme of the French Revolution' was 'to civilize Europe.')[125] Furthermore, the great writers of the nations led each nation into the procession of a gloriously unified civilization – and here, Rosenstock-Huessy would cite Sainte-Beuve's remark that 'no one is a man' who does not know the masterpieces of French and foreign literature.[126] Civilizing means, above all, teaching people to read and write – for the 'illiterate is a poor devil in this enlightened world.'[127] Rosenstock-Huessy's point about literature and nations is supported by the fact that today, the Italian and German governments present themselves to the world through the Dante Aligheri and Goethe societies, cultural/linguistic offices names after their respective national poets. That in the nineteenth century, Shakespeare was repackaged as the English national poet and Cervantes became the voice of Spanish literary genius, further confirms the influence that France's equating of a people with its literature had on other European nations. Of course, the great exception to the rule of the national poet was France itself. But how could France, so full of geniuses, settle on a solitary national poet? It owed its geniuses to a plurality of *les Lumières*.[128]

To put it mildly, France's Napoleonic expansions somewhat problematized this vision of things – for while France could portray itself as the carrier of enlightened ideals to liberate European peoples from their imperial and monarchical masters, Goya's immortal mezzotints of the brutality of the Napoleonic invasions tell another story entirely. And while the relatively young Hegel had welcomed the world soul on a horse, Napoleon had succeeded not so much in bringing the Enlightenment into Germany as in sowing the fateful seeds of German nationalism and laying the foundations for the most explosive of future hostilities.

Nevertheless, just as the nation had been transformed by means of its new associations with liberty and equality, and had given rise to a new entity, nationalism, which at least through the nineteenth century stood in the closest relationship to liberalism and democracy, the meaning of art had undergone a total transformation in its social significance. And that shift stood in the closest connection to the role that reason had played in preparing the ground for the new enlightened class and its social goals. As Rosenstock-Huessy observes, mere reason does not suffice to create the social solidarity a nation needs. The people need to be awoken by the artist, and the artist, to awaken them, must be inspired. Thus what previously had been attributed to the Holy Ghost became the inspired individual.[129] But inspiration means above all awakening oneself to new sensations, to the latest discoveries, inventions, events, artistic creations:

> The art of the nineteenth century is quite different from the art of other periods, of the Italian Renaissance, for example. The use of the same word for both is highly misleading. In the liberal art of the 'French' century in Europe, Reason invested all its faith. The fate and destiny of Reason were trusted to the process of sensuous revelation. A manifest logic seemed to govern the sensations experienced by one genius after the other. One blood, it was supposed, runs through the veins of all the artists who are members of the cult. The pleasures, the excitements, the fashions, the curiosities of genius, are no longer considered to be casual impressions of private individuals. They follow each other – from Chenier to Anatole France, from Beethoven to Strauss, from Byron to Wilde, from Leopardi to d'Annunzio – with the trans-personal logic of evolution.[130]

Thus Rosenstock-Huessy saw it as no mere accident that a society whose sense of reason was essentially scientistic would also have to take its sense of revelation from those who were willing to be as indulgent to the senses as the philosophers were to the mind. We as a species cannot simply give ourselves entirely over to reason, because we are flesh and blood, not merely admixtures of extension (machine) and cognitive functions (the soul, supposedly), as Descartes's bifurcated self of object and subject had portrayed 'man.'

That master of modernity and its paradoxes, Rousseau, had brilliantly encapsulated in his life and writing the need for the unity of reason and passion. He had done so by declaring himself morally superior to any artist, warning of the dangers of the theatre (while composing operas); or to any scientist, complaining that moderns were losing themselves in the machine world (while being a practising botanist). His self was whole but also deeply disturbed – Cartesianism and Rousseauism, says Rosenstock-Huessy, dry out the soul and reduce man to 'a bundle of nerves.'[131] The world that established the cult of the genius and that holds out faith in delivery through scientific progress is the same one that is orienting its citizens each day into the world by bombarding them with disconnected daily alarms classified as 'news.' Hegel had equated reading the morning newspaper with saying prayers – a fascinating equivalence, for it shows precisely the modern faith and its limitation:

> Reason, abstract and unreal, without roots in the soil, without rhythm in its movements, cannot govern its world without submitting to the directing power of sensation. The titillation of our sense of novelty is expensive and ruinous, because world, facts, truth and values lose their roots in the timeless when they are made to depend upon being rediscovered from time to time. Under the dictatorship of Reason, man begins to live like a solitary and one-celled animal. This unicellular life can get nowhere except by eating and swallowing. Multicellular life can depend upon older achievements without eating and digesting them. The modern society of the nineteenth century kills everything which cannot be swallowed in the form of news and sensations. It is unicellular. Now civilization does not form visible cells; its cells consist of generations, ages, periods. The repressive and outstanding feature of the age of Reason is its 'single-aged,' one-generation character. Such an age may go on for two hundred years; but it will always remain a one-generation affair as long as its values depend on reproduction in the form of novelty.[132]

Thus, too, the Age of Reason found its antidote, correlate, and ultimately its reinforcement in a greater (and highly dangerous) monism through its valorization of passion. Robespierre wanted a free and virtuous people to swear their allegiance to the Supreme Being, but this cult did not last, and only a small group can really love reason.

And it was passion, not reason, that made revolution possible. Thus Rosenstock-Huessy correctly points out that while the term 'revolutionary' was used for the first time by the French to describe 'the men who stood *with their reason on the side of the revolution!*'[133] the 'God of the French Revolution [was] the God of passion.'[134] He also underscores how central the emphasis on passion – 'passionate feeling, passionate love, passionate creation' – becomes in French literature, in particular for its understanding of the free man. This emphasis was but the continuation of the revolution, fuelled by a passion for freedom and equality the likes of which had never been known on such a scale; it was also evidence of hatred for every obstacle to freedom's fulfilment: 'Sainte-Beuve described it when he said: "Whereas the classical writers wrote only with the higher and purely intellectual part of their being, today the conditions of the time force the writer to wrest from his nature all and everything that it can sell." "I must express my century," said Balzac.'[135]

What Rosenstock-Huessy sees – correctly, in my view – is that the same monistic process at work in the modern elevation of the sciences (as of the arts) and in the endless search for scientific progress found itself mirrored in the constant array of exhibitions and new schools of art and poetry that appeared throughout the nineteenth and twentieth centuries. This was all part of the same endless journey across space, indifferent to time, with all times collapsed into one space-time matrix, as people searched constantly for sensation and the pursuit of pleasure and novelty. Time was no longer the requisite component of cultivation and care, of what Rosenstock-Huessy considered the most important creative component of human existence, incarnation; it was merely a condition of constancy and surprise. The world now required a diet of daily news; it required new art movements; it required the latest fashion, the latest titillation, the latest discovery, the latest piece of gossip. Once such a mentality begins coursing through society, 'either time is a chain of surprises or it breaks down into a helpless conservatism.'[136]

The French Revolution had seen the elevation of an enlightened class that was able to create the moral environment to accompany the social and economic reality of the bourgeoisie. It succeeded to such an extent that literature became the key to a nation's genius. That being so, the Russian Revolution tells the story of a nation that did not follow the path of having its civilization 'reflect' its social and political struggles, but rather whose 'political life began by detour via culture' and concluded by 'practically abolishing literature' as 'the statistician superseded the novelist' and the poet became but 'a man "in the air."''[137] 'In Europe,' says Rosenstock-Huessy, 'the parties are founded by corporative and social interests. These groups elect and found their organs. In Russia it was the press and the organs of literature which called new parties into life and enabled them to exist.'[138] And whereas the intolerable obstacles to the French commercial classes and *les écrivains* made a political drama of every moment in the wresting of political power away from the first two estates to themselves, the Russian Revolution was, *inter alia*, characterized by its determination to blow away the myths of the French Revolution. And what the French intelligentsia and revolutionaries had set such store on – individual rights, individual freedom and equality, laws, a rational supreme Being, inspiration and genius unsullied by superstition – to the Russian revolutionaries was so much bourgeois nonsense. The one thing the French revolutionaries neglected altogether, and what was most accentuated in the Russian Revolution, was what Rosenstock-Huessy called 'recurrent life' as opposed to 'individual life.' The emphasis on production and 'the material base' was the ongoing link between Marxism and the Russian revolutionaries, one far stronger than the diagnosis of capitalism in crisis given by Marx, which had nothing to do with Russia's social or economic conditions and even less to do with a barely existing capitalist or proletariat class. But it did have a small, dedicated class that had fed off European ideas of progress since their European inception. And it was the extraordinary importance of this class that led Rosenstock-Huessy to say that 'the history of Russian literature is of more importance for the evolution of Russia than the history of any other literature for its own nation.'[139]

Literature was from its inception in Russia primarily political.[140] Western erudition, says Rosenstock-Huessy, was a means of social advancement, and leaders such as Peter the Great (whose reforms were also made possible by the foreign education of his brightest administrators) and Catherine II used theatre and/or essays and journals to advance their reforms. This didn't mean that writing was safe from political surveillance – on the contrary, 'the existence of censorship had led to a real art of reading and writing between the lines.'[141] Nevertheless, while the czars encouraged the accumulation and dissemination of Western ideas to advance Russia (Rosenstock-Huessy reminds his readers that Catherine II corresponded with Voltaire and Rousseau),[142] the intelligentsia with their literary productions – periodicals, magazines, and journals – were an important agent of the even smaller ruling class. But with the quashing of the Decembrist revolt in 1825, which included the hanging of the poet Kondraty Ryleev, the banishment of Pushkin to his estate, and the exile of other men of letters, Czarist Russia had opened a national wound that would only be healed by revolution; the same had occurred in England with the murders of Beckett and More, in France with the slaughter of the Huguenots, and in central Europe with the burning of Huss. What Rosenstock-Huessy referred to as the czars' success since 1697 in Russia was deeply indebted to 'Western techniques.' And the throwing away of the 'freedom of thought, the very instrument that had founded St. Petersburg, the bureaucracy and the army' created a burning hatred from the class that identified with the Decembrist martyrs.

In *The Idiot*, Dostoevsky had famously remarked that beauty would save the world. But he was not talking of the aesthetic beauty of the sensualist or the Platonic beauty of the Ideal. He was talking of what he saw as the incomparable beauty of the overwhelming radiance of love that is not broken but rather strengthened and purified by suffering. That the wives of the exiled Decembrists followed their husbands to Siberia and voluntarily shared their suffering was, for Rosenstock-Huessy, an illustration the kind of beauty that comes out of suffering. The persecution of intellectuals for their willingness to challenge the government had the opposite effect of what the ruling powers had hoped. Far from stopping reading, writing, and thinking, it made the writers and readers think more extreme thoughts. Turgenev 'chooses for himself the name of Nihilist. The innovators had found their shibboleth. Nihil, i.e., nothing, of the old loyalties was to be kept. A complete break was the only condition for a new future.'[143] The gap between the social imagination of the intelligentsia and that of the ruling classes only intensified the resolve of the former: 'no progress in agriculture, no school reform, no constitution offered by the government in later years, could influence the future essentially, because it could not reach, and even less change, the picture of Russia which the revolutionaries had in mind.'[144] Turgenev, in 1867, full of despair, wrote *Smoke*. Nothing had come of the emancipation of the serfs, and he declared the absolute bankruptcy of 'Fathers and Sons,' parties and groups of the better classes of society. He was right. The *'gebildete Gesellschaft,'* the upper classes, were rotten. The intelligentsia had embraced the most radical theories coming out of Europe, to the surprise of Marx, who had always thought that socialism and communism were doctrines best suited to the most industrially advanced societies. In works such as Nikolai Chernyshevsky's *What Is to Be Done* and (again) Turgenev's *Virgin Soil*, the Russian intelligentsia advanced 'a socialism without a capitalist society, a Marxism without a proletariat,' an appeal 'for the intelligentsia *to go among the people*.'[145]

What is essential for understanding the power of Russia's intelligentsia was not simply the imagination they harboured – there has been no dearth of radical imagination in post–Second World War universities in North America and Europe, for example – but their willingness to forsake everything:

> individual conditions, wealth, family, creed . . . Very often they acted as hangman and executioner to their own material interests. Their own families, their own futures, their own intellectual treasures and needs, counted for nothing. Before murdering the Czar or the Grand Duke, they committed moral suicide and became emancipated from all earthly interests. The code radiating from people like Lenin or Savinkov was the code of those who died to themselves ten times over because they clung to their mission. More fanatical than the Spanish Inquisition, they were not interested in their own salvation.[146]

The willingness to die for the future is one of life's greatest powers for leaving an indelible impression on the future. It also meant that the revolutionaries were utterly fearless. And this fearlessness was reflected in how they looked at the French Revolution – with a mixture of respect, as a kind of prelude to the real event to which they were committed, and contempt for its bourgeois limitations. Even the loss of civilization, Rosenstock-Huessy points out, was to the Russan revolutionaries nothing to fear. For civilization, along with liberty, was a bourgeois façade.[147] With the success of Bolshevism, the arts would become a mere matter of class consciousness, a position that took Marx's theory a step beyond Marx himself, who loved the classics of civilization. But in the final throes of pre-revolutionary Russia, it produced Tolstoy and Dostoevsky, two writers who according to Rosenstock-Huessy 'gave back to the West a knowledge of the human soul which makes all French, English and German literature wither in comparison.'[148] Dostoevsky's genius, for him, lay in his ability to extricate 'the types of men who would become the standard bearers of the revolution. To read Dostoevski is to read the psychic history of the Russian Revolution.'[149] Of course, Dostoevsky had tried to direct Russia toward an even more radical solution, a pan-Slavic Church–State fusion (the State becoming Church, as Zossima formulates it in *The Brothers Karamazov*), than that of the nihilists, whom he depicted with astonishing understanding and loathing. But what primarily interested Rosenstock-Huessy about Dostoevsky was that he

> lays the corner-stone for a new building of humanity. In the new house, the prodigal son becomes the basic element. Hell is opened. Mankind, always frightened by hell before, now resolves to bear its presence consciously. The class consciousness of the proletariat, a favourite topic of Marxism, finds its explanation in the fact that the uprooted outlawed stranger, the idiot, the proletarian, have nothing but their consciousness . . .
>
> The revolutionary pure and simple is bodied forth in these novels as an eternal form of mankind.
>
> The Russian Revolution, in proclaiming its permanence, eternalizes the revolutionary, too. The Russians try to use this side of our potentialities for solving the universal economic problem. The destroying features of life impersonated in the 'revolutionary' shall form the basis for a new society which will avoid the casual destructions that came from concealing or ignoring altogether this element of our nature . . . The courage to incorporate a part of hell-fire itself into society and the readiness to use dynamite as the only way to a relative security, is the answer given by Communism to Dostoevski's disclosure of hell within our own bodies.[150]

What Tolstoy adds to this – so suggests Rosenstock-Huessy – is the theme 'of the majesty of the people, not the nation in the Western sense,' but the people as akin to the 'simple Moujik [who] reacts like the ocean, the cornfield and the forest, because it is patient, passive and obedient.'[151]

The French Revolution had been one of individual genius; the Russian Revolution had been, instead, of the mass. Likewise, the Russian revolutionaries had not been interested in crafting wondrous philosophies about the dignity of man. Indeed, there was not one Russian revolutionary philosopher whose contribution to world philosophy came even close to matching those thinkers in France and Germany whose thoughts directly shaped or were shaped by the French Revolution. Given how Marx and his Russian heirs viewed philosophy as merely an ideological mask, this should not surprise us. Thus, too, Kant's view of man as *noumenon* and phenomenon – as a self whose nobility and heights find formulation in the 'the starry skies above me and the moral law within me' – well expresses a view (albeit expressed by a German philosopher) that was tailor-made for the mood and aspirations of the French Revolution. But that same view was utterly irrelevant for the generation of 'martyrs' that wanted to take modern Russia's inert masses and use them to build the world's future with concrete and steel. Such a task would require a unity, 'a mechanisation of nature, with chanting choruses of thousands, with loudspeakers all over the place, with men themselves changed into drops in the ocean or into leaves of grass by the most refined technique mass-hypnotism.'[152] Those wanting to make *that* world were to be uncompromising in the sacrifices they demanded. Those who believed in the importance of the Russian Revolution would never look at literature the same way. And indeed, what we often hear referred to as the 'cultural wars' is really a revamping of the anti-bourgeois emphases of the Russian revolutionaries, except that it has been turned against those who perceive the importance of literature through the grand optic of genius and literature – that is, through the French Revolution.

When Rosenzweig looked at art, his primary concern was to illustrate the Jewish life that artists express extrinsically through rituals and feasts as an interiorization of forces. His position has its counterpoint in Rosenstock-Huessy's analysis of art as an incarnatory power. We might briefly return to Homer by saying that he founded a new type so important in the West that our civilization is inconceivable without muses who not only entertain but also act as seismographs and prophets, as visionaries and bacchic leaders. But it is the interpenetration of art and revolution that has revolutionized the arts themselves and their role in our society and that has made artists the spokespeople of revolutions. In the past twenty years or so there has been much talk of art and its relationship to utopia – of the artist as appellant of the kingdom to come. Rosenstock-Huessy was wary of elevating art too high, precisely *because* of its siren-like powers; nevertheless, he was sensitive to art's real importance as a calling from the agony and suffering of unbearable burdens of past and present to the future Messianic age that was God's promise.

13 Beyond the Prophets of Modernity: Rosenstock-Huessy and Rosenzweig on Nietzsche and Marx

Among the moderns, two men – Nietzsche and Marx – tower above all others as prophets calling for the fashioning of new types of human beings.[1] So it is no surprise that for Rosenstock-Huessy and Rosenzweig, Marx and Nietzsche were by far the most important prophets of their age. That they were both so radically opposed to any kind of transcendence did not make them the slightest bit less eschatological or less driven by a messianic view of life, even if neither was particuarly aware of the eschatological tradition and how they related to it. As has been suggested throughout this book, for both Rosenstock-Huessy and Rosenzweig, transcendence was a Greek trope that had little to do with genuine Redemption. The fact, then, that Marx and Nietzsche were so 'this-sided' and so opposed to a 'God' who was merely the cipher of alienated humanity (Marx) or an otherworldly vampire draining the life out of us (Nietzsche) in no way made Rosenzweig or Rosenstock-Huessy alien to them. On the contrary, in *The Christian Future – or The Modern Mind Outrun*, Rosenstock-Huessy held that Nietzsche and Marx represented a far deeper connection with the messianic aspirations and eschatological orientation of the early twentieth century in general, than nineteenth-century Christian theologians, who were embarrassed to talk about the Last Judgment and who made themselves irrelevant by concerning themselves with morals (who needs theologians for that?) and lives of Jesus.[2]

In his still untranslated *Das Alter der Kirche* (The Age of the Church), Rosenstock-Huessy devoted a chapter to Marx and Nietzsche titled 'The Heart of the World,' in which he declared that it was senseless to take Marx (much like Nietzsche) as an isolated theorist; rather, he had to be seen as a cipher of need and prophecy.[3] Both Marx and Nietzsche, he said, had listened to the heart of the world and had found it cruel and full of terror. Marx had heard the terror of the violence against the dispossessed and disinherited from above, and thanks to socialism, millions of proletarians had become real human beings. Nietzsche, conversely, had heard the unbred mob devouring the spirit from below.[4] It was, said Rosenstock-Huessy, largely thanks to Nietzsche *and* socialism that the generation had survived the Great War and found a future worth living for. In the same vein, he added that Germans would *all* be as 'spiritually atrophied and incurably poisoned' as its nationalists were if not for Marx and Nietzsche.[5] At different times he would argue that Marx and Nietzsche, far from representing the Antichrist, were genuine Christians ready to forgo personal gain in an attempt to realize a future in which the powers of life and human beings would receive their full – and divine – expression.[6]

Rosenstock-Huessy's engagement with Marx and Nietzsche was elaborate and varied, and though he is completely unknown today among scholars of Nietzsche and Marx, he was one of the more interesting interpreters of those two thinkers, having passionately engaged with both throughout his life. Among philosophers and poets, only Goethe was quoted more often than Nietzsche by Rosenstock-Huessy, and it was Nietzsche's promise of a *Gay Science* that he took as a fitting conclusion to *Out of Revolution*. And insofar as his project was closely bound up with revolution, it is not surprising that he engaged so often and so comprehensively with Marx, from his 1914 lectures on the state, in which he thoroughly analysed Marx, through to one of his last public lecture series, The Four Disangelists. Much less on both thinkers is to be found in Rosenzweig, who was, let it be added, affected by both, though much more by Nietzsche than by Marx.

In an early notebook entry, Rosenzweig stated that when he read Nietzsche, he himself was still left hungering after his own path. 'You can't build anything on Nietzsche, as you might on Goethe or nature. Who can possibly be a disciple of Nietzsche, base anything on him? He is neither a foundation, nor all-embracing as nature. He is a scaler of heights and therefore lonely. Who dares follow him? Who has enough conceit for that?'[7] In Nietzsche, Rosenzweig emphasized that that here 'was one man who knew his own life and his own soul like a poet, and obeyed their voice like a holy man, and who was for all that a philosopher.'[8] Later, when Rosenzweig announced that he was writing *The Star of Redemption*, he would again acknowledge Nietzsche's greatness, along with Kant's.[9] In *The Star* itself, he would present Nietzsche's act of self-assertion against philosophy's totalizing claims as one of the steps on the way to the decisive new fusion of philosophy and theology – a precursor to Rosenzweig's recognition that the meta-ethical is a fundamental bloc of the real. Regarding those parts of Nietzsche's thought that Nietzsche himself held so precious – the Dionysian, blond beast, superman, and eternal return – he would say that they simply did not speak to his generation (though some of that was precisely what made Nietzsche attractive to fascists and National Socialists). Yet he also pointed to the fanatical elements of Nietzsche, unfavourably contrasting him with Goethe. Richard A. Cohen in his chapter on Rosenzweig versus Nietzsche excellently grasped what was at stake: 'Nietzsche is too young and too old for Rosenzweig. He is too young in his rebellion against philosophy, which is a rebellion too insistent on himself and himself alone. Peter Pan. But he is too old for life and the love of the neighbour, too demanding of a future far far away, a leap and not a bridge, lightning and thunder but not light and wisdom.'[10]

For Rosenzweig, Nietzsche was the follower of Goethe's prayer to destiny. That prayer pointed to two dangers, which Goethe managed to overleap: that of the sinner 'who prays for anything,' and that of the zealot who prays for too far away:

> The piety of the prayer to one's own destiny borders directly on the prayer of the sinner who presumes he may pray for anything, and on the prayer of the zealot, who, for the sake of the faraway one, which the moment of prayer shows him as necessary, thinks except this one, he is forbidden everything, everything nearest. Goethe did not slip down either of these slopes; he passed through – 'Let someone do the same!' A little illustrated notice is set up on the ridge: following the example of Zarathustra's decline and disappearance, it shows how one can become an immoralist who breaks all the tablets and a tyrant who does violence to his neighbour as to himself for the sake of the second nearest, or to his friends for the sake of his new friends – sinner and zealot in one person. The little notice henceforth warns every traveller who has climbed up to the ridge against wanting to follow Goethe's path a second time, with hopeful trust in his own footsteps, without the wings of faith and love, a pure son of the earth.[11]

But despite such criticism, there was a remarkable twist in Rosenzweig's interpretation of Nietzsche that Rosenstock-Huessy would take up and develop at length throughout his numerous meditations on Nietzsche. The great atheist and Antichrist was seen by Rosenzweig as encountering the living God through his exasperated cry: 'If God existed, how could I bear not to be God.'[12] Nietzsche's valorization of divine freedom – the essence of the living God – was, for Rosenzweig, symptomatic of Nietzsche's having broken out of the limits of philosophical thinking, which at best had rendered God but a meaningless moment within the totality of the All, which had been the real object (according to Rosenzweig) of philosophical thinking for two millennia. Nietzsche, said Rosenzweig, had been the first philosopher to stand eye to eye with the living God: 'The first real human being among the philosophers was also the first who beheld God face to face – even if it was only in order to deny him. For that proposition is the first philosophical denial of God in which God is not indissolubly tied to the world.'[13] In other words, for Rosenzweig, Nietzsche was a negative theologian, and it was this act of the negative – a negation of the would-be God, the pretender God that paved the way for the positive revival of the theology of Judaism – that Rosenzweig undertook. However we dress it, though, the fact is that Rosenzweig's interest in and deployment of Nietzsche always revolved around seeing himself as belonging to the eternal people whereas Nietzsche was a pagan and, his protestations notwithstanding, a Christian, however sympathetic he was to European Jews, and however opposed to anti-Semites (though in the *Antichrist*, his anti-Christianity flipped over into anti-Semitism, in just the manner that Rosenstock-Huessy believed typified the pagan).[14] Nevertheless, insofar as Nietzsche's attack on Platonism was an attack on the very Idealist metaphysics that have become so ubiquitous in the modern world, Rosenzweig was, as we have suggested, able to momentarily team up with him to clear a pathway for talking about the living God.

Rosenzweig's interest in Marx was far more peripheral. He is mentioned neither in *The Star* nor in any of the other key works of his own system, and he is also omitted from the index of Glatzer's collection. Marx does appear in *Hegel und der Staat*, where he is viewed as the most important member of the Hegelian School, as one who takes the master onto side roads before returning him to the main road of history. More significant, though, is that he says Marx 'brought Hegel's system of human community to a point, where it really received form'; furthermore, 'not until Marx was "the great thought of immanence" really carried through.' Rosenzweig compared Marx with Selma Lagerlöf, the very writer whose work was being discussed on that fateful

Leipzig night in 1913. The comparison, though, was at Marx's expense. For Marx had left matters as a mere imitation of the Church.[15] Rosenzweig did not dwell on his judgment, yet it is well worth dwelling on.

There is a Leonard Cohen song, 'Anthem' (on the album *The Future*), that powerfully albeit completely unintentionally captures the essential point that Rosenzweig is making about the Church. It is also the essence of why Levinas is a Rosenzweigian and not a Marxist. 'There is,' sings Cohen, 'a crack in everything / That's how the light gets in.' The Hegelian system of immanence has no crack – which is why, from Rosenzweig's position, it is Godless and faithless. The faithful have been 'cracked' and chipped, wounded and broken, and thus opened up to Redemption. Indeed, without that crack there can be no Redemption. For love is not *sui generis*, it must come from outside; and being cracked and wounded and so on is life's way of forcing us to open ourselves to love's extra radiance. But Hegel has no need of this – once he discovered the Absolute, he dropped his early theological love affair with love. The great triumph of the system is that it already has everything – with time it will dialectically unfold, but nothing gets in that is not already embryonically there. Marx, like the left Hegelians generally, hated Hegel's panlogicism, but that does not mean he avoided it. And this is the real point of the comparison between Lagerlöf's faith and Marx's faith. Marx insisted over and over that he was a scientist and that the fate of the capitalist mode of production was encoded in the formula of commodity production and thus that world bourgeois society would collapse under its own contradictions. Rosenzweig did not need to observe the Russian Revolution to know that the kingdom it sought would not be stormed that way. He simply had no reason to believe that there was some kind of necessary connection between socialism as a solution to the crises of capitalism and the Russian Revolution. He also had no reason to accept that bypassing the nation was a better idea in Marx than in Hegel; thus, just as Hegel's major deficiency as a thinker of the state was that he did not equip us to fathom the fundamental needs and direction of the Germans – needs and direction that stretched from Bismarck to the Great War – Marx's weakness was that he failed to grasp the power and meaning of the nation.[16] Finally, Rosenzweig appreciated that Marx's addition to Hegel was the substitution of society for the state – but for Rosenzweig, Marx remained as imprisoned by the same Rousseauian dialectic as his master.[17]

Marx also comes up in Rosenzweig's *Introduction to the Academic Edition of Hermann Cohen's Jewish Writings*, where he criticizes Marx and

Lasalle for taking up the idea of the messianic and then depriving it of any sense of being a gift of grace, by naturalizing it (i.e., turning it into a drive) as socialism.[18] And in *On Jewish History*, he critically contrasts Marx with Judaism. There, he contends that the Jew is both an aristocrat and a revolutionary, whereas the pagan is merely an aristocrat and the Christian merely a revolutionary. The revolutionary, he says, speaks the *old law* but with the mouth of a prophet. The Jew cannot simply be a socialist, and he must also cease to be a Marxist if he is to be authentically what he is. Moreover, for Rosenzweig – and here he expresses a point that Rosenstock-Huessy will develop in far more detail – Marxism does not really grasp revolution because it does not go deep enough into the motives of revolution: 'The World revolution of 1918 is *un* Marxist, even in Russia. It is doubt, indignation, in short *genuine* revolution. Marx stands in it exactly as isolated as an imperialist among aristocrats of blood.'[19]

As suggested earlier, one metaphysical inheritance that Marx took over from Hegel was his insistence that the real was grounded not in faith but in knowledge. For Hegel, moral and religious faith in something beyond knowledge had been the quick fix for those contemporaries like Schleirermacher, Jacobi, and Schelling and even (as he argued at length in *Faith and Knowledge*) for Fichte and Kant, who had failed to grasp the Absolute through 'the labour of the concept.' In just the same way for Marx, socialism was not an act of faith but an act of historic necessity. Yet as Marxist-Leninists framed every emotional/ psychological/ontological social appeal around the language of class struggle and the goal of communism, Marxists found themselves forced more and more relentlessly to reach into a deeper, more archaic stock of cultural appeals for forming consciences and engendering sacrificial acts of solidarity. Perhaps not surprisingly, the Italian Marxist Antonio Gramsci – who had welcomed the voluntarist strain within Marxism because it freed it from its dogmatic mechanism – stated explicitly that socialism was a religion.[20] What else is one to make of the turn in Marxist-Leninist discourses, which for all all their claims to being based on dialectical material necessities, are trying to build a future around the very elements that constitute Jewish and Christian world and self making – love, faith, martyrdom, and sacrifice?

From Rosenzweig's perspective, Judaism itself had already provided him with that stock, and Marxist theory had the disadvantage of having been developed out of the limited plane of naturalistic metaphysics, its spirit having been infused from some unknown elsewhere – instead of being, as Judaism was, a heritage. Nor did the fact that Marxism was lunging from one crisis to another strengthen its appeal, for compared to Judaism's longevity, Marxism was already looking ephemeral.

In one of the few other references we find to Marx, Rosenzweig notes how strange it is that two authors describe England's exploitative relationship to the world as one of class struggle. He wryly observes that one of the authors had failed to note that in saying this, Marx's notion of class struggle had lost all sense.[21] I think it fair to say that Rosenzweig had gathered that Marx's grounding concepts were incapable of adequately explaining power relations, and that mistakes like this were indicative of a theory's basic weakness.

In his published letters and diaries there are a mere handful of references to Marx. On 22 February 1914, he simply notes that Marx's method emphasizes society and that his world history is a function of social development.[22] In a letter to his parents on 11 September 1916, Marx's name appears in a list of Jews who have left their Jewish community to make broader cultural contributions. On 25 October 1917, he writes to Ernst Baumann, a little less than a fortnight after Bethmann-Hollweg's resignation as chancellor, that he thinks Germany is on its way to revolution – though he adds that perhaps he is too strongly influenced by historical analogy. Rosenzweig sees parliamentary chaos developing out of the single-mindedness of the respective parties in Germany, and the rift between the role of the chancellor and that of the state secretaries, and he points to the absurdity that various party leaders are finding themselves trying to reconcile the canonized Marx with the issue of war credits. He also notes that the important question is state control of the economy and the role that the social democrats must play in stabilizing the rights of individuals against the power of the state. From this letter, it is clear that he thinks the widespread invocation of Marx's name has little to do with the reality of German politics. It is fair to say that Rosenzweig's knowledge of Marx – unlike that of Rosenstock-Huessy – was not based on a deep immersion in Marx's texts. This is suggested by a letter to Gritli on 28 May 1919, in which he says he wants to read some Lasalle and Marx and Engels. But he had picked up enough about Marx to see that he was yet another example of 'atheistic theology,' though Marx had disclosed another dimension to that 'theology,' which Rosenzweig had not canvassed in the essay of that name – that is, he had provided an atheistic theology of the solidarity of the suffering of the producing classes, and of the role of the ruling classes throughout history in contributing to that suffering.

So while we find no shortage of twentieth-century intellectuals declaring themselves to be Marxists, Rosenzweig seems to have been thoroughly unconvinced by Marx's version of history and its privileging of class as the principal springboard for analysis. Some events lend themselves to Marxian theory (the French and English revolutions, the Peasant rebellions in Germany, and Caesarism in Rome); yet it is hard to imagine why any student of European history, when confronted with a seemingly endless number of territorial conflicts, would be inclined to view class as the *primary* cause of Europe's history.

Similar objections can be raised with respect to philosophy. Marx's philosophy inevitably looks pallid beside Hegel and Kant. And Rosenzweig had delved deeply into both Kant and Hegel; he had had the good fortune to have Hermann Cohen as his teacher, and Cohen (in spite of Heidegger's antipathy toward him) was undoubtedly preeminent among Kant scholars of the nineteenth and early twentieth centuries, and, as we have already discussed, he had thrown himself deeply into Hegel's work. No doubt Marx's philosophical shallowness in comparison to both Kant and Hegel is due to them dealing at a level of conceptual and logical analysis that Marx (and Engels) simply never attain. Anyone who reads Hegel's *Science of Logic* or Kant's critical works can only feel bewilderment at the philosophical superficiality of Marx's various comments on Idealism, not to mention Engels's *Dialectics of Nature*. It is true that Benjamin, Adorno, Bloch, and Lukács (among others) held firmly to Marx's distinction between Idealism and materialism, believing it still had philosophical currency. But it is significant that not one single word of these social theorists could in any way be interpreted as making a single contribution to political economy. Indeed, with the possible exception of Bloch – who is no economist but rather, if he can be classified at all, more a historian of ideas – all of these men were 'cultural theorists.' And it is not difficult to argue that their appeal to materialism concealed the fact that their cultural focus remained much more left-Hegelian than strictly Marxist. Moreover, though Rosenzweig broke decisively with Hegel, it is difficult to refute the argument that Hegel makes against philosophies that purport to be materialist – viz., that whatever the subject of a judgment or syllogism, the predicate is necessarily based on a concatenation of concepts whose underlying pattern of meaning is supplied by the governing idea that enables their selection. Nowhere do Adorno, Bloch, or Lukács adequately refute this. The Feuerbachian and Marxian appeal to the immediately given is never true; it is always an appeal to another array of predications and their underlying idea. Thus an appeal to the economic as the material base of the superstructure of culture, including philosophy, is merely an appeal to a different sphere of conceptualizations and ideations that are not a whit more material than Hegel's idealist idea. In his invocation of materialism, Marx cannot overleap the fact that the truths of his claims are always predicated on the truths he makes about the specific economic relations he refers to when trying to demonstrate the reified and hence distorted nature of the bourgeois world by reference to the real material base.

Had Marx simply argued that economic predications provide an important component of the truth of things, his position would not be so palpably false. But the invocation of the material as if it were as obviously immediate – when in fact what Marx means is a *range* of forces that can only be known through scientific (*wissenschaftlich*) analysis – is identical to the blast into the Absolute that Hegel criticized Schelling and his followers for undertaking in his preface to the *Phenomenology of Spirit*. I do not want to equate Rosenzweig's position with Hegel's, because Rosenzweig, like Schelling himself, did not want to remain within the Hegelian system, and both refuse to accept that our concepts are woven into a spherical totality of dialectical development, as Hegel claims, wherein one must, in effect, know *every* thing to know *any* thing. But their disagreement with Hegel stems not from a regression to a 'pre-critical' (to take Kant's term) view of the world – as Feuerbach, Marx, and Engels make when they appeal to a world of objects or matter against ideas – but from the irruptive nature of existence, which from nothing generates something, something as unpredictable as it is unexpected and in defiance of the conceptual symmetries we establish. Neither Schelling nor Rosenzweig lapses back into a metaphysical totalism of the stripe that Marx does when he calls himself a materialist, because Idealisms of every hue – including materialism – are precisely what they are critiquing. To summarize, Marx's critique of Hegel fails to grasp what Hegel himself meant by Idealism, and it subsequently reproduces the very Idealist strand that Rosenzweig rejected – viz., the fantasy that there is a way that all our conceptualizations form a single dialectical pattern conforming to an overarching totalizing 'principle.'[23] The concept of capital – which Marx is able to reduce to a formula of commodity production, which in turn supposedly explains the irrevocable logic of an entire society – functions in Marx in precisely this 'Idealist' manner that Rosenzweig criticizes in *Understanding the Sick and the Healthy.* There he says that the problem with Idealism, as with every ism, is that it is essentialism and that names, not essences, disclose the powers of the world:

> Our enemy is not idealism as such; anti-idealism, irrationalism, realism, materialism, naturalism, and what not are equally harmful. The real cause of the illness is not that reason assumes that 'spirit' is the essence of reality; it is its assumption that it is possible for something to exist beyond reality. Reality, matter, nature, are all terms denoting 'essence' and are just as unacceptable as 'spirit' or 'idea.' All claim to 'be' either reality itself or the essence of reality. All abstract from life. All neglect the fact of names. Consequently all these *isms* fail to conciliate thought and action, which is, after all, the one thing desired. They fail precisely because they are isms, whether 'idealisms' or 'realisms.'[24]

If Rosenzweig's view of history remains fundamentally resistant to any kind of narrative whose 'ground' is formed by an essence or ism – as Marx's historical materialism surely is – there is an even more fundamental resistance on Rosenzweig's part to the kind of eschatology promised by Marx and that (as noted earlier) he criticized in Nietzsche. Most simply put, the revelation of the living God is to love the neighbour. The command is as harsh as it is uncompromising, but it is not in any way an Idealist formulation – indeed, it is the exact opposite of such an Idealist formulation, for the Idealist formulation would have the reality copy the model of an idea, whereas the strength of the divine command is that it leaves unspecified the need of the particular neighbour and hence the loving act that is required in loving each and every neighbour. Marxism, seen in this light, falls precisely under the category that Rosenzweig calls 'the tyrant of heaven.' The tyrant of heaven impatiently overleaps the neighbour in preference to the next but one. The task of the present is thus deferred for the prospect of the future. This was manifest in the history of Marxism. First, it only wanted to love the neighbour who was proletarian; then, only the proletarian who was revolutionary; then, with Lenin, only the revolutionary who was the right kind of revolutionary, a Bolshevik; and then, with Stalin, only the Bolshevik who was the right kind of Bolshevik. A law of such diminishing returns is the exact opposite of the redemptive power of love that is the axis of Rosenzweig's thought. For Rosenzweig this is zealotry, pure and simple:

> The zealot, the sectarian, in short all tyrants of the Kingdom of heaven, instead of accelerating the coming of the Kingdom, sooner delay it; by leaving their nearest unloved and reaching for the second nearest, they are precluded from the multitude of the ones who, moving forward, in a broad front, piece by piece of the ground, each the one nearest to him, conquer, occupy – inspire; and their forestalling, their personal preference for the second nearest does not render any pioneering service to those following; for it remains without effect; the arable land, prematurely ploughed by the zealot, bears no fruit; only when its time has come – and it comes for it, too – only then does its time come.[25]

There are some affinities between Rosenzweig and Rosenstock-Huessy in their respective assessments of Marx and Nietzsche. The fact is, though, that Rosenstock-Huessy is not primarily looking at the gap between these prophets of modernity and the promised kingdom and the role of God's elect, the Jews; but rather to what extent, if any, they are helping to 'realize it.' We have already noted what he says in *The Christian Future* and *Das Alter der Kirche*. It is no exaggeration to say that throughout Rosenstock-Huessy's large corpus there is so much material on both Marx and Nietzsche that one could easily devote a large monograph to the topic of Rosenstock-Huessy's engagement with the two. In what follows, I attempt to give a thorough though far from exhaustive account of that engagement.

As evident in the examples already given, Rosenstock-Huessy often took Marx and Nietzsche as part of the same problematic. And apart from the works already mentioned, there are four main places where he does this: an unpublished but extremely interesting essay titled 'The End of The World or When Theology Slept'; the final section of Volume One of the *Soziologie*, where he provides a fascinating account of how the absence of paternity in Nietzsche is the counterpoint to the absence of maternity in Descartes; the section on the 'Four Disangelists' from the beginning of the Volume Two of the *Soziologie*, where they are discussed in connection with Freud and Darwin; and the public lecture series titled The Four Disangelists, which takes up and develops the theme of the *Soziologie*.

In 'The End of The World or When Theology Slept,' there is a lengthy passage that deserves being quoted in full, for it provides a clear summary of how he positions himself relative to Marx and Nietzsche and to other far better-known twentieth-century theologians, thus enabling us to see why and in what sense his work can accurately be described as that of a 'post-Nietzschean Christian.' It also amplifies much about his understanding of Christianity so that we can understand better his idea of a Christianity without walls, or what we have referred to as Johannine Christianity:

Now, a Christian can be neither a Marxian nor a Nietzschean. However, he may be led to believe that ethical eschatology was saved by Marx in the market place when the temple allowed the flame to die. And we have among us post-marxian Christians like the Dean of Canterbury, like Reinhold Niebuhr, Paul Tillich, Karl Barth.[26] They have been saved because they humbled their theological pride before the infinite challenge of communistic ethics, without succumbing to its finite political tenets.

It is less recognized in this country that we might have to humble ourselves before the eschatological faith of Nietzsche. I am not, never have been, a Nietzschean. But Nietzsche is not merely a tonic in an otherwise Christian world. Nietzsche is a central event in the history of Christianity (and to me, there is no other universal history). Hence, the reader may understand – why when George Morgan published his book 'What Nietzsche Means,' I asked his and 'Christendom's' permission to state the position of post-Nietzschean Christians . . . Post-Nietzschean Christians recognize each other as living in a world completely transformed. The experience of Nietzsche means that we have learned to distinguish forever between the Nomen and the Numen Christianum, between the label Christian Church or Christian World or Christian Spirit, and the powers of the Spirit. We understand why the nomen Christianum could decline without refuting the promises of the New Testament lest the numen Christianum, the powers of faith, love, hope, die. These powers bridge the abysses inside of Man whom we little men have to represent through the ages.

In other words, I believe that the Church is a divine creation and that the Nicene Creed is true, and yet I believe that the Church and the Creed of the future will depend for a new lease on life upon undenominational, nameless and incognito contributions of faith. The inspirations of the Holy Ghost will not remain incarcerated in the walls and partitions of the visible or audible Church. A third form the listening Church, will have to unburden the older form of worship by assembling the faithful to live out their hopes in services within unlabelled, undenominational groups. In these incognito and undenominational situations, we shall have to do repentance for the generations in which theology slept, in which the nominal churches abandoned the eschatological positions of Christianity. By doing so, we may hope to save our places of worship and adoration, and our creeds and hymns, from the powers of this world, in times to come.

When the Churches stripped the 'Last Things' of meaning, especially the 'End of the World,' Nietzsche saved the meaning and whipped the nominal eschatologists. Nietzsche has not abolished Christianity; he has, however, re-invoked the anonymous and incognito life of the Holy Ghost as a power in human society . . . Nietzsche is the Great Divide between the Levite and Good Samaritan, in the realm of our thinking about God, Man, and World.[27]

For Rosenstock-Huessy, Nietzsche is a 'central event in the history of Christianity,' in large part because notwithstanding his attack on 'Christianity,' he reactivated the genuine Christian spirit through his own Christ-like deed, of being the sacrificial victim of his age – an age that, Rosenstock-Huessy argues, had become so sterile and spiritually atrophied that the most Christ-like thing to be done was to attack the Christian phantasm that had become mistaken for genuine Christianity. He returns to this point again and again in his discussion of Christianity. Thus in another unpublished essay on Nietzsche, 'Nietzsche's Untimeliness,' he contrasts what he calls the materialist dogma of Aristotelian-based psychology, which he sees has been so widely absorbed by the moderns with its dependency on a rational unified self, with what Nietzsche rightly saw as the pandemonium and chaos of the self, which is the source of what is greatest in us. For Rosenstock-Huessy, 'man begins with an infinity of men, in himself. To become a person, means to conquer the innumerable masks of life and to restrict them.' And Nietzsche knew this. But the other element in our 'self-ing' is *time*. Rosenstock-Huessy argues that one of Christ's great achievements was to grasp humanity through the triunity of its temporality – 'the past which he shakes off, the future which he creates, and the bridge in between.'[28] This is also what Nietzsche presents constantly in *Thus Spake Zarathustra*. Zarathustra is a bridge to a future in which the powers of the past can rise again, only greater. In the final section of the First Essay of *On the Genealogy of Morals*, Nietzsche implores: 'Must the ancient fire not some day flare up much more terribly, after much longer preparation? More: must not one desire it with all one's might? Even will it? Even promote it?'[29]

For Rosenstock-Huessy, Jesus 'is the case in which the triunity stands before us as lived to perfection . . . Jesus reveals Oneness as triunity: he is the last Jew, the first Christian, and in between the Crucified.' Nietzsche, on the other hand, 'relates triunity to pandemonium, remains this side of triunity, between the innumerable masks: the Singular does not occur at all.'[30] For Rosenstock-Huessy, Nietzsche's madness is the most honest act in an age gone mad, an age that believes itself to have found all the means of peace – the humanist self-certainty of the potency of its Idealism – though it is an age teetering on the verge of the most terrible carnage. For him, Nietzsche's madness is a decision to try to salvage meaning out of the mechanized wars that are to come; he is a prophet of the mayhem of the age into which Rosenstock-Huessy and Rosenzweig were born. He saw the future hell on earth and willingly entered it through his own private madness. His celebration of martial virtues was, for Rosenstock-Huessy, symptomatic of his recognition that war was inevitable as the only way out of the 'witches sabbath' into which Europe was plunging and as the only way to reawaken the necessary virtues that had been lost in peacetime.[31]

In all this, for Rosenstock-Huessy, Nietzsche was Christ-like in that he was a sacrifice born out of love, a love for the future and the past that had been crucified in the nihilism, heartlessness, and folly of the present. Taking the sentence 'the Refutation of God: Refuted is the moral God only' from Nietzsche's notebook – a sentence with which Rosenstock-Huessy and the New Thinkers agreed – he comments:

> He had to annihilate the Platonic and Aristotelian aspect of God, not the living God of Job or Jesus, and in this one sentence, he revealed that he knew it. He smashed the three letters GOD because our Aristotelians and Platonists have mined them, treating GOD as the first cause.
>
> But Nietzsche was forbidden to use such terms as 'Dionysian aspect' of God, 'Platonic aspect of God.' He had to represent the Dionysian aspect of God. Since he was alone in his time, he could not make concessions. Anybody who is alone, has to act like Nietzsche when he wishes to unearth a forgotten aspect of God . . . Nietzsche ceased to ask for a God of the universe. He asked for the God of pandemonium in ourselves . . . Nietzsche called man back into his divinity, at the price of taking away from him all naturalness, all 'Thingness.' If man recognizes his pandemonian origin, he may ascend to heaven. If he insists to remain a thing in nature, he decays.[32]

In this *thing*-ness of modern life – which, says Rosenstock-Huessy in 'Nietzscheana,' is the result of the conquest of space – human beings, who are time-generating creatures (they generate bodies of times, cultures, faiths, new names, new types) are dissolved into itemized, atomized, predictable beings. That is what Nietzsche struggled incessantly against in calling for humanity to 'incarnate his divine, everlasting power, into mind and body.'[33]

For Rosenstock-Huessy, the fact that Nietzsche went mad was not simply part of his biography but an essential component of the truth of the forces to which his life was a response. Nietzsche himself had insisted repeatedly that he read philosophies as symptoms of life's ascending or declining power. In Nietzsche, Rosenstock-Huessy sees the truth of this insight. 'Nietzsche went mad,' he says, 'over his time and for his time. His era was one of prudery, syphilis, progress, humanism, profound scholarship and the idol of Music as God – ersatz – and all these elements of the age converge in Friedrich Nietzsche's life making him a sign to his age that it could not last and had to be overcome.'[34]

That Nietzsche, like Hölderlin, had a fate that was bound up with madness was extremely important for Rosenstock-Huessy. For the madness of such great souls was a deep symptom of the malady of the modern age. And for all Rosenstock-Huessy's appreciation of Nietzsche, there was no escaping the fact that Nietzsche belonged to a time-frame or time-body that was perilous for the human soul. Indeed, with Descartes, he is seen as one of its 'bookends.' And while Nietzsche may seem to be the opposite of the motherless Descartes, with his arid computational take on human existence, 'the merry dancer of life' and Descartes are 'damnably alike.'[35] That is to say, Nietzsche represents the attempt to put soul back into the desouled Cartesian universe (Descartes, says Rosenstock-Huessy, embodied a timepoint, while Nietzsche 'ensouled it')[36] – desouled because everything living is dissolved into the plenum of calculable mechanical forces. Nietzsche was the cry of a living soul against such a world – he 'wanted to be free'; but he, too, remained conditioned by such a world as we have already canvassed in our discussion of the French Revolution; and indeed, Rosenstock-Huessy conceded that Descartes had good reason for his creative act of exigency. And throughout the section from the *Soziologie* titled 'Die Raumnot der Gebildeten' (The Perils of the Intellectual's Spaces), he plays with the maternal imagery of Descartes becoming the mother he did not have. Thus despite his inimicable position to Descartes, Rosenstock-Huessy recognizes him as 'an authentic human being' who hesitated 'with every fibre of his being before finally committing himself' to the new task he had created for the species.[37] And in spite, then, too, of being far closer by nature and temperament to Nietzsche's act of spirit, he portrays them as both running in the same 'one way street' consisting of world, nature, and physics. The difference lies in the directions in which they run. Thus Nietzsche runs from physics to nature to world. The Rosenzweigian criticisms of the triadic dissolution of God, Man, and World resound in Rosenstock-Huessy's account of Descartes and Nietzsche sharing a space that has been forged by the great acts of severance from what Rosenzweig called the original proto-cosmos. Whereas Descartes is portrayed as having had a leg to stand on, and Nietzsche as having had a leg to dance on, each 'one-leggedly' represents the diminishment of the modern soul and the faith that drives it.[38] This is all the harder to see because of the success of the enormous powers of the modern mechanical bodies we inhabit thanks to modern science and the Cartesian vision that played such an enormous role in popularizing and thereby animating that science. But the modern fusion of science and art as the new religion (he cites Goethe's 'who possesses art and science also has religion')[39] does not do the one thing that Nietzsche most wanted to do and did not do, and that Christianity and the other great faiths of the world have always done – incarnate. Just as we saw Rosenzweig take issue with the idolatry of art because it fell far short of the Jewish deployment of art and ritual in the continuous act of incarnation, orientation, and preservation and perpetuation of the Jewish faith across the ages, Rosenstock-Huessy focuses on Nietzsche as the bearer of this modern tragedy whose failure is not so much the 'typical' flaw of premodern tragic figures, but the all too modern one of self-delusion about what we are really doing, as opposed to what we think we are doing.

This was no more evident to Rosenstock-Huessy than in Nietzsche's playing the role of a father to the child to Zarathustra. As he points out, it was not uncommon in the nineteenth century for artists to compare their creative process with giving birth. But a work of art is is not a child. And Rosenstock-Huessy notes how Nietzsche, wanting to distance himself from just being a play actor (like his former mentor, Wagner) also came to distance himself from the maternal metaphors of the artist; he wanted his *Zarathustra* to be seen in its own independence. But the fatherless Nietzsche remained fatherless, the creator of an *intellectual* type; he never became the founder of a living body. Thus, Rosenstock-Huessy observes that despite Nietzsche's emphasis on the cultivaton of types, there was a certain sterility about Nietzsche that he desperately wanted to overcome but never did. Rosenstock-Huessy makes this point very powerfully when he draws attention to the fact that Jacob Burckhardt, whom Nietzsche (again, so desperately) wanted to impress, responded to Nietzsche's incessant talk of his 'son Zarathustra' by muttering, 'I wish you would procreate a living son.'[40]

Just as we saw earlier how Rosenstock-Huessy had seen the power of the gospels coming from their fourfold combination of forces, he also sees that Nietzsche's power mostly came from his alignment with other 'contemporaries' – Freud, Marx, and Darwin – who, taken together, had shocked their contemporaries out of the somnabulance of modernity. Together they formed what Rosenstock-Huessy had designated the 'four disangelists' – which was a none too subtle play on the difference between them and our time. Volume Two of the *Soziologie*, subtitled *The Full Count of the Times*, commences with a section devoted to the 'four disangelists' as his methodological way into 'Our Point in Time.' Thus are his readers alerted from the outset of the volume to the revolutionary nature of our age and the depth of suffering that characterizes it.

For Rosenstock-Huessy, the twentieth century was still caught in a time during which all the certainties of civilization had been torn up. And much of that tearing had been done by the four disangelists. If humanity had been thrown into turmoil by their writings, it was not because they were bad men – on the contrary, in the lecture series of that name, he says that all four disangelists 'were decent people.' Much more decent, he adds with an apt barb, than the academics and scientists of his own time, whose research is driven by money.[41] But because they had mobilized the overthrowing of what previously had passed for bulwarks of civilization – the Church, the ruling class, the family, and the idea of man as the crown of creation – their news was the very bad news that the spirit had left the traditional buildings of civilization. The disangelists, says Rosenstock-Huessy,

> wrote the Gospel before the catastrophe happened, who began at the other end and destroyed and dissolved the humanism and its unholy alliance as idealism with Christianity, who stripped us naked of our complacency as citizens of the academic world; of seminaries, and universities and colleges, and made us into – back into animals, into individuals, into class warriors, and into insane men in a frenzy.[42]

Each of the four disangelists came with his own warning about a part of the old world that was gone forever, and each brought the news that the new world was fraught with catastrophe. Thus while Freud saw the difference between domestic tradition and the disappearance of family ties, he also recognized the need to bury the past;[43] Nietzsche saw that the promise of the coming world wars was a promise of the future; Darwin's's naturalism further assisted in the breakdown of Idealism's dualisms of 'good and evil by emphasizing the inherent necessity of qualitative change';[44] and Marx saw that conflict provided the key for understanding the present:[45]

> These four names denied the achievement of the family (Freud), classes (Marx), history (Nietzsche), of man generally (Darwin). Darwin set out the ground rules of becoming prior to the emergence of humanity. Thus human history became an appendix to natural history. Freud uprooted the rules of chastity of the family and with that destroyed the tribal phase. Nietzsche did away with the achievement of Israel when he, like the Pharonic priests of the stars, preached the eternal return; and Karl Marx annihilated property right and the accumulation of wealth, because he annihilated classes and with that, without seeking it, our native roots.[46]

The impending catastrophe, of course, would turn out to be the century of world wars, and this awakening us to our animality, our individuality, our warlike and frenzied condition was, for Rosenstock-Huessy, a reconnection with the truth of who we are. For him, as it was for Rosenzweig, Idealism was synonymous with essentialism, something hostile to life's complexities, and the four disangelists had – he would say succinctly in the lecture series The Four Disangelists – 'freed us from the equation of Greece and Golgotha.'[47] Just as Christianity 'came into the world against idealism,'[48] the anti-Idealism of the disangelists would help clear the way for the revival of a genuine and timely and hence 'post-Christian' form of Christianity. For Rosenstock-Huessy, Christianity was built on the reality of our nature, and to the extent that it was genuinely Christian and not a Greek or pagan variant, it always recognized, as it did in its originators, that 'man needs frenzy and passion to achieve anything.'[49] Faith, hope, and love are passionate powers, not ideas – they give force to ideas and direction in life because they are the basis of our relationships with our passions and hence ourselves and one another. In this respect, as in so many, Rosenstock-Huessy was expressing a fundamental tenet that had been shared by Christians for more than a millennium – that the classical virtues of wisdom, justice, temperance, and courage are limited, and that the power they may attain derives from the three Christian 'virtues' of faith, hope, and love. Idealism, on the other hand, for Rosenstock-Huessy did not bring reality into connection with the harmony it wanted to achieve. Thus it disabled us and drove us constantly and inevitably further and deeper into wars that would be all the more catastrophic by virtue of the Idealist miasma of denial, appeasement, and all the other suffocating and empty surrogates of love.

The contradiction between what we think we are doing and what we are actually doing is one of the most important lessons of history. The forces of world- and self-making are not, then, merely ideational, but living forces of flesh *and* word; the word calls, the flesh forms. But flesh and word have their own reasons, buried deep within themselves. These secret 'reasons' of life's strivings are invariably missed by philosophers, who tend to look for and thus find symmetries and connections – a relatively simple matter, for the concepts they work with are purer than reality, purer because life's impurities are washed out in the acts of abstraction. But conceptual purity is simply the result of the truncated nature of abstractions. In all of this, Rosenstock-Huessy remains very close to Marx's attack on Idealism (which is not to contradict the earlier point about Marx's thinking also being Idealist, but simply to underscore how his use of totality requires that the more hidden economic relationships always shape ideological ones). And he remains close, as well, to Nietzsche's attack on Platonism as a dominant modality of thought that comes back to the world as a force of deformation because it has had the life ripped out it.

Furthermore, the potencies that develop and accrue over time and across generations are treated by Idealism as subspecies *aeternae;* they are invoked all at once as if we could deploy them all at once. But our powers are distributed through and developed over time. And our solidarity has to be achieved across space if it is to be genuinely effective across time. Hence, for example, for Rosenstock-Huessy (as we saw for Rosenzweig), pacifism is an inflexion of Idealism. But a moral stance such as that of the pacifist, says Rosenstock-Huessy, fails to acknowledge the terrible tragedy of conflict that is the only way in which a peace can be imposed and a new order intervene when an old order has become hell. War is thus, for him, the means by which humanity is forced to get from A to Z, from its complacency and indifference to the Other to genuine solidarity. Marx knew this, and so did Proudhon, whose book *War and Peace* (1861) expresses the truth that 'force is a part of real creation.'[50] And, he continues, it is of the utmost importance not to lose sight of this, and not to pretend – as Idealism does, according to him – that force can be dispensed with. What we must instead do is channel these forces and find, as William James had said, the moral equivalent for war.[51] But at the times the disangelists wrote, there was no occasion for Redemption – the world was too rotten for that. And they sensed the hell into which humanity was being plunged – they revealed hell, and it is our task to take one step further and redeem it. In fact, Rosenstock-Huessy ventures, the Gospel is first written about hell.[52]

To be sure, Rosenstock-Huessy's ideas about war are a long way from liberal consensuses about where force and war fit into life. But that for him is part of the general hypocrisy of the liberal mind and the Idealism that underpins it. The United States, he pointed out in a statement that was far more provocative at the time he made it than it is perhaps today, had had more wars in the previous 150 years than any country in the world, yet it proceeded as if these wars were not part of its reality.[53] In general, then, as we have said, for Rosenstock-Huessy, Idealism not only does not eliminate war, it is one of the great *causes* of war[54] – the result of the conviction of one's own purity through a delusional faith in one's own reason and the implacability of the mind's certitudes. It should go without saying that Rosenstock-Huessy was not advocating war any more than a meteorologist advocates storms. The thing is that having been in the midst of war, he devoted much of his life to examining its significance as both a catastrophic and a creative force; the unity within the two was undoubtedly part of his Goethean heritage, and his work is a rich catalogue of the unity of that fundamental contradiction.

Like Marx, though, and like Hegel, Vico, Montesquieu, and Aristotle, he took our social existence as the given. But far more so than the thinkers just listed, for him the totality of the social was a combination of multiple forces involving the passions themselves and the multiple layers of the past that were still forming us in tandem with the future that was calling us. The economy – which was, for him, never uniform – was a necessary force therein, but no more 'material' for that than any other power that informs and proscribes us. Thus too, for him, revolt was driven not by economic necessity, but by the heart's hatreds in its search for what it loved at the moment that the entire social edifice found itself torn by crises of faith. Thus revolutions were the result of countless forces, long-held repressed memories, resentments, and (frustrated) expectations accumulating over long time scales. From this perspective, Marx's definition of revolution as class struggle obscured the struggle *within* classes over disputes, often of a local kind, and those revolutions now indelibly stamped in the formation of what he called

'Western man' and then a 'planetary consciousness.' It follows that for Rosenstock-Huessy, Marx's theory of revolution was wrong because it oversimplified the relationship between past and future and the role of the passions in overthrowing pasts and forming futures:

If the Marxian revolutionary theory were correct, the revolutions would arise successively in the same territory and in the same nation. Then the march in echelon would be impossible. The French gentry would have overthrown the French monarchy, French bourgeois the gentry, and French workers the bourgeoisie. The Lutheran princes all over Germany would have been beheaded by the 'Junkers,' the Junkers by the German middle classes, and the middle classes by the German Socialists. But that is completely chimerical. Luther's princes revolted for the whole German nation against the Italian pope. The English nation rebelled against the introduction of Continental monarchy into England, where it meant tyranny. The French nation expelled the megalomania which had been nourished by the 'gentilhomme' ever since the British Glorious Revolution; and the Russians expelled European capitalism.

In this way each country could aim at the target of progress in its whole breadth and height. It did not move by simple reaction, what the Marxists call the dialectical process of thesis and antithesis. The pagan and mechanical philosophy of the Socialists made most of them overlook the simple facts and rules of coexistence. The English gentry, in overthrowing Lutheran monarchy, did not fall back into Catholicism. The Russians, in doing away with democracy, have not neglected the obligations imposed upon everybody by the French Revolution. The Russians must cling to national autonomy within their system, the British to Reformation, and the French to Parliament, though for a certain time the Presbyterians or Napoleon or Stalin miss the importance of this inevitable coherence and succession.[55]

From this perspective, the first revolution that self-consciously continued in Marx's image, the Russian Revolution, did not occur because Marx's theory of revolution was true, but because other revolutions had remained unfinished – there was still room for revolutionary necessity. More specifically, the Russian Revolution 'took the guise of an economic revolution because the previous revolutions had stressed other sides of the social order.'[56] For Rosenstock-Huessy, Marx's one-dimensional emphasis certainly was needed because it incorporated a residue of the real that has so far escaped being revolutionized. But his revolutionary theory failed to grasp 'the creative results of revolution'[57] – that is, it failed to grasp how Europe, then the world, had been generated out of the continuity of the fruits of revolution. Russian Marxists wanted the Russian Revolution to be the high and end point of revolution, when in fact, as we have emphasized throughout, for Rosenstock-Huessy it was itself a side effect of the far greater detonation of the Great War, which was the real accumulation of forces not yet quelled and sufficiently integrated over the past thousand years of Europe's revolutionary outbreaks.

Nevertheless, despite these and various other criticisms, Rosenstock-Huessy was not primarily interested in underscoring where Marx went wrong (he was not strictly an anti-Marxist), and he was just as little interested in cheering him on (he was not a Marxist). He *was* interested in living and unassailable contributions, and he *did* believe that more is generated by Marx than what feeds his critics and disciples. He was convinced that for all his many errors as an economist/historian/sociologist, Marx himself and the regimes that bore his name were part of a much greater wave of forces. Unlike the anti-communists, he also was convinced that Marxist regimes, like Marx's ideas, carried within them something both true and necessary and that the truth had to be seen in the context of the much greater picture of the human story going back to the first human beings – or, if one will, Adam. And in both *Out of Revolution* and *Die europäischen Revolutionen* he discussed Marx in the context of the Russian Revolution and the Russian Revolution in light of it being an event that had changed forever at a planetary level our consciousness of labour's social importance.

In *Out of Revolution*, Rosenstock-Huessy wrote that Marx represented 'the last protest against the existing order of things.'[58] For Marx, the revolution was total or not at all, and thus he correctly grasped that it had to be worldwide. In this respect, then, Marx had been driven by the messianic impulse that unites all great revolutionaries – the desire for all to experience the plenitude of their powers – and this is what made Marxism, for Rosenstock-Huessy, an essential contributor to the future. He also wrote that Marx and Engels and Marxism in general had developed 'what Nietzsche called in his last vision "the permanent recurrence of the same." '[59] That is, he referred to a core category in Marxian analysis – social reproduction. But he believed that he himself went far beyond Marx in insisting that revolution is what awakens people to the blindness of this reproduction, that it interrupts mechanical production and creates something new and necessary that the old order cannot do.

Rosenstock-Huessy also cannot agree with Marx's economic theory. He quite rightly takes Marx to task over the theory of immiseration and the labour theory of value, which he points out place far too much weight on industrial labour, just as they mistakenly take congealed labour time as objective. He does not mention Jevons and the economic revolution he led, but the point he makes comes straight out of the revolution that Marx's contemporary economists were engaged in, the key results of which Marx himself systematically ignored – viz., that the pricing mechanism is a signal of consumer interest and want and that business is full of guesses. This is why, in mainstream, marginal utility economic theory, industrial labour power – which Marx makes the *source* of exchange value – is but one of the factors of production. Throughout his entire economic corpus, Marx had focused mainly on producers and their needs, not consumers and their wants (of course he had emphasized the lack of consumption possibilities for the working class), which is to say he had from the beginning had an inadequate and partial view. Thus in Marx's economic theory the entrepreneur, for example, is completely unnecessary; and given that any commodity's value should be calculable from the average number of hours of labour power required for its production, it would take time to come up with the idea/venture. Marx's early polemics, in *The German Ideology*, about artists responding to necessary conditions and hence being thoroughly socially determined, resonate in his view of economic life as completely predictable and calculable. The theory has a certain radical moral attractiveness that makes of employers nothing but thieves. (Marx simultaneously appeals to a higher moral ground, yet he does not want to concede this because morality is merely a superstructural concept.) But the theoretical failure of Marx's model was all too visible in the command economies, which did not need entrepreneurs – and not needing them, they had no incentives for inventiveness, nor for risk, two indispensable qualities for dynamic, consumer-driven economies. What Marx really missed (and this is always the danger when an economist of any political persuasion tries to make all life subject to economic laws) is that value is a quality and that a quality cannot simply be reduced to quantity, even if its production and circulation are measurable quantitatively. For all its failures and crimes, capitalism does not completely eliminate the Holy Spirit on the economic plane. Though admittedly, the price for openness to inspiration (the Holy Spirit) within the sphere of economic cooperation and exchange relationships is the enhanced scale of demonic possibilities, which operate in the vacuums when profit as such is worshipped. Marxian economics wants to eliminate the demonicness of Self-love (the bourgeois), but it does so by killing the Holy Spirit that needs the vehicle of the Self for its own and humanity's enhancement and expansion. This is why for Rosenstock-Huessy a metanomic society also, of necessity, has a polydimensional economy. Indeed, he sees economic polydimensionality as basic to any healthy social fabric. One might say that this is confirmed by the example of China. For China, the most successful heir of the Russian Revolution, has been more successful even than Russia, which is experiencing just that kind of 'humilation' (Rosenstock-Huessy's term) and restoration that is the fate of all revolutionary regimes, because it has more successfully incorporated private property within socialist rule.

Where Rosenstock-Huessy feels an especially strong sense of connection with Marx's economic thinking is in the latter's constant attacks on the Robinsonian views of man that are paraded out again and again in self-serving bourgeois ideologics about proprietal rights and entitlements. The atomized view of the self common to bourgeois economics and liberalism is but a variant of the machine universe and its soul-crushing logic:

> Liberalism owes its very existence to these godfathers: Adam and Robinson Crusoe. Wherever economists begin with human consumption and production, they are doomed to end where liberalism did end: in the World War for a world market. Whoever starts with the Individual must end with the universe. Once the standard unit of power is conceived as one man, enterprising, free, well-equipped, no barrier can be found to his activities. His field is the world.[60]

Yet in spite of such a fundamental agreement, he cannot entirely accept that exchange value is generated solely by the proletariat, or that capitalists are merely a dead weight on society, and that all employer–employee relations under private property are exploitative. Rosenstock-Huessy accepts that the interests of capital and labour are not always identical, and hence there can be war between them; but this is equally true of the relationship between the sexes. He observes that the mistake is in thinking that the struggle can have no resolution other than the elimination of one party – here, the owners of capital. As he points out, in England between 1850 and 1882, 'to the great disappointment of

Marx,' such a peace existed and created an extremely successful period of economic growth. He adds that sometimes growth of one class is at the expense of another class – and sometimes it can even be the wealthy whose living standards decline relatively (e.g., in Germany from 1918 to 1923). And he notes that in Russia under Marxism, the industrial labourers profited at the expense of capitalists and peasants: by the time *Out of Revolution* was published (1938), based on the living wage scale of 1914, the peasants stood at 70 and the industrial proletariat at 135, that is, the industrial proletariat's wages were almost double those of the peasants.

The last point about the industrial labourers profiting from the condition of the peasantry is made in deference to Rosa Luxemburg's idea that the prices of capitalism are low only to the extent that pre-capitalistic markets can be found.[61] The same point, though, pulls Rosenstock-Huessy closer to what political economists call dependency theory. Marx insisted that the search for cheap labour drove capital flows; but he never argued that capital accumulation in highly developed countries depended primarily on resource extraction and the application of 'absolute surplus value' (extraction of a surplus by the sheer force of increased labour time),[62] as occurs in economies with relatively low economic and technological infrastructures; nor did he argue that more complex and well developed levels of infrastructure and technology in more prosperous nations depend on certain regions or nations having cheap labour and a low infrastructure. Indeed, his argument for the necessity of communism was premised on the globe being swept up in more centralized and highly developed technological and economic relationships as relative surplus value expanded. He argued that the world's industrialized workers would be forced to realize that capital accumulation would spiral downwards, along with falling rates of prices, and that the millions upon millions of unemployed workers would simply need to take control of the means of production to eliminate the artifically produced poverty that private ownership had created. In short, Marx – unlike so many twentieth-century Marxists – was not a 'dependency theorist.' And Marx's emphasis on labour-saving technology and the importance of socialization through the development of capital infrastructure was somewhat blurred in Rosenstock-Huessy's appeal to Luxemburg.

Nevertheless, Rosenstock-Huessy is correct to point out that 'liberalism puts to death the old orders of society which cannot compete with its low prices'[63] – something Marx also saw and, unfortunately, greeted with somewhat too enthusiastic applause. Rosenstock-Huessy, by contrast, was far more attuned to the sufferings that modernization itself – through liberalism *and* Marxism – brought to pre-capitalistic life: 'The exploited are the natives of every pre-capitalistic group, class, country.'[64]

As I suggested earlier, the Great War was the irrefutable proof of the commonality of interests between bourgeois and workers, and when Marxist historians interpret that war as proof of Marx's theory of history, they have no choice but to ignore what Rosenstock-Huessy's critique does not:

> The working classes of all the industrialized countries collaborated in the warfare of 1914. The Socialist parties collaborated in the warfare of 1914. The socialist parties had to follow willy-nilly the belligerent instinct of the proletarian masses. Even the great Russian Marxian, Plekhanov fired up at the outbreak of the War. The astonishing fact was often belittled as the result of superstition, atavism, patriotic hypnotism, surprise and similar causes, because it was a terrible shock to Marxian theory and discipline. Nowhere had the masses been better 'Marxians' than in France and Germany. And nowhere did they fight more courageously for their country. A Marxian wrote: 'The failure of all working-class parties in the Great War must be taken as a fact of universal importance, as the result of the former history of the class movement' (Lukács). But it is much simpler to say that labour is not exploited by capitalism, and that the English worker had been repaid by the sacrifice made for his sake in 1846 when the rural interests of England were finally abandoned to secure cheap bread for the cotton workers in Lancashire.[65]

A major divide between Rosenstock-Huessy and all Marxist social theorists of the twentieth century is that the latter never really understood the complex interests behind the Great War, preferring instead far simpler but utterly unconvincing explanations. Typically, they resorted to Lenin's theory of imperialism, exaggerating the importance of disputations over colonial spoils. In keeping with this, the key point of reference for twentieth-century Marxist theoreticians was fascism – a post–Great War phenomenon that sparked the next war. But fascism was always and everywhere an intensification of nationalism – of nationalism injured, defeated, and rancorous – and, again looked at more closely, it displayed the same complex amalgam of class forces as had disproven Marxism in the First World War.[66] Even in his 1914 lecture on Marx in his lectures on state theory, Rosenstock-Huessy had noted how Otto Bauer, the Austrian Marxist writer on nationalism and Marxism, was a necessary corrective to Marx within Marxism.

The 1961 edition of *Die europäischen Revolutionen* repeats much of the discussion in *Out of Revolution;* but in the case of Marx, this work makes a few important points not taken up in the earlier volume. As in *Out of Revolution*, the context is the discussion of the Russian Revolution; and also as in *Out of Revolution,* Rosenstock-Huessy emphasizes the link between the French and Russian revolutions, contending that Marxism alone was capable of taking the fruits of the French Revolution to Russia and that Marx stood in relationship to the ideas of 1789 as Calvin did to Luther: he transferred faith into religion and made the passive active, seeking to actualize philosophy through politics. In Rosenstock-Huessy's view, first, Marx had absorbed and sublated the radical aspirations that reached from Marat to Baboeuf, Saint-Simon, Fourier, and Proudhon by attempting to enter the world's materiality, by entering into the necessities or laws of its struggles, rather than by standing above those struggles as a free thinker. The French Revolution bequeathed to humanity a consciousness of its rights, but Marx fathomed 'man's' being as he was socially produced and reproduced. And he also revealed the worker as the condition of the bourgeois, as the unacknowledged material of the benefits of the bourgeois world. For Marx, the proletariat had no art, no science, no bourgeois rights, no idleness, no religion.[67] Second, the proletariat was formed not by self-consciousness but by labour. The corollary of this in Marxism, according to Rosenstock-Huessy, was that those who did not work were parasites for whom there could be no place in the future society. Third, no one had the right to turn someone into a proletarian. Fourth, all other characteristics besides one's nature as a worker (gender, race, colour, heritage, nationality, creed, party) were extraneous, and no one but workers had rights. And finally, for the proletariat there was only one society – all other social forms, divisions, locations, and connections were secondary and irrelevant.

In all this, it is clear why Marx could not abide trade unions: they were helping maintain and improve the worker's lot in this world, and it was precisely this world that according to Marx had to be brought to an end. In this respect Marx can be compared to the prophets. But, Rosenstock-Huessy notes, the prophets also loved those who had sinned and wished to bring them back into the fold; whereas Marx had no intention of saving the bourgeoisie, for 'he [did] not love the world he [was] describing' – indeed he hated it with every part of his being.[68]

This simple claim might be considered of no theoretical significance whatever. But to make such an easy dismissal as this would be to miss precisely what Rosenstock-Huessy wished to emphasize:

> Because humanity only knows what it loves, and it only knows as much as it loves, love is a practical way of life, which also affects us against our will and consciousness. Marx loved bourgeois society through the deed, through his love which the spirit identified itself with, because he consecrated his life work to knowing it. To recognize something in its essence means to love it. And in that is rooted Marx's mistakes. Religion operates as opium in bourgeois society: but with that one doesn't know what it is otherwise . . . What the proletariat does in and for itself – who can know that? In any case atheism is a bourgeois matter. And only the bourgeois, will take the intellectual effort to occupy themselves with atheism. But Marx is in love with philosophy. And to that extent, he wants reason to rule.[69]

Marxism was purporting to explain what drives people. As a counter, Rosenstock-Huessy posed this simple question: What drives Marx? Behind Rosenstock-Huessy's question stood the full force of the heritage that he claimed as his and Marx's and Nietzsche's and as that of all the revolutionaries – the Christian heritage, which resounds from the Jewish command to love one's neighbour, and the Christian command to love one's enemy, to the psychology of Augustine's insight that love is the gravity that transports us to where we are, to Dante's detailed depiction of the worlds (hellish, purgatorial, and heavenly) created by our love. When Rosenstock-Huessy asked this question, it was hardly an opportune time for a sociologist who wanted to be taken seriously to so unaffectedly move from 'science' to 'emotion.' But the consensus of a given time is not necessarily right, especially when a truth is waiting to break out of the tyranny of that time. Marx's 'science' was riddled with flaws, and Rosenstock-Huessy was interested in the truth of that science – in what it told us not only about Marx but about the world that had responded to him. When Rosenstock-Huessy spoke of Marx's love of philosophy, he was putting his finger on the love of social theorists in the twentieth century who retained the Marxian mode of analysis with ever diminishing deference to the precision of his claims and of the categories whereby they had been formed. This is especially evident in *Das Alter der Kirche*, in which he noted that the social critic heralded a new type whose importance lay in highlighting the significance of society, and not simply the state, as well as the importance of human solidarity.[70]

Finally, let us turn to the discussion of Marx in the lecture series The Four Disangelists. Certainly, Rosenstock-Huessy highlights Marx's weaknesses, and he notes approvingly Proudhon's request to Marx in a letter of 17 May 1846 that they not proclaim a dogma of economics and set themselves up as founders of a new religion; that they remain tolerant and open to the vagaries of reality; and that they not call for the existence of property to be overthrown by violent revolution.[71] But ultimately, Rosenstock-Huessy divides Marx's thought into its living and dead elements. And its living elements are, for him, consistent with what he believes is the one great story/truth that reaches from Adam through the second Adam until his own time and beyond toward the messianic completion of history. As we have indicated, its living elements are these: Marx's general attack on Idealism; his prophetic condemnation of the alienated and diminished life of proletarians in bourgeois society; the destructive heartlessness of the drive for profit; the vision of a world at peace in which humanity's powers are fully developed and expended; the imposition once and for all on human consciousness of the needs of the working class and the unemployed (an argument developed in *Out of Revolution*); and a recognition of the creative dimension of struggle. But what most interests Rosenstock-Huessy in this lecture series are the acts of love that helped form Marx and Marxism:

These are the two things: for war, solidarity; for peace, conversation – which will dominate, because the prophecy of Marx is honorably fulfilled. Honorably, because he has been recognized in his demand for . . . solidarity. Fulfilled, because the nations in their nationalism have come to the end of their rope. Yet, in this honorable fulfillment, there's also a victory of the spiritual tradition of the Bible. Because it is the friendship of Engels and Marx; it is the devotion of Jennie Westfahlen, Marx's wife; it is the faith of the working man in Marx and in the word of Marx that has really allowed us today to see this prophet as a prophet, to know of his existence. Who would mention Marx if he hadn't been put on this pedestal of loyalty, and allegiance, and reverence by the working man? I think he is – has given them this shelter. I think that really all the strikes fought in the last hundred years have been ennobled, have been treated more generously by the fighters, because they had this great program, this great proclamation explaining the strike, every one strike as part of one tremendous outcry for solidarity of the human race in work.

Again, I invite you to – not to be blinded by the Marxians against the greatness of Marx. They never mention the strikes. But after all, the strikes are the real story . . . of the suffering of the working man in the last hundred years. And the working man himself partly has been cheated out of this heroic story . . . I feel today, by his union leaders who are selling him on wages. No strike has ever been fought for wages . . . They have always been . . . fought for the dignity of man and for the solidarity of the workers. And that is a religious item. That is an act of neighborly love and an act of belonging, or – an expression of the deep feeling that all men in this tremendous division of labor are together in one great enterprise, regardless of the place, and the factory, and the individual shop in which they are working. The unity of the process of production all over the world is the other experience of the world wars, which is a triumph of the story of our era, which has said that not only the spirit of man must unite in prayer on Sundays in one – one creed and one faith, but that even our hands may be – by the scientific process – be led in such a way that all production all over the globe is really one. That's incredibly Christian and incredibly ecumenic. I think it's a better ecumenicity than all the ecumenicity of the churches.[72]

Rosenstock-Huessy's assessment of Marx here shows that he saw why Marxism had such a powerful appeal and had become such a powerful historical force. But he was also interested in the fact that Marx's thought was more true than the very theoretical parameters that Marx had established. Rosenstock-Huessy was looking for love's potency in the midst of suffering and catastrophe; that was what Christianity had taught him to look for and why he saw that lifeway was far from dead. Indeed, all the death and suffering, combined with the aspiration and urgency for a messianic future that he had witnessed in the war, is what had convinced him of the ongoing relevance of the cross of reality. Marx and Nietzsche, like Darwin and Freud, had made us contemplate that cross in modern form, but none had really understood their Christian inheritance. As we have suggested earlier, the one great modern social theorist who had recognized this was his hero, Saint-Simon – a figure roundly and unfairly rebuked by Marx as a utopian.

Perhaps the best approach to contrasting Marx with Rosenstock-Huessy is found in the essay 'Revolution, Soziologie, und Universität,' where Rosenstock-Huessy once again declares that though he has learned from the Marxists, he is not a Marxist. But he also says – like Rosenzweig, who coined the term 'absolute empiricism' for the method of *The New Thinking* – that throughout his life he has been 'a passionate empiricist [*leidenschaftlicher Empiriker*] of the last forty years.'[73] Though one should add that in German, the word for passionate is '*leidenschaft*,' which carries within it the word for suffering – *Leiden*. Thus, a freer and possibly more accurate translation of Rosenstock-Huessy's self-description would be 'an empiricist who took the suffering of the last forty years absolutely seriously.'

14 Rosenzweig on Why Allah Is Not Yahweh, the Loving, Revealing, Redeeming God

In the introduction to *The Star of Redemption*, Rosenzweig accounts for Idealism's failure and for the confusion of educated modern men and women who have been beguiled by philosophy into losing their commonsense understanding of God, Man, and World. He explores in Part One the limitations of the proto-cosmic life-worlds of the Greek, Chinese, and Indian civilizations. Then in Part Two he produces a synthesis of philosophy and theology in which he draws attention to the deficiencies of post-Christian Idealism: its horizon does not extend beyond creation; for while it possesses the concept of genesis, it knows nothing of the power of Revelation, for attunement to Revelation requires an attunement to the *logos* itself – not *logos* as ratio, but *logos* as the loving word of the loving God who Himself strives for Redemption. Such a God is not the result of a philosophical account of absolute power, but an attentive hearkening to love's call and to the concession that His love is not something that the mind can fathom and calculate. Also in Part Two of *The Star*, he examines how the God of love and the commandment of love of the neighbour are intrinsically connected to a view of life as a triadic process of Creation, Revelation, and Redemption.

Part Two of *The Star* also examines why Islam must be discarded if one is covenanted, as Jews and Christians are, with the God of Redemption and Revelation. For Rosenzweig, the key critical difference is that Allah displays Himself to His worshippers as a God of might and mercy, but not of love – at least not in the manner that Rosenzweig has traced as being the great gift of Yahweh. I have provided an in-depth treatment of Rosenzweig's critique of Islam elsewhere;[1] but given that he is routinely criticized by scholars (who otherwise hold him in such high esteem) for having embarrassed them, I believe an in-depth account is essential to a clear overview of his thinking. Invariably, Rosenzweig's critique of Islam is criticized for merely repeating prejudices picked up by Hegel or for being the consequence of a systemic need on his part to provide systemic coherence to *The Star*. Thus, not having explored Islam in any depth, he provides a mere caricature of it.[2] I cannot agree with these criticisms, and I have never seen them advanced with any detailed discussion of the Koran or the traditional *hadith* (i.e., what Muslims consider to be sacred Islamic texts). Rosenzweig thought that his discussion of Islam was of major importance but in need of further elaboration, as is clear from a conversation he had with Gertrud Openheim during which he is reported to have asked: 'Have you really not noticed the greatest deficiency in the Star? There isn't enough on Islam?' In 1917, in a letter to Rudolph Ehrenberg, he had written that though he wasn't specifically planning one, he suspected that one day a thick book on Islam would fall from him 'like an overripe fruit.'[3] Thus Rosenzweig himself realized that his treatment of Islam warranted further elaboration; it was a topic to which he had already devoted time, and he intended to devote more. But while his critique of Islam suffers from being too brief and dense, I see it as no less valuable or accurate because of that. The key here is to see it for what it is: a *Jewish* critique of Islam. To put it another way, Rosenzweig enables us to see why a disciple of Yahweh is not a disciple of Allah – and, one might add, vice versa.

In terms of accuracy, Rosenzweig's analysis of Islam is contentious not so much because of the concepts and doctrines he ascribes to Islam, which – as I will emphasize below (shorn of Rosenzweig's polemic) – are the very things that Muslims hold in such high regard. Rather, his analysis is contentious because he is critical of the ends and values that pertain to Islam. Because of the importance of the contrast of different ends between the faiths, that analysis should not simply be dismissed as a polemic bearing little relationship to *The Star*'s overall argument. On the contrary, it is an essential part of a comparison of fundamental qualities that command three different peoples. If one understands *The Star* and anything about Islam, it is more than obvious that Islam issues a challenge that, if it were true, would render lost not only Rosenzweig's life, but also the Jewish and Christian life, not to mention the atheistic or indeed any but the non-Muslim life. In all three faiths, election is construed for its type alone. That this is not liberal – indeed, precisely *because* such a conviction is fraught with political tensions – is one reason why, in the West, liberalism had to impose another kind of law on what had been religiously derived law. (It must be said that a number of works that project liberalism onto Islam are at the very least disingenuous and are deeply revealing about the dangers of hyperpoliticizing academic inquiry.)[4]

Islam typically represents both Christians and Jews as family members who have lost their way and who, through the memory of distant kinship, may be allotted some respect with the faithful, though not equal rights. Jews and Christians should either come back into the fold, or be treated as infidels, or be allowed to quietly practise their faith, while paying special taxes and bearing some restrictions as to the offices they may hold. They are also not permitted to convert souls who already belong to the true faith. Given their common history, and given the claims Muslims make about their God, their prophet, and their faith, it is somewhat disingenuous to insist on core identities that simply are not there.[5] Tellingly – and to repeat a point made earlier – those who believe that all religions lead to the same place and are informed by the same spirit of love and kindness and fraternity, or who wish they did and were, deviate from Rosenzweig in their very first step; for Rosenzweig does not consider the word 'religion' to adequately describe the significance of the covenant established between Yahweh and the Jews. He does, however, see Islam as a religion. Indeed, in 'Jüdische Geschichte im Rahmen der Weltgeschichte' (Jewish History in the Framework of Universal History), he even says that 'Islam is the first "Religion."' This, he adds, is its weakness as well as its strength. For, unlike Jesus and Moses, who did not set out consciously to be 'religious and found a "religion,"'[6] Muslims from the beginning saw themselves in competition with other religions. Muhammad needed to incorporate Moses and the prophets and Christ so that his religion could have the same weight as Christianity and Judaism. It had to win over converts. And, he says, underscoring the very point that is increasingly being made about Islam's early contribution to science and philosophy in today's politically charged debates about Islam,[7] it often did this by being more tolerant and more rational, even serving as a philosophical bridge between ancient Greece and Christendom.[8]

In *The Star*, Rosenzweig emphasizes the religious character of Islam by virtue of the various section headings in his discussion of Islam. Thus he analyses Islam under the rubrics of 'the religion' of reason (*Vernunft*), 'the religion' of necessity, 'the religion' of humanity, 'the religion' of action, 'the religion' of duty, and 'the religion' of progress. He does not treat Christianity as a religion. Moreover, he would have no doubt that those who wish to find the same God of love in Judaism and Islam are tributes to the success of Christianity in bringing all the peoples of the world to the worship of the one (Jewish) God.

That Islam believes in the One God and that it seeks to convert peoples to its cause is, for Rosenzweig, suggestive of its Christian roots. Of course, its renunciation of the Trinity and of Jesus as the Son of God makes it heretical. And Rosenzweig is aware that of all the Christian heresies, Islam has been the most successful competitor and, subsequently, has been a great trial for the Christian faith. This point is made even more explicitly by the Christian sociologist and historian Jacques Ellul, who so appreciated the sections on Islam by Rosenzweig that he had them published in French translation. In *The Subversion of Christianity*, Ellul argues that Christianity was thoroughly refashioned by its response to Islam. That is, Islam attempted to conquer Christian lands with only mixed success, but it did succeed in subverting Christianity from within, as Christians absorbed Islamic concepts and practices such as canon law, theocracy, forced conversion, Holy War (the crusaders as jihadists), slavery, and colonialism.[9] For Rosenzweig, 'the history of Islam has long since ceased to be part of the Christian Church,' but its connection to the Johannine Christian world – this wall-less Church that seeks to make brothers and sisters of all – is another matter. Goethe in *West/East Divan*, with its 'God is the Orient / God is the Occident,' makes such an analysis his imperative.[10]

One might have expected Rosenzweig to raise this very legitimate question: Who is the greater danger, his Islamic brother or his Christian one? In fact, it was the Christian nations whose history of persecution of Jews was so intense that it often compelled Jews to flee to what were often more tolerant Muslim nations.[11] As Rosenzweig reminds his readers, it was the Christians who defined themselves through their eternal hatred of the Jew; and for Jews living in Germany, a Christian nation was the greatest threat to them. Yet for all that, for Rosenzweig, it was the Christian, not the Muslim, who was ruled by the same God. But then, the Christian being also ever a pagan, Rosenzweig implies that there is an affinity between Muslims and Christian peoples (insofar as they succumb to the pagan forces they resuscitate) that is not shared by the Jews.

This is evident in what is probably the most astonishing and prescient aspect of Rosenzweig's critique of Islam – which is evident in the above list of attributes Rosenzweig draws upon to describe Islam. That list is extraordinarily compatible with the major values of modern or enlightened humanism. To any contemporary reader, this at first seems as contrived as it is implausible. Yet its contrivance and implausibility diminishes if one recalls how frequently enlightened thinkers appealed to Islam as a progressive religion; indeed, in their attacks on Christianity, they often saw it as far more compatible with their own deism.[12] Indeed, despite there being plenty of liberal critics of Islam today who point to the incompatibility between modern liberal democracy and Islam as an unreconstructible theopolitics, there are just as many 'liberal' voices who insist on Islam's humanitarian dimensions, especially on the grounds of the role that social justice plays in it and partly, also, because they are disgusted by Christian and Jewish (more specifically Zionist) hypocrisies and their fundamentalisms. One of the great strengths of Rosenzweig's 'absolute empiricism' is that it is able to make sense of such seemingly implausible yet factually true connections.

Because Rosenzweig addresses Islam under the 'enlightened' headings listed above, he is able to undermine the very basis of the more 'progressive' defenders of Islam by addressing – and answering the first part in the negative – the only question that concerns him: Is Islam an authentic teaching of and response to Revelation, or is it a religious assemblage of pagan forces and stratagems? No one would have difficulty with the claim that Voltaire taught neither Revelation nor the revealed God. But alongside the 'concern' that specifying the differences among Yahweh, the Father, and Allah might lead to prejudice and legitimized violence, there is the more thorny issue that Muslims do insist that Allah is a God who has revealed himself and that his Revelation is the truth. Moreover, 'No God but God' means that anything the Jews attribute to Yahweh that is not what the Koran says is of and from Allah only confirms the apostatic nature of the Jewish faith.

The question, then, for Rosenzweig is very simple: Do Allah and Yahweh reveal the same truth? And given his brief, his answer can only surprise those who are indifferent to differences and their importances. But he wants to show in detail that they do not at all teach the same truth – only thus can he silence those for whom one religion is as good as any other, thereby destroying the uniquenes of Judaism. His tactic in demonstrating this involves showing that Yahweh does not reveal what Allah does. At the basis of their differences is the most fundamental one of how divine power is construed in the two traditions. For those who want to understand the revealed God of Judaism and Chrisitianity, matters are somewhat complicated by the fact that all too often, Greek ideas are projected onto Him. One of Rosenzweig's great contributions is to reacquaint his readers – Jews and non-Jews alike – with a theology that is non-Greek. (This can also be said of Rosenstock-Huessy, who renounces the use of the word 'theology' because it itself is Greek.)

The first difference, then, comes from an elementary claim that is consistently followed through in the Koran: Allah is all-powerful. Thus His nature is represented as omnipotent. Such a construction enables the Muslim to argue for the rationality of Allah. But if we use the same logic, Yahweh is *not* omnipotent – at least, if by that term His power is understood to be indicative of the unconditional freedom (i.e., caprice) of His will. In contrast to Allah, Yahweh's power is only comprehensible through paradox. Yahweh loves out of need, but need is, from a strictly reasonable (and Muslim) point of view, a deficiency and hence a weakness. Thus, as Rosenzweig correctly points out, Allah 'is really the Creator who could have abstained from creating.'[13] This is precisely the problem that Rosenzweig had identified in his discussion of the limits of the metaphysics of the proto-cosmic – that is, it leaves God severed from the world. And to emphasize his point, he draws attention to the significance of the Koranic formulation that 'Allah is wealthy without world.' In other words, Allah's omnipotence is conceived exactly in this pagan way, in this way that is only overcome by a God of Revelation, that is, a God that *longs to redeem* the World and Man, that even *needs* to relate to the World and Man. Why or what is this need? It is love.

For Rosenzweig, love is not an essential attribute in Allah. If it were, the claims made about Allah's omnipotence would have to be curtailed. Allah would also not be so despotic were He a lover – but were He less powerful He could not be God, the Muslim argues, with an utterly reasonable argument that mimics philosophy in its substitution of reason for the reality of the loving God. God, then, by definition, for the Muslim, is all-powerful, and this is why Rosenzweig claims that 'His power is shown, like the power of an oriental despot, not in the creating of the necessary nor in the authority to decree the law, but in the freedom for arbitrary action.'

No less provocative is Rosenzweig's charge that while Allah appears to have the attributes of the revealer God, Muhammad has, in fact plagiarized the ideas about Revelation – he speaks of 'this remarkable case of world historical plagiarism.'[14] What leads him to make this accusation is that he believes that Muhammad has misunderstood the fundamental character of Revelation. For Rosenzweig, this is evident in the fact that in Islam, 'creation, revelation, redemption' are construed as a sequence akin to a causal model in which one follows on the other, when in fact, Revelation – at least as it is understood by Jews and Christians – is a relationship involving reversal. That is, Jewish and Christian Revelation is a break with Creation, an intrusion on its order that is distinguishable by being an act of *re-creation*; this act of re-creation also is providential. This difference is no small matter, especially given the Islamic claim that Jews and Christians have fallen away from God's original Revelation and that the Koran is the final Revelation of Allah. At stake, then, are two entirely different conceptions of God's nature, command, and plan – and it helps neither Jews nor Muslims if both those differences are concealed under the term of Revelation. To put it another way, if what appears in the Koran as Revelation *is* Revelation, then what Jews call Revelation is all wrong.

For Rosenzweig, the doctrine of providence is the reversal of Creation that is due to love's salvaging power. It is a recognition that Creation in and of itself is only a first step in what something may become, which in turn involves the recognition that what is lost may be saved, and Creation thus begins anew. The failure to grasp providence in this manner as genuine reversal is, for Rosenzweig, evident in how Islam conceives the world as 'created nature at God's feet,' and it is but a further logical development of Allah as all-powerful.[15] For Rosenzweig, this failure finds itself expressed in the doctrines of *kismet* – predestination – and in the view that God's rule over life involves 'an infinite multiplicity of splintered creative acts' that are 'unconnected among themselves,' as each has 'the span of the entire Creation.'[16] There is in this, it should be stressed, nothing controversial to any Muslim, except perhaps the tone of the formulation. The recent award-winning movie *Slumdog Millionaire* with its overarching theme of 'what is written is written' is utterly orthodox Islam and illustrates precisely what Rosenzweig is talking about.

In contrast to the Muslim view that Allah is required to create every singular thing exactly as if it were itself the universal – and thus never for a moment does Allah not do all, never does he relinquish his power over the world – is the Jewish idea of 'the "renewal" of the world.' This view, says Rosenzweig, 'safeguarded for the individual his relationship with the one Creation and consequently with the unity of existence, precisely because the idea recaptures the singular only in the whole and bases providence on creation.' But, he continues,

the conception of providence in Islam destroys any possibility for such a connection; in the first case, providence, as event of renewal for the act of Creation, fulfils that which is already inaugurated in creation; in the second case, it is an intervention of an essential nature, at every moment, in creation, despite its momentary aspect, and it represents a permanent competition between the creative acts and the unity of the Creation.[17]

Once again, then, Allah's omnipotence points to a very different way of being and responding to creatures in the world than Yahweh's. For the former, one really is totally His, whether or not one adheres to the branch of faith in which *kismet* is operative and every single thing is 'enclosed and included in this whole,' and whether or not the individual is 'at every moment "created" from A to Z.' What is essential to the Redemption that Rosenzweig is tracing is *relationship*, but Allah does not have a *relationship* with His subjects – for relationship is always *mutual responsiveness* and *transformation* through responsiveness – something impossible for an omnipotent God. Thus what relationship there is in Islam is not relationship at all, but a one-way, top-down expression of power. Allah is always *sovereign* over subject. And the pious Muslim finds any other perception of God's role as blasphemous. Many humanist critics of Christianity and Judaism, and even members of the Jewish and Christian faiths, also conceive of their God in this manner, which in part is why Rosenzweig is writing *The Star of Redemption* – because today the real meaning of the God and faith of Redemption has largely been lost. And a major part of that loss is the same Enlightenment cluster of core posits of value – viz., rationality, duty, progress, and so on – which he sees as fundamentally pagan. In the eyes of the loving God, such values must be deprived of their lordly status – indeed, at times they must be thoroughly reversed. It must also be said that just as Allah is not Yahweh, the further Rosenzweig goes into depicting the differences, the clearer it is that Yahweh is not Allah. For the pious Muslim who truly wants what the Koran promises, Rosenzweig's Yahweh must look innocuous and weak, must look exactly as He is depicted in Muslim writings – that is, like a distorted representation of the original.

That Islam, like Christianity, is a religion of colonial conversion is another important line of divide for Rosenzweig. His task is to protect the Jew *as Jew* from both colonialisms, which means he must show and protect the significance of the difference. Again it must be said that Rosenzweig's critics – but not Rosenzweig – are complicit in colonial intolerance; and it shows a remarkable triumph of propaganda as well as astonishing ignorance of history to insist that a non-Zionist Jew writing in the shadow of the tottering Ottoman Empire is a threat to tolerance while ignoring the colonialist legacy of Islam's expansion. No one today ignores the colonization of the Christian nations, though it is remarkable how little general knowledge there is about tensions between those who wished to remain true to the Church's mission, and thus were opposed to colonial enslavement, and those members of the earthly city who used the Church for their objectives. Yet as we have seen and repeat, of the two colonialist faiths, the one forms the necessary ally with the Jew, even though the other may at times – even possibly with greater frequency and length – be the more humane in its treatment of the Jew (if not the Zionist). Yet the Muslim is, in spite of him or herself, from Rosenzweig's perspective, also and ever fundamentally the ally of the pagan – indeed; for the energies that Islam responds to and works with are never, for Rosenzweig, more than the energies of Creation. It is the pagan that the Jew must most stringently define himself in relation to; it is the pagan whom he most seeks to alert the Christian to seeing in his or her own temptation. For what is redemptive in Christianity, for Rosenzweig, comes purely from the Jewish side, for the Jewish faith is the faith of the elect whose entire election is built on nothing less than the revealed promise of Redemption.

It is precisely the Jew's insistence on his or her own election that is so hard for both Muslim and Christian to take; the Christian eliminated the Jew by making him or her someone who has not taken the step, someone who refuses to see that the messiah has come; the Muslim eliminated the Jew by making him or her an apostate. The Christian then accuses the Jew for what he or she refuses to become – not a Christian; the Muslim for what he or she *has* become – a bad Muslim. The difference is significant insofar as while the Jew refuses to accept that Jesus is the messiah – and might well, as Rosenzweig did, find Jesus repellent – and as idolatrous as Christianity is, in some respects at least, from a Jewish perspective, it cannot be denied that it began life as a Jewish sect and thus that it has incorporated some fundamentally Jewish insights – notably, that God loves the weak and the suffering, the broken and the despairing – whereas the inner conversion is invariably meaningful in both Judaism and Christianity insofar as this weakness and brokenness is an openness to God's love. In both, God Himself is involved in the process, suffers with Man. Or as Rosenzweig says: 'Man's shortcomings awaken the love of God more powerfully than man's merits.' But this is 'impossible for Islam to ratify, an absurd idea – and yet it is the central idea of faith; Allah has pity on human weakness, but that he likes it more than strength – this is a divine humility foreign to the God of Mohammed.'[18]

If despite remaining God's servant, Christianity is a (somewhat poor) copy of Judaism that is characterized by its idolatries taking it outside of the eternal and setting it on the path of time; by its creating divisions where Jews experience unity, such as the division between priest and saint; by its taking art one step further away from the faithful re-enactment of worship as life-work; by its making nationhood a matter of politics and faith rather than blood and persistence in God's service, then Islam is a copy of a copy. And Islam is, for Rosenzweig, far closer to Christianity than to Judaism, precisely *because* Christianity has picked up so much paganism along its way. Moreover, in their attunements, and supplications, and obedience, the Christian and Muslim faithful, to the extent they retain their faith, inevitably at some point block out the rays of the living God who tries to touch all men and women, irrespective of their religion. But the Christians do so on the plane of Revelation, the Muslims on that of Creation. At the risk of repetition, for Rosenzweig, in *The Star*, religions themselves are but the false bonds that bind them to what is Other than the living loving God; they ever hold on to the goods of pagan existence that are ever under the judgment of death. But as we have emphasized throughout, in spite of Rosenzweig's critique of Christianity, he does not deny that Christians seek to serve the same God as Jews, and hence, in spite of all their errors, that they are used providentially by God. And central to the act of providence is love, a loving God.

Of course, a Christian or a Muslim will not be able to accept the idea that God has elected only one people of blood to do His will. But that is for them to make their case. Insofar as the Christian God is defined as the same God of love as the Jews worship, for Rosenzweig the power of that love is not wasted, and hence God *does* use, indeed He needs, Christians. It is, however, debatable whether Allah is a God of love at all – that is, whether He commands love and whether His laws are laws of love. Certainly as Rosenzweig understands love, and love as taught in the Jewish and Christian Bibles, he does not think it is commensurate with the all-powerful God of Allah, who has no needs. Love, as we have said, always involves a certain dissolution, a disappearance into more; and hence where love takes place between God and man, 'God enters to the point of denying himself.'[19] That is central to Jews and Christians. But this is not Islam. Allah loves the strong. Muhammad is the perfect man because he is the most excellent: so strong, so exemplary in his deeds, his prayers, his fulfilment of the laws of the Koran, 'a religion of duty'; so virile, 'the religion of action'; so smart – the attributes esteemed so highly are so human and yet, still – so pagan. Yes, says Rosenzweig, 'Islam is the religion of humanity' and hence it claims that Allah sent a prophet to each land,[20] while the Jew's faith is in the promise that Yahweh has made with the Jewish people as His elect. But in being universal, the Muslim – like the Christian – becomes driven, by the logic of universal conversion, to war. To be sure, he concedes, Islam insists on war waged humanely,[21] but it is war nevertheless, which again points to how the logic of the pagan clings to both Islam and Christianity; and it must be said, this is why Rosenzweig – though he became more conciliatory toward Zionism as more of his contemporaries and friends such as Buber and Scholem became Zionists – could not become a Zionist; for the Zionist cannot escape the logic of nations, and war is part of that logic. It is precisely by being God's elect that one can be above it, though the price of 'above-ness' does not and cannot release one from being caught in the crossfire. One is still in life, and Yahweh does not promise his people freedom from suffering, at least until the end of times; He promises Redemption, that is, an end of times.

Ultimately and always, in his comparison between paganism and the Jewish life and hence also in his distinction between Allah and Yahweh, Rosenzweig is concentrating on the nature and 'how' of their love – that is, love from subject to Creator (and revealer and redeemer for the Jew) – and on what *distinguishes* that love from Creator/Revealer/Redeemer for the Jew and for others. For the Jew, Yahweh's love is openness, movement, unpredictability, which is why the coming of the kingdom cannot be squeezed into the schema of progress he finds in Islam and Enlightenment humanism, both of which make of time an 'endless indifference of succession.'[22] Allah's 'love,' on the other hand, remains loveless because it is constrained by the very might that dispenses it: the letting go, the becoming more, the extra residue (ruled out from the start by the conception of His power in the original construction), which is so essential to love as love does not occur. Allah 'gives the revelation to humanity like an objective gift from out of itself.'[23] Allah is all-merciful, which – as Rosenzweig correctly notes – is stated in every *surāh* of the Koran. But there is 'only a love which can move from God to man.'[24] And 'the abundance of this love does not grow; simply once and for all, it has been given to the world; there is no increase in it.'[25] Likewise, for Rosenzweig, this is why in Islam the law, exactly as it operates in Kant (one sees here the extent of Rosenzweig's departure from Hermann Cohen, who sees deep affinities among Judaism, Kant, and reason), is so important: the Jewish law is bound up with love and both are ever in movement; everything in Islam has been decreed in the Koran (and then, as historical necessity forced more laws, the *hadith*); but here is no intrinsically necessary development of the law, just as there is no growth in love:

> Islam has before its eyes such an exact positive image which tells how the world must be transformed by walking the way of Allah; precisely here its work in the world is proven to be pure obedience to a law imposed once and for all upon the will. God's commandments, at least those of the 'Second Table,' which specify the love of the neighbour, have this form without exception: 'Thou Shalt not.' They are capable of wearing the clothing of the law only as prohibitions, only as markers delimiting that which is absolutely inconsistent with love of the neighbour; their positive character, their 'thou shalt,' enters exclusively into the form of the one and general commandment of love. The commandments that are clothed in the coat of positive laws mainly concern laws of worship, of the gestural language where love towards God is expressed, that is to say the carrying into effect of the 'First Table.' The worldly work and above all the highest world is a totally free and unpredictable love; in Islam, on the other hand, it is obedience to 'law' decreed once and for all. Likewise, Islamic law seeks everywhere to go back to the declaration that came immediately from the founder, and develops, precisely for this reason, a strictly historical method, whereas Talmudic and the canonical law attempt to establish their sentences not by resorting to the historical ascertaining facts, but by logical deduction.[26]

Love as freedom, then, as we can see, is central to Rosenzweig's understanding of who God is and what is being prayed and hoped for, and it is no less necessary for God than it is for Man and World. As the revealed law that 'love is as strong as death,' which works with the law of Redemption of 'love thy neighbour,' it is also the key to the entire difference between Jew and pagan and Muslim – and, to repeat a difference of real magnitude, God (Yahweh) Himself is seeking Redemption, and His Redemption is bound up with the Redemption of Man and World. To the pious Muslim, these words are either laughable or contemptible, and in any case they suggest weakness, lack, incoherence, uncertainty, and instability – the panoply of risks and penumbras of faith that Rosenzweig sees as deeply complicit in the Jewish eternal configuration of the star and the God whose radiance it depicts. When we recall the opening words of *The Star,* and the link they establish between the fear of death and cognition of the All, it is evident that the Jewish faith, for Rosenzweig, is bound up with the acceptance of death as a necessary moment in the Redemption of the world and the self.

The reversal of the redemptive path – the beginning, surrender into death, and end, the surrender into life, and the surrender to the Jewish God, these are all acts of love, which is why they are acts of faith or trust. Again Rosenzweig insists that this is easily misunderstood if it is taken in the extrinsic way he holds that it functions in Islam:

> The relationship to the world and God, from which the image of the whole of man follows, in Islam has the precursory signs that are exactly the reverse of true faith; so traditional obedience for the worldly work proceeds from the soul's free submission to God, which is a matter of unceasing reconquest by force of arms. In the arms of Revelation, it is from the simultaneous humble and proud entry of the soul into the peace of the divine love, an entry that took place once and for all, that always sudden, always unforeseen acts of love proceeds, in the place of the saint and the paradoxical form of his piety which deluding and surpassing all expectations scoffs at all imitations. Islam thus substitutes the simply exemplary life of the pious man. Every saintly figure has its absolutely personal traits: to the figure of the saint there belongs the saint's legend. In Islam there are no accounts of the saints: their memory is honoured, but this memory is without content. This piety that simply obeys is based on a free self-denial, laboriously re-conquered at every moment.[27]

Whether Rosenzweig was a saint is debatable. But certainly he made the saint the cornerstone of the Jewish and Christian experiences, implying throughout *The Star* that the Jewish life is a life prepared for sainthood by virtue of its understanding of what God and love are. And what makes the saint has nothing to do with observing the extrinsic practices of faith. Sainthood is what is achieved through the incalculable yet redemptive responses to love's command. By contrast, the specificity of Allah's commands and requirements and models is a large part of why its inductions and appeals are so attractive for people wanting stability, and so powerful – they appeal to our sense of duty, order, and orientation (which is, to be sure, also a large part but for Rosenzweig not the *essential* part of the Jewish faith or Christian Church).

Closely related to this incalculable and interior quality that Rosenzweig esteems so highly is the Jewish/Christian emphasis on the weak and invisible. The parts that seem broken and worthless to the eyes of men and women are the very stuff that God reactivates through His love; these are the bricks and mortar of His kingdom. Likewise these are what remain invisible to those who merely link Creation here with the world to come and who make of that world something just like this one only more pleasurable. Of course there are numerous Christians, quite possibly even the overwhelming majority, who think like this, but for Rosenzweig this merely confirms yet again that Christians constantly lapse into paganism. As in his discussion of Christianity, his discussion of Islam is not based on those who lapse, but on what he sees as the central doctrines and lifeways that issue from its divine decrees.

The Islamic view of life is one whose parts constantly reinforce a view of life that Rosenzweig simply cannot accept. And the belief that all should honour that way of life, as much as the way that he sees has been opened to the Jewish people, is fundamentally at odds with everything he holds important. To anyone who takes the New Thinking or the meaning of Jewish life seriously, any ethical/political attempts that would reduce Revelation and Redemption to the horizon of pagan sensibilities – no matter how liberal or moral one might feel such acts are – would annihilate Jewish life. It is so interesting that Rosenzweig's decision to remain a Jew in the face of Rosenstock-Huessy's and the Ehrenbergs' callings to him to join them in their path as apostates has been applauded, yet his insistence on the divide between Jews and Muslims has tended to be either patronizingly dismissed or outright rebuked. Such charges fail to see what is at stake in the future world to be made. Moreover, as I have implied throughout this chapter, Rosenzweig's critics have never demonstrated that what he actually says about the differences between Islam and Judaism is false. What is extraordinary, and what is such a cipher of our *Zeitgeist,* is that Rosenzweig is criticized so staunchly by people who also do not think Islam is true – but they would rather, for the sake of peace, make all faiths and Gods equal. It is a particular political strategy, another kind of faith, disguised as Reason – an example of what Rosenzweig called 'atheistic theology.' It is, in other words, a purely Idealist tactic – widely deployed and, not surprisingly, believed in by many, especially within the academic world – that would dilute the three historically great contradictory triads with their different Gods, Humans, and World into one reasonable circle.[28] At least the atheist, who would openly exhort Jew and Muslim and Christian to throw off their past and rethink their services to 'humanity,' acknowledges the extent of the problem that has been weaving its way for so many centuries. But what I have called the Idealist representation of the issues is based on ignorance about those issues, mainly due to the desire to transform reality into an idealized version in the hope that such a transmutation will eventually have the world itself accompany it. Rosenzweig simply did not believe this is how reality is made – as if reality were, as the Platonists and positivists hold, a composite or aggregation of things or objects. Moreover, a Muslim's response to Rosenzweig's critique of Islam inevitably must take the dispute to a place very different from the liberal pluralistic one. That place may well be less 'tolerant,' but it is no less important on that account. Rosenzweig's critique, then, far from being something that should provoke embararrasment, should be applauded for its candour and be the kind of starting point for Jewish–Muslim dialogue, in the same way that the blunt and provocative criticisms he and Rosenstock-Huessy made served Jewish–Christian dialogue. The weakness of post–Second World War social theory has been that its fear of any kind of resurgent fascism has contributed to an academic environment in which discussion of the deepest differences is only tolerated if they fit within the liberal template and consensus of what constitutes 'emancipation.' Yet the major differences of faith, of the sort being discussed in *The Star*, cannot be adequately corralled into 'emancipation.'

15 Rosenstock-Huessy on Islam, Confucianism, Taoism, and Buddhism

Islam plays such an important role in the *The Star of Redemption* because that work needs to demonstrate its central conviction: that the Jewish faith is the faith of God's elect; and that the Jewish understanding of Revelation and Redemption is the original truth, the eternal fire from which any other truly revealed faith must take its original orientation. Because Rosenstock-Huessy does not dispute Rosenzweig's central claim, the entire concept of Redemption as something that must be carefully defended philosophically is not a central issue for him. He is far more interested in demonstrating the historical *process* of Redemption, which is why, for him, the Church and hence Christianity is so central to his work.

As with Rosenzweig, Rosenstock-Huessy's position on Islam is not that of the liberal critic of Islam, who either draws attention to discordances between liberal and Islamic principles, or who tries, like the pluralist, to downplay the discrepancies lest discussion of those fundamental differences exacerbate tensions. As we saw earlier, Rosenzweig had drawn attention to the future battle between 'Church and Islam.' As we have also seen, he not only emphasized the contradiction between Judaism and Islam on that note but had also drawn the demarcation lines between those two faiths, just as he had done with Judaism and Christianity.

Rosenstock-Huessy would take up discussing the battle between 'Church and Islam.' Like Rosenzweig – indeed, also like most literate Muslims – he saw that Europe had long been, for all its active pagan energies, a Christian invention, even if the Christian is ever standing on a precipice, occupying a position between (redemptive) life and (pagan) fecundity ending in death. What Rosenzweig had called a future battle between 'Church and Islam' was, for Rosenstock-Huessy, a battle between Johannine Christianity – a deinsitutionalized Church, most of whose members do not even realize they are members – and Islam.

What, for Rosenstock-Huessy, was the case with societies (such as Japan, China, and India) that had not been formed by the Church, but had instead entered into the 'one world' through the revolutions of nations and the explosions of the two world wars, and with what he called other 'pre-Christian remainders,' was also the case with Islam. Like the great non-Christian nations, that great non-Christian religion and political force had been placed on a new footing, most obviously as a result of the formation of Middle Eastern states and the wave of post–Second World War immigration to Europe.

This is the context in which Islam has become reactivated as a serious issue, indeed, as an issue of faith. Of faith that raises the most serious questions about what the West is – for the people of the West are no more important than anyone else, just as, since All Souls' Day, pope and peasant have been viewed as equally created in God's image and have thus been seen by the Church, irrespective of their station/vocation/office/profession, to be equally loved and called to their station, and so on. The question is what kind of world we are making as we draw from and respond to the powers of the past, the crises of the present, and the promise of the future. The hope in the answer is that it will be a better world than one of wars and suffering. Hope, as Rosenzweig so perceptively put it, is the core of Johannine Christianity, for hope is the accompanying mood of the unknown, and modernity's acceleration is one that makes hope an ever necessary condition of soul if we are to counter modernity's other great fabrication – despair.[1]

The above preamble is central to Rosenstock-Huessy's framing of the issue of Islam. It should also suggest that in his discussion of Islam, the thrust of his analysis is not, as it is in Rosenzweig, primarily theological; rather, it is directed at answering the question of Islam's temporality and its place in the forming of the kingdom. Or to say this slightly differently, both Rosenzweig and Rosenstock-Huessy always do theology sociologically, but Rosenstock-Huessy reads the theology *through* the sociology; thus, where Rosenzweig touches on the fit between social formations and matters of faith insofar as they support his analysis of peoples, in Rosenstock-Huessy the question of social formation (and its historical genesis) always occupies central place, alongside language. Thus for him 'Tribes, Realm, People are the aspects of the past, the present, the future of a group consciousness.

They are political time-names.'[2] And the issue of social formation has, for him, reached a stage now where we are forced to speak of a consciousness of a planetary society. This stage is itself part of three millennial events: God becoming man (i.e., the Church's incarnation of Jesus' endowment); the revolutionizing of the world of the second millennium; and the future millennium's promise and prospect of humanity becoming 'complete' (*vollzählig*) by becoming the heir of all the times. Islam now constitutes one large time-body within a greater planetary force field, and as such it must be accommodated and understood. Note, though, that according to Rosenstock-Huessy, if there is to be a great society with a real peace, then its Christian foundations must not be relinquished (and those foundations include Johannine forms of international law based on human rights, freedoms of faith, etc.). This does not mean tearing out the traditions of peoples, root and branch; rather, it means bringing them into metanomic concordance with their respective tensions and discordances. This is why it is so important to understand a key idea we mentioned earlier in Rosenstock-Huessy: that there is no individual salvation, and he has no interest in individuals changing their denomination but *every* interest in the planetary concordance of peoples and institutions to ensure peace and freedom.

When we discussed Rosenzweig's critique of Islam, we set to one side a key fact of its nature: its durability. Rosenstock-Huessy follows Augustine and Dante in his belief that institutions endure only if sustained by love. That is, the continuance and expansiveness of social formations is testament to their loves. This same appreciation had led Rosenzweig to make the following tart comment in *Paralipomenona*, 29 January 1916: 'Augustine, Confessions VIII: The spread of Christianity as proof of its truth – it is good that Islam came' – a neat Jewish retort to the Christian triumphalist, for it drives home that a pagan religion may also endure.

Nevertheless, from the point of view of Augustine's insight – one that Rosenstock-Huessy shares – durability and expansiveness indicate a certain attractiveness and worthiness within Islam,[3] and even that it is providential. To say this, however, is not on its own enough to make it identical with the other revealed religions. But it is an argument for Islam being part of God's plan. This is why Rosenstock-Huessy does not go as far as Rosenzweig by declaring that Islam is *not* a revealed religion of Redemption. Indeed, contrary to Rosenzweig, in his Lectures on Comparative Religion, he tells his students that Islam *is* a revealed religion. But its Revelation must be seen as part of a greater

Revelation.[4] Thus along with the Star of David, 'the sun streaming cross of Christ' and the crescent moon 'have all received their assignments and have been used to strengthen the economy of the spirit.'[5]

Yet for Rosenstock-Huessy, Islam is a Christian heresy,[6] even if Muhammad did not really *know* who Christ was, or what His Church was, because that Church sought to galvanize *all* into neighbours under the one God. Islam continued that project owing to its dissatisfaction with the Church's inability to 'save' those whom Muhammad saw caught up in endless turmoil. And Islam has continued to expand and convert. For Rosenstock-Huessy, Islam is unique for it has brought the tribes that the cross could not penetrate into the one universal history. Moreover, it has done so mainly by recasting tribal elements in a way that has enabled their perpetuity and expansion and that has also enabled a common spiritual purpose to galvanize them in their love of the One God and in the laws of life that have saved them from extinction. What mainly interests Rosenstock-Huessy about Muhammad is that he was a man of the tribe who wanted to bring peace to the warring tribes by constructing one great peaceful tribe under Allah: 'Islam replaced the eon of tribes with the eon of unity, as their own memories were fragmenting and there could no longer be any true tribe in the old world.'[7] Islam's genius was that it knew how to tap into and assuage the needs of tribal peoples long before Christianity could do this: it knew which elements of the tribe to retain and which to transmogrify and prohibit so that peoples of the tribes would be able to continue in a world they recognized as their own. But no longer was it a world that was vulnerable and weak and fragile when confronted with imperialist threats. Islam was able to unite disconnected tribes into armies. Just as the Roman Empire, then, had ultimately been a gift for dying Greek city-states, sparing them from total annihilation, Islam rescued tribes that had never been 'citified': 'From Dakar to Aden, from Persia to Pakistan the tribes owe it to Islam that for 1300 years it has treated them homeopathically: The waves of Islam have galvanised these alliances. It rejuvenates each tiny tribe of one or two thousand souls by providing a heroic, a great survival measure that is larger than life, by means of which chieftains and medicine men can reform themselves.'[8] Moreover, as Rosenstock-Huessy reminds his readers in the *Soziologie*, prior to Islam, the Greek Churches had only converted realms and city-states; Islam, then, was a reaction to this deficit of the Churches of antiquity.[9]

Islam thus is both 'a magnificent monument of the eternal streams' of the tribes[10] and a 'denunciation of the inadequacy of the realms, the

Jews, the Greeks and the Church: they had not pacified the illiterate, temple-less, picture-less, realm-less ancient tribes of the Arabs – or Germans, or Bantus, or indigenes of the islands [*Fischi-insulaner*].'[11] He had made a similar point in his 1957 review of Henri Pierenne's classic *Mohammed and Charlemagne,* where he wrote that his own research into law, language, literature, and liturgy had confirmed Pierenne's thesis that Islam was fundamental in forcing the West – that is, through Charlemagne – 'into far northern intercontinental regions':

> This question has been neglected too long so that Pirenne's thesis seems overdue. For a much more serious task looms before us as soon as we see the break-up of the ancient world as happening from 650 A.D. to 750 A.D. and let the insipid date of 476 disappear. How far are Charlemagne and Muhammed two, the two possible solutions of introducing the non-citified peoples, under the veneer of the Greek-Roman Polis-civilisation, to the worship of One God? Muhammed subjugated the polis to the simple faith of warriors. He freed the tribes from magic and devilry, from tatoo and vendetta. He cleaned but did not open their lips. Charlemagne kept the Roman Catholic veneer and his warrior-bishops changed its creed (filioque), its liturgy and its canons.[12]

He adds, two paragraphs later:

> Pirenne's book has forced upon us a more comprehensive vision of the Dark Ages, so called, during which the ancient polis began to-be replaced by 'the peoples' in the West as Henri Francois Muller has shown in his *Époque Merovingienne* (1945), and where the superstitions of the tribesmen from Africa to India were at least blocked and largely eliminated by the simplifications of the Qur'an.[13]

Given, then, the importance that Rosenstock-Huessy assigns to the relationship between Islam and tribes, it is worth pausing on what he saw as so important in tribes, and why he believed there can be no universal history unless (a) it is inclusive of the universal meaning of tribes, and (b) it acknowledges the role of Islam in bringing those tribes into the one economy of salvation.

For Rosenstock-Huessy, the tribe is the most elemental form of human organization – the original form. It was the first human body of time and thus the condition on which all other social forms took their point of departure. If humans are creatures whose divinity is realized through the creation and redemption of times – a process that facilitates the exploration of their plasticity and the cosmos at large – then the tribes were the beginning of that journey. 'Our history begins with graves,' he says, echoing Vico, before going on to emphasize that with the act of burial the roles between death and life are reversed in such a way that death is transformed so that it is no longer simply the extinction of life, but through the grave becomes placed in service to life.[14] The ability to look the dead in the eye is, for Rosenstock-Huessy, the source of human freedom. Here he means freedom in the sense of opening up and nurturing our creative capacities over time. This is not for him the same as freedom in some moral abstract sense or in the sense of giving appetites their full reign (such a widely held modern view of freedom, from Spinoza to Sade to Bataille and Deleuze, simply reproduces the paradigm of appetitive expansion, as opposed to the much more Nietzschean emphasis on cultivation of types).[15]

The journey of humanity, then, begins when it grasps that it is not simply subject to the world – and to no small extent, this is one more reason why Rosenstock-Huessy sees naturalism as such a devastating spiritual principle, for it dissolves us into and entombs us with the calculable – but instead takes its orientation from something that calls us to make new worlds. The embodiments of that making and the powers that speak beyond the grave are the brave path makers, the heroes, without whose courage, energy, and self-sacrifice the tribe could not survive: 'A tribe is not derived from blood or race, but from the stewardship of past and present through the eyes of the heroes.' Heroes are the original founders, and as such they are, for Rosenstock-Huessy, the first persons of world history.[16]

Just as gods are powers whose names are called upon to give direction in the weaving of selves and worlds, the names of the heroes are the ligaments that enable later generations to clear their way through the thickets and trials of life. The living don masks to represent the heroes here on earth. Everywhere in Rosenstock-Huessy's anthropological excavations of tribes, realms, city-states, and the Israelites we encounter his profound regret at what post-Enlightenment people have lost sight of. It is not that he believes it possible to simply leap back into time; his is not a romantic yearning, for he knows that older lifeways have met with catastrophes, which is why they have not simply endured. But has has a deep sense that life within the modern machine has created its own form of spiritual hell and that the way out requires attentiveness on our part to the other lines of life that endured for so long. One major reason why the West today feels so unsure of itself when confronted with Islam and when faced with obvious contradictions to its own sense of progress – such as the desire of Muslim women to maintain the veil – is that the West feels deeply a sense of loss and rootlessness. This was given early expression in Montaigne's writings about how Europeans should learn from the natives, whose lifeways they were so brutally destroying. This problem is exacerbated in the West by a profound sense of shame over its imperial triumphs and the accompanying death that such triumphs involve – and here, it is interesting that such widespread shame is not replicated in other cultures with imperial pasts, such as Japan and China. Nor is it replicated in Islamic societies. This is one reason why it is so hard to find a common vocabulary for achieving a peace. But the West's readiness to valorize alien traditions also springs from a deep grief: the loss of any sense of its own continuity of the living with the dead.

For Rosenstock-Huessy, 'every tribe,' like every social formation, 'is a force-field.'[17] What for him is constitutive of the particular force field that is the tribe is the spoken matrix that binds together its intrinsic, extrinsic, trajective, and prejective orientations. According to him, four sentences are constitutive of social life in general and hence of all speech. These sentences he refers to as *Grundgesetze jeder Sprache.* Thus:

> The sentence: this is the origin [*Herkommen*] founds the language of the cult of the dead. It establishes what may not come earlier. The sentence – these are the successors, founds the language of propitiation of integrating everything new into the union, whether through a breach of law or as a new warrior. It establishes justice and law. The third sentence – This is adversity and [these are] aliens/ strangers [*Fremde*], founds the language of the science of the use of weapons and technical tactics. The fourth sentence: This is [our] country [*Heimat*][18] establishes the language of poetry and the arts.[19]

As we saw earlier in our discussion of language/speech, it is clear that for Rosenstock-Huessy the practices of the cult, of governance or law making, and of poesy and accumulating knowledge (to take *Wissenschaft* in its broadest sense) are constitutive of human societies; and those practices are founded by speech acts that enable the subsequent callings and engagements of others in the reproduction of these activities. As such they are the openings of trails reaching from past and future, and from inside ourselves as subjects, and from outside into the world. Thus the beginning of our self-realization is a socio-cosmic act first undertaken by the tribes. The tribe finds itself within and confronted by the All; and it is faced, as we all are, with the most elemental poles of orientation – not, he points out in the first volume of the *Soziologie*, with a logical or dialectical triad, but with the quadrilateral facticity of the interpenetrations and crossovers of time and space: 'Truth is the wonder that God holds out a promise to our imagination, when we really speak, call, confess and discern, that is when we simple-mindedly wander on the path of the cult of our predecessors, the rights of our successors, war with nature and the fleeting feet of poetry.'

All social formations are, then, attempts to achieve our inner aim, the becoming (as Nietzsche said) of who we are. That becoming, along with the essential plasticity of humanity, arises from the fact that the creative openings of the world are part and parcel of the creative openings of our selves, or more precisely the time-bodies that form selves and the undergirding commands of language that set us on our way in the initial explorations of the 'All': 'We find the movement into the All written into the heart of the tribes.'[20]

I think it no accident that while Rosenstock-Huessy generally shies away from overtly philosophical terminology, in the *Soziologie* he picks up a manifestly Rosenzweigian term to map out the journey of the human species – a journey that is, for him, the journey of the Holy Spirit or of Revelation itself. When Rosenzweig expresses the formulation of love being as strong as death as the key to Revelation, he does so in the context of a member of the eternal people. And as such, as we have argued in detail, he wants to show how the Jews and *only* the Jews have this particular role of being the eternal people. But Rosenstock-Huessy is interested in how God pours himself into time and how through time we as a species absorb, share, enhance, and express the powers of God. That love is as strong as death, then, is a truth that, while given biblical expression first by the Jews, must be shown to be inscribed into the very heart of humanity from the origin of its undertaking. Thus in the *Soziologie* he writes in the section 'The True Tribe' that 'a whole tribe makes death stronger than love between the sexes, and love towards the heroes stronger than death.'[21] 'The tribe can be defined as an institution to create marriages.'[22] Marriage, he continues, produces the tribe – it is the condition of more life, but the hero speaks from the place of death and inducts tribes into the trail of love that leads beyond death.

While the hero is the saviour of the tribe, and while love for the hero is a means of replenishing the powers of the tribe, the very condition of survival and enhancement is the weak link through which the Holy

Spirit pushes further toward a new formation in order to strengthen the love between peoples. The power of the past is so overwhelming that it becomes – to use an old Marxist term – a fetter on the spirit. For in the tribe the past eventually becomes so strong that it blocks the call of the future. Of course, from the condition of the modern, within which the acceleration of daily life seems like a great juggernaut, the past is a refreshing place, a place of wonder that possesses all the humanity we have lost. But Rosenstock-Huessy is no more an apologist of the present and its numerous pathologies than he is a romantic about the past. Rather, he is an advocate of life as a process of growth. For him, where there is no growth there is sickness and death. For him, the idea that there is a space where rest is both eternal and pleasant is an Idealist fantasy. And this, for him, is why war is not just something that can be meaningfully dismissed on moral grounds. An interesting contrast between Rosenstock-Huessy and the widespread modern Idealist way of seeing things is evident in their respective assessments of the tribe. For Rosenstock-Huessy, the path of war is an essential component of tribal life; tribes must fight their way through the nightmares and monstrous trials of survival. People who live in realms have protracted periods of peace because the realms seek to reconcile 'heaven and earth,'[23] they seek the patterns of the eternal, stability and prosperity. Of course, they too go to war; their eternity does not last, and with the increased power of each social formation, the repercussions from the failure to keep the peace grow ever greater. As Homer reminded his listeners who wished to stave off their own demise, Troy was defeated because its civility was no protection against the powers of rage that its transgression had contributed to unleashing.

With tribes, the path of war is a day-to-day reality, just as war itself within tribal formations is an essential condition of life's perpetuity:

> The war path presumes enemies. The spirit blows in the banners. If the wind swells them, then the spirit blows through the hoards of warriors . . . In war the [the warrior] wages his life on his spirit. That he celebrates the nine scalps of his defeated enemies is spiritual service. The warrior is proud that to honour the spirit he risked his life nine times. To risk one's life is the essense of the warrior; the death of enemies is a secondary matter to him.
>
> War emanates from the uncanny nature of our existence on earth. The true tribe has its homecountry only in the totem pole. Only this eye sees it in a friendly manner. The gazing wilderness enforces war. The warpath is

the escape portal of a tribe surrounded by the bush. When Germany felt itself encircled, World War 1 was unavoidable, and the disaster of tribal madness was the direct consequence.[24]

Being surrounded by life that is unpredictable and dangerous is the basic condition of tribes, for whom the world is an always active field of dangerous threats. Compared to realms and city-states, tribes are much more precarious modalities of survival. Yet they are the original shape of spiritual life, and the path of war is the sacrificial requirement for perpetuating a specific body of life: 'the warpath is the form of the fortress of life';[25] and 'on the warpath, the living generation is willing to keep its own path so straight that it itself is sacrificed. That it is the living victim of this conflict of his tradition with inimical traditions.'[26] Tradition here has nothing to do with romantic longing, or with retaining a museum of something that ennobles us in our more reflective moments when we want to take a break from the mechanical rhythms of our present: it is the very condition of survival, an all or nothing. This staking of the all of a lifeway on the prospect of its nothingness is something that Rosenstock-Huessy treats with genuine awe, and it is why he is so adamantly opposed to equating war with murder: the former is a sacrificial act made for a group's perpetuity, the latter a personal act:

> War is the elimination of a danger to your own law. War is never the same as a murder, or a struggle [or] a fight, a personal fight. War is always something higher because it always tries to protect the way to speak, your spirit. You can't wage war . . . except for your spirit against a foreign spirit.[27]

And in *Letters to Cynthia* he uses a formulation that he will use on many occasions, 'all wars are religious wars':

> Wars are milestones on the road of disclosed directions, beyond the floating shortlivedness of monochron [*sic*] animals. Across the abyss of every individual's passing out of existence, the human soul wishes to invest in lastingness. Her efforts shall make for the perpetuity of life; hence she needs direction . . . The bloody sacrifices of war enable the living to do that which we crave most, to stay in a meaningful path which is longer than 'our own' monochron life, a path which leads from the beginning to the end of time, as it seems to us . . .
>
> The existence of this path is more important to any human than his own physical existence. We ourselves can think of us as human only because

we are placed on this path and because the path has a certain direction. To swerve from this direction, would be the loss of our humanity. In fact, you cannot make people keep direction unless they believe that the salvation of mankind depends on their not swerving one bit to the left or right.

War expresses this certainty within the soldier that the direction of history must be protected from being made crooked by the enemy . . .

. . . All wars . . . are religious wars. There are no others. There may be blasphemous ones; this still is of a religious type. If people did not believe in revealed direction, no wars could occur ever. (Disclosed direction is just another word for 'God,' of course, for the god who governs us and who informs us; but we shall avoid the term.) And because all wars always are and have been and shall be symptoms of the religious character of man in history, all peaces must lead to a new definition of their religion, in the hearts of the survivors. A real peace must make friend and foe of the preceding war share a new religion, a faith, in a direction now revealed authoritatively for both parts of the conflict.[28]

While Rosenstock-Huessy takes war seriously because it has been part of the survival strategy of every time-body that has attempted to establish its direction and ensure its perpetuity, he is just as equally convinced – as we have already noted – that the 'moral equivalent of war' must be found. In the chapter 'A World Without War?' in *Planetary Service*, he argues that such a discovery will only be possible once there is the free flow between borders – that is, when neither of the great power formations of the human spirit that stretch from tribe to nation becomes the primary repository for spiritual nourishment of a group. It is not, for him, a question of voluntary renunciation of such modes of organization; rather, it is creative forms of societies developing through shared interests and energies that make a genuine We.

Rosenstock-Huessy's writings on the tribes, most systematically in the second volume of the *Soziologie*, are lengthy and fascinating, attempting as they do to depict the multitudinous explorations of the All's freedom and its excursions into love's triumphs over death. He comments on the origins and historical significance of the following creations of tribal life: graves, totems, heroes, altars, marriage and the abolition of incest, animal guides, tattoos as early instances of writing, dance and song as a means of group integration, the importance of plainchant and speech, the primordial discernment between play and seriousness, the relationship between warfare and the acquisition of knowledge, the relationship between plainchant, spells, and witchcraft, the powers of metamorphosis, and the relationship between clothing and politics and office and shame. But tribal life is also burdened by its insecurities and fragilities, by threats from powers of greater magnitude, and even by its reliance on what enables them to survive in the first place – viz., the ghosts of the past. For these ghosts are strong enough to guide a tribe, but relatively weak when confronted by circumstances and powers that come from time-bodies that have stored up more future.

In his discussion of Islam, then, Rosenstock-Huessy's most interesting insights stem from his recognition of the kind of time-body out of which it grew and how it tends to reproduce the world from whence it came. That the trace of the tribe is as transparent in the problems that Islam solves as in the solutions it develops is far from simply a means that he uses to 'refute' Islam. It is, in fact, for him, the key to explaining Islam's endurance and power. Of course, to repeat, this is not to say that Islam was never 'civilized' – 'civilization,' for Rosenstock-Huessy as for Nietzsche, was never a word that commanded much respect.[29] It is, however, to say that to simply believe that Islam teaches more or less what Judaism does or what Christianity does is to fail to see how each of these three ways of giving life direction, of binding peoples over time, function. It is to fail to understand the power that makes each what it is. That the countries where Islam is both strong and traditional are countries whose tribal characteristics are generally still strong and whose 'national identity' is often precarious is, from his perspective, perfectly in keeping with what kinds of powers Islam orchestrates.

For Rosenstock-Huessy, this is evident from the beginning in how Islam constructs Moses, Jesus, and Muhammad as tribal chiefs, and from how it insists that Muhammad is the most important because of his place in the lineage. This move retains the idea of there being a lineage of temporal successors to lead each tribe, but it also reverses the process of the tribe by making the last the most important. Yet by making the *last* the supreme legislator for future generations, Muhammad retains the same role as the totem. Muhammad does not grasp that Moses and Jesus articulated principles, not ordinances – hence the importance of the *hadith*, which tries to second-guess the endless variety of possible circumstances resulting in transgressions against Allah, which a reading of the *hadith* can then resolve. But the very needs, indeed crises, that gave birth to the *hadith* are indicative of Islam's failure to construe Allah in any way that resembles the Holy Spirit of the Christians or the moving God of the Jews.

For Muhammad, all creative epochs are essentially indistinguishable so that the Pharaohs, Jesus, and Moses are all basically the same. There are here resonances of Rosenzweig's critique of Islam's (and the Enlightenment's) sequentialist view of historical progress, but the core point for Rosenstock-Huessy is that Islam remains ignorant of the epoch-making nature of time and endowment, as epochs are simply dissolved into a flow so that a unique body of time – apart from that created by Muhammad – is never grasped for what it is. It is as if a veil is thrown over the vastly different temporal creatures, making it impossible for someone whose orientation is dictated by Muhammad to see what really comes from another time. Moses and Jesus are simply other prophets whose followers have become idolatrous, when in fact, for Rosenstock-Huessy, each of them opens up a new pathway of world, self, and human making. In this respect, Muhammad and his immediate followers stand in a paradoxical relationship to Christianity. On the one hand, they had remained outside of the time-body of Christ, and hence though Muhammad was born after Christ, he actually inhabited a pre-Christian time-body. He remained a tribal chief embarking on building an empire. Christ's power, for Rosenstock-Huessy, came at least in part from the fact that he had wanted to rejuvenate each form of social life by recognizing the inherent limit of each, and thus had forsaken trying to attain power for his followers by taking them into these old lions' dens. Christ wanted to make a new humanity possible on the basis of acts that defied the logic of prophets (the Jews), poets/legislators (the Greeks), tribes, and empires. That is why Christ refused to accept the office of king, priest, prophet, or poet – why, that is, he refused to be absorbed into any of the great offices of antiquity. It was because he saw that the fulfilment of humanity lay in the readiness to take on ever new offices and roles, ever new incarnations in accordance with the Holy Spirit, incarnations that were outside the purview of the imagination of the time but that were the very rewards of faith in God's love. For Rosenstock-Huessy, Jesus opened up a new orientation to life precisely *because* he 'did not enter into the life of antiquity, but he stepped out of it . . . Jesus made non-existence the kernel of an almost never ending line of succession of Christs.'[30] Jesus appeared where the basic types of ancient possibilities of humanity were accessible – and then he rejected every one of them by requiring that each office be but a way of momentarily serving the living God. That is why Jesus was able to resist earthly temptation: each of the earthly powers was a potential dead end:

> In place of an organic growth of God's kingdom through the world in tribes, realms, nations, Islam posits a catalogue of messengers of disconnected acts of divine compassion. For him Islam from Adam to Mohammad there were only ever tribes. Each originator of divine truth stood for Mohammad in the same epoch, in the same tribe. That enabled him to become the greatest plagiarist of world history. He simply outcompeted Abraham and Jesus, that he was the leader of 'another' people, and at the same time he was indeed the last prophet. As leader of 'another' people, he was not indebted to anyone but God. As the last prophet, however, he was able to declare his army as the army of all armies. His war path now became the only path, on which all older 'Otherness' is swallowed up in this last prophecy. Through jealousy Mohammad denied the other forms of history. Love of the dead, love of heaven, love of god and love of the neighbour organized the real world of peoples into Scythians and Egyptians, Jews and Greeks. For Mohammad it was all one. God had compassion for all creatures, but he didn't create them in a rich colourful plan of salvation.[31]

That Islam is more singular in its purpose, compared to other religions that emphasize the greater possibilities of life that are generated under different social formations, and that it is hence more unforgiving in what it tolerates, is obvious from the *sharia*, which bears all the hallmarks of tribal law – hallmarks that are tempered but not eliminated by Islam. Thus, for example, the prophet, according to the *hadith,* insists that adulterers be stoned.[32] As a means for ensuring that warriors do not touch one another's wives, this is thoroughly understandable, but as a way of dealing with passion and transgression, it retains the harsh stringencies of tribal necessity. This bringing of the potencies of life *back* into an alignment that does not defy tribal sensibilities is, for Rosenstock-Huessy, part of the same 'colourlessness' he alludes to above. For novelty and difference themselves can be a great threat to tribal life. Rosenstock-Huessy sees this characteristic of tribal conformity preserved in the Islamic understanding of piety:

> The spirits of the dead teachers are also not liberated, like the spirit of the saints, from whose ranks each speaks to us freely. No, the 'pious' of Islam

have colourlessness as their ideal. They are all simply 'pious,' and that's why their dictums [*Aussprüche*] even the most original, are legitimated through a continuous genealogy, i.e. legitimated through the least original thing there is. In the tribe it is precisely familial ancestry, which is the only thing that testifies to the right spirit and this set of norms [*Formelhaftig-keit*].[33]

Just as Rosenzweig had noted that Islam shares some essential emphases that one also finds in the Enlightenment, Rosenstock-Huessy sees that the failure of Islam to adequately denote time as a variable that is not simply a sequential measure but also a means of forming eons, epochs, ages, and creatures is a failure shared by most academicians – 'the academic world has no relationship to living time'[34] – and mechanistic philosophers. This is another reason why contemporary theopolitical discussions of Islam rarely address the all-important issue of *which* time is transported by *which* faith, and vice versa.

For Rosenstock-Huessy, the Church was the great carrier of Christ's teaching not because it was a paragon of virtue but because it worked with the powers of time. He emphasizes this point when he contrasts Islam with the Church, noting that the Church conceded three days of the dead: All Saints' Day (from 854), All Souls' Day (from 998), and a November festival of the dead (November-Totenfest). But, he continues:

Nevertheless the relationship between Church: tribe is different than that between Islam: tribe. The Church retained its freedom to say yes or no to all the powers of time. In Islam this was not the case. The military success of the moment, which the hero embodies in the tribe has remained the yardstick for the caliphs. No follower of Mohammad understands the fruits of our opting out of 'the time,'[35] as the opting out of existence [*Existenz*] in order thereby to step into being [*Dasein*]. The most terrible proof for the Islamic misunderstanding of time are the first four caliphs. These four successors of the prophet were successful conquerors. And they are placed over the place of the four Christan evangelists! In them one knows exactly what it is to be orthodox. With that, Islam retreated back into the old chiefdom of the tribes. Who looks back into the past can only worship success that comes by counting scalps: one must prefer the already spoken to the still unspoken. This fate [*Fatum*], to which the tribes succumb – 'the already said' is the meaning of fate – is simply preserved in Mohammad's kismet. In Islam the most pious is the most unoriginal. He no longer does magic, is no more struck by magic. Islam bequeathed this blessing. The curses of the tribe were silenced. To this extent he came as a liberator.[36]

As this illustrates, the old religious bonds of the tribe are displaced so that the medicine man or tribal practitioner of magic is dispensed with but the more essential bond with the past is retained. Similarly, Muhammad forbids alcohol and thus eliminates the tribal intoxicant, but he also enables the intoxication of the senses by allowing polygamy – thus violating more monogoamous tribal practices and their accompanying kinship structures.[37] Likewise, Muhammad ended the interminable intertribal fighting in the Arab world not by eliminating the path of war but by *expanding* it and giving it a spiritual purpose that would make brothers of all who followed his commands.[38] Both Israel and the Church demanded a much more radical break with the tribal lifeway, and thus Rosenstock-Huessy says that Muhammad 'sealed off the sons of the desert against the preserved truth of the realm which Israel had abrogated (against the temple, astrology, letters, agriculture), he spared them from the treasures of the "polis" of the humanistic sciences and arts which the Church had preserved.'[39] While Islam would eventually make way for some inflow of sciences and the arts, at least among its more 'civilized' denizens, it remained the case that the more open scientists and artists were to the humanist treasures of the Greeks, the more suspicion other Muslims cast on them.[40] It is noteworthy that discussions about the arts and sciences in Islam and the West tend to go back and forth between what either was or was not achieved by Islam in the arts and sciences; those discussions rarely take up the point – one that is central to Rosenstock-Huessy's understanding of a social formation – that what can make something so powerful for its time is precisely its denial and prohibition of certain extrinsic powers: 'The era of Islam is based upon a flight from realm, and city and Judaism and Church into kin and the clan.'[41] What is true of Islam is that even when there was a humanist influx, its followers were for the most part carefully contained. The consequences were twofold: the societies did not continue to become receptive to the fruits of scientific and artistic licence and inquiry that, for good or ill, have given the West much of its shape; and the faith of Islam has not undergone the same kinds of transmutation or (if one takes secularism in a more traditional interpretation and does away with the concept of Johannine Christianity) eventual erosion akin to what happened in the West. In other words, those people who have wanted to make Islam a great contributor to the sciences and the arts have accepted the very humanist game that was originally Greek and then reconfigured on Christian terms, only to be essentially still pagan when used to measure the worth of different peoples.

I have emphasized throughout that for Rosenstock-Huessy, with each form of life the understanding of difference is the key to understanding. And the same principle is at work in his discussion of the basic symbol of Islam, the crescent moon. The moon completes the triad of heavenly bodies of the three faiths of the Book, and according to Rosenstock-Huessy it is deliberately counterposed to the Davidic Star and the Christian Sun. What is important here is the lunar calendar, which Rosenstock-Huessy points out is a further demonstration of Islam's tribal commitment and constituency:

Each year the moon of the Mohammadean year drops out of any cosmic rule. Here seasons are triumphantly ignored. Subsequently one has retained for the believers the husk of a calendar where previously each tribe had its own festivals. Thanks to the moon calendar the feast of Ramadan can occur through all of Africa and Asia at the same time, irrespective of heaven and earth. Now dissolved from heaven and earth, looking only at the ancestory, the old tribe lives in the living. Mohammad broke apart the unity of individual tribes and cast them in a lunar year in an un-living All.[42]

Rosenstock-Huessy further developed some of his ideas about Islam in his 1959 lecture series on American Social History. There, for example, he draws attention to the similarities between Islam and Mormonism: the latter, too, dissolves times and epoch makers into a story of God's messenger and last 'prophet.' Both religions, he says, claim that the true word has been distorted from the more original and much simpler one revealed to them. Indeed, it is this simplification that Rosenstock-Huessy sees as the appeal of both religions, and also as a problem with what they can achieve. For him, both religions want to tailor the truth to fit its peoples (originally the Arabs for Muhammad, North Americans for Joseph Smith), not wanting them to dissolve into something with a much greater and more complex historical past. Hence Muhammad jumps over the entire historical experience of the Jews, Christians, and Greeks so that the Muslim scholar does not need to read Greek or Hebrew to read the Bibles of Jews and Christians in their original language. The Muslim knows that the original book of God is in Arabic (which makes life more difficult for non-Arab Muslims who want to savour God's word) and that what the Jewish and Christian Bibles say must bear the apostatic traces of their scribes. One finds a similar logic in Joseph Smith's strategy for overleaping the experience of Europe and the

Church, justified by his claims that the original Revelation was, for the Americans, in the wilderness. This does indeed give its peoples a sense of their own superiority, but it also truncates the times and hence limits the powers that a people may tap. One should not underestimate how this is a critical difference between what the Jewish Rosenzweig and the Christian Rosenstock-Huessy are doing. Rosenzweig is interested in the power of eternity as revealed to the elect, and thus for him the workings of the Muslims over time cannot provide what he believes is essential for the nourishment of the Jewish people. For Rosenstock-Huessy, God is always working in time. Only the gathering of the times until the end of time will complete the Revelation and provide Redemption. Thus Islam is both an intrinsic part of that gathering and a revelatory component; but to the extent that it fails to understand the Jews and the Christians, it always works with a distorted view of its power in relation to them. And it fails to understand their respective epochal characteristics and the unique array of potencies that each has passed on to its peoples through the ages.

Just as Rosenstock-Huessy sees that Islam's solution to the problem of the ages involved an act of simplification tantamount to extinguishing the ages, he sees that Islam's (and the Mormons') solution to the relationship between the sexes – polygamy – equally brings with it a high cost that deprives it of a more fruitful future. For Rosenstock-Huessy, the achievement of polygamy is that it is a means of creating tighter bonds among group members as families grow in size. But polygamy, while providing security for women, requires women's servitude within the relationship. To the extent that the eventual emancipation of every type is, for Rosenstock-Huessy, the Christian mission, he sees polygamy as a pre-Christian practice.

According to Rosenstock-Huessy, for Islam to enter into the modern world in a genuine living spirit of cooperation, it would have to sacrifice practices from a past time, and in this regard, the treatment of women is a major stumbling block. It would be highly misleading for me to suggest that Rosenstock-Huessy enthusiastically welcomed new developments in feminism during his life, but it would be equally wrong to view him as a staunch traditionalist. He often commented that America had far from solved the 'war between sexes' (a phrase he used regularly enough), and he thought that the ease of divorce in the United States was symptomatic of the corrosiveness of social relations in that country. Nevertheless, when divorce proceedings were brought against King Farouq by his wife, he saw this as an example of the kind of transformation in the Muslim world that was necessary if Islam was ever to enter the modern world as an equal contributor.[43] He did not view such transformations as impossible; indeed, he saw no other way for Islam to become part of the modern world except by coming to terms with its historicity and the requirements of a planetary consciousness, which would require the sacrifice of things past for a messianic future. In the *Soziologie,* he referred to 'the women question' as Islam's 'crucible.'[44]

The difference in the treatment of types by Islam and Christian peoples (naturally, says Rosenstock-Huessy, one must see this as a revolutionary process occurring over time) also has its analogues in their respective attitudes toward proscriptions. The success of Christian nations, for him, can be seen in their expansion of freedoms: 'Christianity has said that . . . the goods of the earth, the things of the earth are indifferent. They can have in themselves no morality one way or the other. You never know. At times, it's right; and at times, it's not right. And it is the human heart that has – decided each time in complete freedom.'[45]

Rosenstock-Huessy is simply repeating Augustine's formulation: 'love God and do what thou will.' Of course, this is not how many Christians see things, but he sees this as a deep confusion within Christian groups about what the real law is. In keeping with this, he holds that prohibitions such as the banning of smoking or drinking on 'religious grounds,' the Christian Scientist's hostility to medicine, Jehovah's Witnesses' opposition to blood transfusions, and the Seventh-day Adventists' banning of meat eating or dancing, are lapses into pre-Christian behaviour. The fact that a people choose to sacrifice an enjoyment is not a sign of lack of faith or a lack of spiritual freedom; rather, when the specific sacrifice is overly valorized and becomes all-important, one no longer understands God's loving free spirit.

In a similar manner, Rosenstock-Huessy compares the role of sacred texts. The good Muslim learns the Koran by heart, but leaving aside that the Church has its catechism, such attempts to shape souls by rote learning, while all too human, and while a typical means of exercising social control, have nothing to do with the real meaning of Christianity. Thus he says simply: 'We cannot understand Christianity by reading the Bible . . . What is the great salvation in theology? Your love for your neighbor.'[46] Again, his position is similar to that of Rosenzweig when the latter emphasizes the attempt by Muhammad to control the spirit by making the word of God something that can be definitively encompassed in a *book* – which only shears that word of its very quality of livingness or spiritedness. The very reverence that is shown for the Book in Islam highlights the awe that comes from the encounter with reading and books. The fact that God chose an illiterate man to read his Book is a telling miracle, one that is as much about the aspirations of Islam as about what its founder valued. By contrast, Christianity was formed in a culture in which books were nothing special. Rosenstock-Huessy repeatedly made the point that had Jesus written a book, he would not have faith in him.[47] The miracle of Islam is that God had an angel have an illiterate man espouse the most beautiful language in the world by having him read His laws and put them into action; the Christian miracle is that Jesus' being and his actions required testimonies – indeed, so many that John writes: 'if they should be written every one, I suppose that even the world itself could not contain the books that should be written' (John 21.25).

Finally, it is worth mentioning a couple of passing remarks that Rosenstock-Huessy makes about Islam – remarks suggesting that, like Rosenzweig, he views Islam as having pagan qualities that appeal deeply to Europeans and Americans. Thus in his Lectures on Comparative Religion, he says that 'by and large, what the actual American believes, is Islam.'[48] As the context indicates, he thinks that the Muslim doctrines of occasionalism and fate (*kismet*) are extremely widespread, and that both doctrines run counter to the providential God of the Jews and Christians. This same point is taken up, and the contrast sharply made, in his lecture 'Liturgical Thinking versus Theology.' Here he draws attention to what he is doing and why he thinks it so important that people understand the meaning of the Christian era.[49] Here we see him engaging in a similar kind of demarcation as Rosenzweig, and, also like Rosenzweig, he expresses himself so that the reader can see the urgency of his task and (of course) the challenge he throws down to peoples of other faiths. And finally, we see clearly how the task he has set is one of Redemption, Redemption of the times – so the great debate between him and Islam concerns this very matter:

> Everybody can understand the Jewish and the Islamic era, but do we understand the principle of Anno Domini?
>
> I wanted to show you that the ambition must be to place all smaller units of time in one large and unique process of God's creation and of God's history with men. If we cannot save the Christian era then all the partial fragmentations, the appearances which are as short-lived as the modern worker . . . will remain un-illuminated.

If time is not one then all time is dead. The question before you is a very simple one: Did God create the whole temporal process as one thought? Or did He really give to every nation and to every man just his little prison-terms: five years here and one day there – and two thousand four hundred working hours.[50]

Because most Christians have no sense anymore of time as the condition of the word becoming flesh, and the fullness of time being the Redemption of the times, he says in the same lecture: *today most Christians are Moslem.*[51] As we have seen from the core elements of Islam that Rosenzweig identified in his discussion of that faith, this was not a conclusion with which Rosenzweig disagreed.

If, then, Rosenstock-Huessy accepts that Islam is part of the 'economy of salvation,' one also needs to add that insofar as he and Rosenzweig concurred on the nature of the Christian 'mission,' his position is not really a departure from Rosenzweig. This is more conspicuous when one takes one's focus away from *The Star* and considers how Islam is touched upon as another power within world history, in 'Die Neue Levante' and 'Globus' – writings that, one is tempted to say, show what by his terms one must call a more 'Christian' set of priorities, or as he puts it – and I translate literally – 'the becoming of the earth into a closed historical space, a "World."'[52]

If, then, both see Islam as intrinsic to the process of forming what Rosenzweig called an ecumene, and if Rosenstock-Huessy makes *more* explicit what is already explicit in Rosenzweig's strictly 'geopolitical' writing, I also want to highlight that Rosenstock-Huessy also retained, like Rosenzweig, a deep concern about the danger that Islam posed to the future. This danger was far more subtle than what may be classified as pertaining to 'the clash of civilizations.' On the contrary, it picks up what is hinted at by Rosenzweig's astute observations of the 'fit' between the large pagan seams at work in the West, which were Greek in origin and were powerfully revived by the philosophers of modernity, who built an Enlightenment upon mechanistic physics involving a revival of Stoic ideas (both Descartes and Spinoza are very open about their Stoic debt) and Epicurean ones (Gassendi was perhaps the most explicitly Epicurean of the modern natural philosophers). (That Kant chose to base his dialectic of practical reason on Epicurean and Stoic morality is an interesting example of Kant's powerful ability to tap the metaphysical currents of his own time.) Rosenstock-Huessy alluded to the danger a number of times in the closing section of the *Soziologie* –

something that was noticed by Georg Müller in his marvellous essay, 'From the Star of Redemption to the Cross of Reality' – viz., the danger of Islam being a genuine impediment to incarnation. And as Müller clarifies, this danger is not incidental but comes back to the construction of the importance of the Book itself, to how God communicates to 'man' in the Koran.

> Neither Judaism nor Christianity, but Islam, is a religion of the book. By making the book an exclusive privilege, any conversation between God and soul is impeded from being a genuine incarnation. 'In Islam, Ishmael, the desert son of Abraham, attacked the Gospel. Mohammed does not understand anything about the transformation of the word. He insists on the simple name of God: Allah is Allah.'[53] And when Islam – through the tradition of Aristotle – contributed to the modern falsehood that there exists a science without preconditions, this is also its failure to appreciate the relationship between God and the *soul-speech* of man. 'A science without preconditions is a phantom without essence. But proof of this thesis is that knowledge does not always presuppose identity. For God, incarnation must be presupposed, otherwise we end in the tautology of the Qu'ran: *Allah Inshallah*, Allah is Allah, and history will be defrauded of its part in continuing creation.'[54] The conversation between Eugen Rosenstock and Franz Rosenzweig is all about the continuing of creation by man in history.[55]

The danger is spelled out even more emphatically some pages later when the connection between a view of a God who is not constantly creating is fused with the (Greek/Enlightenment) mechanistic view of life that threatens to extinguish modern men and women. He emphasizes that 'production and consumption force us to destroy life forms on which we are dependent . . . We become the sacrifice of our own deeds: that's why man has been treated as a resource and material in the concentration camps. He was an object for experiment.' Then he makes the point that total power is a terrible and destructive thing when it is not streaming from the all-loving God. Modern humanity has witnessed one gigantic catastrophe after another in its attempt to impose its will upon life, and in so doing it has produced men of monstrous wills. But no less dangerous is an all-powerful totalizing mechanizing view of life that (as he deals with at length in *Multiformity of Man*) smashes the rhythms of our creaturely existence in order that we may reinsert ourselves as a resource into its never-ending reproductive process.

One minute, he says, we are creating protons and neurons, the next creating a factory producing children. Whether Rosenstock-Huessy is consciously picking up Rosenzweig's aforementioned reference to Goethe's *West/East Divan*'s 'God is the Occident / God is the Orient' is uncertain (and he did not need Rosenzweig to know his Goethe), but he makes the point that the conjunction of East and West is far from simply beneficial; for each category of people has its own pathologies:

> A citizen of the world [i.e., Goethe] has cried out 'Allah does not need to create any more, we create his World.' The relationship between creation and making stands on its head. But Goethe didn't see the creative omnipotence of love as producing, as making. Instead of what Goethe meant by 'producing,' the destructive omnipotence of science declares [it is] creating, [it is] creation. 'Knowledge is supposedly power.'
>
> In the time from 1074–1945 the confusion has been increasingly committed. Humanity should be made, educated, produced according to our will. However, analysis, physics, anatomy, logic and science should create Allah's world.
>
> The world created thus is nevertheless Allah's world. Oh mysterious counsel of Goethe, if Allah is merely Allah, then the world of humanity becomes a factory. But then who creates human beings, not human beings who murmur 'Allah is Allah,' but human beings whom God gave [the capacity] to say what they are suffering.[56]

Thus Rosenstock-Huessy's concern is not simply that as Islam enters into the technological, administrative, legal, and communicative processes generated by the West – processes that now encircle and shape one gigantic social space – it must be sturdy and plastic enough to adjust to the West's powers and freedoms. Even more, he is telling us that the West must be wary that its own deadliest powers not be further fuelled by its absorption of the very strength and determination that made Islam a world religion and a major geopolitical power (strength and determination that, as Rosenzweig rightly saw, had its equivalent in Rome in the form of the Stoics). I hope it is clear that what passes as the usual theological/civilizational apologetics in Western/Islamic 'debate' has a very different inflection here – indeed, a serious one. For it is one that requires all the world's peoples to turn seriously to the traditions that house them, not simply rip them up but *respond* to the tasks that can make us neighbours; no people can simply believe in salvation through either the past or the machine world. The responses required may be at the smallest levels, but they are what make the difference – they are the small pathways and openings of spirit that help deliver real concordance. In his *Soziologie,* to illustrate this point, he offers an example: Arab Muslims wished to honour a deceased Frenchman, so at his burial, to express their grief, they entered the Church, took off their veils, and laid them on his coffin.[57] This fascinating example illustrates our point, which is the difference between what the New Thinking values, what types of events its eye scours out, and how it 'frames' its observations and arguments and the radical liberal paradigm. For there was no 'grand' statement here about women throwing off oppression – indeed, what these women were doing, at least in the brief description we have, was not about anything so abstract as emancipating Muslim women from oppression (something that radical liberals, especially now, feel deeply uncomfortable and conflicted about addressing). Rather, it revolved around the most simple display of genuine love, which, as Rosenstock-Huessy noted here, predominated over 'the montone Koranic verses which sealed the lips of warriors against enchanted verses.'[58]

It is also in this light that we can turn to Rosenstock-Huessy's rather undeveloped but not uninsightful suggestions about how the West can benefit from other religions. For to repeat, he is emphasizing that 'religions, races, lands for the first time ever are now thrown into the one time-space frame, and we are all inevitably changed by this massive influx of previously alien energies and our challenge is to adapt to this "law of the moment"' – here he uses Tillich's term *Kaironomie.*[59]

Rosenzweig had said that he had not written a Philosophy of Religion; this is was equally the case for Rosenstock-Huessy. And just as Rosenzweig had suggested that no one can get to the truth by denying his subjectivity, but rather that his existential placement is the condition of his being able to be any truth at all,[60] Rosenstock-Huessy similarly understood where his audience was coming from. That is why when writing or lecturing in North America and Germany, he wished to open his audience up to far more archaic powers. Thus there are his elaborate and fascinating explorations of the Egyptian gods and society, which demonstrate convincingly that to enter that world without any knowledge of the role or nature of the gods leads to a complete misunderstanding of the meaning of ancient Egypt. Thus, too, in his lectures on Comparative Religion and Universal History, he instructs his students in the power and insights of animism. Animism was especially important to him because in many ways it is the direct opposite of mechanism and hence provides an appreciation of life as a multiplicity of animating forces that vanished long ago from the consciousness of modern men and women (outside of cartoons and childhood tales). Thus, for example, in his Lectures on Comparative Religion, he says of animism:

> These so-called religions of primitive man . . . are very beautiful . . . But they distinguish themselves from your religion, that we at this moment, as you know, deal with . . . dead matter. We dig up uranium. We dig up oil . . . Your and my problem at this moment is . . . that we are overwhelmed by steel and iron, and all kinds of minerals and metals, plastic – that is, by absolutely dead things. And for the first time I think in the history of mankind, you can forget – except for your pet dog, or your chicken – . . . organic nature. That's relegated to the zoo, and to Africa. And you live, actually – if you look around in this room, except for you and me, there's nothing organic. Everything else is on . . . the first level of mere physics. It's just dead. These walls don't breathe. They don't even sweat, they are so carefully taken care of. In a wooden house . . . there is still at least some organic influence of the weather . . . we live much more than the primitive man . . . with the dead corpses. Think of the stench on our roads, on our streets, of our cities, of the gasoline . . . So you become quite immune even to . . . the distinction between death and life. You eat bread that is absolutely dead, this white bread which you eat. It . . . could be steel. It is absolutely worthless, as you know. But you eat it. You believe in death – in dead things.[61]

But while there are still peoples among whom animism has not disappeared completely, and while Rosenstock-Huessy thought those peoples had valuable lessons for us, the two non-Abrahamic religions that he believed offered something necessary to Western men and women in our time were Buddhism and Taoism. As we suggested earlier, he came to see these religions as so important that each occupied a fundamental front of reality. Of course there is the danger that we may become captured by an enormously powerful means of orientation that, if adopted, would absorb us into a one-dimensional and hence fundamentally flawed perspective on life, be it to the neglect of time in both its past and future aspects, or of our imagination, will, and knowledge, or of the external conditions and impediments with which we must deal. We cannot overlook that Rosenstock-Huessy was not an 'expert' on the world's religions and cultures, apart from Christianity and Judaism and the Egyptians and tribes; indeed, he says very little about most of the world's 'religions.' For example, only once in his entire corpus does he refer to Sufism (albeit this is a very positive reference to Sufi prayer); and he makes scant references to Hinduism, which he criticizes sharply for what he sees as its relativism and its rigid cast system,[62] both of which he sees as conspiring against it actively contributing to a universal history. Though, let it be said, he speaks appreciatively on a number of occasions about the powers that the yogi accesses in stages of deep meditation. Even his references to Buddhism and Taoism are quite scanty, considering that he concluded they were valuable for modern men and women's sense of orientation. And he can also be criticized for not appreciating just how valuable some traditions may be in different contexts; for example, Hinduism in Bali appears to be an invaluable and extremely positive force for community integration, whereas Catholicism in the Philippines is a disaster.

Furthermore, like Rosenzweig, he was sceptical of the East/West syncretism that he saw in Steiner, and of those who wanted to usher in the East because they 'have had enough of Western civilization,' much as Rousseau's followers had hoped for salvation in the more 'noble primitive' forms of indigenous peoples.[63]

Yet his system is open enough to undergo constant modification, provided that the case can be made that a lifeway (or challenging and important aspects of it) is genuinely able to aid us in the task of overcoming social death. He emphasized this particular purpose in his various discussions of Abraham, Jesus, Buddha, and Lao-Tse being 'four path breakers' of the spirit. In his 1953 lectures on the Cross of Reality, when speaking of those four, he commented that 'suicide is the challenge of these four founders of the religious regeneration of mankind, because Buddha, Lao-Tzu, Abraham, and Jesus – they have in a strange manner put something in the place of suicide. You can say that the definition of a world religion is a medicine against suicide.'[64] The suicidal threat facing Western men and women that Rosenstock-Huessy had been writing about his entire life (even, as we recall, leading him to write one work titled 'The Suicide of Europe') was largely due to the powers summoned up for the supposed salvation of humankind – its national and international politics, its science, its commercial progress, and the like. Thus he was particularly interested in both Taoism and Buddhism not so much for the private spiritual practices they provided individual Westerners seeking a spiritual answer for their personal journeys, but for the social powers they could apply in order to help all human beings deal with the great forces of modernity that were at work on a planetary scale. Indeed, what particularly appealing to him about both these 'religions' was that both had emerged as responses to crises he saw as directly paralleling those confronting modern men and women. They had, in other words, like Christianity and Judaism, provided a means for us to 'outrun' the modern mind (as the subtitle of *The Christian Future* suggests).

In the case of Taoism, he sees that it had emerged as reaction to the constrictive functionalism of Confucian society. And it was precisely the dominance of a functionalist view of life that he saw as so dangerous to modern life. Max Weber, too, had studied China closely, and I do not think his interest was divorced from the spead of instrumental reasoning that he was so alarmed by. In any case, Rosenstock-Huessy's interest in the relevance of Confucius for alerting us to the kinds of dangers that are confronting us, along with his concern that these ostensibly mundane dangers of instrumental reasoning can easily be lost sight of amidst the more explosive horrors of the world wars, is astonishingly prescient – especially so in the context of the growing number of voices championing the virtues of modern neo-Confucianism as China emerges as a trading superpower. It is, I think, no accident that arguments about Confucianism's contributions invariably have to do with economic growth and production. Thus, what must have struck many of his readers in 1946 as a rather bizarre suggestion that China was invading the West not through theosophy but through John Dewey may well strike readers today as far less strange,[65] especially given that the thought never seems to have occurred to Dewey, even in his letters from China to his children.[66]

The equation, though, is not just between Dewey himself and Confucius, but between two overlapping mindsets that believe that life is essentially functional and capable of being controlled and coordinated provided that the right people of virtue control the right system with the right information. This is very much the model of how managers and policy makers in major institutions in the East and the West present themselves – and it is a mindset that seems so self-assured and so naturally obviously right that it is oblivious to the fact that it could be a major part of the *problem* facing the human race rather than a solution. The depersonalized, integrative, pragmatic, functionalist system is far more totalitarian than anything that either Hegel dreamed of in his perfectly closed developing reason or that those clumsy, halfwitted, murdering, gangster totalitarians of Germany and Russia could have ever come up with. Instead of highlighting the affinities between our contemporary managerialist and policy strategems and those that Rosenstock-Huessy was tracking when he was plotting the elements shared by Confucianism and Dewey, let us simply bear in mind that he was writing in the 1940s. I leave it to the reader to draw the comparisons between what he was saying and the corporate/managerial/policy synthesis of the present global age.

The ideal society envisaged by Dewey was one, says Rosenstock-Huessy, that was a 'scientific, democratic, depersonalizing, cooperative, functional mechanism, in which all individuals are held together by what they call social intelligence.'[67] There is nothing alive and breathing in Dewey's world; there is as little understanding of real love and nourishment as of evil, of how we damage and break one another, of how souls rot and resentments fester, of how we go mad and shriek. Dewey's is a world in which we all fit as harmoniously as polished stones in a mosaic. All of us are members of one great happy discussing vacuous family – the entire world, to take an example that was aired in Rosenstock-Huessy's lifetime, but probably off his radar, as *The Brady Bunch*. That's why, he notes when he criticizes Hitler in *Liberalism and Social Action*, Dewey thinks in vast mechanistic and hence meaningless time scales of millions of years, instead of in the shorter living durations in which creaturely lives struggle and face their ruins or triumphs. Thus, too, speaking of Dewey, he points out that

> for all those truths which only come to life when we feel them as new qualities, for his own heritage of fervent beliefs as listed above, he never has one word to say because personal sacrifice, worship, devotion, exuberance have no representation in his over-plain style. Dewey and his followers are silent about their own motives. They must be silent about the gods since they have cleansed their language from all emphatic elements. ('Millions of years,' a mere quantity, stands for God.)[68]

Immediately after making this point, Rosenstock-Huessy refers to Rosenzweig's comment on Confucius in *The Star* that 'to the honor of the human race it should be mentioned that nowhere but in China has a complete bore like Kongfutse been able to become the "classic model of humanity."'[69] But he adds that Rosenzweig was only half right: Dewey is a major success, impressing people from Turkey through to China, 'and for the same reason as Confucius: both make for boredom, but they make the boredom of depersonalization, of the "cog-in-the-wheel" existence, respectable. That they are able to be impersonal makes them venerable to people who find themselves in an impersonal machine. Argument is useless against success.'[70] He adds that while Dewey himself talks about his faith, the deeper reality of his teaching is drawn from his followers, who hold:

1. Society is God and otherwise there is no god who sends us into the world by calling us by our names.
2. Therefore, human speech is merely a tool, not an inspiration; a set of words, not a baptism of fire.
3. Society includes all men regardless of their evil character. Everybody can be educated or re-educated. The body politic needs no self-purification.
4. The ipse dixit of authority is always out of place. Conflicts can be solved by discussions between equals.[71]

While Dewey's vision was formed by peacetime America of the 1890s – a time when there were no dangers abroad and many lived their lives within the cogs of industry – that environment shared, says Rosenstock-Huessy, the same sense of satisfaction of the triumph over an anarchic, jungle-like world as did Confucius' civilized code. Indeed, he adds, all the essentials of Dewey that made him such an influential figure among American educationists and liberal policy makers are to be found in Confucius, who also was 'impersonal, functional, silent about God, unemphatic, democratic in education.' He continues that Confucius came when the China of the hundred tribes had been welded into one empire: 'Confucius could hold that politics was education, since by that time everybody was inside the Chinese wall of one empire.'[72]

Everything, for both, is about insertion and integration: '"Integration" for him is God.'[73] War and revolt are unmitigated bads to be eliminated. As we have stressed, it is not that Rosenstock-Huessy was preaching that war and revolt are good in themselves; rather, he was saying they are realities that happen when things become so rotten that they cannot be changed by other means: 'in a bad society, it is my duty to disintegrate her still further by taking up arms.'[74] (It is interesting that quite similar sentiments to those Rosenstock-Huessy holds about Dewey and Confucius can be seen in a number of Marxist receptions of Rawls.)

By contrast, 'the Cross explains war and revolution and decay and disintegration and explains why some sacrifice must bridge the gaps which man's abuse of his freedom always rips open.'[75] This, in turn, is why he sees that the cross ultimately animates free peoples because 'free men must shift their allegiance from solidarity and functioning "inside," to rebellion, to reverence, to sacrifice, according to the evils which have to be resisted most urgently.' But for Dewey and for Confucius, this is all raw nature and uncivilized, and what is uncivilized, what is merely natural, must be tamed: 'Birds in cages, waterfalls in gardens and – the climax of Chinese culture – dragons on boudoir tables.'[76] Rosenstock-Huessy does not say this explicitly, but it is clear from his perspective that together across the times and within ostensibly different cultures, Confucius and Dewey conspired to create what Nietzsche called the 'last man,' that blinking know-all moral imbecile whose rule is the triumph of a ceaselessly dull peace and spiritual vacuity.

Throughout I have taken great pains to emphasize the difference between Rosenzweig and Rosenstock-Huessy's approach to life and that of the moralist. In the introduction, I drew attention to the easily overlooked fact that the moral social improvements that have accompanied the interpolation of the radical liberal paradigm into universities, schools, and the heads of journalists, lawyers, policy makers, politicians, and so on have gone hand in hand with the rise of a more litigious and law-bound culture. True, Confucius had warned against the dangers of too many laws. For he believed that good rule stemmed from virtuous leadership, much as Plato had argued and Dewey as well. But I don't think that Rosenstock-Huessy's point is diminished by the fact that Confucius saw the danger of law replacing virtue (so did Plato), for while he did provide a moral vision that was seen as largely irrelevant by the Legalist School, his code of life was still law bound. And the difference between a traditionalist-based society, which China was, and Dewey's America lies in how much more prone the latter society has been to redressing inequalities with new laws. For Rosenstock-Huessy, though, the far more important affinity is an unwarranted faith in a view of life more akin to the polished sphericality of philosophical/contemplative reason (and while much is often made of how unique philosophy was to the Greeks, no one who reads the neo-Confucionist Meng Tsu can accept this without some serious nuances and qualifications).

It is completely understandable that sages of whichever era wish to protect the social body from the horrors of war and revolution. It is, nevertheless, the case that the generations of the future live off the sacrifices that were made in order to excise the cruelties, stupidities, and general rot of past social orders (which is why Rosenstock-Huessy devoted so much time to writing about the history and dynamics of social formations and revolutions). Idealists either always neglect the sacrifices that made the basic freedoms we have today possible or assume that our future can easily be plucked from the improved moral behaviour of society's members.

For Rosenstock-Huessy, then, the great danger of Dewey and Confucius is that they have failed to understand the creative fecundity and necessity of humanity's response to evil – the opening up of new ways of living that take us beyond the integrated totality of wisdom and virtue and into unimagined times and new spaces where love and freer forms of life may flourish. His entire work was based on this, and that is why in *The Christian Future* he pits Oscar Wilde – 'Suffering is really a revelation. One discerns things one never discerned before' – against Dewey, who abandoned 'suffering as our basis of understanding the world.'[77] Thus,

> Confucius and Dewey are very wise, very old, very kind and patient, very sure of being on the inside. Hence, prudence, justice, temperance, industry, self-control are their virtues. Cannot the murderer be improved, the wicked be enlightened, the wars abolished? And revolutions can be avoided. Since man, as they are convinced, can be sure of this, he need not get excited when catastrophes do befall him. They need not make us unhappy since they need not to be. We may overlook them by anticipating the certainty of being inside everything. To them progress is ingress. They mean by it the constant entrance of more and more people into the inside order already familiar. Progress is not the revolutionary beginning of a tradition hitherto unknown but the extension of known qualities. Progress is painless and not the heartrending conflict of previous progress now hardened into tradition and future tradition initiated as progress. To the man who believes that we are creatures, our own accomplishments of yesterday stand in the way of the next accomplishment because the old traditions are sanctified by sacrifices made. But Dewey says that intelligence for millions of years was led astray and has now found itself. Within the frame of millions of years, it is childish to weep over any loss of country, loyalty, love of old; we may keep smiling and this indeed is what we are told.[78]

Of course, this will be very hard for radical liberals to see, for their radicalism has been stripped of the revolutionary component that gave the paradigm its original fire and wrath. Dewey is 'one of the good guys,' a friend of mine said when I raised this issue of Rosenstock-Huessy's criticisms. But this is precisely where the radical liberal paradigm exposes the weakness of its bipolar thinking and of its faith in moral goodness. If I may use an analogy taken from the dynamics of a family model where abuse reigns because of the cruelty of one of the parents: the child (who is a life awaiting fulfilment in its future and whose very future is threatened by routine violation) will not be saved merely by the other parent being a moral model. Unless that parent has the insight to see *early enough* what is happening to the child, and the courage, willingness, and power to stop the abuser, the damage done to the child may be such that it will spend its life damaging others. The allocation of moral responsibility to the abusive parent (whose own story is deeply embedded in the compulsion of violation itself) is really a distraction from the entirety of the process. The healthy, healing, loving family, by comparison, is held together not by its duties and moral allocations, but by necessary self-sacrifice, constant daily gestures of nourishment, and risks of love that no code could ever adequately lay out. It is the constant shifting dynamic of the neighbourly requirements of love that Rosenstock-Huessy and Rosenzweig esteem, not the reasonable articulations of behaviours that (much like Kant's examples in the *Foundation of Metaphysics of Morals*) either state the obvious or sacrifice the obvious to reason's view of virtue itself (the obvious example being Kant's example of how wrong it is to lie to someone even if that person is intent on murder). (Almost daily, newspapers report examples of legal decisions that violate any 'common sense,' but are based on virtuous reasoning.)

The comparison between Dewey and Confucius is, in sum, highly relevant to our situation today, and while we began the book by referring to how Islamic fundamentalism has challenged the West to confront its own roots, as we draw near the conclusion of this book I wish to emphasize that the danger to the West may come far more from within the same tendencies that are common to the West and China, not because they have been absorbed by China's influence – Rosenstock-Huessy never says that for a moment – but rather because civilization rests on the promise of stability, and stability is something deeply craved. Indeed, this very craving is what lies behind that most civilized of activities, philosophy, which prefers the transcendent spherical orb of reason's perpetuity to the messy entanglements of life here on earth. Yet stability as such – the stability of integration and functionalism, in which each person has a place and the system runs smoothly and machine-like – is from the viewpoint of the *eschaton* but a deadly false kingdom: heaven as vacuousness; not life redeemed and infused with love, but life merely drained of everything that might be harmful, dangerous, and potentially lovable. Of course a society that emphasizes stability and integration has its 'benefits' – every system that endures does. Even systems resting on slavery and child labour had 'benefits' – but this doesn't mean they deserve a future.

To return to an earlier point, the reasons why neo-Confucianists are lining up to instruct in the virtues of Confucianism for the modern world are clear from this statement by Rosenstock-Huessy: 'Our modern World Society is as totalitarian in its way as Confucian China was. Our stress on adjustment to environment, the avoidance of conflict, the pragmatic value of truth, our concern for practical success – all are reminiscent of China.'[79] And Lao-Tse's response to the Confucian intricacies of system and ceremony and duties, and the social monism of Chinese imperial inwardness, both have, he thinks, something essential for us in the urgency of our response to 'the colossal coordination' of the intricacies of systems, of duties, that threaten to engulf the modern machine world. Thanks to Lao-Tse, China was able to be saved from spiritual asphyxiation. We moderns, on the other hand, 'still lack a Taoist ear.'[80] And he stresses: 'The safety valve for society is to return from functioning to non functioning, from importance to non-importance'; thus anonymity and vanishing are absolutely necessary today for our survival, just as they were for Lao-Tse's survival.[81] In the 'effortless centre of nonactivity on which all things turn,' Lao-Tse had discovered a cosmic orchestration (Lao-Tse's followers, he adds, 'actually tried to "dance the universe"')[82] that sustains and nourishes us. This effortless centre cannot be found in the endless mechanization of production, endless services, non-stop routines, and the general hurly-burly of modern life, which destroys all life's natural rhythms and injures the most basic human instincts. Lao-Tse's traceless, nameless, weightless life, which leaves behind 'only the joyous feel of some rhythm,' opens a way that he hopes others will follow, for it is a way they need.

That Lao-Tse's reference to 'a way' has Christian affinities is taken up by Rosenstock-Huessy in the *Soziologie*, where he says, in the context of the Tao, that 'to be a Christian is simply, to be on the way.'[83] And he adds: 'whoever is on the way will be somewhat grateful for the Tao of Laotsu.'[84] For 'Tao is the art, to live with endurance [*erträglich*] on the way.'[85] And what he also loves is the contrast of this human pathway of Lao-Tse to a world of mechanical paths:

Instead of the straight highway, on which we roar into the future, in the Tao there opens a humble foot path. That however comes like a redemption [*Erlösung*]: thus near the highway, there must be a footpath, next to the way, a detour. Beside the goal conscious straight stretches of distance, the friends of the 'detour' . . . We travel through the world with the great assignment to reconcile the earth with itself, says Goethe in Faust. Reconciliation, expiation are witnessed by all hearts. We want to be agreeable with ourselves again. This is the main profession of souls. But while upon the great way we also have to endure ourselves, we have to enduringly remain ourselves, so we should become compatible.[86]

For Rosenstock-Huessy, Tao is the medicine the modern needs to salvage him or herself from the excessively functionalized, industrialized, lawbound, and (let us not overlook) morally regulated lives we are building with such alarming rapidity. For this purpose, the Nirvana of Buddhism provides an equally important dimension for our freedom.[87] That his contrast of the Buddha with Lao-Tse, Abraham, and Jesus is shamelessly schematic, providing a fortuitous fourth coordinate to make him a coworker on one front of the cross – Buddha is the founder of a path for dealing with the outward front of reality (Lao-Tse, by contrast, is the inner) – this possibly interferes with his case more than buttressing it. Certainly, it is interesting that the discussion of Lao-Tse in the closing sections of the *Soziologie* only benefits from being released from the burden of systemicity. Yet the representation of Buddha is fascinating provided that we release him from Rosenstock-Huessy's suggestion that he bear the burden of being a sole spiritual pathway into the outer world (spatial). Indeed, a thoughtful friend or editor might well have convinced him to rephrase this, for he himself insisted that the fourfoldness was a way of finding at least four aspects of reality in any given situation, instead of boxing up our understanding within four walls.

Recall from our earlier and somewhat sketchy account of Rosenstock-Huessy and grammar as a social *organon* that is at the basis of our professions. Of course, all living creatures and all professions are unable to escape the various spatial and temporal fronts of life, so there is never the suggestion of pure forms in Rosenstock-Huessy. (Think of how even terms from poetry – elegance, beauty, symmetry, and so on, enter into the penumbra [as a term of appraisal] of mathematical and scientific discourses.) But he does get us to consider how different professions accentuate and deal with different aspects of reality in such a way that they are not isomorphic and hence not able to be all aligned under a totalizing or sovereign principle (the hubris of philosophy and now managerialism). And even these aspects are further subdivided, and on it goes so that, for example, those multiple professions and/or practices that express our inner or mental lives can themselves be subdivided into further forms of the cross. Thus outward epic can be contrasted with and cooperate with the inwardness of lyric and – when time is factored in – with 'backward-looking formula and forward looking drama.'[88]

I am suggesting, then, that Rosenstock-Huessy's cruciform schema is more heuristic than inflexible in principle and that its value can only be gauged by its fruits, not by the metaphysical tightness of argument that leads him to embrace it. Having said all this, it must be added that though he could perhaps have said far more about Buddhism (and this could equally be said about every 'religion' he considers), his cruciform approach provoked in him a rather novel way of construing what spiritually medicinal purpose Buddhism has for the struggling and debilitated modern and postmodern soul. Certainly I am not familiar with anyone else who suggests what he does in *The Christian Future*:

> Through the two central experiences of his life, the Great Renunciation and the Great Enlightenment, Buddha showed the way to mitigate the universal struggle. He taught that man could renounce his own partisanship in the cosmic melee by focussing his whole existence in his eye, his enlightenment, his mental concentration, to the point at which all desire is extinguished. In this way Buddha outdoes those who tend to monopolize life for the outward front, by pushing their very attitude to the ultimate extreme. That attitude, we have seen, consists in treating things or people as objects, i.e. as outside of and opposed to our own living system, and therefore as merely there to be dissected, manipulated, exploited as we please. But if, as Buddha teaches, we empty ourselves wholly into the object we perceive, if we focus our consciousness in absolute objectivity, nothing remains of the greedy vital urges which prompt us to exploit. In Schopenhauer's expression, we have become all eye. When Western man faces the chaos pictured by recent science, and aggravated by its destructive applications, he cannot help accepting something of the Buddha's insight. If future scientists were trained like one gigantic Buddha, science might be brought to diminish rather than increase the world's strife. When a man withdraws from the struggle, he removes a cornerstone on which the whole structure of mutual aggression rests. The self-annihilation of one particle of the frightful will to live mitigates the pressure between all.

> Most of us have found that some degree of restraint, of asceticism, is a way
> of making life less terrible. Actions beget reactions. Do not react, and you
> lessen the conflict, undo the fighting.[89]

The use of Buddha here, although original, reminds me of the intimations of the sort that are to be drawn from late Heidegger and that inspired a Heidegger/Buddhist dialogue. Though it has been shown that Rosenstock-Huessy's metanomic vision involved establishing a multiplicity of openings for dialogue with other traditions – with tribal peoples, and through them (though not only) also with Islam, with Confucianism (notwithstanding the critique), with Taoism, and, of course, with Judaism. In the case of Buddhism, he also emphasized that, like Taoism, it was reacting to a tendency deeply engrained in the Hindu civilization he wished to heal. I have already noted that he said very little about Hinduism beyond that its caste system 'made social divisions almost as deep and fatal as animal ones'[90] and that its proliferation of divinities – its alertness to life's infinitude of powers – was flawed by a lack of unity. As a consequence of this lack of unity, its doctrine of *maya* had been taken over by Buddhism. He also believed that in Hinduism and the philosophy of the Vedas (and it is he who used that word 'philosophy'), the doctrine of *maya* had actually enshrouded the caste system, thereby protecting precisely what had created such cruelty and social horror, leaving unity 'to be found only by "seeing through" *maya* until it vanished altogether and the mind attained the blissful knowledge of Brahma, the Ultimate Being.'[91] Certainly he did not explore what potencies of Hinduism remained once they had been freed from the caste system and the endless relativizing and subsequent terrors at the darker ends of life's spectrums – which is the danger of all polytheisms. And he said repeatedly that we were able to enjoy Greek civilization today precisely *because* it had been shorn of the basis of its social existence – slavery and internecine war. But he did not need to say this for us to be open to the power and beauty of Indian civilization – that is, once it had retransplanted the energies of Creation to within a redemptive context that was the essential condition for a metanomic society. That redemptive act was not something that awaited Judaism and Christianity. On the contrary, Rosenstock-Huessy suggested that just as Lao-Tse had already provided redemptive means in China, Buddha had done the same for India. For while the caste system had not tolerated but rather institutionalized cruelty, Buddha had followed through the logic of cruelty to the *n*th degree.

Recall here those terrible Manu prohibitions against the *chandala* (outcasts), who were only permitted to drink where water had collected in the footprints of animals[92] – a prohibition that Nietzsche would cite enthusiastically as an example of what kind of will would be required to recultivate a higher European type:

> He painted Maya in colors darker than ever: confusion and suffering reign everywhere; everything shoves, lusts, sweats, murders; man is in the fight himself, suffering and making suffer; murder alone makes life possible. Before the Buddha's unflinching all human activity reveals the same pitilessness. Acts never before thought of in this light, like eating and breathing, are seen to be full of violence.[93]

This following through of the meaning of cruelty created a new type, one that spread from India (where it had far less impact) into China and Japan, where it provided spiritual sustenance and an alternative to more brutal orchestrations of powers. (Of course, this does not mean that Buddhism any more than Christianity ever replicated faithfully the life of Buddha – on the contrary, Buddhism also had its military wing, no less cruel and as far from the example of Buddha as the Knight Crusaders slitting the throats of Muslims and Jews were from Christ.) Indeed, much more than Abraham or Lao-Tse or Confucius, who were nowhere near as concerned about suffering as an all-encompassing problem, Buddha and Jesus (recall Romans 8.22: 'the whole universe has been groaning in travail together until now') were the most kindred of spirits precisely because they refused to contribute to the world's suffering (in Jesus' case that of his fellows, in Buddha's that of all animal life). Yet the world they contributed to making has never erased the path of war. And while Rosenstock-Huessy does not say this, I think it worth seriously considering – and a reasonable inference to make from his teaching about incarnation and his recognition of Islam's importance in fusing the tribes by deploying a great path of war – that the real opening with Islam for the future lays precisely in the opposite direction of those who talk all sorts of nonsense about what a peaceful religion Islam is, as if Muhammad (along with Jesus and Buddha, who are bowdlerized in different ways) were yet other warm, cuddly person offering spiritual comfort akin to what might be had from soaking our feet after a hard day's work in a bowl of hot salted water. On the contrary, Islam's enduring contribution is to be found precisely in the ineradicability of our dependency on war and the military type as an eternal feature of social existence, at least until the kingdom has come. Islam shows what a faithful warrior is and what a faithful warrior should fight for – the great peace – and what victory means in warrior terms. Islam is so troubling in its teachings on women and punishment because of the type of world the Koranic warrior was originally fighting to preserve and enhance. The suicide bombers and 'martyrs' (what a revealing difference there is between the Christian and Muslim uses of that term) disclose the deepest need to serve, to love, and to fight the hateful. And while the modern world will never be able to recede back into the vision of the prophet formed by a God unknown to those who dwelled in empire, the prophet whose heart and soul and love were strong and powerful enough to cater even to desert dwellers, that same world is being challenged to find a place for young ensouled men who are willing to stake everything on a future that must include them. Their need is no less ours than that of the serial killer neighbour who is still our neighbour and in need. Though unlike the serial killer, those young ensouled men are part of a clamour of a people to find a place in our time in the one space-time we now all inhabit.

That Muhammad, and Buddha and Confucius and Lao-Tse and Abraham and Jesus, are all founders, is the inescapable condition of our time. That Paracelsus and Copernicus, who according to Rosenstock-Huessy begot Descartes and Newton respectively, likewise found types whose replications were also intrinsic to our world only illustrates the complexity and sheer breadth of incarnation. Our task is not merely to found and replicate valuable forms of life that have been opened up and passed down by testators and founders, but also to seek ways to reconcile those types that will be able to live into the future – and ways, as well, to ensure their concordance. And it is also, and no less, to extinguish what deserves to be extinguished. Such final judgments are themselves directed at whatever simply extinguishes life, and here, Dante's *Divine Comedy* illustrates the principle of Last Judgment perfectly: that judgment delivers over to hell what is but the full and deadly purpose of hellish desire itself. At the same time, all that is living and loving is, in its turn, redeemed. This is as much the meaning of revolution as of Redemption, and its meaning lies at the heart of all that is – and I use this term now in a manner more consistent with Rosenstock-Huessy than with Rosenzweig – genuinely religious: 'for religion,' said Rosenstock-Huessy in a formula as true as it is rare, is 'the power to appropriate a new experience, and to bow to it and give it a new name.'[94] It 'originates in the "mystical marriage" of God, man and world, of I and you, it.'[95] This is why religion is always a task to be done and not simply a past to be venerated. And why, too, it is always a collective engagement based on our mutual dependency, not only in how we associate in the present but also in how we respond to past and future, to the voices of the suffering past and the call of the promised future.

Conclusion: Pagan, Jew, Christian – or, Three Lives in One Love

If there is one statement by Rosenzweig that can be said to sum up his life's work, it is this one, which he wrote to Rudlph Ehrenberg: 'I am remaining a Jew.' Equally, if there is one that sums up Rosenstock-Huessy, it is this one: 'I am an incarnationist.'[1] For Rosenstock-Huessy, the greatness of Christianity was to be found precisely in what it had contributed to what he saw as the grail sought by all forms of life – perpetuity.

For Rosenzweig, the Jews did not need to strive for perpetuity – they were the incarnation of the eternal itself. Thus they did not need to seek ever new forms into which they could be perpetuated. But the price they paid for this – at least until the establishment of Israel (which was purchased at another price, perhaps even more costly) – was their ever dependence on other peoples to create the history in which they partook, and which, as individuals, they too contributed to, but which as a people they did not make and did not *need* to make.

For Rosenstock-Huessy and Rosenzweig, Christianity was the very faith in salvation through striving that Goethe, in Faust, had expressed as being the true doctrine of salvation. What Rosenzweig had seen as Christianity's eternal beginning as it chased ever again after the rays of the eternal star it pursued and sought to dwell within, was, for Rosenstock-Huessy, merely the fact of temporal life that Christianity had grasped better than any other way of life – viz., the need to die into life and thereby to redeem and reaccumulate potencies that would otherwise die with death.

That great vast other that both labelled paganism was the very condition of their own positions. Neither denied this. Paganism was essentially creative life. The pagan life was not, for either man, a morally reprehensible life – and I hope the reader has seen why such an evaluative term carries so little weight for them. The pagan approach to life's energies is multiform, just as the pagan forms are multiform. Indeed, where life has colour and fecundity and joy, paganism is to be found. Indeed, again, all revivals of paganism (even the darkest, such as the Nazis) wish to revive the joyful Pan ('strength through joy' was the Nazi formulation). Here one recalls Rabelais's description of the great weeping that breaks out in the pagan world when it is announced that 'the great Pan is dead.' If, as Rosenstock-Huessy argued, a planetary consciousness will form from the explosions and creations of the great chain of revolutions that reveal the 'way' of Christianity from the Petrine, Pauline, and Johannine Churches, the great influx of energies from around the globe are a great tumult of pagan forces – wondrous, intoxicating, and full of promise but also dangerous and potentially explosive. No one is immune from these forces today, just as none of us today has not been touched in some way by the great revolutions that created the modern nations, modern ideologies, international systems of communication, technology, and commerce, and the two world wars.

Rosenzweig knew that the Jew could not escape from the Christian and pagan; Rosenstock-Huessy went one step further, declaring that we must today live all three lives as one. That can only be done by knowing what those lives are, and Rosenzweig's brilliance was that he disclosed them in such a way that we could discern their respective differences. He used polemics to do this, and he certainly feared the dangers of people's lack of discernment. If he was especially polemical against Islam, that was because he saw that it carried within it elements that were identical to those of other pagan seams of modernity that he saw as particular threats to the redemptive life. But even with his Christian ally he was often hostile, and understandably so. He saw that the great danger Christianity posed was not the tortures of forced conversion ending in death, but much rather the danger that it would extinguish the Jew through its total integration of Jewish existence into a great Christian/pagan hybrid, one in which Redemption would disappear along with the people whose Sabbath, liturgy, holy days, and rituals were a series of living reminders of its promise. And he warned that this would ultimately lead to the extinction of Christianity itself. He certainly believed that the Church had passed through different ages, but he did not think (to borrow Wittgenstein's famous image) that the ladder could be thrown away once we had ascended it – far less could the ground on which it was placed be cut away without consequences. Such talk of grounds and ladders is, of course, metaphorical, and the ground that concerns him is not the rational ground of some philosophical consensus. But let us move to another metaphor, the metaphor of the Jewish people as the seed. Without the seed, there would be no notion of a *tree of humanity* (to recall a metaphor often used by Rosenstock-Huessy) – humanity thus construed as one people under God seeking Redemption through their living growth. As we saw earlier, this was something that Rosenzweig completely convinced Rosenstock-Huessy of. And while there is more than enough material by Rosenstock-Huessy to warrant another book about his views on Judaism (and I am well aware of how scanty I have been on this matter), I have focused on the greater vision that shows how the two – inimical as they were in their faiths – through their very enmity found a new way to bring Jew and Christian in relationship to each other. That not only the pagan as such stands in relationship to them is not something to be disputed. The challenge that confronts us today is *how* the different configurations and potencies of creation – the explosions of types and histories that now, without any conscious intent by anyone, are called upon to demonstrate their contributions to the banquet – are to be reviewed. Our attunements and dialogues are meaningless if they are simply romantic reminders of a past now lost – if they are dead things for museums, mere entertainments in the seemingly endless infantilizing of life whose curse is played out every night on the brain-numbing television shows of the 'developed' nations. How they may serve as vibrant living powers that act as ever more detours from the main path, detours that by their very detouring open up new forms of concordance and joy and love, is the promise and the reason why the pagan is not the enemy of Redemption but the very creative material from which it may take shape.

Postscript

In *Speech and Reality*, in a move that was uniquely his, but was under-taken with a vocabulary that honoured Hans Ehrenberg and Franz Rosenzweig, as well as Eduard Lask and Karl Jaspers, Rosenstock-Huessy provided yet another schematic survey. It essentially summarized the argument he had developed in the first chapter of that book, 'In Defense of the Grammatical Method': that over the past millennium there had been three great revolutions in the social sciences – and he emphasized, as he made this argument, that we engage in the social sciences precisely *because* we are drawn to save society from the perils confronting it. The first such revolution was the metalogical science of theology, undertaken to reconcile the conflicting doctrines of the Church and 'forcing the logic of one-line reasoning to the altitude of the paradoxes with which vital thought deals.'[1] It was known by the historical name of theology, its tool was dialectics, and its concrete field was 'values' (and he adds in brackets 'the gods').[2] The event that forced itself upon those struggling to survive and create a better future was the Crusades. Modern men and women now easily consign Scholasticism to the bin of mumbo-jumbo, but the entire modern university system was formed on its back.

The second science he called meta-esthetics, and its object of inquiry was sense perception ('aesthesis'). And he added that the 'esthetics in the sense of beauty, of the *universalia in re* are part of this quest in so far as the general conditions that bodies in the world of appearance must satisfy, certainly are qualified by the category of beauty, this being the unity of appreciation for our sensuous system.'[3] He declared its task to be 'the coordinating movement of *distant* bodies'; its starting points, Copernicus and Descartes; and its intellectual tool, mathematics.[4] The event – a response into hitherto unchartered territories – was the Thirty Years' War. Salvation, it was hoped, lay in the more predictable and beautiful and sublime (as aestheticians would later add) natural occurrences that were not drenched in the blood and stench of war and in the seemingly endless stupidity of Scholastic logic and gormless zealotry.

If the humanists and reformists had had to struggle to avoid spiritual extinction, in large part because Scholasticism was living on way beyond its vital time, Rosenstock-Huessy and Rosenzweig were but two of the voices clamouring throughout the twentieth century for us not to be drowned in the system of meta-esthetics and its task of studying mere bodies operating through and across space.

The final science he called meta-ethics, which, as we have indicated throughout, also went by the name of metanomics. Its founder was Saint-Simon. But the event that made it a necessary task was what he called simply 'World War.'[5] He deliberately did not precede that term with 'First' or 'Second' because the two wars were part of the same process. Indeed, we are still living in that process. That is why I have written this book: it has been a response and call on my part – a response to Rosenstock-Huessy and Rosenzweig, and a call to others to carry on this new kind of social science, which continues the kind of commitment that the radical liberal paradigm has taken so seriously. But this commitment is now reconfigured in the context of a concrete field that allots an importance to time and speech (and not merely linguistics, of the sort to be found in so much literary theory, post-stucturalist gaming, and analytic philosophy) and to the task of 'synchronizing antagonistic "distemporaries."'[6] It is prepared for and opens up the need for the kind of difficult dialogue and the kind of contradictory alliance that Rosenzweig and Rosenstock-Huessy formed to open a new path (one that is not even seen by Rosenzweig scholars, who read him with so much attention yet who fail to see who and what Rosenstock-Huessy meant in his life and for his own future as a thinker). This is the condition of there being vital futures rather than the various pretexts of unity and tolerance that shut them down and thereby close off all hope, leaving us confronting the haphazard continuance of the war and salvation at the hands of the 'last men,' now joined by the 'last women.'

Notes

Preface

1 Unless I am quoting directly, I will use the name Rosenstock-Huessy throughout. In 1925, Eugen Rosenstock changed his name to Eugen Rosenstock-Huessy, thus adding the family name of his wife to his original surname. While I was tempted throughout to simply refer to him as Rosenstock, as is still often done in Germany today, his insistence on the importance of his chosen name is unequivocal: he wished his deeds on earth to be recalled under the name Rosenstock-Huessy.

2 See his 'Farewell to Descartes' in *Out of Revolution: Autobiography of Western Man* (Norwich: Argo Books, 1969[1938]), 817–30; and *I Am an Impure Thinker* (Norwich: Argo Books, 1970), 17–33.

3 See especially the writings on David Hume and Baruch Spinoza in *The Main Philosophical Writings and the Novel AllWill: Friedrich Heinrich Jacobi*, trans. and intro. George di Giovanni (Montreal and Kingston: McGill-Queen's University Press, 1994).

4 See also the letter to Rudolf Hallo, 27 March 1922, in Franz Rosenzweig, *Gesammelte Schriften, I. Briefe und Tagebucher*, Bd 2: 1919–29, ed. Rachel Rosenzweig and Edith Rosenzweig-Scheinmann (The Hague: Martinus Nijhoff, 1979), esp. 767. See also 'Rosenzweigs Kampf gegen den Religionsbegriff,' in Jörg Kohr, *'Gott selbst muss das letzte Wort sprechen . . .': Religion und Politik im Denken Franz Rosenzweigs* (Freiburg: Karl Alber, 2008), 260–6.

5 Franz Rosenzweig, *Gesammelte Schriften*, III. *Zweistromland. Kleinere Schriften zu Glauben und Denken*, ed. Reinhold Meyer and Annemarie Mayer (Dordrecht: Martinus Nijhoff, 1984), 561–2.

6 In his highly critical review essay 'On Death in Life: Reflections on Franz Rosenzweig,' *Soundings: An Interdisciplinary Journal* 55, no. 2 (Summer

1972), 216–35, Richard L. Rubinstein dismisses *The Star of Redemption* as having no relevance after Auschwitz, 226ff. This piece is as critical an essay on Rosenzweig as has been written. While I disagree with almost all of it, I find it stimulating and provocative. Highly interesting is the comparison it makes between Rozenzweig's irrelevance and the relevance of Marxism and Zionism. Apart from the demise of Marxism as anything more than one piece of academic social theory today, there is one question that, I think, suffices to address Rosenzweig's continuing relevance: Is Jewish existence so bound up with the State of Israel that if that state were to be destroyed, Judaism would be extinguished along with it? If the answer to that question is 'no,' then Rubinstein has hardly refuted Rosenzweig. In contrast to Rubinstein, Levinas definitely felt that Rosenzweig still spoke to Jews after Auschwitz. See his 'The Philosophy of Franz Rosenzweig,' in *In the Time of Nations*, trans. Michael B. Smith (London: Contiuum, 2007); and 'Between Two Worlds,' in *Difficult Freedom: Essays on Judaism*, trans. Seán Hand (Baltimore: Johns Hopkins University Press, 1990). For a more recent assessment of where Rosenzweig fits in the context of Israel, see Fania Oz-Salzberger, 'On Rosenzweig, Israelis, and Europe Today,' *Rosenzweig Jahrbuch* 3: 38–50.

7 Rosenzweig's best student in the area of theopolitics is David Goldmann, who for years has written under the pseudonym 'Spengler' for *Asia Times Online*. One scholarly work that makes a stab at dealing systematically with Rosenzweig's theopolitics is Randi Rashkover's *Revelation and Theopolitics: Barth, Rosenzweig, and the Politics of Praise* (London: T. & T. Clark, 2005). Rashkover's horizons are very much in the radical liberal paradigm discussed below; also, she leaves out the thorny issue of Islam and is not well versed in Rosenstock-Huessy's ideas. The comparison with Barth (which occupies only a small part of the book) is largely fortuitous. Rosenzweig did not think highly of Barth. On the question of theopolitics one must also take issue with Gillian Rose. In her chapter 'Franz Rosenzweig – From Hegel to Yom Kippur,' in *Judaism and Modernity: Philosophical Essays* (Oxford: Basil Blackwell, 1993), at 129, she criticizes Rosenzweig for exchanging political freedom for theosophical freedom 'while remaining on the terrain of idealist philosophy.' Rose is often a powerful and interesting thinker (and in my view, her power grew as she recorded her remarkable response to her illness and confrontation with death). But this particular judgment of Rosenzweig, I think, shows her own tendency at that stage in her writing to engage in an idealization of politics; as well, the essay fails to grasp what Rosenzweig is doing with politics. Also, the rhetorical pejorative use of the term 'theosophy' does not illumine the contribution to collective experience that is made by Rosenzweig.

8 See Wolfram Liebster, 'Franz Rosenzweig und Kornelis Heiko Miskotte. Zu den Anfängen und den Auswirkungen des jüdisch-christlichen Dialoges in den Niederlanden'; and Hendrik Adriaanse, 'Zum Rosenzweig-Bild in K.H. Miskottes Buch "Het wesen der joodse religie,"' both in Wolfdietrich Schmied-Kowarzik, ed., *Der Philosoph Franz Rosenzweig (1886–1929) Internationaler Kongreß – Kassel 1986. Bd I: Die Herausforderung jüdischen Lernens* (Freiburg: Karl Alber, 1988), 425–40 and 441–54. I thank Michael Gormann-Thelen for having alerted me to Miskotte's importance and to the huge importance that *The Star* played for Miskotte. Kornelis Miskotte's *When the Gods Are Silent*, trans. John Doberstein (New York: Harper and Row, [1932]1967), which contains a huge chapter on *The Star of Redemption*, not only refers heavily to Rosenzweig but also shows a genuine appreciation for Rosenstock-Huessy (see esp. 33–6). Miskotte was a Barthian and a Rosenzweigian. Michael Gorman-Thelen made an interesting observation in an e-mail to me on 17 April 2009: 'In his correspondence with Barth, who was Miskotte's master, he tried to convince him over 30 years to read *The Star*. Barth always knew how to evade it. So Miskotte sent Barth a birthday letter for his 70th anniversary which was composed only of quotations from *The Star*. Now, lieber Barth, you have to read *The Star* – this way!'

9 Microfilm: 'Cross of Reality,' 1954, reel 15, item 630.

10 Eugen Rosenstock-Huessy, *The Christian Future – or The Modern Mind Outrun*, intro. Harold Stahmer (New York: Harper and Row, [1947]1966), 10.

11 Ibid., 61.

12 Ibid., 126–7. In keeping with this, among the members of the Rosenstock Gesellschaft whom I have met, as well as North American readers and scholars of Rosenstock-Huessy, a great number – possibly the majority – do not identify themselves in any way as Christians. Which tells us that one does not have to identify oneself as a Christian today to agree with Rosenstock-Huessy about Christianity. This is what Freya von Moltke and Clint Gardner suggest in their editors' introduction to *I Am an Impure Thinker*, where they emphasize the need to translate Rosenstock-Huessy's Christian faith into secular language as well as the appropriateness of Bonhoeffer's 'religionless Christianity' for reading Rosenstock-Huessy (xii).

13 Tillich, Niehbuhr, Harvey Cox, and Martin Marty admired him as well as Miskotte.

14 'Ich bleibe also Jude.' Cf. his letter to Gritli Huessy dated 30 June 1919, in which he writes that he was never reborn as a Jew; rather it was his worldliness (*Weltlichkeit*) that was reborn. What he meant by that was that he saw what it meant to be a Jew in the world, just as he saw what it meant to be a Christian (Rosenstock-Huessy had shown him the latter).

The letter can be found in the collection that has come to be known as the *Gritli Briefe*, that is, the letters that were in the possession of Margrit (Gritli) and Eugen Rosenstock-Huessy. Those letters have been transcribed by Ulrika Von Moltke and edited by Michael Gormann-Thelen and Dr Elfriede Büchsel and are available through the Eugen Rosenstock-Huessy Fund and Argo Books; http://www.argobooks.org/gritli/index. html. An incomplete edition of these letters, with a preface by Rafael Rosenzweig, has also been published: *Die 'Gritli'-Briefe: Briefe an Margrit Rosenstock-Huessy*, ed. Inken Ruhle and Reinhold Mayer (Tubingen: Bilam Verlag, 2002). Any reference to the correspondence between Franz Rosenzweig and Gritli Huessy, and to letters to Rosenstock-Huessy that are included in both collections, will be to the dates of the letters.

15 See Letter to Rudi Ehrenberg, 31 October 1913, in Rosenzweig, *Briefe und Tagebucher*, Bd 1, 133.

16 Wolfgang Ullmann, 'Die Entdeckung des neuen Denkens. Das Leipziger Religionsgespräch und der Briefwechsel über Judentum und Christentum zwischen Eugen Rosenstock und Franz Rosenzweig,' *Stimmstein* 2 (1988): 147–78, trans. Roland Vogt as 'The Discovery of the New Thinking: The Leipzig Conversation on Religion and the Correspondence between Eugen Rosenstock and Franz Rosenzweig about Judaism and Christianity,' in *The Cross and the Star: The Post-Nietzschean Christian and Jewish Thought of Eugen Rosenstock-Huessy and Franz Rosenzweig*, ed. Wayne Cristaudo and Frances Huessy (Newcastle upon Tyne: Cambridge Scholars Publishing, 2009).

17 Letter to Hans Ehrenberg, 26 September 1910, *Briefe und Tagebucher*, Bd 1, 112. I am using Vogt's translation in Ullman, 'The Discovery of the New Thinking.'

18 Microfilm: 'The First Cycle of Letters to Cynthia (Harris): On Tribe, Egypt and Israel in order to find direction in our Era,' 1943, reel 7, item 378, page 173.

19 Wolfgang Ullman, 'The Discovery of the New Thinking,' trans. Roland Vogt, in *The Cross and the Star*, 81–2.

20 That Rosenstock-Huessy suffered great torment during the time that Gritli and Rosenzweig were intimate had also been neglected in the discussions of the story, until 2004, when at the Franz Rosenzweigs 'neues Denken' conference in Kassel, Harold Stahmer read a statement commenting on Rosenstock-Huessy's emotional strain over Freya von Moltke, who had been Rosenstock-Huessy's companion after Gritli's death and who holds the correspondence between the Rosenstock-Huessys relating to this time. Stahmer's contribution, 'Franz, Eugen, and Gritli: "Respondeo *etsi* mutabor,"' is now available in Wolfdietrich

Schmied-Kowarzik, ed., *Franz Rosenzweigs 'neues Denken'*: Bd II: *Erfahrenen Offenbarung in theologos* (Freiburg: Karl Alber, 2006), 1151–68. Having seen some of this correspondence, I think that one should not underestimate how much sacrifice was required by Rosenstock-Huessy for this love to have the shape that it had. In the most detailed attempt at an analysis of the Gritli Briefe (*Letters of Love: Franz Rosenzweig's Spiritual Biography and* Oeuvre in *Light of the Gritli Letters*, [New York: Peter Lang, 2005]) Ephraim Meir overlooks this.

21 Rubinstein even speculates that Adele Rosenzweig's hostile reaction to her son's desire to convert – telling him she would instruct the synagogue authorities to turn him away if he were to present himself at Yom Kippur services (as he told her he would) before his baptism – was of enormous importance in his decision to remain a Jew. Rubinstein, 'On Death in Life,' 221–2.

22 See Rosenstock-Huessy, *I Am an Impure Thinker*, 182–3. For his most comprehensive autobiographical account, see *Ja und Nein: Autobiographische Fragmente aus Anlass des 80. Geburtstags des Autors. Im Auftrag der seinen Namen tragenden Gesellschaft*, ed. Georg Müller (Heidelberg: Lambert Schneider, 1968).

23 Eugen Rosenstock-Huessy, 'What Is Fruitful Is True,' *Soziologie*, Bd 2, *Die Vollzahl der Zeiten* (Stuttgart: W. Kohlhammer Verlag, 1958), 518.

24 Books have been written on Rosenzweig and Levinas (by Robert Gibbs, Robert Cohen, Luc Anckaert), Derrida (Dana Hollander), Barth (Randi Rashkover), Heidegger (Peter Gordon), Buber (forthcoming by Gregory Kaplan), Hermann Cohen, Hans Ehrenberg and Buber (Wolfdietrich *Schmied*-Kowarzik), and Wittgenstein, Buber, and Levinas (Putnam).

25 It is noted by Ullmann, though.

26 See my preface to *The Cross and the Star: The Post-Nietzschean Christian and Jewish Thought of Eugen Rosenstock-Huessy and Franz Rosenzweig*, ed. Wayne Cristaudo and Frances Huessy (Newcastle upon Tyne: Cambridge Scholars Publishing, 2009).

27 For a more detailed critique of Rawls, see Cristaudo, *Power, Love, and Evil: Contribution to a Philosophy of the Damaged* (New York: Rodopi, 2007), ch. 7, 'Love and the Limits of Justice.'

28 A sharp generational divide developed in the 1960s between creative artists who stressed love's transformative power, and the more politicized new left, who went on to become professors, lawyers, judges, and so on. The latter generally eschewed talk of love as naive and worked steadily to gain political power. While the hippie view of love was shallow in retrospect, a vast number of works in film, music, theatre, and literature have

explored the social significance of love and its absence, offering a very, very different way of seeing social evils than the more monodimensional emphasis on social equality that runs through the radical liberal paradigm. This is a central theme throughout *Power, Love and Evil.*

29 For a recent post-structuralist Rosenzweig, go to Eric Santner, 'Beyond Apologetics: Franz Rosenzweig's "Queer Theory" of Anti-Semitism,' in *Franz Rosenzweigs 'Neues Denken,'* Bd 2, 1082–94. The existentialist readings of Freund, Schmied-Kowarzik, and others rest primarily on the importance of the lived and personal (or existential) viewpoint in Rosenzweig's philosophy and on the fact that the philosophy culminates in considerations of how to live. Thus, for example, Rosenzweig would write to Rudolf Stahl that for a philosopher 'there is no other possibility of being objective than honestly starting from one's subjectivity.' 2 June 1927, *Gesammelte Schriften,* I. *Briefe* 2, 1154. But this 'perspectival' starting point and ending point of leaving philosophy as one enters 'into life' should not displace all that stands between them, most notably redemption itself.

30 Post-structuralism is, of course, not all of a piece, and here I focus on the broadest features of a consensus rather than on internal theoretical complexities and nuances and contradictions. French social theory has been of enormous importance in shaping the North American radical liberal paradigm, yet paradoxically, it is often more radical and even less obviously political. Lacan, for example, was never especially political, and Derrida's work became overtly political only after he found a large audience in the United States.

31 The popular American television series *Boston Legal* segued effortlessly from a weekly parade of radical liberal political solutions (repeatedly affirmed by rational juries), to conservative injustices in the United States, to litigation during which victims' achieved redress from the institutions that had caused their problems. Every week in this way, the triumvirate of rights and wealth and law was replayed and the world was made well again. The 'new thinking' would see this as the pagan view of the good life, which is not to say there is nothing good in it, but that it is destined to unravel again and again, to be an eternal return.

32 What in the United States is called 'political correctness' – by those who often object more to the process whereby the spokesperson closes down debate on an issue more than to the content of the radical liberal paradigm – is but one outcome of abstract moralizing. Of course, one can suffer and use the language of the 'politically correct,' and one can be on the post-'68 left and mock it mercilessly (Žižek). But social critics such as John Callahan and Bill Hicks are two extremely powerful and genuinely

moral voices (among others) who did not have a trace of political correctness in them yet generally took a radical liberal stance on things. Especially powerful about them is how their humour is so experiential and so full of their loves and hatreds – they are, I think, much more in the vein of new thinkers.

33 Hans Ehrenberg, *Autobiography of a German Pastor*, trans. Geraint Jones (London: Student Christian Movement, 1943), 8–9.

34 Rosenstock-Huessy, *Out of Revolution*, 5.

35 Rosenzweig, *Gesammelte Schriften, I. Briefe*, Bd 2, 242.

36 For Rosenzweig's brilliant geopolitical portrait of the situation at the time of the First World War, see his 'Globus: Studien zur weltgeschichtlichen Raumlehre,' in *Gesammelte Schriften, III. Zweistromland. Kleinere Schriften zu Glauben und Denken*, ed. Reinhold and Annemarie Mayer (Dordrecht: Martinus Nijhoff, 1984), 313–68.

37 Jacques Derrida, 'Interpretations at War: Kant, the Jew, the German,' *New Literary History* 22, no. 1 (1991): 39–95.

38 Bataille, though, had written a chapter on Islam as a militaristic enterprise in the first volume of *The Accursed Share*. I want to thank Kendall Johnson for reminding me of this when he read through and made invaluable comments on this preface.

39 See *Power, Love, and Evil*, ch. 5, 'Denial and the Elimination of Evil and Evil's Elimination of the Subject in Denial.'

40 See, for example, Alastair Crooke, *Resistance: The Essence of the Islamist Revolution* (London: Pluto Press, 2009).

41 Franz Rosenzweig, *'Innerlicht bleibt die Welt eine': Ausgewaehlte Schriften zum Islam*,' ed. Gesine Palmer and Yossef Schwartz (Berlin: Philo, 2003), 103.

42 Of course, thinkers like René Girard, Northrop Frye, Ivan Illich, Jacques Derrida, and Emmanuel Levinas drew heavily from theological concepts without being theologians, and by the turn of the millennium a new mood was definitely in the air. Studies by Taubes, Agamben, and Badiou on St Paul are now viewed as essential readings for students of social theory. Yet it seems that Taubes alone of the figures just mentioned knew the work of Rosenstock-Huessy. Around the turn of the last century, studies on Judaism as a social force were more common; but typically, those were part of a European anti-Semitic swell, which explains in part why such analyses were later dropped.

43 Reinhold Mayer has an interesting section on the political and specifically anti-Semitic context of Rosenzweig's work in the Lehrhaus and Bible translations that were undertaken. He argues that both can be seen as

forms of political resistance. See Mayer, *Franz Rosenzweig: Eine Philosophie der dialogschen Erfahrung* (München: Chr. Kaiser, 1971), 85–109.

44 Eugen Rosenstock-Huessy, *Judaism Despite Christianity: The Letters on Christianity and Judaism between Rosenstock-Huessy and Franz Rosenzweig,* intro. Harold Stahmer, essays 'About the Correspondence' by Alexander Altmann and Dorothy Emmet, eds. (New York: Schocken Books, 1971), 71.

45 Ibid., 71–2.

46 Rosenstock-Huessy, *I Am an Impure Thinker*, 35.

47 To Rudolf Hallo, 4 February 1923, in *Franz Rosenzweig: Der Mensch und Sein Werk,* Bd 2 (1979), 888–9.

48 Ibid.

49 *Gritli Briefe,* 9 September 1918.

50 Everyone familiar with Hegel knows that *Geist* is translated into English as either 'mind,' 'intellect,' or 'spirit,' and that every translator has a difficult time deciding which term to use. This is precisely because the term often does mean all three. But to the extent that it means spirit, it does not, for Hegel, mean soul in the sense of a capacity or power that belongs to the sacred and is pre- or supra-mindful. Rather, in Hegel the proper realm of the *Geist* is the concept, and the sciences are its proper orb. But if we step outside philosophy, *Geist* can be the living element that gives something life or liveliness, just as we would say that a meeting had spirit, or a performance had spirit, or a person had spirit. Hegel, of course, wanted to destroy anything that smelled of a beyond, a *jenseits.* But it would be incorrect to see Rosenzweig and Rosenstock-Huessy as simply resorting to Platonist, Cartesian, or Kantian kinds of dualism – even though both found *some* parts of Kant methodologically pertinent. In *Der Atem des Geistes* (*The Breath of the Spirit*), Rosenstock-Huessy gives the following positive definition of *Geist,* one that pulls it firmly in the direction of *geistlich*: 'Geist is communal breath.' Rosenstock-Huessy, *Der Atem des Geistes* (Wien: Amandus, 1991), 33.

51 In a later paragraph, the letter discusses another essay of 1918 that Rosenstock-Huessy had only recently sent him. In 'Der Kreuzzug des Sternenbanners,' he argues that the United States has entered the war as a crusader (he likens that country to medieval Christians fighting Muslims), with the Germans playing the devil's role. This crusade is driven by a simplistic kind of humanism that discloses the common spiritual roots the Americans share with France. Microfilm: 'Der Kreuzzug des Sternenbanners,' 1918, reel 1, item 5. Rosenstock-Huessy would write about and lecture in the United States throughout his career and would

always come back to America's image of itself as a leading power with a messianic mission that was both arrogant and humanistic, as well as often naive.

52 Eugen Rosenstock-Huessy, *Die Hochzeit des Krieges und der Revolution* (Würzburg: Patmos-Verlag, 1920; reprint 1965), 14.

53 Ibid., 14.

Introducing Rosenzweig and Rosenstock-Huessy and Their 'Common Life's Work'

1 It appeared on 17 January 1930.

2 Eugen Tannebaum, 'Anleitung zum Judensein: Ein Mensch, Ein Buch, Ein Weg,' *Jüdische Allgemeine Zeitung*, 26 June 1925, 1.

3 Hans Ehrenberg, *Autobiography of a German Pastor,* trans. Geraint Jones (London: Student Christian Movement, 1943), 110.

4 Martin Buber, *Pointing the Way: Collected Essays*, trans. and ed. Maurice Friedman (London: Routledge and Kegan Paul, 1957), 91.

5 *Sammelblätter jüdischen Wissens* February 1930.

6 For a comparison of Benjamin and Rosenzweig, see Stéphane Mosés, 'Walter Benjamin et Franz Rosenzweig' in *La pensée de Franz Rosenzweig*, ed. Arno Münster (Paris: Presses Universitaires de France, 1994). But Benjamin's liking for Rosenzweig appears not to have extended to Rosenstock-Huessy. To Florens Christian Rang, in a letter dated Christmas 1923, Benjamin vehemently wrote: 'What I predicted about Rosenstock-Huessy's failure has now come true. I never welcomed having to look at his name at the beginning of the text. He has crossed it out himself now, in moral terms.' Benjamin, *The Correspondence of Walter Benjamin: 1910–1940*, ed. Gershom Scholem and Theodor Adorno, trans. Manfred Jacobson and Evelyn Jacobson (Chicago: University of Chicago Press, 1994), 204 and 225. It is not exactly clear what Benjamin is referring to. In private conversation with me, Michael Gormann-Thelen has suggested that at the root of Benjamin's hostility to Rosenstock-Huessy was the simple fact of his conversion – that is, Benjamin wanted nothing to do with Jews who had become Christian converts. The immediate background to this comment by Benjamin was the compilation of Florens Christian Rang's *Deutsche Bauhütte* (1924). Rang's book quotes in its introduction a letter from an unknown friend that had inspired him to write the book on German and French relations based on French and German testimonies. The project, of course, was thoroughly dialogical, and that friend was Rosenstock-Huessy. Benjamin had insisted that he would not participate in the project if Rang included a statement by a convert. That is

why, according to Gormann-Thelen, Rang dropped Rosenstock-Huessy's
name from the book's contents.

7 Ibid., 'Notes IV,' 687.

8 For the English translation, see Paul Mendes-Flor, 'Franz Rosenzweig
and His Book *The Star of Redemption*,' in *The Philosophy of Franz Rosenzweig*
(Hanover: University Press of New England, 1988), 20–41 at 40.

9 See her reviews in Franz Rosenzweig, *The New Thinking*, ed. and trans.
Alan Udoff and Barbara Galli (Syracuse: Syracuse University Press, 1999).

10 Karl Löwith, 'Franz Rosenzweig and Martin Heidegger on Temporality and Eternity,' *Philosophy and Phenomenological Research* 3, no. 1 (1942):
53–77. A useful guide to Rosenzweig's literary reception in Germany can
be found in Martin Fricke's *Franz Rosenzweigs Philosophie der Offenbarung:
Eine Interpretation des Sterns der Erlösung* (Würzburg: Königshausen &
Neumann, 2003), 21–34.

11 For Putnam, see his introduction to Franz Rosenzweig, *Understanding the
Sick and the Healthy: A View of World, Man, and God*, trans. Nahum Glatzer
(Cambridge, MA: Harvard University Press, 1999); as well as Hilary Putnam, *Jewish Philosophy as a Guide to Life: Rosenzweig, Buber, Levinas, Wittgenstein* (Bloomington: Indiana University Press, 2008). For Paul Ricouer,
see 'The Figure in *The Star of Redemption*' in his *Figuring the Sacred: Religion, Narrative and Imagination* (Minneapolis: Augsberg Fortress Publishers, 1995).

12 *The Star of Redemption*'s first translator, William Hallo, was not a philosopher, but a scholar of the Near East. Hallo's translation, while mostly serviceable, is sometimes overblown, and at times it makes the text not only
more 'flowery' than it actually is, but almost inscrutable; for example,
he translates the everyday *etwas* (something) and the work-a-day *Nichts*
(nothing) as the more archaic 'Aught' and 'Nought.' But the biggest
problem with Hallo's translation is that he fails to accurately distinguish
between such important cognitive terms as *Vernunft* (reason), *Verstand*
(understanding), and *Denken* (thought), for he treats them as synonymous, thereby erasing some of the building blocks of the German Idealist
tradition from which Rosenzweig emerged and which he critiques in *The
Star*. But Hallo (unlike Galli) does include an index, as well as the extensive notes that accompanied the German edition and that are indispensable for following Rosenzweig. Why Galli dispenses with those notes is
inexplicable, as it makes her translation somewhat less serviceable than
Hallo's. Also, Galli sometimes loses the thread of the German. For some
examples, see Spengler's review in *Asia Times Online*, http://www.atimes.
com/atimes/Front_Page/GK22Aa01.html. Spengler's review of Galli's
translation also has some very perceptive comments on Rosenzweig and

his significance. It has been no easy task choosing which translation to use, for at times Hallo is much the superior; on balance, though, because of her fidelity to the philosophical terminology of the German tradition, I have decided to use Galli's translation – while occasionally departing from her where I have either translated something myself or drawn on Hallo. For the sake of convenience, all references are to the Galli translation, even when I have made minor adjustments.

13 There is some gossip in certain circles familiar with this story of a possible homoerotic connection between Rosenzweig and Rosenstock-Huessy. There is no evidence of this, and the source of the gossip appears to be a fleeting reference by Rosenstock-Huessy to the paganism of their love. What is probably being suggested, instead, is a friendship that persists throughout an adulterous love affair. Generally, Rosenstock-Huessy is highly critical of homosexuality, viewing same-sex love as lacking the consequences of birth. I mention this not because I agree with him (I don't); my point is that his public declarations certainly did not support the rumour (though, of course, that does not preclude anything private). It is a great irony of the spirit that W.H. Auden's high esteem for Rosenstock-Huessy's work led him to proselytize on Rosenstock-Huessy's behalf. Furthermore, I think it fair to say that had Rosenstock-Huessy witnessed the AIDS epidemic he would have had to think about same-sex love in the context of catastrophe and sacrifice – a context that was central to his thinking and that, for him, made all the difference between future founding seriousness and mere play.

14 Mention should also be made of Harold Stahmer's 'Franz Rosenzweig's Letters to Margrit Rosenstock-Huessy, 1917–1922,' *Leo Baeck Institute Yearbook* 34 (1989): 385–409, republished in *The Cross and the Star*. It provides an analysis as well as translations from some important letters. See also Stahmer's 'The Letters of Franz Rosenzsweig to Margrit Huessy: "Franz," "Gritli," "Eugen," and "The Star of Redemption,"' in Wolfdieterich Schmied-Kowarzik, ed., *Der Philosoph Franz Rosenzweig (1886–1929): Internationaler Kongreß – Kassel 1986. Bd I: Die Herausforderung jüdischen Lernens* (Freiburg: Karl Alber, 1988), 109–37; Stahmer, 'Speech is the Body of the Spirit: The Oral Hermeneutic in the Writings of Rosenstock-Huessy,' *Oral Tradition* 2, no. 1 (1987), also republished in *The Cross and the Star*; Ephraim Meier, *Letters of Love: Franz Rosenzweig's Spiritual Biography and Oeuvre in Light of the Gritli Letters* (New York: Peter Lang, 2006); Michael Zank, 'The Rosenzweig–Rosenstock–Huessy Triangle, or, What Can We Learn from *Letters to Gritli*? A Review Essay,' *Modern Judaism* 23 (2003): 74–98; Rivka Horwitz, 'The Shaping of Rosenzweig's Identity According to the Gritli Letters,' in *Rosenzweig als Leser: Kontextuelle Kommentare*

zum Stern der Erlösung, ed. Martin Brasser (Tübingen: Max Niemeyer, 2004), 11–41; and Michael Gormann-Thelen, 'Franz Rosenzweigs Briefe an Margrit (Gritli) Rosenstock: Ein Zwischenbericht mit Drei Dokumenten,' in *The Legacy of Franz Rosenzweig,* ed. Luc Anckaert, Martin Brasser, and Norbert Samuelson (Leuven: Leuven University Press, 2004).

15 This had been building for some time. See especially the letter of 9 March 1924. The cause of the breach between Rosenzweig and the Rosenstock-Huessys is rendered incoherent in Ruhle and Mayer's edition of *Die Gritli Briefe.* Having edited an 822-page book of Rosenzweig's letters to Gritli (and some to Eugen), they relegate the break to a three-line footnote in which Rosenstock-Huessy is made to appear as if he just decides without any real reason to throw a melodramatic tantrum. But the reason why Rosenstock-Huessy is furious is all too evident and understandable if one reads the correspondence during this period (especially from December 1925) that was unavailable in the Ruhle and Mayer edition. One consequence of Gritli's voice being silenced is that any reader has to make conjectures based solely on one voice about the nature of the relationship. Truth cannot be reached in this manner. Unfortunately, this has not prevented some from making claims about the relationship. Thus, for example, in Horwitz's 'The Shaping of Rosenzweig's Identity,' at page 14, we read this blunt and highly misleading summary: 'In 1922 Rosenzweig became paralysed and writing became very difficult for him. In 1924, in a letter to Eugen Rosenstock, he recounts that presumably on account of his illness, Gritli lost interest in him and exclaimed that "she could do no more." She refused to open his letters or to read Rosenzweig's translations of the *Sixty Poems and Hymns of Yehuda Halevi,* although she had read some of the poems at an earlier point.' This passage fails to address the fact that the intimacy of the relationship seems to have long since ceased, due to the marriage as well as to the illness. Nor does Horwitz mention that Gritli continued to write and visit and that she often assisted Franz and Edith. I think that Gritli was becoming tired of what she saw as Franz's controlling behaviour and his fanaticism. Horwitz represents Gritli as cold and heartless – a picture that in no way fits my conversations with the many people who knew her well.

16 Rafael Rosenzweig (Franz and Edith's son) told Rosenstock-Huessy in a letter dated 25 March 1967* that in 1930, Edith had burned Gritli's letters and some of Franz's to Edith because they were too personal. There is also correspondence between Gritli and Eugen Rosenstock in which Gritli reports (in an undated letter, probably from 1925#) that Edith had complained how Franz had not spoken to her for months (this was while he was working with Buber on the Bible translation – itself 'a love story,'

as Gritli suggests in this same letter). In another letter, dated 8 October 1925#, Gritli recounts, having observed Franz's intolerable pedantries and nigglings, that at one point Edith threw herself on the floor and cried 'I am only an animal.' She tells Eugen that she fears that Edith might throw herself out the window, adding that it is not Franz's disease that is behind Edith's misery but his constant 'evil nigglings' ('böse Kleinig-keiten'). Significantly, this letter is from shortly before the break with the Rosenstock-Huessys. And while it appears from Gritli's letters to Eugen Rosenstock-Huessy that Edith is deeply appreciative of her help, it can hardly have helped Edith's self-esteem to be experiencing such treatment in full view of Rosezweig's former beloved.

17 For more on Gritli and Franz and Eugen, see my '"Love Is as Strong as Death": The Triadic Love of Franz Rosenzweig, Eugen Rosenstock-Huessy, and Margrit Rosenstock-Huessy,' paper given at the Persons, Intimacy, and Love Conference in Salzburg, 2007, *Inter-Disciplinary.net*, http://www.inter-disciplinary.net/ptb/persons/pil/pil1/cristaudo%20 paper.pdf. The best review I have seen of this correspondence is by Fried-rich Wilhelm Graf in *Review Zeitschrift für Neuere Theologiegeschichte / Jour-nal for the History of Modern Theology* 10 (2003). Note especially his remark: 'It is not sufficient to view Franz Rosenzweig's commemorative work from the intra-Jewish perspective alone. *Der Stern der Erlösung* must be read diagnostically as a work of a generation, viz. parallel to Paul Tillich's *Kairos*, Friedrich Gogarten's *Zwischen den Zeiten*, and Karl Barth's first *Römerbrief*. The discursive networks between the *Generationsbrüdern* – as Rosenzweig puts it – of the different denominations were closer than the stereotyped talk of the discourse of self-sufficient Jewish minorities suggests. All denominations shared a traumatised German generation of those born in the 1880s, working on the same problems; they all suffered from liberal pluralism and historicist relativism, sought for a new binding absoluteness and hoped for a strong God of action who would heal the spiritual wounds caused by the war.'

18 Franz Rosenzweig, 'The New Thinking,' in *Philosophical and Theological Writings*, ed. and trans. Paul W. Franks and Michael Morgan (Indian-apolis: Hackett, 2000), 127. See Stahmer's articles mentioned earlier, which provide numerous references to the depth of gratitude expressed by Rosenzweig to Rosenstock-Huessy, especially 'Speech Is the Body of the Spirit,' in which he explores the importance of reciprocity between the two. In two letters to Ernst Michel, dated 17 June and 17 July 1947, Rosenstock-Huessy reflects on his leading role as a speech thinker, point-ing out that he had had this central insight in 1912 (four years before

the first draft of *Angewandte Seelenkunde* and more than ten years before its publication). At one point he tells Michel that Rosenzweig, like Hans Ehrenberg, would never have come to speech thinking without his guidance. And in the July letter, where he is feeling the full burden of his intellectual isolation and anonymity, he says: 'Don't forget Franz Rosenzweig studied a full year with me in 1912/13 . . . As with Herder in the case of Goethe, I will probably have to nurse my displeasure.' Both letters can be found through http://www.rosenstock-huessy.com/component/content/article/17-veroeffentlichungen/52-lstimmsteinr.html?directory=5. The *Mitteilungen* are privately printed and are available to members or to anyone who wishes to buy them. *Mitteilungen der Eugen Rosenstock-Huessy Gesellschaft*, 25 April 1977.

19 In the chapter 'Das Versiegen der Sprache' ('The Ebbing of Speech') in *Der Atem des Geistes* (Wien: Amandus, 1991), 27. Rosenstock-Huessy adds the Catholic Ernst Michel to a list of speech thinkers.

20 Letter of 2 April 1923, in Franz Rosenzweig, *Gesammelte Schriften*, Bd I, *Briefe und Tagebuch,* Bd 2, ed. Rachel Rosenzweig and Edith Rosenzweig-Scheinmann (Hague: Martinus Nijhoff, 1979).

21 Franz Töpfer and Urban Wiesing, eds., *Richard Koch und Franz Rosenzweig: Schriften und Briefe zu Krankheit, Sterben und Tod* (Münster: Agenda, 2000), 115.

22 Adele Rosenzweig to Eugen Rosenstock-Huessy, 5 April 1924, in Stahmer 'Franz Rosenzweig's Letters to Margrit Rosenstock-Huessy, 1917–1922,' *Leo Baeck Institute Yearbook* 34 (1989), pp. 385–409. Also in *The Cross and the Star*.

23 See the letter of 4 October 1929 in *Die 'Gritli'-Briefe*.

24 Symptomatically, Dorothy Emmet's and Alexander Altmann's essays on the Rosenstock–Rosenzweig 1916 correspondence are conspicuous by how little they tell their readers about Rosenstock-Huessy; see Franz Rosenzweig, *Judaism Despite Christianity: The Letters on Christianity and Judaism between Rosenstock-Huessy and Franz Rosenzweig*, ed. Eugen Rosenstock-Huessy, trans. Dorothy Emmet, intro. Harold Stahmer (New York: Schocken Books, 1971). Besides their essays, see, for example, Stéphane Mosés, 'On the Correspondence between Franz Rosenzweig and Eugen Rosenstock-Huessy,' in *The German-Jewish Dialogue: A Symposium in Honour of George Mosse*, ed. Klaus Berghahn (New York: Peter Lang, 1996), 109–23; and Wolfdietrich Schmied-Kowarzik, *Franz Rosenzweig: Existentielles Denken und gelebte Bewährung* (Freiburg: Karl Alber, 1991), 121–73. See also Reinhold Mayer's 'Zum Briefwechsel zwischen Franz Rosenzweig und Eugen Rosenstock,' in *Franz Rosenzweig und Hans Ehrenberg:*

Bericht einer Beziehung, Arnoldshainer Text, Bd 42, ed. Werner Licharz and Manfred Keller (Frankfurt am Main: Haag & Herschen, 1986) (which gives a very unflattering and, in my view thoroughly unfair, account of Rosenstock-Huessy); Inken Rühle, *Gott spricht die Sprache der Menschen: Franz Rosenzweig als Jüdischer Theologe – eine Einführung* (Tübingen: Bilam, 2004), 12–36; and Frank Surall, *Juden und Christen – Toleranz in neuer Perspektive: der Denkweg Franz Rosenzweigs in seiner Bezügen zu Lessing, Harnack, Baeck, und Rosenstock-Huessy* (Güterloh: Chr. Kaiser/Güterloher, 2003). Chapter 3 of Graham Ward's *Barth, Derrida, and the Language of Theology* (Cambridge: Cambridge University Press, 1995) also discusses Rosenzweig and Rosenstock-Huessy, but his comments do not show any genuine familiarity with what they are doing. He is simply too quick and too loose in his hurling around of epithets such as 'Hegelian' and 'Gnostic' to do justice to either thinker. Shmuel Hugo Bergman in *Dialogical Philosophy From Kierkegaard to Buber* (New York: SUNY Press, 1991), trans. Arnold Gerstein, has a section on Rosenstock-Huessy, in a very sketchy chapter that is tellingly headed 'Transition' (much as Schelling used to be viewed as a transition to Hegel). Robert Gibbs in *Correlations in Rosenzweig and Levinas* (Princeton: Princeton University Press, 1992) devotes a few pages to some of Rosenstock-Huessy's ideas from *Angewandte Seelenkunde.* The Polish Jesuit Adam Zak, who has written an important book on Rosenzweig's 'speech thinking,' *Vom reinen Denken zur Sprachvernunft: Über die Grundmotive der Offenbarungsphilosophie Franz Rosenzweigs* (Stuttgart: W. Kohlhammer Verlag, 1987), also writes perceptively on Rosenstock-Huessy. See also his 'Erneuerung des Denkens durch Dialog. Anregungen Eugen Rosenstock-Huessys Briefwechsel mit Franz Rosenzweig' in *Dialogdenken-Gesellschaftsethik. Wider die allgegenwärtige Gewalt gesellschaftlicher Vereinnahmung* ed. Angelica Bäumer and Michael Benedikt (Wien: Passagen Verlag, 1991); and 'Die Zeit der Sprache – die Sprache der Zeit. Zum Sprachdenken Eugen Rosenstock-Huessy,' *Orientierung* 1 (1990): 2–6. Both can be found electronically at http://www.cyf-kr.edu.pl/zjzak/ger.htm.

25 Most notably Michael Gormann-Thelen, Harold Stahmer, Georg Müller, and Wolfgang Ullmann. More recently, Gregory Kaplan has begun exploring the relationship; also, *The Cross and the Star* includes an excellent essay by him on Rosenstock-Huessy and Rosenzweig.

26 *The Cross and the Star* includes most of the papers presented at Dartmouth as well as some republished, previously unpublished, and untranslated essays, including pieces by Rosenstock-Huessy on Nietzsche. See also the forthcoming collection of the Frankfurt conference edited by Hartwig Wiedebach, *'Kreuz der Wirklichkeit' und 'Stern der Erlösung'* (Freiburg: Karl Alber, 2010).

27 Rosenstock-Huessy refers to this in *Ja und Nein. Autobiographische Fragmente aus Anlass des 80. Geburtstags des Autors. Im Auftrag der seinen Namen tragenden Gesellschaft*, ed. Georg Müller (Heidelberg: Verlag Lambert Schneider, 1968), 69.

28 On the differences of style, see Michael Gormann-Thelen, 'Orate Thinker versus Literate Thinker: Eugen Rosenstock-Huessy versus Franz Rosenzweig. A Difference Which Makes a Difference,' in *The Cross and the Star*.

29 *Die Soziologie*, Bd 1 (1956), 13.

30 Bejamin Pollock's *Franz Rosenzweig and the Systematic Task of Philosophy* (Cambridge: Cambridge University Press, 2009) takes issue with the anti-totalistic readings of Rosenzweig by demonstrating how Rosenzweig does not so much fracture as reconfigure 'the All.' His reading of Rosenzweig, while in my view conspicuous by what it leaves out or skates over, is a much more 'Germanic' reading of Rosenzweig than is usually found in North American scholarship – that is, it is a very finely honed tracking down of philosophical elements and influences. While the details differ somewhat, it is similar in orientation to interpretations such as Fricke's *Franz Rosenzwegs Philosophie der Offenbarung* (which is, notwithstanding, somewhat more existential than Pollock's interpretation, which is almost devoid of flesh and blood); and Heinz-Jürgen Görtz's far more Hegelian-driven *Tod und Erfahrung: Rosenzweigs 'erfahrende Philosophie' und Hegels 'Wissenshaft der Erfahrung des Bewusstseins'* (Düsseldorf: Patmos Verlag, 1984).

31 The letter is cited in Georg Müller, 'Vom Stern der Erlösung zum Kreuz der Wirklichkeit: Aus Anlaß des Abschlusses der "Soziologie" Eugen Rosenstock-Huessys,' in *Sonderdruck aus: 'Junge Kirche' Protestantische Monatshefte* (Dortmund), 1.

32 Zak, 'Die Zeit der Sprache.'

33 16.161948# 'Review of The Christian Future: Or the Modern Mind Outrun,' *The Christian Century* 9 (11 February 1967), 16.

34 In Germany there is a small and active Rosenstock-Huessy society that publishes the journal *Stimmstein*, which is devoted to materials by, on, or related to Rosenstock-Huessy. But there are very few major works of scholarship exploring his philosophical/sociological work. The most comprehensive of these is Wilfrid Rohrbach's excellent *Das Sprachdenken Eugen Rosenstock-Huessys: Historische Erörterung und systematische Explikation* (Stuttgart: W. Kohlhammer Verlag, 1973). More recently there have been Dominik Klenk's thoughtful doctoral dissertation *Metanomik – Quellenlehre jenseits der Denkgesetze* (Münster: Agenda Verlag, 2003); and Christoph Richter's Master's thesis, *Im Kreuz der Wirklichkeit: Die Soziologie der Räume und Zeiten von Eugen Rosenstock-Huessy* (Frankfurt am

Main: Peter Lang, 2007), which provides a useful overview of Rosenstock-Huessy's *Soziologie.* In English, very little has been written on Rosenstock-Huessy's work. Harold Stahmer's *Speak That I May See Thee: The Religious Significance of Language* (New York: Macmillan, 1968), written forty years ago, has a chapter on Rosenzweig, and his excellent introductions to some of Rosenstock-Huessy's works such as *The Christian Future* and *Speech and Reality* do a fine job of placing Rosenstock-Huessy in the greater tradition of 'speech thinking.' Indeed, all future scholars on Rosenstock-Huessy will owe Harold Stahmer an enormous debt not only for his considerable scholarly excursions into Rosenstock-Huessy, but also for his unflagging efforts to bring him to a wider public. There is also George Morgan, Jr's *Speech and Society: The Christian Linguistic Social Philosophy of Eugen Rosenstock-Huessy* (Gainesville: University Press of Florida, 1987). Morgan had worked with Rosenstock-Huessy, and as a young man he had inspired Rosenstock-Huessy to write *The Christian Future.* He wrote two books during his lifetime. His first, *What Nietzsche Means,* is still one of the most comprehensive and judicious treatments of Nietzsche in English; his second, mentioned above, on Rosenstock-Huessy, he wrote during his retirement and is more crib notes than analysis. Most recently, Clinton Gardner, who had been a student of Rosenstock-Huessy and who set up Argo Press to keep his work alive, has published an interesting work that combines memoir and discussion of some of Rosenstock-Huessy's key ideas (it is especially good on 'the cross of reality' as a 'religionless Christianity' and on comparisons with Russian dialogical thinking). See his *Beyond Belief: Discovering Christianity's New Paradigm* (White River Junction: White River Press, 2008). Gardner had been one of the first soldiers to enter Buchenwald, and that experience completely transformed him. He says in his prologue that 'Buchenwald lies behind everything I say here. In fact, I see this book as one more attempt to answer that difficult question: "How can we speak of God after the Holocaust, after Buchenwald and Ausschwitz?"' 24. A major part of the answer to that, for those who appreciate Rosenstock-Huessy's work, is that he had been trying to get people to serve the living God rather than the dead forces of nationalism in order to stop exactly the kind of horrors that result from such service. Mention should also be made of the theologian Peter Leithart, who has written some excellent pieces on Rosenstock-Huessy, including one on Rosenstock and language in *The Cross and the Star.*

35 Microfilm: 'Bibliography–Biography,' 1959, reel 11, item 524, page 25.

36 See Eugen Rosenstock-Huessy, *Friedensbedingungen der planetarischen Gesellschaft: Zur Ökonomie der Zeit,* ed. and intro. Rudolf Hermeier (Münster: Agenda Verlag, 2001), 204–5. In a letter to Georg Müller# dated 10

October 1965, he says this entire Bloch perversion must be extinguished. He continues by quoting Kierkegaard's 'sin is the reverse of faith': 'Whoever substitutes hope for faith abolishes revelation and sets up philosophy in its place.' Jesus, he says, went to the Cross without hope. That is 'why his faith has the power to free us from hope' and 'the central question is Bloch or Christ.' For Rosenstock-Huessy, Bloch's celebrity in Germany is saddening. Regarding the fourth generation of Feuerbachians, see his letter to Müller, 12 December 1965#, and correspondence. But for the most part he proceeds as if the dominant intellectual currents of his time did not exist – mainly, I think, because he saw them as part of the problem. For their part, Marxist intellectuals ignored him.

37 There are a number of letters to Müller in 1967# expressing irritation at Löwith, but particularly see 28 March 1967.

38 14 September 1966#. However, Rosenstock-Huessy seems to make an exception of György Lukács, whose *History and Class Consciousness* he quotes approvingly in *Die europäischen Revolutionen*. Carola Stern was an influential post–Second World War journalist, broadcaster, and biographer.

39 Edward Mendelson, in *Later Auden* (London: Faber and Faber, 1999), mentions Rosenstock-Huessy's influence on Auden on a number of occasions, but his treatment of Rosenstock-Huessy is not only too brief to be illuminating but also so full of condescension (see especially the put-down on page 261) that he makes it abundantly clear that he thinks Rosenstock-Huessy is not worth the effort. A couple of ideas snatched from *Out of Revolution* give the wildly misleading impression that he has captured the essence of Rosenstock-Huessy and his impact on Auden. No one who reads what Mendelson says about Rosenstock-Huessy and who knows Rosenstock-Huessy's work can come away convinced that Mendelson exerted any reasonable scholarly effort on Rosenstock-Huessy's work. Moreover, Mendelson's claim that Auden had been attracted to Rosenstock-Huessy for a time but had thought the better of it does not at all coincide with what Auden saw fit to say in his Foreword of 1970 (vii–viii) to Rosenstock-Huessy's *I Am an Impure Thinker*. There he writes: 'Half of what I know about the difference between Personal Speech, based upon Proper Names, and Second and First personal Pronouns, words of command, and obedience, summons and response, and the impersonal "objective" as a communication code between individuals, I owe to Rosenstock-Huessy.' Also: 'I first heard of him in, I should guess, 1940 . . . Ever since I have read everything I could lay my hands on.' He concludes: 'Speaking for myself, I can only say that, by listening to Rosenstock-Huessy, I have been changed.' In contrast to Mendelson,

John Fuller in *W.H. Auden: A Commentary* (London: Faber and Faber, 1998) provides numerous references to Rosenstock-Huessy and his influences on Auden. The same kind of uninformed condescension that we encounter in Mendelson can also be found in Mark Lilla's 'A Battle for Religion,' a lengthy review of eleven books on or by Rosenzweig for the *New York Review of Books*, 5 December 2002, 60ff. After making the initial obligatory reference to Rosenstock-Huessy's part in Rosenzweig's conversion, he dismisses him as a kind of theosophist who inspired all the dross in Rosenzweig (which is nonsense – Rosenstock-Huessy's harsh words about Rudolph Steiner in *Die Hochzeit des Krieges und der Revolution* [Würzburg: Patmos-Verlag, 1920; reprint 1965], 111ff, show how little time he had for the kind of 'mysticism' that one associates with theosophy and anthroposophy). Lilla's piece is as vacuous a commentary as has been written on Rosenzweig, which makes perfect sense when one realizes that he treats as dross everything essential to Rosenzweig (see 62).

40 In the foreword to the first volume of his *Soziologie*, Rosenstock-Huessy compares himself with Paracelsus.

41 See his 'Das Nachtgespräch vom 7. Juli 1913. Eugen Rosenstock-Huessy und Franz Rosenzweig,' in *Der Philosoph Franz Rosenzweig (1886–1929) Internationaler Kongreß – Kassel 1986. Bd I: Die Herausforderung jüdischen Lernens*, ed. Wolfdietrich Schmied-Kowarzik (Freiburg: Karl Alber, 1988), 97–104.

42 Rosenstock-Huessy, 'Fritz Mauthner wrote 6000 pages and proved in one and half million words that all words lie.' *Die Sprache des Menschengeschlechts*, I:24. See also Microfilm: 'Der Lebensweg Fritz Mauthners,' 1925, reel, 3, item 166, page 2.

43 Eugen Rosenstock-Huessy, *Soziologie*, Bd I, *Die Übermacht der Räume* (Stuttgart, Berlin, Köln, Mainz: W. Kohlhammer, 1956), 20. He mentions Weber on several occasions in books and lectures. His entry on Weber in *The American Peoples Encyclopedia* makes clear what he thinks the problems with Weber are: 'Taking his cue from the natural sciences, Weber accepted the rigid methodological limitations inherent in atheism; that is, the scientist and his objects are held to be totally separated, and the values of human beings are assumed to have no power over the scientist's mind. He differed from the natural scientists, however, in stressing the uniqueness of each social fact – a uniqueness that renders the usual quantitative methods of physics inapplicable to the social sciences . . . Weber taught that everyone chooses his own value arbitrarily from among a multitude of possible and available values, and that the social world is governed by "chance" (one of Weber's most frequently used terms); and that in fulfilling one's own value one becomes the ideal "type" of this chosen

path – as, for instance, "religious man," "economic man," "patriotic man," and so forth. Even Jesus himself was generalized by Weber into the "charismatic type," and Weber's close friend, Ernst Troeltsch, in regard to "this solution of heroic despair," called him the "modern Machiavelli." Weber saw his own calling in the austere service of his "value-god," the Nation; that is, his ultimate value was the survival of the nation of which, quite by chance, he happened to be born a citizen. Weber embodied the end of the era of Darwinian nationalism which led to two World Wars; his was an immense intellect incapable or unwilling in its intellectualizing to grant the slightest concession to any future of mankind to the faith that enables an individual to escape from the bonds of his "type" and to change and be changed creatively.' See also the remarks in 'Die Ordnung unseres geistigen Lebens' (two entries), Microfilm: 1950, reel 8, page 17.

44 *Europa-Lexicon* (Beck, 2007), 49–50.
45 The claim on revolution is in Peter Sloterdijk and Hans-Jürgen Heinrichs, 'Kantilenen der Zeit: Zur Entidiotisierung des Ich und zur Entgreisung Europas,' in *Lettre Internationale* 36 (1997): 71–7. The claim on speech philosophy and the comparison come from his acceptance speech for the Sigmund-Freud-Preis der Deutschen Akademie für Sprache und Dichtung.
46 Crane Brinton, 'Review of *Out of Revolution: Autobiography of Western Man,*' *Political Science Quarterly* 54, no. 2 (June 1939): 286–8. Rosenstock-Huessy, in turn, savaged Brinton's *Anatomy of Revolution* in *American Historial Review* 44, no. 4 (1939): 882–4.
47 See especially the section on Rosenstock-Huessy in Page Smith, *Killing of the Spirit: Higher Education in America* (New York: Penguin, 1991).
48 See Andreas Leutzsch, *Geschichte der Globalisierung also globalisierte Geschichte: Die historische Konstruktion der Weltgesellschaft bei Rosenstock-Huessy und Braudel* (Frankfurt: Campus, 2009), 64–7.
49 Michael Theunissen, *The Other: Studies in the Social Ontology of Husserl, Heidegger, Sartre, and Buber* (Cambridge, MA: MIT Press, 1984), 411. Ullmann, by contrast emphasizes his grammatical synthesis of psychology, history and sociology, which I think is closer to the mark. See Wolfgang Ullmann, 'Die Entdeckung des neuen Denkens. Das Leipziger Religionsgespräch und der Briefwechsel über Judentum und Christentum zwischen Eugen Rosenstock und Franz Rosenzweig,' *Stimmstein* Das Jahrbuch der Eugen Rosenstock-Huessy Gesellschaft e.V.2 (1988): 147–78. Translated by Roland Vogt as 'The Discovery of the New Thinking: The Leipzig Conversation on Religion and the Correspondence between Eugen Rosenstock and Franz Rosenzweig about Judaism and Christianity,' in *The Cross and the Star: The Post-Nietzschean Christian and Jewish Thought of Eugen Rosenstock-Huessy and Franz Rosenzweig,* ed. Wayne

Cristaudo and Frances Huessy (Newcastle upon Tyne: Cambridge Scholars Publishing, 2009).

50 Rosenstock-Huessy was especially irritated that Thuenissen had missed out on the importance of the years 1912 to 1924 in the formation of his thought. See his letter to Georg Müller, 22 February 1967#. He did not appreciate Theunissen's review of his 'Die Sprache des Menschengeschlechts' in *Görres Gesellschaft Jahrbuch* of 1966.

51 Because of this, I do not think that he privileged his writings over his lectures or spoken words; thus, where I think a point is well made even in an undergraduate or public lecture, I will cite it.

52 See my own 'The Stubborn Jew: Franz Rosenzweig's Gift to Eugen Rosenstock-Huessy,' in *The Cross and the Star*.

53 Horwitz, 'The Shaping of Rosenzweig's Identity,' 12–13. Prior to that, she says: 'Like other Jewish scholars, Glatzer kept a distance from Jews who had converted to Christianity and Eugen Rosenstock-Huessy was a convert to the Christian faith, a *meshumad*. There is a tradition of keeping away from converts. Alexander Altmann, and Gershom Scholem, for example, avoided Rosenstock-Huessy. Altmann wrote about him, but refused to visit him. Ernst Simon was friendly with him in Germany, but later in Israel advised me to avoid him. Only the philosopher Hugo Bergman had a different opinion.' Michael Gormann-Thelen, on the basis of his archival diggings, finds this claim about Glatzer and Altmann 'incredulous.'

54 See Ignaz Maybaum, *Trialogue between Jew, Christian, and Muslim* (London: Routledge and Kegan Paul, 1973), 103. There is not a line of evidence or even the semblance of an 'argument' to support the charge. More recent is the hyperbolic and absurd piece by David J. Wasserstein, 'Now Let Us Proclaim – The Conversions of Franz Rosenzweig,' *Times Literary Supplement*, 27 June 2008. Without bothering with argument or evidence, it preposterously equates Rosenzweig's near conversion with medieval forced conversions that involved torturing and murdering Jews. Wasserstein's fantasy ignores completely not only the utterly different social contexts but also even Rosenzweig's genuine desire to be converted.

55 Rosenstock-Huessy, *Judaism Despite Christianity*, 113.

56 Ibid., 109–10, 112.

57 Ibid., 111–12.

58 Ibid., 157.

59 Ibid., 165–6.

60 Ibid., 159.

61 Ibid., 136

62 Ibid., 160.

63 To Rosenzweig, 29 May 1916, in ibid., 78. See Alexander Altmann's 'Franz Rosenzweig and Eugen Rosenstock-Huessy: An Introduction to their *Letters on Judaism and Christianity*,' in Rosenstock-Huessy, *Judaism Despite Christianity*, 72. That essay, along with Dorothy Emmet's, which follows Altmann's in the same book, first appeared in *Journal of Religion* 24 (October 1944): 258–70.

64 Cited in Stahmer, 'Franz Rosenzweig's Letters,' 397.

65 Cf. Rühle's claim that 'Rosenstock-Huessy appears never to have accepted Rosenzweig's standpoint,' in *Gott spricht die Sprache*, 42. Her argument is based on a complete misinterpretation of Rosenstock-Huessy's use of the term 'despite' in the title he gave to the 1916 correspondence. She contends that the emphasis on the difference is proof of unacceptance. She and others think we must always be 'with' if we wish to accept the other; these people, though, are only indicating their failure to understand the problem the two had solved, and the means by which they solved it. 'Despite' is in the title to indicate a key theme of *The Cross and the Star*, which is, that Rosenzweig acknowledges that Christianity does contain certain truths of revelation, but 'despite this' he was remaining a Jew.

66 Rosenstock-Huessy, *Judaism Despite Christianity*, 176–7.

67 Eugen Rosenstock-Huessy, *The Christian Future – or The Modern Mind Outrun*, intro. Harold Stahmer (New York: Harper and Row, [1947]1966), 182.

68 Edith Rosenzweig, 4 June1955*. I think it is just as likely that Edith had another motive for not wishing to see their publication. She knew that once their friendship was again brought into public light, Gritli's ghost would reappear – which is, of course, exactly what happened. It is also noteworthy that in the 1935 edition of Rosenzweig's *Briefe*, the correspondence between Rosenzweig and Rosenstock-Huessy was assembled into a large Appendix, yet in the 1979 edition it is interspersed throughout, thereby diluting its importance. This suggests that in 1935, Edith and other Jewish people perceived Rosenstock-Huessy's argument with Rosenzweig as helpful to the cause of Jews in Germany in that Rosenzweig and Rosenstock-Huessy had reached an agreement while maintaining their differences. But after the Holocaust, she feared – as she told Rosenstock-Huessy herself – that the arguments put forward by Rosenstock-Huessy that criticized Judaism might be misconstrued as anti-Semitism.

69 Franz Rosenzweig, *The Star of Redemption*, trans. Barbara E. Galli (Madison: University of Wisconsin Press, 2005), 438.

70 Ibid., 438–9. Note as well that this act of Jewish–Christian reconciliation
was also of central importance to the theology of Hans Ehrenberg. In his
Die Heimkehre des Ketzers (*The Homecoming of the Heretic*; 1920) he had argued that the Church, since Luther, had lapsed into an ahistorical form of
Christianity and that it had lost sight of the Jewish roots of its faith. Like
Rosenzweig and Rosenstock-Huessy, Ehrenberg was a member of the
Patmos group, whose approach to religion was one of hoping and waiting – at least on the Christian side – for the fulfilment of a Johannine reli-
gious age in which all would be 'sons of God.' The unconventional nature
of the group can be gauged by Viktor von Weiszäcker's comments about
himself, Buber, and Wittig, the founders of the journal *Die Kreatur,* which
would come out of the Patmos group: 'The Catholic was not a proper
Catholic, the Protestant not a proper Protestant and the Jew not a proper
Jew.' See Viktor von Weiszäcker, 'Die Kreatur, Martin Buber, Jospeh
Wittig,' in *Gesammelte Schriften*, vol. 1 (Frankfurt am Main: Suhrkamp,
1986), 212–18 at 213. In his attempt to bridge Jewish–Christian relations,
Ehrenberg had even suggested to Rosenzweig that he publish *The Star of
Redemption* with a Christian publisher. But for Rosenzweig, the danger
was that Christianity would again try to colonize Judaism. Rosenzweig
and Ehrenberg each saw the other as secretly wanting to become a member of the other's faith. Ehrenberg would speak out against National
Socialism and would try to get his congregation to appreciate Judaism as
an essential fellow faith. After 1927 the Nazis began organizing protests
against him. He would also insist that the only form of conversion that
was permissible for Christians vis-à-vis Jews was through the example
of their own lives. I am grateful to Wolfram Liebster for his marvellous
essay, as yet unpublished, 'Hans Ehrenberg im Kontex der gegenwärtigen
Israeltheologien,' and for 'Ein Judenchrist beginnt den Kirchenkampf:
Bermerkungen zur Geschichtsschreibung des Kirchenkampfes,' in *Sonderdruck aus Jahrbuch für Westfällische Kirchengeschichte*, Bd 79 (1986). For
more on Hans Ehrenberg, see Wolfdietrich Schmied-Kowarzik, *Rosenzweig im Gespräch mit Ehrenberg, Cohen, und Buber* (Freiburg: Alber, 2006);
and Werner Licharz and Manfred Keller, eds., *Franz Rosenzweig und Hans
Ehrenberg: Bericht einer Beziehung*, Bd 42 (Frankfurt am Main: Haag & Herschen, 1986). Note also that Rudi Ehrenberg was convinced that Rosenzweig had made the right decision for himself; indeed, that decision had
helped make Ehrenberg himself a stronger Christian – the faith of each
had been a blessing in its strengthening of the other. See especially the
letter to Rosenzweig from Rudi Ehrenberg, 9 January 1921, in Maria Ehrenberg, 'Rudolf Ehrenbergs Theoretische Biologie und Metabiologie. Hat

der Dialog zwischen Rudolf Ehrenberg und Franz Rosenzweig zu ihrer Entstehung beigetragen?' in *Der Philosoph Franz Rosenzweig*, Bd 1, 159–78.

71 Rosenzweig, *The Star of Redemption*, 405.

72 Franz Rosenzweig, 'Paralipomena,' in *Gesammelte Schriften, Bd III. Zweistromland. Kleinere Schriften zu Glauben und Denken*, ed. Reinhold Meyer and Annemarie Mayer (Dordrecht: Martinus Nijhoff, 1984), 103.

73 Rosenzweig, *The Star of Redemption*, 372–3.

74 Ibid., 407.

75 Ibid., 402.

76 Ibid., 401–2. Cf. Franz Rosenzweig, 'It is Time: Concerning the Study of Judaism, in *On Jewish Learning*, trans. and intro. Nahum N. Glatzer (New York: Noonday Press, 1965): 'Judaism . . . is the goal of the future' (30). This is a pithy expression of his entire life's work.

77 Eugen Rosenstock-Huessy, *Speech and Reality*, intro. Clinton C. Gardner (Norwich: Argo Books, 1970), 42.

78 Rosenzweig, *Judaism Despite Christianity*, 71.

79 Ibid., 172

80 Ibid., 154.

81 Unpublished letter, *Rosenstock-Huessy to Gritli, 1.11.1924. Again I thank Michael Gormann-Thelen for his detective work.

82 Leo Weismantel, ed., 'Zwölf Bücher,' *Die Zwölf Wegbereiter. Ein Almanach persönlicher Beratung für das Jahr 1921* (Munich: Verlag der Arbeitsgemeinschaft, 1921), 43–5. Same title in microfilm: reel 2, item 111. This piece was all but forgotten until reproduced by Michael Gormann-Thelen in Luc Anckaert, Martin Brasser, and Norbert Samuelson, eds., *The Legacy of Franz Rosenzweig: Collected Essays* (Leuven: Leuven University Press, 2004), 76–7.

83 Again, I am grateful to Michael Gormann-Thelen for bringing this to my attention.

84 Franz Rosenzweig, *Franz Rosenzweig Briefe* (Berlin: Schocken, 1935), 638. Ullmann, 'The Discovery of the New Thinking,' also draws attention to this at the conclusion of his essay *The Cross and the Star*, 101–3. It is a great pity that the English edition of *Judaism Despite Christianity* does not contain any traces of this reference. Clearly, Rosenstock-Huessy never thought that the reference would mean much to his postwar American readers.

85 The information about Barth and the cries for help comes from Wolfram Liebster's discussion of René Süss's study on Karl Barth and the Jews. Wolfram Liebster, 'Buchbesprechung und Wiedergabe des Buches "Een genadeloos bestaan (Eine gnadenlose Existenz); Karl Barth over het

Joodse Volk" von Rene Suess,' in *Wolfram Liebster: Theologie im Lichte des Neuen Denkens* (Ahrweiler: Wahrlich Druck 2010), 121–31. I am deeply thankful to Michael Gormann-Thelen for showing me this.

86 In her preface to *Hitler and Israel*, in *Beiheft Stimmstein: Hitler und Israel oder vom Gebet, Hitler and Israel or On Prayer,* ed. Eugen Rosenstock-Huessy Gesellschaft, intro. Cynthia Harris, Jochen Lübbers, Bas Leenman, and Adam Żak (Mössingen-Talheim: Talheimer, 1992), 15, Rosenstock-Huessy's friend Cynthia Harries asks this question: 'How did it happen, then, that the Christians went on to develop their virulent anti-Semitism, culminating in Hitler's concentration camps?' In *Out of Revolution: Autobiography of Western Man* (Norwich: Argo Books, 1993, intro. Page Smith; Providence: Berg Publishers, 1993, intro. Harold Berman), Rosenstock-Huessy does talk of Christianity's anti-Jewish outbreaks being desperate acts of self-preservation in moments of extreme crisis, though not – as is evident below – to be justified on that account: 'The fifteenth century offers a good example of Jewish persecutions at a time when Christianity was frightened by the approaching downfall of its visible unity. The fear of Reformation and dissolution spread all over Europe between 1450 and 1517, and led to violent pogroms. The pogroms were the lightning-rod that protected the Papacy; they averted Luther's Reformation for fifty years. The same could perhaps be said of Czarist Russia. There, too, the Jews were one of the lightning-conductors of the regime. These atrocities of a senescent institution fighting for a longer span of life are always peculiarly insulting and outrageous. But as mankind's propensity to war is not explained by condemning iniquitous wars, neither are persecutions explained by condemning iniquitous persecutions.' *Out of Revolution*, 227. In the same work, he compares Hitler to Giovanni Capistrano, the anti-Semite, who burned Jews and led a crusade against the Turks and who 'had a tremendous following between 1445 and 1455, delay[ing] the Reformation for another fifty years by defending the dictatorship of a ruthless papacy.' Ibid., 601.

87 Ibid., 225.

88 Ibid., 228.

89 My emphasis.

90 Harries, *Hitler and Israel or On Prayer*, 20.

91 Ibid.

92 Rosenstock-Huessy, *Out of Revolution*, 216.

93 Ibid., 217.

94 A little later down the page, without naming him directly, Rosenstock-Huessy refers to a 'great Jewish scholar' (i.e. Rosenzweig) who had characterized 'the follies of pagan philosophy' as 'crude pagan superstition.'

95 Rosenzweig, *The Star of Redemption*, 97ff. The implication is found by
comparing the task of the Pauline mission, which must then win over
pagan souls. See the discussion elsewhere in this volume on Rosenzweig's three ages of the Church.

96 'Die jüdischen Antisemiten oder die akademische Form der Judenfrage,' 9.

97 Rosenstock-Huessy's own translation of 'Die jüdischen Antisemiten
oder die akademische Form der Judenfrage,' in *Frankfurter Hefte* (1951):
8–17; and Rosenstock-Huessy, *Das Geheimnis der Universität: Wider den
Verfall von Zeitsinn und Sprachkraft*, ed. Georg Müller (Stuttgart: W. Kohlhammer Verlag, 1958), 44–55. Same title in microfilm: 1958, reel 9, item
442, page 17. Niemoeller, as Ehrenberg emphasizes in his 'Open Letter'
to him in 1943 (*Autobiography of a German Pastor*, 38ff) became the face of
Christian resistance to Nazism in Great Britain during the War. He was
a complex figure, acting at a complex time. Ehrenberg's letter draws
out these complexities. Nevertheless, Niemoeller's relationship to the
Jews has become a source of great embarrassment to his memory. In his
extremely critical essay, Robert Michaels writes: 'At the Prussian Synod
of the Confessing Church held at Berlin in September 1935, Niemoeller
unsuccessfully argued for an expression of brotherly support for Jewish
Christians. Yet Niemoeller's actions during this period were leavened
with hostility to Jewish Jews. Niemoeller himself admitted that even his
defence of baptized Jews was tainted, because it was only "scriptural,
ecclesiastical, and theological rather than ethical or humanitarian." His
Sätze zur Arierfrage, published in November 1933, confirmed that his
support of converted Jews was disagreeable. It was, in fact, as he wrote,
"a matter of real self-denial to champion their cause." Moreover, in the
same year, he advocated a separate Protestant Church for the baptized
Jews. At his trial in 1938, he stated in his defence that even baptized
"Jews were alien and uncongenial to him." That God had revealed
himself in the Jew, Jesus, was to Niemoeller a "painful and grievous
stumbling-block [that] has to be accepted." From the pulpit, until his
incarceration, his silence about the Jews was thundering. As in his hesi-
tating defence of the baptized, he was most likely influenced both by
his enthusiasm for the Nazis' national revival and by his theological
anti-Semitism. So at the very time that Niemoeller was begrudgingly
defending the so-called non-Aryan Christians, he was acquiescing in the
Nazi onslaught against the Jewish Jews. With the exception of a mild
exhortation to his parishioners in June 1933 to love one's neighbour be
he Christian or Jew, and a sermon in 1935, Niemoeller stood publicly
silent on the status and condition of the Jewish Jews.' Robert Michaels,
'Theological Myth, German Antisemitism, and the Holocaust: The Case

of Martin Niemoeller,' *Holocaust and Genocide Studies* 2, no. 1 (1987): 105–22 at 112.

98 'All true prayer,' writes Rosenstock-Huessy, again in a manner no different in its emphasis than one finds in Rosenzweig, 'begins with establishing distance between two poles: one, the sacrifice of a mortal's own ideas and ideals, i.e., his self-will, thus making room for God's will by repentance; the other a majesty of light, future, creativity. Prayer is the act by which the potential between the two poles, God and man, is enhanced or enlarged; the hollowness of man and the glory of God both are increased.' *Hitler and Prayer* (Stimmstein, Talheimer, 1992), 30.

99 Rosenstock-Huessy, *Judaism Despite Christianity*, 45–6. In the same volume, one should read all of 44–8 by Altmann.

100 Rosenstock-Huessy, *Out of Revolution*, 220–1.

101 Ibid., 220. Again, this was pre-Israel. 'Unable' here does not mean due to lack of ability but rather due to obedience to faith in being the elect.

102 Ibid., 226.

103 Acording to Rosenstock-Huessy, Rosenzweig 'was the first to speak of the revolutionary fact of the exposure of the three groups [Jews, Pagans, and Christians] to each other.' Rosenstock-Huessy, 'Die jüdischen Antisemiten,' 8. That Rosenzweig's insight was rather novel can be gauged by Rosenstock-Huessy's remark in *Out of Revolution:* 'As far as I know, the Jews in 1789 did not discriminate in their language between Pagans and Christians. They did not believe in the genuineness of the Christian faith.' *Out of Revolution*, 216.

104 See microfilm: 'Stahl, Gambetta, Marx: Drei europäischen Juden,' 1924, reel 2, item 138, page 62.

105 Rosenstock-Huessy, *Out of Revolution*, 218.

106 'Ehrlos – Heimatlos,' in *Die Hochzeit*, 246; also in *Die Sprache des Menschengeschlechts*, vol. 2, 109.

107 'Ehrlos – Heimatlos,' in *Die Hochzeit*, 249; also in *Die Sprache des Menschengeschlechts*, vol. 2, 114.

108 This is why a judgment such as Frank Surrall's that a free conversation between Rosenzweig and Rosenstock-Huessy, as partners, never took place misses the point that it took place over their respective lifetimes. Surrall, *Juden und Christen – Toleranz in neuer Perspektive: der Denkweg Franz Rosenzweigs in seiner Bezügen zu Lessing, Harnack, Baeck, und Rosenstock-Huessy* (Gütersloh: Chr. Kaiser/Gü, 2003), 254.

109 Though Rosenstock-Huessy rightly noted, in his 1954 undergraduate lecture series on Greek philosophy, that Plato does not take this tack in the *Symposium*. There we see the celebration of difference – albeit not without poor old Agathon, the tragic poet fresh from celebrations of winning a

festival, being humiliated, and Socrates giving a speech that integrates and synthesizes everything in a manner that attempts to demonstrate the underlying philosophical concordance that the other speakers have not completely realized.

110 Rosenstock-Huessy, *Ja und Nein*, 71–2.

111 Rosenzweig got the idea of establishing a symbol for his system from Rosenstock-Huessy's 'cross of reality.' *The Star of Redemption* was originally conceived as a counterpart or counterpole (*Gegenstück*) to Rosenstock-Huessy's cross of reality. See letter of 22 August 1918 in *Gritli Briefe*, transcribed by Ulrika Von Moltke, ed. Michael Gormann-Thelen and Dr Elfriede Büchsel (Eugen Rosenstock-Huessy Fund and Norwich: Argo Books). http://www.argobooks.org/gritli/index.html. The most recent edition of Rosenstock-Huessy's *Soziologie*, edited by Michael Gormann-Thelen, Ruth Mautner, and Lise van der Molen, bears the title *Im Kreuz der Wirklichkeit: Eine nach-goethische Soziologie* (Tübingen: Talheimer, 2008–9). The edition has created controversy within the Rosenstock-Huessy Gesellschaft, and not the least of the controversies revolves around the title change. I am part of an editorial team involved in translating the *Soziologie*, and Rosenstock-Huessy's heirs have expressed their desire that we translate the 1956–8 edition. Thus throughout I have referred to the earlier edition. However, the title of the new edition has some justification, and it is certainly the case that Rosenstock-Huessy often referred to his enterprise under that title.

112 Paul Franks and Michael Morgan, eds., *New Thinking in Philosophical and Theological Writings* (Indianapolis: Hackett, 2000), 112.

113 See Rosenstock-Huessy, 'Die Bahnbrecher,' in *Soziologie*, Bd 1, *Die Übermacht der Räume* (Stuttgart: W. Kohlhammer Verlag, 1956), 204ff. This contains the essential material for what would become chapter 7 of *The Christian Future*. Rudi Ehrenberg would tell Rosenstock-Huessy that he was uncomfortable about Buddhism and Taoism being part of 'the cross of reality,' fearing that he had relativized revelation. 18 February 1947*.

1. Which Spirit to Serve? The Stirring of the Living Loving God

1 One possible exception to this might be the liberal tradition (understood in its British sense as a constitutional form of rights-based democratic government). Though even here, Mill and Tocqueville were certainly alert to this problem. Nevertheless, much twentieth-century liberal thinking is more concerned with fighting the twin evils of totalitarian thinking than with the mechanization of the world and self. On the other hand, for many twentieth-century social theorists of both the left and the right,

liberalism proceeds on the same metaphysical basis as the mechanistic philosophies and ways of thinking that create the problem; it follows that these are part of the problem, not the solution. Liberal democratic societies contain hordes who are afflicted by depression, addiction, and anomie – a circumstance that hardly entitles us to think we have discovered the correct fit between our social needs and our political institutions. Rosenstock-Huessy certainly thought along these lines; hence, while an enemy of totalitarianism, he was by no means convinced that liberalism was the way out.

2 Eugen Rosenstock-Huessy, *Soziologie*, Bd 1, *Die Übermacht der Räume* (Stuttgart: W. Kohlhammer Verlag, 1956), 315–29.

3 Eugen Rosenstock-Huessy, *Soziologie*, Bd 2, *Die Vollzahl der Zeiten* (Stuttgart: W. Kohlhammer Verlag, 1958), 560ff.

4 Hans Ehrenberg, *Autobiography of a German Pastor*, trans. Geraint Jones (London: Student Christian Movement, 1943), 114.

5 Ibid., 21–2.

6 An idea of their interests can be gathered by some of their major works – for example, Rudolf Ehrenberg's most important publications: *Theoretische Biologie. Vom Standpunkt der Irreversibilität des eelmentaren Lebensvorganges* (Berlin: Julius Springer 1923); *Der Lebenslauf. Eine biologisch-metabiologische Vorlesung* (Heidelberg: Lambert Schneider, 1946); and *Metabiologie* (Heidelberg: Lambert Schneider, 1950). For more on Rudi Ehrenberg, see Rudolf Hermeier, ed., *Jenseits all unsres Wissens wohnt Gott. Hans Ehrenberg und Rudolf Ehrenberg zur Erinnerung* (Moers: Brendow Verlag, 1987); Heinz-Jürgen Görtz, '*Der Stern der Erlösung* als Kommentar: Rudolf Ehrenberg und Franz Rosenzweig,' in *Franz Rosenzweig als Leser. Kontextuelle Kommentare zum Stern der Erlösung*, ed. Martin Brasser (Tübingen: Niemeyer, 2004); idem, 'Rudolf Ehrenbergs Gedanke des "Lebens,"' *Theologie und Philosophie* 78 (2003): 811–96; Maria E. Ehrenberg, 'Rudolf Ehrenbergs theoretische Biologie und Metabiologie. Hat der Dialog zwischen Rudolf Ehrenberg und Franz Rosenzweig zu ihrer Entstehung beigetragen?' in *Der Philosoph Franz Rosenzweig*, Bd 1. Richard Koch's central work is *Die ärztliche Diagnose. Beitrag zur Kenntnis des ärztlichen Denkens* (Wiesbaden: Bergmann, 1917, 1920); a second edition then appeared as *Ärztliches Denken. Abhandlungen über die philosophischen Grundlagen der Medizin* (München: Bergmann, 1923), and then again as *Das Als-Ob im ärztlichen Denken* (München: Rösl & Cie., 1924). See also Frank Töpfer und Urban Wiesing, eds., *Richard Koch und Franz Rosenzweig: Schriften und Briefe zu Krankheit, Sterben, und Tod* (Münster: Agenda, 2000). Viktor von Weiszäcker is the best known of the three, and Suhrkamp has published a ten-volume edition of his *Gesammelte Schriften*. His writings range across

medical anthropology; sociology of medicine; clinical studies on a range of medical issues such as perception, dreams, the muscular system, the heart, nutrition, pyschosomatic illness, and the nervous system; as well as the philosophy of nature and biology. He has a short 'reflection piece' on Rosenzweig in Bd 1 (Frankfurt am Main: Suhrkamp, 1986), 413–14. See also, at 398–9 of that same volume, his comment on the Rosenstock-Huessy/Rosenzweig 1916 correspondence. See also Wolfgang Jacob, 'Viktor von Weiszäcker und Franz Rosenzweig,' in *Der Philosoph Franz Rosenzweig,* Bd 1; Hartwig Wiedebach, 'Apologie gegen sich selbst. Zur Antilogik der Person bei Viktor von Weizsäcker und Franz Rosenzweig,' in *Religious Apologetics: Philosophical Arguments*, ed. Yossef Schwartz and Volkhard Krech (Tübingen: Mohr Siebeck, 2004).

7 Eugen Rosenstock-Huessy, *Heilkraft und Wahrheit: Konkordanz der Politischen und kosmischen Zeit* (Moers: Brendow, 1952; Wien: Amandus, 1991), 158.

8 Microfilm: 'Biology and the Life of Life,' 1946, reel 8, item 404, pages 3 and 4.

9 I think it very interesting and significant that this way of thinking was also important among Jews in the years before the Holocaust. Thus, for example, in *Gemeindeblatt der Deutsch-Israelistischen Gemeinde zu Hamburg* (26 September 1935), the lead article on the front page – just above Hans Liebeschütz's review of the *Die Briefe Franz Rosenzweig* – is titled 'Wachsende Kräfte' (Growing Forces). This short piece goes on to speak of the slumbering forces and capacities that the Jews in Germany need to awaken. In keeping with this, Liebeschütz's review speaks of the power (*Macht*) that can be felt in Rosensweig's writings.

10 Microfilm: Eugen Rosenstock-Huessy and Richard Koch, '"Einleitung" to *Theophrast von Hohenheim. Fünf Bücher über die unsichtbaren Krankheiten,'* 1923, reel 2, item 125, page 9.

11 Eugen Rosenstock-Huessy and Joseph Wittig, *Das Alter der Kirche. Kapitel und Akten*. 3 Bde (Münster: Agenda, 1998), 733. The chapter is titled 'Der Annus Acceptus des Thephrast von Hohenheim (Paracelsus).'

12 The other volumes in the series were Diderot's *D'Alembert's Dream*, ed. and intro. Koch and C.S. Gutkind; *Kant: The Organism*, ed. and intro. Viktor von Weiszäcker; a work on Hobbes; and another on Lamarck and Darwin. They give a good indication of the importance of 'materiality' in the new thinking and its anti-dualism.

13 Microfilm: Rosenstock-Huessy and Koch, '"Einleitung" to *Theophrast von Hohenheim. Fünf Bücher über die unsichtbaren Krankheiten,'* in *Theophrast von Hohenheim*. Microfilm: 1923, reel 2, item 125. Thus one essay dealing with him is titled 'A Classic and a Founder,' included in *The Rosenstock-Huessy*

Papers (Norwich: Argo Books, 1981). It was never edited and is merely a reproduction of Rosenstock-Huessy's original typewritten pages. Frances Huessy has recently completed a much more thorough edit – as yet unpublished – with accompanying notes on Paracelsus, to make a much more readable manuscript. Paracelsus is discussed in many of Rosenstock-Huessy's writings and lectures. He also wrote the entry on Paracelsus in *The American Peoples Encylopedia.*

14 Rosenstock-Huessy, *Soziologie,* Bd 2, 692ff.

15 Eugen Rosenstock-Huessy, *The Star of Redemption,* trans. Barbara E. Galli (Madison: University of Wisconsin Press, 2005), 230–1.

16 Franz Rosenzweig, *Gesammelte Schriften,* I. *Briefe und Tagebucher,* Bd 1: 1900–18, ed. Rachel Rosenzweig and Edith Rosenzweig-Scheinmann (The Hague: Martinus Nijhoff, 1979), 37.

17 Eugen Rosenstock-Huessy, *Der Atem des Geistes* (Wien: Amandus, 1991), 32.

18 Ibid., 278. Cf. also his 'Protestantismus und Seelenführung' ('Protestantism and Soul-leading') in *Protestantismus als Kritik und Gestaltung,* ed. Paul Tillich (Darmstadt: Otto Reichl, 1929), which begins by contrasting the living powers of the soul with the moralistic, rationalistic position he opposes.

19 Eugen Rosenstock-Huessy, *Out of Revolution,* 721.

20 Ibid., 720.

21 Eugen Rosenstock-Huessy, *The Christian Future – or The Modern Mind Outrun,* intro. Harold Stahmer (New York: Harper and Row, [1947]1966), 155.

22 Rosenstock-Huessy, *Out of Revolution,* 473.

23 For example, in 'Militia Academica': 'The social home asks students for a cooperative fellowship between irreconcilable opponents, because we are going to have a society of "totality by diversity." Universal truth about nature was accessible to one single philosophical mind who could stamp his ideas upon millions of obedient other minds. But as soon as you transfer this philosophical domination to questions of society, family, race, government, education you end in fascism. Mussolini could be called by "l'Impero l'unico cervello d'Italia," the only brain of Italy. This is the clerical error and heresy of a scientific age, extending principles of natural science to social life. We are dictators over nature because we can unite and move against it like one man. But man becomes a slave as soon as society is treated like nature.' Microfilm: 'Militia Academica,' 1933 and 1980, reel 6, item 296, pages 8 and 9.

24 See especially 'Liturgical Thinking,' in *Rosenstock-Huessy Papers,* vol. 1.

25 See Chris Hutton, *Race and the Third Reich* (Cambridge: Polity Press, 2005).

26 Microfilm: 'Circulation of Thought,' 1954, reel 16, item 634, page 20.
27 Microfilm: 'The Rise and Fall of Nationalism and Internationalism,' 1939, reel 6, item 331, page 3.
28 Rosenzweig, *The Star of Redemption*, 444.
29 Ibid., 403.
30 For many of the English, God is a silly concept and they find it genuinely bewildering that anyone could ever have taken it seriously. Examples include Christopher Hitchens, Richard Dawkins, and Martin Amis. Their take on God is expressed with much greater wit but no less intellectual force by the English comedian Ricky Gervais. All of them, however, present God as a silly but dangerous joke. What they are all scorning, however, is a widespread literalist and thoughtless faith, one that is as 'empirically' faithful to the Bible in its own way as the 'scientistic' minds that mock it. When Ricky Gervais and Rowan Williams, the Archbishop of Canterbury, engaged in a radio discussion about 'God,' it was obvious that they did not share a common language. Bill Hicks, the late and great American comic, also spent much of his time satirizing Christian literalists and bigots, yet he would add sincerely: 'I believe there's a LIVING GOD WHO WILL TALK DIRECTLY F**NG TO YOU! . . . I believe that God is Love, and that he created us and that we are his beloved children . . . I also believe forgiveness is the key to healing our perceptions and allowing us to remember god and his everlasting love for us.' Bill Hicks, *Love All the People: Letters, Lyrics, Routines* (London: Constable, 2004), 195 and 275. Hicks is the new thinkers' comedian.
31 See especially Eugen Rosenstock-Huessy, 'In Defense of the Grammatical Method,' in *Speech and Reality*, (Norwich: Argo Books, 1970). For Rosenstock-Huessy, 'religion is a power, and therefore it is not a system.' Microfilm: 'Comparative Religion,' 1954, reel 15, item 633, page 11.
32 Rosenzweig, *The Star of Redemption*, 103.
33 Ibid., 103–4.
34 Ibid., 108.
35 Ibid., 113.
36 Rosenzweig reminds his readers that there have been several enlightenments: the campaign against pagan myths; the Renaissance against scholasticism; 'the enlightenment against "the webs that reason spins"'; and the Enlightenment 'against credulity based on experience, [which] became slowly but surely historical critique of experience' (ibid., 117).
37 It is interesting that none of the commentaries by Samuelson, Moses, and Freund are very illuminating regarding the 'Introduction of Part Two of *The Star*.' No doubt this is in part because the introduction is a section of

the book more likely than most to completely baffle the reader. It is indeed a brief, dense commentary on the state of affairs of nineteenth- and early-twentieth century theology and philosophy; but keep in mind that Rosenzweig's move to language as a sign of the miracle was the critical move that united him and Rosenstock-Huessy.

38 Rosenzweig, *The Star of Redemption*, 110 in Hallo's translation (120 in Galli).
39 See chapter 2 of Nietzsche's *Twilight of the Idols*.
40 *Franz Rosenzweig zum 25. Dezember 1926 glueckwuensche zum 40. Geburtstag*. Published on the Centenary of Franz Rosenzweig's Birth by the Leo Baeck Institute (New York: Leo Baeck Institute, 1987).
41 Ibid.

2. The Basis of the New Speech Thinking

1 Eugen Rosenstock-Huessy, *Judaism Despite Christianity: The Letters on Christianity and Judaism between Rosenstock-Huessy and Franz Rosenzweig*, intro. Harold Stahmer (Tuscaloosa: University of Alabama Press, 1969; New York: Schocken Books, 1971), 29 May 1916, 78.
2 Ibid., letter #2, 82.
3 Microfilm: 'Philosophy and the Social Sciences,' 1942, reel 7, item 373, page 1.
4 Adam Zak, 'Die Zeit der Sprache – die Sprache der Zeit. Zum Sprachdenken Eugen Rosenstock-Huessy,' *Orientierung* 1, no. 1 (1990): 2–8 at 8.
5 *New Thinking*, in Franks and Morgan, *Philosophical and Theological Writings*, 110.
6 *Briefe an Gritli*, 7 February 1919.
7 Rosenstock-Huessy, *Judaism Despite Christianity*, 19 November 1916, 142.
8 Rosenzweig to Rosenstock in Rosenstock-Huessy, *Judaism Despite Christianity* [n.d.], 167.
9 Microfilm: 'Biology and the Life of Life,' 1946, reel 8, item 433, page 4.
10 Microfilm: 'Circulation of Thought,' 1954, reel 16, item 634, page 22.
11 Eugen Rosenstock-Huessy, *Soziologie*, Bd 2: *Die Vollzahl der Zeiten* (Stuttgart: W. Kohlhammer Verlag, 1958), 299. For his most developed critique of theology, see his *Heilkraft und Wahrheit: Konkordanz der Politischen und Kosmischen Zeit* (Moers: Brendow, 1952; Wien: Amandus, 1991), especially (but not only) the chapter 'Heilsgeschichte wider Theologie / Eine Denkschrift zur Person.'
12 Franz Rosenzweig, *The Star of Redemption*, trans. Barbara E. Galli (Madison: University of Wisconsin Press, 2005), 116.

13 In Rosenzweig, Heraclitus is clearly an exception, as he is for Rosenstock-Huessy, who sees (as does Rosenzweig) that it is with Parmenides that things become cut off from what Rosenstock-Huessy calls 'the aboriginality of humanity.'

14 Rosenzweig, *The Star of Redemption*,10.

15 Ibid., 10.

16 Ibid., 11.

17 *New Thinking*, Franks and Morgan, 111.

18 Rosenzweig, *The Star of Redemption*, 16.

19 Ibid., 17–18.

20 Ibid., 18. Galli correctly renders Rosenzweig's *Denken* as 'thinking,' not as 'reasoning,' which is Hallo's translation. It is precisely the opening up of thought against reason's hegemony that is essential to Rosenzweig and 'his precursors.'

21 Much has been written of Rosenzweig's debt to Schelling since Else Freund's *Franz Rosenzweig's Philosophy of Existence*, trans. Stephen Weinstein and Robert Israel (The Hague: Martinus Nijhoff, [1933]1979), but an excellent analysis is provided by Wolfdietrich Schmied-Kowarzik, a philosopher who has written extensively on both Schelling and Rosenzweig, in 'Vom Totalexperiment des Glaubens. Kritisches zur positiven Philosophie Schellings und Rosenzweigs' in *Der Philosoph Franz Rosenzweig (1886–1929)*, Bd 2.

22 *New Thinking*, 120–1.

23 Ibid., 138.

24 Franz Rosezweig, *Understanding the Sick and the Healthy: A View of World, Man, and God*, ed. and trans. Nahum Glatzer (Cambridge, MA: Harvard University Press, 1999), 57.

25 Ibid., 40.

26 Rosenzweig, *The Star of Redemption*, 24. One must not underestimate the huge importance of another New Thinker, Hans Ehrenberg, in Rosenzweig's construction of *The Star of Redemption*. In a letter to Ernst Simon in August 1922, Rosenzweig says that Ehrenberg was 'my real teacher.' *Gesammelte Schriften*, I. *Briefe und Tagebucher*, Bd 1: 1900–18, ed. Rachel Rosenzweig and Edith Rosenzweig-Scheinmann (The Hague: Martinus Nijhoff, 1979), 808ff. It had been Hans Ehrenberg in *Die Parteiung der Philosophie* (with its appendix, 'Studium wieder Hegel und die Kantianer') and *Die Geschichte des Menschen unserer Zeit* – both of which appeared in 1911 – who originally argued that the true logic was a metalogic because it problematized the relationship between reality and reason in a way that destroyed all pan-logicism. Rosenstock-Huessy also uses the terms

'metalogic,' 'metaethic,' and 'metaesthetic' in *Speech and Reality* for his own efforts to break out of traditional, philosophical/theological enclosures. See his chapter 'In Defense of the Grammatical Method' in *Speech and Reality*.

27 Rosenzweig, *The Star of Redemption*, 21.
28 Ibid., 20.
29 Ibid., 22.
30 Ibid., 21.
31 Eugen Rosenstock-Huessy, 'Die Rasse der Denker,' in *Die Sprache des Menschengeschlechts: Eine leibhaftige Grammatik in vier Teilen*, Bd 1 (Heidelberg: Lambert Schneider, 1963/4), 619.
32 'Liturgical Thinking,' in *Rosenstock-Huessy Papers*, vol. 1 (Norwich: Argo Books, 1981), 14.
33 This does not mean there are no overlaps. Indeed there are – see my 'Rosenstock-Huessy: Before, During, and After Post-Modernism,' *Revue Roumaine de Philosophie* 48, nos. 1–2 (2004): 190–203. Among the major thinkers who usually fall under the rubric 'post-structuralist,' Derrida comes the closest to New Thinking, especially in his later work – if, that is, we see his attack on logocentrism as an attack on a deformed version of the *logos* (as ratio). But his politics still share the predominantly left-Hegelian orientation. Bruno Bauer's 'critical criticism,' while lampooned by Marx, finds its resonances throughout the Frankfurt School as well as in Derrida's politics.
34 *Ereignis* – 'event' – is a key term in Heidegger as well, notwithstanding the claims he makes about the importance of language. But in large part, because of his concern with Being rather than names, he does not proceed with it as Rosenstock-Huessy does.
35 Rosenstock-Huessy, *Die Sprache des Menschengeschlechts*, Bd 1, 739. The point about compulsion, about having to speak, is well made in the opening section of Michael Gormann-Thelen, 'Orate Thinker versus Literate Thinker,' in *The Cross and the Star: The Post-Nietzschean Christian and Jewish Thought of Eugen Rosenstock-Huessy and Franz Rosenzweig*, ed. Wayne Cristaudo and Frances Huessy (Newcastle upon Tyne: Cambridge Scholars Publishing, 2009).
36 The translation is from Eugen Rosenstock-Huessy, *Practical Knowledge of the Soul*, trans. Mark Huessy and Freya von Moltke (Norwich: Argo Books, 1988), 19. Gormann-Thelen suggests in 'Ornate Thinker versus Literate Thinker' that 'a better translation might be "The Soul's Know-How."'
37 I think that Rosenstock-Huessy has correctly underscored where his and Rosenzweig's New Thinking differs fundamentally from Wittgenstein and from Husserlian phenomenology; yet it is true that the later

Wittgenstein was trying to carry out a kind of diagnostics of sick reason, as Rosenstock-Huessy himself implies above with more than a little contempt. This can be seen as comparable to what Rosenzweig is doing in *Understanding the Sick and the Healthy*. This point, at least, was put by Hilary Putnam in his introduction to that book (reprinted as chapter 1 of *Jewish Philosophy as a Guide to Life* [Indianapolis: Indiana University Press, 2008]). But Putnam's enthusiasm for the similarities between Rosenzweig and Wittgenstein skates over how the problem of language in Rosenzweig is inseparable from the problem of creation, revelation, and redemption and the great act of solidarity across the times of the Jewish life, which is not Wittgenstein's concern at all. In his *Jewish Philosophy*, Putnam has a chapter on 'Rosenzweig on Revelation and Romance,' but it does not address the relationship between language and revelation.

38 Of course, we might qualify this in the case of Heidegger, who is happy to resume where philosophy broke off from Heraclitus, Anaxagoras, and Parmenides – for whom, that is, there has been a two-thousand-year-old error. Rosenstock-Huessy and Rosenzweig are equally critical of the Platonic legacy; but unlike Heidegger, they note that the Platonic legacy has had formidable institutional opponents in Church and synagogue. Hence too, while they themselves are opposed to the machine age in which we find ourselves enmeshed, they think that the powers to counter it are far more ready to hand than Heidegger concedes. The grimness of Heideggeran politics is largely a function of its lack of interest in opening up new bodies of time for future generations. Heidegger and his followers are far more 'me generational' than Rosenstock-Huessy or Rosenzweig.

39 Franz Rosenzweig, *Judaism Despite Christianity: The Letters on Christianity and Judaism between Rosenstock-Huessy and Franz Rosenzweig*, ed. Eugen Rosenstock-Huessy, trans. Dorothy Emmet (New York: Schocken Books, 1971), 147–8.

40 Ibid., 147.

41 Eugen Rosenstock-Huessy, *Der Atem des Geistes* (Wien: Amandus, 1991), 66.

42 Ibid., 26–7.

43 Ibid., 27.

44 According to Rosenstock-Huessy, for the French, 'the war was the answer and the pendant to 1870'; for the English, it was a continuation of the 'crusade against the continental Napoleon'; for the Germans, it was partly a second 1870 and partly a continuation of Moltke's defensive war of the German people and in that sense a continuation of the Thirty Years' War; for the Prussians, it was the Seven Years' War reprised; for the Austrians, it brought back memories of 1742–8 and Maria Theresa; and for the

smaller states, it was a struggle for existence conducted through alliances that were essential to their preservation. Meanwhile the Russians, having missed the revolutionary waves of the nineteenth century, were now conducting their own revolution, which had begun in 1905; 33ff.

45 Microfilm: 'Greek Philosophy,' 1956, reel 16, item 641, page 12.

46 Eugen Rosenstock-Huessy, *Die Hochzeit des Kriegs und der Revolution* (Würzburg: Patmos-Verlag, 1920; reprint 1965), 53.

47 Microfilm: 'The Secret of the University,' 1950, reel 8, item 427.

48 Rosenstock-Huessy, *Die Hochzeit*, 53.

49 This seems to me to go to the heart of what separates Rosenstock-Huessy and Rosenzweig's dialogical thinking from Habermas's 'communicative action.'

50 Eugen Rosenstock-Huessy, *Ja und Nein. Autobiographische Fragmente aus Anlass des 80. Geburtstags des Autors. Im Auftrag der seinen Namen tragenden Gesellschaft*, ed. Georg Müller (Heidelberg: Verlag lambert Schneider, 1968), 21.

51 Microfilm: 'Four Disangelists,' 1954, reel 16, item 635, lecture 2, page 23.

52 See *Stimmstein*, vol. 3, 20. Letter from Eugen Rosenstock-Huessy to Piet Tommissen, 9 March 1951. In his public lecture series 'Die Gesetze der christlichen Zeitrechnung' (microfilm: reel 18, item 660, page 471), without naming him directly – saying he refused to name him so that he would not contribute further to his fame – he called Schmitt 'the greatest scum amongst German jurists.' He also called him 'scum' in print in 'Die Interims des Rechts' (microfilm: reel 11, item 559, page 10).

53 See the section '"Love Thine Enemy" in Politics,' in *Out of Revolution: Autobiography of Western Man* (Norwich: Argo Books, Page Smith, 1993; Providence: Berg Publishers, 1993), 459–62. Michael Gormann-Thelen, in his essay-style footnote on Schmitt and Rosenstock-Huessy in the second volume of *Das Alter der Kirche. Kapitel und Akten* (Münster: Agenda, 1998), 398–401, quite rightly sees an important difference between them: that is, Schmitt thinks in terms of power politics in the context of spatial politics, whereas Rosenstock-Huessy is primarily interested in transformation and temporality as the bases of political life. Schmitt claimed to be a Catholic, yet there is nothing especially Christian in his view of politics. His political impulses (as expressed by his choice of whom to serve) are tribal and pagan, and his politics focus on loyalty, decision making, and territoriality – not, as with Rosenstock-Huessy, on love and sacrifice and self-dissolution to engender a new form of life.

54 Eugen Rosenstock-Huessy, *The Origin of Speech* (Norwich: Argo Books, 1981), 82.

55 Rosenstock-Huessy, *Ja und Nein*, 98.

56 Ibid., 101.
57 Rosenstock-Huessy, *Speech and Reality* (Norwich: Argo Books, 1970), 19.
58 Ibid., 122–3.
59 Rosenstock-Huessy, *Ja und Nein*, 34.
60 Eugen Rosenstock-Huessy, *I Am an Impure Thinker*, ed. Freya von Moltke and Clint Gardner (Norwich: Argo Books, 1970), 108.
61 Rosenstock-Huessy, *Die Sprache des Menschen Geschlechts*, Bd 2 (Heidelberg: Lambert Schneider, 1964), 612. The German reads: 'Die unerhörte Behauptung der Denker geht dahin, daß sie erst denken, und dann erst das, was sie denken, mit Hilfe der Sprache als ihres Werkzeuges, uns verraten.' It is the use of *unerhörte* and *verraten* that makes it so delicious because the one word captures such fundamentally different, even contrary tones and ideas, and Rosenstock-Huessy means all the contraries: *unerhörte* can be translated as 'unbelievable/unheard/impermissible/terrific/scandalous' and *verraten* as 'disclose' or 'betray.'
62 Rosenzweig, *The Star of Redemption*, 119.
63 Ibid., 157.
64 Ibid., 157.
65 Ibid., 58.
66 Ibid., 59.
67 Ibid., 157.
68 *The New Thinking*, 125–6.
69 Rosenstock-Huessy, *Soziologie*, Bd 2, 342.

3. Grammatical Organons in Rosenstock-Huessy and Rosenzweig

1 Eugen Rosenstock-Huessy, *Ja und Nein. Autobiographische Fragmente aus Anlass des 80. Geburtstags des Autors. Im Auftrag der seinen Namen tragenden Gesellschaft*, ed. Georg Müller (Heidelberg: Verlag Lambert Schneider, 1968), 37 and 43.
2 See especially chapter 1 of Eugen Rosenstock-Huessy, *The Origin of Speech* (Norwich: Argo Books, 1981).
3 Microfilm: 'Make Bold to be Ashamed,' 1953, reel 16, item 632, lecture 1, page 9.
4 Eugen Rosenstock-Huessy, *The Fruit of Lips, or, Why Four Gospels?* ed. Marion Davis Battles (Pittsburgh: Pickwick Press, 1978), 86. Of course Rosenstock-Huessy does not deny that machines may assist us with our lives, but when we ourselves become mechanized in our speech we become dead to ourselves and our own powers.
5 Ibid. Eric Voegelin had also maintained that gnosis is a spiritual pathology of the modern. But for Voegelin, gnosis was really about trying to

actualize heaven on earth, a product of the mind or spirit soaring above the order of the real and seeking to reinject the abstract or vision into a world in which it cannot fit. Voegelin's idea is a useful antidote to those who think that heaven can be successfully stormed. But the danger of Voegelin's appeal to the real is that it is ultimately an appeal to a static present that is every bit as much an abstraction as the feared future – as if the order that is there is a genuine order to be found in life, instead of a process in which the residues of evil are constantly being generated in all manner of ways, and not just or even primarily by utopian (gnostic) dreamers. Rosenstock-Huessy's point about gnosticism is, I think, an insightful one dealing with the most urgent problem: we become deadened through the circulation of dead words.

6 Rosenstock-Huessy, *Practical Knowledge of the Soul*, trans. Mark Huessy and Freya von Moltke (Norwich: Argo Books, 1988), 17.

7 Rosenstock-Huessy, *Ja und Nein*, 32.

8 Ibid., 24.

9 Ibid., 25.

10 Ibid., 26.

11 Ibid., 32.

12 Ibid., 26.

13 Ibid., 22. I have translated *Vorstellung* as it is used here as 'introduction,' which follows on from the previous discussion. But in the final line – taken from Schopenhauer's work of that name – Rosenstock-Huessy is playing with the fine line that exists between the terms 'representation,' 'imagination,' 'idea,' and 'introduction' (Schopenhauer's book's title is translated either as *The World as Will and Representation* or *The World as Will and Idea*). Indeed, *Vorstellung* has an important philosophical pedigree in German idealism. For Kant, it is the basis of concepts and intuitions (*Anschauungen*). For Hegel, it is the preliminary form of the concept before it is specified and developed as idea; thus he associates it with feelings and maintains that its proper sphere of expression is art. Rosenstock-Huessy goes back to the much more basic, everyday use of the term, as in *sich vorstellen*, 'to introduce oneself,' which also has resonances of presentation, as in, 'I would like to present myself, to show you myself, to be in your circle.' One might add that this initial act of presentation is the condition of *re*-presentation, of the *Stellung* – the condition/position/emplacement – that is set before us.

14 Rosenstock-Huessy, *Practical Knowledge of the Soul*, 40.

15 Eugen Rosenstock-Huessy, *Speech and Reality*, intro. Clinton C. Gardner (Norwich: Argo Books, 1970), 41.

16 Eugen Rosenstock-Huessy, *Out of Revolution: Autobiography of Western Man* (Norwich: Argo Books, 1993; Providence: Berg Publishers, 1993), 707.

17 Ibid., 716.

18 Ibid., 717.

19 Eugen Rosenstock-Huessy, *Practical Knowledge of the Soul*, 42.

20 Ibid., 41–2.

21 Microfilm: *The First Cycle of Letters to Cynthia (Harris): On Tribe, Egypt, and Israel in Order to Find Direction in Our Era*, reel 7, item 378, 162.

22 Franz Rosenzweig, *The Star of Redemption,* trans. Barbara E. Galli (Madison: University of Wisconsin Press, 2005), 146–56.

23 Ibid., 146.

24 Ibid., 120.

25 Ibid., 121.

26 Ibid., 166.

27 Ibid., 166.

28 Ibid., 162–3.

29 Ibid., 35 and 45.

30 Ibid., 34.

31 Jean Paul Sartre, *Being and Nothingness*, trans. Hazel Barnes (New York: Washington Square Press, 1966), 49. There are affinities between Sartre's idea of freedom and its relationship to nothingness – e.g. 'Freedom is precisely the nohtingness which is *made-to-be* at the heart of man and which forces human reality *to make itself* instead of *to be*' (568) and Rosenzweig's use of the 'No' as the move of redemption. But Sartre could never find a body large and worthy enough to facilitate his freedom. Curiously, though, toward the end of Sartre's life, and through his friendship with Benny Lévy, a former Maoist, who became an orthodox Jew, Sartre, who had previously supported the Jews on political grounds, came to appreciate the power of the Jewish idea of redemption.

32 Ibid., 45.

33 I think the most illuminating discussion is in Robert Gibbs, *Correlations in Rosenzweig and Levinas* (Princeton: Princeton University Press, 1994), 67–79. See also Inken Rühle, *Gott spricht die Sprache der Menschen: Franz Rosenzweig als Jüdischer Theologe – eine Einführung* (Tübingen: Bilam, 2004), 216–37; and Martin Fricke, *Franz Rosenzweigs Philosophie der Offenbarung: eine Interpretation des Sterns der Erlösung* (Würzburg: Königshausen & Neumann, 2003), 173–83.

34 Rosenzweig, *The Star of Redemption*, 137.

35 See Pt 2 of my *The Metaphysics of Science and Freedom: From Descartes to Kant to Hegel* (Aldershot: Avebury, 1991).

36 Rosenzweig, *The Star of Redemption*, 163.
37 Ibid., 163.
38 Ibid., 248.
39 In his *Critique of Pure Reason*, Kant famously distinguishes between 'thread' (*Leitfaden*) and *organon*. That is part of his formalism, which proceeds in a way that does not 'infect' *a priori* forms with content. By contrast, Rosenzweig's analysis of the form is content bound. In this respect at least, Rosenzweig remains more a Hegelian than a Kantian. Indeed, the procedure here of grammatical category generating category is patently and deeply reminiscent of Hegel's *Science of Logic*.
40 Rosenzweig, *The Star of Redemption*, 137.
41 Ibid., 139.
42 Ibid., 139.
43 Ibid., 139–40. The difference between Rosenstock-Huessy and Rosenzweig on this point cannot go unnoticed. For the intrinsic encounter between speaker and world that is the key to Rosenzweig's grammatical analysis adopts a speculative or disinterested stance from the outset, the very thing that Rosenstock-Huessy refuses (quite rightly, in my view) to do.
44 Rosenzweig, *The Star of Redemption*, 142.
45 Ibid., 164.
46 Rosenstock-Huessy, *Ja und Nein*, 71–2.
47 Heidegger and Sartre, for him, belong to the old paradigm because they do not pay enough attention to language.
48 Ignaz Maybaum, *Trialogue between Jew, Christian, and Muslim* (London: Routledge & Kegan Paul, 1973), 7.
49 Ibid., 11.
50 Rosenstock-Huessy, 'St Augustine by the Sea.' Microfilm: June 1962, reel 18, page 12.
51 Sydney Rome and Beatrice Rome, eds., *Philosophical Interrogations: Interrogations of Martin Buber, John Wild, Jean Wahl, Brand Blanshard, Paul Weiss, Charles Hartshorne, Paul Tillich* (New York: Holt, Rinehart and Winston, 1964), 31–5.
52 Rome and Rome, *Philosophical Interrogations*, 31–2. His criticism is also expressed in a letter to Buber, where it is very clear that Rosenstock-Huessy distinguishes between humanists and Christians not on the basis of what people think they are doing but rather on the basis of their entire acts and expressions. Thus he says to Buber: 'The incognito of the third in your execution doesn't change the fact that it bears the other two with it. Your Christian crown witnesses are, to be sure, Christians in their souls, but when it comes to thought they are merely Greek, above all Schweitzer

and Bultmann. The anti-Pauline affect condemns the complete theology to remain a legal theology, which means to offer a merely supplementary safeguard and to come too late for the life of faith. Had Jesus not had to come forty years before the fall of Jerusalem, then the Law and Paul would not have been necessary. In both belief is neither "*Pistis*" nor "*Emuna*," but the creative sacrifice, a spiritual rebirth out of love for the neighbour.' Martin Buber, *Briefwechsel aus Sieben Jahrzehnten, 1918–1938*, Bd III (Gütersloh: Gütersloher Verlag, 1972), letter 242, 25 December 1951, 298–9.

53 Derrida, *Specters of Marx: The State of the Debt, the Work of Mourning, and the New International,* translated by Peggy Kamuf (New York: Routledge, 1994), xix.

54 Along with Rosenstock-Huessy, another thinker – a near contemporary of his – who did appreciate this and wrote about it was Ivan Illich.

55 I think that a completely unintentional confirmation of my point comes from Bill Readings, *The University in Ruins* (Cambridge, MA: Harvard University Press, 1996). He commences by outlining the capitalist nature of the transformations taking place in the modern university. Wanting no truck with old-style humanists who rage against the destruction of a humanist education, he calls on his readers to accept the institution as ruined and to work within its ruins. His stance is a hybrid that recognizes the ubiquity of the market while standing up for the radical gesture. Oblivious to the idealism of the stance (and using dialogical language rather than content), he declares: '"Thinking together" is a dissensual process; it belongs to dialogism rather than dialogue'; 192. And accepting the lack of social mission of the university, his concluding sentence is – to use the term in its old Marxist sense – a model of idealism: 'Therein lies both the freedom and the enormous responsibility of Thought at the end of the twentieth century, which is also the end of what has been the epoch of the nation state'; 193. If Kant and Fichte had come back to life, they could not have said it better. And the final act of renunciation of the nation-state is the culminating gesture of the mind's utter sovereignty (even though it is intended to say something about global capitalism). For the nation-state remains the greatest humanist contribution to incarnation – it is true that it is in all sorts of crises, but to pronounce its death is extremely premature.

56 Rome and Rome, *Philosophical Interrogations*, 32–3.

57 Ibid., 33.

58 Ibid., 34–5.

59 Rosenstock-Huessy, *Ja und Nein*, 72–3.

60 Kornelis Miskotte, *When the Gods Are Silent,* trans. John Doberstein (New York: Harper and Row, [1932]1967), 34.

4. On God as an Indissoluble Name and an Indispensable Pole of the Real

1 Franz Rosenzweig, *Understanding the Sick and the Healthy: A View of World, Man, and God,* ed. and trans. Nahum N. Glatzer (Cambridge, MA: Harvard University Press, 1999), 91.

2 There is no small irony (and I think it cannot have been unconscious) that Rosenzweig makes fear of death the main drive behind the attempt to grasp the All. In doing so, he turns the tables on a philosopher like Epicurus, arguing that Judaism and Christianity are both built on the acceptance of death.

3 In *The Star of Redemption,* Hegel's naive praise of the proof of the ontological argument is said to be its death blow. See Franz Rosenzweig, *The Star of Redemption,* trans. Barbara E. Galli (Madison: University of Wisconsin Press, 2005), 24. It is naive because God himself is missing from what it is that is proved.

4 Rosenzweig, *Understanding the Sick and the Healthy,* 44.

5 The despair in *Being and Time,* so patent in the role of anxiety and 'worried-ness' (*Sorge,* very misleadingly translated as 'care' by Macquarie and Robinson) as sources of the world's disclosure to *Dasein,* while taken by Heidegger as part of the ontological structure of *Dasein,* is an astounding depiction of the German people between the World Wars; in just the same way, the dark political intimations of that work suggest a voluntarist and decisive resolve of heroics as their means of salvation. This does not mean that *Being and Time* cannot be read in other ways – quite clearly it can – but the historicity of its mood encapsulates its ontological delineations. The question of Heidegger and National Socialism – a question I discussed in 'Heidegger's Political Judgement: Nazism and After,' *Australian Journal of Political Science* 12, no. 2 (1990): 289–308, and in 'Heidegger and Cassirer: Being, Knowing, and Politics,' *Kant Studien* 82, no. 4 (1991): 469–83, has now grown into a minor industry. Those who wish to preserve the philosophy from the political suggest in effect that the philosophy was better than the man and his politics – which is certainly not how either Rosenstock-Huessy or Rosenzweig want to see and do philosophy: if a philosophy leads one to catastrophic decisions, then there must be something catastrophically wrong with the philosophy. The test of an idea is its incarnation, not its logical or poetic purity. Of the countless works about Heidegger and Nazism, by far the most illuminating is, I think, Johannes Fritsche, *Historical Destiny and National Socialism in Heidegger's Being and Time* (Berkeley: University of California Press, 1999), which explores the deep affinities between the language of *Being and Time* and the conservative nationalist language of his contemporaries in Germany.

6   Eugen Rosenstock-Huessy, *I Am an Impure Thinker*, ed. Freya von Moltke and Clint Gardner (Norwich: Argo Books, 1970), 90.
7   Ibid., 83–4.
8   Ibid., 82.
9   Microfilm: 'Greek Philosophy,' 1956, reel 16, item 641, page 17.
10 Ibid., page 24.
11 Hans Ehrenberg, *Disputation: I, Fichte* (Munich: Drei Masken Verlag, 1923).
12 Ibid., 6–25.
13 Rosenzweig, *Understanding the Sick and the Healthy*, 73.
14 Ibid., 71.
15 Eugen Rosenstock-Huessy, *Speech and Reality*, intro. Clinton C. Gardner (Norwich: Argo Books, 1970), 174.
16 Rosenstock-Huessy, *I Am an Impure Thinker*, 42.
17 Rosenzweig, *Understanding the Sick and the Healthy*, 72. A very similar point to that being made by Rosenzweig and Rosenstock-Huessy on names can be found in Alan Bennett's *The History Boys*. The scene concerns the recitation of the Hardy poem 'Drummer Hodge' about the war grave of Drummer Hodge: 'yet portion of that unknown plain / Will Hodge forever be, / His homely Northern breast and brain Grow to some Southern Tree, / And strange-eyed constellations reign His stars eternally.' After the student reciting the poem notes the parallels between Brooke's 'There's some corner of a foreign field / In that dust a richer dust concealed' and Hardy's lines, Hector, the teacher, responds: 'Though Hardy is better because he is more detailed.' Then he adds: 'Anything about his name? The important thing is, he *has* a name. Say Hardy's writing about the Zulu Wars. Or later, or . . . the Boer War, possibly. And these were the first campaigns when soldiers, common soldiers were commemorated. The names of the dead were recorded and inscribed on war memorials. Before this, soldiers – private soldiers – were all unknown soldiers. And so far from being revered, there was a firm in the 19th century, in Yorkshire of course, which swept up their bones from the battlefields of Europe in order to grind them into fertilizer. So, thrown, into a common grave he may be, he's still Hodge, the Drummer. Lost boy though he is, on the far side of the world, he still has a name.' He might have gone on to say that because he had a name he had the prospect of redemption – as indeed he is redeemed in the very deployment of the name that is used by life to enhance life through the act of commemoration.
18 Rosenzweig, *Understanding the Sick and the Healthy*, 86.
19 Ibid.
20 Ibid., 87.
21 Ibid., 87.

22 Ibid., 88.
23 Ibid., 88.
24 Ibid., 89.
25 Rosenzweig, *The Star of Redemption*, 25.
26 Ibid., 22.
27 Ibid., 405.
28 Ibid., 26.
29 Ibid., 26.
30 Ibid., 27.
31 Ibid., 28.
32 Rosenstock-Huessy, *I Am an Impure Thinker*, 26.
33 Ibid., 29.
34 Regina M. Schwartz, *The Curse of Cain: The Violent Legacy of Monotheism* (Chicago: University of Chicago Press, 1997).
35 Jonathon Kirsch, *God Against the Gods: The History of the War between Monotheism and Polytheism* (Harmondsworth: Penguin, 2005).
36 Michael York, *Pagan Theology: Paganism as a World Religion* (New York: NYU Press, 2005).
37 N.A. Berdyaev, 'Polytheism and Nationalism,' *Journal Put'* 43 (April–June 1934): 3–16, at Berdyaev Online Bibliotek Library, http://www.berdyaev.com/berdiaev/berd_lib/1934_391.html. In contemporary social theory, Slavoj Žižek and Eric Santner argue that polytheism is not so great and monotheism not so bad.
38 Eugen Rosenstock-Huessy, *Out of Revolution: Autobiography of Western Man*, intro. Harold Berman (Providence: Berg Publishers, 1993, 722–3.
39 Ibid., 725.
40 Ibid., 723.
41 Ibid., 726.
42 Ibid., 727–8.

5. The Sundered and the Whole: Rosenzweig's Distinction between Pagans and the Elect

1 Interview with Gil Anidjar conducted by Nermeen Shaikh of AsiaSource, http://www.asiasource.org/news/special_reports/anidjar5.cfm.
2 The question of Israel's political wars with its Arab neighbours is here completely irrelevant, for Israel did not exist as a state when Rosenzweig was writing. And even if one were to construe Rosenzweig's more favourable statements on Zionism as somehow a kind of endorsement of Israel *avant la lettre*, the conflict – at least from the Israeli standpoint – is

mainly about Jewish survival, not the elimination of another religion *qua* religion. Israelis have every interest in retaining their country, but none in converting Muslims; and except as it relates to their right to territorial existence, they have as little interest in what most Muslims believe as they have in what Seventh-day Adventists or Buddhists believe. This is not to deny that most Arab Muslims do not see it that way – which itself points to a deep difference between Judaism and Islam.

3 Franz Rosenzweig, Briefe an die Eltern, 17 February 1917, in *Franz Rosenzweig, Der Mensch und Sein Werk. Gesammelte Schriften*, Bd 1, *Briefe und Tagebücher*, 350. Cf. also letter to Eugen Rosenstock-Huessy, Anfang März 1917, in *Gritli Briefe*; 'Jüdische Geschichte im Rahmen der Weltgeschichte,' *Gesammelte Schriften*, Bd III, *Zweistromland. Kleinere Schriften zu Glauben und Denken*, ed. Reinhold Meyer and Annemarie Mayer (Dordrecht: Martinus Nijhoff, 1984), 545.

4 Given how Anidjar magically transforms Jesus' 'love thine enemy' into the origin of enmity of the neighbour, it is clear that for him, extermination and difference must go together: 'With Jesus, then, we witness the becoming-enemy of the neighbor.' Gil Anidjar, *The Jew, the Arab: A History of the Enemy* (Stanford: Stanford University Press, 2003), 19. Besides turning black into white through such eristics, *The Jew, the Arab* is simply breathtaking in its absence of Arab self-understanding. In his book, the conflict between Jews and Arabs is not to be understood by exploring history and the words and speeches of Jews and Arabs but exclusively through European thought: Jews and Arabs, for Anidjar, are at war solely because of Europeans. That is how he can justify the constant resort to Schmitt, Derrida, and the rest of his European canon as somehow providing the key to this story. The little matter of the Ottomans – not to mention pre-Ottoman relations between Jews and Muslims – might as well never have happened.

5 There is nothing amiss in noting that peoples have friends and enemies – that is more or less true for all. The problem arises when this is transformed into the norm for all political decision making. It fails to take into account the *value* of enemies and of enmity in general, except simply as obstacles to be eliminated. But this is to say that Schmitt is no 'speech thinker' (nor are those who follow him). And he thinks it is impossible to love one's enemies. That this is simply wrong is confirmed by the lives of those two inimical friends, Rosenzweig and Rosenstock-Huessy.

6 *Gritli Briefe*, 2 July 1919, 360.

7 In *Judaism Despite Christianity: The Letters on Christianity and Judaism between Rosenstock-Huessy and Franz Rosenzweig*, ed. Eugen Rosenstock-Huessy, trans. Dorothy Emmet (New York: Schocken Books, 1971),

Rosenstock-Huessy refers to the third act of the relationship between himself and Rosenzweig (the first two being the 1913 conversation, the second the 1916 correspondence), 71–6. The third act came in 1920 when Rosenzweig insisted to Rudolf Hallo that the community of all those who confess – as opposed to those who merely think timelessly – embraces all believers: 'Sprache ist doch mehr als Blut' (speech is more than blood). Franz Rosenzweig, letter 339, 6 October 1929, in Franz Rosenzweig, *Briefe* (Berlin: Schocken Verlag, 1935). That statement might seem to contradict the argument in *The Star of Redemption*, though it is the line between Jew and Christian in that book. According to Rosenstock-Huessy, Hallo had been 'toying with baptism,' under Rosenstock-Huessy's influence, but had then become quite fanatical in his Judaism and in his pivotal role in the Jewish *Lehrhaus*. Confronted by the excessive zeal of his reconverted Jewish friend, Rosenzweig declared: 'The walls have fallen. Where we met, where Eugen and I met, no antiquated walls separate man and man . . . "For those who have awakened the cosmos has become a community" [Herakleitos]. Our communion – which I tried to resist between 1913 and 1917 – is safe. Judaism, Christianity, Creation: what has happened to us with regard to all three is the living faith, and no [mere] orthodoxy can chain this stream of life, which must achieve our resurrection from the cemeteries of Germany and of Europe. How the shape of this resurrection may *look*, is no proper cause for worry. We have to live it' (*Briefe*, 381ff). And to Eugen's wife Margrit, Franz wrote on 15 June 1920: 'It is a great act of mercy that God once has uprooted me out of life during my life. From July to September, 1913 I was quite willing to die – to let everything within myself die. But this may not be made into a rule. Most men simply live their life's fate, or destiny, and nothing more. It is the extraordinary in us that God, in our case, has not only spoken to us through our lives; in addition he has made the life around us fall down like the wings of a theatrical decoration, and on the empty stage he has spoken to us. We have to know that this is something peculiar, and we must construe no hard and fast rule from it.' *Judaism Despite Christianity*, 76.

8 Franz Rosenzweig, *The Star of Redemption*, trans. Barbara E. Galli (Madison: University of Wisconsin Press, 2005) 31, 49, 72.

9 Ibid., 33.

10 Ibid., 32.

11 Ibid., 35.

12 Ibid., 35.

13 Ibid., 37.

14 Ibid., 37.

15 Ibid., 39.

16 Ibid., 39.

17 Ibid., 42.

18 Many are listed later in our discussion of Islam. Matters are not helped by thinking – as several Rosenzweig scholars seem to do – that Redemption for Rosenzweig is a kind of fusion of (neo-Platonist, or let us say, pagan) mysticism with ethics. Much of the discussion on Cabala in Rosenzweig makes this mistake, for Cabala – which does, to be sure, provide *some material* for Rosenzweig, as it did for Schelling, especially in the account of God's creation – is the incorporation of neo-Platonist elements in Judaism (much like Sufism is the incorporation of neo-Platonist and neo-Aristotelian elements in Islam). It is these elements that I think confuse some scholars about what Cabala meant for Rosenzweig. Claims such as this one – 'for, in Rosenzweig's perception, the essence of the *Weltanschauung* which he arrogates to Paganism lies in its taking the world given in our sense perception as it is given, i.e. in terms of its own significance – it does not recognize any reference point that transcends it' – are pretty well wrong on everything and rest on the mistaken idea that God's transcendence is all-important for Rosenzweig. See Manfred Vogel, *Rosenzweig on Profane/Secular History* (Atlanta: Scholars Press, 1996). The frequent and sometimes overstrained comparisons between Rosenzweig and Levinas also seem to me to usually miss the point. In fact, both tendencies (Rosenzweig as mystic / Rosenzweig as ethicist) – which do indeed express widespread academic emphases, interests, and orientations – tell me far more how deeply pagan (which for Rosenzweig is not a simple contradiction to the Christian) academic institutions are and how difficult it seems for people residing in them to think outside the pagan box. Throw in art and politics alongside mysticism and ethics and there we have the major elements of the pagan's more philosophical conception of the good life.

19 Rosenzweig, *The Star of Redemption*, 432. Paganism accounts for both belief and non-belief in an afterlife. Neither Rosenzweig nor Rosenstock-Huessy believes in an afterlife, at least in the (neo-Platonist or 'Egyptian') sense that so many (including so-called Christians) ascribe to. Rosenstock-Huessy believed that such ideas of an afterlife have been countenanced in the Church for the 'childish' – that is, for those who take literally what is intended as merely a sign about how to live this life. That sign is not meant as a 'fact' about the afterlife. What is all-important is the *how* of one's life as an openness to love, faith, and hope, and as a response to life in which dying to the good (and dead things) of the world is an active component. What is *not* important is the childish idea one has

about the rewards for being a good boy or girl. The questions 'Is there a God?' and 'Is there a heaven?' demonstrate the intellectual/Greek/disinterested orientation to life that forecloses the love and response of the life responding to revelation.

20 Franz Rosenzweig, 'On Being a Jewish Person,' *Commentary*, November 1945, 77. I have used this translation rather than the one provided by Glatzer in *Franz Rosenzweig: His Life and Thought* (Indianapolis: Hackett, 1998). The word translated here as 'trust' is *Vertrauen*, which Glatzer translates as 'confidence.' *Vertrauen* can be translated as both, and indeed, the trust being spoken of here is one that is backed up by assuredness. But I think that 'confidence' has too many resonances in English, resonances that to my ear at least do not quite convey what I think Rosenzweig is talking about.

21 In *The New Thinking*, Rosenzweig says somewhat gleefully – clearly, he is taking a potshot at Steiner and the disciples of Blavatsky and the like – that in his analysis in *The Star of Redemption*, 'things go badly for the favorites of modernity, the "spiritual religions of the Far East."' 120.

22 Rosenzweig, *The Star of Redemption*, 46.

23 Ibid., 43.

24 Ibid., 221.

25 Ibid., 45–6.

26 Eugen Rosenstock-Huessy, *The Christian Future – or The Modern Mind Outrun*, intro. Harold Stahmer (New York: Harper and Row, [1947]1966), 176–8. This was very much to the bewilderment and consternation of Rudi Ehrenberg.

27 Microfilm: 'Comparative Religion,' 1954, reel 15, item 633, page 1.

28 Rosenzweig, *The Star of Redemption*, 46.

29 Ibid., 46–7.

30 Ibid., 47.

31 Ibid., 52.

32 Ibid., 53.

33 Ibid., 53.

34 Ibid., 54.

35 Ibid., 54.

36 Ibid., 55.

37 Gilles Deleuze and Félix Guattari, *A Thousand Plateaus: Capitalism and Schizophrenia*, trans. Brian Massumi (Minneapolis: University of Minnesota Press, 1987), 7–8.

38 Rosenzweig, *The Star of Redemption*, 60.

39 Ibid., 61–2.

40 Eugen Rosenstock-Huessy, *Ja und Nein. Autobiographische Fragmente aus Anlass des 80. Geburtstags des Autors. Im Auftrag der seinen Namen tragenden Gesellschaft*, ed. Georg Müller (Heidelberg: Verlag Lambert Schneider, 1968), 40.

41 Rosenzweig, *The Star of Redemption*, 63.

42 Ibid., 64.

43 E.g., Rosenstock-Huessy, *The Christian Future*, 115; *Israel and Prayer*.

44 Rosenzweig, *The Star of Redemption*, 65.

45 Ibid., 67. The collision between China and Tibet can be grasped precisely in these terms. This, however, is not simply to support China's position. China has been driven by the messianism of Marxism, and its critique of Buddhism is linked strongly to the feudal structures that Buddhism consolidated in Tibet. The Dalai Lama is a symbol of world peace, and his speeches are full of references to love. Yet one can hardly say that Tibet's past social structures grew out of a desire for social redemption in Rosenzweig's sense. However one judges China, its drive for modernization continued the revolutionary and redemptive logic of Marxism, and like every revolutionary movement, it has been compromised and contained by its own history and local pressures and contradictions.

46 Rosenzweig, *The Star of Redemption*, 66.

47 Ibid., 66.

48 Ibid., 75.

49 Ibid., 80.

50 Ibid., 81.

51 Ibid., 82.

52 Ibid., 84.

53 Ibid., 86.

54 Ibid., 90.

55 Ibid., 96.

56 Ibid., 97.

57 Ibid., 100.

58 Hence Else Freund, in *Franz Rosenzweig's Philosophy of Existence: An Analysis of The Star of Redemption*, divides her analysis into the triad of thinking, faith, and faith thinking.

59 Rosenzweig, *The Star of Redemption, 104*.

60 Ibid., 105.

61 Ibid., 105.

62 Bernard Knox, introductory essay in Homer, *The Iliad*, trans. Robert Fagles (New York: Penguin, 1990), 44.

63 Rosenzweig, *The New Thinking*, 130.

64 Ibid., 130.
65 Rosenzweig, *The Star of Redemption*, 124.
66 Ibid., 130–1.
67 Ibid., 241.
68 Ibid., 240.
69 Microfilm: 'Comparative Religion,' 1954, reel 15, item 633, page 21.
70 Rosenzweig, *The Star of Redemption*, 124.
71 Ibid., 131.
72 Ibid., 133.
73 Ibid., 280.
74 Ibid., 169.
75 See particularly his letter to Rudolph Hallo of late January 1923, Franz Rosenzweig, *Briefe und Tagebücher Gesammelte Schriften*, Bd 1, 885f, where he reconciles being a good Jew with being a good German, and how the former helps the latter.
76 Rosenzweig, *The Star of Redemption*, 124.
77 Ibid., 415.
78 Ibid., 176.
79 Ibid., 177–8.
80 Ibid., 256.
81 Ibid., 185.
82 Ibid., 196.
83 One would be hard pressed to find a more succinct formulation of the liberal pluralistic interpretation of Rosenzweig than in the title of Katrin Kirchner's *Franz Rosenzweigs Theorie der Erfahrung: Ein Beitrag zur Überwindung totalitrer Denkstruktures und zur Begründung einer Kultur der Pluralität* (Würzburg: Könighaus und Neumann, 2005); (i.e., Franz Rosenzweig's Theory of Experience: A Contribution to the Overcoming of Totalitarian Thought Sructures and towards a Grounding of Cultural Plurality). The book, though, is more sensitive to Rosenzweig's theology than the title might suggest.
84 Rosenzweig, *The Star of Redemption*, 221.
85 Ibid., 304–5.
86 Ibid., 305.

6. Rosenstock-Huessy's Incarnatory Christianity

1 Eugen Rosenstock-Huessy, *Out of Revolution: Autobiography of Western Man* (Norwich: Argo Books, 1993; Providence: Berg Publishers, 1993), 235.
2 William Empson, *Milton's God* (Abingdon: Greenwood, 1979).

3 See my 'Will, Pride, and Enslavement in Milton's *Paradise Lost,*' which
  shows, contrary to readings that transform him into either a proto-liberal
  or radical – a member of the devil's party, as Blake put it – that Milton is
  steeped in the Reformist vision of humanity and God. Wayne Cristaudo
  and Peter Poiana, *Great Ideas in the Western Literary Canon* (Lanham: University Press of America, 2003).
4 The deployment of animals by nations to represent them shows a deep-
  seated awareness of this archaic truth.
5 See, especially, chapter 4 of Wayne Cristaudo, *Power, Love and Evil: Contribution to a Philosophy of the Damaged* (New York: Rodopi, 2007).
6 Cf. Eugen Rosenstock-Huessy, *Practical Knowledge of the Soul,* trans. Mark
  Huessy and Freya von Moltke (Norwich: Argo Books, 1988), 11.
7 Eugen Rosenstock-Huessy, *Heilkraft und Wahrheit: Konkordanz der Politischen und Kosmischen Zeit* (Wien: Amandus, 1991), 191.
8 Emil Fackenheim, *God's Presence in History: Jewish Affirmations and Philosophical Reflections after Auschwitz* (New York: NYU Press, 1970), 69–70.
  Levinas's 'Useless Suffering,' trans. Richard Cohen, can be found in Robert Bernasconi and David Wood, eds., *The Provocation of Levinas: Rethinking the Other* (London: Routledge, 1988), see esp. 162–4.
9 Rosenstock-Huessy was a fierce opponent of what Weber called 'instru-
  mentalist reasoning' and Heidegger called 'calculative thinking.' And his
  lectures are replete with barbs about the destruction this kind of thinking
  was playing in the world at large and in the universities with their grant
  culture. Two especially powerful attacks on this kind of thinking are his
  The Multiformity of Man (Norwich: Argo Books, 1973), and 'Kirche und
  Arbeit – Eine Rede,' *Die Kreatur* 2, ed. Martin Buber, Joseph Wittig, and
  Victor von Weizsäcker (Berlin: Verlag Lambert Schneider, 1927–8, 158–80.
  Microfilm: reel 4, item 204.
10 Booklet to CD/DVD *Here Is What Is,* by Daniel Lanois (Red Floor Records). A nice piece of serendipity was involved when I came across a
  piece in *Rolling Stone* (19 March 2009) on U2's recent album, *No Line on
  the Horizon,* which Eno and Lanois had produced. One track, 'Moment of
  Surrender,' for Eno, gained much of its power from a busted electronic
  drum kit that required certain compensations by the band's drummer,
  Adam Mullen, on the high hat. For Eno, this was a 'miracle.' '"These . . .
  guys," he says with a smile, "they're supposed to be so spiritual – they
  don't spot a miracle when it hits them in the face"' (56). I mention this to
  highlight that it is precisely this aspect of existence – expressed by such
  terms as 'miracle,' 'grace,' and 'providence' – that is the basis for the orientations of Rosenzweig and Rosenstock-Huessy, and that it is nothing
  otherworldly and is completely experiental.

11 Hence the first volume of his *Soziologie* is titled *Die Übermacht der Räume* (The Dominance of Spaces), and he devotes much time to highlighting the differences between the spaces of war and those of play. His writings on revolution demonstrate how and why the spaces of war can be both necessary and fecund, which is not to say that these writings are calls to arms. In *Speech and Reality*, intro. Clinton C. Gardner (Norwich: Argo Books, 1970), he lists revolution, anarchy, decadence, and war as four great social diseases/evils (12–13). But even though revolution is a disease, revolutions have been indispensable to improving our lives on earth. That said, taking a moral stand for or against revolution as a social disease no more cures it than telling someone he or she should or should not have measles.

12 See Rosenstock-Huessy's discussion of Romanticism in his postscript to *Ja und Nein. Autobiographische Fragmente aus Anlass des 80. Geburtstags des Autors. Im Auftrag der seinen Namen tragenden Gesellschaft*, ed. Georg Müller (Heidelberg: Verlag Lambert Schneider, 1968); see also *Soziologie*, Bd 1, 277ff.

13 Microfilm: 'Faculty Address on the Potential Christians of the Future,' 1941, reel 7, item 358, pages 11 and 12.

14 Eugen Rosenstock-Huessy, *The Christian Future – or The Modern Mind Outrun*, intro. Harold Stahmer (New York: Harper and Row, [1947]1966), 100.

15 Microfilm: 'Comparative Religion,' 1954, reel 15, item 633, page 6. Note here that the reading of the Bible, though not literal, is thoroughly experiential. This is how both Rosenzweig and Rosenstock-Huessy see the Bible. Note as well, though it is true that many Christians read the Bible literally, nowhere does the Bible privilege a literalist reading. Let us remember this later when we compare Islam to the Jewish and Christian faiths. Muhammad supposedly read the precise word of God, and as a consequence the hermenutical direction of mainstream Islam – be it Sunni or Shia – is based on ensuring that *that* word is repeated precisely. This is the only way to ensure that God's word is followed – hence the importance of rote learning in Koranic schools. It also is why, while some minor streams within Islam are not literalist, that religion's stronger impetus *is* literalist. It is also why the *hadith* provide so many examples of the lives of the prophet – so that he can be quite literally followed. For Rosenstock-Huessy, only a madman would literally try to model his life on Jesus. That was not Jesus' purpose – he *had* to live his life his way, and each person must follow the Holy Spirit in the way the situation demands. Finally, though the Bible is a sacred book, God even in the Bible

is a moving spirit of future promise who at all times demands that the distinction be drawn between spirit and letter.

16 Microfilm: 'Comparative Religion,' 1954, reel 15, item 633, page 8. And in his 'Circulation of Thought' lecture to his undergraduates: 'I don't believe in another world or another Heaven, I think it must be right here. God – Jesus – . . . didn't create two worlds: one for the dead and one for the living. He created one world, as we all profess in our Creed. So the dead are here, very much alive. So the . . . Christian peoples have always acted on one assumption . . . : our values are our forbears.' Microfilm: 'Circulation of Thought,' 1954, reel 16, item 634, page 4. But this does not mean that Rosenstock-Huessy thought that the term 'go to heaven' is meaningless. For more on heaven, see, for example, the later argument at these microfilms: 'Circulation of Thought,' 1956, reel 16, item 640, page 6; and 'Comparative Religion,' 1954, reel 15, item 633, page 13. In this last set of lectures, Rosenstock-Huessy discusses 'heaven' at length. Also pertinent are the frequent references in *Letters to Cynthia* and the *Lectures on Greek Philosophy*. What happens to the soul after death only concerns Rosenstock-Huessy to the extent that it contributes to the salvation of humankind. He eschews speculation as a waste of time. Life does what it does – that is all we can know.

17 See microfilm: 'Faculty Address on the Potential Christians of the Future,' 1941, reel 7, item 358, page 19.

18 Rosenstock-Huessy, *The Christian Future*, 100.

19 Ibid., 100–1.

20 Microfilm: 'Before and After Karl Marx. Prophesies Fulfilled and Unfulfilled,' 1954, reel 9, item 467, page 23.

21 Rosenstock-Huessy, *The Christian Future*, 99.

22 Eugen Rosenstock-Huessy, *Die Gesetze der christlichen Zeitrechnung*, ed. Rudolf Hermeier and Jochen Lübbers (Münster: Agenda, 2004), 280.

23 Eugen Rosenstock-Huessy, *Judaism Despite Christianity: The Letters on Christianity and Judaism between Rosenstock-Huessy and Franz Rosenzweig*, intro. Harold Stahmer (New York: Schocken Books, 1971), 104.

24 3 February 1946*. Interestingly, this letter also spells out that this same error had been made by Altmann in his discussion of the 1916 correspondence. Thus he also writes of his relationship with Rosenzweig: 'In Leipzig, I had as my student an older, far superior thinker (who is now famous all over the world, and who died in 1929). This man probed into my faith and my thinking, unexpectedly. And I threw him, converted him, changed his whole life. This event is described in the "Journal of Religion," October 1944 by a man [Altmann] whom I do not know at

all. But he declares that at that time, 1912/13, I was the embodiment of a Kierkegaardian thinker.' I also think that this claim to have converted Rosenzweig fully supports the argument in my first chapter: Rosenstock-Huessy is saying explicitly that Rosenzweig's becoming a Jew was the *successful completion* of Rosenstock-Huessy's attempt to convert him.

25 Rosenstock-Huessy, *The Christian Future*, 108.

26 Ibid., 98.

27 Ibid., 108.

28 Ibid., 109.

29 Ibid., 109–10.

30 Eugen Rosenstock-Huessy, *I Am an Impure Thinker*, ed. Freya von Moltke and Clint Gardner (Norwich: Argo Books, 1970), 69.

31 Ibid., 72.

32 Ibid., 73.

33 Ibid., 74.

34 Rosenstock-Huessy, *The Christian Future*, 108.

35 Ibid., 72. He references Jean Guitton, *Le temps et l'eternité chez Plotin et Saint Augustine* (Paris: Vrin, 1933), 359.

36 Mark 10.18; Matthew 19.17; Luke 18.19.

37 Karl Löwith, 'Review of *The Christian Future*,' *Church History* 15, no. 3 (1946): 248–9.

38 On 28 October 1919, Karl Barth informed Eduard Thurnysen that he had read 'Europe's Suicide,' which Rosenstock-Huessy had sent him, and that he had enjoyed it like a 'hearty lunch.' *Karl Barth–Eduard Thurneysen: Briefwechsel*, Bd 1, 1913–1921 (Zürich: Theologischer Verlag, 2000), 348. The next day, Rosenstock-Huessy wrote to Barth saying that he had just read the preface of Barth's *Letter to the Romans* and that he was looking forward eagerly to reading the whole thing. Throughout the rest of 1919 and 1920, Rosenstock-Huessy wrote to him on several occasions. The original correspondence is in the Karl Barth archive in Basel, but the Rosenstock-Huessy archive in Basel also has copies. I provide a much more detailed account of Barth and Rosenstock-Huessy in 'Rosenstock-Huessy's Anti-Transcendent Critique of Karl Barth,' in *The Cross and the Star*, 277–89.

39 Unpublished letter from Rosentock-Huessy to Barth, 18 November 1919#.

40 'Brief an *** [Letter to Karl Barth]' (1920), in *Tumult*, vol. 20 (Wien: Turia u. Kant, 1995), 9–15.

41 Ibid., 10.

42 Ibid., 10.

43 Ibid., 11.

44 Ibid., 11.

45 Rosenstock-Huessy, *Ja und Nein*, 81. Rosenzweig says that Barth is a Greek systematic thinker, 83.

46 This translation is from Nathan Glatzer and can be found in his introduction to Franz Rosenzweig, *Understanding the Sick and the Healthy: A View of World, Man, and God*, ed. and trans. Nahum N. Glatzer (Cambridge, MA: Harvard University Press, 1999), 33.

47 Franz Rosenzweig and Jehuda Halevi, *Translating, Translations, and Translators*, trans. Barbara Galli (Montreal and Kingston: McGill-Queen's University Press, 1995), 204–5.

48 For Rosenstock-Huessy there are two points of agreement that he says are put 'admirably well' by Brunner. '1. That the world waits for the twelve apostles again, and that this time it is not only declericalized but frankly dechristianized. 2. That labor and marriage would still be mysteries of creation and would have to be explored if the world were perfect, whereas the State does belong to the realm of fallen nature only.' Microfilm: 'Comments on the Document by Emil Brunner, The Ethical Reality and Function of the Church,' 1942, reel 7, item 366, page 1.

49 Ibid., 1.

50 Ibid., 2–3.

51 See Rosenstock-Huessy, *Soziologie*, Bd 2, *Die Vollzahl der Zeiten* (Stuttgart: W. Kohlhammer Verlag, 1958), 595ff.

52 Ibid., 600.

53 Of course, Rosenstock-Huessy is not saying that the ascetic begins with Anthony. But Anthony *coins* this type in Christendom.

54 Rosenstock-Huessy, *Soziologie*, Bd 2, 601.

55 Ibid., 604–5.

56 For example, *Die Gesetze der christlichen Zeitrechnung*, 410; and Eugen Rosenstock-Huessy, *Die europäischen Revolutionen und der Charakter der Nationen*, rev. ed. (Moers: Brendow Verlag, 1961), 525.

57 Cf. 'Athanasius ... was for 40 years hated by the emperors, because he exalted the Son of Man over the son of Zeus, or Jupiter, on the throne of Rome. God-likeness would have equaled Caesar and Jesus. The divinity of Christ exalted Christ over ... the life of the Caesars.' Microfilm: 'Universal History,' 1949, reel 16, item 627, page 20. Also microfilm 'Universal History,' 1954, reel 16, item 637, page 16, where the point about the divinization of Hitler is made.

58 Rosenstock-Huessy, *The Christian Future*, 106.

59 Microfilm: 'Universal History,' 1949, reel 15, item 627, page 17.

60 Rosenstock-Huessy reminds his readers in *The Christian Future* that this was a Frankish piece of politics, remote from Roman intentions, that would subsequently be used by the Eastern Church against Rome. See *The Christian Future*, 152ff. For Rosenstock-Huessy, a major difference between Eastern and Western Christianity involves the historical dynamism of the latter and the ahistorical reading of Christianity of the former – a reading that he maintains was fundamental in the character of Eastern Europe and that would be important for the Russian revolutionaries' view of Christianity.

61 Rosenstock-Huessy, *Soziologie*, Bd 2, 607.

62 Ibid., 607.

63 Microfilm: 'The Terms of the Creed,' 1955, reel 9, item 488, page 10.

64 A neat illustration of what Rosenstock-Huessy is talking about can be found in a song about the life and teachings of St Jerome by Dion (who as a youth had had been a pop sensation with hits such as 'The Wanderer'). The song is called 'The Thunderer' and appears on the album *Son of Skip James*. Dion 'translates' St Jerome's life and teachings into the concise idiom of the blues.

65 Rosenstock-Huessy, *Soziologie*, Bd 2, 611.

66 Microfilm: 'Universal History,' 1949, reel 15, item 627, page 12.

67 Rosenstock-Huessy, *Soziologie*, Bd 2, 611.

68 Ibid., 759.

69 Ibid., 759.

70 Ibid., 616.

71 See Wayne Cristaudo, 'The Weight of Love and Evil in Augustine,' in *St Augustine: His Relevance and Legacy*, ed. Wayne Cristaudo and Heung-wah Wong (Adelaide: ATF, 2010).

72 Philip Schaff, *History of the Christian Church* (Grand Rapids: Eerdman, 1965), vol. 3, 650–3, maintains that the phrase was coined during the religious wars by Ruperthus Meldenius. The mistake was also pointed out in Marion Davis Battles, ed., *The Fruit of Lips, or, Why Four Gospels?* (Pittsburgh: Pickwick Press, 1978), 47n29. But whoever provided the exact formulation, it is Augustinian in its spirit.

73 Rosenstock-Huessy, *Soziologie*, Bd 2, 687. He uses the phrase in the context of making sense of the confessional relationship wherein the confessor has authority over the listener (the penitent) while being subordinate to the penitent's salvation. The cooperation between the two is what holds the power, and in this respect each is necessary for the salvation of the other. But this particular relationship serves as an illustration of

the more general principle of salvation through surrender to love's power.

74 See Rosenstock-Huessy, *I Am an Impure Thinker*, 35ff.

75 Battles, *The Fruit of Lips*, 2–3. A German version – with some minor diffences – is in Rosenstock-Huessy, *Die Sprache des Menschengeschlechts: Eine leibhaftige Grammatik in vier Teilen* (Heidelberg: Lambert Schneider, 1963–4); and many of the points made in *The Fruit of Lips* are covered in Rosenstock-Huessy, *Soziologie*, Bd 2.

76 Battles, *The Fruit of Lips*, 4.

77 It is a telling point that in the entire corpus of Plato, slaves are nameless, even in *Meno*, where a slave boy helps Socrates answer a geometry problem.

78 Ibid., 66.

79 Ibid., 70.

80 'The name of Jesus in the ancient Church consisted of four parts – Jesus, Christus, God's Son, Saviour. The four Greek initials of his four names were read as ICHTHYS, (ἰχθύς fish). The four Gospels reproduced this name. Matthew the sinner knew the Lord to be his personal saviour (soter), Mark knew him from the first as the Son of God (υἱς θεοῦ), Luke saw in him the 'Christ' who converted Paul to whom Jesus never had spoken, to Paul, Jesus could not 'be Jesus' but Christ exclusively, and John, the kindred spirit, understood him as an older brother – that is, he thought of him as "Jesus," personally. 1, Saviour; 2, Son of God; 3, Christ; 4, Jesus, were the aspects under which the four Evangelists wrote.' Battles, *The Fruit of Lips*, 41.

81 Ibid., 132.

82 Ibid., 53.

83 Ibid., 129.

84 Ibid., 131.

85 Franz Rosenzweig, *The Star of Redemption*, trans. Barbara E. Galli (Madison: University of Wisconsin Press, 2005), 374.

86 Ibid., 374.

87 Rosenstock-Huessy, *Soziologie*, Bd 2, 16–19.

88 Clinton Gardner has provided an excellent account of the Cross of Reality in *Beyond Belief: Discovering Christianity's New Paradigm* (White River Junction: White River Press, 2008). He also provides an extremely useful diagram as an appendix.

89 Rosenstock-Huessy, 'Die Mythen um die Zahl Vier und die Metaphysick,' in *Soziologie*, Bd 1: *Die Übermacht der Räume* (Stuttgart: W. Kohlhammer Verlag, 1956), 266–76.

90 Rosenstock-Huessy, 'Kants Disziplin,' in ibid., 280–4.
91 Rosenstock-Huessy, *Speech and Reality*, 52.
92 Microfilm: 'Dr. Johnson's Cat and the Assimilation of Reality,' 1936, reel 6, item 311, page 1.
93 Rosenstock-Huessy, *The Christian Future*, 168.
94 Ibid., 166.
95 Microfilm: 'What Is New about Sociology?' reel 8, item 438, pages 1 and 4.
96 Ibid., 1.
97 Ibid., 2.

7. The Ages of the Church and Redemption through Revolution

1 Franz Rosenzweig, *The Star of Redemption*, trans. Barbara E. Galli (Madison: University of Wisconsin Press, 2005), 299.
2 Ibid., 299.
3 Ibid., 301.
4 Ibid., 302.
5 Ibid., 294–5.
6 Ibid., 303. Note that Rosenzweig says of the Eastern Church that 'it is not a new church.'
7 Ibid., 295.
8 Ibid., 302–3. Rosenzweig does not mention Kant in this respect, but I think it clear that Kant's great metaphysical questions 'What can I know?' 'What should I do?' and 'What may hope?' completely destroy the traditional Christian understandings of faith and love. Kant champions himself in the preface to the *First Critique* for having limited knowledge to make room for faith (*Glauben*) – but the faith that is left is a purely rational one that rests on the possibility of a noumenal self of moral freedom. The faith that is preserved is the faith in the humanist idea of moral freedom. That this faith is unrecognizable from the traditional view of faith is patently conspicuous in the way it exists in complete disconnection from love. Traditional faith, by contrast, is nothing if it is not part of the triumvirate with love as its main guiding power. But in Kant, love has been relegated to the realm of appearances to ensure that its morally heteronomous character does not infect the rational moral subject. Moreover, love is just one more appetite in the admixture of living forces, all of which *should* be bent before the moral sovereignty of the pure and dutiful will. What to Kant is a shimmering triumph, the interior equivalent of the starry skies, is from a traditional view merely the vacuity of faith without incarnation, God without love, and humanity reposing in the sublimity of its own grandiose chatter about its dignity.

9 Rosenzweig, *The Star of Redemption*, 286.

10 Ibid., 286.

11 Franz Rosenzweig, *Gesammelte Schriften*, Bd III, *Zweistromland. Kleinere Schriften zu Glauben und Denken*, ed. Reinhold Meyer and Annemarie Mayer (Dordrecht: Martinus Nijhoff, 1984), 588.

12 Letter to Gerturde Oppenheim, 5 February 1917, in *Gesammelte Schriften*, Bd I, 344–5, my translation.

13 If I may be permitted an anecdote, in a recent class of mine in Hong Kong, the Turkish Consul stated – without batting an eye or seeing any need to elaborate – 'The European Union is a Christian club.'

14 Eugen Rosenstock-Huessy, *Soziologie*, Bd 2, *Die Vollzahl der Zeiten* (Stuttgart: W. Kohlhammer Verlag, 1958), 256.

15 Ibid., 257. He adds: 'Hitler's destructive war against God has made contemporaries of the Jews, thus the last pre-Christian time, the time of Israel and the time of the Church . . . Jews, Catholics, Protestants are contemporaries since 1933.'

16 Anidjar's statement that with Christianity begins 'the becoming enemy of the neighbour,' as if prior to or outside of Christianity there was no enmity, only serves to show how muddled partisan idealist thinking is. Gil Anidjar, *The Jew, the Arab: A History of the Enemy* (Stanford: Stanford University Press, 2003), 19.

17 Rosenstock-Huessy, *Soziologie*, Bd 2, 49–50.

18 Ibid., 116.

19 Ibid., 121.

20 Eugen Rosenstock-Huessy, *Out of Revolution: Autobiography of Western Man* (Norwich: Argo Books, 1993; Providence: Berg Publishers, 1993), 530.

21 Ibid., 536.

22 Ibid., 536.

23 Ibid., 539.

24 Ibid., 457.

25 Ibid., 473.

26 Ibid., 457.

27 Ibid., 32.

28 Ibid., 714.

29 Ibid., 365.

30 Ibid., 365.

31 But this does not mean he is not marshalled into the cause for radical political purpose. See, for example, Slavoj Žižek's *In Defense of Lost Causes*, or the writings of La Clau and Mouffe.

32 Jacques Derrida, *Specters of Marx: The State of the Debt, the Work of Mourning, and the New International* (London: Routledge, 1994), 65.

33 The Kantian thread of the radical liberal paradigm was not primarily
by choice but rather by necessity. The generation that came of age in the
1960s and 1970s most certainly had the will to change its world; but even
in the most difficult of postwar economic times, there was no catastrophe
big enough to galvanize people into launching a genuine, life-and-death
revolutionary struggle. Also, the working class shared few if any of the
goals of the radical liberal paradigm. Revolt thus occurred primarily at
the level of ideas, and could be most effective in those social domains that
were receptive to transformation through ideas.
34 Rosenstock-Huessy, *Out of Revolution*, 699.
35 Ibid., 564.
36 Ibid., 716–17.
37 Ibid., 739.
38 Ibid., 475–6.
39 Ibid., 652.
40 Ibid., 473.
41 Ibid., 467.
42 Ibid., 475–6.
43 Ibid., 563.
44 Eugen Rosenstock-Huessy, *The Christian Future – or The Modern Mind
Outrun*, intro. Harold Stahmer (New York: Harper and Row, [1947]1966),
62–3.
45 Ibid., 75.

8. The Modern Humanistic Turn of the French Revolution in Rosenstock-Huessy

1 Eugen Rosenstock-Huessy, *Out of Revolution: Autobiography of Western
Man* (Norwich: Argo Books, 1993; Providence: Berg Publishers, 1993), 145.
By liberalism, he clearly means the love of freedom as expressed, for example, in Pericles' great funeral speech in Thucydides.
2 Ibid., 144–5.
3 Ibid., 236.
4 Ibid., 217.
5 Ibid., 217.
6 Ibid., 217.
7 Ibid., 407.
8 Ibid., 407. This is not to deny that Luther also followed Paul in demanding that Christian subjects obey their princes. But the timing of Luther's
plea to the peasants to stop their rebellion was as pertinent to his call

for an end to bloodshed as was his attempt to Christianize princes. Furthermore, a central tenet of Rosenstock-Huessy's hermeneutics of the Christian faith is the temporality of every utterance – except, perhaps, the imperative to love, though even that carries the temporal requirement that one be attentive to the loving act that is required at the time of action.

9 Ibid., 409.
10 Ibid., 217.
11 Ibid., 217.
12 Cf. ibid., 237, 77, 78. See also the entire chapter 'Wiederetdeckung des Juden' (The Rediscovery of the Jews) in Hans Ehrenberg, *In der Schule Pascals* (Heidelberg: Lambert Schneider, 1954).
13 Ibid., 78. And see also, again, 'Die Wiederetdeckung des Juden.'
14 Ibid., 153.
15 Ibid., 152.
16 Microfilm: 'Abelard: in Contributions to The American People's Encyclopedia,' reel 11, item 545, page 2.
17 Rosenstock-Huessy, *Out of Revolution*, 153.
18 Ibid., 155.
19 Ibid., 156.
20 Ibid., 175.
21 Ibid., 158.
22 Ibid., 159.
23 Ibid., 157.
24 Ibid., 161–2.
25 Ibid., 162.
26 Ibid., 163. Surprisingly, nowhere in the chapter does Rosenstock-Huessy mention the earlier literary master, Rabelais, whose mid-sixteenth-century attack on the University of Paris, the French clergy, French lawyers, and, indeed, all the holders of privilege of his contemporaries reflects the same candour and power that Dante's *Divine Comedy* had directed against the scourges of his age. Rabelais reveals the degeneneracy of the French Church and State well before the St Bartholomew massacre and the centralization of the French state.
27 Ibid., 167.
28 Regarding the building of Versailles, Rosenstock-Huessy writes: 'The "esprit," the inspiration of this realm, worked passionately to overcome all natural obstacles. The fountains of Versailles were wrested from a dry and waterless soil! The Duke of Saint-Simon, chronicler of Versailles, speaks of the glorious pleasure of enslaving nature. And nature was enslaved. The physical and the social traditions of France were overshadowed by

the Kings' domination over nature. And what was the ultimate goal of this new power established in an arbitrary centre? The new standard was expressed by Richelieu in his Testament: "Le but de mon ministère a été de rendre à la Gaule les frontières que lui a destinées la nature, de rendre aux'Gaulois un roi Gaulois, de confondre la Gaule avec la France, et partout où fut Fancienne Gaule d'y rétablir la nouvelle." This was already the regeneration of a pre-Christian order of things.' In ibid., 158.

29 Rosenstock-Huessy does not mention this, but it is, I think, highly supportive of his argument.

30 See the Letter to Regius, January 1642, in Descartes, *Philosophical Letters*, trans. and ed. Anthony Kenny (Oxford: Clarendon, 1970), 126–7.

31 Rosenstock-Huessy, *Out of Revolution*, 187–8.

32 Ibid., 188.

33 See especially Book VI of *The Discourse*. See also Descartes's Letter to Huygens, 31 January 1642, in which he discusses Father Bourdin's objections to his *Meditations*: 'It is now a prisoner in my hands . . . Every day I call my council of war about it . . . Perhaps these scholastic wars will result in my *World* being brought into the world.' Descartes, *Philosophical Letters*, 131.

34 Descartes's advice to Frans Burman is apposite: 'A point to note is that you should not devote so much effort to the *Meditations* and to metaphysical questions, or give them elaborate treatment in commentaries and the like. Still less should one do what some try and do, and dig more deeply into these questions than the author did. He has dealt with them quite deeply enough. It is sufficient to have grasped them once in a general way, and then to remember the conclusion. Otherwise, they draw the mind too far away from physical and observable things, and make it unfit to study them. Yet it is just these physical studies that it is most desirable for men to pursue, since they would yield abundant benefits for life.' René Descartes, *Conversations with Burman*, trans. John Cottingham (Oxford: Clarendon, 1976), para. 48. Also, in a letter to Princess Elizabeth of 28 June 1643, he writes that the chief rule he has always observed in his studies is 'never to spend more than a few hours a day in the thought[s] which occupy the imagination' – that is, in scientific thought, which requires the imaginative construction of models to test against reality – and 'a few hours a year on those which occupy the pure intellect' – that is, on metaphysics. Descartes, *Philosophical Letters*, 141–2. That (especially analytical) philosophy undergraduate classes around the world systematically ignore this and set up Descartes's metaphysical arguments for eighteen-year-olds to cut their teeth on only confirms, for me, why Rosenstock-Huessy was so suspicious of any approach to philosophy that treats

arguments as timeless things in themselves, instead of – as it is in most philosophy generated during revolutionary times – urgent acts of speech conducted at a particular moment for the most serious of purposes. In my own *The Metaphysics of Science and Freedom* (Aldershot: Gower, 1991), I provide a lengthy analysis of why Descartes's metaphysics is meaningless without the revolution he was undertaking in physics, and how its crafting was undertaken mainly for political purposes. Notwithstanding arguments about God and immortality, its content is utterly unreligious; and while it is superficially scholastic, it is merely a scaffold to support the view of the universe as lawful, and the mind as a set of cognitive functions enabling the collection of data. His dualism is no more susceptible to the criticisms of his more monistic materialist critics such as Hobbes because it is meaningless – in more contemporary parlance, a category mistake – to dissolve matters of method into a search for material causes.

35 It also, as he says to Mersenne on 28 January 1641, 'contains all the foundations of my Physics, But please do not tell people for that might make it harder for supporters of Aristotle.' Descartes, *Philosophical Letters*, 94. The metaphysics might come first in the system, but it *serves* the physics. Rosenstock-Huessy, in *Out of Revolution*, 156, rightly says that Descartes's *Discourse on Method* 'establishes a philosophy which keeps away from any servitude to theology.' Cf. Julien de La Mettrie, *Man and Machine*, trans. Gertrud Bussey (Illinois: Open Court, 1935), 148 – 'the distinction of the two substances, thus is plainly but a . . . ruse of style, to make theologians swallow a poison, hidden in an analogy which strikes every body else and which they alone fail to notice.'

36 'I cannot forgive Descartes,' writes Pascal. 'In his whole philosophy he would like to do without God: but he could not help allowing him a flick of the fingers to set the world in motion; after that he had no more need for God.' Blaise Pascal, *Pensees,* trans. A.J. Krailsheimer (Harmondsworth: Penguin, 1966), 355.

37 See René Descartes, *Philosophical Writings of Descartes*, 2 vols., trans. John Cottingham, Robert Stoothoff, and Dugald Murdoch (Cambridge: Cambridge University Press, 1985), I:97.

38 Microfilm: 'There Are No Synonyms,' 1944, reel 8, item 387, page 1.

39 Ibid., 5.

40 Ibid., 2.

41 Microfilm: 'Greek Philosophy,' 1956, reel 16, item 641, page 14.

42 Rosenstock-Huessy, *Speech and Reality,* intro. Clinton C. Gardner (Norwich: Argo Books, 1970), 39.

43 Ibid., 25.

44 Rosenstock-Huessy, *Out of Revolution*, 186–7.

45 Ibid., 188–9.
46 Ibid., 194.
47 Ibid., 194.
48 Ibid., 195.
49 Ibid., 193.
50 Ibid., 240.
51 Ibid., 243.
52 Rosenstock-Huessy points out that 'the first two bodies to be transferred to the Pantheon on Mount St. Geneviève were those of Voltaire and Rousseau.' Ibid., 179.
53 Ibid., 179.
54 See Paul Corcoran, *Before Marx: Socialism and Communism in France, 1830–48* (New York: St Martin's Press, 1983).
55 Rosenstock-Huessy, *Out of Revolution*, 180–1.
56 Ibid., 180.
57 Ibid., 182.
58 Ibid., 184.
59 Microfilm: 'Liturgical Thinking,' reel 8, item 424, page 1.
60 Consider, for example, J.L. Talmon's classic *The Origins of Totalitarian Democracy* (New York: Norton, 1970).
61 Rosenstock-Huessy, *Out of Revolution*, 190.
62 The importance of social biorhythms – 'time is living rhythms'; see Rosenstock-Huessy, *Die europäischen Revolutionenen*, 33 – is an interesting and important aspect of Rosenstock-Huessy's studies of human societies and revolutions. As early as 1919, he had written of the patterns that one can see in every fourth to fifth generation; see 'Der Neubau der deutschen Rechstgeschichte'; microfilm: 1920, reel 2, item 95. And in his work on the Church with Jospeh Wittig, as in his early versions of his study of revolutions, he had been struck by the intergenerational rhythms. This had in turn alerted him to the importance of Matthew's gospel regarding this issue. In 1946 he realized that he had a precursor in Giuseppi Ferrari, who had identified four phases of a revolution – preparatory, revolutionary, reactionary, conciliatory – in his *Theory of Revolutions*, and who had anticipated Rosenstock-Huessy's six revolutionary phases: conflict, despair, faith, pride, humiliation, fulfilment (Rosenstock-Huessy, *Out of Revolution*, 486). For Rosenstock-Huessy, these phases are common to all revolutions and thus enable one to draw asymmetrical correspondences (see especially ibid., 664) between the time periods of the different revolutions. Like Rosenstock-Huessy, Ferrari noted that revolutions had a cumulative character. He also saw that past lessons become forgotten as

social toxicities build up, thus often forcing yet another explosion. For Rosenstock-Huessy, the generational development is a Christian idea that finds itself expressed at the beginning of Matthew's gospel. As Rosenstock-Huessy reads him, Matthew has grasped that a catastrophe occurs after every fourteen generations that, as Thomas Hardy puts it, leads to 'the precipice of an epoch.' Rosenstock-Huessy, *Heilkraft und Wahrheit: Konkordanz der Politischen und Kosmischen Zeit* (Wien: Amandus, 1990), 115. Rosenstock-Huessy found Croce's dismissal of Ferrari as a crackpot to be a typical liberal prejudice stemming from liberalism's general failure to deal with time as a living, and not merely mechanical, power. According to Rosenstock-Huessy, Ferrari had predicted an economic revolution (i.e., the Russian Revolution) in 1917 and had predicted that in 2000 the world would either perish or be forced to find a new paradigm. For an overview of his position on Ferrari, see 'Der Datierungszwang und Giuseppi Ferrari' in *Das Geheimnis der Universität: Wider den Verfall von Zeitsinn und Sprachkraft,* ed. Georg Müller (Stuttgart: W. Kohlhammer Verlag, 1958), 35–43. I think it fair to say that Rosenstock-Huessy mainly wants us to consider seriously, rather than dogmatically deploy (as if it could turn social scientists into the children of Nostradamus), the idea of generational buildup and breakdown and social explosions.

63 Rosenstock-Huessy, *Out of Revolution,* 237.

64 Ibid., 146–7.

65 Ibid., 146.

66 'Some order is required by which Europe be organized economically as America and Russia are already organized.' Ibid., 640. In 1938 he thought that the prospects of this were 'dim' and that Britain and France were burdened by different histories that made it difficult for them to achieve cooperation. Given the ongoing squabbling between France and Britain in the EU, his awareness of the tensions is reasonable enough. In 1938 he speculated that 'the common administration of Africa' might bring Europe together – though, here, too, he saw Europe as more interested in division. What is interesting about this conjecture is that Europe has abandoned its responsibilities to its former colonies and by and large has left a ruin of Africa. It is the largest aid donor in the world, yet its protectionist policies have rendered much of that aid little more than a token. That said, Europe certainly realizes that it has responsibilities, and ultimately it wants to change the world politically through the application of 'soft power.' Rosenstock-Huessy would, I think, be somewhat sceptical of Europe's tacit dependency on the United States' hard power while promoting itself as offering an alternative. And while one can find much to

commend in the European Union's efforts to entice and retain members by insisting on democratic behaviour as a condition of membership, one does not need to be a complete cynic to see how abstract ideas are often a substitute for real actions.

9. Beyond the Idol of the Nation, Part 1: Rosenstock-Huessy in the Aftermath of the Great War

1 Desmond Dinan, *Ever Closer Union: An Introduction to European Integration* (New York: Palgrave Macmillan, 1999).
2 Cf. Eugen Rosenstock-Huessy, 'Schluß, 1 c,' *Soziologie*, Bd 1: *Die Übermacht der Räume* (Stuttgart: W. Kohlhammer Verlag, 1956). And for a Romantic reading of Rosenzweig, see Ernest Rubenstein, *An Episode of Jewish Romanticism: Franz Rosenzweig's* The Star of Redemption (Albany: SUNY Press, 1999). But, as with post-structuralist and existentialist readings of Rosenzweig, such a reading, while it helps delineate similar concerns that Rosenzweig shares with a particular group, can be quite misleading if it pays too little attention to the dialogical and the redemptive, not to mention the specific task of the Jewish and Christian peoples.
3 Eugen Rosenstock-Huessy, *The Christian Future – or The Modern Mind Outrun*, intro. Harold Stahmer (New York: Harper and Row, [1947]1966), 82.
4 Eugen Rosenstock-Huessy with Joseph Wittig, *Das Alter der Kirche. Kapitel und Akten*. 3 Bde (Münster: Agenda, 1998), I:55.
5 Ibid., 54.
6 Marion Davis Battles, ed., *The Fruit of Lips, or, Why Four Gospels?* (Pittsburgh: Pickwick Press, 1978), 33.
7 Eugen Rosenstock-Huessy, *Out of Revolution: Autobiography of Western Man* (Norwich: Argo Books, 1993; Providence: Berg Publishers, 1993), 485.
8 Microfilm: 'The Rise and Fall of Nationalism and Internationalism,' 1939, reel 6, item 331, page 4.
9 Rosenstock-Huessy, *Out of Revolution*, 6.
10 Ibid., 605.
11 Ibid., 640.
12 Ibid., 515.
13 Eugen Rosenstock-Huessy, *Die Hochzeit des Kriegs und der Revolution* (Würzburg: Patmos-Verlag, 1920; reprint 1965), 105.
14 Rosenstock-Huessy, 'Menschheit und Menschengeschlect,' in *Hochzeit*, 299.
15 See Rosenstock-Huessy, 'Goethe und Bismarck,' in *Hochzeit*. It would be misleading to imply that Rosenstock-Huessy thought that Bismarckian

politics was all wrong. In *Soziologie, Bd 2: Die Vollzahl der Zeiten* (Stuttgart: W. Kohlhammer Verlag, 1958), at 97, he acknowledges that from 1865 to 1879 Bismarck was a great statesman. But after 1879, his political judgment deteriorated 'until he ended with fanciful plans of the German Reich and a totally ruined constitution.' Passing over the socialist laws, he refers to 'one criminal act that has remained unreproached by Bismarck historians, which set the mould for all the concentration camps of the Nazis.' He then notes the case of the liberal parliamentarian Eduard Lasker, whose love of liberty so incensed Bismarck that when he died in the United States, and the American congress asked Bismarck to publicly express its condolences, he refused to do so. To link Bismarck to National Socialism on the basis of the Lasker case seems a stretch; rather, Rosenstock-Huessy uses this example to highlight that Bismarck could see in Lasker only an 'enemy,' and that on an occasion requiring that friend/enemy thinking be transcended, he refused to do so. In this way, he entrenched a friend/enemy politics that would be disastrous for Germany.

16 Rosenstock-Huessy, *Hochzeit*, 153.

17 Ibid., 243.

18 This was how he formulated it in his retrospective summing up of *Hochzeit* in 'Die jüdischen Antisemiten oder die akademische Form der Judenfrage.' Microfilm: 1951, reel 9, item 442, page 15.

19 Rosenstock-Huessy, *Hochzeit*, 156. Cf. Rosenstock-Huessy, *Friedensbedingungen der planetarischen Gesellschaft: Zur Ökonomie der Zeit*, ed. Rudolf Hermeier (Münster: Agenda Verlag, 2001), 122.

20 Microfilm: 'Abbau der politischen Lüge,' 1924, reel 2, item 138, page 66.

21 Microfilm: 'Industrievolk,' 1924, reel 2, item 139, page 4. For a more detailed discussion of this side of Rosentock-Huessy's work, see Willibald Huppuch, *Eugen Rosenstock-Huessy (1888–1973) und die Weimarer Republik: Erwachsenenbildung, Industriereform, und Arbeitslosenproblematik* (Hamburg: Dr Kovač, 2004).

22 See Rosenstock-Huessy's 'Europa und Christheit'; microfilm: 1919, reel 1, item 60; and 'The Next Homer,' microfilm: 1944, Reel 1, item 385.

23 *Tumult*, no. 21.

24 *Tumult*, vol. 20, ed. Frank Böcelman, Dieter Kampfer, and Walter Seitter (Wien: Turian und Kant, 1995), 20–3.

25 Ibid., 23.

26 Eugen Rosenstock-Huessy, 'Lehrer oder Führer? Zur Polychrome des Menschen,' in *Die Sprache des Menschengeschlechts*, Bd 2 (Heidelberg: Lambert Schneider, 1964), 136–56. In his 1958 Münster Lectures, *Die Gesetze der christlichen Zeitrechnung*, ed. Rudolf Hermeier and Jochen Lübben

(Münster: Agenda, 2002), at 377, Rosenstock-Huessy writes: 'All the heroes of the will, these monstrous men of will, are people who misuse the will, raise the will of a moment in time over themselves to become an idol . . . Fichte and Hitler – that's the same thing. All German idealism ends in the divization of a firmly set will [des einmal gesetzten Willens].'

27 Rosenstock-Huessy, *Out of Revolution*, 445. He adds – and this is very easy to misinterpret – that 'the Nazis themselves are no militarists.' This is bound to be understood very differently by a Prussian than by an English-speaking reader. Given what he says here about Nazism and its dangers, it is clear he is trying to say that the National Socialists are not driven by a military code of honour.

28 Ibid., 444–5.

29 Indeed, the closeness was such that the two of them collaborated for a time. See Werner Picht, ed., *Die Arbeitsgemeinschaft, Monatsschrift für das gesamte Volkshochschulwesen* (Leipzig: Quelle and Meyer, 1920).

30 23 April 1962#. Michael Gormann-Thelen has informed me in private conversation that Picht 'was one of the very few who had to write the diary of the German Army during WWII. He edited selections of it at many times in just those countries the German Army had invaded.'

31 *Gritli Briefe*, 19 October 1917. Rosenzweig says he could understand Picht's anti-Semitism had it been on religious grounds; because it was on racial grounds, he held Picht in utter contempt.

32 See Georg Picht in Günther Neske, ed., *Erinnerung an Martin Heidegger*, (Pfullingen: Günther Neske Verlag, 1977), 197–205; Rüdiger Safranski, *Ein Meister aus Deutschland. Heidegger und seine Zeit* (München: Hanser Verlag 1994, 271); Alois Prinz, *Beruf Philosophin oder die Liebe zur Welt: die Lebensgeschichte der Hannah Arendt* (Basel: Beltz Goldberg, 1998), 81; and Heinrich Petzet in *Encounters and Dialogues with Martin Heidegger, 1929–1976*, trans. Emad Parvis and Kenneth Maly (Chicago: University of Chicago Press, 1993). I first learned of this from Andreas Moeckel in his e-mail of 12 May 2007 to the Rosenstock-Huessy Gesellschaft. Michael Gormann-Thelen kindly discussed the matter with me at great length and with great insight.

33 As far as I know, the only time Arendt mentions Rosenstock-Huessy is in a letter to Jaspers (19 November 1948), where she says she has received an 'even crazier letter' from him that she could not understand. See Hannah Arendt and Karl Jaspers, *Correspondence, 1926–1929*, ed. Lotte Kohler and Hans Saner, trans. Robert Kimber and Rita Kimber (New York: Harcourt Brace Jovanovich, 1992), 122. I know of no mention of Arendt by Rosenstock-Huessy, but I am sure that her work on revolutions would

have driven him quite crazy (his frame of reference is simply much vaster than hers), and I can well imagine him writing her a letter pointing out all her errors.

34 Klemens von Klemperer, *German Incertitudes, 1914–1945: The Stones and the Cathedral* (Westport: Greenwood Publishing, 2001), 81.

35 Ibid., 82. Klemperer continues: 'The design of Rosenstock, after 1923 professor at the University of Breslau, was, as he later explained, to enrich life in the factory by the rhythm of communal life. He also took great interest in the work camp movement in Silesia which aimed at bringing together workers, peasants, and students as well as captains of industry in a vita communis that would help solve the many economic and social problems of the area so much afflicted by the World War. In the course of this undertaking he met up with the Youth Movement in Silesia and also with a group of men, Helmuth James von Moltke and his friends, who during the Third Reich would form the oppositional "Kreisau Circle." It was upon Rosenstock's initiative that in September 1927 Moltke got in touch with Heinrich Brüning, then Reichstag representative for Electorial District 7 (Breslau), in order to obtain financial backing for the work. In many ways Rosenstock became Moltke's mentor, and after Helmuth's death remained closely connected with the family.' After Margrit Huessy's death, Helmuth's widow, Freya von Moltke, would become Rosenstock-Huessy's faithful companion.

36 Rosenstock-Huessy, *Out of Revolution*, 20.

37 Ibid., 624.

38 Eugen Rosenstock-Huessy, *Judaism Despite Christianity: The Letters on Christianity and Judaism between Rosenstock-Huessy and Franz Rosenzweig*, intro. Harold Stahmer, ed. Alexander Altmann and Dorothy Emmet (New York: Schocken Books, 1971), 47.

39 Franz Rosenzweig to Eugen Rosenstock-Huessy, *Gritli Briefe*, 30 April 1917.

40 Franz Rosenzweig to Eugen Rosenstock-Huessy, 30 April 1917, in ibid.

41 Rosenstock-Huessy, *Out of Revolution*, 715.

42 Ibid., 718.

43 Ibid., 496. 'European History is the sequence of these equations between universal and particular, between local rights and federal government. The oldest form of this equation is, on one side, the Emperor of Holy Rome marching on his laborious way through the Continent as the sole and universal judge, and, on the other, the Lords of the Manor asking absolute loyalty, including the vendetta from their knaves, chaplains and children.' Ibid., 499.

44 Ibid., 718.

10. Beyond the Idol of the Nation, Part 2: Rosenzweig on Hegel

1 See especially Haggai Dagan, 'The Motif of Blood and Procreation and Blood in Franz Rosenzweig,' *AJS Review* 26, no. 2 (2002), 241–9. Dagan rightly points out that the motif of blood in Rosenzweig is deployed in emphatic opposition to the 'earth' (esp. 246–7); and he rightly draws out how Rosenzweig emphasizes 'pure existence (as expressed in blood and propagation), which he places before ethics or reason,' 249.

2 Franz Rosenzweig, 'Atheistic Theology,' in *Philosophical and Theological Writings*, trans. and ed. Paul W. Franks and Michael Morgan (Indianapolis: Hackett, 2000), 18.

3 See also Michael Mack, 'The Politics of Blood,' chapter 8 of his *German Idealism and the Jew: The Inner Anti-Semitism of Philosophy and German Jewish Responses* (Chicago: University of Chicago Press, 2003). Mack provides a very astute reading of how Rosenzweig's blood community of the Jew 'undermines German idealism's attempt to translate the body into the body politic. The state sets out to glorify its power by shedding blood in order to gain possession of yet-to-be-conquered land.'

4 Franz Rosenzweig, *Gesammelte Schriften*, Bd 3, *Zweistromland. Kleinere Schriften zu Glauben und Denken*, 553.

5 See Jörg Kohr *'Gott selbst muss das letzte Wort sprechen . . .': Religion und Politik im Denken Franz Rosenzweigs* (Freiburg: Karl Alber, 2008), 54ff.

6 Franz Rosenzweig, 'Volksschule und Reichsschule,' in *Gesammelte Schriften*, Bd III, *Zweistromland*, 371–411. The work was also referred to as the 'Putzianum.'

7 Rosenzweig, *Gesammelte Schriften*, Bd 3, *Zweistromland*, 314. See also Paul Mendes-Flohr, 'Franz Rosenzweig and the Crisis of Historicism,' in *The Philosophy of Franz Rosenzweig* ed. Paul Mendes-Flohr (Hanover: University Press of New England, 1988), 138–61. Mendes-Flohr offers a good discussion of Rosenzweig's geopolitical war writings. See also Francesco Paolo Ciglia, 'Zwischen homerischem und biblischem Weltbild: Rosenzweigs Europa-Gedanke,' *Rosenzweig Jahrbuch*, 3: 127–39.

8 Ibid.

9 Rosenzweig, *Gesammelte Schriften*, Bd 1, Briefe an Eltern, 17 August 1916.

10 Ibid.

11 Ibid., 1 September 1916. Cf. Cordula Hufnagel, *Die kultische Gebärde: Kunst, Politik, Religion im Denken Franz Rosenzweigs* (Freiburg: Karl Alber, 1994), 88–9.

12 Cf. ibid., 88–9.

13 Rosenzweig, Briefe an Eltern, 12 August 1916. Cf. Hufnagel, *Die kultische Geärde*, 88–9.

14 Rosenzweig, *Briefe an Eltern*, 1 September 1916.

15 Ibid.

16 I agree with Peter Eli Gordon, who argues in *Rosenzweig and Heidegger: Between Judaism and German Philosophy* (Berkeley: University of California Press, 2003) that this text is important for understanding Rosenzweig and should not be treated simply as a work on Hegel. However, while Gordon's book is particularly good in its discussion of the relationship between Christians and Jews in Hegel's early thought, anyone who reads his book and mine will see that we disagree strongly about the book's meaning. That is in no small part to do with where Gordon ends up taking Rosenzweig and where I believe he is going. I am much less impressed by Heidegger than Gordon; I am also much more interested in how social bodies work over time – that is to say, I am more impressed by what Rosenzweig and Rosenstock-Huessy disclose as sociologists than by what philosophers like Heidegger do.

17 Karl Rosenkranz's *Hegels Leben* is a faithful rendition of his master; Rudolph Haym's *Hegel und seine Zeit* is a savage liberal critique; Dilthey's depiction of the romantic strands in the young Hegel is to be found in his *Die Jugendgeschichte Hegels und andere Abhandlungen zur Geschichte des Deutschen Idealismus*.

18 Significantly, only now with the Rosenzweig renaissance does the book look like it will be translated, but not because it is seen by Hegel scholars as throwing strong philosophical light on Hegel's political understanding. Rather, it is because Rosenzweig scholars see it as a key to Rosenzweig's philosophical development. It is worth noting that Hegel scholars generally dismiss Rosenzweig's reading of Hegel, largely because Hegel is being read so differently in the aftermath of the Second World War. The immediate postwar generation generally read Hegel through the prism of totalitarianism: Was he a totalitarian, or did he have something to offer a liberal state that recognizes the need for collective representation? It is clear that in *Open Society and Its Enemies*, Karl Popper put him in the totalitarian camp, but that reading in the Anglo-American world was overthrown as Kaufmann (*Hegel*, 1965) and Avineri (*Hegel's Theory of the Modern State*, 1974) offered a much more benign version of Hegel – one that has largely taken hold in the avalanche of Hegel studies coming out of Britain and North America over the past fifteen years. These latter studies tend to reflect what has become the rather orthodox academic view of politics – one that emphasizes substantive rights and community membership. I think that the rereading has had much to do with the fact that Hegel's polarities of self/individual and collective totality/state took on much more prominence and made much more sense in the context of

the ideological polarization of liberalism and totalitarianism than they did in the context of a much more 'nationalist'-driven agenda experienced in the penumbra of the Great War. Hegel simply looks far less useful when one is thinking about nationalism. In France, by contrast, Hegel has remained the *bête noire*, especially in Deleuze and Foucault, whose political armoury is utterly – in spite of all their grand gestures and genuine animosities toward Hegel himself – left Hegelian, that is to say, they remain overdetermined by the negative.

19 This point, once pretty well universally held, has become a source of scholarly contention. For what it is worth, I think the ideas are so patently related to Schelling's themes that even if Hegel had composed it, he was being simply a philosophical clone of Schelling.

20 Letter of 2 February 1933 in Franz Rosenzweig, *Gesammelte Schriften, Briefe und Tagebucher*, Bd 2, 889.

21 Franz Rosenzweig, *Hegel und der Staat* (Munich: R. Oldenbourg, 1920; Reprint Aalen: Scientia, 1962), Bd I, xiii.

22 Ibid., Bd I, xii.

23 The Hubertus Treaty, signed by Prussia, Saxony, and Austria at the end of the Seven Years' War, involved the retention of existing pre-War borders.

24 Briefe an die Mutter, 19 October 1918, *Gesammelte Schriften Briefe und Tagebucher*, Bd 1, 615. Regarding the many periods of Rosenzweig expressing frustration, see the letter to Rosenstock-Huessy, *Briefe und Tagebucher*, Bd 1, 29 July 1917.

25 *Gritli Briefe*, 9 November 1918. Cf. 28 February 1919, where he says: 'now we are going to war with the Bolsheviks, seen personally, one would have to certainly wish this.'

26 Ibid., 9 July 1917.

27 Ibid., 12–13 November 1917.

28 Franz Rosenzweig, *Gesammelte Schriften*, Bd III, *Zweistromland. Kleinere Schriften zu Glauben und Denken,*552.

29 See Briefe an die Eltern, 9 September 1914 and 10 January 1915, Bd 1. Cf. Kohr, *'Gott selbst muss das letzte Wort sprechen . . .,'* 62ff.

30 Rosenzweig's *Hegel und der Staat* shows Meinecke's hand all over it, both in its method and in its general assessment of Bismarck and Prussia and Hegel. The postwar editions, however, show a willingness to abandon the cosmopolitan faith that was so important to Meinecke. Also, Rosenzweig had expressed to his parents in 1917 his belief that Meinecke's major weakness was that he thought too much in terms of individual states rather than in terms of state alliances. Brief an die Eltern, 1 October 1917, *Briefe und Tagebucher*, Bd 1, 459.

31 Meinecke's assessment was that 'whoever surrendered completely to the
   spirit of Hegel's theory always stood in danger of transforming actual life
   in this world into a phantasmagoria – stood in danger, too, in terms of our
   basic theme here, of forcefully and prematurely imposing the universal
   element onto the life of the state and nation.' This indicates the extent to
   which Meinecke and Rosenzweig concurred in their assessment of Hegel;
   it could also pass as an accurate summary of *Hegel und der Staat*. See
   Friedrich Meinecke, *Cosmopolitanism and the National State*, trans. Robert
   Kimber, intro. Felix Gilbert (Princeton: Princeton University Press, 1970),
   202. Mention should also be made of Meinecke's contribution to the collection of essays for Rosenzweig's 40th birthday, in which he writes: 'I remember, dear Mr. Rosenzweig, a moving conversation with you about six
   or seven years ago, when we were walking together across the Leipziger
   Place. Just as my eye caught sight of the Count of Brandenburg, you ut-
   tered those words which struck me so powerfully. We were still shaken
   by the collapse of 1918, and you expressed the opinion that the spiritual
   basis and assumptions of your work on Hegel were entirely shattered –
   or at least seriously threatened – and so too was your confidence in the
   stability and continuity of the humanistic Protestant culture of Germany
   and the survival of the State which had been founded on it . . . Much was
   broken for the Liberals in 1860, when Bismarck did not create German
   unity by means of liberalism, but through "Blood and iron."' In *Franz
   Rosenzweig zum 25. Dezember 1926 glueckwuensche zum 40. Geburtstag* (New
   York: Leo Baeck Institute, 1987), 36.
32 Rosenzweig, *Hegel und der Staat*, II:82.
33 According to Gordon in *Rosenzweig and Heidegger*, 114, Rosenzweig's attitude toward Hegel in *Hegel und der Staat* is one of ambivalence in which
   there is more love than hatred. Gordon supports his interpretation (see his
   n71) by reference to Rosenzweig's scolding of Lasson for praising Hegel
   too much, whereas, for Rosenzweig, loving meant keeping an awareness
   of one's difference from the object of the study. I think it quite disingenuous of Rosenzweig to imply that he who leaves Hegel's thoughts on
   politics as a historical rubble of shifting contradictions and political and
   social errors loves Hegel more than a disciple. Gordon rightly picks up
   on Rosenzweig's failure to offer comment on Hegel's attitude toward the
   Jews. But I see the silence as being broken in the general tone of the work.
   To me, *Hegel und der Staat* reads like a coroner present at the autopsy of
   a putrid corpse. The coroner is trying to be objective in the reporting,
   but every so often he is unable to withhold the odd comment about the
   stench. I am also somewhat surprised that Otto Pöggeler in 'Between

Enlightenment and Romanticism: Rosenzweig and Hegel,' 107–23 in *The Philosophy of Franz Rosenzweig*, ed. Paul Mendes Flohr, also passes over the tone and hence I think makes rather superficial comparisons between the two. More accurate is Stéphane Mosès in *System and Revelation: The Philosophy of Franz Rosenzweig*, trans. Catherine Tihanyi (Detroit: Wayne State University Press, 1992), 30–2. Mosès, at 32, also cites Eric Weil's *Hegel and the State* regarding the anti-Hegelian tone of Rosenzweig's book. Weil's book is one of the best apologies for Hegel as a state theorist. It has a much more 'liberal' view of Prussia than Rosenzweig, but it does not seem to me to circumvent the deeper criticism of Rosenzweig that questions the abstract nature of the matrix underpinning its construction of the state. See also Mosès's 'Hegel beim Wort genommen: Gescichtskritik bei Franz Rosnzweig,' in Gotthard Fuchs und Hans Hermann Henrix, eds., *Zeitgewinn: Messianisches Denken nach Franz Rosenzweig* (Frankfurt am Main: Knecht Verlag, 1987), 67–95.

34 Rosenzweig, *Hegel und der Staat*, I:4–5.

35 Ibid., I:8.

36 Ibid., II:169.

37 The lengthy section on the Philosophy of Right in *Hegel und der Staat* is especially instructive – and damning – as it traces how Hegel seems desperate to fit bits of the system's bric-a-brac – property, morality, the ethical life, family, civil society – into a political structure all dancing upon the (Rousseauian) will.

38 Rosenzweig, *Hegel und der Staat*, II:49.

39 Hence to Rosenstock-Huessy he writes, in 1916, the interesting comment that while Hegel might belong to the ten most important men, he does not belong to the ten most important Germans; Franz Rosenzweig, *Judaism Despite Christianity, Judaism Despite Christianity: The 'Letters on Christianity and Judaism' between Rosenstock-Huessy and Franz Rosenzweig*, ed. Eugen Rosenstock-Huessy, trans. Dorothy Emmet (New York: Schocken Books, 1971), 168 (undated letter of 1916).

40 Rosenzweig, *Hegel und der Staat*, II:243.

41 Franz Rosenzweig, *Gesammelte Schriften* I, *Briefe und Tagebucher*, Bd 1: 1900–18, ed. Rachel Rosenzweig and Edith Rosenzweig-Scheinmann (The Hague: Martinus Nijhoff, 1979), 25. Entry for 9 February 1906.

42 The testimonies can be found in the German Jewish newspaper *Der Orden Bne Biss: Mitteilungen der Grosslosse für Deutschland*, Berlin, March 1930, no. 3, available at the Leo Baeck Archives in New York City. See also Michael Brocke, 'Franz Rosenzweig und Gerhard Scholem,' in *Sondedruck aus Juden in der Weimar Republik*, ed. Walter Grab and Julius

Schoeps (Stuttgart: Burg Verlag, 1986). For Scholem, Rosenzweig's German/Jewish harmony was a major source of disagreement between them. Rosenzweig, as Brocke points out, saw Scholem as a nihilist, as someone wanting all or nothing, whereas he saw himself as building his life around the 'something' (*etwas*); see ibid., 132–6. Scholem also saw Rosenzweig's Judaism as suffering from a form of protestant-pietistic-churchliness. Ibid.,143.

43 That Marx had famously remarked to Engels (January 1868) how irritated he was that Hegel was treated like a dead dog was, I think, a pretty fair assessment of a philosophical climate that was becoming increasingly re-attuned to Kant – as Otto Liebmann put it 'Back to Kant!'

44 Eugen Rosenstock-Huessy, 'Hegel und unser Geschlecht,' *Der Neue Merkur* 8 (1924–5), also in *Friedensbedingungen der planetarischen Gesellschaft: Zur Ökonomie der Zeit,* ed. and intro. Rudolf Hermeier (Münster: Agenda Verlag, 2001), 286–9.

45 Eugen Rosenstock-Huessy, *Die europäischen Revolutionen und der Charakter der Nationen,* rev. ed. (Moers: Brendow Verlag, 1961), 428. In his discussion of the Austro-Hungarian Empire, Rosenstock-Huessy is quite laudatory, seeing it as having accomplished a great deal, especially in its management of so many different national groups for so long. But that is very different from the kind of Romanticism supported by Schlegel, which is a retreat into the past that blinds one to more contemporary destabilizing forces.

46 For Rosenstock-Huessy's discussion of Schlegel, see esp. *Die europäischen Revolutionen*, 432–3. For Rosenstock-Huessy, if Hegel's sin was to sacrifice the colourful, complex world of reality to the grey simplicity of logic, Schlegel's was to have sacrificed his dream of a humanity united by history to a particular realm that was somehow supposed to embody it. Idolatry in both cases. In *Out of Revolution*, Schlegel and Hegel are both treated more kindly, I suspect because to an American audience in 1938, neither name meant much at all.

47 Rosenstock-Huessy, *Die europäischen Revolutionen*, 430.

48 Ibid., 430.

49 Ibid., 431.

50 Eugen Rosenstock-Huessy, *Die Hochzeit des Kriegs und der Revolution* (Würzburg: Patmos, 1920), 8.

51 Ibid., 9.

52 *Gritli Briefe*, 11 September 1917.

53 That is, Germany and Austro-Hungary.

54 Rosenstock-Huessy, *Die europäischen Revolutionen*, 434–5.

11. Beyond the Idol of Art, Part 1: Rosenzweig and the Role of Art in Redemption

1 Not Book XI, as Findlay's translation of the *Encyclopedia* wrongly has it. The citation is important because it so powerfully demonstrates the arc that reaches from Aristotle (and before him Parmenides and Plato) to Hegel. Note that *nous* and *noesis* can be translated as 'mind,' 'reason,' 'thought,' or 'intelligence,' hence the cognitive distinctions that take on such importance for the moderns are not yet differentiated by the ancients. 'And thinking in itself deals with that which is best in itself, and that which is thinking in the fullest sense with that which is best in the fullest sense. And thought thinks on itself because it shares the nature of the object of thought; for it becomes an object of thought in coming into contact with and thinking its objects, so that thought and object of thought are the same. For that which is capable of receiving the object of thought, i.e. the essence, is thought. But it is active when it possesses this object. Therefore the possession rather than the receptivity is the divine element which thought seems to contain, and the act of contemplation is what is most pleasant and best. If, then, God is always in that good state in which we sometimes are, this compels our wonder; and if in a better one this compels it yet more. And God is in a better state. And life also belongs to God; for the actuality of thought is life, and God is that actuality; and God's self-dependent actuality is life most good and eternal. We say therefore that God is a living being, eternal, most good, so that life and duration continuous and eternal belong to God; for this is God' (1072b-18–30); translated by W.D. Ross.

2 See 'General Observation on the Whole System,' in F.W.G. Schelling, *System of Transcendental Idealism* (1800), trans. Peter Heath (Charlottesville: University Press of Virginia, 1978), 233.

3 Friedrich Nietzsche, 'Reason in Philosophy,' in *Twilight of the Idols,* in *The Portable Nietzsche,* trans. Walter Kaufmann (New York: Viking, 1968), section 5.

4 See Josef Chytry, *The Aesthetic State: A Quest in Modern German Thought* (Berkeley: University of California Press, 1989); and J.M. Bernstein, *The Fate of Art: Aesthetic Alienation from Kant to Derrida and Adorno* (Cambridge: Polity Press, 1992). Note Bernstein: 'Art and politics are one: this speculative and apoeitic proposition is the volitional analogue of Adorno's governing speculative proposition that art and philosophy are one,' 273. Note also that Chytry's work bridges art and the state, whereas Bernstein's betrays the neo-Hegelian thrust of so much twentieth-century radical social theory, which sees the state as part of the problem but

nevertheless remains committed to an aesthetic politics. For Rosenzweig, this valorization of art and politics is the result of people being forced to embrace the phantasmic because there is nothing substantial for them to hang on to and embrace.

5 Menke perfectly albeit unintentionally expresses its promise and dead end: 'Art is not sovereign in that it tears down the boundaries separating aesthetic and nonaesthetic experience, thereby proving itself to be the direct overcoming of reason. It is instead sovereign in that, as a discourse of merely particular validity, it represents a crisis for our functioning discourses. The aporias of the traditional romantic view of the sovereignty of art can only be resolved by combining two theses: (1) the subversion rather than the overcoming of reason; and (2) the thesis, which can be found in Adorno, that it is not the contents but the effects, consequences, or repercussions of art that are the foundations of this critique. Taken together, these two claims outline an understanding of aesthetic sovereignty – as an aesthetic generated critique of reason – that not only does not violate the autonomy of the enactment of aesthetic experience, but is actually premised upon it.' Christophe Menke, *The Sovereignty of Art*, trans. Neil Solomon (Cambridge, MA: MIT Press, 1998), xiii.

6 Franz Rosenzweig, *The Star of Redemption*, trans. Barbara E. Galli (Madison: University of Wisconsin Press, 2005), 158.

7 Ibid., 159.

8 Ibid., 159.

9 Ibid., 205.

10 Ibid., 209.

11 Ibid., 382.

12 'Anleitung zum jüdischen Denken,' in Franz Rosenzweig, *Zweistromland, Gesammelte Schriften*, Bd 3, 615. The translation is found in Leora Batnitzky, *Idolatry and Representation: The Philosophy of Franz Rosenzweig Reconsidered* (Princeton: Princeton University Press, 2000), 100. Chapter 4 of that work provides a good account of Rosenzweig and art.

13 Rosenzweig, *The Star of Redemption*, 375.

14 Ibid., 376.

15 Ibid., 262.

16 Ibid., 312.

17 Thus, for example, 'Rosenzweig provides us with what we might term a "philosophical mystical" doctrine.' Kenneth Hart Green, 'The Notion of Truth in Franz Rosenzweig's *The Star of Redemption:* A Philosophical Inquiry,' *Modern Judaism* 7, no. 3 (1987): 297–323 at 318.

18 Rosenzweig, *The Star of Redemption*, 223.

19 Ibid., 209.

20 Ibid., 209.
21 Ibid., 209–10.
22 Ibid., 262–3.
23 Ibid., 263.
24 One cannot help but see the parallels with Plato, who belittles epic and tragic and dramatic poetry in comparison with the great new example of spiritual expression – his own dialogues.
25 Rosenzweig, *The Star of Redemption*, 263.
26 Ibid., 263.
27 Ibid., 265.
28 Ibid., 266.
29 Ibid., 219.
30 Ibid., 219.
31 Ibid., 269.
32 Ibid., 312.
33 Ibid., 323–4 and 361–2.
34 Ibid., 363.
35 Ibid., 376.
36 Ibid., 378.
37 Ibid., 378.
38 Ibid., 383.
39 Ibid., 393.
40 Ibid., 394.
41 Ibid., 395. Actually, this is not true of churches outside Europe. I have witnessed the most extraordinary dancing in a Catholic Philippine church.
42 Ibid., 395.
43 Ibid., 395.
44 Ibid., 399.
45 Ibid., 399–400.
46 Ibid., 400.

12. Beyond the Idol of Art, Part 2: Rosenstock-Huessy and Art in Service to Revolution

1 Microfilm: 'Lingo of Linguistics,' 1966, reel 18, item 654, pages 21 and 22.
2 Eugen Rosenstock-Huessy, *Soziologie*, Bd 2: *Die Vollzahl der Zeiten* (Stuttgart: W. Kohlhammer Verlag, 1958), 313.
3 For the Wilder quote, see microfilm: 'Greek Philosophy,' 1956, reel 16, item 641, page 9. In this lecture he says that 'unfortunately today the best things are only in poetry, not in philosophy.' The following citations from

the lectures are telling enough about his taste and his reasons: 'If *Mourning Becomes Electra* is the expression of our time, gentlemen, I certainly have for the last 40 years nothing to do with it. I have always tried to write off *The Decline of the West*. This happened when I was born, so to speak, *The Decline of the West*. But you still eat it all up. You read Proust, and – and you read O'Neill . . . And – James Joyce and – and all these assassinations of the corpse of Western man, because there's no epics, there's no drama, and there's no lyrics in all this. It's just all analysis.' Microfilm: 'Circulation of Thought,' 1954, reel 16, item 634, page 21. And this: 'You must find heroes from Greek tragedy, or from Shakespeare, or from Goethe, or from Dostoevski to work with. And it won't be Mr. Kafka, either. But you are in such an all-time low, gentlemen, that you are no longer . . . able . . . to feel this electrifying power . . . to be exposed to somebody like Dante.' Microfilm: 'Universal History,' 1957, reel 17, item 643, page 19. On Proust he is more conciliatory in *Out of Revolution: Autobiography of Western Man* (Norwich: Argo Books, 1993; Providence: Berg Publishers, 1993); see 238f, 246f, and 474. But in 'Die Gesetze der christlichen Zeitrechnung' (microfilm: reel 18, item 660, page 250), he despairs of modern literature and mentions Flaubert, Proust, Wilde, and Poe as examples of how sick the nineteenth century is. In his 'Lectures on Greek Philosophy,' however, he says, 'Who is Proust? I do not care for his book. But I do very much care that such men like Proust still exist who say something different.' What he really could not stand was the idea of the author as hero, and of aesthetics as a primary factor in assessing the truth of something. Microfilm: 'Greek Philosophy,' 1956, reel 16, item 641, page 23.

4 Rosenstock-Huessy, *Out of Revolution*, 98.

5 Ibid., 98.

6 Eugen Rosenstock-Huessy, *Die Sprache des Menschengeschlechts: Eine leibhaftige Grammatik in vier Teilen* (Heidelberg: Lambert Schneider, 1963–4), I:24.

7 Rosenstock-Huessy, *Out of Revolution*, 162.

8 Thus in *Out of Revolution*, he writes: 'An American statesman, defying Europe and European imperialism, exclaimed: "Happy the country that has no history. America has not much of it, and should try to have even less." He was a man who had come from Europe and with ardent love had adopted the new world as his country. He is seconded by a modern sophisticate of infinite timeliness, the hero of Joyce's *Ulysses*, who exclaims: "History is the nightmare from which I will awake." These words may help us to decipher the prehistoric of the modern masses. They don't bother about Church and State. The monotony of their life is not to be

interrupted by crusades of the soul or reforms of the mind. They long for the ritual of a primitive clan.' Ibid., 118–19. See also microfilm: 'Universal History,' 1957, reel 17, item 643, page 10.

9 Ibid., 9.
10 Eugen Rosenstock-Huessy, *Soziologie*, Bd 1: *Die Übermacht der Räume* (Stuttgart: W. Kohlhammer Verlag, 1956), 100.
11 Eugen Rosenstock-Huessy, *Soziologie*, Bd 2: *Die Vollzahl der Zeiten* (Stuttgart: W. Kohlhammer Verlag, 1958), 216.
12 Ibid., 507.
13 Ibid., 409, 505, 508.
14 Ibid., 507.
15 Microfilm: 'The Artist and His Community,' 1940, reel 7, item 333, page 18.
16 Cf. microfilm: 'Cross of Reality,' 1953, reel 15, item 630, page 1. Here Rosenstock-Huessy is specifically talking about literature, and specifically about Homer; but as will be clear from what follows, it fits his view of all important art.
17 Rosenstock-Huessy, *Out of Revolution*, 436.
18 Rosenstock-Huessy, *Die Sprache des Menschengeschlechts*, II:773.
19 Ibid., 776.
20 Rosenstock-Huessy, *Soziologie*, Bd 2, 212.
21 Ibid., 216.
22 'Gedenken' usually means commemoration or remembrance, but here I think Rosenstock-Huessy is emphasizing more its second-order character, rather than commemoration as such.
23 Rosenstock-Huessy, *Soziologie*, Bd 2, 213.
24 Ibid., 235.
25 Ibid., 481.
26 Ibid., 483.
27 Ibid., 234.
28 Ibid., 215.
29 Ibid., 224.
30 Ibid., 497.
31 Ibid., 498.
32 Ibid., 217.
33 Ibid., 217.
34 Ibid., 219.
35 'All art of the poet involves producing a short time which effects endlessly.' Ibid., 253.
36 Ibid., 223ff.

37 Ibid., 213. Of course, the same accusation can be made against the Christian view of life. But Rosenstock-Huessy would argue that Christianity, as an historical force, is rarely a pure form, and that its uniqueness lies in universalizing neighbourly love and redemption, and that where it has been successful in its undertaking and true to its mission it has been open to the Other as a divine creature. That is why, for him, the Christian mission is not about destroying other life ways, but rather about salvaging them in the context of a universal future peace.

38 Ibid., 213, 222.

39 Ibid., 213, 228.

40 Ibid., 213, 225.

41 Ibid., 213, 226. Rosenstock-Huessy's thinking here seems to reflect Rosenzweig's on the association between the indefinite 'something' and the mathematical view of reality.

42 Ibid., 213, 225.

43 Ibid., 213, 221.

44 Ibid., 213, 235.

45 Ibid., 213, 244ff, and *The Next Homer*.

46 Microfilm: 'Mad Economics or Polyglot Peace,' 1944, reel 7, item 384, page 24.

47 Rosenstock-Huessy, *Soziologie*, Bd 2, 249.

48 Rosenstock-Huessy, *Soziologie*, Bd 2, 212–49.

49 Rosenstock-Huessy, *Out of Revolution*, 509.

50 Ibid., 506.

51 Ibid., 500–1.

52 Ibid., 500–1.

53 'Protestants and Dante's Christians easily meet. They are not in a deadly opposition. The very existence of the imperial period of Christianity prevented – in Luther's days – the Reformation from destroying the unit of our faith totally and forever. For Roman Catholicism contained many more layers than popery against which Luther raged, and especially a strong imperial and monastic admixture' Ibid., 514.

54 Ibid., 507.

55 Ibid., 508.

56 Note here and elsewhere that where Rosenstock-Huessy pauses on 'holy days,' he is engaging in what he had so early in his career announced as the 'calendar method.' A new innovation or victory is ensconced in time for future generations to commemorate the fact that a new direction in the human journey has been marked. Of course, generations later, many, perhaps all, the journeyers will have forgotten the 'why' of their holiday

(even the word we use to designate the rest day from the normal rhythms of time has its Jewish/Christian resonances). Rosenstock-Huessy uses calendars the way a forensic scientist reconstructs an event out of residual materials.

57 Ibid., 506.
58 Ibid., 505.
59 Ibid., 507.
60 Ibid., 509.
61 Ibid., 509.
62 Ibid., 508.
63 Ibid., 510.
64 Ibid., 511.
65 Ibid., 509.
66 Ibid., 534.
67 Ibid., 512.
68 Ibid., 517.
69 Ibid., 517.
70 Ibid., 518.
71 Ibid., 518–19.
72 Ibid., 527.
73 Ibid., 528.
74 Ibid., 548. Every visitor to the Renaissance wing of a European art gallery or Renaissance church can see the great faith and hope that was invested in this Mother when surveying seemingly endless depictions of the Holy mother and child. Jörg Traeger's *Renaissance und Religion: Die Kunst des Glaubens im Zeitalter Raphaels* (München: C.H. Beck, 1997) does not mention Rosenstock-Huessy, but it makes an independent and thorough case for he argument developed by Rosenstock-Huessy regarding the revolutionary role played by the Church in the thirteenth and fourteenth centuries and the role of art in representing that revolution. Just like Rosenstock-Huessy, Traeger emphasizes that the interpretation of the Renaissance as primarily a pagan reaction against the Church (as argued by, for example, Burckhardt and Nietzsche) finds itself utterly contradicted by the overwhelming evidence of the great majority of examples of Renaissance art. The point both he and Rosenstock-Huessy emphasize is that the internal revolutionary agenda came from within the Church itself – the mother, represented in all these paintings, giving birth to the new child who is open to the earth.
75 Ibid., 573ff.
76 Ibid., 577ff.
77 Ibid., 584ff.

78 Ibid., 528.
79 Ibid., 551.
80 Ibid., 550.
81 Ibid., 552.
82 Ibid., 575.
83 Ibid., 576.
84 Ibid., 577.
85 Ibid., 577.
86 Ibid., 578–80.
87 Ibid., 585.
88 Ibid., 592.
89 Ibid., 587.
90 Ibid., 583–4.
91 Ibid., 586.
92 See *Paradiso*, XII, 140–1.
93 Margaret Reeves, *The Influence of Prophecy in the Later Middle Ages: A Study in Joachism* (Oxford: Clarendon, 1969), 3.
94 One should also note that Joachim's deep hostility to religious literalism, as opposed to seeing religion as a stock of symbols for making sense of and giving orientation to life on earth, makes him a precursor of Rosenstock-Huessy and Rosenzweig. As Bernard McGinn says, 'for the abbot of Fiore the list of history's villains is nothing else than the sum total of literalist exegesis.' *The Calabrian Abbot: Joachim of Fiore and the History of Western Thought* (New York: Macmillan, 1985), 126.
95 Rosenstock-Huessy, *Out of Revolution*, 586–7.
96 Ibid., 597–8.
97 Ibid., 297.
98 Percy Scholes, *Music and Puritanism: With an Appendix on Dancing and Puritanism* (Vevey: Sauberlin & Pfeiffer, 1934).
99 Ibid., 420.
100 Ibid., 417–18.
101 Ibid., 363.
102 Ibid., 414.
103 Ibid., 414. It is true, of course, that Hegel argued a similar point about the connection between German philosophy and the Reformation.
104 Ibid., 420–1.
105 Ibid., 421.
106 Ibid., 442ff. Rosenstock-Huessy also investigates Germany's exaltation of the State and Hitler as a 'religious' phenomenon in the context of the German Reformation. He sees Hitler as a throwback to the pre-Reformation type – as the result of the disappearance of 'High Magistrates,' men who

were called upon in their daily work to profess their faith before God. The three greatest achievements of Germany – its civil service, its universities, and its music – had all been sacrificed on the religion of race.

107 Ibid., 424–5.

108 Ibid., 432.

109 Ibid., 432.

110 Ibid., 433.

111 Ibid., 432.

112 Ibid., 434.

113 Ibid., 434.

114 Ibid., 436.

115 Ibid., 183.

116 Ibid., 169.

117 Ibid., 171.

118 Ibid., 174–5.

119 Ibid., 126.

120 Ibid., 175.

121 Ibid., 176.

122 Ibid., 198–9.

123 Ibid., 178.

124 One should emphasize here that Rosenstock-Huessy's statement is neither polemical nor apologetic. His analysis of the term 'Europe' is thoroughly philological, based merely on his attentiveness to its discursive deployment throughout the last millennium.

125 Ibid., 147.

126 Ibid., 199.

127 Ibid., 248.

128 Cf. Vercors's comparison of German musicians and French writers in *Le silence de la mer*.

129 Rosenstock-Huessy, *Out of Revolution*, 170.

130 Ibid., 250.

131 Rosenstock-Huessy often refers to modern men and women being bundles of nerves. In his 'Liturgical Thinking,' he provides an early example of the use of the term 'postmodern' as he makes an interesting comparison between 'postmodern man' and the 'person' of the Reformation: '"Postmodern" man differs widely from the men of the Renaissance, viz are analyzed as bundles of nerves. Schizophrenia is rampant. We are torn and often we break down. In 1500, every layman claimed to be a "person." Before, "person" in canon law meant a dignitary, a bishop perhaps, or an abbot, or a princely person. Persons had status and authority. They

had something to say, to administer, to answer for. A person was always responsible for a functioning part of the whole community, he held an office of some kind.' Microfilm: 'Liturgical Thinking,' 1949, reel 8, item 424, page 1. Deleuze and Guattari's description of the modern condition in *Capitalism and Schizophrenia* is, I think, identical to Rosenstock-Huessy's. But unlike Rosenstock-Huessy, they see no choice but to fight it on its own mechanistic terms; thus they seek a flight in a positive form of schizophrenia. Their decision and hence the models of 'self' and 'society' they work with suggest to me how deeply imbued they are in the French tradition.

132 Rosenstock-Huessy, *Out of Revolution*, 251–2.
133 Ibid., 129.
134 Ibid., 246.
135 Ibid., 245.
136 Ibid., 54, 212–13.
137 Ibid., 94.
138 Ibid., 54.
139 Ibid., 53.
140 Ibid., 54.
141 Ibid., 54.
142 Ibid., 55.
143 Ibid., 57.
144 Ibid., 59.
145 Ibid., 58.
146 Ibid., 59.
147 Ibid., 59.
148 Ibid., 91.
149 Ibid., 91.
150 Ibid., 92–3.
151 Ibid., 94.
152 Ibid., 115.

13. Beyond the Prophets of Modernity: Rosenstock-Huessy and Rosenzweig on Nietzsche and Marx

1 It is noteworthy that when Leninism, Stalinism, and Maoism were still revolutionary forces, references to 'the new socialist man' were commonplace in communist discourses. But since Marx has become more strictly an academic prerogative, such incarnatory aspirations have completely disappeared from those who still deploy Marx. Instead, those who

summon his name have returned to the far more 'Greek'/philosophical activity of ethical politics. Jacques Derrida's belated decision to engage with Marx in *Specters of Marx*, after the fall of the Soviet Union, was widely welcomed, especially by his North American and British academic supporters. Particularly revealing about *Specters* was that Marx had been marshalled into the project of seeking justice. Derrida had succeeded in fusing politics with ethics by associating Marx with Levinas; yet he totally ignored the fact that Marx had fought bitterly against those who wanted to interpret his work or the communist movement in those terms. Indeed, it is hard to imagine any social philosopher writing a book on Marx so wilfully contrary to Marx's method and explicit intentions. Nevertheless, the same fate that befell Marx more or less befell Nietzsche. Nietzsche's enormous popularity in the latter part of the twentieth century, especially among North American and French social theorists, had nothing to do with his overt political project (which had been a major part of early-twentieth-century discourse, during which his legacy was divided mainly among artists – especially Expressionists, Dadaists and Surrealists – and fascists and Nazis). The North American reading of Nietzsche, following Walter Kaufmann's politically innocuous and often highly dubious renditions of Nietzsche to make him palatable to a post–Second World War North American readership, has with one or two exceptions seemed wilfully blind to Nietzsche's importance to the Nazi project of creating supermen. Kaufman correctly brought out Nietzsche's hatred of anti-Semites, but his claim that Nietzsche was systematically abused and misread by the Nazis is hardly convincing when one reads someone like Bauemler, who was a Nazi but not a philosophical dunce. Had it not been for his political allegiances, Bauemler's book on Kant's *Critique of Judgment* would still count as a crucial contribution to scholarship. Kaufmann confuses quality of mind with quality of soul.

2 Karl Marx and Friedrich Nietzsche kept the flames of eschatology alive.' Eugen Rosenstock-Huessy, *The Christian Future – or the Modern Mind Outrun*, intro. Harold Stahmer (New York: Harper and Row, [1947]1966), 70.

3 The term 'Age' has many associations. I think that one of the most important for this book is 'seniority.'

4 Eugen Rosenstock-Huessy with Joseph Wittig, *Das Alter der Kirche. Kapitel und Akten*. 3 Bde (Münster: Agenda, 1998), I:57–8, 62.

5 Ibid., 58.

6 Ibid., 59.

7 Nahum Glatzer, *Franz Rosenzweig: His Life and Thought* (Indianapolis: Hackett, 1998), 5.

8 Franz Rosenzweig, *The Star of Redemption*, trans. Barbara E. Galli (Madison: University of Wisconsin Press, 2005), 9. *The Star*'s section on Nietzsche does little more than repeat Rosenzweig's earliest impressions of Nietzsche – that his uniqueness was his unity, and it was *his*.

9 Letter to Gertrude Oppenheim, 27 August 1918, in Glatzer, *Franz Rosenzweig*, 81.

10 Richard Cohen, *Elevations: The Height of the Good in Rosenzweig and Levinas* (Chicago: University of Chicago Press, 1994), 87–8.

11 Rosenzweig, *The Star of Redemption*, 304.

12 Ibid., 18.

13 Ibid., 18.

14 See, especially, Friedrich Nietzsche, *The Anti-Christ*, in *The Portable Nietzsche*, trans. Walter Kaufmann (New York: Viking, 1968), section 60: 'Really there should not be any choice between Islam and Christianity, any more than between an Arab and a Jew.'

15 An English translation of the conclusion can be found in Franz Rosenzweig, *Philosophical and Theological Writings*, trans. Paul Franks and Michael Morgan (Indianapolis: Hackett Publishing, 2000), 76. See also Rosenzweig, *Hegel und der Staat* (Munich: R. Oldenbourg, 1920; reprint Aalen: Scientia, 1962), II:200ff. Cf. Wolfgang Ullmann, 'The Discovery of the New Thinking: The Leipzig Conversation on Religion and the Correspondence between Eugen Rosenstock and Franz Rosenzweig about Judaism and Christianity,' in *The Cross and the Star: The Post-Nietzschean Christian and Jewish Thought of Eugen Rosenstock-Huessy and Franz Rosenzweig*, ed. Wayne Cristaudo and Frances Huessy (Newcastle upon Tyne: Cambridge Scholars Publishing, 2009).

16 Of the numerous problems that confronted Marx's prophecies, the one that would have by far the most impact in helping generate its opposite was Marx's short-sightedness regarding the nation. This lack of understanding of the myth of the nation – as Mussolini would call it – would be decisive for Mussolini, as well as for other Italian Marxists and anarcho-syndicalists who followed him, as they invented a new political movement. The real moment of truth for Marx's claim that class interests are more powerful than national differences came when the working classes of Europe supported war, often with great enthusiasm. The Austrian Marxist Otto Bauer had sought to salvage Marx; and Rosenstock-Huessy in his 1914 lecture series 'State Theory of the Present' discussed Bauer's contribution to Marxism. Microfilm: 'Vorlesungen Staatstheorien der Gegenwart,' 2nd and 3rd series, 1914, reel 1, item 26, page 6.

17 Rosenzweig, *Hegel und der Staat*, II:201–2.

18 Ibid., 186.

19 Franz Rosenzweig, *Gesammelte Schriften*, III. *Zweistromland. Kleinere Schriften zu Glauben und Denken*, ed. Reinhold Meyer and Annemarie Mayer (Dordrecht: Martinus Nijhoff, 1984), 565.

20 'Our religion becomes once again history; our faith becomes once again man, his will and activity.' And on the same page he calls on those 'socialists . . . who have a living faith.' Pedro Cavalcanti and Paul Piccone, eds., *History, Philosophy, and Culture in the Young Gramsci* (St Louis: Telos Press), 70.

21 Rosenzweig, *Gesammelte Schriften*, III. *Zweistromland*, 83.

22 Franz Rosenzweig, *Gesammelte Schriften*, Bd 1: *Briefe und Tagebücher*, ed. Rachel Rosenzweig und Edith Rosenzweig-Scheinmann (The Hague: Martinus Nijhoff, 1979), 153.

23 I argued this at agonizing length in my PhD, submitted to the University of Adelaide in 1988: 'The Metaphysics of Science and Freedom: Shifting Scopes in the Foundations of Descartes, Kant, Hegel and Marx.'

24 Franz Rosenzweig, *Understanding the Sick and the Healthy: A View of World, Man, and God*, ed. and trans. Nahum N. Glatzer (Cambridge, MA: Harvard University Press, 1999), 57.

25 Rosenzweig, *The Star of Redemption*, 289–90.

26 At Four Wells there is an interesting letter by Tillich, who is somewhat surprised by the high esteem Rosenstock-Huessy had for Nietzsche, indicative I think of how tainted Nietzsche had become through his Nazi reception. Tillich, 25 March 1944*.

27 'The End of the World, or When Theology Slept' in *The Cross and the Star*, 5–6. See also microfilm: 1941, reel 7, item 356, pages 2–3.

28 'Nietzsche's Untimeliness,' in *The Cross and the Star*, 22. See also microfilm: 1942, reel 7, item 370, page 2.

29 Friedrich Nietzsche, *On the Genealogy of Morals* and *Ecce Homo*, in *Basic Writings of Nietzsche*, trans. Walter Kaufmann (New York: Vintage, 1989), 54, para. 17.

30 'Nietzsche's Untimeliness,' *The Cross and the Star*, 23. See also microfilm: 1942, reel 7, item 356, page 3.

31 Microfilm: 'Nietzscheana,' 1942, reel 7, item 369, page 16.

32 'Nietzsche's Untimeliness,' in *The Cross and the Star*, 24.

33 Microfilm: 'Nietzscheana,' 1942, reel 7, item 369, page 15.

34 Ibid., page 1.

35 Eugen Rosenstock-Huessy, *Soziologie*, Bd 1: *Die Übermacht der Räume* (Stuttgart: W. Kohlhammer Verlag, 1956), 318. Though I provide

references from this section on Descartes and Nietzsche from the final section of volume 1 of the *Soziologie*, I will use Jurgen Lawrenz's translations, which can be found in Cristaudo and Huessy, eds., *The Cross and the Star.*

36 Ibid., 315.
37 Ibid., 324.
38 Ibid., 325.
39 Ibid., 319.
40 Ibid., 329.
41 Microfilm: 'Four Disangelists,' 1940, reel 16, item 135, lecture 1, page 9.
42 Ibid., II:2. Rosenstock-Huessy speaks with deep affection for a man whom he says (with some exaggeration) that he has never spoken about at length before (by this time he was in his mid-sixties.
43 In *Soziologie*, Bd 1, 303ff, Rosenstock-Huessy devotes a section to 'Sigmund Freud and the Violence of the Times.' For Rosenstock-Huessy, Freud is the last of the individualists whose analysis rests on an attempt to centre and stabilize the ego. In his view, Freud was attempting to reconcile the conflicting forces of the ego, the id, the superego, and the outerworld. What Freud left out, however, was *his own* place in the system – why he was doing what he was doing, why it was important, and what it cost him. That is to say, he did not ask the central question of the New Thinking: Who (or what power) was he responding to by his discovery? This is the central question of scientific incarnation that Rosenstock-Huessy poses in his essay 'Datives Denken' in *Heilkraft und Wahrheit: Konkordanz der Politischen und Kosmischen Zeit* (Moers: Brendow, 1952; Wien: Amandus, 1991), in which he makes this provocative remark: 'Paul is the first normal modern scientist. He knows whom he serves and whom he has believed'; 102. That is to say, all science is developed through successors following in the tracks of and expanding on the truths that the founders of the science they serve have garnered through their original incursions into one part of reality and the sacrifices that have been required to make the incursion. According to Rosenstock-Huessy, Freud as a founder of psychoanalysis had undertaken a great act of incursion, but his own treatment of the soul did not disclose the very act of his own and his successors' very existence. Again, this is yet one more symptom of the modern failure to appreciate time's role in our incarnatory acts.
44 Eugen Rosenstock-Huessy, *Soziologie*, Bd 2: *Die Vollzahl der Zeiten* (Stuttgart: W. Kohlhammer Verlag, 1958), 20.
45 Ibid., 17–18.
46 Ibid., 258.

47 Rosenstock-Huessy, 'Four Disangelists.' See also his 'Unser Zeitpunkt (Nach Darwin, Marx, Freud und Nietzsche)' in *Soziologie*, Bd 2, 13–20.

48 Rosenstock-Huessy, 'Four Disangelists,' page 8.

49 Ibid., 1:15.

50 Ibid., 2:6.

51 See 'The Soul of William James,' in Eugen Rosenstock-Huessy, *I Am an Impure Thinker*, ed. Freya von Moltke and Clint Gardner (Norwich: Argo Books, 1970).

52 Ibid., 2:19.

53 Ibid., 2:2.

54 Ibid.

55 Eugen Rosenstock-Huessy, *Out of Revolution: Autobiography of Western Man* (Norwich: Argo Books, 1993; Providence: Berg Publishers, 1993), 464–5.

56 Ibid., 732.

57 Ibid., 736.

58 Ibid., 73.

59 Ibid., 75.

60 Ibid., 184.

61 Ibid., 88.

62 According to Marx, developed capitalist economies are instead driven by the increased circulation of commodities over time (what he calls 'relative surplus value') and by the broadening markets that result. The increase in relative surplus value is ultimately caused by the requirement that labour displace technology. For Marx, this requirement is what portends the 'logical' end of capitalism. For (and this is sheer scholastism) commodity production depends on surplus value, which is provided solely by labour power supplied by living workers, whereas labour technology is the storing of 'dead labour.' Thus he argues that the accumulation of displaced living labour will inevitably bring about a revolutionary consciousness owing to the absolute poverty of those who have been dispossessed; not only that, but falling profits (a result of the dependency on labour-saving technology, which cannot generate sufficient surplus value, dependent as that is on living labour power) will cause another crisis in the endless boom-and-bust cycle that charactizes capitalism, which in turn will lead to a collapse from which capitalism cannot recover. This theory is contained in embryo in Marx's pre-economic work of 1843, 'A Contribution to a Critique of Hegel's Philosophy of Right: Introduction,' but Marx did not complete it until the volume 3 of *Capital*, in which he spelled out the 'law' of the falling rate of profit.

63 Ibid., 88.

64 Ibid., 89. He cites Rosa Luxemburg: 'Capitalism is the first form of economy with the powers of propaganda, a form with the tendency to expand over all the earth and to eliminate other forms of production. At the same time, it is the first economy which cannot exist without using the other forms as its alimentary soil and milieu.'

65 Ibid., 89–90.

66 Nicos Poulantzas, *Fascism and Dictatorship: The Third International and the Problem of Fascism* (London: New Left Books, 1974), is the classic Marxist study of fascism. Neither nationalism nor ideology is seriously examined in Poulantzas's study. Rather, his interest lies in the mechanical push and pull of class forces. Many Marxists objected to the structural Marxism represented by Poulantzas and his teacher Althusser, maintaining that they had erased agency from the equation in a way that Marx had not. Far more compelling, but also far less rigid in its Marxism, is Franz Neumann's study of the Nazi state, *Behemoth: The Structure and Practice of National Socialism, 1933–1944* (Lanham: Ivan R. Dee, [1944]2009).

67 Marx also makes the interesting point that the rich have practically abolished religion for themselves insofar as they are indifferent to God. And that one only recommends belief in God to those who lack the divinities of art and science. Hence the proletariat must be atheist in order to resist the 'opiate' of the religion on offer in the bourgeois world. See Eugen Rosenstock-Hueassy, *Die europäischen Revolutionen und der Charakter der Nationen*, rev. ed. (Moers: Brendow Verlag, 1961), 458.

68 Ibid., 460.

69 Ibid., 461.

70 Rosenstock-Huessy, *Das Alte der Kirche*, 56.

71 Rosenstock-Huessy, 'Four Disangelists,' pages 11–13. Rosenstock-Huessy sees no contradiction between this request of Proudhon's and what he says about war elsewhere. That is because Rosenstock-Huessy's thought shares the same paradoxical relationship to violence and revolution – there are times when it is inescapable and then one must adapt without hatred of the enemy to the severity of the task at hand. But that is very different from developing a doctrine based on the idea of the necessity of war *against* a group (the ruling class), or nations, or race etc.

72 Rosenstock-Huessy, 'Four Disangelists,' page 16.

73 Eugen Rosenstock-Huessy, 'Revolution, Soziologie, und Universität,' *Werbeheft* (W. Kohlhammer Verlag, 1960), 3–11. See also 'An die Russen. Naturforschung oder Gesellschaftslehre?' and 'Die Fortschritte der

Gesellschaft und die Soziologie,' *Frankfurter Hefte* (1959), on microfilm: reel 10, item 518, page 5.

14. Rosenzweig on Why Allah Is Not Yahweh, the Loving, Revealing, Redeeming God

1 A different version of the material used in this chapter can be found in my own 'Franz Rosenzweig's "Troubling" Critique of Islam,' *Rosenzweig Jahrbuch*, Bd 2 (Freiburg: Karl Alber, 2007), 43–86. In that same volume, Gesine Palmer has written a response to my article. I appreciate and am flattered by her critical tribute; even so, I think her piece misses the essential point, for she is adopting what is now the conventional 'liberal' academic position, which focuses less on Islamic texts and real history and states and more on the dangers that threaten if people fan the flames of intercultural hatred. I do not dispute that this is a serious concern and that adopting such a position involves certain moral commitments and decisions that are worth taking seriously. But it bypasses the real problem of values that unequivocally are not only different but also conflicting. Instead of commencing with the real differences and thinking about what can be done to address them, one sets up a smokescreen of pretended unity. For any genuine dialogue to take place, genuine differences and areas that cannot be compromised must be discussed. My problem with radical liberal (post-Rousseauian) politics is that they repeat Rousseau's basic error – they assume a harmony that must in fact be created. And the great problem confronting us all today is how we can produce a concordance that does not yet exist.

2 Besides my piece, there are three notable exceptions. The first two are Matthias Lehmann, 'Franz Rosenzweig's Kritik des Islams im *Stern der Erlösung*,' *Jewish Studies Quarterly* 1, no. 4 (1993–4): 340–68; and Spengler, 'Franz Rosenzweig and the Abrahamic Religions,' *First Things: The Journal of Religion, Culture, and Public Life*, October 2007, http://www.firstthings. com/article.php3?id_article = 5428, also published in Wayne Cristaudo and Frances Huessy, eds., *The Cross and the Star: The Post-Nietzschean Christian and Jewish Thought of Eugen Rosenstock-Huessy and Franz Rosenzweig* (Newcastle upon Tyne: Cambridge Scholars Publishing, 2009). But by far the best essay on Islam and Rosenzweig that I am aware of is one that compares Rosenzweig with Rosenstock-Huessy in terms of how they differ on Islam: Georg Müller, 'From the Star of Redemption to the Cross of Reality,' in *The Cross and the Star*, 49–71. More typical comments include these: Peter Elli Gordon's aside in 'Rosenzweig Redux: The Reception of German-Jewish Thought,' *Jewish Social Studies* 8, no. 1,

http://www.iupress.indiana.edu/journals/jss/jss8–1.html: 'I leave aside the troublesome fact that Rosenzweig's "pluralism" appears to exclude Islam'; and Michael Oppenheim's foreword to Barbara Galli's translation of *The Star of Redemption* (Madison: University of Wisconsin Press, 2005), where he writes: 'There are passing gratuitous comments on Indian and Chinese religions, [and] disparaging appraisals about Islam,' xiii. For Robert Gibbs, Rosenzweig's 'constant use of Islam in Part II reflects an embarrassing prejudice.' According to him, Rosenzweig 'has not taken history half seriously enough.' Gibbs, *Correlations in Rosenzweig and Levinas* (Princeton: Princeton University Press, 1992), 113. Gibbs then goes on to discuss Rosenzweig's historiographical method. The charge of historical ineptness is, Gibbs suggests, supposedly an open-and-shut case. Yet astonishingly, he does not deal with any of Rosenzweig's specific claims, which he claims can be refuted by historical evidence; nor does he devote any time to Islamic history. Then there are lengthier attempts to address this supposed prejudice of Rosenzweig's, the most significant being Gesine Palmer, 'Vorwort' and Yossef Schwartz's 'Nachwort' to their edition of his writings on Islam, *Innerlich bleibt die Welt eine: Franz Rosenzweig, Ausgewaehlte Schriften zum Islam* (Berlin: Philo, 2003). Despite the length of the essays, their responses and silences are the same as those of the other critics mentioned above. Schwartz's afterword follows Shlomo Pines's 'Der Islam im "Stern der Erlösung"' in *Eine Untersuchung zu Tendenzen und Quellen Franz Rosenzweigs*, in *Hebräische Beiträge zur Wissenschaft des Judentums*, 3–5 (1987–9): 138–48, in its claim that Rosenzweig has simply regurgitated Hegel and not looked first-hand at the evidence. (Pines's piece is cited widely by Rosenzweig's critics, but always to make the same point about Hegel.) None of those who use Pines's work to establish guilt by association show that Hegel, let alone Rosenzweig, is actually wrong. What they are doing is neatly summarized by Spengler in his review of Palmer's and Schwartz's book. Taking as his title a comment by Palmer, 'Oil on the Flames of Civilizational War,' he makes this point: 'Palmer and Schwartz view the text as if it were an unexploded shell left over from World War I, and set out to defuse it. To make a long story short, they reduce Rosenzweig's critique of Islam to a mere philosophical construct, claiming that his philosophical system needed a pigeon-hole for a pagan alternative to Judeo-Christian thought, and he found Islam handy.' http://www.atimes.com/atimes/Front_Page/EL02Aa01.html, 2 December 2003. Yet none of these criticisms engages with what Rosenzweig actually says or why he says it. At a Rosenzweig conference in Jerusalem in October 2006, Schwartz was reported in the *Jerusalem Post* as having said that Rosenzweig had not read any of the *hadith*. The claim has no supporting evidence to justify it; indeed, it flies in the face of Rosenzweig's own account of his reading materials and activities, which included learning Arabic. I find just as fanciful as the claim that Rosenzweig has not read the *hadith*, the implication that if one has read the *hadith* then one would see that Rosenzweig is wrong. As anyone who has looked at the *hadith* knows, most of it concerns specific prescriptions for daily conduct that are based on the prophet's model. But the *hadith* also provides evidence to support Rosenzweig's claim about Islam and Holy War (see the section on *jihad* in Book 4 of *Al Bukhari*), and indeed, the extremely orthodox reading of Islam that he deploys in *The Star*.

3 Franz Rosenzweig to Hans Ehrenberg, 23 February 1917, in *Gesammelte Schriften, I. Briefe und Tagebucher.* Bd 1: 1900–18, ed. Rachel Rosenzweig and Edith Rosenzweig-Scheinmann (The Hague: Martinus Nijhoff, 1979), 353.

4 Not untypical of the genre is Reza Aslan, *No God But God: The Origins, Evolution, and Future of Islam* (London: Arrow, 2005), which renders the pre-Islamic world as a multicultural ideal, while presenting Muhammad's overthrow of that world as an even more liberal act. The term *egalitarian* is central to Aslan's hagiographic narrative. My objection is not that a case cannot be made for the centrality of social justice in Islam – it *is* central – but that the term is highly misleading if it floats too freely without a more thorough explication of the social formation, priorities, and human relationships from which the faith emerges. The importance of the warrior code in Islam is barely touched on by Aslan. Perhaps the most famous North American popularizer of Islam is Karen Armstrong, whose narrative is equally dedicated to eliminating any details that might alert her readers to just how central war was to the sacred founding narrative of Islam. But given that the point of her exercise is to get people to believe that religions are basically all of a piece, this is not surprising.

5 Ignaz Maybaum, in *Trialogue between Jew, Christian, and Muslim* (London: Routledge and Kegan Paul, 1973), takes a much more conciliatory approach. See also his 'Das Gesetz: Franz Rosenzweigs Ringen mit den Jüdischen Traditionen,' *Emuna* 2 (1970): 82–8. He bases his approach on the commonality of monotheism. Rosenzweig, however, holds that 'not Monotheism but the Torah makes the Jews.' Briefe an Gertrud Oppenheim, 30–31 May 1917, *Briefe und Tagebucher.* Bd 1, 414.

6 Franz Rosenzweig, 'New Thinking,' in *Philosophical and Theological Writings,* trans. Paul Franks and Michael Morgan (Indianapolis: Hackett Publishing, 2000), 130–1.

7 See, for example, Jonathon Lyons, *The House of Wisdom: How the Arabs Transformed Western Civilization* (London: Bloomsbury, 2009). Lyons tells

his readers at every opportunity how backward Christian lands and peoples were compared to the civilized Islamic empires. He believes that by arguing along these lines he is refuting those who look down on their Arab neighbours – see especially page 123. He doesn't realize that his emphasis on science, wealth, and power actually leads to the exact opposite conclusion – that is, by his 'logic,' American and European cultures are in fact 'superior' to those which lack their science and technology. Rosenzweig is not interested in such a blatantly materialist scale of values.

8 Franz Rosenzweig, *Gesammelte Schriften*, III. *Zweistromland. Kleinere Schriften zu Glauben und Denken*, ed. Reinhold Meyer and Annemarie Mayer (Dordrecht: Martinus Nijhoff, 1984), 547.

9 See chapter 5 of Jacques Ellul, *The Subversion of Christianity*, trans. Geoffrey W. Bromiley (Grand Rapids: Eerdmans Publishing, 1986).

10 Rosenzweig had made this point in 'Die neue Levante,' in *Gesammelte Schriften*, III. *Zweistromland*, 312.

11 The most even-handed study on this topic is, I think, Mark R. Cohen, *Under the Crescent and the Cross: The Jews in the Middle Ages* (Princeton: Princeton University Press, 1994).

12 This point has been addressed by the Muslim apostate Ibn Warraq, who has adopted a pseudonym as a consequence of death threats he has received for his critiques of Islam. This is all the more interesting when we consider that Warraq is a strong supporter of a rational, scientific approach to life and is genuinely perplexed by why such prominent Enlightened figures have been so supportive of Islam. See Warraq, *Why I Am Not a Muslim* (New York: Prometheus Books, 1995), 17ff. Rosenzweig, I think, answers that question.

13 Franz Rosenzweig,*The Star of Redemption*, trans. Barbara E. Galli (Madison: University of Wisconsin Press, 2005), 128.

14 Ibid., 128.

15 Ibid., 133.

16 Ibid., 134. Of course, the concept of election would also find Christian adherents in Calvinism. This, though, for Rosenzweig only demonstrates how easy it is for Christians to lose sight of revelation.

17 Ibid., 134.

18 Ibid., 180.

19 Ibid., 180.

20 Ibid., 179.

21 Ibid., 231–2.

22 Ibid., 243.

23 Ibid., 179.

24 Ibid., 179.

25 Ibid., 179.
26 Ibid., 232–3.
27 Ibid., 233–4.
28 Spengler, 'Tin-Opener Theology from Turkey,' *Asia Times Online*, 3 June 2008, http://www.atimes.com/atimes/Middle_East/JF03Ak02.html, contains a fascinating discussion of Felix Koerner's appraisal of a theological circle operating out of Ankara University whose members are seeking ways to make Islam compatible with the modern world. Koerner noted that this circle 'subsume[s] the whole of Koranic theology under the single intention of influencing people's behavior. Consequently, they are what should be called ethical reductionis[ts].' See Koerner, *Revisionist Koran Hermeneutics in Contemporary Turkish University Theology: Rethinking Islam* (Wurzburg: Ergon Verlag, 2005), 84. We may add that this is precisely what will have to be to make Islam completely palatable to modern Western sensibilities – unless, of course, Islam succeeds in converting the West away from the ethical sensibility that gives it its present socially 'spiritual' orientation. Spengler also refers to Muhammad Tahir, 'The Pope's Special Forces,' in Ummah Pulse.com, 29 February 2008, http://ummahpulse.com/index.php?option=com_content&task=view&id=345&Itemid=97, which presents a much more orthodox Islamic point of view that is contemptuous of what Koerner and the Ankara circle wish to do. My point is that by far the dominant view on the subject of faith that we find in academic works today is 'ethically reductionist.' The fact is that there are millions upon millions of Jews, Christians, and Muslims who – much to what would have disappointed Kant and the other fathers and followers of the faith of modern humanism – do not subscribe to ethical reductionism. Hence it does little good to treat matters of faith *as if* they could be so reduced. They may be *converted*, but that is a very different matter from being reduced. But the interesting point is that the modern ethical reductionist is reluctant to concede that his or her own faith also is based on the tacit acceptance (a) that conversion is a good thing and (b) that he or she is a proselytiser.

15. Rosenstock-Huessy on Islam, Confucianism, Taoism, and Buddhism

 1 See my own discussion on Munch's 'The Scream' in *Power, Love, and Evil: Contribution to a Philosophy of the Damaged* (New York: Rodopi, 2007), 8. See also Geoffrey Hawthorne's appropriately titled book, *Enlightenment and Despair: A History of Social Theory* (Cambridge: Cambridge University Press, 1987).

2 Eugen Rosenstock-Huessy, *Soziologie,* Bd 2, *Die Vollzahl der Zeiten* (Stuttgart: W. Kohlhammer Verlag, 1958), 209.
3 One recalls the same resort to durability as a demonstration of providence in Dante's argument for Rome's historical importance for salvation in *De Monarchia.*
4 'Islam is, of course, a religion inside our own . . . It tends to restore the true religion to all the faithful. It's a universal religion, in this sense . . . Islam is a part of revealed religion.' Microfilm: 'Comparative Religion,' 1954, reel 15, item 633, page 16.
5 Rosenstock-Huessy, *Soziologie,* Bd 2, 378.
6 Microfilm: 'American Social History,' 1959, reel 17, item 644, page 5.
7 Rosenstock-Huessy, *Soziologie,* Bd 2, 375. Cf. Hugh Kennedy's recent book, *The Great Arab Conquest: How the Spread of Islam Changed the World We Live In* (London: Phoenix Books, 2007), 38: 'In some ways the early Muslim leadership set out to destroy or at least reduce the loyalty to tribe. The Muslim community, the umma, was to be a new sort of tribe, based not on descent but on commitment to the new religion, the acceptance [that] Allah was the one true God and that Muhammad was his prophet.'
8 Rosenstock-Huessy, *Soziologie,* Bd 2, 374.
9 Ibid., 373.
10 Ibid., 373.
11 Ibid., 374.
12 Eugen Rosenstock-Huessy, 'Review of *Henri Pirenne, Mohammed and Charlemagne*' in *The Muslim World* 47 (1967): 74–5. Microfilm: 'Review, Henri Pirenne, Mohammed and Charlemagne,' 1959, reel 10, item 505, pages 1–2.
13 Ibid.
14 Rosenstock-Huessy, *Soziologie,* Bd 2, 155.
15 Nietzsche esteemed Spinoza, and both Bataille and Deleuze esteemed Nietzsche, but Nietzsche's admiration for the aristocracy has no parallels in any of the other three mentioned here. Nietzsche, and again unlike the others mentioned here, thought mainly in terms of cultivating types over time. This is why Deleuze's radical democratic reading of Nietzsche is – to put it mildly – a '68 rewriting of Nietzsche that makes Nietzsche sound far less potent, not to mention dangerous, than he actually is.
16 Rosenstock-Huessy, *Soziologie,* Bd 2, 158.
17 Ibid., 341.
18 In my translation of *Heimat,* I have followed the usage of Australian Aborigines.
19 Ibid., 341.

20 Ibid., 372. In his discussion of the tribes, Rosenstock-Huessy wants, *inter alia*, to dwell on the original pathmakers of life who spread across the earth, the ancestors not just of contemporary tribal peoples but of *all* peoples. Thus he says that 'in truth the entire existence of tribes from beginning to end is the migration of peoples [*Völkerwanderung*].' And 'the most far wandering tribe is the truest tribe.' The indigenous tribes that still exist today have all in some way been curbed by the need for security, compelled to hide themselves from imperial or some other alien encroachment. Ibid., 372. The most awful proof of this is the vulnerability of indigenous peoples when confronted with technically advanced societies. There is nothing Darwinian behind such a statement – on the contrary, the capacity of modern humanity to 'live mechanically' and to surive technology's consequences is a rather dubious and debilitating honour. Sensitivity and vulnerability are not vices, any more than insensitivity and brute survival are virtues.

21 Ibid., 332.

22 Eugen Rosenstock-Huessy, 'Tribalism,' *Exodus Quarterly* 2 (Fall 1959): 9.

23 Rosenstock-Huessy, *Soziologie*, Bd 2, 355–6.

24 Ibid., 356.

25 Microfilm: 'Universal History,' 1954, reel 16, item 637, page 19.

26 Ibid.

27 Microfilm: 'Universal History,' 1957, reel 17, item 643, page 9.

28 Microfilm: 'First Cycle of Letters to Cynthia (Harris),' reel 7, item 378, page 131.

29 Consider the following from his lecture 'American Social History' (microfilm: 1959, reel 17, item 644, page 3): 'I had to listen to a speech the poor Queen Elizabeth II had to make . . . She dared to say to . . . her countrymen, "Let us enjoy our accumulated civilization." Now that's the end of any empire . . . Neither the word "civilization," nor "enjoy," nor "accumulated," . . . is able to hold people together in a panic, and in a fearsome moment. That's the end of the world.'

30 Rosenstock-Huessy, *Soziologie*, Bd 2, 259.

31 Ibid., 374.

32 See the section on stoning in *Al Bukhari,* vol. 8, and note how the prophet insists that punishment must be carried out – on earth Allah's law must prevail over human mercy.

33 Rosenstock-Huessy, *Soziologie*, Bd 2, 375.

34 Ibid., 375.

35 Rosenstock-Huessy is using 'the time' in the sense of a time body.

36 Rosenstock-Huessy, *Soziologie*, Bd 2, 376–7.

37 Ibid., 377.

38 See Hugh Kennedy's citation of Arab leaders thanking Muhammad for how he stopped intertribal fighting and created unity between tribes, in *The Great Arab Conquest*, 47.

39 Rosenstock-Huessy, *Soziologie*, Bd 2, 377.

40 Cf. Toby Huff's discussion of the consequences flowing from the lack of anything resembling a 'neutral space' (or public space akin to what would later be called civil society) in *Islam The Rise of Early Modern Science: Islam, China, and the West* (Cambridge: Cambridge University Press, 1993).

41 Rosenstock-Huessy, *Soziologie*, Bd 2, 378.

42 Ibid., 377.

43 Microfilm: 'American Social History,' 1959, reel 17, item 644, page 5.

44 Rosenstock-Huessy, *Soziologie*, Bd 2, 735.

45 Microfilm: 'American Social History,' 1959, reel 17, item 644, page 13.

46 Microfilm: 'Circulation of Thought,' 1954, reel 1, item 634, page 20.

47 For example, microfilm: 'Greek Philosophy,' 1956, reel 16, item 641, page 15.

48 Microfilm: 'Lectures on Comparative Religion,' 1954, reel 15, item 633, page 18.

49 Microfilm: 'Liturgical Thinking versus Theology,' 1952, reel 9, item 452, page 9.

50 Microfilm: 'Liturgical Thinking versus Theology,' 1952, reel 9, item 452, page 9.

51 Ibid., 8.

52 Globus, *Zweistromland: Kleinere Schriften zu Glauben und Denken*, Franz Rosenzweig: Der Mensch und sein Werk, *Gesammelte Schriften*, Bd 3, 314.

53 Rosenstock-Huessy, *Soziologie*, Bd 2, 619.

54 Ibid., 696.

55 This is included in *The Cross and the Star*, translated by Roland Vogt. The original essay was entitled 'Vom Stern der Erlösung zum Kreuz der Wirklichkeit: Aus Anlaß des Abschlusses der "Soziologie" Eugen Rosenstock-Huessys,' in *Sonderdruck aus: 'Junge Kirche' Protestantische Monatshefte* (Dortmund).

56 Rosenstock-Huessy, *Soziologie*, Bd 2, 711–12.

57 Ibid., 735. Rosenstock-Huessy's use of the word *zogen*, suggesting they were pulled or drawn into the Church, is a marvellously astute choice, emphasizing, as it does, that there was something at work stronger than their own will. And his point is very much that they responded rather than initiated – they did not enter into a place that was easy or 'natural' for them to be in. On the contrary, they were pulled into a place that traditionally housed apostates and idolaters and that contained all the symbolism of God that is an affront to Allah's law about false representation.

58 Ibid., 735. This depiction of the Koran might sound polemical, but it is simply a fact that Muhammad was hostile to contemporary Arabic poetry. And Rosenstock-Huessy is also emphasizing that the Koran is built upon a warrior's code – again I don't know how anyone who reads the Koran with its exhortations of war, rules for distribution of booty, and correct warrior conduct cannot see this, unless they are determined not to see it.

59 Ibid., 736–8.

60 This is the core of Fricke's interpretation of Rosenzweig.

61 Microfilm: 'Comparative Religion,' 1954, reel 15, item 633, page 12. An interesting anecdote: the *China Morning Post* reported this year that a number of childen in Hong Kong are phobic about touching the earth or living animals.

62 Microfilm: 'Universal History,' 1954, reel 16, item 637, page 7; and 'Universal History,' 1957, reel 17, item 643, page 7. Also Rosenstock-Huessy, *The Christian Future*, 176f.

63 Microfilm: 'Cross of Reality,' 1953, reel 15, item 630, page 11. Also see 'Die Bahnbrecher,' in *Soziologie*, Bd 1, 221ff.

64 Microfilm: 'Cross of Reality,' 1953, reel 15, item 630, page 21.

65 Eugen Rosenstock-Huessy, *The Christian Future – or The Modern Mind Outrun*, intro. Harold Stahmer (New York: Harper and Row, [1947]1966), 42–3.

66 Ibid., 44.

67 Ibid., 44–5.

68 Ibid., 45.

69 Ibid., 45. There is a slightly different translation of the sentence in Galli's version of *The Star*, 83.

70 Rosenstock-Huessy, *The Christian Future*, 46.

71 Ibid., 46.

72 Ibid., 46.

73 Ibid., 48.

74 Ibid., 48.

75 Ibid., 48.

76 Ibid., 50.

77 Ibid., 56.

78 Ibid., 50.

79 Ibid., 180.

80 Ibid., 178–80.

81 Ibid., 178–80.

82 Ibid., 180.

83 Rosenstock-Huessy, *Soziologie*, Bd 2, 723.

84 Ibid., 722.

85 Ibid., 722.
86 Ibid., 722.
87 On the relationship to the Tao and nirvana to freedom, see *The Christian Future*, 181.
88 Eugen Rosenstock-Huessy, *Speech and Reality*, intro. Clinton C. Gardner (Norwich: Argo Books), p. 79 – backward-looking formula being the indicative mood of the scientist and continuous present of the historian.
89 Rosenstock-Huessy, *The Christian Future*, 179.
90 Ibid., 176. In *Soziologie*, Bd 2, 736, he makes the point that while the castes have been India's curse, we moderns are able to prise virtues from their vices by finding ways for human beings to take a custodial role in nature to preserve different species of animals and plant life from extinction and thus free them from the 'electron World All.' Of course, this is exactly what has happened with the stance of environmentalists and animal rights activists striving to preserve species and to educate the public about the dangers to different species through our way of life. Though rarely, I suspect, if ever, has the idea been linked to Hinduism.
91 Rosenstock-Huessy, *The Christian Future*, 176.
92 With breathtaking ignorance or shameless disregard for the truth, Walter Kaufmann, while doing all in his power to make Nietzsche palatable for comfortable, peace-loving, economically prosperous North Americans, argued that Nietzsche was actually criticizing the Laws of Manu!
93 Ibid., 176–7.
94 Microfilm: 'Comparative Religion,' 1954, reel 15, item 633, page 7.
95 Eugen Rosenstock-Huessy, *Practical Knowledge of the Soul*, trans. Mark Huessy and Freya von Motke (Norwich: Argo Books, 1981), 44.

Conclusion: Pagan, Jew, Christian – or, Three Lives in One Love

1 Eugen Rosenstock-Huessy, *Soziologie*, Bd 2, *Die Vollzahl der Zeiten* (Stuttgart: W. Kohlhammer Verlag, 1958), 113.

Postscript

1 Eugen Rosenstock-Huessy, *Speech and Reality*, intro. Clinton C. Gardner (Norwich: Argo Books, 1970), 39.
2 Ibid., 44.
3 Ibid., 38.
4 Ibid., 44.
5 Ibid., 44.
6 Ibid., 44.

Bibliography

I am grateful to the heirs of Rosenstock-Huessy and the Rosenstock-Huessy Gesellschaft for access to unpublished materials from Four Wells in Norwich, Vermont, and Bielefeld, Germany. All material that comes from the archive at Four Wells, now held at Baker Library, Dartmouth College, is referred to as *, any material from the Rosenstock-Huessy archives at Bielefeld by #. I am also grateful to the Leo Baeck Institute in New York for access to material from Rosenzweig. Any material from the Leo Baeck collection is cited with §.

All references to 'Microfilm' refer to *The Collected Works of Eugen Rosenstock-Huessy on DVD* (Norwich: Argo Books, 2005) and provide the title, publishing date, reel and item number, and page number if required (e.g., Microfilm: 'Cross of Reality,' 20 January 1954, reel 15, item 630, page 25). For all titles, see *A Guide to the Works of Eugen Rosenstock-Huessy*, http://www.argobooks.org/collected/a_guide_to_the_works.html.

Collected Published and Unpublished Works of Eugen Rosenstock-Huessy

The Collected Works of Eugen Rosenstock-Huessy on DVD. Norwich: Argo Books, 2005. For all titles, see *A Guide to the Works of Eugen Rosenstock-Huessy*, http://www.argobooks.org/collected/a_guide_to_the_works.html. Note that all the works of Rosenstock-Huessy, with the exception of letters listed as being from the Rosenstock-Huessy archives, are available on the DVD of the *Collected Works*. The further listing of major Works of Rosenstock-Huessy in English and German below does not include all works cited in text and endnotes, only his major works.

Major Published Works of Rosenstock-Huessy in English

The Christian Future – or The Modern Mind Outrun. Introduction by Harold
   Stahmer. New York: Harper and Row, [1947]1966.
The Fruit of Lips, or, Why Four Gospels? Edited by Marion Davis Battles. Pitts-
   burgh: Pickwick Press, 1978.
Hitler and Prayer, in Beiheft *Stimmstein: Hitler und Israel oder vom Gebet, Hitler
   and Israel or On Prayer*. Edited by the Eugen Rosenstock-Huessy Gesellschaft
   with Introductions by Cynthia Harris, Jochen Lübbers, Bas Leenman, and
   Adam Żak. Mössingen-Talheim: Talheimer, 1992.
I Am an Impure Thinker. Edited by Freya von Moltke and Clint Gardner. Fore-
   word by W.H. Auden. Norwich: Argo Books, 1970.
*Judaism Despite Christianity: The Letters on Christianity and Judaism between
   Rosenstock-Huessy and Franz Rosenzweig*. Introduction by Harold Stahmer.
   Essays 'About the Correspondence' by Alexander Altmann and Dorothy
   Emmet, eds. Tuscaloosa: University of Alabama Press, 1969. New York:
   Schocken Books, 1971.
The Multiformity of Man. Norwich: Argo Books, 1973.
The Origin of Speech. Introduction by Harold M. Stahmer, editor's postscript by
   Hans R. Huessy. Norwich: Argo Books, 1981.
Out of Revolution: Autobiography of Western Man. New York: William Morrow,
   [1938]1969. Norwich: Argo Books, with introduction by Page Smith, 1993.
   Providence: Berg Publishers, 1993, with introduction by Harold Berman.
Practical Knowledge of the Soul. Translated by Mark Huessy and Freya von
   Moltke. Norwich: Argo Books, 1988.
Rosenstock-Huessy Papers. Vol. 1. Norwich: Argo Books, 1981.
'Rosenstock-Huessy's Engagement with Nietzsche.' In *The Cross and the Star:
   The Post-Nietzschean Christian and Jewish Thought of Eugen Rosenstock-Huessy
   and Franz Rosenzweig*. Edited by Wayne Cristaudo and Frances Huessy.
   Newcastle upon Tyne: Cambridge Scholars Publishing, 2009.
Speech and Reality. Introduction by Clinton C. Gardner. Norwich: Argo Books,
   1970.

Major Works of Rosenstock-Huessy in German

Das Alter der Kirche. Kapitel und Akten. 3 Bde. Co-authored by Joseph Wittig.
   Berlin: Lambert Schneider, 1927–8. New edition, Münster: Agenda, 1998.
Angewandte Seelenkunde. Darmstadt: Röther Verlag, 1924.

Der Atem des Geistes. Moers: Brendow, 1951; Wien: Amandus, 1991.

'Brief an *** [Letter to Karl Barth]' (1920). In *Tumult*, vol. 20. Wien: Turia u. Kant, 1995, 9–15.

Die europäischen Revolutionen und der Charakter der Nationen [1951]. Revised edition *Die Europäischen Revolutionen und der Charakter der Nationen* [1961]. Foreword by Karl Deutsch. Biographical note by Rudolph Hermeier. Moers: Brendow Verlag, 1987. Reprint of the 1961 edition.

Friedensbedingungen der planetarischen Gesellschaft: Zur Ökonomie der Zeit. Edited and introduced by Rudolf Hermeier. Münster: Agenda Verlag, 2001.

Das Geheimnis der Universität: Wider den Verfall von Zeitsinn und Sprachkraft. Essays and addresses, 1950–7. Edited by Georg Müller, with a contribution by Kurt Ballerstedt, 'Leben und Werk Eugen Rosenstock-Huessys.' Stuttgart: W. Kohlhammer Verlag, 1958.

Heilkraft und Wahrheit: Konkordanz der Politischen und kosmischen Zeit. Moers: Brendow, 1952; Wien: Amandus, 1991.

Herzogsgewalt und Friedensschutz: Deutsche Provinzialversammlungen des 9–12 Jahrhunderts. Aalen: Scientia Verlag, 1969.

Die Hochzeit des Kriegs und der Revolution. Würzburg: Patmos-Verlag, 1920; reprint 1965.

Vom Industrierecht. Rechtssystematische Fragen. Festgabe für Xaver Gretener. Berlin: H. Sack, 1926.

Ja und Nein. Autobiographische Fragmente aus Anlass des 80. Geburtstags des Autors. Im Auftrag der seinen Namen tragenden Gesellschaft. Edited by Georg Müller. Heidelberg: Verlag Lambert Schneider, 1968.

Königshaus und Stämme in Deutschland zwischen 911 und 1250. Leipzig: Felix Meiner, 1914; Aalen: Scientia Verlag, 1965.

Im Kreuz der Wirklichkeit: Eine nach-goethische Soziologie. Foreword by Irene Scherer. Afterword by Michael Gormann-Thelen. Edited by Michael Gormann-Thelen, Ruth Mauthner, Lise van der Molen. Mössingen-Talheim: Talheimer, 2009.

Soziologie I. Die Kräfte der Gemeinschaft. Berlin and Leipzig: Walter de Gruyter, 1925.

Soziologie, Bd 1: Die Übermacht der Räume. Stuttgart: W. Kohlhammer Verlag, 1956.

Soziologie, Bd 2: Die Vollzahl der Zeiten. Stuttgart: W. Kohlhammer Verlag, 1958.

Die Sprache des Menschengeschlechts: Eine leibhaftige Grammatik in vier Teilen. Heidelberg: Lambert Schneider, 1963–4.

Werkstattaussiedlung, Untersuchungen über den Lebensraum des Industriearbeiters: In Verbindung mit Eugen May und Martin Grünberg. Berlin: Julius Springer Verlag, 1922.

Writings of Franz Rosenzweig in English

Cultural Writings of Franz Rosenzweig. Edited and translated by Barbara E.
   Galli. Syracuse: Syracuse University Press, 2000.
Franz Rosenzweig: His Life and Thought. Presented by Nahum Glatzer. New
   foreword by Paul Mendes-Flohr. Indianapolis: Hackett, 1998.
Franz Rosenzweig and Jehuda Halevi: Translating, Translations, and Translators.
   Translated by Barbara Galli. Foreword by Paul Mendes-Flohr. Montreal and
   Kingston: McGill-Queen's University Press, 1995.
God, Man, and the World: Lectures and Essays. Edited and translated by Barbara
   E. Galli. Syracuse: Syracuse University Press, 1998.
'On Being a Jewish Person.' *Commentary,* November 1945.
On Jewish Learning. Translated and introduced by Nahum N. Glatzer. New
   York: Noonday Press, 1965.
*Judaism Despite Christianity: The 'Letters on Christianity and Judaism' between
   Rosenstock-Huessy and Franz Rosenzweig.* Edited by Eugen Rosenstock-
   Huessy. Translated by Dorothy Emmet. New York: Schocken Books, 1971.
Philosophical and Theological Writings. Translated and edited by Paul W. Franks
   and Michael Morgan. Indianapolis: Hackett, 2000. Includes 'The New
   Thinking.'
The Star of Redemption. Translated by William W. Hallo. New York: Holt, Rine-
   hart and Winston, 1971. New translation by Barbara E. Galli. Madison: Uni-
   versity of Wisconsin Press, 2005.
Understanding the Sick and the Healthy: A View of World, Man, and God. Edited
   and translated by Nahum N. Glatzer. Cambridge, MA: Harvard University
   Press, 1999.

German Editions of Works by Franz Rosenzweig

Franz Rosenzweig, Der Mensch und sein Werk. Gesammelte Schriften. Bde I–IV.
   The Hague: Martinus Nijhoff, 1976–84.
   I. *Briefe und Tagebucher.* Bd 1: 1900–18. Bd 2: 1919–29. Edited by Rachel
      Rosenzweig and Edith Rosenzweig-Scheinmann with the cooperation of
      Bernhard Casper. The Hague: Martinus Nijhoff, 1979.
   II. *Der Stern der Erlösung.* Introduction by Reinhold Mayer. The Hague: Mar-
      tinus Nijhoff, 1976 [4th ed.].
   III. *Zweistromland. Kleinere Schriften zu Glauben und Denken.* Edited by Rein-
      hold Meyer and Annemarie Mayer. Dordrecht: Martinus Nijhoff, 1984.
   IV. *Sprachdenken im Obersetzen.* Bd 1: *Jehuda Halevi. Funfundneunzig Hym-
      nen und Gedichte.* Edited by Rafael N. Rosenzweig. Dordrecht: Martinus

Nijhoff, 1983. Bd 2: *Arbeitspapiere zur Verdeutschung der Schrift*. Edited Rachel Bat Adam. Dordrecht: Martinus Nijhoff, 1984.

Die 'Gritli'-Briefe: Briefe an Margrit Rosenstock-Huessy. Edited by Inken Ruhle and Reinhold Mayer. Preface by Rafael Rosenzweig. Tubingen: Bilam Verlag, 2002. (This is not the complete edition.)

Gritli Briefe (complete edition). Transcribed by Ulrika Von Moltke. Edited by Michael Gormann-Thelen and Dr Elfriede Büchsel. Eugen Rosenstock-Huessy Fund and Argo Books. http://www.argobooks.org/gritli/index.html.

Hegel und der Staat. Munich: R. Oldenbourg, 1920. Reprint Aalen: Scientia, 1962.

'Innerlich bleibt die Welt eine': ausgewählte Texte zum Islam. Edited by Gesine Palmer and Yossef Schwartz. Berlin: Philo, 2003.

Der Stern der Erlösung. Frankfurt am Main: Suhrkamp, [1988] 1996.

Other Works on or Relevant to Rosenstock-Huessy and/or Rosenzweig

Adriaanse, Hendrik. 'Zum Rosenzweig-Bild in K.H. Miskottes Buch "Het wesen der joodse religie."' In *Der Philosoph Franz Rosenzweig (1886–1929) Internationaler Kongreß – Kassel 1986*. Bd I: *Die Herausforderung jüdischen Lernens*. Edited by Wolfdietrich Schmied-Kowarzik. Freiburg: Karl Alber, 1988. 441–53.

Anckaert, Luc. *A Critique of Infinity: Rosenzweig and Levinas*. Dudley: Peeters, 2006.

Anckaert, Luc, Martin Brasser, and Norbert Samuelson, eds. *The Legacy of Franz Rosenzweig: Collected Essays*. Leuven: Leuven University Press, 2004.

Anidjar, Gil. Interview conducted by Nermeen Shaikh of AsiaSource. http://www.asiasource.org/news/special_reports/anidjar5.cfm.

– *The Jew, the Arab: A History of the Enemy*. Stanford: Stanford University Press, 2003.

Barth, Karl. *Karl Barth–Eduard Thurneysen: Briefwechsel*, Bd 1, 1913–21. Zürich: Theologischer Verlag, 2000.

Batnitzky, Leora. *Idolatry and Representation: The Philosophy of Franz Rosenzweig Reconsidered*. Princeton: Princeton University Press, 2000.

Benjamin, Walter. *Selected Writings*. Vol. II, *1927–1934*. Edited by Michael W. Jennings, Howard Eiland, and Gary Smith. Translated by Rodney Livingstone et al. Cambridge, MA: Belknap Press, 1999.

– *The Correspondence of Walter Benjamin: 1910–1940*. Edited by Gershom Scholem and Theodor Adorno. Translated by Manfred Jacobson and Evelyn Jacobson. Chicago: University of Chicago Press, 1994.

Bergman, Shmuel Hugo. *Dialogical Philosophy from Kierkegaard to Buber*. Albany: SUNY Press, 1991.

Bieberich, Ulrich. *Wenn die Geschichte gottlich ware: Rosenzweigs Auseinandersetzung mit Hegel*. St Ottilien: EOS Verlag, 1990.

Bienenstock, Myriam. 'Rosenzweig's Hegel.' *Owl of Minerva* 23, no. 2 (Spring 1992): 177–82.

Brakelmann, Günter. *Hans Ehrenberg. Ein judenchristliches Schicksal in Deutschland*. Teil 1: *Leben, Denken, und Wirken 1883–1932*. Teil 2: *Widerstand, Verfolgung, und Emigration 1933–1939*. Schriftenreihe der Hans-Ehrenberg-Gesellschaft, Bde 3 und 4. Waltrop, 1997–9.

Brinton, Crane. 'Review of *Out of Revolution: Autobiography of Western Man*,' *Political Science Quarterly* 54 (1939): 286–8.

Brocke, Michael. 'Franz Rosenzweig und Gerhard Scholem.' In *Sondedruck aus Juden in der Weimar Republik*. Edited by Walter Grab and Julius Schoeps. Stuttgart: Burg Verlag, 1986.

Bryant, Darrol M., and Hans Huessy, eds. *Eugen Rosenstock-Huessy: Studies in His Life and Thought*. Toronto: Edwin Mellen, 1986.

Buber, Martin. *Briefwechsel aus Sieben Jahrzehnten, 1918–1938*. Bd III. Gütersloh: Gütersloher Verlag, 1972.

– *Pointing the Way: Collected Essays*. Edited and translated by Maurice Friedman. London: Routledge and Kegan Paul, 1957.

Casper, Bernhard. *Das dialogische Denken: Franz Rosenzweig, Ferdinand Ebner, und Martin Buber*. Freiburg: Karl Alber, 2002.

Ciglia, Francesco Paolo. 'Zwischen homerischem und biblischem Weltbild: Rosenzweigs Europa-Gedanke.' *Rosenzweig Jahrbuch* 3: 127–39.

Cohen, Richard A. *Elevations: The Height of the Good in Rosenzweig and Levinas*. Chicago: University of Chicago Press, 1994.

Cristaudo, Wayne. 'Eugen Rosenstock-Huessy: Before, During, and After Post-Modernism.' *Revue Roumaine de Philosophie* 48, nos. 1–2 (2004): 190–203.

– 'Franz Rosenzweig's "Troubling" Critique of Islam.' *Rosenzweig Yearbook*, Bd II. Freiburg: Karl Alber, 2007. 43–86.

– *Power, Love, and Evil: Contribution to a Philosophy of the Damaged*. New York: Rodopi, 2007.

– '"Love Is as Strong as Death": The Triadic Love of Franz Rosenzweig, Eugen Rosenstock-Huessy, and Gritli Huessy.' *Inter-Disciplinary.net*, http://www.inter-disciplinary.net/ptb/persons/pil/pil1/cristaudo%20paper.pdf.

– 'Philosophy, Christianity, and Revolution in Eric Voegelin and Eugen Rosenstock-Huessy.' *European Legacy* 4, no. 6 (December 1999): 58–74.

– 'Redemption and Messianism in Franz Rosenzweig's *The Star of Redemption*.' In *Messianism, Apocalypse, Redemption: 20th Century German Thought*. Edited by Wendy Baker and Wayne Cristaudo. Introduction by Wayne Cristaudo. Adelaide: Australian Theological Forum, 2006.

– 'Revolution and the Redeeming of the World: The Messianic History of Eugen Rosenstock-Huessy's *Out of Revolution.*' In *Messianism, Apocalypse, Redemption: 20th Century German Thought.* Edited by Wendy Baker and Wayne Cristaudo. Introduction by Wayne Cristaudo. Adelaide: Australian Theological Forum, 2006.

– 'Rosenzweig and Rosenstock's Critiques of Idealism: The Common Front of Contrary Allegiances.' In *Franz Rosenzweigs Neues Denken.* Edited by Wolfgang Schmied-Kowarzik. Freiburg: Karl Alber, 2006.

Cristaudo, Wayne, and Frances Huessy, eds. *The Cross and the Star: The Post-Nietzschean Christian and Jewish Thought of Eugen Rosenstock-Huessy and Franz Rosenzweig.* Newcastle upon Tyne: Cambridge Scholars Publishing, 2009.

Dagan, Haggai. 'The Motif of Blood and Procreation and Blood in Franz Rosenzweig.' *AJS Review* 26, no. 2 (2002): 241–9.

Derrida, Jacques. 'Interpretations at War: Kant, the Jew, the German.' *New Literary History* 22, no. 1 (Winter 1991): 39–95.

Dressler, Stephan. 'Viktor von Weizsäcker: Medizinische Anthropologie und Philosophie.' Wien, Berlin: 1989. (*Überreuter Wissenschaft, Wiener Studien zur Medizin, Geschichte, und Philosophie 1*).

Ehrenberg, Hans. *Autobiography of a German Pastor.* Translated by Geraint Jones. London: Student Christian Movement, 1943.

– *In der Schule Pascals.* Heidelberg: Lambert Schneider, 1954.

Ehrenberg, Maria. 'Rudolf Ehrenbergs Theoretische Biologie und Metabiologie. Hat der Dialog zwischen Rudolf Ehrenberg und Franz Rosenzweig zu ihrer Entstehung beigetragen?' In *Der Philosoph Franz Rosenzweig*, Bd 1.

– *Theoretische Biologie. Vom Standpunkt der Irreversibilität des eelmentaren Lebensvorganges.* Berlin: Julius Springer, 1923.

– *Der Lebenslauf. Eine biologisch-metabiologische Vorlesung.* Heidelberg: Lambert Schneider. 1946.

– *Metabiologie.* Heidelberg: Lambert Schneider. 1950.

Franz Rosenzweig zum 25. Dezember 1926 glueckwuensche zum 40. Geburtstag. Published on the Centenary of Franz Rosenzweig's Birth. New York: Leo Baeck Institute, 1987.

Freund, Else. *Die Existenzphilosophie Franz Rosenzweigs: ein Beitrag zur Analyse seines Werkes 'Der Stern der Erlösung.'* Hamburg: Meiner, 1959.

Fricke, Martin. *Franz Rosenzweigs Philosophie der Offenbarung: eine Interpretation des Sterns der Erlösung.* Würzburg: Königshausen & Neumann, 2003.

Fuller, John. *W.H. Auden: A Commentary.* London: Faber and Faber, 1998.

Gardner, Clint. *Beyond Belief: Discovering Christianity's New Paradigm*. White River Junction: White River Press, 2008.

Gibbs, Robert. *Correlations in Rosenzweig and Levinas*. Princeton: Princeton University Press, 1994.

Gordon, Peter Eli. *Rosenzweig and Heidegger: Between Judaism and German Philosophy*. Berkeley: University of California Press, 2003.

– 'Science, Finitude, and Infinity: The End of Neo-Kantianism and the Birth of Existentialism.' *Jewish Social Studies* 6, no. 1 (1999): 30–53.

– 'Rosenzweig Redux: The Reception of German-Jewish Thought.' *Jewish Social Studies* 8, no. 1 (2001): 1–57.

Gormann-Thelen, Michael. 'Franz Rosenzweigs Briefe anMargrit (Gritli) Rosenstock: Ein Zwischenbericht mit Drei Dokumenten.' In *The Legacy of Franz Rosenzweig*. Edited by Luc Anckaert, Martin Brasser, and Norbert Samuelson. Leuven: Leuven University Press, 2004.

– ed. 1998. *Nachwort to Hans Ehrenberg: Die Parteiung der Philosophie: Studien wider Hegel und die Kantianer*. Essen: die blaue Eule, 1911.

Görtz, Heinz-Jürgen. *Franz Rosenzweigs neues Denken: eine Einführung aus der Perspektive christlicher Theologie*. Würzburg: Echter, 1992.

– 'Rudolf Ehrenbergs Gedanke des "Lebens."' *Theologie und Philosophie* 78 (2003): 811–96.

– '*Der Stern der Erlösung* als Kommentar: Rudolf Ehrenberg und Franz Rosenzweig.' In *Franz Rosenzweig als Leser. Kontextuelle Kommentare zum Stern der Erlösung*. Edited by Martin Brasser. Tübingen: Niemeyer, 2004.

– *Tod und Erfahrung. Rosenzweigs 'erfahrende Philosophie' und Hegels 'Wissenschaft der Erfahrung des Bewußtseins*.' Düsseldorf: Patmos Verlag, 1984.

Graf, Friedrich Wilhelm. 'Review of the *Gritli Briefe*.' *Zeitschrift für Neuere Theologiegeschichte / Journal for the History of Modern Theology* 10 (2003).

Green, Hart Kenneth. 'The Notion of Truth in Franz Rosenzweig's *The Star of Redemption: A Philosophical Inquiry*.' *Modern Judaism* 7 (1987): 297–323.

Greenberg, Yudit Kornberg. *Better Than Wine: Love, Poetry, and Prayer in the Thought of Franz Rosenzweig*. Foreword by Elliot R. Wolfson. Atlanta: Scholars Press, 1996.

Guttmann, Julius. *Philosophies of Judaism: The History of Jewish Philosophy from Biblical Times to Franz Rosenzweig*. Translated by David W. Silverman. Philadelphia: Jewish Publication Society, 1964.

Hermeier, Rudolf, ed. *Jenseits all unseres Wissens wohnt Gott. Hans Ehrenberg und Rudolf Ehrenberg zur Erinnerung*. Moers: Brendow Verlag, 1987.

Hollander, Dana. *Exemplarity and Chosenness: Rosenzweig and Derrida on the Nation of Philosophy*. Stanford: Stanford University Press, 2008.

Horwitz, Rivka. 'The Shaping of Rosenzweig's Identity According to the Gritli Letters.' In *Rosenzweig als Leser: Kontextuelle Kommentare zum* Stern der Erlösung. Edited by Martin Brasser. Tübingen: Max Niemeyer, 2004. 11–41.

Hufnagel, Cordula. *Die kultische Gebärde: Kunst, Politik, Religion im Denken Franz Rosenzweigs*. Freiburg: Alber, 1994.

Huppuch, Willibald. *Eugen Rosenstock-Huessy (1888–1973) und die Weimarer Republik: Erwachsenenbildung, Industriereform, und Arbeitslosenproblematik*. Hamburg: Dr Kova, 2004.

Jacob, Wolfgang. 'Viktor von Weiszäcker und Franz Rosenzweig.' In *Der Philosoph Franz Rosenzweig. 1886–1929: Internationaler Kongress, Kassel 1986*. Vol. 1. Freiburg: Karl Alber, 1988. 179–86.

Jäger, Lorenz. *Messianische Kritik: Studien zu Leben und Werk von Florens Christian Rang*. Köln: Böhlau, 1998.

Kaplan, Gregory. 'Politics, Theology, Race, and Religion in the 1916–1924 Dialogue of Franz Rosenzweig and Eugen Rosenstock-Huessy.' In *The Weimar Moment*. Edited by Len Kaplan and Rudy Koshar. Lanham: Lexington Books, forthcoming.

– 'Sovereignty and Sacrifice in the Writings by Franz Rosenzweig and Eugen Rosenstock-Huessy.' In *The Cross and the Star: The Post-Nietzschean Christian and Jewish Thought of Eugen Rosenstock-Huessy and Franz Rosenzweig*. Edited by Wayne Cristaudo and Frances Huessy. Newcastle upon Tyne: Cambridge Scholars Publishing, 2009.

Kirchner, Katrin. *Franz Rosenzweigs Theorie der Erfahrung: Ein Beitrag zur Überwindung totalitrer Denkstruktures und zur Begründung einer Kultur der Pluralität*. Würzburg: Könighaus und Neumann, 2005.

Klemperer, Klemens von. *German Incertitudes, 1914–1945: The Stones and the Cathedral*. Westport: Greenwood Publishing, 2001.

Klenk, Dominik. *Metanomik. Quelenlehre jenseits der Denkgesetze*. Münster: Agenda Verlag, 2003.

Koch, Richard. *Die ärtzliche Diagnose. Beitrag zur Kenntnis des ärtzlichen Denkens*. Wiesbaden: Bergmann, 1917, 1920.

– *Ärztliches Denken. Abhandlungen über die philosophischen Grundlagen der Medizin*. München: Bergmann, 1923.

– *Das Als-Ob im ärtzlichen Denken*. München: Rösl & Cie. 1924.

Kohlenberger, Helmut, Wilfrid Gärtner, and Michael Gormann-Thelen, *Rosenstock-Huessy. Tumult*, vol. 20. Vienna: Turia and Kant, 1995.

Kohr, Jörg. *'Gott selbst muss das letzte Wort sprechen . . .': Religion und Politik im Denken Franz Rosenzweigs*. Freiburg: Karl Alber, 2008.

Lehmann, Matthias. 'Franz Rosenzweig's Kritik des Islams im *Stern der Erlösung*.' *Jewish Studies Quarterly* 1, no. 4 (1993–4): 340–68.

Leithart, Peter. 'The Relevance of Eugen Rosenstock-Huessy.' *First Things: The Journal of Religion, Culture, and Public Life*, 28 June 2007. http://www.first things.com/onthesquare/2007/06/the-relevance-of-eugen-rosenst.
– 'The Social Articulation of Time in Eugen Rosenstock-Huessy.' *Modern Theology* 26, no. 2 (March 2010): 197–219.
Leutzsch, Andreas. *Geschichte der Globalisierung als globalisierte Geschichte. Die historische Konstruktion der Weltgesellschaft bei Rosenstock-Huessy und Braudel.* Frankfurt: Campus Verlag, 2009.
Lévinas, Emmanuel. 'Between Two Worlds.' In *Difficult Freedom: Essays on Judaism.* Translated by Seán Hand. Baltimore: Johns Hopkins University Press, 1990.
– 'The Philosophy of Franz Rosenzweig.' In *In the Time of Nations.* Translated by Michael B. Smith. London: Continuum, 2007.
Licharz, Werner, and Manfred Keller, eds. *Franz Rosenzweig und Hans Ehrenberg: Bericht einer Beziehung,* Bd 42. Frankfurt am Main: Haag & Herchen, 1986.
Liebster, Wolfram. 'Franz Rosenzweig und Kornelis Heiko Miskotte. Zu den Anfängen und den Auswirkungen des jüdisch-christlichen Dialoges in den Niederlanden'. In *Der Philosoph Franz Rosenzweig (1886–1929) Internationaler Kongreß – Kassel 1986.* Bd I: *Die Herausforderung jüdischen Lernens.* Edited by Wolfdietrich Schmied-Kowarzik. Freiburg: Karl Alber, 1988. 425–40.
– 'Die Kirche als das Zwischenreich. Hans Ehrenbergs Beitrag zur Ekklesiologie im Dialog mit Franz Rosenzweig. Eine Studie zu Hans Ehrenbergs theologischem Erstlingswerk.' In *Berliner Theologische Zeitschrift* 8, no. 1 (1991): 76–93.
Lilla, Mark. 'A Battle for Religion.' *New York Review of Books.* 5 December 2002. 60ff.
Löwith, Karl. 'Franz Rosenzweig and Martin Heidegger on Temporality and Eternity.' *Philosophy and Phenomenological Research* 3, no. 1 (1942): 53–77.
– 'Review of *The Christian Future.*' *Church History* 15, no. 3 (1946): 248–9.
Mack, Michael. *German Idealism and the Jew: The Inner Anti-Semitism of Philosophy and German Jewish Responses.* Chicago: Chicago University Press, 2003.
Maybaum, Ignaz. 'Das Gesetz: Franz Rosenzweigs Ringen mit den Jüdischen Traditionen.' *Emuna* 2 (1970): 82–8.
– *Trialogue between Jew, Christian, and Muslim.* London: Routledge and Kegan Paul, 1973.
Mayer, Reinhold. *Franz Rosenzweig: Eine Philosophie der dialogschen Erfahrung.* München: Chr. Kaiser, 1971.
– 'Zum Briefwechsel zwischen Franz Rosenzweig and Eugen Rosenstock.' In *Franz Rosenzweig and Hans Ehrenberg: Bericht einer Beziehung.* Arnoldshainer

Text, Bd 42. Edited by Werner Licharz and Manfred Keller. Frankfurt am Main: Haag & Herschen, 1986.

Meier, Ephraim. *Letters of Love: Franz Rosenzweig's Spiritual Biography and Oeuvre in Light of the Gritli Letters.* New York: Peter Lang, 2006.

Mendes-Flor, Paul, ed. *The Philosophy of Franz Rosenzweig.* Hanover: University Press of New England, 1988.

Miskotte, Kornelis. *When the Gods Are Silent.* Translated by John Doberstein. New York: Harper and Row, [1932]1967.

Morgan, George. *Speech and Society: The Christian Linguistic Social Philosophy of Eugen Rosenstock-Huessy.* Gainsville: University Press of Florida, 1987.

Mosès, Stéphane. 'On the Correspondence between Franz Rosenzweig and Eugen Rosenstock-Huessy.' In *The German-Jewish Dialogue: A Symposium in Honour of George Mosse.* Edited by Klaus Berghahn. New York: Peter Lang, 1996. 109–23.

– 'Walter Benjamin et Franz Rosenzweig.' In *La pensée de Franz Rosenzweig.* Edited by Arno Münster. Paris: Presses Universitaires de France, 1994.

– 'Hegel beim Wort genommen: Gescichtskritik bei Franz Rosenzweig.' In *Zeitgewinn: Messianisches Denken nach Franz Rosenzweig.* Edited by Gotthard Fuchs und Hans Hermann Henrix. Frankfurt am Main: Knecht Verlag, 1987.

– *System and Revelation: The Philosophy of Franz Rosenzweig.* Translated by Catherine Tihanyi. Detroit: Wayne State University Press, 1992.

Müller, Georg. 'Der Sprachdenker Eugen Rosenstock-Huessy.' *Evangeslische Theologie* 14 (1954): 314–33.

– 'Eugen Rosenstock-Huessy und Nikolai Berdjaev.' *Kyrios* (1966): 174–85.

– 'Das neue Sprachdenken.' *Neue deutsche Hefte* 9 (1957): 538–48.

– 'Zum Problem der Sprache. Erwägungen im Anschluß an das Sprachdenken Eugen Rosenstock-Huessys.' *Kerygma und Dogma* 2 (1956): 139–54.

– 'Vom *Stern der Erlösung* zum *Kreuz der Wirklichkeit*: Aus Anlaß des Abschlusses der "Soziologie" Eugen Rosenstock-Huessys.' In *Sonderdruck aus der 'Junge Kirche' Protestantische Monatshefte.* Dortmund: 1959. Translated in *The Cross and the Star: The Post-Nietzschean Christian and Jewish Thought of Eugen Rosenstock-Huessy and Franz Rosenzweig.* Newcastle upon Tyne: Cambridge Scholars Publishing, 2009.

Münster, Arno, ed. *La pensée de Franz Rosenzweig.* Paris: Presses Universitaires de France, 1994.

Oz-Salzberger, Fania. 'On Rosenzweig, Israelis, and Europe Today.' *Rosenzweig Jahrbuch* 3: 38–50.

Pines, Shlomo. 'Der Islam im "Stern der Erlösung."' In *Eine Untersuchung zu Tendenzen und Quellen Franz Rosenzweigs, in Hebräische Beiträge zur Wissenschaft des Judentums* 3–5 (1987–9): 138–48.

Pollock, Benjamin. *Franz Rosenzweig and the Systematic Task of Philosophy*. Cambridge: Cambridge University Press, 2009.

Putnam, Hilary. *Jewish Philosophy as a Guide to Life: Rosenzweig, Buber, Levinas, Wittgenstein*. Indianapolis: Indiana University Press, 2008.

Rashkover, Randi. *Revelation and Theopolitics: Barth, Rosenzweig, and the Politics of Praise*. London: T. & T. Clark, 2005.

Ricoeur, Paul. *Figuring the Sacred: Religion, Narrative, and Imagination*. Minneapolis: Augsberg Fortress Publishers, 1995.

Rohrbach, Wilfrid. *Das Sprachdenken Eugen Rozenstock-Huessys: Historische Erörterung und systematische Explikation*. Stuttgart: W. Kohlhammer Verlag, 1973.

Rome, Sydney, and Beatrice Rome, eds. *Philosophical Interrogations: Interrogations of Martin Buber, John Wild, Jean Wahl, Brand Blanshard, Paul Weiss, Charles Hartshorne, Paul Tillich*. New York: Holt, Rinehart and Winston, 1964.

Rose, Gillian. *Judaism and Modernity: Philosophical Essays*. Oxford: Basil Blackwell, 1993.

Rubenstein, Ernest. *An Episode of Jewish Romanticism: Franz Rosenzweig's* The Star of Redemption. Albany: SUNY Press, 1999.

Rubinstein, Richard L. 'On Death in Life: Reflections on Franz Rosenzweig.' *Soundings: An Interdisciplinary Journal* 55, no. 2 (Summer 1972): 216–35.

Rühle, Inken. *Gott spricht die Sprache der Menschen: Franz Rosenzweig als Jüdischer Theologe – eine Einführung*. Tübingen: Bilam, 2004.

Samuelson, Norbert M. *A User's Guide to Franz Rosenzweig's* The Star of Redemption. Richmond: Curzon, 1999·

Santner, Eric. 'Beyond Apologetics: Franz Rosenzweig's "Queer Theory" of Anti-Semitism.' In *Franz Rosenzweigs 'Neues Denken,'* Bd 2: 1082–94.

– *On the Psychotheology of Everyday Life: Reflections on Freud and Rosenzweig*. Chicago: University of Chicago Press, 2001.

Schmied-Kowarzik, Wolfdietrich. *Franz Rosenzweig: Existentielles Denken und gelebte Bewährung*. Freiburg: Karl Alber. 1991.

– ed. *Franz Rosenzweigs 'Neues Denken.'* Bd 1: *Selbstbegrenzendes Denken – in Philosophos*. Bd 2: *Erfahrene Offenbarung – in Theologos*. Freiburg: Karl Alber, 2006.

– ed. *Der Philosoph Franz Rosenzweig (1886–1929): Internationaler Kongress – Kassel; 1986*. Bd 1: *Die Herausforderung jüdischen Lernens*. Bd 2: *Das neue Denken und seine Dimensionen*. Freiburg: Karl Alber, 1988.

– *Rosenzweig im Gespräch mit Ehrenberg, Cohen, und Buber*. Freiburg: Alber, 2006.

Schoeps, Hans-Joachim. *The Jewish-Christian Argument: A History of Theologies in Conflict*. London: Faber and Faber, 1963.

Smith, Page. *Killing of the Spirit: Higher Education in America*. New York: Penguin, 1991.

Spengler. 'Franz Rosenzweig and the Abrahamic Religions.' *First Things: The Journal of Religion, Culture, and Public Life*, October 2007, http://www.firstthings.com. Also in *The Cross and the Star: The Post-Nietzschean Christian and Jewish Thought of Eugen Rosenstock-Huessy and Franz Rosenzweig*. Edited by Wayne Cristaudo and Frances Huessy. Newcastle upon Tyne: Cambridge Scholars Publishing, 2009.

Stahmer, Harold. 'Franz, Eugen, and Gritli: "Respondeo *etsi* mutabor."' In *Franz Rosenzweigs 'neues Denken': Bd II: Erfahrenen Offenbarung in theologos*. Edited by Wolfdietrich Schmied-Kowarzik. Freiburg: Karl Alber, 2006. 1151–68.

– 'Franz Rosenzweig's Letters to Margrit Rosenstock-Huessy, 1917–1922.' *Leo Baeck Institute Yearbook* 34 (1989): 385–409. Also in *The Cross and the Star: The Post-Nietzschean Christian and Jewish Thought of Eugen Rosenstock-Huessy and Franz Rosenzweig*. Edited by Wayne Cristaudo and Frances Huessy. Newcastle upon Tyne: Cambridge Scholars Publishing, 2009.

– *'Speak That I May See Thee': The Religious Significance of Language*. New York: Macmillan, 1968.

– 'The Letters of Franz Rosenzsweig to Margrit Huessy: "Franz," "Gritli," "Eugen," and "The Star of Redemption."' In *Der Philosoph Franz Rosenzweig (1886–1929): Internationaler Kongress – Kassel; 1986. Bd 1: Die Herausforderung jüdischen Lernens*. Edited by Wolfdieterich Schmied-Kowarzik. Freiburg: Karl Alber, 1988. 109–37.

– 'Speech is the Body of the Spirit: The Oral Hermeneutic in the Writings of Rosenstock-Huessy.' *Oral Tradition* 2, no. 1 (1987): pp. 301–22. Also in *The Cross and the Star: The Post-Nietzschean Christian and Jewish Thought of Eugen Rosenstock-Huessy and Franz Rosenzweig*. Edited by Wayne Cristaudo and Frances Huessy. Newcastle upon Tyne: Cambridge Scholars Publishing, 2009.

Stahmer, Harold, and Michael Gormann-Thelen. 1998. 'Rosenstock-Huessy, Eugen (1888–1973).' *Theologische Realenzyklopädie*. Vol. 29. Berlin: Walter de Gruyter.

Stimmstein: Mitteilungsblätter der Eugen Rosenstock-Huessy Gesellschaft. Norwich: Argo Books.

Surall, Frank. *Juden und Christen – Toleranz in neuer Perspektive: der Denkweg Franz Rosenzweigs in seiner Bezügen zu Lessing, Harnack, Baeck, und Rosenstock-Huessy*. Gütersloh: Chr. Kaiser/Gü, 2003.

Tannebaum, Eugen. 'Anleitung zum Judensein: Ein Mensch, Ein Buch, Ein Weg.' *Jüdische Allgemeine Zeitung* 26 (June 1925): 1.

Thaler, Jürgen. *'Ein Kriseln geht durch unsere schüttere Zeit': zur Transformation des Karnevals in den Schriften von Florens Christian Rang (1864–1924).* Wien: WUV-Universität-Verlag, 1996.

Theunissen, Michael. *The Other: Studies in the Social Ontology of Husserl, Heidegger, Sartre, and Buber.* Cambridge, MA: MIT Press, 1984.

Töpfer, Franz, and Urban Wiesing, eds. *Richard Koch und Franz Rosenzweig: Schriften und Briefe zu Krankheit, Sterben, und Tod.* Münster: Agenda, 2000.

Ullmann, Wolfgang. 'Die Entdeckung des neuen Denkens. Das Leipziger Religionsgespräch und der Briefwechsel über Judentum und Christentum zwischen Eugen Rosenstock und Franz Rosenzweig.' *Stimmstein* 2, *Jahrbuch der Eugen Rosenstock-Huessy-Gesellschaft.* Edited by Bas Leenman et al. Moers: Brendow Verlag, 1988. Translated by Roland Vogt as 'The Discovery of the New Thinking: The Leipzig Conversation on Religion and the Correspondence between Eugen Rosenstock and Franz Rosenzweig about Judaism and Christianity.' In *The Cross and the Star: The Post-Nietzschean Christian and Jewish Thought of Eugen Rosenstock-Huessy and Franz Rosenzweig,* ed. Wayne Cristaudo and Frances Huessy. Newcastle upon Tyne: Cambridge Scholars Publishing, 2009.

Vogel, Manfred. *Rosenzweig on Profane/Secular History.* Atlanta: Scholars Press, 1996.

Vogel, Paul, ed. *Viktor von Weizsäcker: Arzt im Irrsal der Zeit; eine Freundesgabe zum 70. Geburtstag am 21.4.1956.* Göttingen: Vandenhoeck & Ruprecht, 1956.

Ward, Graham. 'Forms of Logocentrism among Barth's Contemporaries.' In *Barth, Derrida, and the Language of Theology.* Cambridge: Cambridge University Press, 1995.

Wasserstein, David J. 'Now Let Us Proclaim – The Conversions of Franz Rosenzweig.' *Times Literary Supplement,* 27 June 2008.

Weismantel, Leo, ed. *'Zwölf Bücher.' Die Zwölf Wegbereiter. Ein Almanach persönlicher Beratung für das Jahr 1921.* Munich: Verlag der Arbeitsgemeinschaft, 1921.

Weiszäcker, Viktor von. 'Die Kreatur, Martin Buber, Joseph Wittig.' *Gesammelte Schriften,* vol. I. Frankfurt am Main: Suhrkamp, 1986. 212–18.

Wiedebach, Hartwig. 'Apologie gegen sich selbst. Zur Antilogik der Person bei Viktor von Weizsacker und Franz Rosenzweig.' In *Religious Apologetics: Philosophical Argumentation.* Edited by Yossef Schwartz and Volkhard Krech. Tübingen: Mohr Siebeck, 2004. 531–50.

– *'Kreuz der Wirklichkeit' und 'Stern der Erlösung.'* Freiburg: Karl Alber, 2010.

Zak, Adam. 'Die Zeit der Sprache – die Sprache der Zeit. Zum Sprachdenken Eugen Rosenstock-Huessy,' *Orientierung* 1 (1990): 2–8.

– 'Erneuerung des Denkens durch Dialog. Anregungen Eugen Rosenstock-Huessys Briefwechsel mit Franz Rosenzweig.' In *Dialogdenken-Gesellschaftsethik. Wider die allgegenwärtige Gewalt gesellschaftlicher Vereinnahmung*. Edited by Angelica Bäumer and Michael Benedikt. Wien: Passagen Verlag, 1991.
– *Vom reinen Denken zur Sprachvernunft: Über die Grundmotive der Offenbarungsphilosophie Franz Rosenzweigs*. Stuttgart: W. Kohlhammer Verlag, 1987.
Zank, Michael. 'The Rosenzweig–Rosenstock Triangle, or, What Can We Learn from *Letters to Gritli*? A Review Essay.' *Modern Judaism* 23 (2003): 74–98.
Žižek, Slavoj, Eric L. Santner, and Kenneth Reinhard. *The Neighbor: Three Inquiries in Political Theology*. Chicago: University of Chicago Press, 2006.

Index

1968 or radical liberal paradigm, xx–xxii, xxiv–xxvi, xxix–xxx, 244–5, 439, 445–7, 459, 461, 465, 519, 552

Abelard, Pierre, 260
Abraham, 31, 33, 99, 185, 200, 206, 429, 437, 441, 449, 452, 453
Absolute Empiricism, 64, 163, 213, 399, 405
Academy of Labour, 9, 284
Adorno, Theodor, 9–10, 45, 92, 110, 117, 377, 468, 536
adult education, xiii, 240, 284–5, 287
Aeschylus, 170
aesthetics. *See* art
Africa, xxiv, 294, 357, 420, 432, 440, 525
Agamben, Giorgio, 34, 244, 293, 312, 466
Alexandrian grammar, 82–6, 106
All Saints' Day, 341, 430
All Souls' Day, 241, 340–2, 345, 417, 430
Allah, 132. *See also* chapters 14 and 15 *passim*, 551, 556, 558, 559
Althusser, Louis, xxii, 550

Altmann, Alexander, 13, 25, 289–90, 467, 473, 480, 481, 486, 513, 529
American Constitution, 108, 274
American Revolution, 241
analytic philosophers, 66, 459
Anidjar, Gil, 138–40, 504–5, 519
Anthony, St, 209–12, 215, 515
anthropological turn, xii, 143
anti-Semitism, xxiv, xxix, 12, 21–4, 25–6, 30, 142, 150, 287–8, 298–9, 303, 305, 355, 373, 465–6, 481, 484, 485, 528, 529, 546
anti-transcendent, 54, 204–5
Aquinas, St Thomas, 79, 261, 345
Aragon, Lois, 310–11
Arendt, Hannah, 11, 288, 528
Aristotle, 10, 34, 79, 128, 134, 135, 161–3, 176, 225, 260–1, 265, 269, 311, 330, 389, 437, 523, 535
Arius, 207, 212, 213
art, 36, 48–50, 89, 92, 93, 133, 141, 152, 162, 164, 165, 170, 171, 175, 176, 295, chapters 11 and 12 *passim*, 540, 542; architectural space of Church, 321–2; dance, 322, 326, 385, 426; music, 90, 281, 286,

313, 316–18, 320, 321, 328, 353,
354, 355, 356, 357, 384, 464, 543;
painting, 328, 345, 349, 350–3;
poetry: lyric and epic, 90, 118, 168,
222, 316–31, 335–7, 338, 357, 364,
422–3, 449, 537, 559; tragedy and
drama, 90, 168, 170, 221, 247, 316,
322, 330–1, 385, 450, 537, 538
Athanasius, 211–15, 515
atheism, 114, 115, 122, 131, 133, 151,
178, 190, 289, 397, 478; Rosenzweig's 'atheistic theology,' 292–3,
376, 414, 529
Auden, W.H., 10, 477–8
Augustine, St, 102, 189, 209, 211,
215–17, 224, 229, 244, 252, 256, 275,
338, 397, 418, 434, 500, 514, 516
Austrian and Austro-Hungarian
Empire, 277, 304, 306, 353, 535

Bach, J.S., 354–5
Bacon, Francis, 134
Badiou, Alain, 466
Bakhtin, Mikhail, 50
Bakunin, Mikhail, 62
Barth, Karl, xiii, 21–2, 40, 51, 54, 204,
205–6, 207, 209, 218, 381, 461, 462,
464, 472, 474, 483, 514
Bataille, Georges, 66, 421, 466, 557
Bauer, Bruno, 494
Bauer, Otto, 399, 550, 555
Bayle, Pierre, 178
Beaumarchais, Caron de, 359
Beethoven, Ludwig van, 193, 354–5,
362
Benjamin, Walter, 4, 9, 244, 377, 468
Bennett, Alan, 503
Berdyaev, Nikolai, 9, 132, 504
Bergman, Hugo, 474, 480
Bergson, Henri, 130

Berman, Harold, 11, 504
Bethmann-Hollweg, Theobald von,
294, 376
biology. *See* energy
Bismarck, Otto von, 282, 305, 309,
374, 526, 532, 533
Bloch, Ernst, 9, 377, 477
Blum, Emil, 27–8
Bodin, Jean, 258
Bolshevism, 26, 234, 241, 247, 283–4,
289, 298, 306–7, 348, 367, 379, 532
Bonaparte, Napoleon, 74, 277, 301–2,
361–2, 390, 495
Bonhoeffer, Dietrich, 51
Book of Manu, 168
Borgia, Cesare, 252–8
Brahma. *See* Hinduism
Brandeis, George, 50
Breton, André, 310–11
Brinton, Crane, 11, 479
Brunner, Emil, 206–9, 218, 515
Buber, Martin, 3, 6, 9, 50, 105–8,
111–13, 206, 315, 411, 464, 468, 469,
471, 474, 479, 482, 500, 501, 511
Buddha, xiv, 33, 169, 441, 449, 453
Buddhism, 50, 168–70, 190, 324, 440,
441, 449–50, 453, 487, 509, 556
Bultmann, Rudolf, 500
Burckhardt, Jacob, 163, 386

calendar, 13, 57, 141–2, 224, 347, 432,
541
Calvin, Jean, 209, 396, 555
Camp William James, 9, 284
Campbell, Joseph, 132
Camus, Albert, 50, 187, 359
Carnap, Rudolf, 116
Cartesian. *See* Descartes
Cassirer, Ernst, 325
Castoriadis, Cornelius, 260

catastrophe, xxi, xxiv–xxvi, 36, 43, 67, 68, 71, 73, 75, 77, 148, 175, 188–9, 193–4, 195–6, 214, 220, 248, 251, 282–4, 295, 309, 386–7, 399, 421, 437, 446, 470, 519, 524
Chesterton, G.K., 325
China, xxiv, 143, 146, 148–9, 152–3, 168, 212, 218, 393, 417, 422, 442–5, 447, 448, 451–2, 509
Christian eternal hatred of the Jew, 13, 22, 32, 404
Christians, rays of the star, 15, 25, 455
Church of Rome, 209, 221, 238, 263, 343–4, 352–3, 358; and Petrine Church, 24, 230–5, 238, 254, 320, 352
Churchill, Winston, 326
Cluny, 242, 245, 341–3
Cohen, Hermann, xxvi, 4, 52, 128, 374, 377, 412, 464
Cohen, Leonard, 374
Cohen, Richard, 4, 372
Cold War, 76, 308
commerce, xxvii, 48–9, 456
communism, 45, 49, 108, 131, 366, 368, 375, 394
Confucianism. *See* Confucius
Confucius, 166, 169, 446–9, 451, 454, 456–7
Constantine, Emperor, 208, 211, 214
creation and Islam, 406–10, 417–18
creation and tribal life, 422–3
creation, xvi, 16, 19, 29, 45, 53–5, 59, 65–7, 76, 78–9, 86, 93–8, 100–1, 103–4, 110, 122, 128, 132, 136, 141–2, 145, 147, 149–50, 154, 156, 158, 160, 163–4, 169, 171, 174, 175–7, 179, 181, 185, 194, 197, 199, 224, 228, 235, 242, 250, 252–3, 255,

264, 277, 315, 319–20, 329, 334, 349, 357, 362, 364, 381, 386, 388, 401, 406–10, 414, 417–18, 421, 435, 437, 438, 451, 457, 495, 506, 507, 515
creature, 65–7, 167, 175–7, 181–2, 186, 189, 193–4, 197, 218, 222, 237, 242, 254, 320, 328, 408, 420, 428, 430, 437, 443, 446, 449, 540
Cromwell, Oliver, 247
Cross of Reality, 8, 13, 33, 155, 225–8, 399, 437, 441, 462, 476, 487, 517, 539, 552, 559

Dadaism, 45, 66, 264, 310, 546
Dante, 31, 209, 238, 329–30, 337–40, 342, 343–4, 348, 351, 353, 361, 397, 418, 453, 521, 538, 541, 556
Darwin, Charles, 272, 380, 386–7, 399, 479, 489, 549, 557
dative, 549
David, Larry, 152
De Man, Paul, xxi
death, xiv, xxiii, 4–5, 24, 34, 39–40, 51, 60, 77–8, 85, 103, 108, 112, 134, 141, 150, 159, 163, 169, 173–4, 177–82, 188, 192, 198, 200–1, 203, 205, 208, 216, 253, 282, 285, 288, 311, 318, 321, 333, 342, 359, 399, 410, 423–6, 440, 455–6, 460, 461, 502, 513
deism, 127, 178–9, 271, 405
Deleuze, Gilles, xxx, 39, 66, 160, 421, 531, 544, 557
democracy, xxviii, xxxiii, 49, 131, 236, 256, 276, 277, 280, 340–1, 343, 362, 405, 524
Derrida, Jacques, xiii, xxvi, xxx, 11, 71, 109, 244, 293, 312, 464–6, 494, 505, 545

Descartes, René, xi, xxxi, 36, 41, 46,
47, 63, 71, 74–5, 134–5, 188, 197,
254, 264–7, 269–72, 274–7, 333, 363,
380, 384–5, 436, 453, 458, 460, 521,
522, 523, 548
Deutsch, Karl, 10
Die Kreatur, 6, 9, 54, 66, 132, 482
Dilthey, Wilhelm, 296, 531
Dinan, Desmond, 279
disangelist, 76, 371, 380, 386–7, 389,
398, 496, 551
Dostoevsky, Fyodor, xxv, 38, 50–3,
325, 366, 367–8, 538
Dreyfus, Alfred, 235, 255

Ebner, Ferdinand, 6, 50
Egypt, 12, 169, 200, 218–19, 224, 236,
331, 429, 439–40, 507
Ehrenberg, Hans, xv–xvii, xxiii, 3, 6,
21, 38–9, 41, 51, 52, 118, 259, 265,
414, 458, 464, 473, 481–2, 485, 493
Ehrenberg, Rudi, xv–xviii, 6, 39,
51–2, 402, 482, 487, 488, 508
Einstein, Albert, xxxi, 46
election (Jewish), xxx, 129, 141–2,
149–50, 244, 402, 409, 555
Eliot, T.S., 325
Emmet, Dorothy, 473, 481
Empedocles, 264
endowment, 194, 199, 240, 283,
308–9, 418, 428
enemy, xxi, 76, 77, 79, 286, 336, 397,
426, 488, 496, 505, 519, 526–7, 551
energy, 39–41, 109, 187, 267, 283, 285,
421
Engels, Friedrich, 62, 376–8, 391, 398,
534
English Revolution, 346, 353, 377
Enlightenment, 45, 46, 53, 92, 98, 148,
172, 184, 195, 251, 271–2, 276, 277,

300, 301, 305, 362, 408, 411, 421,
428, 430, 436, 437, 450, 491; and
paradigm shift, 172
Eno, Brian, 193
Epicurean, 34, 115, 163, 502
epoch, 44, 75, 108, 112, 200, 216, 223,
282, 294, 319, 325, 341, 349, 351,
428–30, 432–3, 501, 524
equality, xx, xxvi, xxxii, xxxiii, 178,
183, 243, 257, 273, 276–8, 360, 362,
364–5, 465
Erasmus, 35, 261
eschatology (also *eschaton*), xvii,
xviii, xix, xxiv, 136, 199, 244, 250,
251, 339, 351, 370, 379, 381–2, 448,
546
ethics, xxix, 13, 37–8, 42, 46–7, 53, 61,
62, 64, 88, 90, 110, 124–5, 151, 171,
295, 380, 414, 459, 485, 507, 529,
534, 545, 555–6
Euripides, 170
Europe, xxiii, xxiv, xxvii, xxx,
xxxii, 27, 45, 52, 75, 92, 116, 131,
154, 198, 200, 209, 211, 218, 222,
223, 235, 237, 249, 256, 258–63,
266, 272, 277–82, 284, 290, 293,
294, 301, 307–9, 320–2, 330, 341,
343–4, 348, 352, 356, 358, 361–2,
365–7, 377, 383, 391, 416–17,
422, 432, 435, 452, 466, 484, 503,
506, 514, 516, 525, 529, 538, 539,
542, 544, 547, 554
European Union, 278, 518, 525
event, 67–8, 84–5, 104, 117, 120, 143,
159, 174, 180, 204, 208–9, 216, 220,
237, 244–5, 257, 262, 267, 331–2,
334, 360, 367, 377, 381–2, 391, 407,
418, 439, 458–9, 494, 513, 541
evil, xxvi, xxix, 23, 43, 78, 108–9, 150,
185–92, 209, 217, 224, 245, 296,

387, 443–6, 465, 472, 487, 498,
512
Expressionism, 45

faith, hope, and love, xix, 197, 224,
248, 254, 258, 339, 387
fanatic. *See* zealot
fascism, xx, xxiv, xxv, xxix, 26, 32,
37, 52, 77, 131–2, 243–4, 249–50,
284–5, 289, 312, 395, 415, 490, 550
Ferrari, Giuseppi, 12, 524–5
festival, xxxiv, 98, 223, 257, 322–3,
430, 432, 486. *See also* ritual
Feuerbach, Ludwig, xii, 9, 62, 73,
116, 143, 354, 377–8, 477
Fichte, J.G., 25, 46, 75, 118, 285, 296,
354, 375, 501
Foucault, Michel, xxii, xxvi, 39, 63,
126, 244, 264, 272, 312, 531
Founding, 33, 44, 83, 87, 194, 199,
225, 241, 252, 344, 361, 470, 554
Francis of Assisi, St, 110, 200, 209,
241, 242, 247, 344, 348, 349, 351, 353
Frederick the Great, 27
freedom, xxvi, xxxii, 35, 36, 37, 41,
42, 43, 45, 48, 62, 68, 70, 84, 90, 126,
130, 134, 146, 147, 148, 153, 167,
178, 185, 187, 209, 215, 232, 237,
239, 240, 242, 243, 266, 273–8, 303,
311, 334, 346–7, 364–5, 366, 373,
406, 411–12, 418, 421, 426, 430, 434,
438, 445–6, 449, 461, 499, 501, 518,
520, 560
French Revolution, xxvi, xxviii,
25, 127, 236, 241–3, 245–6, 254,
chapter 8 *passim*, 293, 346–7, 358,
360–1, 364–5, 367, 368–9, 384, 390,
396
Freud, Sigmund, 26, 192, 386–7, 399,
548–9

Freund, Elsa, 4, 465, 491, 493, 509
Friedrich, Carl, 10
Fries, Jakob, 296, 354
Futurism, 310

Gambetta, Léon, 26
geistig, xxxii, 48, 479; *geistlich*, xxxii,
48, 467
generations, xxii, xxviii, 29, 31, 52,
96, 104, 108, 171, 183, 189, 192, 195,
200, 209, 216, 245, 264, 285, 327,
363, 381, 388, 421, 427, 445, 472,
495, 524, 541
Genesis, xvi, 96, 100, 101, 102, 103,
129, 141, 315, 318
Gilgamesh, 169
Glatzer, Nahum, 12–13, 373, 469,
480, 508
Gnosticism, 43, 84, 107, 112, 113, 162,
183, 315, 351, 474, 497
Gobineau, Arthur de, 79
Goethe, J.W., xviii, xxxi, xxxiii, 6,
123, 167, 204, 231–5, 282, 295, 306,
328, 338, 353, 356–8, 361, 371, 372,
385, 389, 404, 438, 449, 455, 473,
526, 538; and Johannine Church,
233–6, 245, 320
Gordon, Peter, 4, 464, 530, 533, 552
Gormann-Thelen, Michael, 83, 462,
463, 468, 471, 474, 475, 479, 483,
487, 494, 496, 528
Gospels, 112, 204, 215, 221, 386, 517
Gramsci, Antonio, 110, 375
Great War. *See* World War One
Greece, 12, 58, 143, 146, 148–9, 161,
163, 218, 221, 231, 332, 387, 403
Gregory VII (Pope), 237–8, 258,
343–4, 346–7, 349, 353
Gregory of Nyssa, 198
Groethuysen, Bernard, 273

Guattari, Felix. *See* Deleuze, Gilles

Guelphs, 247, 338, 340, 344, 347–9, 353

Guitton, Jean, 203

Habermas, Jürgen, 9, 10, 66, 496

Halevi, Jehuda, 16, 17, 471

Haller, Karl Ludwig von, 301

Hallo, Rudolf, xxxii, 6, 297, 305, 460

Hamann, J.G., xii, 126

Hardy, Thomas, 503, 524

Harnack, Adolf von, 30, 474

Hayek, Friedrich von, 160

Haym, Rudolf, 296, 301, 531

Hegel, G.W.F., xii, xxiv, xxxii, xxxiii, 6, 7, 35, 46, 61, 62, 65, 66, 69, 70, 75, 80, 92, 94, 99, 103, 112, 115, 116, 123, 124, 139, 144, 163–4, 251, 285, chapter 10 *passim*, 311, 317, 321, 346, 354, 362–3, 373–5, 377–8, 389, 402, 442, 467, 474, 498, 500, 502, 530, 531–6, 543, 547, 553

Heidegger, Martin, xii, xxi, xxxiv, xxxvii, 4, 7, 9, 11, 34, 50, 53, 66, 70, 71, 77, 79, 96, 112, 116–17, 138, 191, 204, 243, 264, 287, 311–12, 377, 451, 464, 494, 495, 500, 502, 511, 530–1, 533

Heilsgeschichte, 184, 217, 250, 307, 308

Henry IV, Holy Roman Emperor, 237

Henry IV (King of France), 261

Heraclitus, 73, 116–17, 492, 495

Herder, J., 123, 195, 354, 473

hero, 133–5, 168, 170, 258, 329, 331–3, 337, 339, 356, 399, 419, 421, 423, 426, 430, 479, 502, 527, 538–9

Hesiod, 132, 172

Hillman, James, 132

Hinduism, 149, 153, 154, 168–70, 190, 216, 441, 451, 560

Hitler, Adolph, 22–4, 26, 32, 34, 39, 46, 77, 186, 192, 212, 286, 288, 291, 308, 356, 443, 484, 515, 519, 527, 543

Hobbes, Thomas, 489, 523

Hölderlin, Friedrich, 287–8, 384

Holocaust, xiii, xxiv, xxv, 14, 23, 26, 32, 54, 106, 151, 186, 192, 288, 476, 481, 485, 489

Holy War, 139, 404

Homer, 118, 167, 172, 321, 329–32, 334–9, 358, 369, 424, 540

Horwitz, Rivka, 12, 471, 480

Huessy, Gritli, xviii, xxix, 5, 20, 57–9, 287, 298, 376, 462–4, 471–2, 481

Hugo of St Victor, 241–2

Huguenots, 261–3, 366

humanism, xvii, xix, xxxii, 22, 24, 26, 45, 47, 56, 105–13, 195, 202, 218, 219, 248, 259, 335, 337, 361, 384, 386, 405, 411, 467, 556

Huss, Johann, 209, 352, 366

Husserl, Edmund, 50, 63, 66, 68–71, 264, 479, 494

Hutton, Chris, 46

Idealism, xxvii, 4, 35–8, 50, 52, 53, 59, 64, 69, 71, 79, 80, 94, 98, 112, 113, 120, 141, 147, 160–1, 163, 176, 182, 267, 285, 297, 305–7, 311–13, 335–9, 383, 386, 387, 388, 389, 398, 401, 498, 501, 527, 530

idolatry, xxx, xxxi, 15–16, 24, 32, chapter 1 *passim*, 51, 54, 60, 70, 89, 132, 164–5, 175, 212–13, 235, 244, 254, 280, 282, 287–8, 292–3, 385, 409–10, 428, 535, 559

imperative, 83, 85, 86, 91, 92, 104, 107, 120, 207

Incarnation, xiv, xv, xvii, 12, 32, 58,
  70, 79, 82, 109–10, 118, 163, 199,
  201, 202, 206–8, 236, 250, 283, 288,
  321, 329, 338, 364, 385, 418, 428,
  437, 452, 453, 455, 501, 502, 518, 549
incognito and non-denominational
  Christianity, 320, 381–2
India, 143, 146, 148, 149, 152–3,
  156–7, 166, 168, 315, 401, 417, 420,
  451, 452, 552, 560
indicative mood, 83, 84, 86, 92, 560
Innocent III, 247
Islam, xiii, xxvi–xxviii, xxxiii, 13,
  94, 95, 98, 107, 137–41, 149, 150,
  157, 172, 175, 176, 182, 215, 220,
  244, 278, 330, chapters 14 and 15
  passim, 456, 461, 466, 505, 507, 512,
  546, 551–6
Israel, xiii, xvii, 24, 27, 32, 146, 221,
  235–6, 242, 247, 387, 431, 455, 461,
  480, 504, 519

Jacobi, Friedrich, xii, 35, 296, 375
Jacoby, Felix, 288
James, William, 130–2, 389
Jefferson, Thomas, 178, 275
Jerome, St (Hieronymous), 209, 215,
  516
Jesuits, 262–3
Jesus, xiv, 33, 131, 190, 196, 197, 204,
  212, 213, 214, 217, 220, 221, 224,
  247, 252–3, 269, 273, 309, 323, 342,
  351, 370, 382–3, 403–4, 409, 418,
  427–9, 435, 452, 505, 512, 517
Jewish *Lehrhaus*, xiii, 3, 466, 506
Jews: as coals in God's fire, 14,
  25, 149, 163, 173, 319; as eternal
  people, 13, 14, 17–18, 30, 88, 103,
  293, 373, 423; as prisoners of God,
  25; as remainder, 150

Job, 129, 185, 383
Johannine Christianity, 13, 234,
  235, 236, 245, 254, 320, 352, 354,
  356, 381, 404, 417–18, 431, 456,
  482
John, St, 34, 38–9, 221, 238, 320, 352,
  435
Joyce, James, xxxiv, 325–6, 538, 539
Jung, Carl, 132
justice, xx, xxii, xxiii, 38, 43, 109, 117,
  132, 137, 139, 159, 178, 188, 190,
  295, 338–40, 342–4, 387, 405, 422,
  446, 465, 474, 545, 553

Ka (Egyptian), 219
Kafka, Franz, 34, 325, 538
Kampfer, Dietrich, 10
Kant, Immanuel, xxvi, 7, 19, 20, 28,
  37–8, 45, 46, 52, 61, 66, 70, 74, 75,
  94, 99, 100, 115, 125–7, 134–5, 139,
  146, 158, 185, 187, 203, 219, 225,
  244, 267, 269, 272, 275–6, 285, 295,
  296, 311–12, 368, 371, 375, 377–8,
  411–12, 436, 447, 467, 498, 501, 518,
  534, 546, 556
Kleist, Heinrich von, 320
Kierkegaard, Søren, 50, 51, 52, 53, 62,
  73, 99, 127, 198, 203, 206, 266, 303,
  474, 477
Klemperer, Klemens, 288, 528
Knox, Bernard, 172
Koch, Richard, 6, 39–41, 44, 488
Kohr, Jörg, 294

Lagarde, Paul de, 285, 305
Lanois, Daniel, 193, 511
Lao-Tse. *See* Tao and Taoism
Lasson, Georg, 571
Last Judgment, 195, 241–2, 244,
  338–9, 341–2, 353, 370, 453

Left Hegelian, 9, 109, 293, 374, 377, 494, 531, 536

Leibniz, Gottfried, 134, 139, 269

Leipzig night, xv, xvi, xvii, 374, 463, 479

Lenin, Vladimir (*also* Leninism), 109, 165, 367, 375, 379, 395, 545

Levinas, Emmauel, xiii, xxi, 4, 37, 46, 47, 145, 151, 191, 374, 461, 464, 466, 507, 511, 545

liberalism, 48, 111, 126, 137, 140, 148, 153, 179, 256, 274, 277, 305, 355, 362, 393, 395, 402–3, 443, 487–8, 520, 524, 531, 533

liberty. *See* freedom

Lincoln, Abraham, 69, 79, 200

Liszt, Franz, 355

liturgy, 32, 304, 315, 317–19, 331, 341–2, 345, 420, 435, 456

living, loving, revealing God, xxxiii, 6, 24–5, 29, 32, chapter 1 *passim*, 70, 98, 102, 104, 124–5, 132, 135, 137, 144, 145, 151–4, 157–9, 160–2, 164, 165, 168, 170–80, 183, 217, 251, 314, 373, 379, 401, 404–6, 408–10, 413–14, 419, 428, 429, 437, 476, 485, 487

Locke, John, 75, 134

Louis XIV, 256, 262

love as strong as death, 40, 77, 103, 141, 173, 177, 180–2, 200, 216, 253, 318, 412, 423, 426, 472

Löwith, Karl, 4, 9, 204, 477

Lucretius, 35

Ludendorf, Erich, 26

Lukács, György, 306, 377, 395, 477

Luther, Martin, 22, 35, 110, 206, 209, 238, 241, 246–7, 258, 261, 275, 338, 340, 352–8, 393, 396, 482, 484, 520, 541

Lyotard, Jean-François, xxx, 312

Machiavelli, Niccolò, 257–8

Mahler, Gustav, 355

Malebranche, Nicholas, 265

Mao Tse-tung, xxvi, 34, 212, 499, 545

Martel, Charles, 256

Marty, Martin, 9, 462

Martyr, 192, 205, 207, 333, 342, 366, 369, 375, 453

Marx, Karl, xii, xxvi, xxx, xxxiv, 26, 30, 48, 62, 66, 87, 110, 134, 136, 139, 143, 217, 243, 245, 250, 255, 274, 284, 288, 298, 300, 365–8, chapter 13 *passim*, 424, 444, 461, 477, 494, 501, 509, 534, 545–7, 550

Mass, 326, 342, 345

mathematics, 97, 127, 145, 219, 263, 267, 269–70, 315, 330, 335, 449, 458, 540

Mauthner, Fritz, 11, 478

Maya, 166, 170, 451–2

Maybaum, Ignaz, 106, 480, 554

mechanistic, xi, 26, 35–6, 39, 45–7, 49, 50, 52, 63, 70, 84, 86, 87, 100, 115, 116, 133–4, 164, 187, 188, 198, 199, 202, 211, 251, 255, 264–5, 267, 276–7, 285, 310, 357, 369, 375, 392, 430, 436–7, 443, 448, 487, 497, 544

Meinecke, Friedrich, 297, 299, 300, 532

meta-ethical, 53, 61, 64, 88, 92, 124–7, 143, 144, 161, 164, 166, 167, 168, 170, 266, 317, 372, 459

meta-logical, 126, 162

metanomics, 18, 88–9, 393, 418, 451, 459

metaphysics, xii, xvi, 35, 41, 45, 50, 60, 92, 97, 116, 117, 124–7, 134, 143, 144, 146, 148, 152, 161–2, 164, 166, 168–9, 187, 202, 225, 265, 267,

269–70, 271, 296, 311, 373, 375, 378, 406, 436, 450, 487, 518, 522–3
Michel, Ernst, 9, 472–3
Michelangelo, 136, 348, 350, 353
Middle Ages, 50, 143, 163, 210, 231, 238, 245–6, 308, 554
Milton, John, 35, 135, 185, 353, 510
mind. *See* reason
miracle, 100, 159, 163, 172, 173, 199, 210, 224, 265, 270, 435, 491, 511
Miskotte, Kornelius, xiii, 113, 462
modernity, xxvii, xxxi, 34–6, 70, 115, 116, 119, 135, 204, 219, 333, 355, 363, 380, 386, 417, 441, 456, 461, 508
Moltke, Freya von, 462, 494
Moltke, Helmuth James von, 528–9
Montaigne, Michel de, 34, 422
Montesquieu, Baron de, 254, 276, 301–2, 359, 389
morals. *See* ethics
More, St Thomas, 209
Moses, 31, 55, 99, 127, 209, 403, 427–8
Mosès, Stephan, 98, 533
Mozart, Wolfgang Amadeus, 354–5
Muhammad, chapter 14 *passim*, 419, 427, 428, 431–2, 434, 452, 453, 553, 556, 558, 559
Müller, Georg, 8, 13, 204, 287, 437, 474
Müller, Johannes, 283
Munch, Edvard, 36
Muslim. *See* Islam
mysticism, 70, 107, 112, 154, 156, 315, 478, 507
myth, 23–4, 53, 62, 123, 148, 152, 154, 156, 162, 166, 168, 188, 195–7, 199, 214, 219, 225, 231, 235, 245, 258, 283, 289, 330–1, 337, 346, 365, 491, 547

names, xiv, xxii, 46, 65, 67, 69, 86, 102, 111, chapter 4 *passim*, 143, 184, 196, 209, 267, 268, 312, 315, 332, 336, 361, 379, 384, 387, 421, 444, 477, 494, 503
National Socialism. *See* Nazism
nationalism, xv, 23, 26–7, 54, 106, 132, 195, 256, 277, chapters 9 and 10 *passim*, 360, 362, 395–6, 398, 476, 479, 502, 531, 550
naturalism, 24, 50, 55, 63, 66, 68, 115, 125, 130, 134, 143, 146, 201, 219, 313, 375, 379, 387, 421
Naumann, Friedrich, 294
Nazism, xxv, xxx, 13, 23–4, 39, 46, 77, 132, 138, 191–2, 271, 287–91, 312, 327, 337, 456, 482, 485, 502, 526–7, 546, 548, 550; Rosenstock-Huessy and, 285–91
neighbour, love thy, xx, xxix, 22, 24, 37, 41, 42, 44, 103, 104, 107, 137, 141, 144, 145, 154, 169, 173, 176, 182–3, 218, 234–6, 251–3, 283, 304, 336, 372, 379, 397, 401, 412, 419, 429, 438, 447, 453, 485, 501, 505, 540
neo-Hegelian. *See* Left Hegelian
neo-Platonism, 102, 154, 162, 176, 203, 507
Neumann, Franz, 550
New Thinking, xi, xiii, xix, xx, xxi, xxiii, xxiv, xxv, xxvi, xxviii, xxxiv, 6, 21, 33, 34, 38–9, 41, 44, 54, chapter 2 *passim*, 82–5, 105, 118, 131, 322, 399, 414, 439, 465–6, 489, 494, 508, 549; compared with radical liberal paradigm, xx–xxix. *See also* Speech Thinking
Newton, Isaac, 99, 100, 265, 269–70, 453

Nibelungen, 285, 337
Nicene Creed, xviii, 212, 214, 381
Niebuhr, Reinhold, 10, 381
Niemöller, Martin, 25, 485
Nietzsche, Friedrich, xii, xxxi, xxxiii,
    6, 19, 30, 35–8, 40, 45, 50, 51, 52–3,
    55, 61, 64, 66, 73, 74–5, 125, 126,
    127, 134, 136, 143, 163, 168, 169,
    183, 204, 234, 249, 250–2, 259, 266,
    275, 288, 311, 312, 354–5, chapter
    13 *passim*, 420, 423, 427, 445, 452,
    474, 476, 542, 545–6, 548, 557,
    560–1
Nihilism, xxi, 37, 169, 252, 314, 382,
    534
Noah, 241–2, 248

Odilo of Cluny, 242, 244, 342, 343,
    351–2
Ottoman Empire, xxiv, xxviii, 244,
    408, 505

pagan, xii, 10, 13, 23–6, 30, 49, 103,
    105, 111, 112, 124, 132, chapter 5
    passim, 184, 187, 194, 199, 212, 223,
    231, 232, 233, 235, 251–3, 257, 259,
    261, 264–5, 268, 283, 320, 322–4,
    333, 339, 344, 349, 373, 375, 387,
    390, 404–6, 408–12, 414, 416, 418,
    431, 435, 436, 455–7, 465, 470, 484,
    486, 491, 496, 507, 542, 553
Paine, Thomas, 253
pantheism, 122, 178
Papal Revolution, 237, 241–2, 343–4,
    346–7
Paracelsus, 10, 40, 41, 44, 75, 453,
    478, 489–90
Parmenides, 61, 65, 116–17, 204, 492,
    495, 535
particular, 158–62, 166–8, 176, 529

Pascal, Blaise, 259, 263–6, 273–4, 523
Patmos Group, 54, 113, 206, 287, 482
Paul, St, xv, xvii, 38, 60, 129, 205, 214,
    237–8, 258, 275, 354, 466, 500, 517,
    520, 549
Pauline Church, 231–3, 235, 238, 254,
    320, 352, 354, 456, 484, 500
Peirce, Charles, 83
Petzet, Heinrich, 287
Philo of Alexandria, 162
philosophy, critique of, chapters 2,
    3, and 4 *passim*, 140, 142–3, 171,
    178, 198, 204, 206, 222, 248, 269–70,
    335–6, 371–2, 374–5, 467, 470, 500,
    522–3, 536–7
Picasso, Pablo, 310–11
Picht, Georg, 287–9
Picht, Werner, 287, 528
Plato and Platonism, 28–30, 35, 60–1,
    81, 102–3, 117, 119, 128–9, 162–3,
    176, 193, 203–5, 213, 218, 224, 330,
    334, 336, 366, 373, 383, 388, 415,
    445, 486, 495, 517, 535, 537
Plesssner, Helmuth, 288
Plotinus, 162
pluralism, 38, 130, 137, 164, 178,
    414–15, 472, 552
politics, 91–2, 180, 228–9, 249, 257,
    278, 280, 294, 300, 334, 347, 348,
    427
polytheism, 132, 164, 169, 170, 451
post-Christian, xv, 210, 387, 401
postmodernist. *See* post-structuralist
post-structuralist, xxi, xxx, 37, 50, 66,
    70, 109, 117, 142, 250, 264, 290, 450,
    465, 494, 526, 544
priest, 15, 238, 410
Prinz, Alois, 287–8
Proclus, 162
Protagoras, 28, 119, 166

Proudhon, Pierre, 388, 396, 398, 551
Proust, Marcel, 195, 325, 538–9
providence, xxi, 46, 55, 172, 176, 177,
    184, 191, 192, 194–5, 208, 224, 294,
    407, 410, 511, 556. See also *Heilsge-
    schichte*
Prussia, 298, 301, 305–8, 485, 495,
    527, 532, 533
Psalms, 103, 141, 317–18
public law, 249
public, 241, 333–7
Putnam, Hilary, 4, 58, 66, 469, 494–5
Pythagoras, 163

Rabelais, François, 115, 261, 456, 521
radical liberal. *See* 1968 paradigm
Rang, Florens Christian, 6, 9
Raphael, 345, 349, 350, 353, 542
Rawls, John, xx–xxi, 444
Readings, Bill, 501
reason, critique of, xi, 38, 62, 79–80,
    125–9, 135, 146, 159, 188, 195, 218,
    254, 267, 269–70, 311, 362–4, 397,
    406, 414, 447, 493, 499, 511
Redemption, xiii, xx, 15–17, 23,
    30–2, 36, 40–1, 54, 55, 88, 93–6, 98,
    100–1, 103, 105, 137, 141–4, 146,
    149–50, 152–8, 163, 166, 170–1,
    174–6, 179, 184, 189, 191, 195, 199,
    204, 216, 251, 259–60, 315, 323–4,
    333, 374, 408–9, 412, 416, 433,
    435–6, 451, 453, 457, 465, 495, 499,
    507, 526, 540; triple, of God, Man,
    and World, 149, 153, 181–2
Reformation, 22, 196, 214, 231, 241,
    261, 286, 347, 349, 352–6, 390, 484,
    541, 543, 544
Regius, Henricus, 265
relativism, xv, xxxi, 67, 69, 119, 441,
    472

Renaissance, xvii, 35, 163, 231, 233,
    242, 245–6, 252, 275, 340, 347, 349,
    352–3, 362, 491, 542, 544
Renouvier, Charles, 130
responsiveness, xi, 71–6, 96, 135, 178,
    182, 217, 408
Revelation, xx, 4, 15–17, 41, 53–5,
    59, 72, 76–8, 88, 93–5, 98, 100, 101,
    105, 137–8, 140–1, 146, 149, 153,
    156, 168, 173–8
Ricoeur, Paul, 4
ritual, 31, 98, 135–6, 141, 154, 173,
    175, 197, 221, 223, 326, 331, 341,
    369, 385, 456, 539. *See also* festival
Roman Empire, 162, 209–11, 219,
    223, 232, 237, 252, 254, 438, 556
Romanticism, 36, 275, 277, 280, 283,
    305, 512, 533, 535
root words, 99, 101
Rosenzweig, Edith, 5, 14, 21, 471–2,
    481
Rousseau, Jean Jacques, xxvi, 19, 20,
    34, 139, 234, 241, 243, 248, 254, 266,
    272–6, 301–2, 359–60, 363, 365,
    374, 441, 534, 552
Rubinstein, Richard, 152, 461, 464
Russian Revolution, xxvi, xxviii,
    245–6, 271, 325, 346, 348, 364–5,
    367–9, 374, 390–1, 393, 396, 495,
    516, 524

sacrifice, 36, 55, 99, 109, 157, 164, 183,
    196, 197, 202, 204, 207–8, 230, 234,
    243, 246, 248, 258, 265, 276, 281,
    286, 290, 302, 332–4, 343, 347, 369,
    375, 382–3, 395, 421, 425, 433–4,
    437, 443, 444–7, 464, 470, 485–6,
    496, 501, 535, 543, 549
Sade, Marquis de, 46, 421
Safranski, Rüdinger, 287–8

saint, 15, 110, 168, 194, 202, 207, 339, 341, 410, 413, 429
Saint-Simon, Claude Henri de Rouvroy, 228, 396, 399, 459
Salvation, 184, 194, 198, 205, 216–18, 224, 236, 264, 307, 351, 358, 367, 418, 426, 429, 434, 438, 441, 455, 459, 502, 513, 516; economy of, 155, 218, 420, 436. *See also* redemption
Samuelson, Norbert, 98, 491
Sartre, Jean-Paul, 50, 97, 359, 499, 500
Saussure, Ferdinand de, 11, 79
Savigny, Friedrich Carl von, xvi
Schelling, F.W.J., 62–3, 116, 118, 123, 146–7, 225, 296, 297, 311, 354, 375, 378, 474, 493, 507, 531
Schestow, Leo, 9
Schlegel, Friedrich, 306, 308–9, 535
Schleiermacher, Friedrich, 53
Schlink, Bernard, 186
Schmitt, Carl, 77, 140, 258, 496, 505
Scholem, Gershom, 4, 411, 468, 480, 534
Schopenhauer, Arthur, 53, 61, 75, 127, 190, 266, 354, 450, 498
Schweitzer, Albert, 30, 500
Searle, John, 11
Shakespeare, William, 35, 229, 353, 361, 538
Silesia, 210, 528
Simon, Ernst, 3, 21, 480
sin. *See* evil
Sloterdijk, Peter, 11, 479
Smith, Page, 11
socialism, 27, 108, 374–5
Socrates, 29, 119, 129, 303, 486, 517
solidarity, xxv, 52, 78–9, 224, 242, 271, 273, 344, 346–7, 362, 375, 388, 398–9, 445, 495
Song of Songs, 103, 141, 177, 318

Sophocles, 170
soul, xiii, xiv, xxiii, xxv, xxxii–xxxiii, 23, 27, 30, 49–51, 58, 60, 77, 83, 89–90, 93, 95, 103, 131, 134–5, 159, 171, 177, 181, 182, 195, 199–205, 210, 216, 220, 222, 227, 231–3, 242, 251, 263, 266, 270, 274, 312, 315, 318, 321–4, 327–9, 338, 340, 342–3, 346, 347, 351, 355–6, 362–3, 367, 371, 384–5, 403, 417, 419, 425, 434, 443, 449–50, 453, 467, 484, 490, 500, 513, 539, 546, 549
sovereignty: of man, 185; of reason, 38, 79; of self, 35, 44, 79, 134, 135, 143, 166
space, 38, 43, 57, 73, 86, 89–91, 104, 109, 118, 194, 209, 226, 228, 237, 249, 254, 263, 270, 272, 275, 276, 283, 316–17, 321, 330, 334, 337, 347, 364, 383, 384–5, 423–4, 436, 438–9, 446, 453, 459, 511–12, 558; playing space, 196, 209, 334–5, 427
Speech Thinking, xi, xviii, 33, chapter 2 *passim*, 92, 106, 113, 473, 474, 476. *See also* New Thinking
Spengler (pseudonym for David Goldmann), 461, 469, 553, 555
Spengler, Oswald, 282
Spinoza, Baruch, xxxi, 36, 46, 50, 115–16, 121–2, 123–5, 134, 139
stages of life, 201–2
Stahl, Friedrich Julius, 26
Stahmer, Harold, 463, 470, 474, 476
Stalin, Joseph, and Stalinism, xxvi, 34, 76, 165, 212, 379, 390, 545
Star of Redemption, synopsis, 140–2
star: Davidic, 31–3, 419, 432; eternal, 455; and human face, 32, 37
state, 49, chapter 10 *passim*; Jewish statelessness, 234, 296, 299
Steiner, Rudolf, 283, 441, 478, 508

Stern, Carola, 9–10

Stoic, 163, 436, 438

suffering, xv, xxii–xxiii, 31–2, 61, 74, 92, 150, 186, 189–92, 207, 211, 224, 228, 229, 251, 253, 281–2, 323, 335, 341, 366, 369, 376, 386, 395, 399–400, 409, 411, 417, 438, 446, 452, 454, 534; sociology as science of, 229–30

Sufism, 441, 507

Surrealism, 66, 310, 546

Susman, Margaret, 4, 9

Tannebaum, Eugen, 3

Tao and Taoism, 14, 33, 149–50, 154, 168–70, 216, 440–2, 448–9, 451, 487, 560

Taubes, Jacob, 10, 466

testator, 201–2, 453

Thayer, Abbot, 329

The All, xxii, 60, 61, 80, 123–5, 143, 144, 161, 171, 177, 181, 329, 335, 373, 413, 423, 426, 475, 502

The Nothing: Eastern religions and nothingness, 146, 147, 152, 153, 154, 168–9, 171; and nothingness, 51, 128, 169, 171, 192, 312, 425; nothing will come from nothing dogma, 128, 144, 146–7, 499

theology, 49–50, 53, 54, 58, 59, 93, 122, 126, 128, 141, 143, 172–7, 184, 195, 204–7, 244, 248, 260–2, 269–70, 292, 354, 358, 361, 370, 372–3, 376, 380–1, 401, 406, 414, 417, 434, 435, 438, 458, 466, 476, 481, 485, 491, 493, 500, 510, 523

theopolitics, xiii, xxviii, xxix, xxxvii, 405, 461

Theosophy, 54, 138, 152, 442, 461, 478

Theunissen, Michael, 11–12, 480

Thirty Years War, 74, 459, 495

Tillich, Paul, 51, 381, 439, 462, 548

time-body, 18, 109, 111, 118, 148, 194, 237, 283, 384, 418, 420, 426–8, 495, 497–8. *See also* epoch

Tolstoy, Leo, 234, 367–8

Torah, 172, 554

totality, xxx, 3, 61, 65, 147, 162, 169, 180, 181, 297, 303, 307, 309, 313, 316, 334, 354, 373, 378, 388–9, 446, 490, 531

Transcendent, xiv, 22, 205, 208, 447

trauma, 73–4, 92, 96, 472

Treitschke, Heinrich von, 302

tribe, 24–5, 77, 149, 210–11, 217–20, 267–8, 289–91, 326–7, 330–1, 332–3, 387, 419–32, 451, 496, 557, 558

Trinity, 157, 207, 351, 404

Troeltsch, Ernst, 30, 479

Tzara, Tristram, 311

Ullmann, Wolfgang, xv–xvii, 464, 474

Universal History, xxx, 32, 148, 184, 213, 216, 218, 245, 291, 381, 403, 419–20, 439, 441. See also *Heilsgeschichte*

universals, 47, 104, 158–61, 165–7, 168, 176, 260

University of Paris, 260–1, 269, 360, 521

Utopia, 225, 234, 310, 369, 399, 498; art and, 310, 369

Vahinger, Hans, 115

Vico, Gambatista, 12, 71, 389, 421

victim, 31, 109, 185, 191, 221, 223–4, 244, 251, 382, 425, 465

Victor II, Pope, 247

vocative, 83, 85, 86, 107, 138, 336

Voegelin, Eric, 351, 497

Voltaire, 50, 139, 265–6, 271–2, 276, 359–60, 365, 405, 523

Wagner, Richard, 288, 314–15, 354–5, 385
Walzer, Michael, xxi
war: role of, 74–8; as social disease, 84, 198, 245, 295, 512
war-path, 210, 424, 429
warrior, 76, 152, 210, 335, 386, 420, 422, 424, 429, 453, 554, 559
Weber, Max, 11, 442, 478–9, 511
Weizsäcker, Viktor von, 6, 9, 39, 489, 511
Whig, 219, 245, 271, 272
Wilde, Oscar, 362, 446, 539
Wilder, Thornton, 325
Wilhelm II (Kaiser), 195, 298
Wittgenstein, Ludwig, xi, 66–71, 116, 212, 456, 464, 494–5

Wittig, Joseph, 230, 482, 511, 524
World War One, xxiii–xxix, 9, 26, 27, 48, 71, 73, 75, 108, 142, 173, 206, 236, 281, 282, 393, 425, 459, 466, 528
World War Two, xix, xx, xxv, xxvii, xxviii, xxix, 3, 9, 75, 113, 142, 186, 198, 279, 286, 289, 297, 367, 531

Yahweh, 129, 131, 136, 152, chapter 14 *passim*. *See also* living, loving, revealing God
Yoga, 150, 155, 170, 441

Zak, Adam, 8, 57, 474
Zealot, 22, 183, 223–4, 235, 283, 372, 378, 380, 459
Zionism, xiii, 20, 106, 113, 138, 235, 303, 411, 461, 504
Žižek, Slavoj, 109, 465, 504, 519

www.ingramcontent.com/pod-product-compliance
Lightning Source LLC
Chambersburg PA
CBHW051251200725
29844CB00007B/96